Hardball Legends and Journeymen and Short-Timers

Hardball Legends and Journeymen and Short-Timers

333 Illustrated Baseball Biographies

Written and Illustrated by
RONNIE JOYNER

McFarland & Company, Inc., Publishers
Jefferson, North Carolina, and London

LIBRARY OF CONGRESS CATALOGUING-IN-PUBLICATION DATA

Joyner, Ronnie.
Hardball legends and journeymen and short-timers : 333 illustrated baseball biographies / written and illustrated by Ronnie Joyner.
p. cm.
Includes index.

ISBN 978-0-7864-7052-5
softcover : acid free paper ∞

1. Baseball players—United States—Biography. 2. Baseball—United States—History—20th century. I. Title.
GV865.A1J69 2012 796.3570922—dc23 [B] 2012007785

BRITISH LIBRARY CATALOGUING DATA ARE AVAILABLE

Cover illustration by Ronnie Joyner

Manufactured in the United States of America

McFarland & Company, Inc., Publishers
Box 611, Jefferson, North Carolina 28640
www.mcfarlandpub.com

CONTENTS

ACKNOWLEDGMENTS

The bio-illustrations featured in this book were produced continually from 1997 through 2011, and were published in a variety of publications. The graphic nature of these illustrations does not lend itself to traditional bibliographic forms of reference notation, but conscientious efforts were made within the text to give credit when information used or quoted was uniquely tied to specific sources. Credits for ordinary data like statistics or game details were impossible to accommodate in this graphic presentation. That information, nonetheless, was as important as any to the storytelling.

The following sources were of great value in fleshing out the details: *The New York Times*, *The Washington Post*, *The Chicago Tribune*, *The Los Angeles Times*, *The Sporting News*, *Baseball Digest*, *The Baseball Encyclopedia*, *Sports Illustrated*, The Associated Press, United Press International, Topps, baseballinwartime.com, sabr.org, retrosheet.org, baseballlibrary.com, baseball-almanac.com, and baseball-reference.com.

Gratitude must also be expressed to the countless authors of other books, magazines, periodicals, websites, interviews—and all other manner of baseball writing—whose recording of baseball history was also invaluable.

Lastly, thanks go out to Sumner G. Hunnewell, Jr., for his hard work in compiling the index.

PREFACE

Hello baseball fans! Or is it art fans? Maybe you're both. If you are, then you're a lot like me. What follows in this book are 333 illustrated biographies of baseball players, mostly major leaguers, written and drawn by me. These illustrations are the confluence of two of my favorite things—baseball and art—and I am lucky to have found a way to squeeze two of my biggest passions into one activity.

People have referred to my work as caricatures, or cartoons, or other similar categorizations, but none of those descriptions really seem to hit the mark. The dominant element of my graphic biographies is the player portrait. Since these portraits do not exaggerate the players' facial features in a comical way, the term "caricature" never really fit. And while these graphic biographies are peppered with small cartoons, the overriding element is still the portrait, thereby rendering the term "cartoon" inadequate in defining them. And then there's the text. There is a lot of text in most of my pieces, so it seemed important to reference that in whatever term I settled on to describe my work. Sometime between 2000 and 2005 I started to use the term "bio-illustration" to describe my graphic biographies, and that seemed to be the perfect resolution.

There's no denying that my bio-illustrations owe everything to the great newspaper sports cartoonists of the early- to mid–20th century. Sports cartooning for newspapers was already a nearly-extinct art form by the time I started creating my bio-illustrations in 1997. Bill Gallo was still keeping the genre alive up at *The Daily News* in New York, but for the most part the era of newspaper sports cartoonists had long since been laid to rest by 1997. And when Gallo himself passed away at age 88 in May of 2011, it could be viewed as the official last gasp of a bygone art form—at least on a mainstream level. Sure, there will always be a few hard-headed people who continue to work enthusiastically in the old style, but it most likely will be enjoyed only by niche audiences. And you never really know. If there ever comes a day when the masses tire of all the busy, over-the-top, hi-tech graphics splashed everywhere, good old-fashioned sports cartooning might find its way back into the mainstream.

While sports cartooning has likely been around as long as there have been sports (imagine a cave drawing of Cro-Magnon skull bad-hopping through legs of surprised Neanderthal 1st baseman), the "modern" age of sports cartooning for newspapers can be traced to the early 1900s as an offshoot of the editorial cartoon. It was artists like Bob Edgren, E.W. Kemble, Thomas A. Dorgan ("Tad"), Burris Jenkins, Jr., and Rube Goldberg who began to inject life into rather drab newspaper layouts with their flashy illustrations. Limitations in the newspaper printing technology of the time led to less-than-stellar results in reproducing photographs. Yet the crisp black-and-white high-contrast nature of these artists' illustrations reproduced very well, making them jump off the page for readers whose eyes were weary of wall-to-wall text and mushy, detail-void halftones.

The golden age of the sports cartoon was the 1930s, '40s, and into the mid–'50s as the genre was elevated by talented artists like Leo O'Mealia, Bob Coyne, Tom Paprocki ("Pap"), John Pierotti, Lenny Hollreiser, Alan Maver, Lou Darvas, Karl Hubenthal, Murray Olderman, and the granddaddy of them all, Willard Mullin. This is just a small sampling of the sports cartoonists working in that period. Most papers had an artist on staff in the pre–TV boom era of newspapers, and the competition among them resulted in amazing advancements in technique, layout, and creativity.

As television grew in popularity in the mid–1950s, newspaper readership began to decline—in the process taking down many of the sports cartoonists who'd come to prominence during the glory days. Some took to writing sports columns to supplement their dwindling illustration assignments. Some began drawing traditional editorial cartoons. Some got out of the business all together. By the 1970s there were just a handful of sports cartoonists holding down the fort, like the great Bruce Stark of *The Daily News*, but the writing was on the wall.

While I have worked diligently for the last 15 years to keep the old style alive, my bio-illustrations have generally been seen by relatively small audiences in the grand scheme of things. Still, I have received numerous comments on how much my work reminds them of the cartoons they saw in the sports pages of their youth, and to me that is the ultimate compliment.

One way in which my bio-illustrations differ from those of golden age sports cartoonists is the amount of text. My bio-illustrations feature much more text. Years ago I sent a few samples of my work to legendary sports cartoonist Murray Olderman to seek his opinion as to where I could improve. Not one to lavish false praise on any artist, Mr. Olderman commented that while my illustration technique was very good, my work would benefit by reducing the amount of text. That was sage advice from an illustrative point of view—which was Mr. Olderman's intent—but I felt it wasn't the best direction for me. Here's why:

The contemporary artists of the golden age of sports cartooning were documenting current events. That allowed them to be much briefer with the text. For example, when Lou Darvas wanted to illustrate the great year reliever Jim Konstanty had just logged for the 1955 Yankees, he was able to do so with a large portrait, a handful of cartoons, and just a few blurbs of text. My bio-illustrations, on the other hand, almost always recount the entire career of the featured player.

My bio-illustrations are said to have a vintage look. I chalk that up to two things—my illustration style and the media I use. My style is a by-product of countless childhood hours spent poring over the works of the sports cartooning masters, then trying to emulate their techniques. End result: my work looks more like that of the sports artists of the 1940s and '50s than that of many other present-day artists who are influenced more by modern trends, like the manga style, for example. And, the media in which I work also contribute greatly to the vintage look. All of the bio-illustrations in this book were produced using now-antiquated media commonly used by sports cartoonists of the past.

Approximately 90 percent of the bio-illustrations in this compilation were produced on Duoshade board. The remainder were done on coquille board. Duoshade was a cartoonist's staple for decades until discontinued around 2009 by the product's only manufacturer. Demand for Duoshade declined significantly over the last decade with the advancement of computer graphics. Eventually, the only artists left using the stuff were crusty old timers who refused to let go, and there simply weren't enough of us to save Duoshade from extinction. Duoshade artists suddenly found themselves scrambling to find sources who still had "new old stock." Now, to the best of my knowledge, there are no stashes left, and Duoshade has gone the way of the dinosaur.

Duoshade was really an ingenious product. It was a bristol board with barely-visible lines printed at 45-degree angles. First, the cartoonist inked the black line-work of his drawing onto the Duoshade board. Most guys used a combination of brushwork and pen work. I pretty much strictly use a brush—a Windsor-Newton Series-7 Number-1 sable. Then, the artist painted on clear developer where he wanted the gray tones to appear. There were two different developers with Duoshade—one bottle activated the light tone lines, and the second bottle activated the dark tone lines. The end result was an illustration with a dynamic range of tones that was actually "camera-ready" line art. This allowed the piece to be enlarged or reduced without any loss of quality. In other words, a Duoshade illustration reproduced wonderfully in the newspaper regardless of size, and that couldn't always be said about newspaper halftone photos.

Coquille board had all the reproduction benefits of Duoshade, but it had quite a different look. Illustrations done on coquille board have a much softer look than that of a Duoshade illustration. This is because coquille board drawings utilize a soft black pencil to achieve the gray tones. As with Duoshade, the artist first inked his black line-work, then used the black pencil to render the tonal areas. Coquille board had a pebbly finish to it, so the pencil only took to the high areas of the rough finish. Light pressure gave the artist light gray tones, while heavier pressure gave him darker grays—but the nature of the pebbly finish ensured that the grays would never be too dark.

As with Duoshade, a completed coquille board cartoon is camera-ready, meaning the cartoonist could rest easy in the belief that his work would not be compromised by a production glitch. There are manufacturers who still make coquille board, but none make the "fine" grade used by the artists of the golden age. The fine grade was ideal for creating all the subtle tones necessary for a good portrait. The "coarse" grade that's still produced will do, and I've used it on a number of pieces in this book, but it's a far cry in quality from the original fine grade.

All this shop talk about artist's media wouldn't mean beans if I had to use these materials to illustrate backyard grills, lawn mowers, or washing machines in the newspaper's weekend sales insert. Instead, I'm using these materials to illustrate baseball history. It's hard to say what I enjoyed more while growing up—playing baseball or drawing. I have notebooks filled with baseball cards that I collected avidly from 1970 to 1975. But I also have notebooks stuffed to capacity with my childhood drawings of ballplayers and comic book superheroes. In any case, whatever dreams I had of playing ball beyond high school evaporated quickly after tearing up my knee playing centerfield in my senior year. My art, on the other hand, always gave me better opportunities for advancement than did my baseball skills. So I set my sights on a career in art and ventured off to the University of Maryland to get the necessary schooling.

My love of baseball history led me to dedicate my abilities to documenting the colorful stories and characters of the game. As for who to draw, I never really cared whether a ballplayer I was illustrating had a 20-year career or a 20-minute career. My personal compulsion was to choose subjects based on interesting story lines, and I found those could come from Hall of Famers (the Legends from the title of this book), the everyday players (the Journeymen), or the cup-of-coffee guys (the Short-Timers). And while almost all of the bio-illustrations in this collection are of major league players, there are, however, an assortment of interesting exceptions—minor leaguers, negro leaguers, female players, entertainers, et al.

My bio-illustrating began when the folks at the Washington Baseball Historical Society asked me to contribute to their quarterly newsletter. The historical society was a group dedicated to preserving the legacy of the Washington Senators. This was a very exciting opportunity for me because having been born in Washington, D.C., and raised in the nearby Maryland suburbs, I was a rabid Senators fan until their departure for Texas when I was nine years old.

Within a few years I was creating bio-illustrations for publications of the St. Louis Browns Historical Society, the Philadelphia Athletics Historical Society, and the Boston Braves Historical Society. This eventually led to my work with *Sports Collectors Digest*, a weekly memorabilia publication out of Iola, Wisconsin. *SCD* ran one of my bio-illustrations every week. No longer confined to drawing only Senators, Browns, Athletics, or Braves, the sky was the limit—and it is my bio-illustrations for all of the aforementioned publications that make up the bulk of what is in this book.

I like a lot of pictures in the baseball books I read. Yet here I've already violated my own axiom with this long, picture-less preface. So enough said—page forward and enjoy. And in the words of 1950s Reds outfielder Jim Greengrass (was there ever a better baseball name?), many happy innings!

ASSORTED LEGENDS, JOURNEYMEN, AND SHORT-TIMERS

Wally MOON

SHOOT FOR THE MOON AND YOU MIGHT VERY WELL BECOME A STAR! THAT CERTAINLY PROVED TO BE THE CASE FOR 1954 N.L. ROOKIE OF THE YEAR WALLACE WADE MOON! WALLY HAD STARRED IN BASEBALL AND BASKETBALL FOR TEXAS A&M, THEN LABORED FOR FOUR YEARS IN THE CARDINALS FARM SYSTEM WHEN HE MADE A FATEFUL DECISION! UNINVITED, HE REPORTED TO CARDS SPRING TRAINING IN ST. PETERSBURG AND TOLD THE ST. LOUIS BRASS THAT HE'D QUIT THE GAME IF THEY DIDN'T GIVE HIM A REAL SHOT TO PROVE THAT HE BELONGED ON THEIR BIG LEAGUE ROSTER! IN A HIGH STAKES GAME OF CHICKEN, THEY BLINKED -- AND WALLY WENT ON TO HAVE SUCH A FINE SPRING THAT THEY HAD NO CHOICE BUT TO WRITE HIS NAME IN THEIR OPENING DAY LINEUP! UNFORTUNATELY, WALLY'S PLACE ON THE ROSTER MADE OBSOLETE A ST. LOUIS LEGEND -- THE GREAT ENOS SLAUGHTER -- SO "COUNTRY" WAS DEALT AWAY TO THE NEW YORK YANKEES! CARDS FANS WEREN'T SO SURE ABOUT THE SWITCH, AND THEY VOICED THEIR OPINIONS WITH A "WE WANT SLAUGHTER" CHANT AS WALLY STEPPED UP FOR HIS FIRST CAREER AT-BAT! MOMENTS LATER THE CHANT TURNED INTO CHEERS FOR WALLY WHEN HE DEPOSITED A PAUL MINNER PITCH INTO THE BUSCH STADIUM SEATS! IT WAS A GREAT BEGINNING TO WHAT WOULD TURN INTO A FINE 12-YEAR BIG LEAGUE CAREER IN WHICH WALLY HIT .289 WITH 1,399 HITS AND 142 HOMERS! A SPEEDY OUTFIELDER WITH A STRONG ARM, WALLY WAS A GOLD GLOVE WINNER AND A 3-TIME ALL-STAR! A DEVOUT CHRISTIAN, WALLY FOUND THE PERFECT JOB WHEN HE RETIRED FROM PLAYING -- HE BECAME THE ATHLETIC DIRECTOR AND BASEBALL COACH AT JOHN BROWN U. -- A CHRISTIAN COLLEGE IN HIS HOME STATE OF ARKANSAS!

WALLY WAS DEALT TO THE LOS ANGELES DODGERS PRIOR TO THE 1959 SEASON, AND IT TURNED OUT TO BE A REBIRTH FOR HIM! HIS BATTING AVERAGE SOARED WHILE PLAYING FOR L.A., AND HIS DODGERS WON THREE WORLD SERIES CROWNS DURING HIS YEARS WITH THE CLUB! AND PLAYING IN THE COLISEUM WITH ITS SHORT BUT TALL LEFTFIELD WALL GAVE BIRTH TO THE "MOON SHOT" -- A NATIONAL SENSATION IN '59 WHEN THE DODGERS WON THEIR FIRST TITLE IN LOS ANGELES! A LEFTY HITTER, WALLY RETOOLED HIS SWING AND BECAME ADEPT AT POPPING HIGH FLIES -- MOON SHOTS -- OVER THE TALL OPPOSITE FIELD WALL! FITTINGLY, WALLY MOON TALLIED THE QUIRKY COLISEUM'S FINAL RUN IN 1961!

Billy SOUTHWORTH

WILLIAM HAROLD SOUTHWORTH WAS BORN ON MARCH 9, 1893, IN HARVARD, NEBRASKA! "BILLY" GREW UP IN COLUMBUS, OHIO, AND IT WAS THERE THAT HE LAID THE FOUNDATION FOR A LIFETIME AFFAIR WITH THE GAME OF BASEBALL! IN SPITE OF HIS FATHER'S RESERVATIONS, BILLY TIRELESSLY CHASED HIS DREAM OF MAKING IT TO THE BIG LEAGUES! HIS EFFORTS PAID OFF IN 1913 WHEN HE MADE HIS DEBUT AS AN OUTFIELDER WITH THE CLEVELAND INDIANS! ONE OF THE HIGH POINTS OF BILLY'S CAREER CAME 13 YEARS LATER WHEN HE HIT .320 WITH 16 HOMERS AND 99 RBIs WHILE SPLITTING THE SEASON BETWEEN THE GIANTS AND CARDINALS! BILLY'S CONTRIBUTION HELPED PUSH THE CARDS TO THE PENNANT, AND ONCE IN THE SERIES HE HELPED LIFT HIS CLUB TO VICTORY OVER THE YANKEES! BILLY BATTED .345 IN THE SERIES, AND HIS 3-RUN HOMER IN GAME TWO NAILED DOWN THE WIN FOR GROVER CLEVELAND ALEXANDER! NOT GIFTED WITH SUPERLATIVE TALENT, BILLY ETCHED OUT A FINE 13-YEAR CAREER THROUGH HARD WORK AND HUSTLE! "I HAD TO HUSTLE," HE SAID, "BECAUSE I WAS A SMALL FELLOW. I KNEW I HAD TO PUT OUT THAT MUCH MORE THAN A FELLOW WITH BETTER PHYSICAL EQUIPMENT." BILLY APPLIED THAT SAME WORK ETHIC IN LATER YEARS WHEN HE BEGAN HIS CAREER AS A MANAGER! HE LED THE CARDINALS TO THREE STRAIGHT PENNANTS FROM 1942-44, WINNING IT ALL IN 1942 AND '44! AN OFFER OF $50,000 LURED BILLY TO JOIN BOSTON IN 1946, AND TWO SHORT YEARS LATER THE BRAVES REAPED THE BENEFIT -- THEIR FIRST FLAG IN 34 YEARS! DESPITE GREAT SUCCESS ON THE BALLFIELD, BILLY'S LIFE WAS NOT WITHOUT HARDSHIP! HIS SON, BILLY JR., A MINOR LEAGUE M.V.P. BALLPLAYER, COMPLETED A FULL TOUR OF DUTY PILOTING B-17s OVER WAR-RAVAGED EUROPE, ONLY TO BE TRAGICALLY KILLED STATESIDE WHILE PILOTING A DISABLED B-29 ON FEBRUARY 15, 1945! SENIOR FORGED AHEAD, AND WAS POSTHUMOUSLY ELECTED TO THE HALL OF FAME IN 2008!

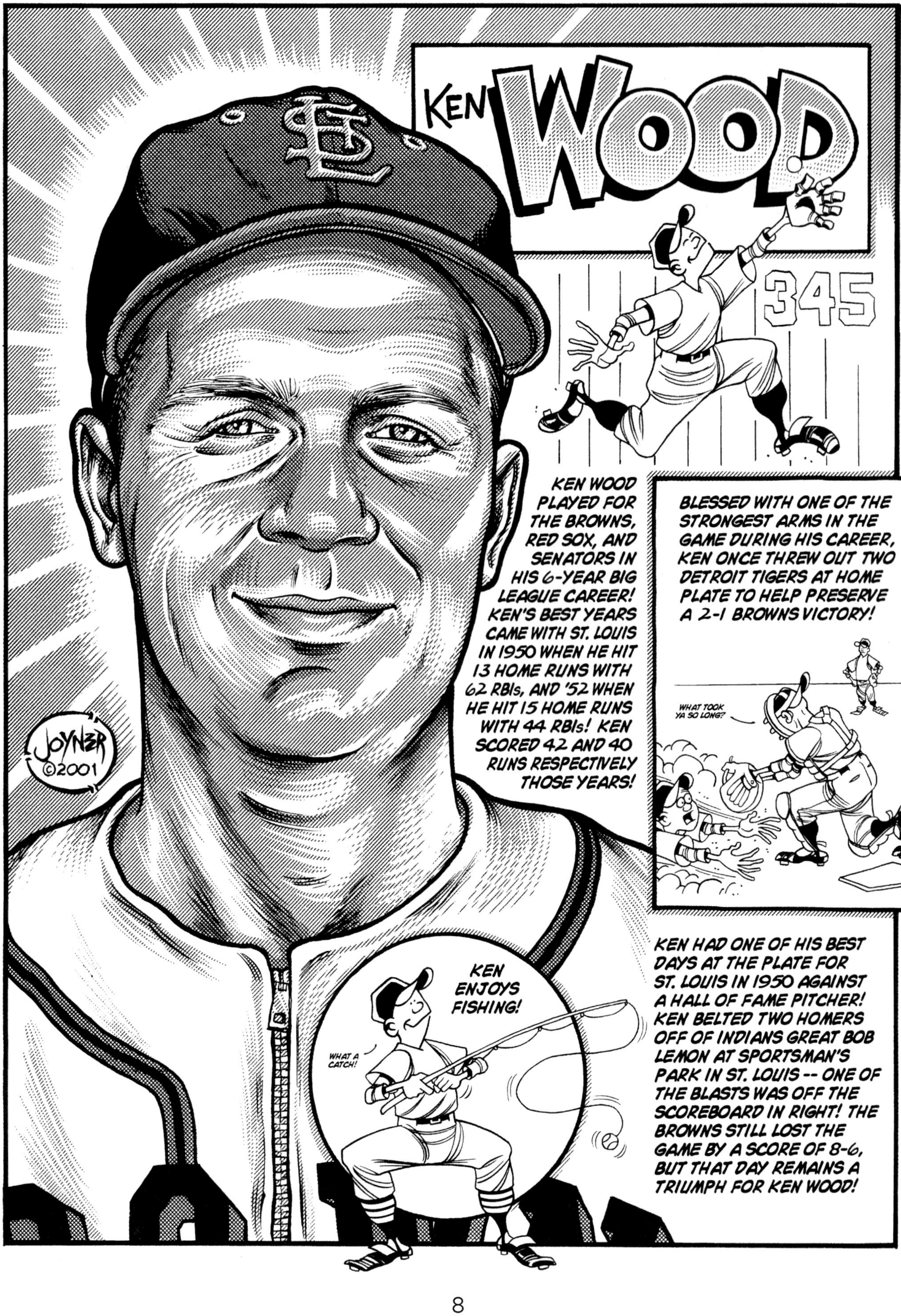
KEN WOOD
345
KEN WOOD PLAYED FOR THE BROWNS, RED SOX, AND SENATORS IN HIS 6-YEAR BIG LEAGUE CAREER! KEN'S BEST YEARS CAME WITH ST. LOUIS IN 1950 WHEN HE HIT 13 HOME RUNS WITH 62 RBIs, AND '52 WHEN HE HIT 15 HOME RUNS WITH 44 RBIs! KEN SCORED 42 AND 40 RUNS RESPECTIVELY THOSE YEARS!
BLESSED WITH ONE OF THE STRONGEST ARMS IN THE GAME DURING HIS CAREER, KEN ONCE THREW OUT TWO DETROIT TIGERS AT HOME PLATE TO HELP PRESERVE A 2-1 BROWNS VICTORY!
WHAT TOOK YA SO LONG?
JOYNER ©2001
KEN ENJOYS FISHING!
WHAT A CATCH!
KEN HAD ONE OF HIS BEST DAYS AT THE PLATE FOR ST. LOUIS IN 1950 AGAINST A HALL OF FAME PITCHER! KEN BELTED TWO HOMERS OFF OF INDIANS GREAT BOB LEMON AT SPORTSMAN'S PARK IN ST. LOUIS -- ONE OF THE BLASTS WAS OFF THE SCOREBOARD IN RIGHT! THE BROWNS STILL LOST THE GAME BY A SCORE OF 8-6, BUT THAT DAY REMAINS A TRIUMPH FOR KEN WOOD!

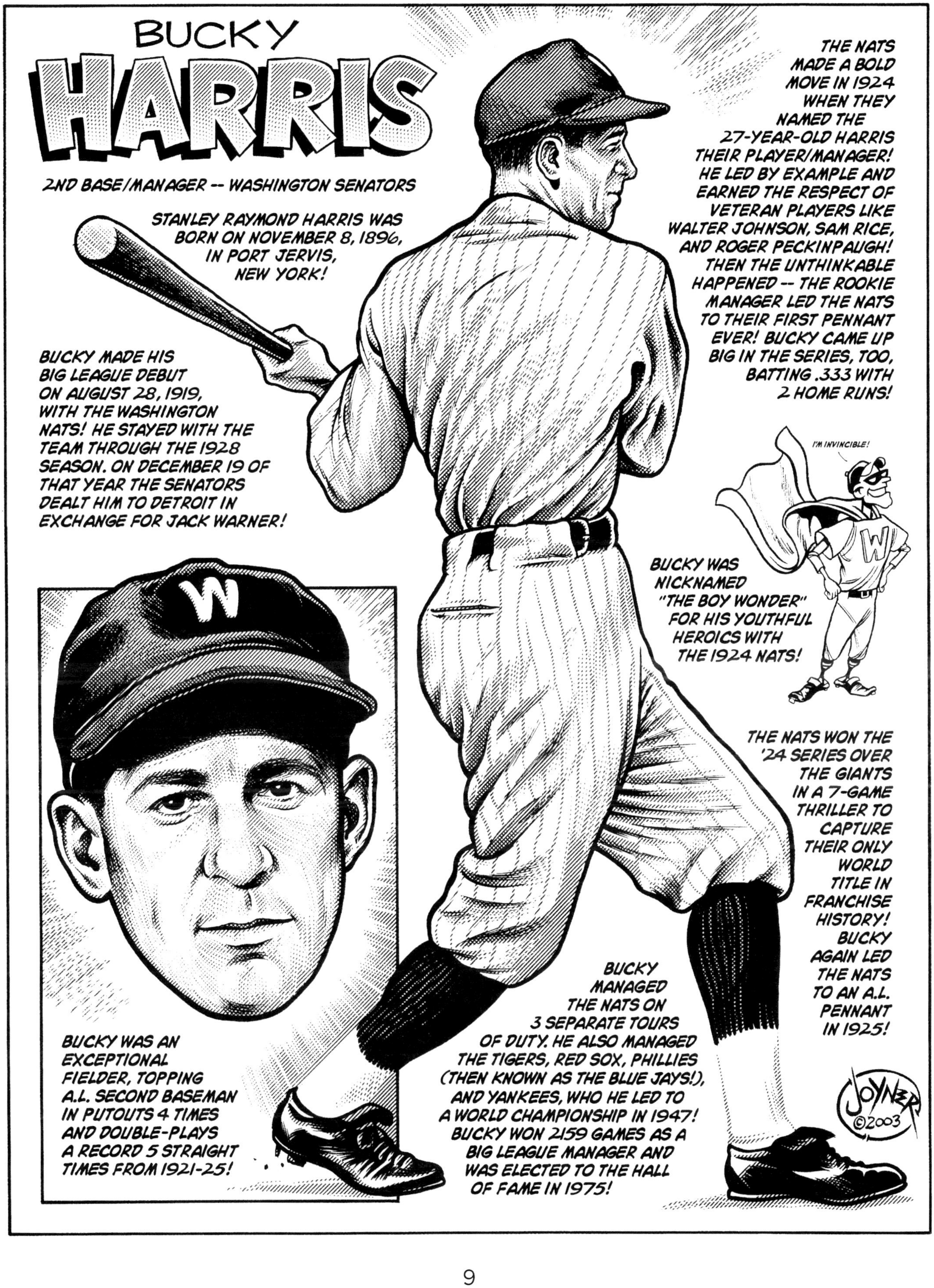
BUCKY HARRIS
2ND BASE/MANAGER -- WASHINGTON SENATORS
STANLEY RAYMOND HARRIS WAS BORN ON NOVEMBER 8, 1896, IN PORT JERVIS, NEW YORK!
BUCKY MADE HIS BIG LEAGUE DEBUT ON AUGUST 28, 1919, WITH THE WASHINGTON NATS! HE STAYED WITH THE TEAM THROUGH THE 1928 SEASON. ON DECEMBER 19 OF THAT YEAR THE SENATORS DEALT HIM TO DETROIT IN EXCHANGE FOR JACK WARNER!
THE NATS MADE A BOLD MOVE IN 1924 WHEN THEY NAMED THE 27-YEAR-OLD HARRIS THEIR PLAYER/MANAGER! HE LED BY EXAMPLE AND EARNED THE RESPECT OF VETERAN PLAYERS LIKE WALTER JOHNSON, SAM RICE, AND ROGER PECKINPAUGH! THEN THE UNTHINKABLE HAPPENED -- THE ROOKIE MANAGER LED THE NATS TO THEIR FIRST PENNANT EVER! BUCKY CAME UP BIG IN THE SERIES, TOO, BATTING .333 WITH 2 HOME RUNS!
I'M INVINCIBLE!
BUCKY WAS NICKNAMED "THE BOY WONDER" FOR HIS YOUTHFUL HEROICS WITH THE 1924 NATS!
THE NATS WON THE '24 SERIES OVER THE GIANTS IN A 7-GAME THRILLER TO CAPTURE THEIR ONLY WORLD TITLE IN FRANCHISE HISTORY! BUCKY AGAIN LED THE NATS TO AN A.L. PENNANT IN 1925!
BUCKY WAS AN EXCEPTIONAL FIELDER, TOPPING A.L. SECOND BASEMAN IN PUTOUTS 4 TIMES AND DOUBLE-PLAYS A RECORD 5 STRAIGHT TIMES FROM 1921-25!
BUCKY MANAGED THE NATS ON 3 SEPARATE TOURS OF DUTY. HE ALSO MANAGED THE TIGERS, RED SOX, PHILLIES (THEN KNOWN AS THE BLUE JAYS!), AND YANKEES, WHO HE LED TO A WORLD CHAMPIONSHIP IN 1947! BUCKY WON 2159 GAMES AS A BIG LEAGUE MANAGER AND WAS ELECTED TO THE HALL OF FAME IN 1975!
JOYNER ©2003

Chuck STOBBS

ON APRIL 7, 1953, 23-YEAR-OLD WASHINGTON SENATORS LEFT-HANDER CHUCK STOBBS SERVED UP A GOPHER BALL TO PROLIFIC YOUNG YANKEE SLUGGER MICKEY MANTLE. NO SHAME IN THAT -- THE MICK WAS CLOUTING ROUND-TRIPPERS AT A PRETTY HEALTHY RATE BY 1953. BUT CHUCK KNEW THIS ONE WAS DIFFERENT. THE BALL WAS STILL AIRBORNE AS MANTLE ROUNDED SECOND BASE, AND CHUCK HUNG HIS HEAD AS HIS GLOVE SLIPPED QUIETLY OFF HIS HAND AND FELL TO THE MOUND. IT WAS ALMOST AS IF HE KNEW THAT THIS WAS A DUBIOUS MOMENT -- ONE THAT WOULD BE WITH HIM FOREVER. AND THAT'S EXACTLY WHAT HAPPENED. WHAT SET THIS HOMER APART FROM ALL OTHERS WAS ITS LENGTH. IT COMPLETELY LEFT GRIFFITH STADIUM, TRAVELING A DISTANCE ESTIMATED AT 565 FEET. THE BLAST WAS BIG NEWS IN THE SPORTS PAGES, AND THE REPORTING OF IT SPAWNED A NEW PHRASE -- THE "TAPE MEASURE" SHOT -- SUPPOSEDLY COINED BY WASHINGTON SPORTSWRITER SHIRLEY POVICH. NOW, WHENEVER THE NAME OF CHUCK STOBBS IS MENTIONED, IT IS LIKELY IN CONJUNCTION WITH THE RETELLING OF THE TALE OF MANTLE'S 565-FOOT BOMB. IT'S AN UNFAIR FATE FOR STOBBS, A LEGENDARY 3-SPORT ATHLETE IN VIRGINIA'S TIDEWATER AREA AND A MAN WHO WOULD WIN 107 GAMES OVER 15 BIG LEAGUE SEASONS. BUT SUCH CAN BE THE CRUELTY OF BASEBALL HISTORY (SEE: MERKLE, FRED; BUCKNER, BILL; BRANCA, RALPH; MAYS, CARL; OWEN, MICKEY; DAVIS, WILLIE; ETC.).

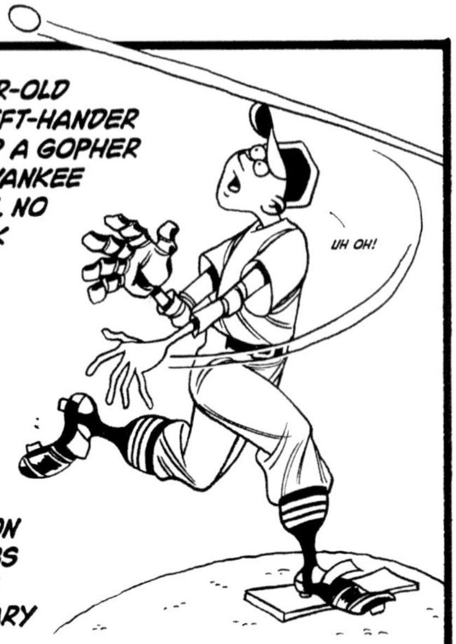

"THE WIND HELPED CARRY IT," CHUCK SAID IN THE 1990 BOOK 'WHEN THE CHEERING STOPS.' "THE PAPERS HAD A BOX TO SHOW WHERE THE BALL WENT. NATIONAL BOHEMIAN BEER, THE SPONSOR OF OUR GAMES, PUT A BIG BASEBALL UP ON THE SCOREBOARD WHERE IT HIT. BUCKY HARRIS, OUR MANAGER, GOT SORE AND MADE THEM TAKE IT DOWN. EVERY TIME A NEW TEAM CAME IN, THE PLAYERS WOULD POINT AND ASK, 'IS THAT WHERE HE HIT IT?' AND I'D SAY, 'YEAH, THAT'S IT.' WHADDAYA GONNA DO? AFTER A WHILE I GOT OVER IT AND DIDN'T MIND ANSWERING THE QUESTIONS -- DEPENDING ON HOW PEOPLE ASKED. IF HE HIT IT 600 FEET OR 320 FEET, IT DIDN'T COUNT ANY MORE OR LESS. I GUESS SOME PEOPLE ARE ALWAYS GONNA REMEMBER THAT HOMER, BUT THERE'S SO MUCH MORE (TO MY CAREER)."

CHUCK STOBBS IS AS GOOD AN EXAMPLE AS YOU'LL EVER FIND OF HOW BITTERSWEET THE LIFE OF A BIG LEAGUER CAN BE. HE MADE IT TO THE SHOW AND WON OVER 100 GAMES, YET HE IS ETERNALLY DOGGED BY THE 565-FOOTER. AND HE STILL DREAMS OF WHAT IT WOULD BE LIKE HAD HE JUST CAUGHT A BREAK AND BEEN A HERO. BUT HIS DREAMS ARE OFTEN RUINED BY HIS STAR-CROSSED REALITY -- LIKE IN '49 WHEN HE PITCHED A GEM FOR BOSTON AGAINST THE NATS WITH THE PENNANT ON THE LINE. RELIEVED BY 20-GAME WINNERS MEL PARNELL AND ELLIS KINDER, THE SOX BLEW THE LEAD AND LOST, 2-1. "THEN THE YANKS BEAT US TWICE AND WE LOST THE PENNANT BY ONE GAME," SAID CHUCK. "HECK, IF WE HADN'T BLOWN THE GAME AGAINST WASHINGTON, I COULDA BEEN A HERO."

Joe DeMaestri

BORN ON SUNDAY, DECEMBER 9, 1928, IN SAN FRANCISCO, CALIFORNIA, JOSEPH PAUL DeMAESTRI WAS 22 YEARS OLD WHEN HE BROKE INTO THE BIG LEAGUES WITH THE 1951 CHICAGO WHITE SOX! "PAUL RICHARDS WAS THE MANAGER," JOE TOLD BASEBALL DIGEST BACK IN 2003, "AND HE WAS THE SMARTEST, TOUGHEST, MOST INTENSE MANAGER I EVER PLAYED FOR. NO CONVERSATION. NO WORDS OF ENCOURAGEMENT. SELDOM A SMILE. BUT HE WAS ALWAYS TWO, THREE INNINGS AHEAD." 1952 SAW THE YOUNG SHORTSTOP MOVE TO THE BROWNS WHERE ROGERS HORNSBY WAS THE MANAGER! HORNSBY WAS HATED BY THE BROWNIE PLAYERS, AND SUBSEQUENTLY FIRED IN MIDSEASON! "WE ALL CHIPPED IN AND GAVE OWNER BILL VEECK A TROPHY FOR LIBERATING US," JOE RECALLED. JOE WAS DEALT TO THE PHILADELPHIA ATHLETICS THE NEXT SEASON, BEGINNING A SEVEN YEAR RUN WHERE HE WAS THE A'S REGULAR SHORTSTOP! AFTER MANY YEARS IN THE SECOND DIVISION, JOE WAS TRADED TO THE YANKEES WHERE HE WOULD SOON ENJOY THE BOUNTIFUL HARVEST OF THE BRONX BOMBERS' WINNING WAYS!

JOE WAS KNOWN FOR HIS SURE-HANDED GLOVEWORK!

"STENGEL WOULD SLEEP ON THE BENCH BEHIND THOSE DARK GLASSES," JOE SAID OF THE HALL OF FAME YANKEE SKIPPER. "IT DIDN'T MAKE ANY DIFFERENCE. HE DIDN'T HAVE TO SAY ANYTHING WITH THE KIND OF TEAM HE HAD. I COULD HAVE MANAGED THOSE TEAMS." JOE WAS PART OF THE 1960 A.L. CHAMPION YANKS WHO LOST TO THE PIRATES ON BILL MAZEROSKI'S BIG HOMER, AND HE WAS ALSO WITH THE 1961 CLUB THAT WON IT ALL AGAINST THE REDS! ACCORDING TO JOE, JOINING THE YANKEES WAS "THE BEST MOVE I EVER MADE. TWO YEARS, TWO WORLD SERIES."

Max Bishop

2ND BASE
PHILADELPHIA A's

CONNIE MACK PAID A STAGGERING $50,000 TO OBTAIN MAX FROM THE ORIOLES IN 1924!

MAX FREDERICK BISHOP WAS BORN ON SEPTEMBER 5, 1899, IN WAYNESBORO, PA! THE LAD LEFT HIGH SCHOOL IN 1918 TO JOIN JACK DUNN'S BALTIMORE ORIOLES -- AN ALL-TIME GREAT BALLCLUB THAT WON SEVEN CONSECUTIVE INTERNATIONAL LEAGUE PENNANTS FROM 1919 THROUGH 1925! MAX MISSED OUT ON THE LAST TWO ORIOLES TITLES WHEN HE JOINED CONNIE MACK'S PHILADELPHIA A's FOR THE 1924 SEASON, BUT HE WAS SOON REWARDED WITH THREE STRAIGHT ATHLETICS PENNANTS FROM 1929-31 AND TWO WORLD SERIES CROWNS IN 1929 AND '30!

MAX CONTRIBUTED GREATLY TO THE ATHLETICS' SUCCESS AS A TOP-NOTCH LEADOFF MAN WHO EXCELLED AT GETTING ON BASE, SETTING THE TABLE FOR SLUGGERS LIKE FOXX, SIMMONS AND COCHRANE! MAX HAD AN UNCANNY ABILITY TO COAX WALKS, A TALENT THAT EARNED HIM THE NICKNAME "CAMERA EYE"! MAX'S GLOVE AT SECOND BASE WAS ALSO A KEY TO PHILADELPHIA'S GOLDEN AGE, SOLIDIFYING THEIR DEFENSE UP THE MIDDLE WITH HIS 4-TIME LEAGUE-LEADING LEATHER-WORK!

MAX WAS BELOVED IN PHILADELPHIA FOR HIS TREMENDOUS ABILITY ON THE BALLFIELD, BUT IT WAS HIS QUIET, GENTLEMANLY DEMEANOR THAT TRULY ENDEARED HIM TO THE FANS! THAT MADE IT ESPECIALLY DIFFICULT FOR A's FAN TO SEE HIM DEALT TO THE RED SOX IN 1934 WHEN MR. MACK BROKE UP THE A's DYNASTY! MAX PLAYED FOR BOSTON IN 1934-35 BEFORE RETURNING TO THE ORIOLES IN 1936 AND SCOUTING FOR THE TIGERS IN 1937! MAX LATER MANAGED THE NAVAL ACADEMY BASEBALL TEAM FOR 24 YEARS, COMPILING AN EYE-POPPING RECORD OF 306-143!

STAR SECOND BASEMAN -- DETROIT TIGERS
EDDIE MAYO
THIRD BASEMAN EDDIE MAYO MADE HIS FIRST BIG LEAGUE APPEARANCE IN 1936 WITH THE NEW YORK GIANTS SPELLING TEAMMATE TRAVIS JACKSON IN 40 GAMES! EDDIE'S ROOKIE YEAR TURNED OUT TO BE A MEMORABLE ONE AS HIS GIANTS WON THE NATIONAL LEAGUE PENNANT AND EDDIE ENJOYED THE THRILL OF APPEARING IN HIS FIRST WORLD SERIES! EDDIE SPENT 1937-38 IN BEANTOWN AFTER THE GIANTS DEALT HIM STRAIGHT UP FOR BEES INFIELDER MICKEY HASLIN! AFTER SOME SEASONING IN THE MINORS FROM 1939-42, EDDIE JOINED THE PHILADELPHIA A's FOR 1943!
HOW'S THIS, KID?!
EQUIPMENT
20
EDDIE PLAYED 128 GAMES FOR THE 1943 A's, BUT HE MOVED ON TO BIGGER AND BETTER THINGS THE NEXT SEASON WHEN HE JOINED THE DETROIT TIGERS! SHIFTING TO 2ND BASE, EDDIE SAW ACTION IN A CAREER-HIGH 154 GAMES AND RAISED HIS AVERAGE 30 POINTS! EDDIE ALSO LED ALL A.L. 2ND-SACKERS IN TURNING DOUBLE-PLAYS IN 1944!
HEY -- HOW'D YOU DO THAT?!
JOYNER ©2003
EDDIE KNOCKED OUT 7 HITS IN THE 1945 WORLD SERIES!
I LIKE THE BIG STAGE!
7
EDDIE WAS JUST GETTING WARM IN '44! HE HIT A CAREER-HIGH .285 WITH 10 LONG BALLS IN 1945 WHILE CONTINUING HIS STELLAR PLAY AT 2ND! HIS SOLID PLAY AND LEADERSHIP HELPED HIS TIGERS WIN THE AMERICAN LEAGUE PENNANT IN 1945! THEY THEN TOOK THE WORLD SERIES FROM THE CUBS IN A 7-GAME NAIL-BITER IN WHICH EDDIE HIT .250! IN A PECULIAR WARTIME FOOTNOTE, EDDIE WAS SELECTED TO THE 1945 A.L. ALL-STAR TEAM, BUT THE GAME WAS CANCELLED DUE TO WWII TRAVEL RESTRICTIONS! HIS FINE 1945 SEASON WAS CAPPED NICELY WHEN THE SPORTING NEWS NAMED HIM THE MOST VALUABLE NON-PITCHER IN THE A.L.! EDDIE SPENT 3 MORE SOLID YEARS AS A PLAYER FOR THE TIGERS BEFORE MOVING ON TO MANAGING THE TOLEDO MUD HENS AND COACHING WITH THE RED SOX AND PHILLIES!

IRV HALL
IRVIN GLADSTONE HALL WAS BORN ON OCTOBER 17, 1918, IN ALBERTON, MARYLAND! IRV, SLENDER AT 5-FOOT-11-INCHES AND 160 LBS, BECAME THE ATHLETICS' FULL-TIME SHORTSTOP IN 1943 AFTER FINISHING SECOND IN BATTING WITH WILLIAMSPORT OF THE EASTERN LEAGUE IN 1942! PHILADELPHIA OWNER-MANAGER CONNIE MACK BROUGHT IN IRV BY SIGNING HIM TO A $2,500 SALARY WITH A $1,200 BONUS! MR. MACK GOT MORE THAN HIS MONEY'S WORTH WHEN YOUNG IRV TURNED IN A FINE ROOKIE SEASON, DEMONSTRATING STELLAR GLOVE WORK WHILE BATTING .256!
IRV GRADUATED WITH A B.S. DEGREE IN MECHANICAL ENGINEERING IN 1981 -- 35 YEARS AFTER BEGINNING WORK ON THE DEGREE AT JOHNS HOPKINS IN 1946!
BETTER LATE THAN NEVER!
IRV MADE HIS BIG LEAGUE DEBUT IN THE 1943 SEASON-OPENER, A 7-5 LOSS AT WASHINGTON! HELD HITLESS IN THAT GAME AS WELL AS THE NEXT, IRV FINALLY REGISTERED HIS FIRST HIT ON APRIL 23RD WHEN HE SINGLED OFF BOSTON'S JOE DOBSON IN A 5-0 WIN AT SHIBE PARK! A FAVORITE OF CONNIE MACK, IRV WENT ON TO BE A FIXTURE IN THE A's INFIELD THROUGH THE 1945 SEASON! IRV, EQUALLY PROFICIENT AS A SHORT-STOP OR SECOND-SACKER, ALWAYS EXHIBITED SLICK FIELDING AND WAS PARTICULARLY ADEPT AT THE PIVOT WHEN EXECUTING A TWIN-KILLING!
IRV WAS STEADY WITH THE BAT, HITTING .261 FOR HIS CAREER IN THE MAJORS! HE AVERAGED ABOUT 50 RBIs PER SEASON, AND NONE WAS MORE IMPORTANT THAN THE ONE HE SENT HOME ON SEPTEMBER 9, 1946! ON THAT DAY, IRV HIT A 9TH-INNING SINGLE TO SCORE HAL PECK, DRIVING IN THE ONLY RUN IN DICK FOWLER'S DRAMATIC 1-0 NO-HITTER AGAINST THE ST. LOUIS BROWNS! AMAZINGLY, IT WAS FOWLER'S FIRST START AFTER RECENTLY RETURNING FROM THE ARMY!
JOYNER ©2006

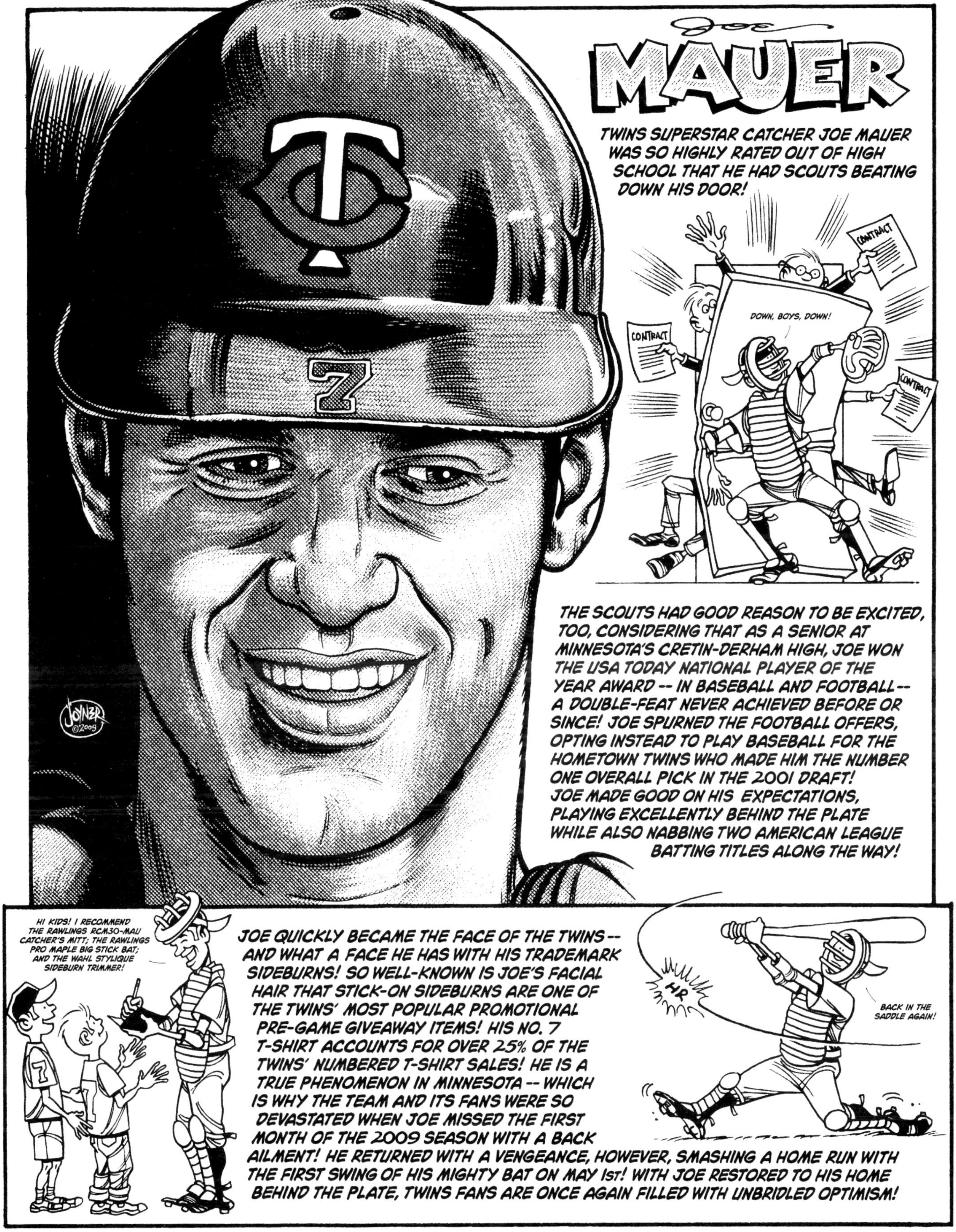
JOE MAUER
TWINS SUPERSTAR CATCHER JOE MAUER WAS SO HIGHLY RATED OUT OF HIGH SCHOOL THAT HE HAD SCOUTS BEATING DOWN HIS DOOR!
CONTRACT
DOWN, BOYS, DOWN!
CONTRACT
CONTRACT
THE SCOUTS HAD GOOD REASON TO BE EXCITED, TOO, CONSIDERING THAT AS A SENIOR AT MINNESOTA'S CRETIN-DERHAM HIGH, JOE WON THE USA TODAY NATIONAL PLAYER OF THE YEAR AWARD -- IN BASEBALL AND FOOTBALL -- A DOUBLE-FEAT NEVER ACHIEVED BEFORE OR SINCE! JOE SPURNED THE FOOTBALL OFFERS, OPTING INSTEAD TO PLAY BASEBALL FOR THE HOMETOWN TWINS WHO MADE HIM THE NUMBER ONE OVERALL PICK IN THE 2001 DRAFT! JOE MADE GOOD ON HIS EXPECTATIONS, PLAYING EXCELLENTLY BEHIND THE PLATE WHILE ALSO NABBING TWO AMERICAN LEAGUE BATTING TITLES ALONG THE WAY!
JOYNER ©2009
HI KIDS! I RECOMMEND THE RAWLINGS RCM30-MAU CATCHER'S MITT; THE RAWLINGS PRO MAPLE BIG STICK BAT; AND THE WAHL STYLIQUE SIDEBURN TRIMMER!
JOE QUICKLY BECAME THE FACE OF THE TWINS -- AND WHAT A FACE HE HAS WITH HIS TRADEMARK SIDEBURNS! SO WELL-KNOWN IS JOE'S FACIAL HAIR THAT STICK-ON SIDEBURNS ARE ONE OF THE TWINS' MOST POPULAR PROMOTIONAL PRE-GAME GIVEAWAY ITEMS! HIS NO. 7 T-SHIRT ACCOUNTS FOR OVER 25% OF THE TWINS' NUMBERED T-SHIRT SALES! HE IS A TRUE PHENOMENON IN MINNESOTA -- WHICH IS WHY THE TEAM AND ITS FANS WERE SO DEVASTATED WHEN JOE MISSED THE FIRST MONTH OF THE 2009 SEASON WITH A BACK AILMENT! HE RETURNED WITH A VENGEANCE, HOWEVER, SMASHING A HOME RUN WITH THE FIRST SWING OF HIS MIGHTY BAT ON MAY 1st! WITH JOE RESTORED TO HIS HOME BEHIND THE PLATE, TWINS FANS ARE ONCE AGAIN FILLED WITH UNBRIDLED OPTIMISM!
HR
BACK IN THE SADDLE AGAIN!

Ted LEPCIO

FROM SETON HALL'S ESTEEMED CORRIDORS OF HIGHER LEARNING BURST INFIELDER TED LEPCIO, READY TO TACKLE THE BUSINESS WORLD WITH HIS BACHELOR'S DEGREE -- BUT ONLY AFTER HE FIRST TOOK A SHOT AT PRO BASEBALL! TED WAS A STANDOUT ON SETON HALL'S BASEBALL TEAM, HELPING HIS 1950 SQUAD WIN THE NCAA DISTRICT II CHAMPIONSHIP THAT QUALIFIED THEM FOR THE COLLEGE WORLD SERIES! TED WAS REWARDED FOR HIS COLLEGE EXCELLENCE BY BEING ELECTED TO THE PIRATES' HALL OF FAME IN '73! THE RED SOX SIGNED TED TO A BIG BONUS, AND THEN ASSIGNED HIM TO THEIR CLASS-B AFFILIATE IN 1951! BY THE END OF 1952, TED WAS ALREADY COMPLETING HIS FIRST YEAR IN THE BIGS, HAVING HIT A RESPECTABLE .263 WITH FIVE HOMERS IN 84 GAMES! TED SETTLED NICELY INTO HIS ROLE AS RED SOX UTILITY MAN, AVERAGING .244, EIGHT LONG BALLS, AND 74 GAMES PER YEAR FROM '53 THROUGH '58! A HUMBLE MAN AT HEART, TED TOLD THE BOSTON GLOBE, "IT DIDN'T MATTER IF YOU WERE A BIG STAR. EVERYBODY WENT THROUGH THE SAME AGONY. YOU GOT THE SAME BLISTERS ON YOUR HANDS, AND YOU SUFFERED THE SAME HUMILIATION WHEN YOU STRUCK OUT."

TED MIGHT HAVE HAD HIS FAIR SHARE OF WHIFFS, BUT HE ALSO HAD A PENCHANT FOR THE BIG HIT! TED COUNTS THE FOUR GRAND SLAMS HE CLUBBED AMONG THE HIGHLIGHTS OF HIS CAREER -- AND NONE WAS MORE SATISFYING THAN THE ONE HE HIT ON MAY 5, 1959! DEALT BY THE SOX TO THE TIGERS JUST THREE DAYS EARLIER, TED MADE HIS DETROIT DEBUT AGAINST HIS FORMER BOSTON MATES -- AND MADE THEM PAY WHEN HE SMASHED A FOUR-RUN FOUR-BAGGER! BACK SURGERY FORCED TED TO CALL IT QUITS AFTER THE '61 SEASON, BUT HE WENT ON TO TO A LONG AND BOUNTIFUL CAREER IN SALES! MUCH OF TED'S POST-BASEBALL SALES SUCCESS CAN BE ATTRIBUTED TO THE WARM AND FRIENDLY DISPOSITION HE EXHIBITED DURING HIS PLAYING DAYS -- TRAITS THAT SERVED HIM WELL IN HIS SECOND CAREER AS A SALESMAN! NOWADAYS, TED CAN OFTEN BE SPOTTED AT FENWAY PARK WERE HE'S BEEN A BOSOX SEASON TICKET HOLDER FOR OVER 30 YEARS!

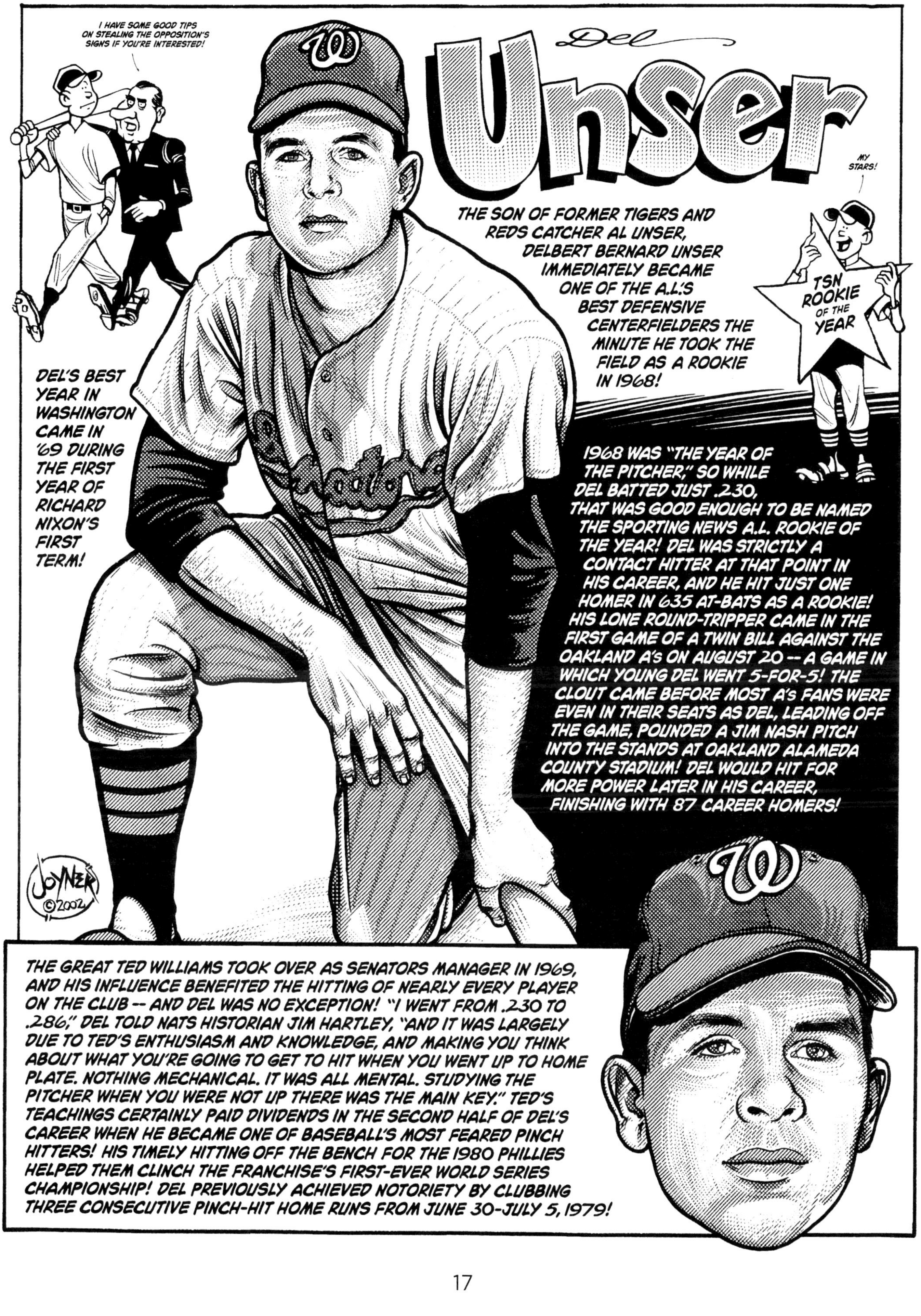

I HAVE SOME GOOD TIPS ON STEALING THE OPPOSITION'S SIGNS IF YOU'RE INTERESTED!
Del Unser
THE SON OF FORMER TIGERS AND REDS CATCHER AL UNSER, DELBERT BERNARD UNSER IMMEDIATELY BECAME ONE OF THE A.L.'S BEST DEFENSIVE CENTERFIELDERS THE MINUTE HE TOOK THE FIELD AS A ROOKIE IN 1968!
MY STARS!
TSN ROOKIE OF THE YEAR
DEL'S BEST YEAR IN WASHINGTON CAME IN '69 DURING THE FIRST YEAR OF RICHARD NIXON'S FIRST TERM!
1968 WAS "THE YEAR OF THE PITCHER," SO WHILE DEL BATTED JUST .230, THAT WAS GOOD ENOUGH TO BE NAMED THE SPORTING NEWS A.L. ROOKIE OF THE YEAR! DEL WAS STRICTLY A CONTACT HITTER AT THAT POINT IN HIS CAREER, AND HE HIT JUST ONE HOMER IN 635 AT-BATS AS A ROOKIE! HIS LONE ROUND-TRIPPER CAME IN THE FIRST GAME OF A TWIN BILL AGAINST THE OAKLAND A'S ON AUGUST 20 -- A GAME IN WHICH YOUNG DEL WENT 5-FOR-5! THE CLOUT CAME BEFORE MOST A'S FANS WERE EVEN IN THEIR SEATS AS DEL, LEADING OFF THE GAME, POUNDED A JIM NASH PITCH INTO THE STANDS AT OAKLAND ALAMEDA COUNTY STADIUM! DEL WOULD HIT FOR MORE POWER LATER IN HIS CAREER, FINISHING WITH 87 CAREER HOMERS!
JOYNER ©2002
THE GREAT TED WILLIAMS TOOK OVER AS SENATORS MANAGER IN 1969, AND HIS INFLUENCE BENEFITED THE HITTING OF NEARLY EVERY PLAYER ON THE CLUB -- AND DEL WAS NO EXCEPTION! "I WENT FROM .230 TO .286," DEL TOLD NATS HISTORIAN JIM HARTLEY, "AND IT WAS LARGELY DUE TO TED'S ENTHUSIASM AND KNOWLEDGE, AND MAKING YOU THINK ABOUT WHAT YOU'RE GOING TO GET TO HIT WHEN YOU WENT UP TO HOME PLATE. NOTHING MECHANICAL. IT WAS ALL MENTAL. STUDYING THE PITCHER WHEN YOU WERE NOT UP THERE WAS THE MAIN KEY." TED'S TEACHINGS CERTAINLY PAID DIVIDENDS IN THE SECOND HALF OF DEL'S CAREER WHEN HE BECAME ONE OF BASEBALL'S MOST FEARED PINCH HITTERS! HIS TIMELY HITTING OFF THE BENCH FOR THE 1980 PHILLIES HELPED THEM CLINCH THE FRANCHISE'S FIRST-EVER WORLD SERIES CHAMPIONSHIP! DEL PREVIOUSLY ACHIEVED NOTORIETY BY CLUBBING THREE CONSECUTIVE PINCH-HIT HOME RUNS FROM JUNE 30-JULY 5, 1979!

Art MAHAFFEY

ARMED WITH A BLAZING FASTBALL AND HERALDED BY THE PHILADELPHIA PRESS AS "THE NEXT ROBIN ROBERTS," RIGHT-HANDER ART MAHAFFEY MADE HIS BIG LEAGUE DEBUT WITH THE PHILLIES ON JUNE 30, 1960! ARMED ALSO WITH A PICK-OFF MOVE THAT TEAMMATE JOHNNY CALLISON CALLED "THE BEST I'VE EVER SEEN," ART PROCEEDED TO PROVE CALLISON'S CLAIM BY PICKING OFF THE FIRST THREE BATTERS TO REACH BASE OFF HIM!

THE 6-FOOT-ONE 185-POUND CINCINNATI NATIVE ATTENDED WESTERN HILLS HIGH SCHOOL -- THE SAME SCHOOL THAT PRODUCED SINGERS ANDY WILLIAMS AND DORIS DAY, NOT TO MENTION THE GREAT PETE ROSE! ART PROVIDED THE PHILS FANS WITH THRILLS FROM THE GET-GO, WINNING SEVEN OF THE FOURTEEN GAMES HE APPEARED IN WHILE FINISHING THIRD IN VOTING FOR N.L. ROOKIE-OF-THE-YEAR! ART WAS AT HIS UNHITTABLE BEST EARLY THE NEXT SEASON WHEN HE SET A PHILLIES RECORD BY FANNING 17 CUBBIES ON APRIL 23, 1961! ART MADE THE ALL-STAR TEAM IN 1962 AND '63, BUT A SHOULDER INJURY ROBBED HIM OF HIS GREAT HEATER THEREAFTER!

ART PITCHED THROUGH THE PAIN WITH THE '64 AND '65 PHILLIES BEFORE FINISHING HIS BIG LEAGUE DAYS WITH THE 1966 CARDINALS! ONE OF THE MOST MEMORABLE MOMENTS IN ART'S CAREER IS ALSO ONE OF THE MOST MEMORABLE IN THE STORIED SAGA OF THE PHILLIES! ON SEPTEMBER 21, 1964, REDS ROOKIE CHICO RUIZ LED CINCINNATI TO A 1-0 WIN OVER THE PHILS WHEN HE STOLE HOME OFF ART WITH TWO OUT IN THE 6TH -- WITH SLUGGER FRANK ROBINSON ON DECK! THE LOSS WAS THE FIRST OF TEN-IN-A-ROW THAT ENDED UP COSTING THE PHILS THE PENNANT! DESPITE HIS BRIEF CAREER, ART PUNCHED OUT A LOT OF BATSMEN! IN FACT, HE'S EIGHTH ON THE PHILS' ALL-TIME LIST OF PITCHERS WITH THE MOST TEN-STRIKEOUT GAMES! FOLLOWING BASEBALL, ART BECAME A FINE GOLFER AND ENJOYED A LONG, SUCCESSFUL SECOND CAREER IN INSURANCE!

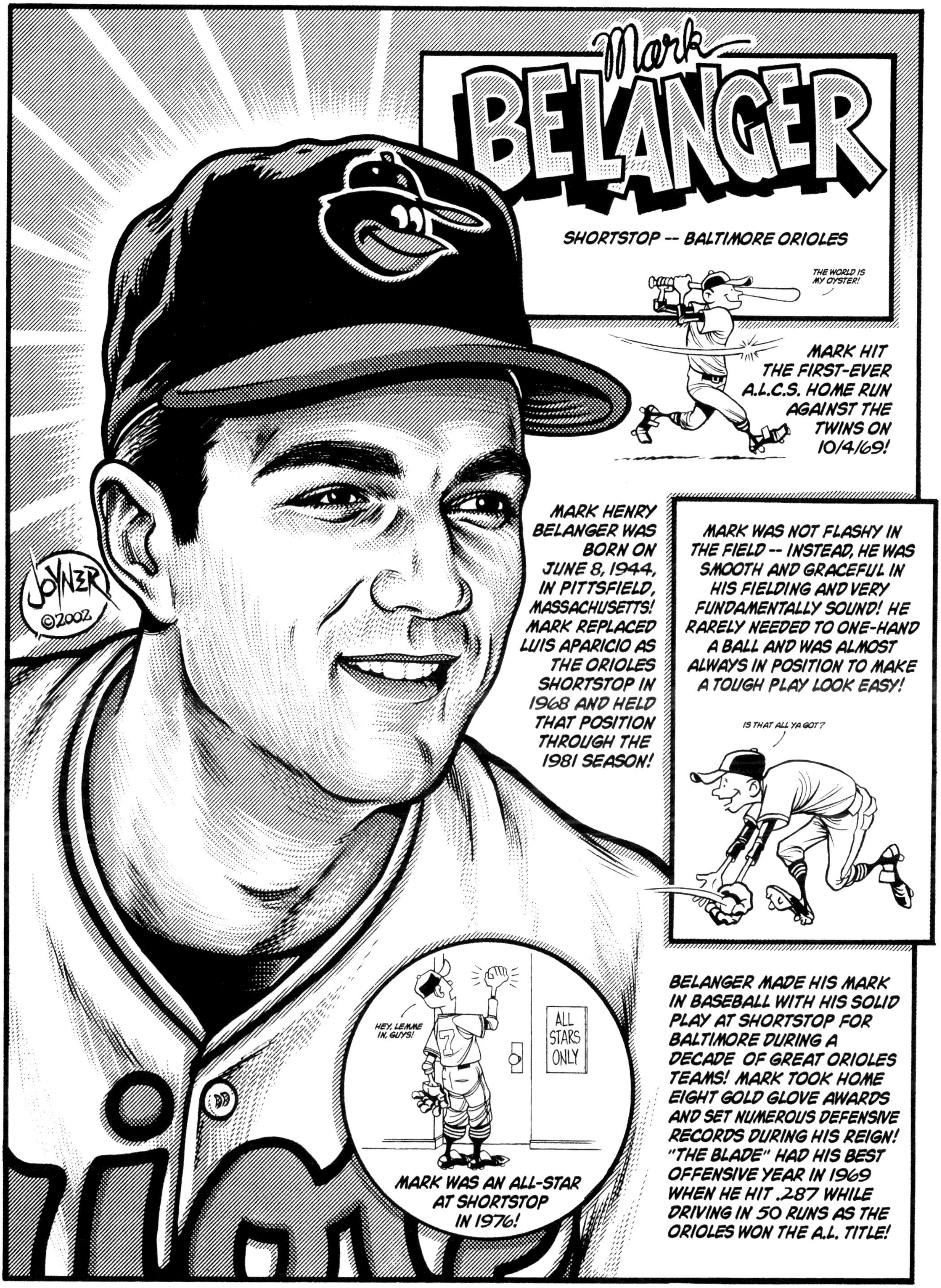

Mark
BELANGER
SHORTSTOP -- BALTIMORE ORIOLES
THE WORLD IS MY OYSTER!
MARK HIT THE FIRST-EVER A.L.C.S. HOME RUN AGAINST THE TWINS ON 10/4/69!
MARK HENRY BELANGER WAS BORN ON JUNE 8, 1944, IN PITTSFIELD, MASSACHUSETTS! MARK REPLACED LUIS APARICIO AS THE ORIOLES SHORTSTOP IN 1968 AND HELD THAT POSITION THROUGH THE 1981 SEASON!
MARK WAS NOT FLASHY IN THE FIELD -- INSTEAD, HE WAS SMOOTH AND GRACEFUL IN HIS FIELDING AND VERY FUNDAMENTALLY SOUND! HE RARELY NEEDED TO ONE-HAND A BALL AND WAS ALMOST ALWAYS IN POSITION TO MAKE A TOUGH PLAY LOOK EASY!
IS THAT ALL YA GOT?
JOYNER ©2002
HEY, LEMME IN, GUYS!
ALL STARS ONLY
MARK WAS AN ALL-STAR AT SHORTSTOP IN 1976!
BELANGER MADE HIS MARK IN BASEBALL WITH HIS SOLID PLAY AT SHORTSTOP FOR BALTIMORE DURING A DECADE OF GREAT ORIOLES TEAMS! MARK TOOK HOME EIGHT GOLD GLOVE AWARDS AND SET NUMEROUS DEFENSIVE RECORDS DURING HIS REIGN! "THE BLADE" HAD HIS BEST OFFENSIVE YEAR IN 1969 WHEN HE HIT .287 WHILE DRIVING IN 50 RUNS AS THE ORIOLES WON THE A.L. TITLE!

Butch
HOBSON
CLELL "BUTCH" HOBSON WAS BORN ON AUGUST 17, 1951, IN TUSCALOOSA, ALABAMA! BUTCH, LIKE HIS DAD BEFORE HIM, WAS A ROUGH-AND-TUMBLE QUARTERBACK FOR THE ALABAMA CRIMSON TIDE UNDER LEGENDARY COACH BEAR BRYANT! BUTCH WAS ALSO A STAR PLAYER FOR ALABAMA'S BASEBALL TEAM, AND IT WAS IN BASEBALL THAT BUTCH DECIDED TO PURSUE HIS DREAM OF MAKING IT TO THE MAJORS! ON SEPTEMBER 7, 1975 -- JUST TWO YEARS AFTER HIS LAST YEAR AT ALABAMA -- BUTCH REALIZED HIS DREAM WHEN HE MADE HIS BIG LEAGUE DEBUT WITH THE BOSTON RED SOX! BUTCH BECAME THE SOX'S REGULAR THIRD SACKER IN 1977, AND IT PROVED TO BE A BREAKOUT SEASON FOR HIM AS HE CLOUTED 30 LONG BALLS AND DROVE IN 112 RUNS! PLAYING WITH THE SAME ALL-OUT GO-FOR-BROKE STYLE HE'D DEMONSTRATED ON THE GRIDIRON WITH ALABAMA, BUTCH BECAME A FENWAY PARK FAVORITE! HE WOULD REMAIN IN BOSTON THROUGH THE 1980 SEASON, TALLYING ANOTHER 56 DINGERS FOR THE SOX BEFORE FINISHING HIS BIG LEAGUE PLAYING DAYS WITH THE 1981 ANGELS AND THE 1982 YANKEES!
I'M OKAY, COACH! WHAT INNING IS IT?!
MAYBE YOU BETTER SIT OUT FOR A PLAY, KID!
BUTCH IS TOUGH AS NAILS, AIN'T HE?!
WHILE BUTCH'S GUNG-HO STYLE WAS THRILLING TO WATCH, THE DOWNSIDE WAS IT OFTEN LEFT HIM INJURED! HE WAS A GAMER, THOUGH, AND ALWAYS ENDURED THE PAIN IN ORDER TO PLAY THE GAME HE LOVED! BUTCH'S INJURIES DEFINITELY SHORTENED WHAT COULD HAVE BEEN A LONG AND BRILLIANT CAREER AS A PLAYER, BUT HIS DIVING, SLIDING, AND ROLLICKING BRAND OF BASEBALL HAS LEFT AN INDELIBLE MARK ON ALL THOSE WHO WERE FORTUNATE ENOUGH TO WATCH HIM PLAY! AFTER A SUCCESSFUL RUN MANAGING IN THE MINORS, BUTCH SKIPPERED THE RED SOX FROM 1992-94, BUT WAS LET GO AS THE SOX STRUGGLED THROUGH A REBUILDING PERIOD! HE IS CURRENTLY THE MANAGER OF THE SOUTHERN MARYLAND BLUE CRABS OF THE INDEPENDENT ATLANTIC LEAGUE!
JOYNER ©2008

BERNIE
ALLEN
INFIELD -- WASHINGTON SENATORS
AN ALL-AROUND ATHLETE, BERNIE WAS WAS A QUARTERBACK AT PURDUE UNIVERSITY!
'SCUSE ME -- JUST PASSING THROUGH!
UMMMMPH!
P
BERNIE WAS PUT IN THE PURDUE ATHLETIC HALL OF FAME IN 1999!
BERNIE BROKE IN WITH THE MINNESOTA TWINS IN 1962! HE HAD A BIG YEAR AS A ROOKIE PLAYING IN A CAREER-HIGH 159 GAMES AND HITTING CAREER-HIGHS IN HOME RUNS WITH 12, TRIPLES WITH 7, RBIs WITH 64, AND BATTING AVERAGE AT .264!
POW!
JOYNER ©2003
AFTER 5 SEASONS WITH THE TWINS IN WHICH BERNIE HIT .318 AGAINST THE SENATORS, THE NATS WENT AND ACQUIRED ALLEN ON DECEMBER 3, 1966! THE SURE-HANDED KID FROM OHIO WAS A MAINSTAY OF THE NATS INFIELD THROUGH 1971!
HEY -- THAT AIN'T FAIR!

Joe Cunningham

ON JULY 1, 1954, 22-YEAR-OLD CARDINALS 1ST BASEMAN "JERSEY" JOE CUNNINGHAM, PLAYING IN JUST HIS SECOND BIG LEAGUE GAME, SLAMMED TWO HOME RUNS OFF THE GREAT WARREN SPAHN! HE'D ALSO HOMERED THE DAY BEFORE IN HIS MAJORS DEBUT -- A 3-RUN CLOUT OFF THE REDS' ART FOWLER! IT WAS QUITE A BEGINNING FOR THE YOUNGSTER FROM SADDLE RIVER, NEW JERSEY, AND HE EXCITEDLY TOLD THE SCRIBES, "MAN, WAIT UNTIL POP HEARS ABOUT THIS! I HAVEN'T HAD TIME TO CALL HIM YET!"

JOE COOLED TO A MORE HUMAN PACE FOLLOWING HIS BIG DEBUT, BUT STILL FINISHED WITH A SOLID ROOKIE YEAR BY HITTING .284 WITH ELEVEN LONG BALLS AND 50 RBIs! DESPITE HIS OBVIOUS ABILITY TO SWING THE BAT, THE PRESENCE OF STAN MUSIAL PREVENTED JOE FROM BECOMING A REGULAR WITH THE CARDS! HE SETTLED INTO THE ROLE OF HANDYMAN, CONSISTENTLY DELIVERING CLUTCH PINCH HITS, AS WELL AS SPELLING THE AGING MUSIAL WHEN NEED BE! JOE WAS INCREDIBLY GOOD IN HIS HANDYMAN ROLE, CONSTANTLY FRUSTRATING OPPONENTS WITH HIS UNCANNY ABILITY TO COME OFF THE BENCH AND DELIVER A GAME-WINNING HIT!

JOE WAS PLAYING OUTFIELD BY 1958 IN AN EFFORT TO GET MORE PLAYING TIME! WHILE NO THREAT TO ANY OF TRIS SPEAKER'S OLD RECORDS OUT THERE (JOE'S OWN WORDS), THE SHIFT DID ALLOW HIM TO SEE MORE ACTION! HE RESPONDED BY HITTING .312 WITH 12 HOMERS IN '58, THEN .345 IN 1959! JOE FINISHED SECOND IN HITTING TO HANK AARON THAT YEAR, EARNING HIM HIS ONLY TRIP TO THE ALL-STAR GAME!

JOE LATER WENT ON TO PLAY WITH THE WHITE SOX AND SENATORS, BUT IT WAS IN ST. LOUIS WHERE HE WAS TRULY LOVED BY THE MEDIA AND THE FANS -- ESPECIALLY THE LADIES DAY CROWDS AT OLD BUSCH STADIUM!

Bennie DANIELS

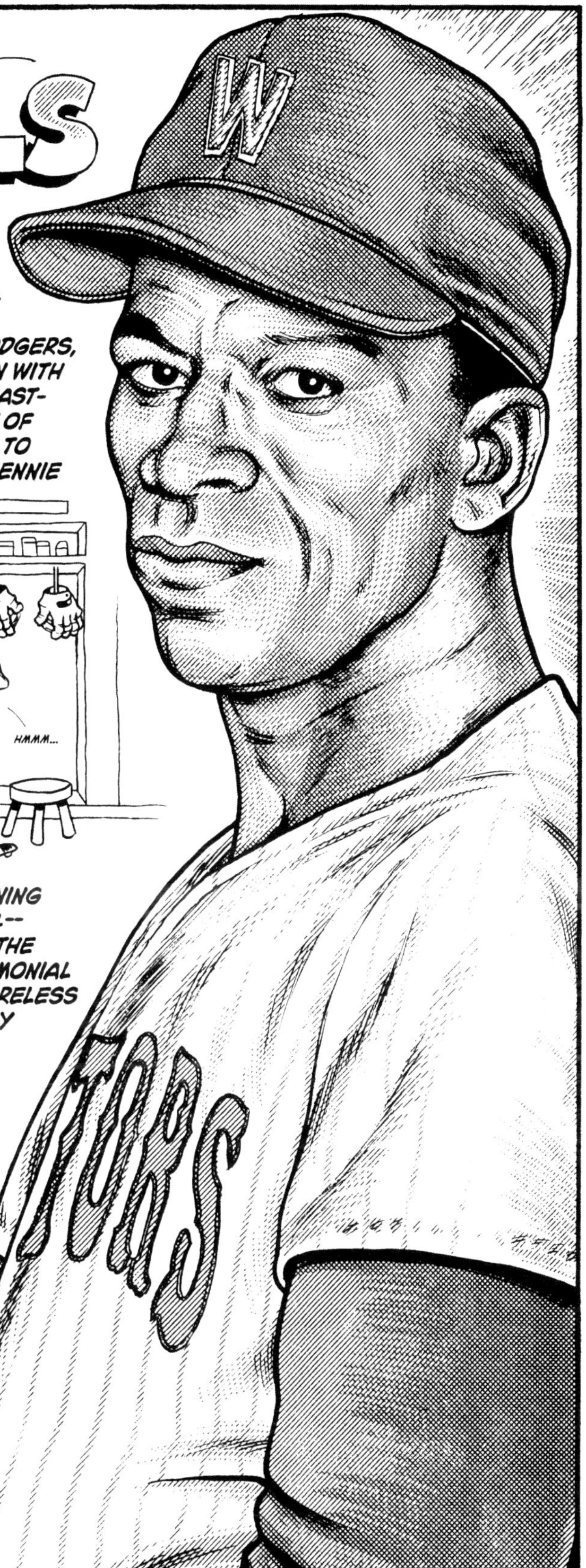

BORN ON JUNE 17, 1932, IN TUSCALOOSA, ALABAMA, PIRATES PITCHER BENNIE DANIELS MADE HIS BIG LEAGUE DEBUT ON SEPTEMBER 24TH, 1957, IN THE LAST GAME EVER PLAYED AT EBBETS FIELD! BENNIE PITCHED SEVEN STRONG INNINGS AGAINST THE DODGERS, BUT TOOK THE TOUGH 2-0 LOSS! HE SAW LIMITED ACTION WITH THE BUCS OVER THE NEXT THREE YEARS, BUT HIS GOOD FAST-BALL AND EXCELLENT SINKER MADE HIM A PRIME TARGET OF WASHINGTON SENATORS EXECUTIVES AS THEY PREPARED TO BUILD AN EXPANSION TEAM FOR 1961! THEY ACQUIRED BENNIE PRIOR TO THAT SEASON, AND THE MOVE PROVED TO BE VERY SUCCESSFUL AS THE BIG RIGHT-HANDER BECAME THE ACE OF THE STAFF BY WINNING 12 BALLGAMES! BENNIE WAS THE FULL PACKAGE, TOO, SUPERBLY FIELDING HIS POSITION WHILE ALSO PROVING TO BE A LEGITIMATE THREAT WITH THE BAT! BENNIE WAS A RARE BREED -- AN AMBIDEXTROUS THROWER! HE WAS OFTEN SEEN WARMING UP LEFT-HANDED IN THE BULLPEN -- WITH GOOD STUFF, TOO! BENNIE CLOSED OUT ANOTHER OLD BALLPARK WHEN HE WAS WASHINGTON'S STARTER IN THEIR LAST GAME AT GRIFFITH STADIUM ON THE 21ST OF SEPTEMBER, 1961! HE THEN HELPED OPEN THEIR NEW PARK, D.C. STADIUM (LATER RENAMED R.F.K. STADIUM), BY STARTING AND WINNING THE FIRST GAME EVER PLAYED THERE ON APRIL 9TH, 1962-- A 4-1 VICTORY OVER THE DETROIT TIGERS! BENNIE TOOK THE MOUND FOLLOWING PRESIDENT JOHN F. KENNEDY'S CEREMONIAL FIRST PITCH, THEN PROCEEDED TO HOLD THE TIGERS SCORELESS FOR THE FIRST FIVE INNINGS! DETROIT SCORED THEIR ONLY RUN OF THE GAME IN THE 6TH FOLLOWING AN ERROR, BUT BENNIE SHUT THE DOOR AFTER THAT! HE WENT THE FULL NINE, EVEN HELPING HIMSELF TO ONE SINGLE IN THREE TRIPS TO THE PLATE! IT WAS A GREAT DAY FOR BENNIE, AS WELL AS THE HUGE CROWD OF 44,383 WHO BRAVED THE RAIN TO WATCH THE OPENING OF THE THEN STATE-OF-THE-ART FACILITY! THE "NEW" NATS HAVE SINCE CLOSED THE CURTAIN ON BASEBALL AT R.F.K, BUT THE GREAT OLD BEER-STAINED MEMORIES REMAIN!

Paul
BLAIR
CENTERFIELD -- BALTIMORE ORIOLES
PAUL'S RANGE ALLOWED HIM TO PLAY VERY SHALLOW IN CENTER!
YOU MAY CALL ME SHALLOW... BUT I CALL YOU OUT!
PAUL L.D. BLAIR WAS BORN ON FEBRUARY 1, 1944, IN CUSHING, OKLAHOMA! HE CAME UP WITH THE ORIOLES IN '64 AND STAYED WITH THEM UNTIL '76!
PAUL FIT RIGHT IN WITH THE GREAT ORIOLES TEAMS OF THE 1960s AND '70s THAT WERE BUILT ON GREAT PITCHING AND DEFENSE! HIS INCREDIBLE SKILL IN THE FIELD WON HIM EIGHT COVETED GOLD GLOVES!
MY FAVORITE COLOR? GOLD!
JOYNER © 2002
HOLY COW! THAT'S A SHOT THAT'D MAKE OL' BOOGER TAKE NOTICE!
PAUL HIT A 430-FOOT HR IN GAME 3 OF THE 1966 WORLD SERIES!
PAUL WAS IN THE ORIOLES TOP FIVE ALL-TIME IN TWELVE OFFENSIVE CATEGORIES WHEN HE LEFTAFTER THE 1976 SEASON! HE WAS A TOP PERFORMER IN THE POST-SEASON, TOO, APPEARING IN 53 PLAYOFF AND WORLD SERIES GAMES! PAUL SET A RECORD FOR MOST HITS IN A 5-GAME WORLD SERIES WITH 9 IN 1970! HIS BIGGEST YEAR CAME IN 1969 WHEN HE HIT .285 WITH 26 HOME RUNS AND 76 RBIs!

Billy HUNTER

WILLIAM GORDON HUNTER WAS BORN ON JUNE 4TH, 1928, IN PUNXSUTAWNEY, PENNSYLVANIA! BILLY'S FLASHY GLOVEWORK AND GREAT TEAM SPIRIT MADE HIM ONE OF THE DODGERS' TOP CANDIDATES TO SUCCEED PEE WEE REESE! AN M.V.P. SEASON AT FT. WORTH IN 1952 PUT BILLY AT THE TOP OF EVERY G.M.'S WANT LIST, BUT IT WAS THE ST. LOUIS BROWNS WHO GOT HIM WHEN BILL VEECK SENT $150,000 IN CASH AND PLAYERS TO PRY THE KID AWAY FROM BROOKLYN! WITH THAT, BILLY BECAME THE HIGHEST PRICED ROOKIE IN TEAM HISTORY!

BILLY PLAYED IN EVERY GAME FOR THE BROWNS IN 1953, SPARKLING ON DEFENSE WHILE HITTING WELL ENOUGH TO MAKE THE ALL-STAR TEAM! "I WAS IN THE TOP TEN IN HITTING AT THE END OF JUNE," BILLY SAID! "I ALWAYS JOKE THAT I MUST NOT HAVE GOT ANOTHER HIT THE REST OF THE YEAR BECAUSE I ENDED UP AT .219!" ONE HIT HE DID GET, HOWEVER, WAS A BIG ONE IN THE ANNALS OF THE ST. LOUIS BROWNS! "I HIT THE LAST HOME RUN IN BROWNIE HISTORY," BILLY RECALLED! "IT WAS MY ONLY HOME RUN OF THE SEASON."

BILLY WENT WITH THE TEAM WHEN IT MOVED TO BALTIMORE THE NEXT SEASON, THEN SPENT 1955-56 IN YANKEE PINSTRIPES! FOLLOWING HIS PLAYING DAYS, BILLY WAS A LONGTIME ORIOLES COACH AND ALSO MANAGED THE RANGERS! HE THEN WENT ON TO COACH BASEBALL AT TOWSON UNIVERSITY FOR MANY YEARS, LATER RISING TO THE POST OF ATHLETIC DIRECTOR!

WHEN TOLD OF A DAY WITH THE '53 BROWNS WHEN HE GATHERED SEVEN HITS IN A DOUBLEHEADER AGAINST CHICAGO, BILLY LAUGHED AND SAID, "I REMEMBER A LOT OF TIMES WHEN I HAD NO HITS IN A DOUBLE-HEADER! I REMEMBER A SERIES AGAINST DETROIT LATER IN MY CAREER WITH THE YANKEES. I HIT 12 LINE DRIVE OUTS. 0-FOR-12! I LEFT THE DUGOUT FOR MY POSITION IN THE FIELD AND SLID INTO SECOND BASE -- JUST TO SEE WHAT IT WOULD FEEL LIKE!"

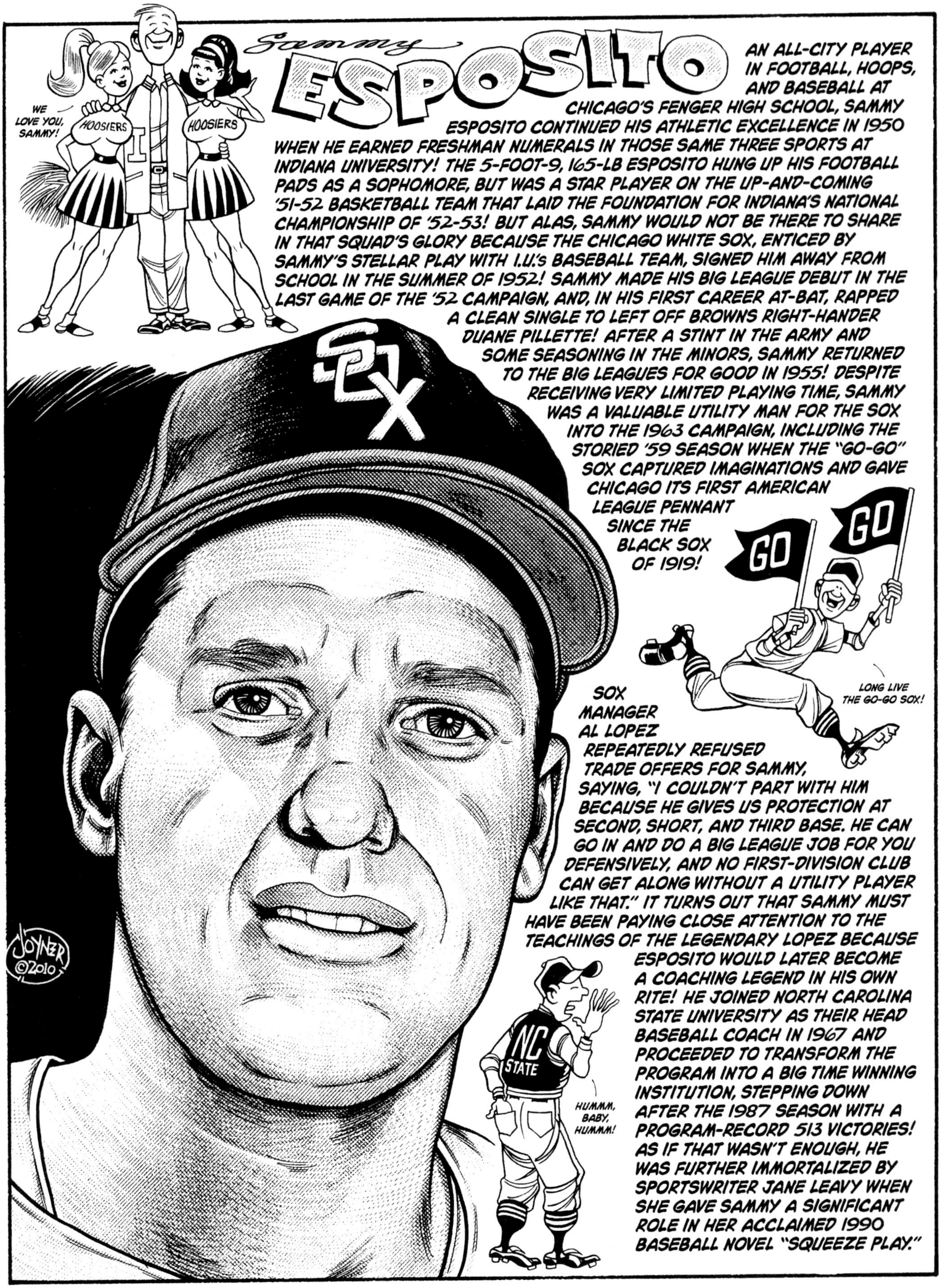
Sammy ESPOSITO
WE LOVE YOU, SAMMY!
HOOSIERS
HOOSIERS
AN ALL-CITY PLAYER IN FOOTBALL, HOOPS, AND BASEBALL AT CHICAGO'S FENGER HIGH SCHOOL, SAMMY ESPOSITO CONTINUED HIS ATHLETIC EXCELLENCE IN 1950 WHEN HE EARNED FRESHMAN NUMERALS IN THOSE SAME THREE SPORTS AT INDIANA UNIVERSITY! THE 5-FOOT-9, 165-LB ESPOSITO HUNG UP HIS FOOTBALL PADS AS A SOPHOMORE, BUT WAS A STAR PLAYER ON THE UP-AND-COMING '51-52 BASKETBALL TEAM THAT LAID THE FOUNDATION FOR INDIANA'S NATIONAL CHAMPIONSHIP OF '52-53! BUT ALAS, SAMMY WOULD NOT BE THERE TO SHARE IN THAT SQUAD'S GLORY BECAUSE THE CHICAGO WHITE SOX, ENTICED BY SAMMY'S STELLAR PLAY WITH I.U.'S BASEBALL TEAM, SIGNED HIM AWAY FROM SCHOOL IN THE SUMMER OF 1952! SAMMY MADE HIS BIG LEAGUE DEBUT IN THE LAST GAME OF THE '52 CAMPAIGN, AND, IN HIS FIRST CAREER AT-BAT, RAPPED A CLEAN SINGLE TO LEFT OFF BROWNS RIGHT-HANDER DUANE PILLETTE! AFTER A STINT IN THE ARMY AND SOME SEASONING IN THE MINORS, SAMMY RETURNED TO THE BIG LEAGUES FOR GOOD IN 1955! DESPITE RECEIVING VERY LIMITED PLAYING TIME, SAMMY WAS A VALUABLE UTILITY MAN FOR THE SOX INTO THE 1963 CAMPAIGN, INCLUDING THE STORIED '59 SEASON WHEN THE "GO-GO" SOX CAPTURED IMAGINATIONS AND GAVE CHICAGO ITS FIRST AMERICAN LEAGUE PENNANT SINCE THE BLACK SOX OF 1919!
SOX
GO
GO
LONG LIVE THE GO-GO SOX!
SOX MANAGER AL LOPEZ REPEATEDLY REFUSED TRADE OFFERS FOR SAMMY, SAYING, "I COULDN'T PART WITH HIM BECAUSE HE GIVES US PROTECTION AT SECOND, SHORT, AND THIRD BASE. HE CAN GO IN AND DO A BIG LEAGUE JOB FOR YOU DEFENSIVELY, AND NO FIRST-DIVISION CLUB CAN GET ALONG WITHOUT A UTILITY PLAYER LIKE THAT." IT TURNS OUT THAT SAMMY MUST HAVE BEEN PAYING CLOSE ATTENTION TO THE TEACHINGS OF THE LEGENDARY LOPEZ BECAUSE ESPOSITO WOULD LATER BECOME A COACHING LEGEND IN HIS OWN RITE! HE JOINED NORTH CAROLINA STATE UNIVERSITY AS THEIR HEAD BASEBALL COACH IN 1967 AND PROCEEDED TO TRANSFORM THE PROGRAM INTO A BIG TIME WINNING INSTITUTION, STEPPING DOWN AFTER THE 1987 SEASON WITH A PROGRAM-RECORD 513 VICTORIES! AS IF THAT WASN'T ENOUGH, HE WAS FURTHER IMMORTALIZED BY SPORTSWRITER JANE LEAVY WHEN SHE GAVE SAMMY A SIGNIFICANT ROLE IN HER ACCLAIMED 1990 BASEBALL NOVEL "SQUEEZE PLAY."
JOYNER ©2010
NC STATE
HUMMM, BABY, HUMMM!

Don MONEY

DON MONEY WAS BORN ON JUNE 7, 1947, IN WASHINGTON, D.C., BUT HIS FAMILY RELOCATED TO THE SMALL TOWN OF LA PLATA, MARYLAND, JUST IN TIME FOR HIS JUNIOR YEAR! DON, NICKNAMED "BROOKS" AFTER HIS BOYHOOD IDOL BROOKS ROBINSON, STARRED IN BASEBALL FOR LA PLATA HIGH, BATTING .512 AS A SENIOR WHILE PITCHING AND PLAYING SHORTSTOP! SHORTLY AFTER GRADUATION, PIRATES SCOUT SYD THRIFT SIGNED DON TO A CONTRACT, STARTING THE YOUNGSTER ON THE ROAD TO HIS DREAM OF PLAYING BIG LEAGUE BALL! ALSO HELPING IN THE DEVELOPMENT OF YOUNG DON'S SKILLS WERE THE TWO YEARS THAT HE SPENT IN THE CHARLES-ST. MARY'S (CHASM) LEAGUE -- A MARYLAND SEMI-PRO LEAGUE THAT DON SAID PROVIDED A "MORE COMPETITIVE LEVEL" OF PLAY! DON WAS DEALT TO THE PHILLIES IN THE WINTER OF 1967, AND ON APRIL 10, 1968 -- JUST THREE YEARS AFTER HIS LAST CHASM GAME -- DON MADE HIS MAJOR LEAGUE DEBUT WITH THE PHILS! PLAYING MOSTLY AT THIRD BASE, DON PARLAYED HIS FINE GLOVE AND LIVELY BAT INTO A 16-YEAR BIG LEAGUE CAREER THAT INCLUDED FOUR ALL-STAR APPEARANCES! DON WENT FROM THE PHILLIES TO THE BREWERS IN 1973, AND IT WAS IN MILWAUKEE THAT HE ENJOYED HIS GREATEST SUCCESS, INCLUDING A 25-HOMER SEASON IN 1977 AND AN A.L. PENNANT IN '82! A FAVORITE OF THE BREWER FANS, DON WAS THE TEAM M.V.P. TWICE DURING HIS YEARS IN MILWAUKEE! HE WAS NOT WITHOUT HIGHLIGHTS IN PHILLY, HOWEVER, INCLUDING CHRISTENING THE NEWLY-OPENED VETERANS STADIUM WITH ITS 1ST-EVER HOME RUN, CLUBBED OFF BILL STONEMAN ON APRIL 10TH OF 1971!

GEORGE "SHOTGUN"

SHUBA

GEORGE THOMAS SHUBA WAS BORN ON DECEMBER 13, 1924, IN YOUNGSTOWN, OHIO -- 12 YEARS AFTER HIS PARENTS LEFT CZECHOSLOVAKIA IN SEARCH OF GREENER PASTURES IN AMERICA! GEORGE QUICKLY DISCOVERED THOSE GREENER PASTURES IN THE FORM OF BASEBALL DIAMONDS, AND IT WAS THERE THAT HE HONED HIS BAT INTO A LETHAL WEAPON! HIS UNCANNY ABILITY TO SPRAY LINE DRIVES SOON EARNED HIM A VERY APPROPRIATE NICKNAME -- SHOTGUN!

SHOTGUN, OFTEN RIBBED BY HIS TEAMMATES FOR NOT BEING VERY GOOD IN THE OUTFIELD, USED HIS GLOVE TO HELP CARL ERSKINE GAIN HIS FIRST BIG LEAGUE WIN! YEARS LATER, AFTER ERSKINE REMINDED SHOTGUN OF HIS GREAT SHOETOP CATCH, GEORGE SAID, "YEAH, I REMEMBER THAT PLAY -- I TRAPPED THE BALL!"

GEORGE PLAYED HIS ENTIRE 7-YEAR BIG LEAGUE CAREER WITH THE BROOKLYN DODGERS, BUT NOT BEFORE LOGGING 4-1/2 YEARS ON THE BROOKLYN FARM! HIS .389 AVERAGE AT MOBILE IN '48 DEMANDED THAT HE BE CALLED UP, AND HE FINALLY DEBUTED WITH A 2-HIT GAME AGAINST THE GIANTS AT EBBETS FIELD ON JULY 2ND, 1948! SHOTGUN'S BEST SEASON WITH BROOKLYN WAS 1952 WHEN HE PLAYED IN A CAREER-HIGH 92 GAMES AND BATTED .305 WITH 9 LONG BALLS AND 40 RBIS! SHOTGUN WAS A VERY RELIABLE PINCH-HITTER FOR THE DODGERS, AND ONE OF THE TRUE HIGHLIGHTS OF HIS CAREER WAS HIS PINCH-HOMER IN THE OPENER OF THE 1953 WORLD SERIES -- THE FIRST N.L. PINCH-HOMER EVER HIT IN A SERIES! SHOTGUN, HOWEVER, IS MOST PROUD OF THE ROLE HE PLAYED ON OPENING DAY OF '46 WHEN HE GREETED HIS MONTREAL ROYALS TEAMMATE, JACKIE ROBINSON, WITH BASEBALL'S "FIRST INTERRACIAL HAND-SHAKE" FOLLOWING A HOME RUN BY THE TRAILBLAZER!

Paul
CASANOVA
CATCHER
WASHINGTON SENATORS
DON'T EVEN THINK ABOUT IT!
PAUL HAD A CANNON FOR AN ARM AND LED ALL A.L. CATCHERS IN DOUBLE PLAYS 3 TIMES!
PAULINO ORTIZ "PAUL" CASANOVA WAS BORN ON NEW YEAR'S EVE IN 1941 IN COLON MATANZAS, CUBA! HE SPENT 10 YEARS IN THE MAJOR LEAGUES, BREAKING IN WITH THE A.L. WASHINGTON SENATORS IN 1965! PAUL TURNED IN A FINE ROOKIE SEASON IN 1966 WINNING THE SPORTING NEWS ALL-STAR CATCHER AWARD!
PAUL CAUGHT ALL 22 INNINGS OF THE LONGEST GAME IN AMERICAN LEAGUE HISTORY -- A 6-5 NATS WIN OVER THE CHICAGO WHITE SOX ON JUNE 12, 1967! PAUL WAS THE HERO DRIVING IN THE WINNING RUN AT 2:43 IN THE MORNING OF JUNE 13!
ZZZZZZZZZZZZZZZ
JOYNER ©2002
PAUL WAS AN ALL STAR IN 1967!
ALL-STAR 1967
CASSIE WAS BIG -- 6'4" -- AND HAD A LITTLE POP IN HIS SWING! HIS BEST SEASON CAME IN 1966 WHEN HE HIT .254 WHILE HITTING 13 HOME RUNS! HE HAD ANOTHER FINE YEAR IN 1967 AS HE BATTED .248 AND HIT 9 LONG BALLS! PAUL STUCK WITH THE NATS FOR 4 MORE SEASONS UNTIL HE WAS TRADED TO THE BRAVES IN EXCHANGE FOR HAL KING ON DECEMBER 2, 1971! HE PLAYED SPARINGLY WITH ATLANTA UNTIL HE RETIRED FROM THE GAME IN 1974!

Pete
REISER
A NAME SOMETIMES LOST IN THE SHADOW CAST BY OTHERS WITH GAUDY STATS, "PISTOL" PETE REISER WAS A FIVE-TOOL OUTFIELDER WHOSE STAR BLAZED HOT AND BRIGHT -- BUT FLAMED OUT ALL TOO SOON! HE DAZZLED AS A ROOKIE IN 1941 WHEN HE LED THE N.L. IN BATTING, SLUGGING, DOUBLES, TRIPLES, AND RUNS SCORED! PETE'S DESTINY OF SUPERSTARDOM WAS DERAILED, HOWEVER, BY DEVASTATING INJURIES SUFFERED FROM THE ALL-OUT RECKLESS STYLE OF PLAY FOR WHICH HE WAS KNOWN! HIS GREATNESS IS NOT MEASURED BY NUMBERS IN A RECORD BOOK, BUT RATHER BY THE STORIES TOLD BY OLD MEN WHO ONCE SAW HIM PLAY!
I HAD NO IDEA IT WAS A MOVING VIOLATION TO RUN FROM HOME TO FIRST IN 3.6 SECONDS!
I'M ACTUALLY A SIX-TOOL PLAYER, IF YOU COUNT HOW HANDY I AM WITH THIS RAKE!
ONE MAN WHO SAW PETE PLAY UP CLOSE WAS HIS SKIPPER, LEO DUROCHER -- AND LEO WASN'T JUST PAYING LIP SERVICE WHEN HE SPOKE GLOWINGLY ABOUT PETE! "PETE REISER MIGHT JUST HAVE BEEN THE BEST BALLPLAYER I EVER SAW," LEO TOLD BOB ORTMAN OF THE SAN DIEGO EVENING TRIBUNE IN '75! "AT THE AGE OF 22 HE HIT .343 TO LEAD THE LEAGUE IN BATTING. THE NEXT YEAR HE WAS HITTING .380 IN JULY WHEN HE RAN INTO A FENCE AND BUSTED HIMSELF UP. REISER WAS EVERY BIT AS GOOD AS MAYS -- MIGHT HAVE BEEN BETTER. HE HAD MORE POWER THAN WILLIE, LEFT AND RIGHT BOTH. HE COULD THROW AS GOOD AS WILLIE -- AT LEAST AS GOOD -- AND HE COULD THROW RIGHT-HANDED AND LEFT-HANDED. YOU THINK MAYS COULD RUN IN HIS HEYDAY? YOU THINK MANTLE COULD RUN? NAME WHOEVER YOU WANT, AND REISER WAS FASTER. HE RAN DOWN TO 1st BASE IN 3.6 AND 3.7 -- AND BELIEVE ME, THERE HAS NEVER BEEN ANYONE BEFORE OR SINCE WHO COULD DO THAT. PETE REISER HAD EVERYTHING ... BUT LUCK."
JOYNER ©2011
OH, GIVE ME LAND, LOTS OF LAND, UNDER BROOKLYN SKIES ABOVE... DON'T FENCE ME IN!
PETE KNEW HIS ALL-OUT STYLE OF PLAY HAD ROBBED HIM OF A LONG CAREER! "IT WAS MY WAY OF PLAYING," HE WOULD SAY. "THAT'S THE WAY IT HAD TO BE. I COULDN'T PLAY ANY OTHER WAY."

Bob Aspromonte

One of the first major league stars for the city of Houston, Bob Aspromonte was the everyday 3rd-sacker for the Colt .45s (later renamed the Astros) for the first six years of their existence -- 1962-67! Bob was an excellent glove man and played 57 consecutive errorless games at the hot corner in 1962 -- a National League record for third basemen! Bob, a Brooklyn kid, broke into the bigs at age 18 with his hometown Dodgers! He was the last active Brooklyn player when he logged his final season in 1971! Bob's brother, Ken, was also a big league infielder -- a veteran of six teams from 1957-63! Both were graduates of Brooklyn's famed Lafayette High -- the same school that produced the great Sandy Koufax! While Bob could muscle up now and then, he wasn't exactly a power hitter -- he collected just 60 homers in his 13-year career! But that's what makes this next story so amazing! After nine-year-old Arkansas Little Leaguer Billy Bradley was blinded by a bolt of lightning in 1962, it was his idol, Bob Aspromonte, who came to visit him in the hospital! Billy asked Bob if he would hit a home run for him in that night's ballgame! In his last at-bat of the game, Bob hit one into the seats as Billy lay in bed listening on the radio -- to which Colt .45s announcer Gene Elston exclaimed, "This one's for you, Bill Bradley!" Bob visited Billy on two other occasions when the youngster was in Houston for surgeries on his damaged eyes! Each time Billy asked Bob if he'd hit another homer for him, and each time Bob delivered -- and grand slams, no less! These surgeries eventually restored Billy's sight, but in a cruel twist of fate Bob was blinded when a car battery exploded in his face in 1974! A specialist was called in -- Baylor University opthalmologist Dr. Louis Girard -- the same surgeon who had restored Billy's sight over a decade earlier! In a true miracle, Dr. Girard was able to restore 40 percent of Bob's vision! Bob went on to be a successful restaurateur and beer distributor, while Billy Bradley became an executive with Merrill Lynch in Memphis!

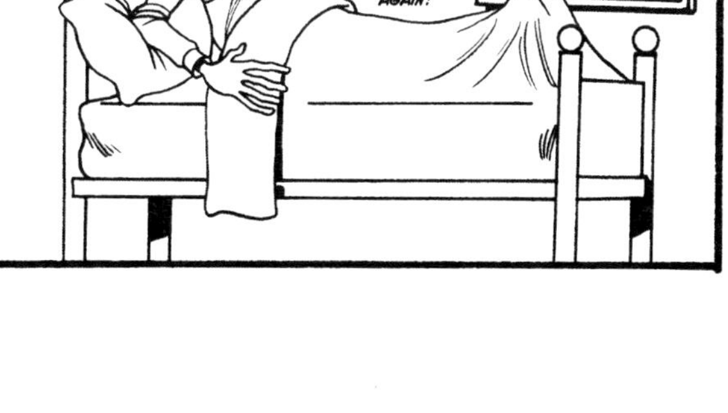

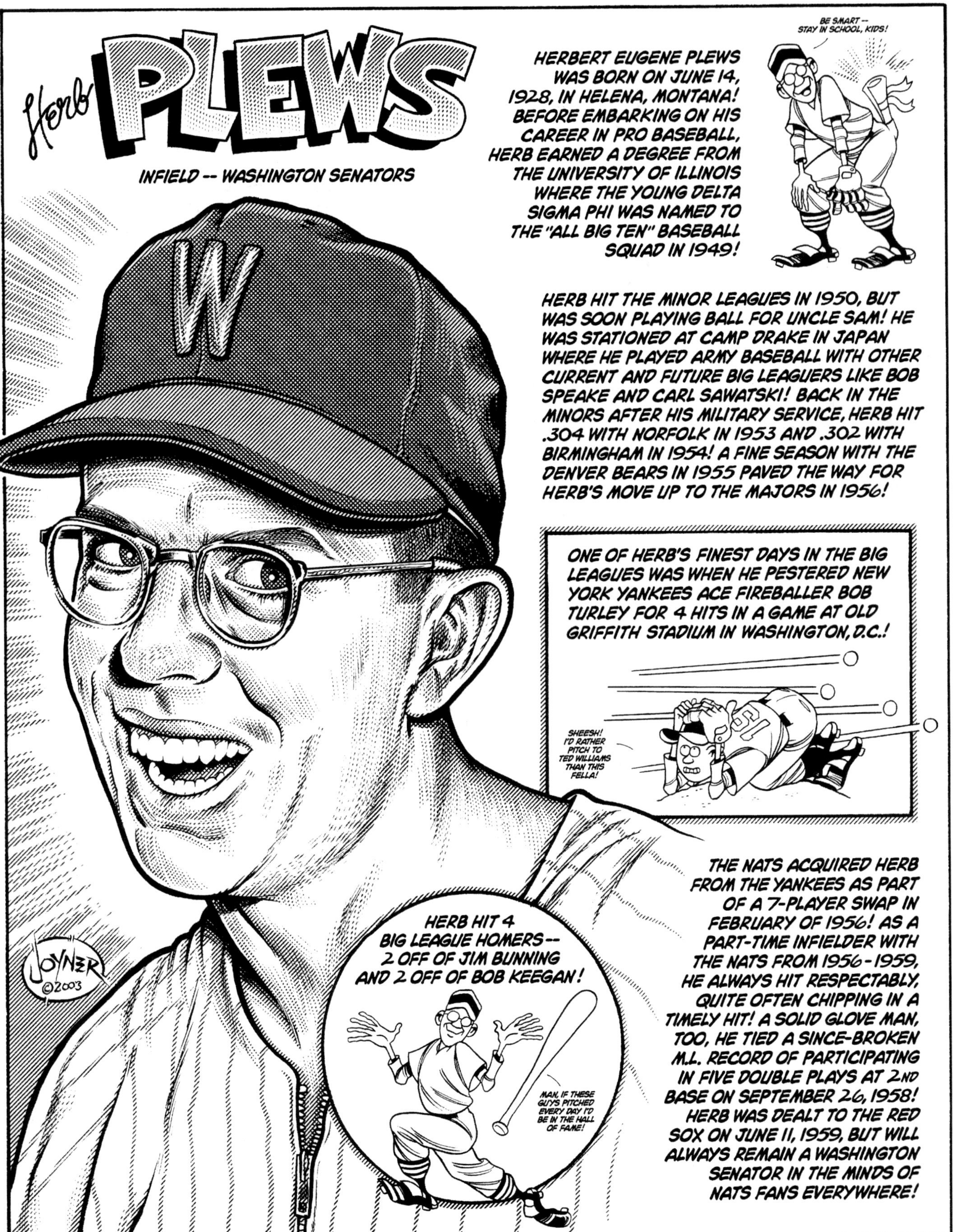
HERB PLEWS
INFIELD -- WASHINGTON SENATORS
HERBERT EUGENE PLEWS WAS BORN ON JUNE 14, 1928, IN HELENA, MONTANA! BEFORE EMBARKING ON HIS CAREER IN PRO BASEBALL, HERB EARNED A DEGREE FROM THE UNIVERSITY OF ILLINOIS WHERE THE YOUNG DELTA SIGMA PHI WAS NAMED TO THE "ALL BIG TEN" BASEBALL SQUAD IN 1949!
BE SMART -- STAY IN SCHOOL, KIDS!
HERB HIT THE MINOR LEAGUES IN 1950, BUT WAS SOON PLAYING BALL FOR UNCLE SAM! HE WAS STATIONED AT CAMP DRAKE IN JAPAN WHERE HE PLAYED ARMY BASEBALL WITH OTHER CURRENT AND FUTURE BIG LEAGUERS LIKE BOB SPEAKE AND CARL SAWATSKI! BACK IN THE MINORS AFTER HIS MILITARY SERVICE, HERB HIT .304 WITH NORFOLK IN 1953 AND .302 WITH BIRMINGHAM IN 1954! A FINE SEASON WITH THE DENVER BEARS IN 1955 PAVED THE WAY FOR HERB'S MOVE UP TO THE MAJORS IN 1956!
ONE OF HERB'S FINEST DAYS IN THE BIG LEAGUES WAS WHEN HE PESTERED NEW YORK YANKEES ACE FIREBALLER BOB TURLEY FOR 4 HITS IN A GAME AT OLD GRIFFITH STADIUM IN WASHINGTON, D.C.!
SHEESH! I'D RATHER PITCH TO TED WILLIAMS THAN THIS FELLA!
HERB HIT 4 BIG LEAGUE HOMERS -- 2 OFF OF JIM BUNNING AND 2 OFF OF BOB KEEGAN!
MAN, IF THESE GUYS PITCHED EVERY DAY I'D BE IN THE HALL OF FAME!
THE NATS ACQUIRED HERB FROM THE YANKEES AS PART OF A 7-PLAYER SWAP IN FEBRUARY OF 1956! AS A PART-TIME INFIELDER WITH THE NATS FROM 1956-1959, HE ALWAYS HIT RESPECTABLY, QUITE OFTEN CHIPPING IN A TIMELY HIT! A SOLID GLOVE MAN, TOO, HE TIED A SINCE-BROKEN M.L. RECORD OF PARTICIPATING IN FIVE DOUBLE PLAYS AT 2ND BASE ON SEPTEMBER 26, 1958! HERB WAS DEALT TO THE RED SOX ON JUNE 11, 1959, BUT WILL ALWAYS REMAIN A WASHINGTON SENATOR IN THE MINDS OF NATS FANS EVERYWHERE!
JOYNER ©2003

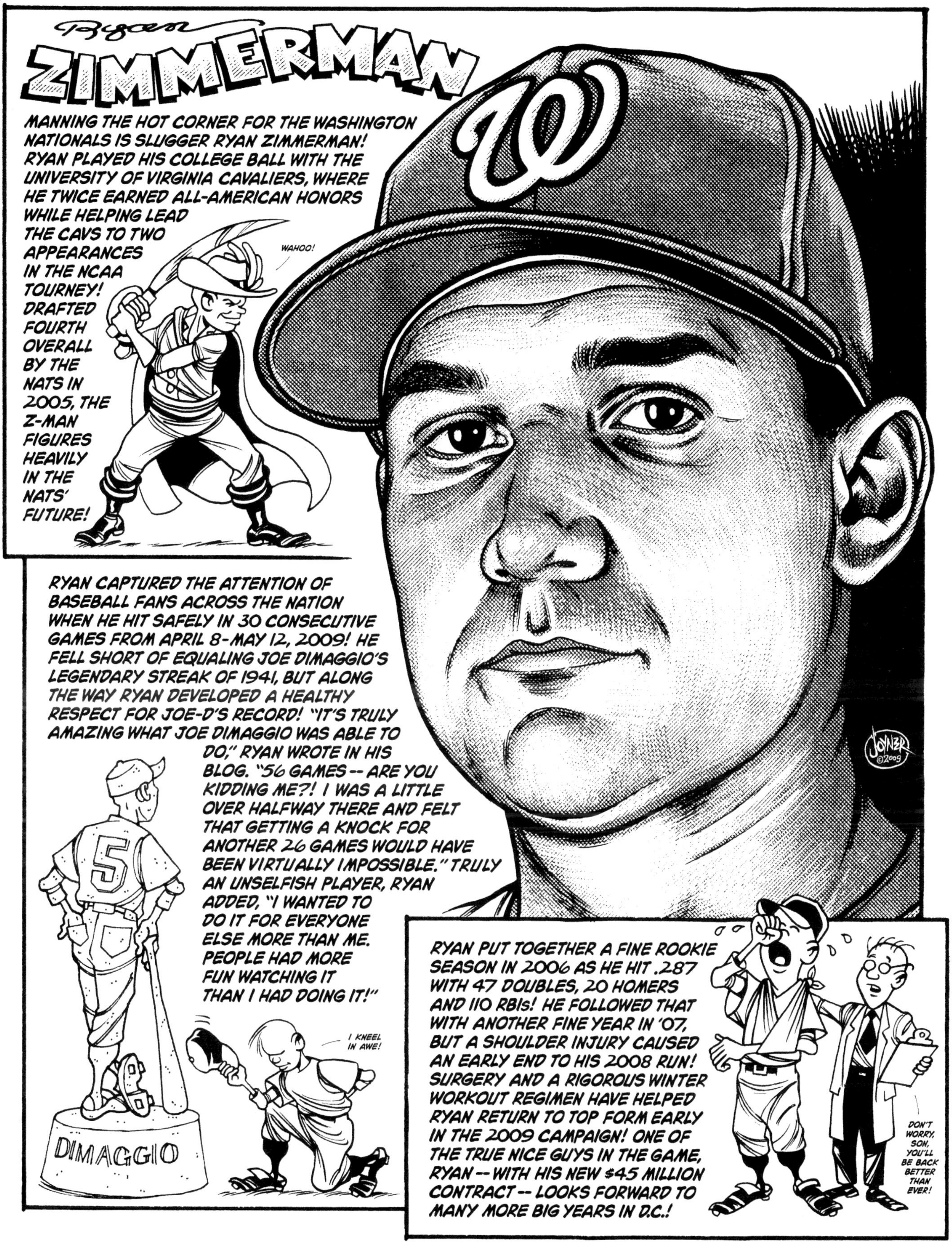
Ryan
ZIMMERMAN
MANNING THE HOT CORNER FOR THE WASHINGTON NATIONALS IS SLUGGER RYAN ZIMMERMAN! RYAN PLAYED HIS COLLEGE BALL WITH THE UNIVERSITY OF VIRGINIA CAVALIERS, WHERE HE TWICE EARNED ALL-AMERICAN HONORS WHILE HELPING LEAD THE CAVS TO TWO APPEARANCES IN THE NCAA TOURNEY! DRAFTED FOURTH OVERALL BY THE NATS IN 2005, THE Z-MAN FIGURES HEAVILY IN THE NATS' FUTURE!
WAHOO!
RYAN CAPTURED THE ATTENTION OF BASEBALL FANS ACROSS THE NATION WHEN HE HIT SAFELY IN 30 CONSECUTIVE GAMES FROM APRIL 8-MAY 12, 2009! HE FELL SHORT OF EQUALING JOE DIMAGGIO'S LEGENDARY STREAK OF 1941, BUT ALONG THE WAY RYAN DEVELOPED A HEALTHY RESPECT FOR JOE-D'S RECORD! "IT'S TRULY AMAZING WHAT JOE DIMAGGIO WAS ABLE TO DO," RYAN WROTE IN HIS BLOG. "56 GAMES -- ARE YOU KIDDING ME?! I WAS A LITTLE OVER HALFWAY THERE AND FELT THAT GETTING A KNOCK FOR ANOTHER 26 GAMES WOULD HAVE BEEN VIRTUALLY IMPOSSIBLE." TRULY AN UNSELFISH PLAYER, RYAN ADDED, "I WANTED TO DO IT FOR EVERYONE ELSE MORE THAN ME. PEOPLE HAD MORE FUN WATCHING IT THAN I HAD DOING IT!"
JOYNER ©2009
5
DIMAGGIO
I KNEEL IN AWE!
RYAN PUT TOGETHER A FINE ROOKIE SEASON IN 2006 AS HE HIT .287 WITH 47 DOUBLES, 20 HOMERS AND 110 RBIs! HE FOLLOWED THAT WITH ANOTHER FINE YEAR IN '07, BUT A SHOULDER INJURY CAUSED AN EARLY END TO HIS 2008 RUN! SURGERY AND A RIGOROUS WINTER WORKOUT REGIMEN HAVE HELPED RYAN RETURN TO TOP FORM EARLY IN THE 2009 CAMPAIGN! ONE OF THE TRUE NICE GUYS IN THE GAME, RYAN -- WITH HIS NEW $45 MILLION CONTRACT -- LOOKS FORWARD TO MANY MORE BIG YEARS IN D.C.!
DON'T WORRY, SON, YOU'LL BE BACK BETTER THAN EVER!

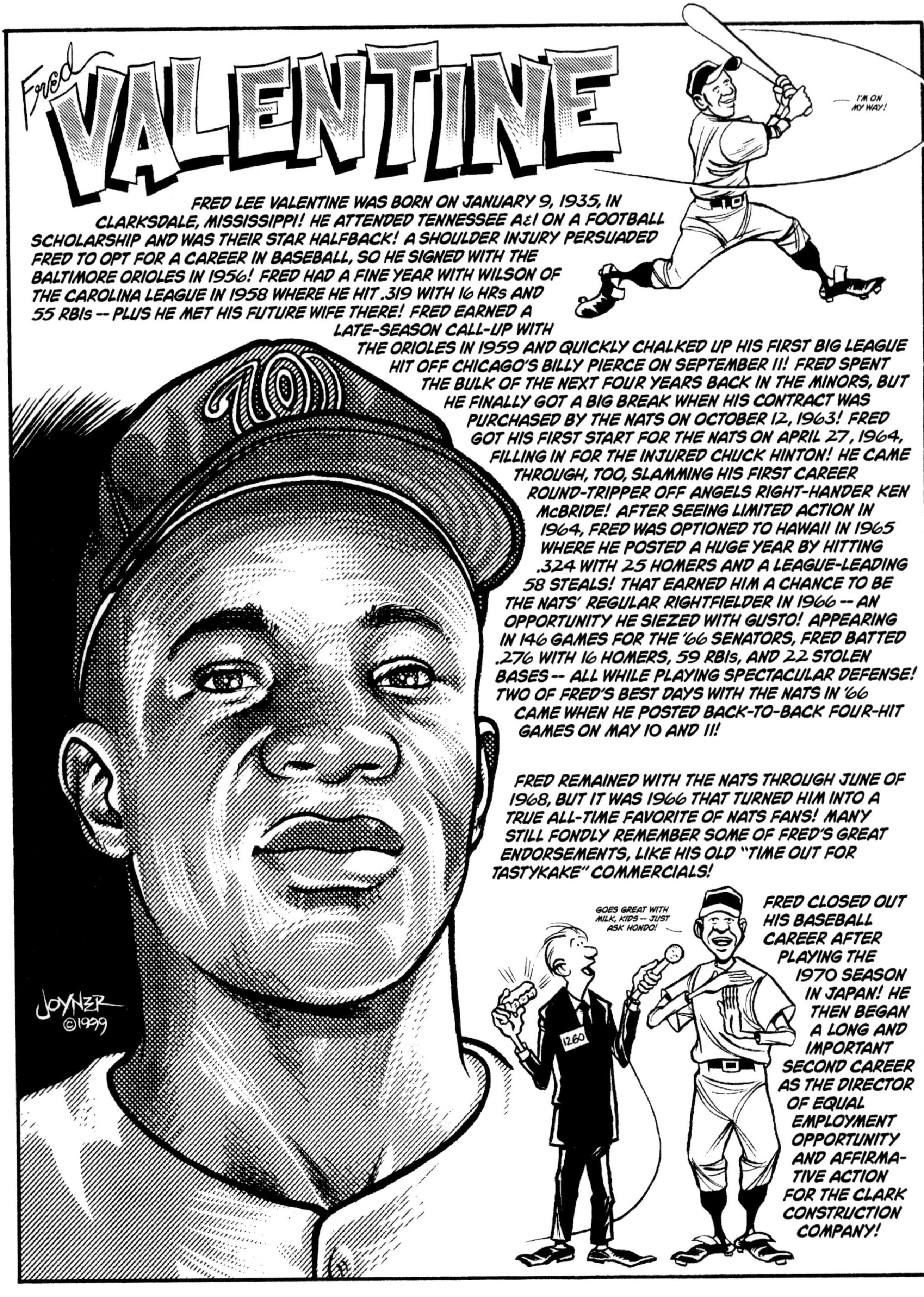
Fred VALENTINE
— I'M ON MY WAY!
FRED LEE VALENTINE WAS BORN ON JANUARY 9, 1935, IN CLARKSDALE, MISSISSIPPI! HE ATTENDED TENNESSEE A&I ON A FOOTBALL SCHOLARSHIP AND WAS THEIR STAR HALFBACK! A SHOULDER INJURY PERSUADED FRED TO OPT FOR A CAREER IN BASEBALL, SO HE SIGNED WITH THE BALTIMORE ORIOLES IN 1956! FRED HAD A FINE YEAR WITH WILSON OF THE CAROLINA LEAGUE IN 1958 WHERE HE HIT .319 WITH 16 HRs AND 55 RBIs -- PLUS HE MET HIS FUTURE WIFE THERE! FRED EARNED A LATE-SEASON CALL-UP WITH THE ORIOLES IN 1959 AND QUICKLY CHALKED UP HIS FIRST BIG LEAGUE HIT OFF CHICAGO'S BILLY PIERCE ON SEPTEMBER 11! FRED SPENT THE BULK OF THE NEXT FOUR YEARS BACK IN THE MINORS, BUT HE FINALLY GOT A BIG BREAK WHEN HIS CONTRACT WAS PURCHASED BY THE NATS ON OCTOBER 12, 1963! FRED GOT HIS FIRST START FOR THE NATS ON APRIL 27, 1964, FILLING IN FOR THE INJURED CHUCK HINTON! HE CAME THROUGH, TOO, SLAMMING HIS FIRST CAREER ROUND-TRIPPER OFF ANGELS RIGHT-HANDER KEN McBRIDE! AFTER SEEING LIMITED ACTION IN 1964, FRED WAS OPTIONED TO HAWAII IN 1965 WHERE HE POSTED A HUGE YEAR BY HITTING .324 WITH 25 HOMERS AND A LEAGUE-LEADING 58 STEALS! THAT EARNED HIM A CHANCE TO BE THE NATS' REGULAR RIGHTFIELDER IN 1966 -- AN OPPORTUNITY HE SIEZED WITH GUSTO! APPEARING IN 146 GAMES FOR THE '66 SENATORS, FRED BATTED .276 WITH 16 HOMERS, 59 RBIs, AND 22 STOLEN BASES -- ALL WHILE PLAYING SPECTACULAR DEFENSE! TWO OF FRED'S BEST DAYS WITH THE NATS IN '66 CAME WHEN HE POSTED BACK-TO-BACK FOUR-HIT GAMES ON MAY 10 AND 11!
FRED REMAINED WITH THE NATS THROUGH JUNE OF 1968, BUT IT WAS 1966 THAT TURNED HIM INTO A TRUE ALL-TIME FAVORITE OF NATS FANS! MANY STILL FONDLY REMEMBER SOME OF FRED'S GREAT ENDORSEMENTS, LIKE HIS OLD "TIME OUT FOR TASTYKAKE" COMMERCIALS!
JOYNER ©1999
GOES GREAT WITH MILK, KIDS -- JUST ASK HONDO!
1260
FRED CLOSED OUT HIS BASEBALL CAREER AFTER PLAYING THE 1970 SEASON IN JAPAN! HE THEN BEGAN A LONG AND IMPORTANT SECOND CAREER AS THE DIRECTOR OF EQUAL EMPLOYMENT OPPORTUNITY AND AFFIRMATIVE ACTION FOR THE CLARK CONSTRUCTION COMPANY!

Ed Mickelson

FILLING IN FOR STAN MUSIAL WHO WAS SICK IN BED WITH A TEMPERATURE OF 103°, ED MICKELSON BANGED OUT HIS FIRST BIG LEAGUE HIT ON SEPTEMBER 21, 1950! "MY FIRST TIME AT BAT," RECALLED ED, "AGAINST THE GREAT WARREN SPAHN, I HIT A SINGLE TO LEFT FIELD. WE GOT ONLY ONE MORE HIT THAT DAY IN A 5-0 LOSS. IT WAS SPAHN'S 21ST VICTORY OF THE SEASON."

ED WAS THE FIRST PICK AMONG 8,500 PLAYERS IN THE MINOR LEAGUE DRAFT IN 1954, MAKING HIM A PORTLAND BEAVER IN THE P.C.L.!

IT WAS A GREAT 1950 SEASON AT MONTGOMERY THAT EARNED ED HIS CALL-UP TO THE CARDINALS AND HIS SHOT TO SPELL STAN THE MAN! ED HIT .417 FOR THE REBELS THAT SEASON WITH 21 HOMERS AND 102 RBIs! BORN ON SEPTEMBER 9, 1926, IN OTTAWA, ILLINOIS, EDWARD ALLEN MICKELSON PUT TOGETHER A FANTASTIC MINOR LEAGUE CAREER THAT, AS FATE WOULD HAVE IT, DID NOT TRANSLATE INTO THE FULL-TIME BIG LEAGUE TRIAL THAT HE TRULY DESERVED! ED ALWAYS GAVE HIS ALL, THOUGH, AND FROM 1946 THROUGH '57 HE DISTINGUISHED HIMSELF IN GREAT MINOR LEAGUE TOWNS LIKE DECATUR, POCATELLO, COLUMBUS, LYNCHBURG, NEW ORLEANS, ROCHESTER, SAN ANTONIO, SHREVEPORT AND PORTLAND! ED'S MOTTO OF "WIN SOME, LOSE SOME, AND SOME ARE RAINED OUT!" HELPED HIM EMBRACE HIS FATE AS A CAREER MINOR LEAGUER!

ED APPEARED IN 5 GAMES WITH THE '50 CARDS; 7 GAMES WITH THE '53 BROWNS; AND 6 GAMES WITH THE '57 CUBS! HE MADE HISTORY ON SEPTEMBER 27, 1953, AS THE BROWNIES PLAYED THEIR LAST GAME IN FRANCHISE HISTORY -- A 2-1 LOSS TO THE WHITE SOX! "JOHNNY GROTH HIT A DOUBLE," ED REMEMBERED, "AND I HIT A SINGLE TO DRIVE HIM HOME. I HAD BECOME A TRIVIA QUESTION -- WHO DROVE IN THE LAST BROWNS RUN!"

Rick DEMPSEY

SELECTED IN THE 15TH ROUND OF THE 1967 FREE AGENT DRAFT BY MINNESOTA, RICK DEMPSEY MADE HIS DEBUT AS A LATE-SEASON CALL-UP FOR THE TWINS IN 1969 WHERE HE RAPPED OUT THREE HITS IN SIX AT-BATS! WHILE USED SPARINGLY BY THE TWINS THROUGH THE 1972 SEASON, RICK MADE THE MOST OF HIS SITUATION BY ABSORBING AS MUCH KNOWLEDGE AS POSSIBLE ABOUT THE ART OF CATCHING! HE WAS DEALT TO THE YANKS PRIOR TO THE '73 CAMPAIGN WHERE HE CONTINUED TO LEARN THE ROPES AS A BACK-UP TO THE GREAT THURMAN MUNSON! FINALLY ENJOYING THE FRUITS OF THE BOMBERS' LONG-RUNNING REBUILDING PROGRAM AND PREPARING FOR A POSSIBLE TRIP TO THE '76 PLAYOFFS, RICK WAS DEVASTATED WHEN HE LEARNED HE HAD BEEN TRADED TO THE ORIOLES ON JUNE 15, 1976! THE DEAL, HOWEVER, TURNED OUT TO BE THE BEST THING THAT EVER HAPPENED TO RICK, AS HE IMMEDIATELY BECAME THE ORIOLES NUMBER-ONE CATCHER -- A JOB HE WOULD OWN FOR THE NEXT 10-1/2 YEARS! RICK WAS THE BIRDS' CATCHER WHEN BALTIMORE LOST THE 1979 SERIES TO THE PIRATES, BUT HE WAS REDEEMED WHEN HIS ORIOLES DEFEATED THE PHILLIES IN THE '83 SERIES -- WITH RICK NABBING M.V.P. HONORS! RICK POCKETED ANOTHER WORLD SERIES RING IN 1988 AS A BACK-UP TO MIKE SCIOSCIA WHILE WITH THE DODGERS! RICK WAS BACK IN THE HEADLINES TWO YEARS LATER WHEN HE KNOCKED THE CHAW OUT OF LENNY DYKSTRA'S MOUTH IN A BRAWL AT HOME PLATE!

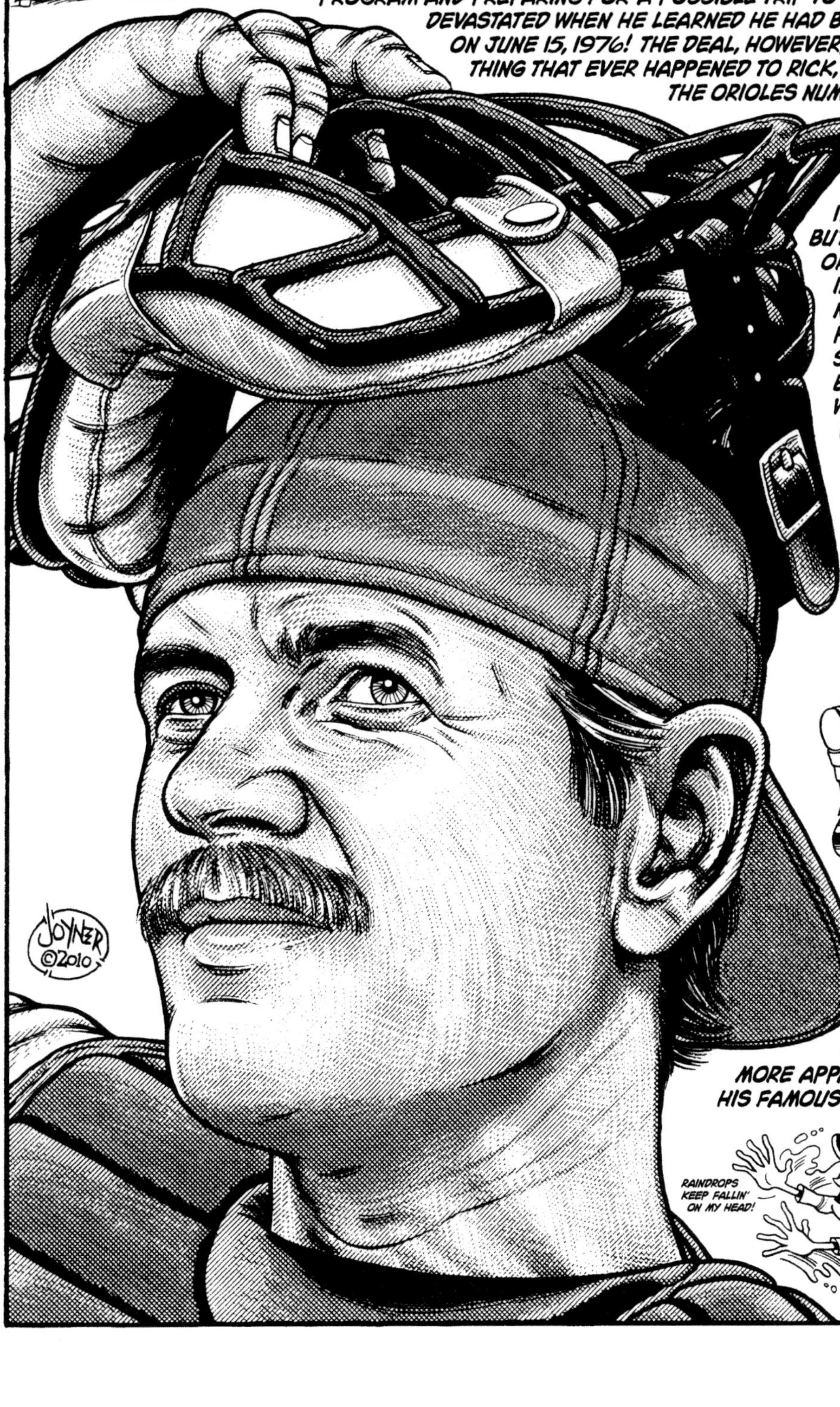

RICK'S DUST-UP WITH DYKSTRA WAS ACTUALLY WAY OUT OF CHARACTER FOR HIM! HE WAS KNOWN MORE FOR HIS GREAT SENSE OF HUMOR, WHICH WAS NEVER MORE APPARENT THAN WHEN HE PUT ON HIS FAMOUS RAIN DELAY THEATER ON THE RAIN-SOAKED TARPAULIN!

Shane VICTORINO

THE PHILLIES KNEW WHEN THEY STOLE SHANE VICTORINO FROM THE DODGERS VIA THE RULE 5 DRAFT THAT THEY WERE NOT ONLY GETTING A FINE PLAYER, BUT ALSO A FELLOW OF GREAT CHARACTER! IN FACT, SHANE PROVED HIS INTEGRITY YEARS EARLIER WHEN HE BECAME AN EAGLE SCOUT AS A TEEN! THE HAWAIIAN BORN AND RAISED CENTERFIELDER WAS A FOUR-SPORT STAR AT ST. ANTHONY'S HIGH, AND EVEN REJECTED A FOOTBALL SCHOLARSHIP TO THE UNIVERSITY OF HAWAII TO ENTER THE MINOR LEAGUES! HIS CHOICE PROVED TO BE A WISE ONE, AND BY 2008 SHANE WAS USING HIS SPEED, POWER, AND LEADERSHIP TO HELP THE PHILS TO THEIR FIRST CHAMPIONSHIP SINCE 1980! NICKNAMED THE "FLYIN' HAWAIIAN" BECAUSE OF HIS BLAZING SPEED, SHANE SWIPED 36 BAGS DURING THEIR CHAMPIONSHIP YEAR OF 2008!

TO GO WITH HIS WORLD SERIES RING, OTHER 2008 ACHIEVEMENTS FOR SHANE INCLUDE A PERSONAL BEST .293 BATTING AVERAGE, A 14-GAME HITTING STREAK, AND A GOLD GLOVE AWARD!

SHANE WAS AT THE CENTER OF WHAT MAY HAVE BEEN THE PIVOTAL MOMENT IN THE PHILLIES' RUN AT THE 2008 WORLD SERIES -- GAME THREE OF THE NATIONAL LEAGUE CHAMPIONSHIP SERIES AGAINST THE DODGERS IN LOS ANGELES! AFTER GOING 2-FOR-5 WITH FOUR RBIs IN THE PHILS' GAME TWO WIN, DODGERS RIGHT-HANDER HIROKI KURODA GREETED SHANE WITH A FASTBALL FIRED AT HIS HEAD! THE PITCH BARELY MISSED, AND SHANE ANGRILY GESTURED TO KURODA THAT PITCHING INSIDE WAS OKAY -- BUT NOT AT THE HEAD! THIS INCENSED THE DODGER PLAYERS AND FANS, AND LOS ANGELES WENT ON TO WIN THE GAME -- BUT SHANE ULTIMATELY SILENCED THEM FOR GOOD WITH A BACK-BREAKING 8TH-INNING 2-RUN HOMER THAT HELPED PHILLY TO VICTORY IN GAME FOUR! THEIR SPIRIT BROKEN, THE DODGERS WOULD BE ELIMINATED IN GAME FIVE! THE FIRE THAT SHANE DEMONSTRATED THAT DAY ISN'T UNUSUAL FOR HIM -- HE DOES IT DAY-IN AND DAY-OUT FOR THE PHILS, MAKING HIM A FAN FAVORITE IN THE CITY OF BROTHERLY LOVE!

Marty MALLOY

.228-HITTING PRIMA DONNAS REFUSING TO GIVE A KID AN AUTOGRAPH... MILLIONAIRE PLAYERS FIGHTING BILLIONAIRE OWNERS FOR MORE MONEY... HALF A WEEK'S PAY FOR A DAD TO TAKE HIS FAMILY TO A BALLGAME... THESE WERE JUST A FEW OF THE REASONS THAT RENOWNED ALABAMAN WRITER AND BASEBALL FAN PAUL HEMPHILL DECIDED TO TURN HIS BACK ON BIG LEAGUE BALL. THE YEAR WAS 1993. FOR PURE, OLD SCHOOL BASEBALL, HEMPHILL DECIDED TO TURN HIS ATTENTION TO THE MINOR LEAGUES AND THE NEARBY CLASS-A MACON BRAVES. THERE, BURIED DEEP IN THE BUSHES, HEMPHILL DISCOVERED A SCRAPPY, HUSTLING, SLICK-FIELDING, UNDERSIZED SECOND BASEMAN WHO PLAYED THE GAME WITH A TENACITY AND PASSION THAT HARKENED BACK TO THE GLORY DAYS OF THE GAME. THE KID'S NAME WAS MARTY MALLOY. HEMPHILL FOLLOWED YOUNG MARTY THROUGHOUT HIS THIRD YEAR IN PRO BALL, THE '94 SEASON AT DURHAM, AND CHRONICLED IT IN THE ACCLAIMED BOOK "THE HEART OF THE GAME." IN THE BOOK, HEMPHILL DETAILED HOW MARTY BATTLED THROUGH THE RIGORS OF THE MINORS -- AND PERSEVERED. A THREE-SPORT ATHLETE AT FLORIDA'S TRENTON HIGH SCHOOL, MARTY WENT ON TO STAR IN BASEBALL AT SANTE FE COMMUNITY COLLEGE IN GAINSVILLE BEFORE SIGNING WITH THE BRAVES IN 1992. MARTY HIT .315 IN ROOKIE BALL AT IDAHO FALLS BEFORE MOVING ON TO MACON WHERE HEMPHILL FIRST SAW HIM DURING INFIELD PRACTICE. DRAWN TO HIM IMMEDIATELY, HEMPHILL WROTE THAT MARTY WAS "FRAIL AND LOOSE-JOINTED AT FIVE TEN AND 160 POUNDS, WEARING AN OLD-FASHIONED CREW CUT, TRYING TO SPROUT A MUSTACHE, HOLLERING AND SLAPPING HIS GLOVE AND PIROUETTING OUT OF THE THE WAY OF IMAGINARY BASE RUNNERS AS HE SPUN ON THE DOUBLE-PLAY PIVOT." SOON AFTERWARDS, HEMPHILL, HIS BASEBALL SPIRITS LIFTED BY MARTY'S SPUNK, PROCLAIMED, "LO, JUST WHEN BASEBALL APPEARED TO BE COMMITTING SUICIDE, HERE CAME HUCK FINN TO PLAY SOME BALL."

BURIED IN THE BRAVES' TALENT-RICH FARM SYSTEM, MARTY PAID HIS DUES, BUT FINALLY BEAT THE ODDS BY GETTING CALLED UP ON SEPTEMBER 6, 1998. IN THE SECOND AT-BAT OF HIS BIG LEAGUE DEBUT THAT DAY, MARTY, WHO HAD ALL OF 33 LONG BALLS IN 2,900 MINOR LEAGUE AT-BATS, HOMERED INTO THE METS BULLPEN TO GIVE HIS BRAVES A 2-0 LEAD. "NO WORDS CAN DESCRIBE THIS FEELING," MARTY SAID AFTER THE GAME. HE WAS BACK IN THE MINORS THE NEXT YEAR UNTIL RETURNING FOR A BRIEF MAJOR LEAGUE STINT WITH THE MARLINS IN 2002. HE FINALLY HUNG UP HIS SPIKES AFTER THE 2003 MINOR LEAGUE SEASON. WHILE HIS TIME IN THE SHOW WAS BRIEF, MARTY'S TIME IN "THE GAME" WAS LONG AND EXCITING. HE GAVE HIS ALL, WHICH IS WHY HE'LL ALWAYS SYMBOLIZE THE HEART OF THE GAME.

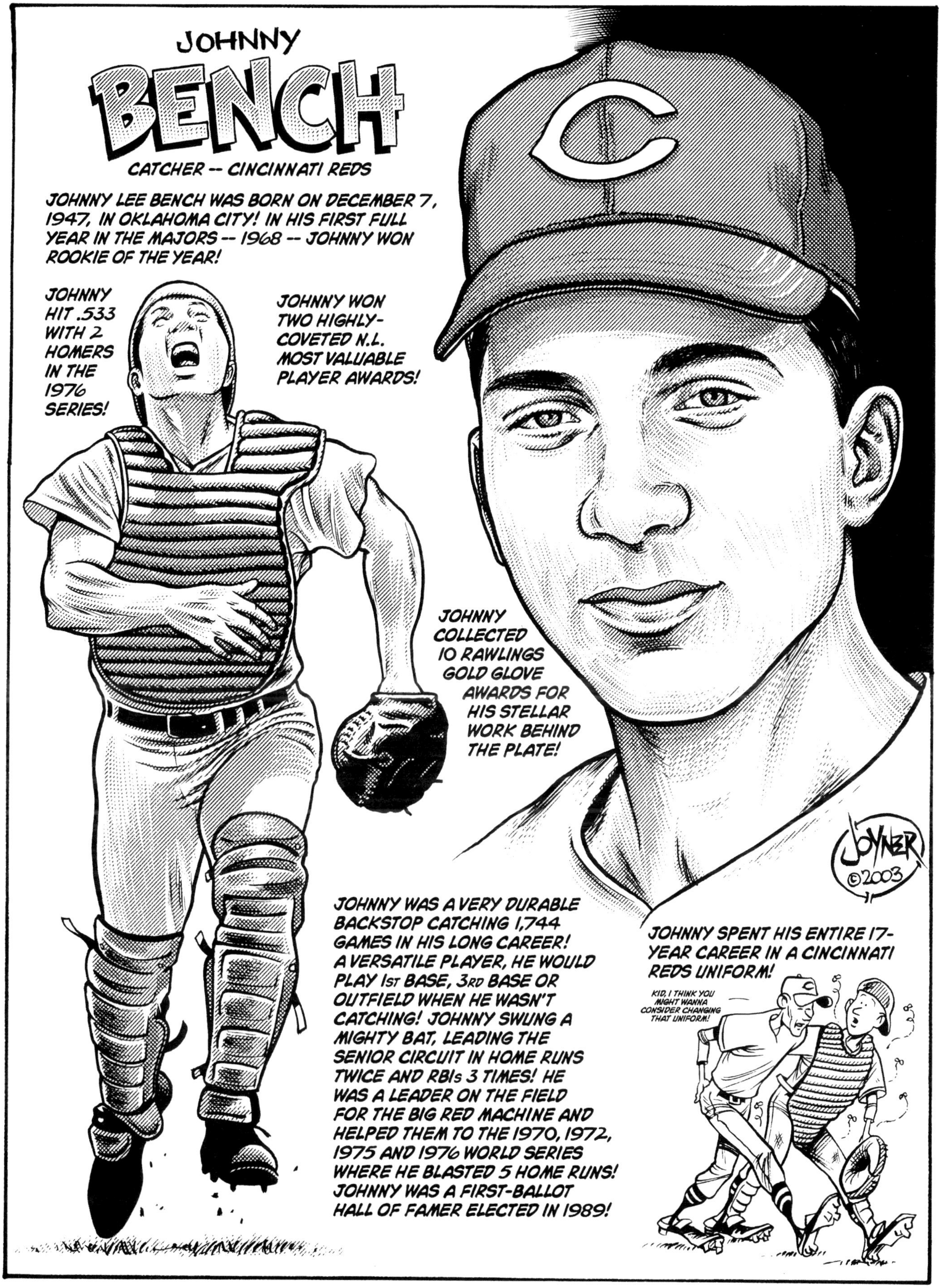
JOHNNY
BENCH
CATCHER -- CINCINNATI REDS
JOHNNY LEE BENCH WAS BORN ON DECEMBER 7, 1947, IN OKLAHOMA CITY! IN HIS FIRST FULL YEAR IN THE MAJORS -- 1968 -- JOHNNY WON ROOKIE OF THE YEAR!
JOHNNY HIT .533 WITH 2 HOMERS IN THE 1976 SERIES!
JOHNNY WON TWO HIGHLY-COVETED N.L. MOST VALUABLE PLAYER AWARDS!
JOHNNY COLLECTED 10 RAWLINGS GOLD GLOVE AWARDS FOR HIS STELLAR WORK BEHIND THE PLATE!
JOYNER ©2003
JOHNNY WAS A VERY DURABLE BACKSTOP CATCHING 1,744 GAMES IN HIS LONG CAREER! A VERSATILE PLAYER, HE WOULD PLAY 1st BASE, 3rd BASE OR OUTFIELD WHEN HE WASN'T CATCHING! JOHNNY SWUNG A MIGHTY BAT, LEADING THE SENIOR CIRCUIT IN HOME RUNS TWICE AND RBIs 3 TIMES! HE WAS A LEADER ON THE FIELD FOR THE BIG RED MACHINE AND HELPED THEM TO THE 1970, 1972, 1975 AND 1976 WORLD SERIES WHERE HE BLASTED 5 HOME RUNS! JOHNNY WAS A FIRST-BALLOT HALL OF FAMER ELECTED IN 1989!
JOHNNY SPENT HIS ENTIRE 17-YEAR CAREER IN A CINCINNATI REDS UNIFORM!
KID, I THINK YOU MIGHT WANNA CONSIDER CHANGING THAT UNIFORM!

Albie PEARSON

ALBERT GREGORY PEARSON, THE OVERACHIEVING 5-FOOT-5-INCH 1958 A.L. ROOKIE OF THE YEAR, STOOD AS A HERO TO THE "SMALL MAN" IN HIS EARLY YEARS! NOW, WELL INTO IN HIS SENIOR YEARS, HE STANDS AS A HERO TO "EVERY MAN." FOLLOWING HIS COLORFUL NINE-YEAR CAREER AS A BIG LEAGUE OUTFIELDER, ALBIE DEDICATED HIS LIFE TO HELPING ABUSED AND NEGLECTED BOYS THROUGH HIS "FATHER'S HEART RANCH" IN DESERT HOT SPRINGS! COUNTLESS BOYS HAVE BEEN GIVEN A NEW START THANKS TO ALBIE, TO WHICH HE SAYS, "WHEN YOU SEE A LIFE CHANGED BY THE POWER OF GOD, THE POWER OF LOVE, IT'S WORTH EVERY GAME I EVER PLAYED."

LITTLE ALBIE WAS BORN ON SEPTEMBER 12, 1938, IN ALHAMBRA, CA! HIS GROWTH WAS STUNTED DUE TO A CONGENITAL SPINAL CONDITION -- BUT THAT JUST SERVED TO FUEL HIS COMPETITIVE FIRE! HE LETTERED IN BASEBALL, FOOTBALL, TRACK, AND BASKETBALL AT EL MONTE HIGH SCHOOL -- AND THAT DREW THE ATTENTION OF THE RED SOX ORGANIZATION WHO SIGNED HIM IN 1953! UNABLE TO CRACK THE BOSTON LINEUP, ALBIE WAS DEALT TO THE SENATORS PRIOR TO HIS STELLAR ROOKIE CAMPAIGN OF 1958! ALBIE'S GREATEST YEARS CAME WITH THE ANGELS OF THE EARLY-TO-MID '60s! HIS STEADY BAT, SPEED ON THE BASES, EXCELLENT OUTFIELD RANGE, AND CANNON-ARM PLACE HIM SECURELY ALONGSIDE SOME OF THE GREATEST EVER TO WEAR ANGELS FLANNELS!

ALBIE'S POPULARITY WITH ANGELS FANS ONCE LED TO AN OFFSEASON JOB AS A LATE-NIGHT DISC JOCKEY! IT DIDN'T LAST LONG, HOWEVER -- BUT NOT FOR LACK OF LISTENERS! "I COULDN'T STAND THE HOURS," SAID ALBIE. "ALL I WANTED TO DO WAS PLAY GOLF!"

ALBIE WAS PAIRED WITH MARILYN MONROE FOR A PRE-GAME CHARITY EVENT IN THE SPRING OF '62! HE RECALLED SEEING "SADNESS" IN HER EYES, BUT ALBIE, WHO WAS ALWAYS VERY RELIGIOUS, GOT LOST IN THE MOMENT AND MISSED THE CHANCE TO OFFER HER ANY COUNSEL. MONTHS LATER, SHE WAS DEAD. IT WAS AT THAT MOMENT THAT ALBIE PLEDGED TO DO ALL HE COULD TO HELP OTHERS AVOID THE SAME FATE!

BILLY'S 12 HITS IN THE 1953 WORLD SERIES NETTED HIM THE SERIES' BIG AWARD -- MOST VALUABLE PLAYER!
Billy Martin
I'M GONNA NEED A BIGGER TROPHY CASE!
WHEN 2ND-YEAR YANKEE MANAGER CASEY STENGEL NEEDED A NEW SPARKPLUG PLAYER FOR HIS CLUB AS THEY HEADED INTO THE 1950 CAMPAIGN, HE IMMEDIATELY THOUGHT OF A SCRAPPY, TOUGH KID WHO HAD PLAYED FOR HIS P.C.L. OAKLAND OAKS TEAM BACK IN 1948 -- 21-YEAR-OLD BILLY MARTIN! BILLY'S HUSTLING, AGGRESSIVE STYLE OF PLAY HELPED SPARK THE YANKEES TO PENNANTS IN EACH OF HIS SEVEN SEASONS IN PINSTRIPES FROM 1950-57! THE ONLY YEAR THAT NEW YORK DIDN'T WIN THE PENNANT IN THAT SPAN WAS 1954 -- THE YEAR THAT BILLY WAS IN THE U.S. ARMY! BILLY'S ACHIEVEMENTS ON THE BALLFIELD ARE MANY, IN PARTICULAR HIS RECORD-SETTING 12 HITS IN THE 1953 WORLD SERIES, BUT PERHAPS THE MOST MEMORABLE IMAGE OF BILLY -- ASIDE FROM HIS FREQUENT FISTFIGHTS -- WAS HIS LUNGING, SERIES-SAVING CATCH OF JACKIE ROBINSON'S BASES-LOADED INFIELD POP IN THE 7TH INNING OF GAME SEVEN OF THE 1952 FALL CLASSIC!
I HAD IT ALL THE WAY!
BILLY'S FINE ON-FIELD ABILITY CAME TO BE OVERSHADOWED BY THE MANY NOTORIOUS FIGHTS HE WAS INVOLVED WITH AS A PLAYER AND MANAGER! HERE ARE A FEW OF HIS GREATEST HITS: BILLY WHIPPED JIMMY PIERSALL UNDER THE FENWAY PARK STANDS BEFORE A GAME IN 1952; HE, ALONG WITH A NUMBER OF HIS YANKEE TEAMMATES, WAS INVOLVED IN A BRAWL AT THE COPACABANA CLUB -- AN INCIDENT THAT LED THE YANKS TO TRADE HIM IN 1957; WHILE WITH THE REDS IN 1960 BILLY BROKE THE CHEEKBONE OF CUBS PITCHER JIM BREWER IN A FIGHT ON THE MOUND AT WRIGLEY; AS A MANAGER WITH THE TWINS IN 1969 BILLY PUNCHED OUT HIS OWN PITCHER, DAVE BOSWELL, HOSPITALIZING HIM; IN 1979 BILLY SUFFERED HIS FIRST OF MANY FIRINGS AS YANKEE SKIPPER AFTER BEATING UP A MARSHMALLOW SALESMAN!
PIERSALL
BREWER
JACKSON
TAKE A NUMBER, BOYS!
JET PUFF MARSHMALLOW
JOYNER ©2005

Chuck HINTON

CHARLES EDWARD HINTON, JR. WAS BORN ON MAY 3, 1934, IN ROCKY MOUNT, NORTH CAROLINA! ALWAYS POSSESSING EXTRAORDINARY ATHLETIC ABILITY, CHUCK BECAME A MULTI-SPORTS SUPERSTAR AT BOOKER T. WASHINGTON HIGH SCHOOL! EVENTUALLY FOLLOWING IN HIS BROTHER CHECO'S FOOTSTEPS, CHUCK ATTENDED SHAW UNIVERSITY IN RALEIGH, DISTINGUISHING HIMSELF IN BASEBALL, FOOTBALL, AND BASKETBALL! BASEBALL WAS CHUCK'S TRUE PASSION, SO HE PURSUED HIS DREAM OF PLAYING BIG LEAGUE BALL BY ATTENDING AN OPEN MAJOR LEAGUE TRYOUT AT GRIFFITH STADIUM IN 1956! CHUCK BLEW AWAY ALL THE SCOUTS, BUT OPTED TO SIGN WITH THE BALTIMORE ORIOLES! AFTER A BRIEF STINT WITH PHOENIX OF THE ARIZONA-MEXICO LEAGUE, CHUCK DID A 2-YEAR STINT WITH UNCLE SAM! UPON HIS DISCHARGE, CHUCK RESUMED HIS MINOR LEAGUE CAREER, BLAZING A QUICK PATH TO THE SHOW!

THE NEW WASHINGTON SENATORS SNATCHED CHUCK FROM THE ORIOLES ORGANIZATION IN THE EXPANSION DRAFT ON NOVEMBER 14, 1960! CHUCK OPENED THE 1961 SEASON ON LOAN TO CINCINNATI'S TRIPLE-A TEAM IN INDIANAPOLIS, BUT HIS HOT HITTING THERE DEMANDED THAT THE SENATORS CALL HIM UP -- QUICKLY! ON MAY 14, 1961, CHUCK ACHIEVED HIS DREAM BY PLAYING IN HIS FIRST BIG LEAGUE GAME AND GETTING HIS FIRST CAREER HIT -- A SINGLE OFF BOSTON'S BILLY MUFFETT! WITH THAT CHUCK WAS ON HIS WAY TO A FINE 11-YEAR MAJOR LEAGUE CAREER PLAYING WITH THE INDIANS AND ANGELS IN ADDITION TO HIS FOUR YEARS IN WASHINGTON! IN HIS CAREER CHUCK COLLECTED 1,048 HITS, 113 HOME RUNS, 130 STOLEN BASES, AND WAS AN AMERICAN LEAGUE ALL-STAR IN 1964! FOLLOWING HIS PLAYING DAYS CHUCK COACHED BASEBALL AT HOWARD UNIVERSITY FOR 28 YEARS, LEADING THEM TO MULTIPLE MEAC CHAMPIONSHIPS!

CHUCK WAS THE LAST SENATOR TO BAT OVER .300 WHEN IN 1962 HE POSTED THE BEST ALL-AROUND OFFENSIVE YEAR BY ANY EXPANSION SENATOR -- .310 WITH 25 2Bs, 17 HRs, 75 RBIs, AND 28 SBs!

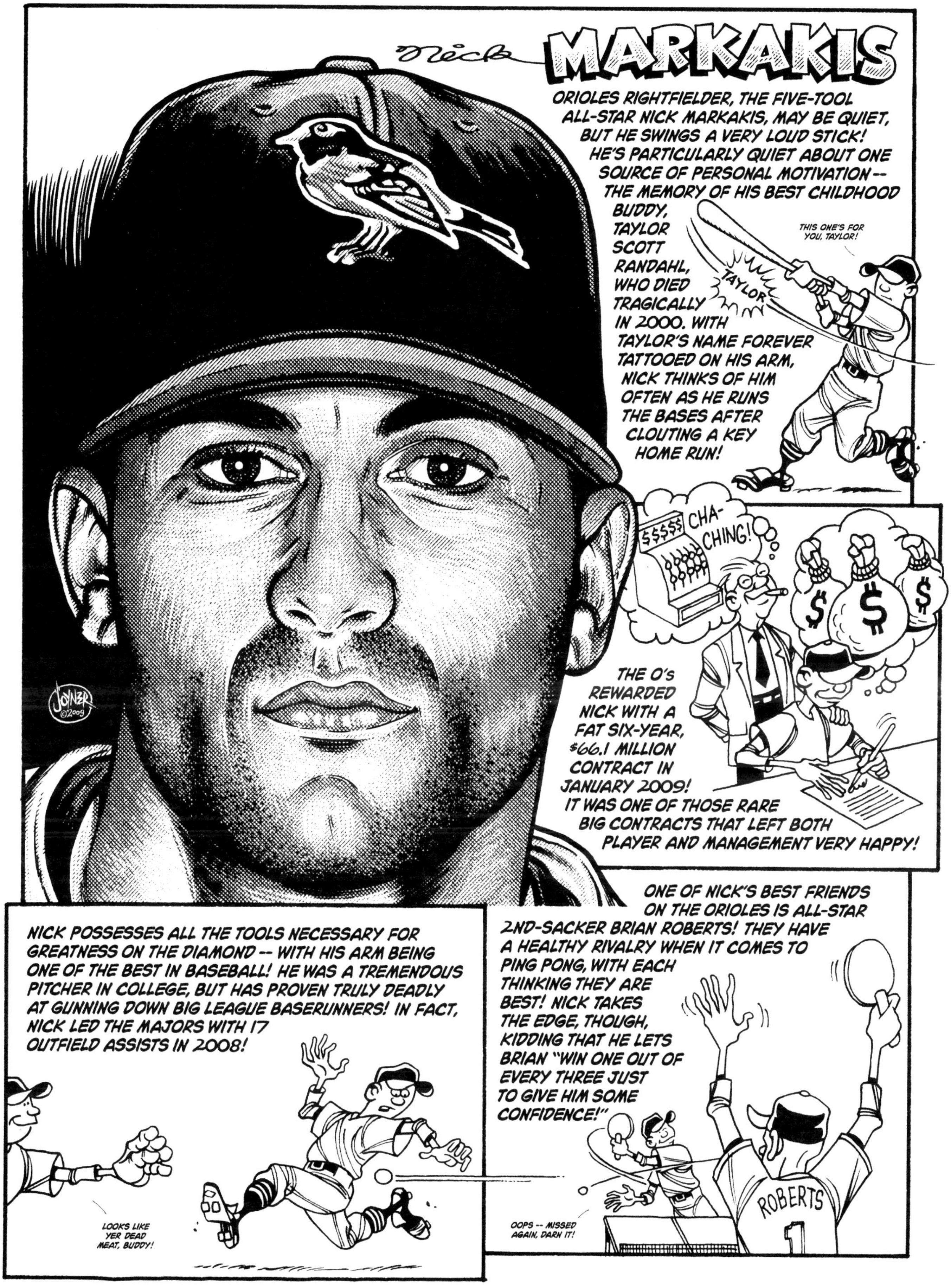

Nick MARKAKIS
ORIOLES RIGHTFIELDER, THE FIVE-TOOL ALL-STAR NICK MARKAKIS, MAY BE QUIET, BUT HE SWINGS A VERY LOUD STICK! HE'S PARTICULARLY QUIET ABOUT ONE SOURCE OF PERSONAL MOTIVATION -- THE MEMORY OF HIS BEST CHILDHOOD BUDDY, TAYLOR SCOTT RANDAHL, WHO DIED TRAGICALLY IN 2000. WITH TAYLOR'S NAME FOREVER TATTOOED ON HIS ARM, NICK THINKS OF HIM OFTEN AS HE RUNS THE BASES AFTER CLOUTING A KEY HOME RUN!
THIS ONE'S FOR YOU, TAYLOR!
TAYLOR
JOYNER ©2009
$$$$$
CHA-CHING!
$
$
$
THE O's REWARDED NICK WITH A FAT SIX-YEAR, $66.1 MILLION CONTRACT IN JANUARY 2009! IT WAS ONE OF THOSE RARE BIG CONTRACTS THAT LEFT BOTH PLAYER AND MANAGEMENT VERY HAPPY!
NICK POSSESSES ALL THE TOOLS NECESSARY FOR GREATNESS ON THE DIAMOND -- WITH HIS ARM BEING ONE OF THE BEST IN BASEBALL! HE WAS A TREMENDOUS PITCHER IN COLLEGE, BUT HAS PROVEN TRULY DEADLY AT GUNNING DOWN BIG LEAGUE BASERUNNERS! IN FACT, NICK LED THE MAJORS WITH 17 OUTFIELD ASSISTS IN 2008!
LOOKS LIKE YER DEAD MEAT, BUDDY!
ONE OF NICK'S BEST FRIENDS ON THE ORIOLES IS ALL-STAR 2ND-SACKER BRIAN ROBERTS! THEY HAVE A HEALTHY RIVALRY WHEN IT COMES TO PING PONG, WITH EACH THINKING THEY ARE BEST! NICK TAKES THE EDGE, THOUGH, KIDDING THAT HE LETS BRIAN "WIN ONE OUT OF EVERY THREE JUST TO GIVE HIM SOME CONFIDENCE!"
OOPS -- MISSED AGAIN, DARN IT!
ROBERTS
1

Ossie BLUEGE

NATIONALS THIRD BASEMAN OSSIE BLUEGE ENJOYED AN 18-YEAR CAREER IN WASHINGTON (1922-39), BUT IT ALMOST DIDN'T HAPPEN BECAUSE OF RUMORS THAT THE 3RD-SACKER HAD A BUM KNEE! JOE ENGEL, THE 29-YEAR-OLD NATIONALS SCOUT AND FORMER PITCHER, HAD A SOLUTION! HE CHALLENGED YOUNG OSSIE TO A FOOTRACE -- WITH A NATS CONTRACT BEING THE PRIZE! THE RACE WAS NO CONTEST AS OSSIE WON EASILY, PROVING THE SOUNDNESS OF HIS KNEE AND EARNING HIM A CONTRACT! BY LOSING TO OSSIE, HOWEVER, ENGEL ACTAULLY WON BIG AS HE WOULD SPEND MUCH OF THE NEXT TWO DECADES WITNESSING HIS SIGNEE SPARKLE DEFENSIVELY WHILE COLLECTING 1,751 BASE KNOCKS! OSSIE ALSO APPEARED WITH THE NATS IN THREE WORLD SERIES, INCLUDING THE CLUB'S ONE AND ONLY CHAMPIONSHIP IN 1924! ALAS, OSSIE'S ON-FIELD SUCCESS DID NOT TRANSLATE TO BIG DOLLARS, SO HE MOONLIGHTED AS AN ACCOUNTANT WITH SOME OF WASHINGTON'S BEST HOTELS AS CLIENTS! FEARFUL THAT HIS WORK CRUNCHING NUMBERS MIGHT DAMAGE HIS BATTING EYE, NATS FRUGAL OWNER CLARK GRIFFITH ORDERED OSSIE TO QUIT! OSSIE'S MEAGER SALARY WITH THE NATIONALS, HOWEVER, PROHIBITED HIM FROM OBEYING GRIFFITH'S DEMAND! IT TURNED OUT THAT OSSIE'S HANDINESS WITH NUMBERS WOULD LATER BENEFIT THE NATS AS HE WOULD SERVE AS THE FRANCHISE'S COMPTROLLER FROM 1948-56! FOLLOWING HIS PLAYING DAYS, OSSIE MANAGED THE NATS FROM 1943-47, WHICH INCLUDED 2ND-PLACE FINISHES IN 1943 AND '45! HE MOVED ON TO BECOME FARM DIRECTOR IN 1948, A POSITION HE HELD FOR NINE YEARS! BY THE TIME HE RETIRED FROM BASEBALL IN 1971, HE HAD SERVED THE NATIONALS/TWINS FRANCHISE FOR 50 YEARS! OSSIE WAS A MODEL OF CONSISTENCY ON THE FIELD, AND HIS QUIET AND WHOLESOME DEMEANOR SET A GREAT EXAMPLE FOR HIS YOUNG FANS AROUND WASHINGTON! HE NEVER DRANK OR SMOKED, A STARK CONTRAST TO MANY OF THE ROUGH-AND-TUMBLE CHARACTERS HE PLAYED WITH AND AGAINST!

OSSIE'S YOUNGER BROTHER, OTTO, PLAYED BRIEFLY WITH THE REDS IN 1932 AND 1933!

HAL MANDERS

PITCHER -- DETROIT TIGERS

HAL'S COUSIN IS HALL OF FAMER BOB FELLER!

HAROLD CARL MANDERS WAS BORN ON JUNE 14, 1917, IN WAUKEE, IOWA! FOLLOWING A FINE HIGH SCHOOL CAREER, HAL STUDIED MEDICINE AT THE UNIVERSITY OF IOWA WHILE ALSO STARRING AS A PITCHER WITH THE HAWKEYES! WITH ONLY ONE YEAR OF COLLEGE REMAINING, HAL WAS LURED AWAY WHEN THE DETROIT TIGERS SIGNED HIM IN 1939! HAL SHOWED WHY HE WAS A TOP-NOTCH PROSPECT BY MAKING THE TEXAS LEAGUE ALL-STAR TEAM WITH BEAUMONT IN 1939 AND '40! 15 VICTORIES AT KNOXVILLE IN '41 AND A SPOT ON THE SOUTHERN LEAGUE ALL-STAR TEAM WAS FINALLY ENOUGH TO EARN HAL A SEPTEMBER CALL-UP IN 1941 WHERE HE PROVED HE HAD THE GOODS BY PITCHING TO A 1-0 RECORD WITH A 2.35 E.R.A. IN 8 GAMES!

HAL ONCE SET AN IOWA HIGH SCHOOL RECORD BY STRIKING OUT 21 BATTERS IN A 7-INNING GAME!

HAL STARTED THE 1942 SEASON WITH THE TIGERS AND WAS 2-0 IN 18 RELIEF APPEARANCES BEFORE WORLD WAR II INTERVENED! CLASSIFIED 3-A FOR HIS BACKGROUND IN AGRICULTURE, HAL LEFT BASEBALL AND RETURNED TO DO ESSENTIAL FARMING ON HIS FARM IN IOWA FOR THE DURATION OF THE WAR! HAL RETURNED TO THE TIGERS IN 1946, BUT WHEN THEY TRADED HIM TO THE CUBS AND CHICAGO REFUSED TO PAY HIM A FAIR WAGE, HAL WALKED AWAY FROM THE GAME FOR GOOD AND RETURNED TO HIS FARMS!

HAL WAS A VERY SUCCESSFUL FARMER WHO RAISED CORN, SOYBEANS, PURE BRED HOGS, AND BEEF CATTLE! PRESIDENT RONALD REAGAN RECOGNIZED HAL'S FARMING EXPERTISE AND NAMED THE FORMER HURLER TO THE NATIONAL ADVISORY COUNCIL ON RURAL DEVELOPMENT IN 1987! HAL, ALWAYS A COMPETITOR, TOOK ON HIS NEW JOB WITH THE SAME VIGOR HE ONCE USED TO CUT DOWN BATTERS!

Rocky BRIDGES

ROCKY BRIDGES WAS A VALUABLE UTILITY MAN FOR ELEVEN BIG LEAGUE SEASONS BEFORE BEGINNING A LONG SECOND CAREER AS A MINOR LEAGUE MANAGER! THROUGHOUT IT ALL, ROCKY WAS THE SCRIBES' GO-TO GUY FOR WITTY WISECRACKS AND CLEVER QUOTES THAT WOULD ADD COLOR TO THEIR STORIES AND COLUMNS! HERE'S A SAMPLING OF THE WORLD ACCORDING TO ROCKY ... ON PLAYING FOR SEVEN DIFFERENT TEAMS IN ELEVEN YEARS: "MY WIFE HAD TO WRITE ME IN CARE OF COMMISSIONER FORD FRICK. HE WAS THE ONLY ONE WHO KNEW WHERE I WAS. AND IT'S A GOOD THING I STAYED IN CINCINNATI FOR FOUR YEARS -- IT TOOK ME THAT LONG TO LEARN HOW TO SPELL IT." ... ON HIS FACE: DODGER TEAMMATE PEE WEE REESE ONCE ASKED ROCKY, "DOES THAT FACE HURT YOU?" ROCKY REPLIED, "YOU'RE NO MONA LISA." ROCKY WAS APPARENTLY ABSENT THE DAY THEY EXPLAINED THAT MONA LISA WAS FAMOUS FOR HER CURIOUS SMILE AND HER VERY 'ORDINARY' LOOKS ... ON HIS WEAK HITTING ABILITY: "THERE USED TO BE A RULE AGAINST HITTING OR WALKING ME. THEY HAD A LOT GOING FOR THEM IF I SWUNG." ... ON HIS SIGNING BONUS: "BONUS? I HAD TO TAKE A TROLLEY DOWN TO MEET DODGER SCOUT TOM DOWNEY AND SIGN THE CONTRACT. THAT COST ME A NICKEL. I WALKED BACK BECAUSE I FIGURED THAT I HAD SPENT ENOUGH ON THE DEAL ALREADY." ... ON HIS ALL-STAR SEASON WITH THE '58 NATS: "I WAS HITTING .307 AT THE BREAK, BUT THEN I CHECKED OUT FRANK LARY'S FASTBALL ON MY JAW. THE TROUBLE WITH HAVING A WIRED JAW IS THAT YOU CAN NEVER TELL WHEN YOU'RE SLEEPY -- YOU CAN'T YAWN." ... ON HIS DISLIKE FOR EATING SNAILS: "I LIKE FAST FOOD." ... ON HIS FIRST YEAR MANAGING IN THE MINORS: "I MANAGED GOOD, BUT BOY DID THEY PLAY BAD." ... ON MANAGING AN EXHIBITION GAME AGAINST A JAPANESE TEAM: "AN HOUR AFTER THE GAME, YOU WANT TO GO OUT AND PLAY THEM AGAIN." ... ON BANNING HIS PLAYERS FROM EATING SUNFLOWER SEEDS: "THAT'S FOR BIRDS TO EAT. I'M AFRAID MY PLAYERS MIGHT START MOULTING OR GOING TO THE BATHROOM ON NEWSPAPERS." ... ON GIANTS SHORTSTOP JOSE GONZALES, WHO CHANGED HIS NAME TO URIBE GONZALES, AND THEN TO JOSE URIBE: "HE'S THE ULTIMATE PLAYER TO BE NAMED LATER." ... ROCKY ON THE UNIVERSAL NATURE OF MAN: "THERE ARE THREE THINGS THE AVERAGE MAN THINKS HE CAN DO BETTER THAN EVERYBODY ELSE -- BUILD A FIRE, RUN A HOTEL, AND MANAGE A BASEBALL TEAM."

LEE ELIA

LEE ELIA WAS AN INFIELDER WITH THE WHITE SOX AND CUBS DURING THE MID- TO LATE-60s, BUT IT'S HIS STINT AS CUBS SKIPPER IN 1982-83 FOR WHICH HE'S BEST REMEMBERED. WITH HIS PLAYERS COMING UNDER WHAT HE FELT WAS UNFAIRLY-HARSH SCRUTINY FROM THE CHICAGO FANS AND MEDIA, LEE BATTERED A GROUP OF REPORTERS WITH A PROFANITY-LACED TIRADE FOLLOWING A TOUGH ONE-RUN LOSS TO THE DODGERS ON APRIL 29, 1983. LEE'S RANT MADE NEWS IMMEDIATELY, BUT THE LEGEND OF IT HAS GROWN IN STATUS IN EACH SUBSEQUENT YEAR. WHAT FOLLOWS IS SOME OF THE TRANSCRIPT OF LEE'S EPIC TIRADE -- BLEEPED, HOWEVER, FOR MASS CONSUMPTION.

"WE GOT ALL THESE SO-CALLED BLEEPIN' FANS THAT COME OUT HERE AND SAY THEY'RE CUB FANS, THAT ARE SUPPOSED TO BE BEHIND YOU, RIPPIN' EVERY BLEEPIN' THING YOU DO! I HOPE WE GET BLEEPIN' HOTTER THAN BLEEP -- JUST TO STUFF IT UP THEM 3,000 BLEEPIN' PEOPLE THAT SHOW UP EVERY BLEEPIN' DAY! THEY CAN KISS MY BLEEPIN' BLEEP RIGHT DOWNTOWN -- AND PRINT IT! WHAT THE BLEEP AM I SUPPOSED TO DO? GO OUT THERE AND LET MY BLEEPIN' PLAYERS GET DESTROYED EVERY DAY AND BE QUIET ABOUT IT? FOR THE BLEEPIN' NICKEL-AND-DIME PEOPLE THAT SHOW UP? THE MOTHER-BLEEPERS DON'T EVEN WORK! THAT'S WHY THEY'RE OUT AT THE BLEEPIN' GAME! THEY OUGHT TO GO OUT AND GET A BLEEPIN' JOB AND FIND OUT WHAT IT'S LIKE TO GO OUT AND EARN A BLEEPIN' LIVING! 85 PERCENT OF THE BLEEPIN' WORLD IS WORKING! THE OTHER 15 PERCENT COME OUT HERE! IT'S A BLEEPIN' PLAYGROUND FOR THE BLEEP-SUCKERS! RIP 'THEM' MOTHER-BLEEPERS LIKE (YOU'RE RIPPING) THE BLEEPIN' PLAYERS! WE GOT GUYS BUSTIN' THEIR BLEEPIN' BLEEPS, AND THEM BLEEPIN' PEOPLE BOO! AND THAT'S THE CUBS? THEY TALK ABOUT THE GREAT BLEEPIN' SUPPORT THAT THE PLAYERS GET AROUND HERE. I HAVEN'T SEEN IT THIS BLEEPIN' YEAR! EVERY TIME WE LOSE A BLEEPIN' CLOSE GAME, IT'S MAGNIFIED. WHY DID THIS GUY BUNT? THAT GUY POP UP? OR THIS GUY THROW A WILD PITCH? THAT'S BASEBALL, FELLAS. THAT'S HOW RUNS ARE SCORED. THAT'S THE DIFFERENCE BETWEEN VICTORY AND DEFEAT. THE BLEEPIN' CHANGES THAT HAVE HAPPENED IN THE CUB ORGANIZATION ARE MULTI-FOLD. ALRIGHT, THEY DON'T SHOW BECAUSE WE'RE 5-AND-14. AND, UNFORTUNATELY, THAT'S THE CRITERIA OF THEM DUMB 15 MOTHER-BLEEPIN' PERCENT THAT COME OUT TO DAY BASEBALL! THE OTHER 85 PERCENT ARE EARNING A LIVING! I TELL YOU, THERE'S SOME BLEEPIN' PROS OUT THERE THAT WANNA PLAY THIS GAME. BUT YOU'RE STUCK IN A BLEEPIN' STIGMA OF THE BLEEPIN' DODGERS, AND THE PHILLIES, AND THE CARDINALS, AND ALL THAT CHEAP BLEEP! ALL THESE MOTHER-BLEEPIN' EDITORIALS ABOUT CEY, AND BLEEPIN' PHILLY-ITIS, AND ALL THAT BLEEP -- IT'S SICK! WE GOT 143 BLEEPIN' GAMES LEFT! WHAT I'M TRYIN' TO SAY IS DON'T RIP THEM BLEEPIN' GUYS OUT THERE. IF YOU WANNA RIP SOMEBODY, RIP MY BLEEPIN' BLEEP! BUT DON'T RIP THEM BLEEPIN' GUYS 'CAUSE THEY'RE GIVIN' EVERYTHING THEY CAN GIVE! AND RIGHT NOW, THEY'RE TRYIN' TO DO MORE THAN GOD GAVE 'EM, AND THAT'S WHY WE MAKE THE SIMPLE MISTAKES. ONCE WE HIT THAT BLEEPIN' GROOVE, IT'LL FLOW-- THE TALENT'S THERE. I DON'T KNOW HOW TO MAKE IT ANY CLEARER TO YOU. I'M FRUSTRATED. IT'D BE DIFFERENT IF I WAS IN THIS ROOM EVERY DAY AND SAW A BUNCH OF GUYS THAT DIDN'T GIVE A BLEEP. THEY DO GIVE A BLEEP, AND IT'S TOUGH." LONG LIVE LEE BLEEPIN' ELIA FOR TELLIN' IT LIKE IT BLEEPIN' IS!

Bob
UECKER
INDICATIONS THAT HE WAS NOT DESTINED TO BECOME A BASEBALL ALL-STAR WERE THERE FROM THE VERY BEGINNING FOR FUNNY-MAN BOB UECKER. "ROLAND HEMOND OF MILWAUKEE SIGNED ME FOR A $3,000 BONUS," HE SAID. "THAT BOTHERED MY DAD AT THE TIME BECAUSE HE DIDN'T HAVE THAT KIND OF DOUGH TO LAY OUT. FINALLY, HE SCRAPED IT UP AND GOT ME TO LEAVE HOME."
YOU'RE NOT GOING TO BRING HIM BACK, ARE YOU MR. HEMOND?
$
$
MIL.
AFTER SPENDING 1962-63 WITH THE BRAVES, BOB JOINED THE CARDINALS IN 1964 WHERE HIS .198 AVERAGE HELPED BRING A WORLD TITLE TO ST. LOUIS! BOB SAW NO ACTION IN THE SERIES, BUT HE DID HIS PART TO KEEP HIS TEAMMATES LOOSE -- LIKE SHAGGING FLIES WITH A TUBA, FOR EXAMPLE, BEFORE GAME ONE AT SPORTSMAN'S PARK!
I GOT IT! I GOT IT!
USING A CLEVER, SELF-DEPRICATING SENSE OF HUMOR, BOB TURNED HIMSELF INTO A BONA FIDE TV AND FILM STAR FOLLOWING THE CONCLUSION OF HIS PLAYING DAYS! IN THE MEANTIME, BOB WAS ALSO MAKING A FINE NAME FOR HIMSELF AS A PLAY-BY-PLAY MAN FOR THE BREWERS -- A JOB HE HAS NOW HELD FOR NEARLY FOUR DECADES! BOB WAS ELECTED TO THE BASEBALL HALL OF FAME AS A BROAD-CASTER IN 2003! UNABLE TO PLAY IT STRAIGHT AT HIS INDUCTION CEREMONY, BOB SAID, "I HOPE THIS DOESN'T COME OFF AS SOUR GRAPES, BUT I REALLY THINK I SHOULD BE GOING IN THE HALL AS A PLAYER."
SHHHHHH...
HALL OF FAME
PLAYERS
ENTRANCE
JOYNER ©2011

Sam Mele

SABATH ANTHONY "SAM" MELE WAS BORN ON JANUARY 21, 1923, IN ASTORIA, NEW YORK! SAM WAS A QUEEN'S PARK BASEBALL LEGEND LONG BEFORE HE MOVED ON TO THE BIGGER STAGE OF THE MAJOR LEAGUES!

SAM ATTENDED NEW YORK UNIVERSITY WHERE HE STARRED IN BASEBALL AND BASKETBALL, EVENTUALLY LEADING THE NYU BASKETBALL SQUAD TO AN APPEARANCE IN THE 1943 NCAA TOURNAMENT! SAM SERVED IN THE MARINES DURING WORLD WAR II, THEN BEGAN HIS PRO BASEBALL CAREER WITH LOUISVILLE AND SCRANTON IN 1946! SAM MADE QUITE A SPLASH AS A ROOKIE OUTFIELDER WITH THE RED SOX IN 1947 WHEN HE HIT .302 WITH 12 HOMERS AND 73 RBIs!

INJURIES SLOWED SAM IN 1948 PRECIPITATING HIS TRADE TO THE WASHINGTON SENATORS IN 1949! HE REBOUNDED FOR THE 1950 NATS BY HITTING .274 WITH 12 LONG BALLS AND 86 BATTED IN! SAM HIT .274 AGAIN THE NEXT SEASON FOR WASHINGTON WHILE LEADING THE A.L. WITH 36 TWO-BAGGERS! HE WAS DEALT TO THE WHITE SOX EARLY IN THE NEXT SEASON, AND IN A GAME AGAINST BOSTON ON JUNE 10, 1952, SAM BELTED A 3-RUN HOMER AND A 3-RUN TRIPLE -- IN THE SAME INNING! SAM CONCLUDED HIS BIG LEAGUE PLAYING DAYS IN 1956, AND BY 1961 HE HAD RISEN TO THE POSITION OF MANAGER OF THE MINNESOTA TWINS -- A JOB HE HELD FOR SEVEN YEARS! SAM COMPILED A .548 WINNING PERCENTAGE IN HIS REIGN AS TWINS SKIPPER, LEADING THE CLUB TO A PENNANT IN 1965 AND EARNING THAT YEAR'S MANAGER OF THE YEAR AWARD!

LINCECUM

WITH A PITCHING DELIVERY THAT CAN ONLY BE DESCRIBED AS VIOLENT, "TINY" TIM LINCECUM HAS BEEN EVISCERATING MAJOR LEAGUE BATTERS SINCE HE HIT THE BIGS IN MAY OF 2007! CONSIDERED BY MOST SCOUTS TO BE TOO SMALL AT 5'-10" AND 160-LBS, NINE CLUBS PASSED ON TIM BEFORE THE GIANTS TOOK HIM WITH THE 10TH PICK OF THE 2006 AMATEUR DRAFT! ELEVEN SHORT MONTHS LATER TIM STRUCK OUT THE SIDE IN HIS DEBUT AGAINST THE PHILS, PROVING ONCE AND FOR ALL THAT SIZE DOESN'T MATTER!

TIM'S MOTION INVOLVES A MEDIUM-HEIGHT LEG KICK FOLLOWED BY ROTATION, TORQUE, AND AN EXPLOSIVE DRIVE OFF THE SLAB! ONE OF THE KEYS TO TIM'S SUCCESS IS HIS INCREDIBLY LONG STRIDE TOWARD THE PLATE -- SOME 7-1/2 FEET! THAT'S 129% OF HIS HEIGHT -- THE AVERAGE PITCHER'S STRIDE IS ABOUT 82% OF HIS HEIGHT! TIM DEVELOPED HIS UNIQUE STYLE BY LEARNING FROM HIS FATHER, CHRIS, WHO USED VIDEO, LAWS OF PHYSICS, AND INNOVATIVE TRAINING TECHNIQUES TO GET MAXIMUM EFFICIENCY FROM TIM'S UNDERSIZED FRAME!

TIM'S 18-WIN SEASON OF 2008 EARNED HIM A SPOT ON THE N.L. ALL-STAR TEAM, BUT THE FLU KEPT HIM FROM BEING ABLE TO PLAY! HE MADE UP FOR IT IN 2009 WHEN HE STARTED THE MID-SUMMER CLASSIC FOR THE NATIONAL LEAGUERS!

IN SPITE OF HIS SMALL STATURE, IT SHOULD COME AS NO SURPRISE THAT TIM HAS EXCELLED IN THE MAJORS! FOR STARTERS, AS A SENIOR TIM LED HIS HIGH SCHOOL TEAM TO A STATE TITLE, THEN LIT UP PAC-10 HITTERS FOR THREE YEARS AS THE ACE FOR THE UNIVERSITY OF WASHINGTON -- OFTEN HITTING 100-MPH ON THE RADAR GUN! SINCE COMING TO THE GIANTS, TIM HAS CONTINUED TO OVERMATCH THE COMPETITION WITH HIS BLISTERING TWO-SEAM FASTBALL, BIG-BREAKING CURVE, AND LETHAL CHANGE-UP! TIM WON THE 2008 CY YOUNG AWARD AND IS MAKING ANOTHER BID TO NAB THE SAME HARDWARE HERE IN 2009! "IT'S A GREAT ACHIEVEMENT FOR ME," TIM TOLD ESPN ABOUT WINNING THE CY YOUNG AWARD, ADDING, "IT'S A GREAT HONOR FOR ME TO JOIN THAT ELITE CLASS OF ATHLETES." IT MAY BE A LITTLE EARLY TO ORDER TIM'S H.O.F. PLAQUE, BUT THE GUYS IN COOPERSTOWN MAY WANT TO KEEP THEIR SCULPTOR ON CALL!

Jim GREENGRASS

JIM GREENGRASS -- PERHAPS THERE HAS NEVER BEEN A BETTER BASEBALL NAME. AND WHILE THERE HAVE BEEN BETTER PLAYERS, JIM GREENGRASS WAS PRETTY DARN GOOD. JIM WAS A STRONG-ARMED 16-YEAR-OLD THIRD-SACKER WHEN HE WAS SIGNED BY FAMED YANKEE SCOUT PAUL KRICHELL IN 1944. IN ADDITION TO HIS TIME AT THE HOT CORNER DOWN ON THE YANKEE FARM, JIM ALSO PLAYED SHORTSTOP AS WELL AS TRYING HIS HAND AT PITCHING IN 20 GAMES WHILE WITH MUSKEGON IN 1950. JIM WAS CONVERTED TO AN OUTFIELDER IN 1952 THANKS TO GREAT TUTELAGE FROM HIS BEAUMONT MANAGER, THE FORMER GREAT REDS CENTER-FIELDER HARRY CRAFT. THE YANKS DEALT JIM TO THE REDS LATE THAT SEASON, AND GREENGRASS JOINED CINCY IN TIME TO PLAY IN 18 GAMES. THAT WAS JUST ENOUGH TIME FOR JIM TO SERVE NOTICE THAT HE COULD CLOUT THE BALL AS HE SLAMMED FIVE ROUND-TRIPPERS AND 24 RBIs IN JUST 68 AT-BATS. IN 1991 JIM TOLD BASEBALL DIGEST ABOUT HIS BIGGEST THRILL IN BASEBALL -- HIS FIRST CAREER HOMER, HIT ON SEPTEMBER 15, 1952, IN A TENSE WIN OVER THE 1st-PLACE DODGERS. "THE DODGERS WALKED TED KLUSZEWSKI TO GET TO ME, THE ROOKIE," SAID JIM. "CHARLIE DRESSEN, THE DODGER MANAGER, CALLED TULSA, WHERE I'D BEEN PLAYING, FROM THE DUGOUT TO GET AN OPINION ON HOW TO PITCH TO ME. JOHNNY RUTHERFORD WAS THE PITCHER, AND THE SECOND PITCH HE THREW I HIT IN THE UPPER DECK FOR A GRAND SLAM AND WON THE GAME, 4-0. I DON'T THINK I TOUCHED THE GROUND FOR THREE WEEKS AFTER I HIT THAT BALL." JIM PROVED HIS FAST START IN THE FALL OF '52 WAS NO FLUKE WHEN HE CLUBBED 20 HOMERS WITH 100 RBIs IN 1953, FOLLOWED BY 27 BOMBS AND 95 RBIs IN 1954. TRUE STARDOM MAY HAVE AWAITED JIM, BUT A BADLY BROKEN ANKLE SUFFERED AGAINST PITTSBURGH DEVELOPED INTO A CHRONIC CASE OF THROMBOPHLEBITIS, A CONDITION WHICH EFFECTIVELY ENDED HIS BIG LEAGUE CAREER FOLLOWING THE 1956 SEASON. JIM STILL HAD A FEW THRILLS FOR FANS BEFORE HANGING UP HIS SPIKES, LIKE THE HOME RUN HE HIT IN HIS FIRST AT-BAT AS A PHILLIE FOLLOWING HIS TRADE TO THEM IN 1955. INSTEAD OF BEING BITTER ABOUT HIS TOUGH BREAK, JIM STILL LOVES THE GAME ENDS ALL HIS LETTERS BY WISHING "MANY HAPPY INNINGS!"

CHRISTMAN

IT TOOK A ROCK-SOLID INFIELD TO HELP THE ST. LOUIS BROWNS FINALLY CAPTURE WHAT WOULD PROVE TO BE THE FRANCHISE'S ONE-AND-ONLY PENNANT! IT HAPPENED IN 1944 -- A TIME WHEN BIG LEAGUE ROSTERS WERE HIT HARD BY THE LOSS OF THEIR BEST PLAYERS TO THE U.S. WAR EFFORT! THE BROWNS INFIELD CONSISTED OF GEORGE McQUINN AT 1st, DON GUTTERIDGE AT 2nd, VERN STEPHENS AT SHORT, AND 30-YEAR-OLD MARK CHRISTMAN AT THE HOT CORNER! IN JUST HIS FIRST YEAR AS A REGULAR PLAYER, THE SURE-HANDED CHRISTMAN LED ALL A.L. 3rd BASEMEN WITH A .972 FIELDING AVERAGE IN 1944! MARK CONTRIBUTED GREATLY WITH THE BAT, TOO, HITTING .271 WITH 56 RUNS SCORED AND 83 DRIVEN IN! MARK GAVE INSIGHT INTO THE '44 SEASON IN "EVEN THE BROWNS," BILL MEAD'S CLASSIC 1978 BOOK ABOUT WARTIME BASEBALL! "WHEN I WAS TRADED TO THE BROWNS (IN MAY OF '39), I WAS READY TO QUIT BASEBALL," MARK RECALLED. "I WAS WORRIED ABOUT GOING TO A CLUB THAT COULDN'T WIN. THEY HAD PRACTICALLY SET A RECORD FOR LOSSES IN 1939." AFTER BEING USED SPARINGLY SINCE THEY'D ACQUIRED HIM, MARK FINALLY GOT A CHANCE TO PLAY DAILY DURING A TWO-WEEK WINDOW IN AUGUST OF 1943 AS THEY AWAITED THE ARRIVAL OF ELLIS CLARY, THEIR NEW 3rd BASEMAN. "THE FIRST NIGHT I HIT TWO TRIPLES. I HIT WELL, AND I NEVER GOT OUT OF THE LINEUP THE REST OF THE YEAR -- OR THE NEXT THREE YEARS." MARK'S CONTRIBUTION WAS AN IMPORTANT PART OF THE BROWNIES' IMPROBABLE PENNANT, BUT HE WAS QUICK TO CREDIT THE TEAM CHEMISTRY OF THE '44 CLUB! "THE GUYS WERE LOOSEY-GOOSEY THAT SEASON -- KIDDING, LAUGHING, AND JOKING. THERE WASN'T A GUY ON THE BALLCLUB THAT DIDN'T LIKE THE NEXT GUY. (MANAGER LUKE) SEWELL KEPT TELLING US WE HAD THE POTENTIAL TO WIN THE PENNANT. IT HELPED. IT KEPT US GOING ALL THE TIME." THE BROWNIES LOST THE WORLD SERIES TO THE CARDINALS, BUT THEY FOREVER SEALED A UNIQUE PLACE FOR THEMSELVES IN HISTORY! MARK WAS PROUD OF THAT, AND HE ALWAYS LOVED THE GAME -- EVEN AFTER HIS BIG LEAGUE CAREER WAS OVER AND HE WAS AGAIN TOILING IN THE MINORS! "I FEEL JUST AS GOOD ABOUT IT TODAY AS WHEN I WAS PLAYING FOR MAPLEWOOD HIGH SCHOOL," MARK SAID IN 1951. "GUESS I ALWAYS WILL, TOO."

MARK'S YOUNGER BROTHER WAS PITCHIN' PAUL CHRISTMAN, AN AN ALL-AMERICAN FOOTBALL PLAYER AT THE UNIVERSITY OF MISSOURI WHO WAS LATER A KEY MEMBER OF THE LEGENDARY BACK-FIELD OF THE 1947 NFL CHAMPION CHICAGO CARDINALS!

RALPH
McLEOD
RALPH ALTON McLEOD WAS BORN ON OCTOBER 19, 1916, IN NORTH QUINCY, MASSACHUSETTS! UNBEKNOWNST TO YOUNG RALPH, HIS NEXT DOOR NEIGHBOR WAS FRED DOE, A FORMER PITCHER! "HE WAS A GRUMPY OLD GUY," REMEMBERS RALPH. "I HARDLY EVER SPOKE TO HIM. HE WAS ALWAYS PUTTERING AROUND IN THE YARD. IF I EVER HIT THE BALL OVER IN HIS YARD, HE YELLED AT ME. I NEVER THOUGHT HE THOUGHT MUCH OF ME." BUT MR. DOE DID, IN FACT, THINK HIGHLY OF RALPH, AND HE USED HIS BRAVES CONTACTS TO GET RALPH SIGNED IN 1936! RALPH JOINED McKEESPORT AND HIT A ROBUST .326! HE MOVED UP TO COLUMBIA OF THE SOUTH ATLANTIC LEAGUE IN 1937 AND POSTED A SOLID .312 AVERAGE! IT WAS ON TO HARTFORD OF THE EASTERN LEAGUE IN 1938 WHERE THE SPEEDY OUTFIELDER'S .331 MARK EARNED HIM A SEPTEMBER CALL-UP! RALPH SPENT '39 THROUGH '40 SHUTTLING BETWEEN HARTFORD, TORONTO, AND ST. PAUL! BOSTON RECALLED HIM ONCE IN THE MIDDLE OF '39, BUT HE NEVER GOT IN A GAME! A LONG STINT IN THE INFANTRY DURING WORLD WAR II ENDED RALPH'S HOPES OF RETURNING TO BASEBALL! "YOU LOSE FIVE SEASONS AND YOU CAN'T GO BACK TO THE CALIBER WHEN YOU LEFT," SAYS RALPH. BASEBALL LOST A GOOD MAN WHEN RALPH McLEOD HUNG UP HIS SPIKES!
RALPH ENJOYED A BIG LEAGUE "CUP OF COFFEE" WHEN HE APPEARED IN SIX GAMES WITH THE BOSTON BEES AT THE TAIL-END OF THE '38 SEASON! IN SEVEN OFFICIAL AT-BATS, RALPH CONNECTED FOR ONE SINGLE AND ONE DOUBLE FOR A CAREER AVERAGE OF .286!
CUP O' JOE? DON'T MIND IF I DO!
JOYNER ©2007
RALPH'S FIRST BIG LEAGUE HIT CAME OFF PAUL DEAN IN THE OPENER OF A SCHEDULED TWIN BILL IN BOSTON ON SEPTEMBER 21, 1938 -- THE DAY THE GREAT HURRICANE OF 1938 HIT NEW ENGLAND! POOR CONDITIONS FORCED THE NIGHTCAP TO BE CALLED OFF IN THE 3RD INNING! "I THINK I BLOOPED ONE OVER THE FIRST BASEMAN," SAYS RALPH. "PART OF THE OUTFIELD FENCE BLEW DOWN. THEY HAD TO STOP THE GAME AND MAKE UP NEW GROUND RULES. BALLS HIT TO CENTER ENDED UP FOUL IN LEFT!"
I AIN'T AFRAID OF NO HURRICANE!
RALPH WAS A MEMBER OF THE QUINCY FIRE DEPARTMENT FROM 1948 THROUGH 1980!

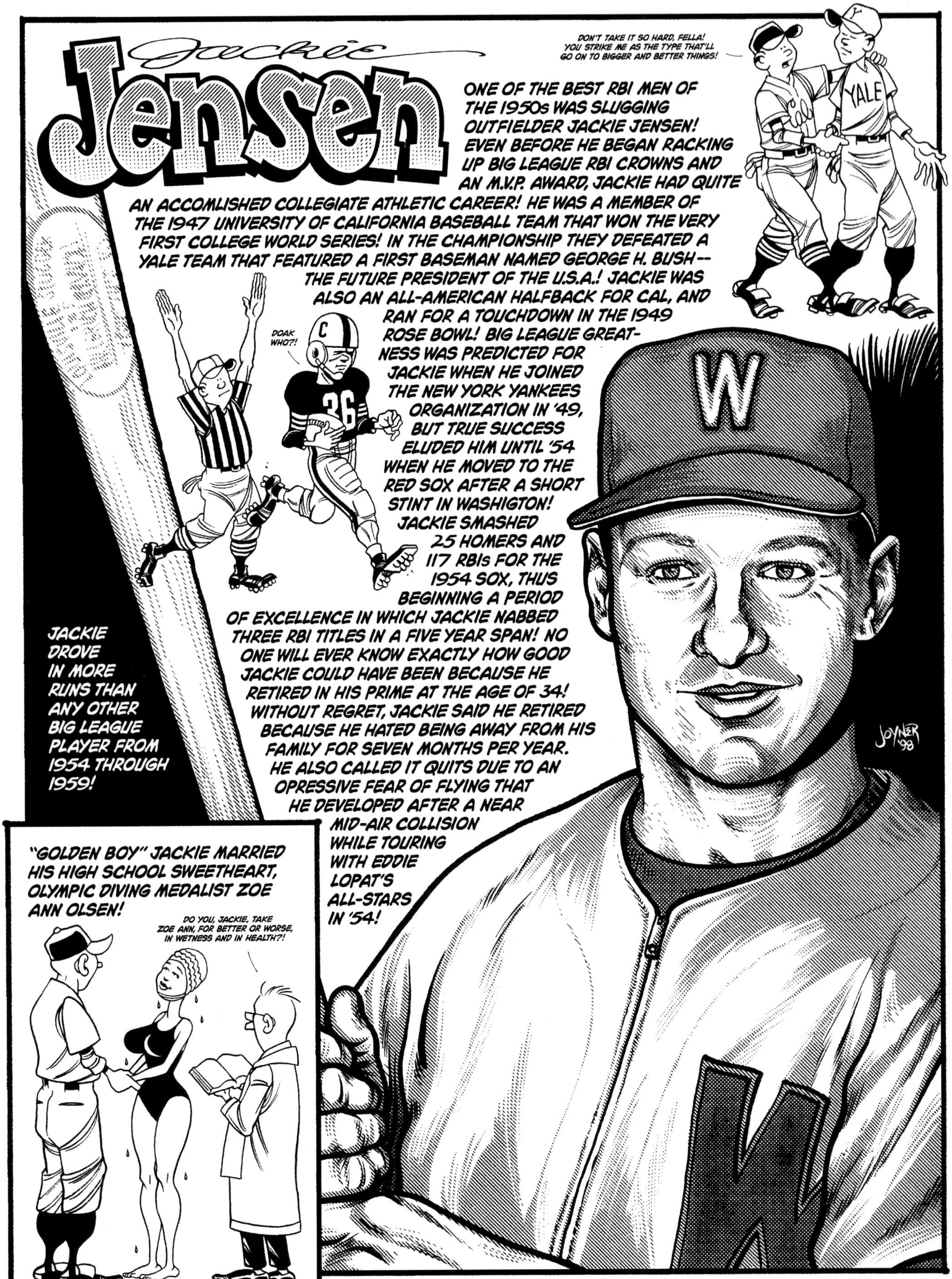
Jackie
Jensen
DON'T TAKE IT SO HARD, FELLA! YOU STRIKE ME AS THE TYPE THAT'LL GO ON TO BIGGER AND BETTER THINGS!
YALE
ONE OF THE BEST RBI MEN OF THE 1950s WAS SLUGGING OUTFIELDER JACKIE JENSEN! EVEN BEFORE HE BEGAN RACKING UP BIG LEAGUE RBI CROWNS AND AN M.V.P. AWARD, JACKIE HAD QUITE AN ACCOMLISHED COLLEGIATE ATHLETIC CAREER! HE WAS A MEMBER OF THE 1947 UNIVERSITY OF CALIFORNIA BASEBALL TEAM THAT WON THE VERY FIRST COLLEGE WORLD SERIES! IN THE CHAMPIONSHIP THEY DEFEATED A YALE TEAM THAT FEATURED A FIRST BASEMAN NAMED GEORGE H. BUSH -- THE FUTURE PRESIDENT OF THE U.S.A.! JACKIE WAS ALSO AN ALL-AMERICAN HALFBACK FOR CAL, AND RAN FOR A TOUCHDOWN IN THE 1949 ROSE BOWL! BIG LEAGUE GREATNESS WAS PREDICTED FOR JACKIE WHEN HE JOINED THE NEW YORK YANKEES ORGANIZATION IN '49, BUT TRUE SUCCESS ELUDED HIM UNTIL '54 WHEN HE MOVED TO THE RED SOX AFTER A SHORT STINT IN WASHIGTON! JACKIE SMASHED 25 HOMERS AND 117 RBIs FOR THE 1954 SOX, THUS BEGINNING A PERIOD OF EXCELLENCE IN WHICH JACKIE NABBED THREE RBI TITLES IN A FIVE YEAR SPAN! NO ONE WILL EVER KNOW EXACTLY HOW GOOD JACKIE COULD HAVE BEEN BECAUSE HE RETIRED IN HIS PRIME AT THE AGE OF 34! WITHOUT REGRET, JACKIE SAID HE RETIRED BECAUSE HE HATED BEING AWAY FROM HIS FAMILY FOR SEVEN MONTHS PER YEAR. HE ALSO CALLED IT QUITS DUE TO AN OPRESSIVE FEAR OF FLYING THAT HE DEVELOPED AFTER A NEAR MID-AIR COLLISION WHILE TOURING WITH EDDIE LOPAT'S ALL-STARS IN '54!
DOAK WHO?!
C
36
W
JACKIE DROVE IN MORE RUNS THAN ANY OTHER BIG LEAGUE PLAYER FROM 1954 THROUGH 1959!
JOYNER '98
"GOLDEN BOY" JACKIE MARRIED HIS HIGH SCHOOL SWEETHEART, OLYMPIC DIVING MEDALIST ZOE ANN OLSEN!
DO YOU, JACKIE, TAKE ZOE ANN, FOR BETTER OR WORSE, IN WETNESS AND IN HEALTH?!

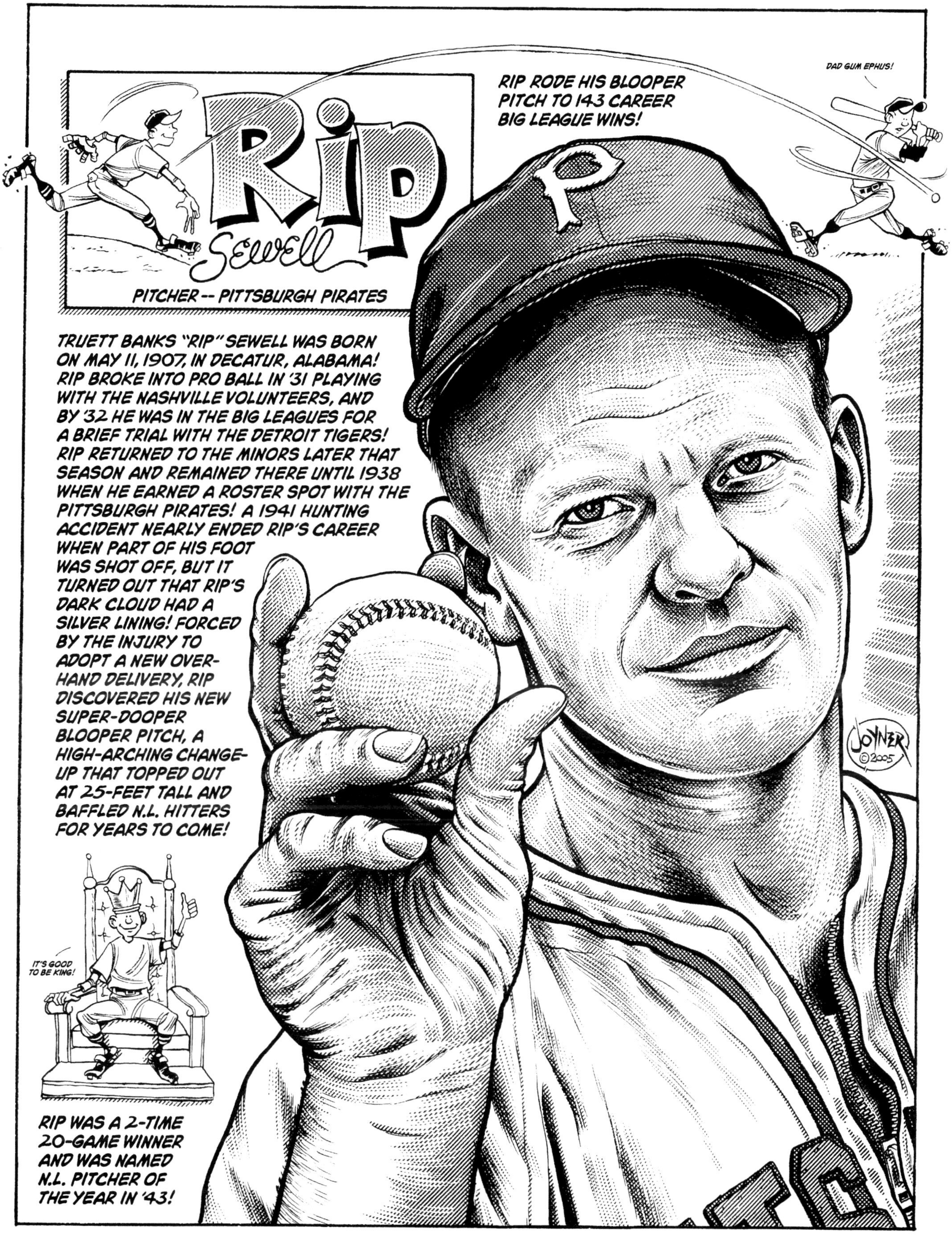
RIP
SEWELL
PITCHER -- PITTSBURGH PIRATES
RIP RODE HIS BLOOPER PITCH TO 143 CAREER BIG LEAGUE WINS!
DAD GUM EPHUS!
TRUETT BANKS "RIP" SEWELL WAS BORN ON MAY 11, 1907, IN DECATUR, ALABAMA! RIP BROKE INTO PRO BALL IN '31 PLAYING WITH THE NASHVILLE VOLUNTEERS, AND BY '32 HE WAS IN THE BIG LEAGUES FOR A BRIEF TRIAL WITH THE DETROIT TIGERS! RIP RETURNED TO THE MINORS LATER THAT SEASON AND REMAINED THERE UNTIL 1938 WHEN HE EARNED A ROSTER SPOT WITH THE PITTSBURGH PIRATES! A 1941 HUNTING ACCIDENT NEARLY ENDED RIP'S CAREER WHEN PART OF HIS FOOT WAS SHOT OFF, BUT IT TURNED OUT THAT RIP'S DARK CLOUD HAD A SILVER LINING! FORCED BY THE INJURY TO ADOPT A NEW OVERHAND DELIVERY, RIP DISCOVERED HIS NEW SUPER-DOOPER BLOOPER PITCH, A HIGH-ARCHING CHANGE-UP THAT TOPPED OUT AT 25-FEET TALL AND BAFFLED N.L. HITTERS FOR YEARS TO COME!
IT'S GOOD TO BE KING!
RIP WAS A 2-TIME 20-GAME WINNER AND WAS NAMED N.L. PITCHER OF THE YEAR IN '43!
JOYNER ©2005

Danny LITWHILER

BORN ON AUGUST 31, 1916, IN THE PENNSYLVANIA DUTCH ENCLAVE OF RINGTOWN, DANIEL WEBSTER LITWHILER SPENT A LIFETIME IN BASEBALL! USED PRIMARILY AS AN OUTFIELDER, DANNY MADE A REAL SPLASH WHEN HE JOINED THE 1940 PHILS AS AN AUGUST CALL-UP AND BATTED .345 WITH FIVE HOMERS IN 36 GAMES! IN '42 HE AMAZED BASEBALL FANS BY BECOMING THE FIRST EVER TO PLAY AN ENTIRE SEASON WITHOUT MAKING AN ERROR! DANNY PLAYED IN THE 1943 AND '44 WORLD SERIES WITH THE CARDINALS, BLASTING A ROUND-TRIPPER IN GAME FIVE OF THE '44 CLASSIC! HE ALSO PLAYED WITH THE BOSTON BRAVES AND CINCINNATI REDS BEFORE MOVING INTO A LONG AND SUCCESSFUL CAREER AS A COLLEGE COACH WITH FLORIDA STATE AND MICHIGAN STATE UNIVERSITIES! DANNY WAS AN INNOVATOR, TOO, INVENTING MANY GAME-IMPROVING CREATIONS LIKE THE RADAR GUN AND A PRODUCT NOW CALLED "DIAMOND GRIT," USED TO QUICKLY DRY WET INFIELDS!

WHILE DANNY'S TIME WITH THE BRAVES WAS BRIEF, HE REMEMBERS THOSE YEARS FONDLY! "BILLY SOUTHWORTH AND I WERE FRIENDS SINCE I'D PLAYED FOR HIM WITH THE CARDINALS. HE'D JOINED BOSTON IN 1946 AND BROUGHT ME THERE AS SOON AS I GOT OUT OF THE ARMY. ONE DAY WE WERE PLAYING THE REDS AND EWELL BLACKWELL WAS PITCHING. HE HAD A WICKED SIDEARM DELIVERY AND WAS ON TOP OF HIS GAME. I KNEW I WOULDN'T BE IN THE LINEUP SINCE BLACKWELL WAS A RIGHT-HANDER AND I ALSO HIT FROM THE RIGHT SIDE, BUT I TOLD BILLY HE SHOULD PLAY ME BECAUSE BLACKWELL NEVER GAVE ME ANY TROUBLE. IT WAS TRUE, BUT THE FACT OF THE MATTER WAS THAT I'D NEVER HIT AGAINST BLACKWELL! BILLY STILL KEPT ME OUT OF THE LINEUP, BUT HE CALLED ON ME LATE IN THE GAME TO PINCH HIT. SO I WENT UP THERE AND GOT A GOOD LOOK AT WHY BLACKWELL WAS SO TOUGH! HE CAME IN WITH A CURVEBALL THAT HAD ME ON MY HEELS, BUT I HIT A SPINNER OFF THE END OF THE BAT FOR A LUCKY TRIPLE. BILLY WAS LAUGHING WHEN I GOT TO THIRD AND SAID, 'NO TROUBLE WITH BLACKWELL, HUH?!' HE HAD A GOOD SENSE OF HUMOR, AND I FOUND OUT JUST HOW FUNNY HE COULD BE IN MAY OF 1948. WE WERE HEADED FOR THE PENNANT, BUT BILLY CAME TO ME AND SAID, 'I HATE TO TELL YOU THIS, DANNY, BUT WE NEED A LEFT-HANDED HITTER.' HIS PLATOON SYSTEM AGAIN! SO THEY TRADED ME TO THE REDS AND I MISSED OUT ON THE PENNANT, BUT I STILL REALLY ENJOYED MY TIME PLAYING UNDER BILLY IN BOSTON."

EDDIE

BASINSKI

EDWIN FRANK BASINSKI WAS BORN IN BUFFALO, NEW YORK, ON NOVEMBER 4, 1922! RAIL-THIN AT 6-FOOT-1 AND 170 LBS WITH COKE-BOTTLE GLASSES, EDDIE DID NOT LOOK THE PART OF THE BALLPLAYER, BUT HE WORKED TIRELESSLY TO OVERCOME PEOPLE'S MISCONCEPTIONS ABOUT HIM! EDDIE DID NOT PLAY HIGH SCHOOL OR COLLEGE BASEBALL, PLAYING INSTEAD IN THE COMPETITIVE LOCAL SUMMER LEAGUES! WHEN HE MADE HIS BIG LEAGUE DEBUT WITH THE BROOKLYN DODGERS ON MAY 20, 1944, EDDIE HAD YET TO EVEN APPEAR IN THE MINORS! STILL, HE RAPPED OUT A TRIPLE ON THE SECOND PITCH THROWN TO HIM! THINKING INSIDE-THE-PARK HOMER, EDDIE SAID THIRD BASE COACH LEO DUROCHER "HAD TO TACKLE ME AS I RAN AROUND THIRD! I FELL DOWN AND JUST BARELY GOT BACK!"

"RIPLEY'S BELIEVE IT OR NOT" WAS SO IMPRESSED WITH EDDIE'S UNORTHODOX PATH TO THE BIG LEAGUES THAT THEY FEATURED HIM IN A CARTOON, DECLARING HIS AMAZING ACHIEVEMENT "A TEN MILLION TO ONE SHOT!"

EDDIE'S REPUTATION AS A VERY ACCOMPLISHED VIOLINIST PRECEDED HIM TO BROOKLYN, BUT NOT EVERYONE WAS A BELIEVER -- INCLUDING MANAGER LEO DUROCHER! A CHALLENGE WAS MADE FOR EDDIE TO PROVE HIS CHOPS, WHICH HE DID BY PLAYING FOR THE ENTIRE TEAM IN THE CLUBHOUSE WHILE DRESSED IN HIS DODGERS UNIFORM! "WELL, I'LL BE A SON OF A BITCH," SAID LEO "THE KID CAN PLAY!" AND WITH THAT, LEO HAD TO BUY EDDIE A NEW SUIT WORTH $85! IN TIME, EDDIE PROVED HE COULD PLAY BALL AS WELL HE PLAYED THE VIOLIN! HE WAS SLICK IN THE FIELD WITH A BAZOOKA FOR AN ARM, AND NO SLOUCH WITH THE BAT, EITHER, HITTING IN 18 STRAIGHT IN '45!

PEE WEE REESE RETURNED FROM THE WAR IN 1946, SO EDDIE WAS SENT TO ST. PAUL WHERE HE HAD AN ALL-STAR SEASON! HE LANDED BRIEFLY WITH THE '47 PIRATES BEFORE MOVING ON TO PLAY OVER A DECADE IN THE PACIFIC COAST LEAGUE! EDDIE WAS A REAL IRON MAN IN PORTLAND, AT ONE TIME PLAYING IN EVERY INNING OF EVERY GAME FOR 557 STRAIGHT GAMES!

BROOKS ROBINSON
THIRD BASE
BALTIMORE ORIOLES
FEEEEED ME!
THE REDS NICKNAMED BROOKS "HOOVER" AFTER HIS PERFORMANCE IN THE 1970 SERIES!
BROOKS CALBERT ROBINSON WAS BORN ON MAY 18, 1937, IN LITTLE ROCK, ARKANSAS! HE SPENT 23 YEARS AS THE ORIOLES 3RD BASEMAN!
BROOKS CARRIED THE O's TO A WORLD SERIES TITLE IN 1970 WITH FANTASTIC PLAYS IN THE FIELD AND A GAUDY .429 AVERAGE WITH 2 HRS AT THE PLATE vs. THE REDS!
I'M FINE, BOYS, JUST DON'T LET BOOG GET ON!
JOYNER ©2002
OUR HERO!
BROOKS LED THE BIRDS --AND THE LEAGUE-- IN RBIs WITH 118 IN 1964!
BROOKS SET THE STANDARD FOR DEFENSIVE PLAY AT THE HOT CORNER WINNING GOLD GLOVE AWARDS FROM 1960 THROUGH 1975! HE WAS SOLID AT THE PLATE, TOO, HITTING A RESPECTABLE .267 LIFETIME WITH 268 HOMERS! BROOKS PLAYED CLUTCH BALL IN THE POSTSEASON, HITTING .348 LIFETIME IN 18 A.L.C.S. GAMES, AS WELL AS .263 WITH 3 HRS IN 21 WORLD SERIES GAMES! HE WAS ELECTED TO THE HALL OF FAME IN 1983!

I LOVE THIS GAME SO MUCH I'D PLAY IT FOR NOTHING!
Andy
Pafko
ANDY WAS A FINE OUTFIELDER WITH VERY STRONG THROWING ARM, OFTEN SAVING GAMES WITH HIS TOP-NOTCH DEFENSIVE ABILITY!
OUTFIELD -- CHICAGO CUBS
ANDREW PAFKO WAS BORN ON FEB. 25, 1921, IN BOYCEVILLE, WISCONSIN! "HANDY ANDY" MADE HIS DEBUT WITH THE CUBS ON SEPTEMBER 24, 1943, DRIVING IN FOUR RUNS WITH A DOUBLE AND A SINGLE IN A 7-4 WIN OVER THE PHILLIES! ANDY SPENT THE NEXT SEVEN YEARS AS A VERY PRODUCTIVE PLAYER WITH CHICAGO, HIS BEST SEASON COMING IN 1950 WHEN HE EXPLODED FOR 36 CIRCUIT BLASTS! BROOKLYN ACQUIRED ANDY'S SERVICES PARTWAY THROUGH THE 1951 CAMPAIGN, AND HE MADE A MAJOR CONTRIBUTION TO THE DODGERS' RUN AT THE PENNANT BY HITTING 30 LONG BALLS! BUT ANDY HAD A CLOSE-UP LOOK AT THE DODGER HEART-BREAK OF '51 AS HE HELPLESSLY WATCHED GIANTS HERO BOBBY THOMSON'S PENNANT-WINNING HOME RUN SAIL INTO THE POLO GROUNDS SEATS!
I KNEW SUKEY SHOULDA GONE WITH LABINE!
JOYNER ©2005
ANDY JOINED THE BRAVES IN 1953 AND QUICKLY BECAME A FAVORITE OF THE MILWAUKEE FANS! A WELCOME SIGHT WITH HIS DISTINCTIVE BATTING STANCE, ANDY TREATED THE BRAVES FANS TO CLUTCH HITTING FOR 7 SEASONS!
HOME IS WHERE THE CHEESE IS!
ANDY DEVELOPED HIS STRONG HANDS AND WRISTS BY MILKING COWS ON HIS FATHER'S DAIRY FARM IN WISCONSIN!
ANDY, I TOLD YOU NO MORE COWS IN THE ON-DECK CIRCLE!

Al NAPLES
SHORTSTOP -- ST. LOUIS BROWNS
IN HIS MID-TEENS, AL WAS ON A POWERHOUSE CLUB THAT PLAYED AGAINST TOP-FILGHT SEMI-PRO TEAMS, NEGRO LEAGUE TEAMS, AND THE HOUSE OF DAVID!
HOUSE OF DAVID
HOLY MOSES -- WHAT WAS THAT?!
ON JUNE 25, 1949, 19-YEAR-OLD STATEN ISLAND BORN ALOYSIUS FRANCIS NAPLES FOUND HIMSELF SUDDENLY IN THE BIG LEAGUES -- WITHOUT EVER HAVING PLAYED A DAY IN THE MINORS! AL WAS A STAR SHORTSTOP FOR GEORGETOWN UNIVERSITY'S BASEBALL TEAM WHERE HE WAS MENTORED BY THE TEAM'S SKIPPER, LEGENDARY FORMER WASHINGTON SENATORS FIRST BASEMAN JOE JUDGE!
AL -- HAVE I EVER TOLD YOU ABOUT THE 1924 WORLD SERIES WHEN I HIT .385?!
THE BROWNS HAD SEEN AL WORKOUT AT GEORGETOWN A FEW TIMES WHEN ST. LOUIS WAS IN WASHINGTON TO PLAY THE NATS! IN DESPERATE NEED OF A SHORTSTOP, THE BROWNS PLUCKED YOUNG AL FROM THE G.U. ROSTER, SIGNED HIM, AND QUICKLY FLEW HIM UP TO BOSTON WHERE ST. LOUIS WAS IN THE MIDST OF A SERIES AGAINST THE RED SOX! AL STARTED THE NEXT DAY AND LASHED A DOUBLE IN HIS FIRST BIG LEAGUE AT-BAT -- A SCREAMER DOWN THE RIGHTFIELD LINE AGAINST BOSTON ACE MEL PARNELL! AL PLAYED AGAIN THE NEXT DAY, BUT THOSE TWO GAMES WOULD BE THE TOTALITY OF HIS MAJOR LEAGUE CAREER!
JOYNER ©2006
THIS MAKES FINAL EXAMS LOOK EASY!
2B
AFTER PLAYING OUT THE REST OF THE SEASON AT SPRINGFIELD OF THE THREE-I LEAGUE, AL OPTED TO RETURN TO HIS STUDIES! HE THEN EMBARKED ON A LONG CAREER AS A MATH TEACHER -- AND SCHOOL BASEBALL COACH!

Dick GROAT

FROM 1956 THROUGH 1962, THE PITTSBURGH PIRATES HAD ONE OF BASEBALL'S ALL-TIME BEST DOUBLE-PLAY COMBINATIONS IN SECOND BASEMAN BILL MAZEROSKI AND SHORTSTOP DICK GROAT! AS A MEMBER OF THE HALL OF FAME, MAZ WILL BE ETERNALLY REMEMBERED, BUT GROAT'S EXCELLENCE IS OFTEN FORGOTTEN! BORN IN WILKINSBURG, PENNSYLVANIA, DICK WAS A PIRATES FAN WHILE GROWING UP AND WAS THRILLED TO SIGN WITH THEM IN 1952! DICK WAS SMART AND KNEW JUST WHERE TO PLAY ALL THE N.L. HITTERS -- SOMETHING THAT ALLOWED HIM TO LEAD THE LEAGUE IN PUTOUTS FOUR TIMES IN SEVEN YEARS! DICK WAS A COMPLETE BALLPLAYER -- A HARD WORKER AND HUSTLER! 1960 TURNED OUT TO BE A MAGICAL YEAR FOR THE PIRATES AND DICK AS THE CLUB WON THE WORLD SERIES WHILE GROAT BAGGED A BATTING TITLE AND THE N.L. M.V.P. AWARD!

DICK CONTINUED TO PLAY TOP-NOTCH BALL FOR THE BUCS IN 1961 AND '62, BUT PITTSBURGH BROKE HIS HEART BY TRADING HIM TO THE CARDINALS! DETERMINED TO SHOW THEM THAT THEY'D MADE A MISTAKE, DICK PLAYED GREAT IN ST. LOUIS! WHILE THE BUCS FADED WITHOUT HIS LEADERSHIP, THE CARDINALS THRIVED WITH DICK AND WON THE 1964 WORLD SERIES!

PRIOR TO HIS BIG LEAGUE BASEBALL CAREER, DICK WAS A 2-TIME ALL-AMERICAN BASKETBALL PLAYER FOR DUKE UNIVERSITY! HE ALSO PLAYED IN THE NBA BEFORE FOCUSING SOLELY ON HARDBALL! DICK SPENT 1953 AND '54 IN THE ARMY WHERE HE LED HIS FT. BELVOIR BASE TO CHAMPIONSHIPS IN BOTH SPORTS -- THE FIRST TIME THAT HAD EVER BEEN DONE! AS GOOD AS HE WAS IN BASEBALL, DICK WAS PROBABLY BETTER AT HOOPS! HIS DUKE JERSEY WAS THE FIRST TO BE RETIRED AT CAMERON INDOOR STADIUM, AND DICK HAS BROADCAST PITT PANTHER GAMES FOR THE LAST 30 YEARS!

BRANT ALYEA

GARRABRANT RYERSON ALYEA WAS BORN ON DECEMBER 8, 1940, IN PASSAIC, NEW JERSEY! AT 6-FOOT-3 AND 215 POUNDS, BRANT USED HIS POWERFUL BUILD TO STAR IN BASKETBALL AND BASEBALL AT HOFSTRA COLLEGE! CINCINNATI REDS SCOUT CHUCK WARD LIKED BRANT'S POWER AND SIGNED THE YOUNG SLUGGER IN 1962! ALYEA QUICKLY DISPLAYED THE POWER THAT HAD ATTRACTED WARD BY UNLOADING 32 BOMBS AS A ROOKIE WITH GENEVA OF THE NEW YORK-PENN LEAGUE! THE SENATORS NABBED BRANT IN THE 1ST-YEAR PLAYER DRAFT OF 1962, AND HE EARNED HIS FIRST BIG LEAGUE CALL-UP AT THE END OF THE 1965 SEASON AFTER CLOUTING 27 HOMERS FOR HAWAII!

BRANT'S FIRST MAJOR LEAGUE AT-BAT CAME AS A PINCH-HITTER IN A GAME AGAINST THE CALIFORNIA ANGELS ON SEPTEMBER 12TH! BRANT BELTED THE FIRST PITCH THROWN TO HIM INTO THE LEFTFIELD SEATS FOR A 3-RUN HOMER! HE WAS THE FIRST AMERICAN LEAGUER TO ACCOMPLISH THIS FEAT!

THE RIGHT-HANDED SWINGING OUTFIELDER WAS OFTEN PLATOONED AGAINST LEFT-HANDED PITCHING, THEREBY LIMITING HIS AT-BATS AS A NAT TO JUST 400 FROM 1965-69! BRANT STILL MANAGED TO CLOUT 19 LONG BALLS IN THAT TIME SPAN, HOWEVER, WITH HIS BEST NATS SEASON BEING 1969 WHEN HE WENT DEEP 11 TIMES! BRANT'S BEST OVERALL SEASON WOULD COME IN 1970 FOLLOWING HIS TRADE TO THE TWINS WHEN HE BATTED .291 WITH 16 ROUND-TRIPPERS AND 60 RBIs! WHILE PLAYING WINTER BALL IN THE LATE 60'S, BRANT AND HIS GIRLFRIEND HAD A SON, BUT JUST FOUR MONTHS LATER THEY WERE SEPARATED BY THE REVOLUTION IN NICARAGUA! THE SITUATION MADE IT IMPOSSIBLE FOR BRANT TO SEE HIS SON-- FOR 18 YEARS! THEY FELL OUT OF TOUCH, BUT WERE HAPPILY REUNITED IN 1985 WHEN BRANT ALYEA JR SLIPPED OUT OF NICARAGUA TO JOIN THE TORONTO BLUE JAYS MINOR LEAGUE SYSTEM! "BRANT HAS BEEN THROUGH SO MUCH ADVERSITY," SENIOR SAID PROUDLY, "AND HE OVERCAME IT. I SEE NOTHING BUT GOOD THINGS FOR HIM NOW." IT WAS A GREAT END TO A TOUGH CHAPTER IN BRANT'S LIFE!

FRANK Saucier

THE ANSWER TO AN OFT-ASKED TRIVIA QUESTION -- FRANK SAUCIER IS, IN FACT, THE ONLY BIG LEAGUER TO BE PINCH-HIT FOR BY A MIDGET! INSTEAD OF VIEWING THE INCIDENT AS A HUMILIATION, FRANK HAS ALWAYS BEEN VERY MATTER-OF-FACT ABOUT IT, SAYING, "I NEVER CONSIDERED THE 'MIDGET CAPER' INFAMOUS OR AN INJUSTICE (TO ME). IT WAS LIKE AN ACT IN A CARNIVAL OR CIRCUS. A GREAT PIECE OF SHOWMANSHIP. AND, OF COURSE, IT WAS THE EASIEST MONEY I EVER MADE." IRONICALLY, IT WAS FRANK'S AMAZING HITTING ABILITY THAT PUT HIM IN THE POSITION TO BE PINCH-HIT FOR BY A MIDGET. A PROLIFIC PLAYER AT MISSOURI'S WASHINGTON HIGH SCHOOL AND WESTMINSTER COLLEGE, FRANK BEGAN MAKING A NAME FOR HIMSELF IN THE PRO RANKS WHEN HE HIT .348 AT BELLEVILLE IN 1948! HE BATTED .446 AT WICHITA FALLS IN 1949, THEN NOTCHED A .343 AVERAGE AT SAN ANTONIO IN 1950 -- GOOD ENOUGH TO WIN THE SPORTING NEWS MINOR LEAGUE PLAYER OF THE YEAR AWARD! FRANK JOINED THE ST. LOUIS BROWNS IN JULY OF 1951, BUT INJURIES ESSENTIALLY LIMITED HIM TO PINCH-HITTING AND PINCH-RUNNING DUTIES! BECAUSE OF THAT, FRANK TOTALED JUST 14 AT-BATS FOR THE '51 BROWNIES, HIS ONLY SAFETY A BOOMING DOUBLE OFF MUNICIPAL STADIUM'S LEFT-CENTERFIELD WALL AGAINST INDIANS RIGHT-HANDER MIKE GARCIA ON AUGUST 7!

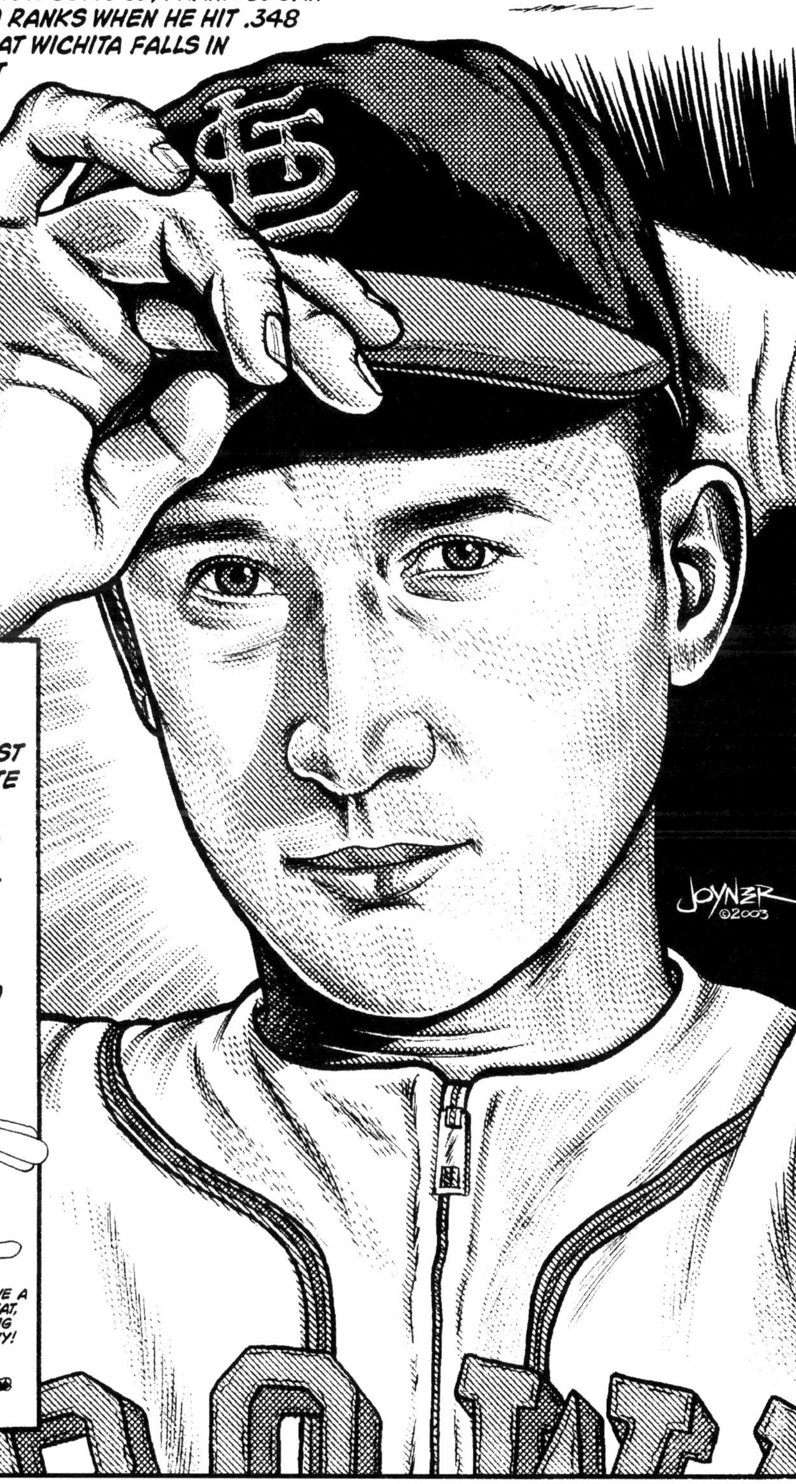

DUE TO A SEVERE ARM INJURY, FRANK WAS QUITE SURPRISED WHEN HE FOUND HIMSELF STARTING IN RIGHT AND BATTING LEADOFF IN THE SECOND GAME OF A TWIN-BILL AGAINST DETROIT AT AUGUST 19! IT ALL BECAME QUITE CLEAR, HOWEVER, WHEN FRANK, PREPARING FOR HIS FIRST AT-BAT, HEARD EDDIE GAEDEL ANNOUNCED AS A PINCH-HITTER OVER THE SPORTSMAN'S PARK P.A. SPEAKERS! OUT OF THE DUGOUT POPPED THE 3-FOOT-7-INCH TALL GAEDEL, WHO PROCEEDED TO DRAW A 4-PITCH BASE ON BALLS -- AND THE REST IS HISTORY! FRANK PLANNED ON RETURNING TO THE BROWNS IN 1952, BUT HIS CAREER WAS INTERRUPTED BY THE KOREAN WAR! FRANK, WHO'D ALSO SERVED IN WORLD WAR II, NEVER RETURNED TO PRO BASEBALL, INSTEAD WORKING IN THE OIL BUSINESS WHERE HE ENJOYED GREAT SUCCESS! FRANK REGRETS NOTHING, SAYING, "I WOULDN'T CHANGE A THING."

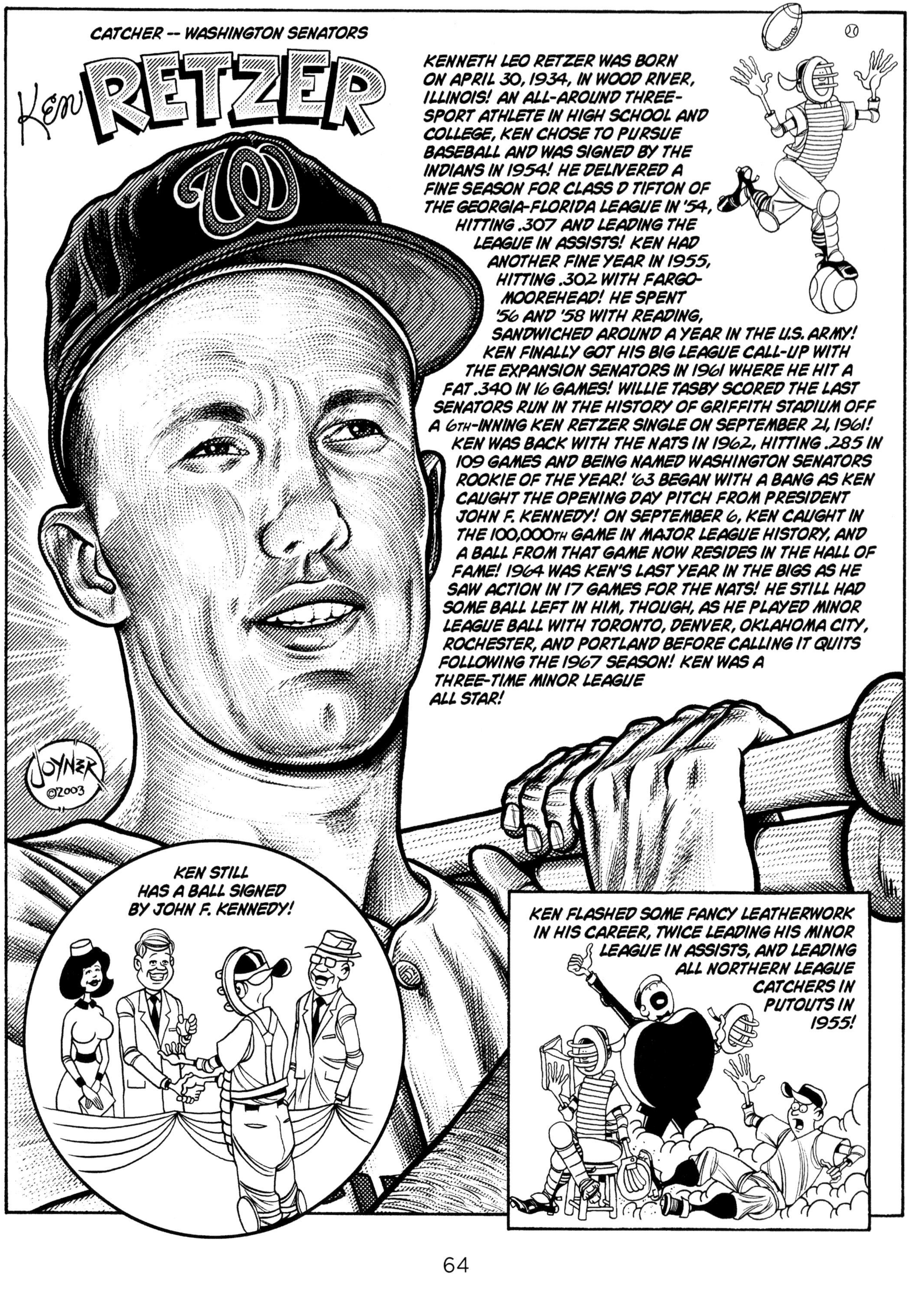
CATCHER -- WASHINGTON SENATORS
Ken RETZER
KENNETH LEO RETZER WAS BORN ON APRIL 30, 1934, IN WOOD RIVER, ILLINOIS! AN ALL-AROUND THREE-SPORT ATHLETE IN HIGH SCHOOL AND COLLEGE, KEN CHOSE TO PURSUE BASEBALL AND WAS SIGNED BY THE INDIANS IN 1954! HE DELIVERED A FINE SEASON FOR CLASS D TIFTON OF THE GEORGIA-FLORIDA LEAGUE IN '54, HITTING .307 AND LEADING THE LEAGUE IN ASSISTS! KEN HAD ANOTHER FINE YEAR IN 1955, HITTING .302 WITH FARGO-MOOREHEAD! HE SPENT '56 AND '58 WITH READING, SANDWICHED AROUND A YEAR IN THE U.S. ARMY! KEN FINALLY GOT HIS BIG LEAGUE CALL-UP WITH THE EXPANSION SENATORS IN 1961 WHERE HE HIT A FAT .340 IN 16 GAMES! WILLIE TASBY SCORED THE LAST SENATORS RUN IN THE HISTORY OF GRIFFITH STADIUM OFF A 6TH-INNING KEN RETZER SINGLE ON SEPTEMBER 21, 1961! KEN WAS BACK WITH THE NATS IN 1962, HITTING .285 IN 109 GAMES AND BEING NAMED WASHINGTON SENATORS ROOKIE OF THE YEAR! '63 BEGAN WITH A BANG AS KEN CAUGHT THE OPENING DAY PITCH FROM PRESIDENT JOHN F. KENNEDY! ON SEPTEMBER 6, KEN CAUGHT IN THE 100,000TH GAME IN MAJOR LEAGUE HISTORY, AND A BALL FROM THAT GAME NOW RESIDES IN THE HALL OF FAME! 1964 WAS KEN'S LAST YEAR IN THE BIGS AS HE SAW ACTION IN 17 GAMES FOR THE NATS! HE STILL HAD SOME BALL LEFT IN HIM, THOUGH, AS HE PLAYED MINOR LEAGUE BALL WITH TORONTO, DENVER, OKLAHOMA CITY, ROCHESTER, AND PORTLAND BEFORE CALLING IT QUITS FOLLOWING THE 1967 SEASON! KEN WAS A THREE-TIME MINOR LEAGUE ALL STAR!
JOYNER ©2003
KEN STILL HAS A BALL SIGNED BY JOHN F. KENNEDY!
KEN FLASHED SOME FANCY LEATHERWORK IN HIS CAREER, TWICE LEADING HIS MINOR LEAGUE IN ASSISTS, AND LEADING ALL NORTHERN LEAGUE CATCHERS IN PUTOUTS IN 1955!

BABE MARTIN

BABE CREDITS HIS PAL DOM DIMAGGIO FOR ADVICE THAT HELPED HIM STICK WITH THE 1948 RED SOX AS THEIR RARELY-USED THIRD CATCHER. "KID," SAID DOM, "IF YOU WANT TO MAKE THIS BALLCLUB, LEAVE YOUR SHIN GUARDS ON WHEN YOU TAKE BATTING PRACTICE, FINISH HITTING, THEN GO BACK AND CATCH." BABE LISTENED TO DOM -- AND IT WORKED!

THE 1944 WORLD SERIES FEATURED PERENNIAL FRONT-RUNNERS, THE ST. LOUIS CARDINALS, AGAINST AN UNLIKELY OPPONENT -- PERENNIAL CELLAR-DWELLERS, THE ST. LOUIS BROWNS! SEATED ON THE BROWNIE BENCH THROUGHOUT THE WORLD SERIES WAS 24-YEAR-OLD BORIS MICHAEL "BABE" MARTIN! THE BROWNS WERE IN A DOGFIGHT FOR THE A.L. PENNANT IN LATE-SEPTEMBER OF 1944, SO THEY LOOKED TO THEIR DOUBLE-A AFFILIATE IN TOLEDO FOR SOMEONE WHO COULD HELP! THERE THEY SAW BABE -- THE AMERICAN ASSOCIATION M.V.P. WITH A .350 AVERAGE AND 14 LONG BALLS! BABE SAW HIS FIRST BIG LEAGUE ACTION ON SEPTEMBER 25, AND HE SHOWED WHAT HE COULD DO WITH THE LUMBER BY RAPPING OUT TWO HITS IN THREE AT-BATS IN A BROWNIE VICTORY OVER BOSTON! BABE SAW HIS ONLY OTHER ACTION TWO DAYS LATER WHEN HE SINGLED IN A 9TH-INNING PINCH-HITTING APPEARANCE! "I PLAYED WELL, GOING 3-FOR-4," BABE SAID, "AND I WAS ABLE TO WATCH THE SERIES IN UNIFORM FROM THE BENCH, BUT I WAS NOT ELIGIBLE TO PLAY BECAUSE I WAS NOT ON THE ROSTER BEFORE SEPTEMBER 1st." THERE WAS ONE MORE CONDITION BABE HAD TO ABIDE BY! "I WAS NOT ALLOWED TO OPEN MY MOUTH UNDER ANY CIRCUMSTANCE," HE TOLD BASEBALL HISTORIAN BILL NOWLIN. "THOSE WERE THE ORDERS." BABE HAD BEEN IN THE U.S. NAVY ONLY ONE YEAR EARLIER, SO IT WAS DARN NEAR A MIRACLE THAT HE WAS IN A POSITION TO HELP THE BROWNIES TO A PENNANT IN '44! A RUPTURED LEFT QUAD FORCED HIM OFF UNCLE SAM'S ROSTER, BUT A SPECIAL BRACE ENABLED BABE TO PLAY FOR TOLEDO -- AND ULTIMATELY THE BROWNS! IT WAS TOUGH FOR BABE TO BE A SILENT SPECTATOR IN THE SERIES, BUT HE WAS, NONETHELESS, THANKFUL TO BE ABLE TO SEE ST. LOUIS' STREETCAR SERIES FROM THE BEST SEAT AT SPORTSMAN'S PARK!

BABE WAS THE SON OF PROFESSIONAL WRESTLER "IRON MIKE" MARTIN! LIKE HIS FATHER, BABE LEARNED THE ART OF WRESTLING AND BOXING, AND SPENT MANY YEARS AS A WRESTLING REFEREE! BABE ALSO PICKED UP EXTRA MONEY FROM TIME TO TIME AS A CLUB BOXER! BABE, WELL INTO HIS 80s, IS STILL A TOUGH GUY WITH BICEPS LIKE PYTHONS AND FISTS LIKE HAMMERS! HE RECENTLY FENDED OFF FOUR STREET THUGS WHO TRIED TO ROB HIM! HE K.O.'D THE FIRST THUG WITH A SHORT RIGHT, THEN WATCHED THE OTHERS FLEE AS HE LOADED UP HIS POWERFUL LEFT!

Rube OLDRING

SITTING BEHIND FIRST BASE AT PHILADELPHIA'S COLUMBIA PARK COULD BE QUITE DANGEROUS IN 1906 THANKS TO THE WILD HEAVES OF BAZOOKA-ARMED A's THIRD BASEMAN REUBEN HENRY "RUBE" OLDRING! RUBE COMMITTED 16 ERRORS -- MOSTLY THE THROWING VARIETY -- IN JUST 49 GAMES AT THE HOT CORNER THAT SEASON! THE 22-YEAR-OLD FROM BRIDGETON, NEW JERSEY, SHOWED A LOT OF POTENTIAL, HOWEVER, SO A's OWNER CONNIE MACK DECIDED TO MOVE THE KID TO THE OUTFIELD FOR THE 1907 CAMPAIGN! MR. MACK INFORMED RUBE OF THE SWITCH BY ENCLOSING A SHORT NOTE IN THE ENVELOPE THAT HELD OLDRING'S NEW CONTRACT! IT READ, "FROM THIS DAY ON YOU WILL BE MY CENTERFIELDER. YOU WILL HAVE ALL THE ROOM YOU WANT AND WILL NOT HAVE TO THROW THE BALL OVER ANYBODY'S HEAD." IT PROVED TO BE A SHREWD MOVE BECAUSE RUBE SPENT THE NEXT TEN SEASONS IN THE A's OUTFIELD -- SEASONS THAT INCLUDED FOUR A.L. PENNANTS AND THREE WORLD SERIES CROWNS! RUBE HELPED PUSH THE A's TO THE FIRST OF THOSE SERIES TITLES WHEN HE POSTED A CAREER YEAR IN 1910, FINISHING IN THE TOP TEN IN THE A.L. IN BATTING AVERAGE, SLUGGING PERCENTAGE, HITS, TOTAL BASES, DOUBLES, TRIPLES, AND HOMERS! THE A's REPEATED AS WORLD CHAMPIONS IN 1911, AND RUBE AGAIN POSTED A FINE SEASON BY HITTING .297! PHILLY WON THE FINAL WORLD SERIES OF THEIR MINI-DYNASTY IN 1913, AND WHILE RUBE BEGAN TO SHOW SIGNS OF SLIPPING, THE FANS STILL NAMED HIM THE MOST POPULAR PLAYER IN THE CITY, AND AWARDED HIM A BRAND NEW CADILLAC!

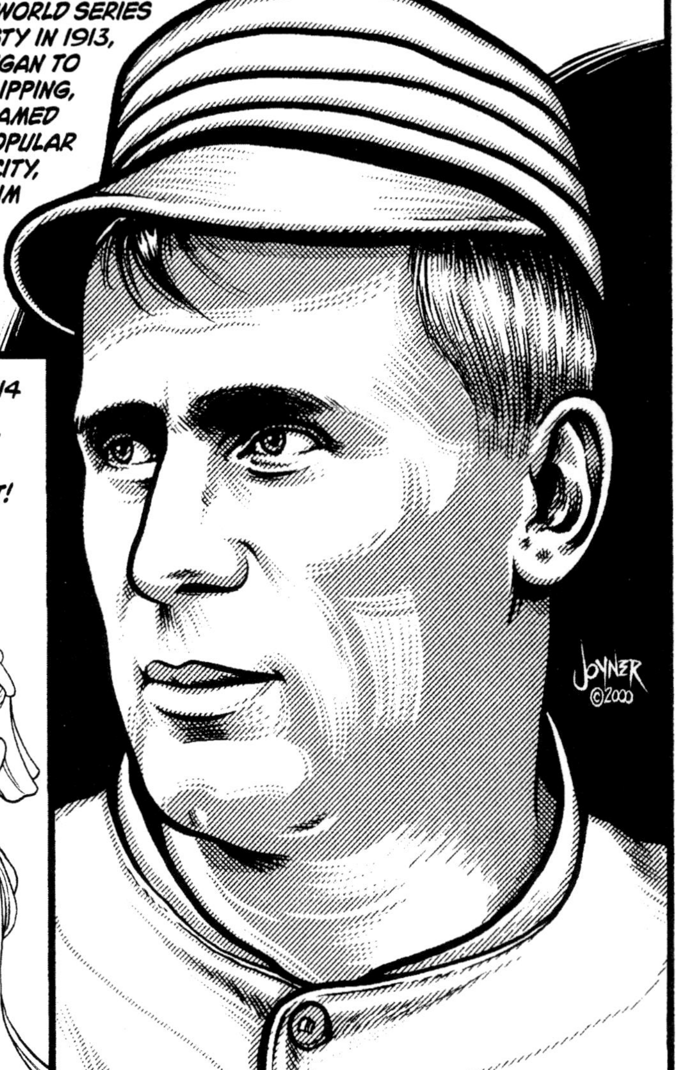

TEAM-WIDE POOR PLAY CAUSED THE A's TO LOSE THE 1914 WORLD SERIES TO THE BRAVES! LIKE HIS TEAMMATES, RUBE WAS TERRIBLE IN THE SERIES, BUT HE HAD UNIQUE CIRCUMSTANCES UPON WHICH HE COULD PIN HIS LOUSY PLAY -- HE WAS BUSY TRYING TO BECOME A POLYGAMIST! JUST PRIOR TO GAME ONE OF THE SERIES, RUBE ANNOUNCED HIS ENGAGEMENT TO HANNAH THOMAS! THINGS GOT STICKY, HOWEVER, WHEN HELEN OLDRING, RUBE'S ESTRANGED COMMON-LAW WIFE, SAW THE ANNOUNCEMENT IN THE NEWSPAPER AND CAME FORWARD! FANS SOON GOT WIND OF THE SCANDAL, AND THEY RODE RUBE THROUGH THE ENTIRE SERIES! "I KNOW I DIDN'T PLAY AS I SHOULD," RUBE LATER SAID, "AND I ATTRIBUTE IT TO THIS TROUBLE." RUBE CLEARED IT UP, AND HE AND HANNAH WERE WED FOR 47 YEARS!

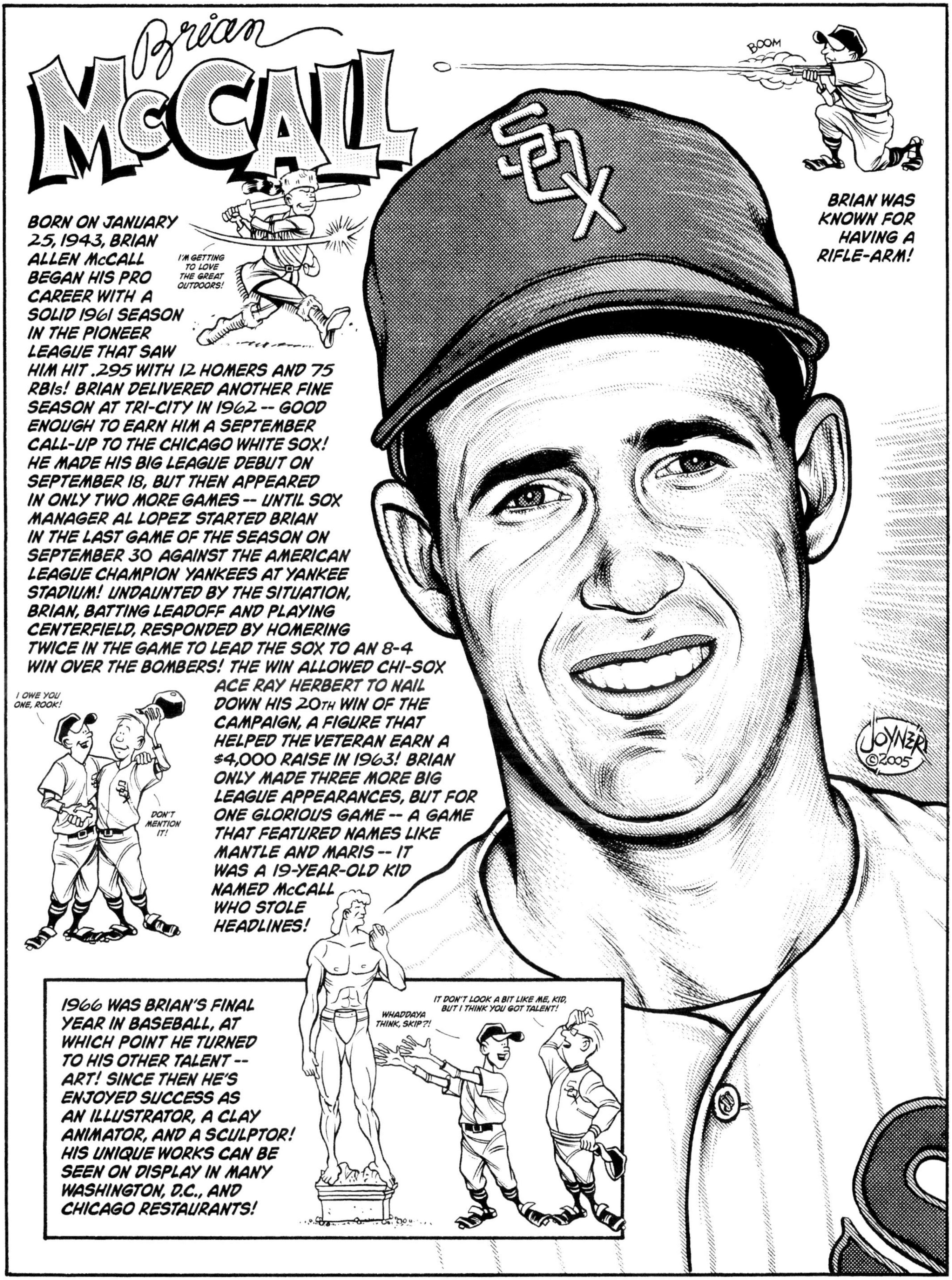
Brian
McCALL
BOOM
BRIAN WAS KNOWN FOR HAVING A RIFLE-ARM!
BORN ON JANUARY 25, 1943, BRIAN ALLEN McCALL BEGAN HIS PRO CAREER WITH A SOLID 1961 SEASON IN THE PIONEER LEAGUE THAT SAW HIM HIT .295 WITH 12 HOMERS AND 75 RBIs! BRIAN DELIVERED ANOTHER FINE SEASON AT TRI-CITY IN 1962 -- GOOD ENOUGH TO EARN HIM A SEPTEMBER CALL-UP TO THE CHICAGO WHITE SOX! HE MADE HIS BIG LEAGUE DEBUT ON SEPTEMBER 18, BUT THEN APPEARED IN ONLY TWO MORE GAMES -- UNTIL SOX MANAGER AL LOPEZ STARTED BRIAN IN THE LAST GAME OF THE SEASON ON SEPTEMBER 30 AGAINST THE AMERICAN LEAGUE CHAMPION YANKEES AT YANKEE STADIUM! UNDAUNTED BY THE SITUATION, BRIAN, BATTING LEADOFF AND PLAYING CENTERFIELD, RESPONDED BY HOMERING TWICE IN THE GAME TO LEAD THE SOX TO AN 8-4 WIN OVER THE BOMBERS! THE WIN ALLOWED CHI-SOX ACE RAY HERBERT TO NAIL DOWN HIS 20TH WIN OF THE CAMPAIGN, A FIGURE THAT HELPED THE VETERAN EARN A $4,000 RAISE IN 1963! BRIAN ONLY MADE THREE MORE BIG LEAGUE APPEARANCES, BUT FOR ONE GLORIOUS GAME -- A GAME THAT FEATURED NAMES LIKE MANTLE AND MARIS -- IT WAS A 19-YEAR-OLD KID NAMED McCALL WHO STOLE HEADLINES!
I'M GETTING TO LOVE THE GREAT OUTDOORS!
I OWE YOU ONE, ROOK!
DON'T MENTION IT!
JOYNER ©2005
1966 WAS BRIAN'S FINAL YEAR IN BASEBALL, AT WHICH POINT HE TURNED TO HIS OTHER TALENT -- ART! SINCE THEN HE'S ENJOYED SUCCESS AS AN ILLUSTRATOR, A CLAY ANIMATOR, AND A SCULPTOR! HIS UNIQUE WORKS CAN BE SEEN ON DISPLAY IN MANY WASHINGTON, D.C., AND CHICAGO RESTAURANTS!
WHADDAYA THINK, SKIP?!
IT DON'T LOOK A BIT LIKE ME, KID, BUT I THINK YOU GOT TALENT!

Grady
SIZEMORE
INDIANS ALL-STAR CENTERFIELDER GRADY SIZEMORE BRINGS INCREDIBLE ATHLETICISM TO THE DIAMOND! IN ADDITION TO POWER, SPEED, AND EXCELLENT DEFENSIVE SKILLS, GRADY PLAYS WITH AN ALL-OUT STYLE THAT HARKENS BACK TO THE GOLDEN AGE OF THE GAME! IT'S THE SAME STYLE THAT HE USED TO SET ALL-TIME RECORDS IN RUSHING AND PICKS AT CASCADE HIGH SCHOOL IN EVERETT, WASHINGTON! MEANWHILE, GRADY ALSO HIT THE BOOKS TO THE TUNE OF AN IMPRESSIVE 3.85 GPA!
OUTTA MY WAY, BUB, I GOTTA GET TO A TEST!
GRADY'S HUSTLE AND HUMBLE DEMEANOR HAVE MADE HIM A FAVORITE WITH TEAMMATES AND FANS ALIKE! HIS MOVIE STAR GOOD LOOKS HAVE MADE HIM PARTICULARLY POPULAR WITH THE INDIANS' FEMALE FAN BASE -- A GROUP THAT HAS COME TO BE CALLED "GRADY'S LADIES!"
MRS. SIZEMORE
YOO HOO, GRADY! HOW DOES MY NEW T-SHIRT LOOK?
TAKING NOTE OF GRADY'S POPULARITY WITH WOMEN, THE INDIANS MARKETING DEPARTMENT HAD "MRS. SIZEMORE" T-SHIRTS PRINTED AND OFFERED FOR SALE AT JACOBS FIELD! NEEDLESS TO SAY, THEY WERE AN INSTANT HIT AND SOLD EXTREMELY WELL!
JOYNER ©2009
TOM VERDUCCI OF SPORTS ILLUSTRATED ONCE WROTE OF HOW GRADY ARRIVES TO THE BALLPARK IN STYLE, SHOWING UP IN HIS "1966 LINCOLN CONTINENTAL CONVERTIBLE, THE ONE WITH THE SUICIDE DOORS AND THE THE EIGHT-TRACK TAPE PLAYER. HE TURNS UP THE DOORS OR THE BEATLES AND STEERS HIS LAND YACHT TO JACOBS FIELD TO PUT IN ANOTHER HARD DAY'S NIGHT."
DON'T WORRY, BABY-- YOU'RE THE ONLY TRUE GRADY'S LADY!
CONTINENTAL

Red
BOROM
EDWARD J. "RED" BOROM WAS BORN ON OCTOBER 30, 1915, IN SPARTANBURG, SOUTH CAROLINA! RED GREW UP IN ATLANTA WHERE THE BASEBALL COMPETITION WAS STIFF, AND BY THE TIME HE GRADUATED FROM BOYS HIGH IN 1934, THE LEFTY-SWINGING, RIGHTY-THROWING KID HAD TURNED HIMSELF INTO A WELL-RESPECTED, SMOOTH-FIELDING MIDDLE INFIELDER! THE NEXT TEN YEARS SAW RED DO SOME HARD TRAVELING AS HE WAS CONSTANTLY ON THE MOVE IN PURSUIT OF HIS DREAM TO MAKE IT TO THE BIG LEAGUES! HE PLAYED IN MINOR LEAGUE TOWNS LIKE KNOXVILLE, TALLASEE, CLEVELAND (MISSISSIPPI), MERIDIAN, MONROE, MONTGOMERY, GREENVILLE, AND TYLER! HIS OFFSEASONS WERE FILLED BY WORKING ALL TYPES OF VARIOUS JOBS IN AN EFFORT TO MAKE ENDS MEET -- ONCE EVEN SERVING AS A DEPUTY SHERIFF! RED ENTERED THE SERVICE IN '43 AND PLAYED ON A CRACK ARMY BASEBALL TEAM AT FT. RILEY, BUT SEVERE MIGRAINE HEADACHES CAUSED HIM TO BE DISCHARGED IN MARCH OF 1944! JUST AS RED WAS STARTING TO BELIEVE THAT HIS DREAM OF MAKING IT TO THE MAJORS WAS OVER, HE WAS ASKED TO JOIN THE DETROIT TIGERS AT THEIR WARTIME SPRING TRAINING CAMP IN EVANSVILLE, INDIANA! JUST TWO MONTHS LATER, ON APRIL 30, RED COLLECTED HIS FIRST HIT, A SHARP SINGLE OFF ALLIE REYNOLDS IN A 4-2 TIGER WIN! RED APPEARED IN ONLY SEVEN GAMES FOR THE '44 TIGERS, SPENDING MOST OF THE SEASON AT BUFFALO, BUT HE WAS BACK WITH THE TIGERS IN '45, PLAYING IN 55 GAMES AND HELPING DETROIT TO A WORLD SERIES TITLE! RED HAD A NUMBER OF HIGHLIGHTS IN '45, LIKE HIS FIVE STRAIGHT HITS OFF BOB FELLER, AND HIS 5-HIT DAY AGAINST THE YANKEES! BUT RED SAYS HIS GREATEST MOMENT CAME AS A PINCH-RUNNER, STANDING ON THIRD BASE WHEN HANK GREENBERG WALLOPED A DRAMATIC GRAND SLAM TO WIN THE PENNANT ON THE LAST DAY OF THE SEASON!
JOYNER ©2008
30
THERE IT GOES! ATTA BOY, HANK!

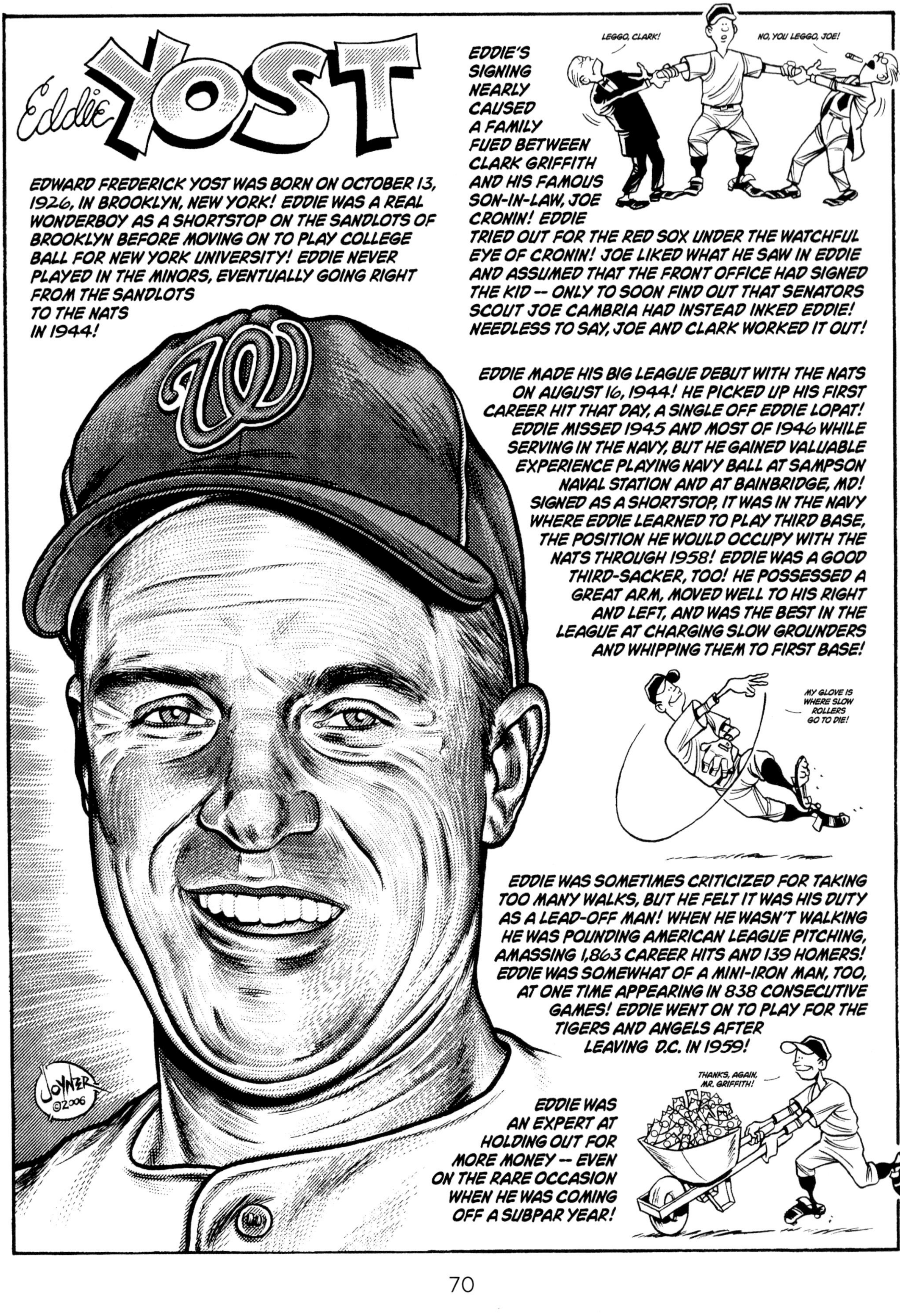
Eddie YOST
EDWARD FREDERICK YOST WAS BORN ON OCTOBER 13, 1926, IN BROOKLYN, NEW YORK! EDDIE WAS A REAL WONDERBOY AS A SHORTSTOP ON THE SANDLOTS OF BROOKLYN BEFORE MOVING ON TO PLAY COLLEGE BALL FOR NEW YORK UNIVERSITY! EDDIE NEVER PLAYED IN THE MINORS, EVENTUALLY GOING RIGHT FROM THE SANDLOTS TO THE NATS IN 1944!
EDDIE'S SIGNING NEARLY CAUSED A FAMILY FUED BETWEEN CLARK GRIFFITH AND HIS FAMOUS SON-IN-LAW, JOE CRONIN! EDDIE TRIED OUT FOR THE RED SOX UNDER THE WATCHFUL EYE OF CRONIN! JOE LIKED WHAT HE SAW IN EDDIE AND ASSUMED THAT THE FRONT OFFICE HAD SIGNED THE KID -- ONLY TO SOON FIND OUT THAT SENATORS SCOUT JOE CAMBRIA HAD INSTEAD INKED EDDIE! NEEDLESS TO SAY, JOE AND CLARK WORKED IT OUT!
LEGGO, CLARK!
NO, YOU LEGGO, JOE!
EDDIE MADE HIS BIG LEAGUE DEBUT WITH THE NATS ON AUGUST 16, 1944! HE PICKED UP HIS FIRST CAREER HIT THAT DAY, A SINGLE OFF EDDIE LOPAT! EDDIE MISSED 1945 AND MOST OF 1946 WHILE SERVING IN THE NAVY, BUT HE GAINED VALUABLE EXPERIENCE PLAYING NAVY BALL AT SAMPSON NAVAL STATION AND AT BAINBRIDGE, MD! SIGNED AS A SHORTSTOP, IT WAS IN THE NAVY WHERE EDDIE LEARNED TO PLAY THIRD BASE, THE POSITION HE WOULD OCCUPY WITH THE NATS THROUGH 1958! EDDIE WAS A GOOD THIRD-SACKER, TOO! HE POSSESSED A GREAT ARM, MOVED WELL TO HIS RIGHT AND LEFT, AND WAS THE BEST IN THE LEAGUE AT CHARGING SLOW GROUNDERS AND WHIPPING THEM TO FIRST BASE!
MY GLOVE IS WHERE SLOW ROLLERS GO TO DIE!
EDDIE WAS SOMETIMES CRITICIZED FOR TAKING TOO MANY WALKS, BUT HE FELT IT WAS HIS DUTY AS A LEAD-OFF MAN! WHEN HE WASN'T WALKING HE WAS POUNDING AMERICAN LEAGUE PITCHING, AMASSING 1,863 CAREER HITS AND 139 HOMERS! EDDIE WAS SOMEWHAT OF A MINI-IRON MAN, TOO, AT ONE TIME APPEARING IN 838 CONSECUTIVE GAMES! EDDIE WENT ON TO PLAY FOR THE TIGERS AND ANGELS AFTER LEAVING D.C. IN 1959!
EDDIE WAS AN EXPERT AT HOLDING OUT FOR MORE MONEY -- EVEN ON THE RARE OCCASION WHEN HE WAS COMING OFF A SUBPAR YEAR!
THANKS, AGAIN, MR. GRIFFITH!
JOYNER ©2006

ART JOHNSON

ARTHUR HENRY JOHNSON WAS BORN ON JULY 16, 1916, IN WINCHESTER, MASSACHUSETTS! "THE BRAVES WERE WERE ALWAYS MY FAVORITE TEAM," ART RECALLED, "AND LITTLE DID I DREAM THAT SOMEDAY I WOULD HAVE THE HONOR OF PLAYING FOR THEM!"

ART JOINED THE PROFESSIONAL RANKS IN 1938 WITH ERIE OF THE MID-ATLANTIC LEAGUE! 1939 SAW HIM LOG TIME WITH EVANSVILLE AND HARTFORD, BUT IT WAS THE LEFT-HANDER'S 17-WIN SEASON WITH HARTFORD IN 1940 THAT GOT THE ATTENTION OF THE BIG LEAGUE BRAVES! INCIDENTALLY, ART'S BROTHER, CARL, WAS ALSO A MINOR LEAGUE SOUTHPAW!

CALLED UP TO CASEY STENGEL'S BEES LATE IN THE 1940 CAMPAIGN, ART SAW HIS FIRST BIG LEAGUE ACTION ON SEPTEMBER 22ND IN A RELIEF APPEARANCE AGAINST THE GIANTS! ART DREW HIS FIRST STARTING ASSIGNMENT ONE WEEK LATER, ALSO AGAINST NEW YORK! "THE FIRST BATTER I FACED WAS JOHNNY RUCKER," REMEMBERED ART. "HE GROUNDED TO ME AND I THREW HIM OUT AT FIRST BASE." ART WAS BACK WITH THE BRAVES IN 1941 WHERE HE PITCHED IN 43 GAMES -- 18 OF THEM AS A STARTER! HIS FIRST MAJOR LEAGUE WIN CAME IN RELIEF ON MAY 17, A 6-3 VICTORY OVER THE CARDINALS! ART CHUCKED 2-2/3 SCORELESS INNINGS AND WAS THE PITCHER OF RECORD WHEN BABE DAHLGREN SMASHED A 12TH-INNING 3-RUN HOME RUN! ART WOULD WIN SIX MORE GAMES IN '41, HIS 3.53 ERA IN 183 INNINGS A TESTAMENT TO HIS EFFECTIVENESS! ART APPEARED IN FOUR MORE GAMES FOR THE BRAVES IN 1942 BEFORE VOLUNTEERING FOR SEA DUTY IN WWII!

ART NEVER RETURNED TO THE BIGS AFTER THE WAR, BUT HE HAS NO REGRETS! "I WOULD LIKE TO BE REMEMBERED AS THE KID FROM WINCHESTER WHO PLAYED BALL WHEN IT WAS A GAME," SAYS ART. "A YOUNG KID WHO PLAYED ON THE SAME FIELDS AS BABE RUTH, JOE DIMAGGIO, TED WILLIAMS AND STAN MUSIAL. A KID WHO PLAYED FOR THE LOVE OF THE GAME."

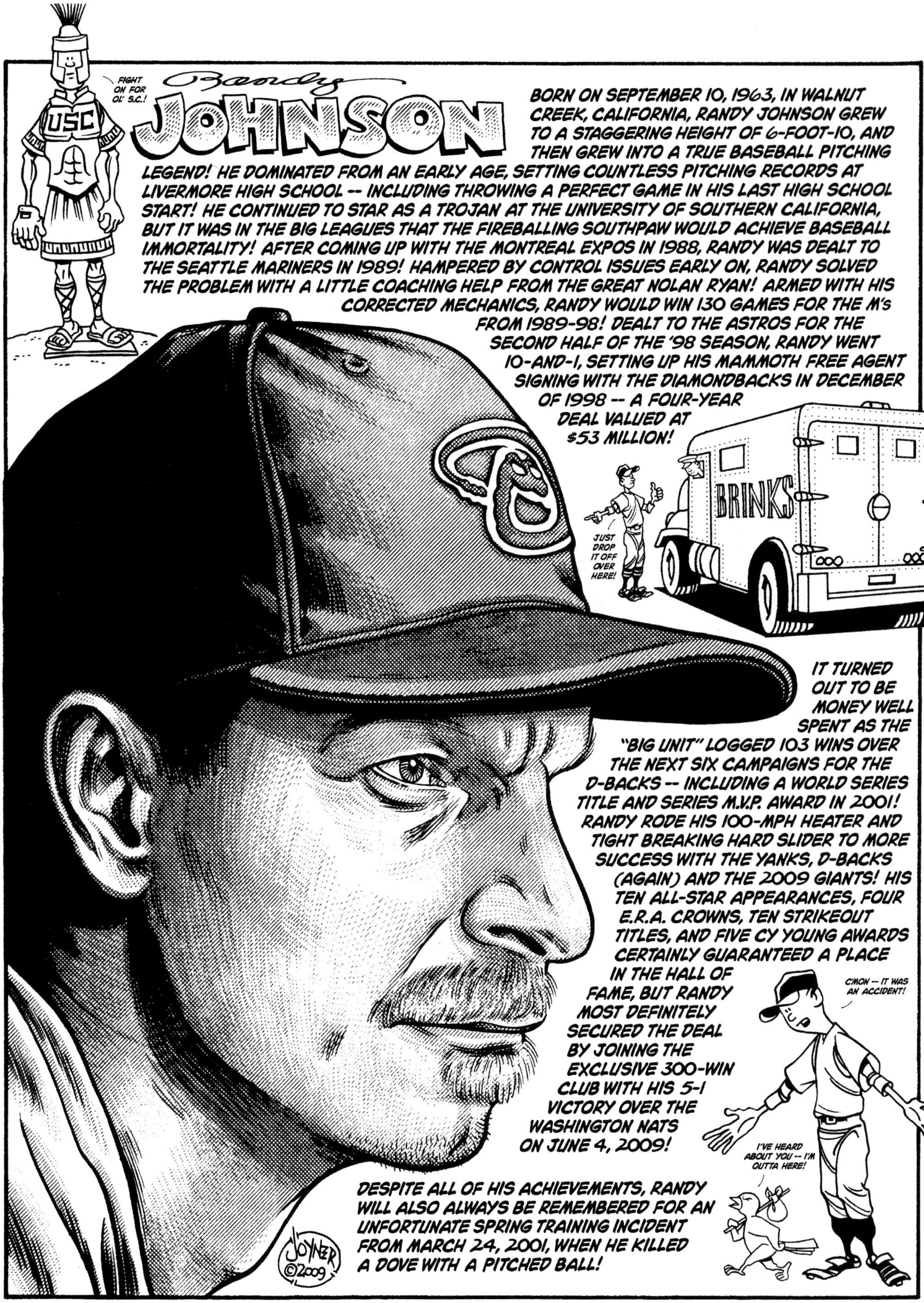

FIGHT ON FOR OL' S.C.!
USC
Randy
JOHNSON
BORN ON SEPTEMBER 10, 1963, IN WALNUT CREEK, CALIFORNIA, RANDY JOHNSON GREW TO A STAGGERING HEIGHT OF 6-FOOT-10, AND THEN GREW INTO A TRUE BASEBALL PITCHING LEGEND! HE DOMINATED FROM AN EARLY AGE, SETTING COUNTLESS PITCHING RECORDS AT LIVERMORE HIGH SCHOOL -- INCLUDING THROWING A PERFECT GAME IN HIS LAST HIGH SCHOOL START! HE CONTINUED TO STAR AS A TROJAN AT THE UNIVERSITY OF SOUTHERN CALIFORNIA, BUT IT WAS IN THE BIG LEAGUES THAT THE FIREBALLING SOUTHPAW WOULD ACHIEVE BASEBALL IMMORTALITY! AFTER COMING UP WITH THE MONTREAL EXPOS IN 1988, RANDY WAS DEALT TO THE SEATTLE MARINERS IN 1989! HAMPERED BY CONTROL ISSUES EARLY ON, RANDY SOLVED THE PROBLEM WITH A LITTLE COACHING HELP FROM THE GREAT NOLAN RYAN! ARMED WITH HIS CORRECTED MECHANICS, RANDY WOULD WIN 130 GAMES FOR THE M's FROM 1989-98! DEALT TO THE ASTROS FOR THE SECOND HALF OF THE '98 SEASON, RANDY WENT 10-AND-1, SETTING UP HIS MAMMOTH FREE AGENT SIGNING WITH THE DIAMONDBACKS IN DECEMBER OF 1998 -- A FOUR-YEAR DEAL VALUED AT $53 MILLION!
JUST DROP IT OFF OVER HERE!
BRINKS
IT TURNED OUT TO BE MONEY WELL SPENT AS THE "BIG UNIT" LOGGED 103 WINS OVER THE NEXT SIX CAMPAIGNS FOR THE D-BACKS -- INCLUDING A WORLD SERIES TITLE AND SERIES M.V.P. AWARD IN 2001! RANDY RODE HIS 100-MPH HEATER AND TIGHT BREAKING HARD SLIDER TO MORE SUCCESS WITH THE YANKS, D-BACKS (AGAIN) AND THE 2009 GIANTS! HIS TEN ALL-STAR APPEARANCES, FOUR E.R.A. CROWNS, TEN STRIKEOUT TITLES, AND FIVE CY YOUNG AWARDS CERTAINLY GUARANTEED A PLACE IN THE HALL OF FAME, BUT RANDY MOST DEFINITELY SECURED THE DEAL BY JOINING THE EXCLUSIVE 300-WIN CLUB WITH HIS 5-1 VICTORY OVER THE WASHINGTON NATS ON JUNE 4, 2009!
C'MON -- IT WAS AN ACCIDENT!
I'VE HEARD ABOUT YOU -- I'M OUTTA HERE!
DESPITE ALL OF HIS ACHIEVEMENTS, RANDY WILL ALSO ALWAYS BE REMEMBERED FOR AN UNFORTUNATE SPRING TRAINING INCIDENT FROM MARCH 24, 2001, WHEN HE KILLED A DOVE WITH A PITCHED BALL!
JOYNER ©2009

Ken McMullen

A "THROW-IN" BY THE DODGERS IN THE DEAL THAT BROUGHT FRANK HOWARD TO WASHINGTON, KEN McMULLEN TURNED OUT TO BE REAL BARGAIN, EXPERTLY MANNING THE HOT CORNER FOR THE NATS FROM 1965 THROUGH 1969, WHILE AVERAGING 17 HOMERS AND 65 RBIs IN THAT TIMEFRAME! SIGNED OUT OF CALIFORNIA'S OXNARD HIGH SCHOOL IN 1960 FOR A $60,000 BONUS, THE DODGERS HAD HIGH EXPECTATIONS FOR KEN, ESPECIALLY AFTER HE WON THE AMERICAN ASSOCIATION M.V.P. AWARD IN 1962, BUT HE FAILED TO HIT ENOUGH TO STICK WITH LOS ANGELES AFTER SHORT TRIALS IN 1962, '63, AND '64! INSTALLED AS THE SENATORS EVERYDAY THIRD BASEMAN IN 1965 BY NATS SKIPPER GIL HODGES, KEN MADE THE MOST OF HIS OPPORTUNITY BY SMASHING 18 LONG BALLS! THE GREAT TED WILLIAMS OFFERED THE SAME ADVICE TO ANYONE WHO ASKED HIM FOR THE KEY TO GOOD HITTING -- "GET A GOOD PITCH TO HIT." KEN'S PHILOSOPHY IN 1965 COULDN'T HAVE BEEN MORE DIFFERENT. "I'M UP THERE TO HIT, AND I DON'T CARE WHERE THE BALL IS PITCHED -- JUST SO I CAN GET MY BAT ON IT," HE TOLD WASHINGTON POST SPORTSWRITER BUS HAM DURING HIS BREAKOUT SEASON OF 1965. "I'M NOT GOING TO STAND THERE WAITING FOR MY PITCH OR UNTIL IT'S IN THE GROOVE. THEY TOLD ME FOR YEARS I HAD POTENTIAL TO HIT WELL, BUT I USED TO TAKE TOO MANY STRIKES. NOW I GO UP THERE AGGRESSIVELY AND IF I HIT TO RIGHT OR RIGHT-CENTER, THAT'S ALL RIGHT WITH ME." KEN DID FINE BY HIS NEW APPROACH, TOO, RIGHT THROUGH THE 1968 SEASON WHEN, IRONICALLY, TED WILLIAMS -- MR. GET-A-GOOD-PITCH-TO-HIT -- JOINED THE NATS AS THEIR NEW MANAGER FOR 1969! KEN, ALWAYS WELL-LIKED AND EASY-GOING, KEPT HIS AGGRESSIVE STYLE, YET STILL WAS ABLE TO INTEGRATE MUCH OF WHAT TED PREACHED ABOUT HITTING! THE RESULT WAS A CAREER YEAR FOR KEN -- .278 WITH 19 LONG BALLS AND 87 RUNS DRIVEN IN!

KEN MOVED ON FROM D.C. IN 1970 AND DIVIDED THE NEXT SEVEN YEARS AMONG THE ANGELS, DODGERS AND A'S. BY '77, KEN'S LAST YEAR IN THE MAJORS, HE WAS SERVING MOSTLY IN THE CAPACITY OF DESIGNATED HITTER AND PINCH HITTER FOR THE BREWERS! KEN HAD NO WAY OF KNOWING IT, BUT HE WAS ABOUT TO HAVE HIS LAST BIG LEAGUE AT-BAT AS HE STRODE TO THE PLATE TO PINCH HIT IN THE 8TH INNING AGAINST THE MARINERS ON SEPTEMBER 14! ALL KEN DID WAS POLE A 2-RUN HOMER OFF TOM HOUSE! IT WAS THE 156TH, AND LAST, HOMER OF KEN'S FINE CAREER! IT WAS A GREAT WAY TO END THE CAREER OF A CLASS GUY! KEN THEN RETURNED TO VENTURA COUNTY TO RUN THE FAMILY BUSINESS!

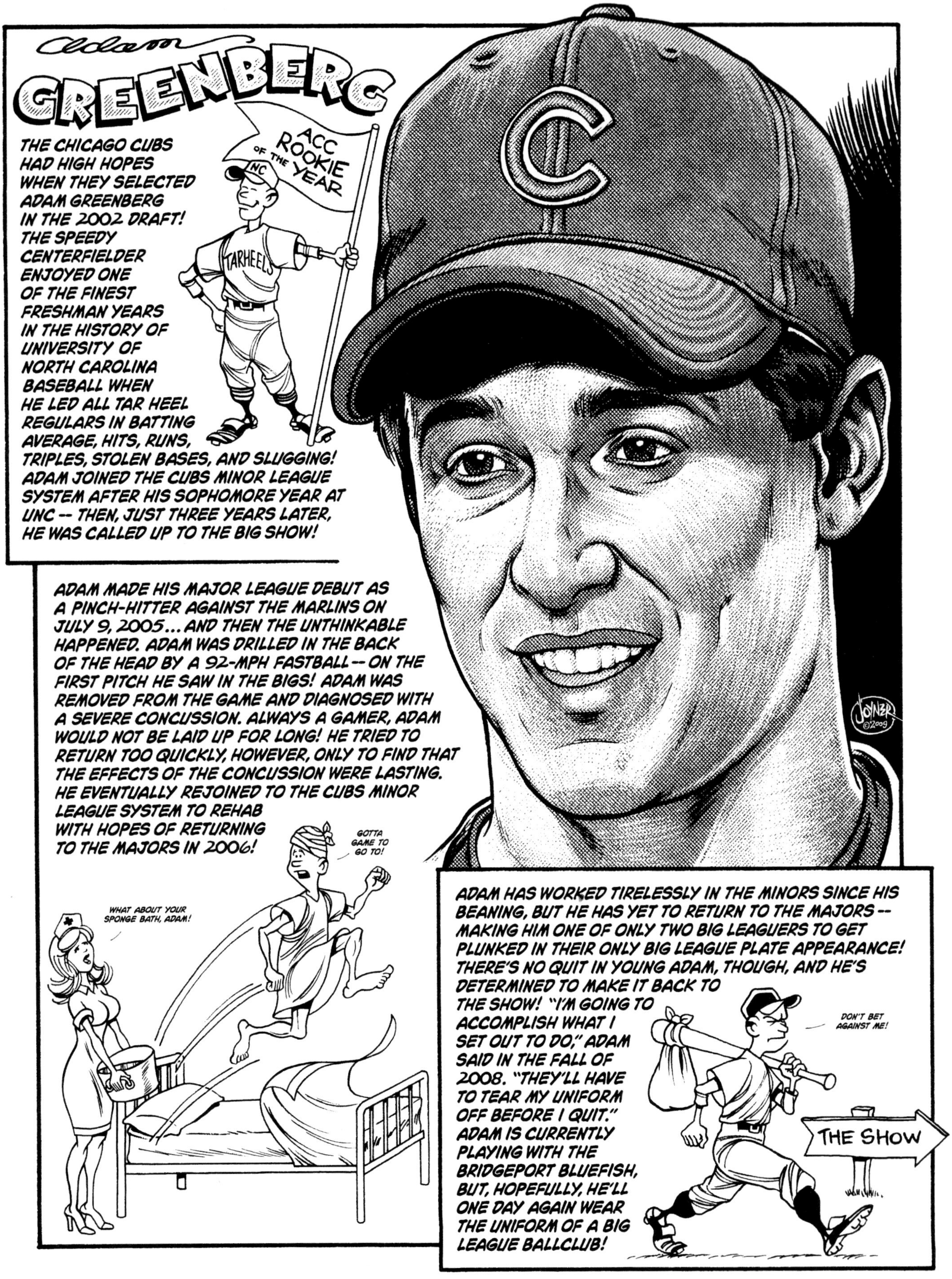
Adam
GREENBERG
ACC ROOKIE OF THE YEAR
NC
TARHEELS
THE CHICAGO CUBS HAD HIGH HOPES WHEN THEY SELECTED ADAM GREENBERG IN THE 2002 DRAFT! THE SPEEDY CENTERFIELDER ENJOYED ONE OF THE FINEST FRESHMAN YEARS IN THE HISTORY OF UNIVERSITY OF NORTH CAROLINA BASEBALL WHEN HE LED ALL TAR HEEL REGULARS IN BATTING AVERAGE, HITS, RUNS, TRIPLES, STOLEN BASES, AND SLUGGING! ADAM JOINED THE CUBS MINOR LEAGUE SYSTEM AFTER HIS SOPHOMORE YEAR AT UNC -- THEN, JUST THREE YEARS LATER, HE WAS CALLED UP TO THE BIG SHOW!
C
JOYNER ©2009
ADAM MADE HIS MAJOR LEAGUE DEBUT AS A PINCH-HITTER AGAINST THE MARLINS ON JULY 9, 2005... AND THEN THE UNTHINKABLE HAPPENED. ADAM WAS DRILLED IN THE BACK OF THE HEAD BY A 92-MPH FASTBALL -- ON THE FIRST PITCH HE SAW IN THE BIGS! ADAM WAS REMOVED FROM THE GAME AND DIAGNOSED WITH A SEVERE CONCUSSION. ALWAYS A GAMER, ADAM WOULD NOT BE LAID UP FOR LONG! HE TRIED TO RETURN TOO QUICKLY, HOWEVER, ONLY TO FIND THAT THE EFFECTS OF THE CONCUSSION WERE LASTING. HE EVENTUALLY REJOINED TO THE CUBS MINOR LEAGUE SYSTEM TO REHAB WITH HOPES OF RETURNING TO THE MAJORS IN 2006!
GOTTA GAME TO GO TO!
WHAT ABOUT YOUR SPONGE BATH, ADAM!
ADAM HAS WORKED TIRELESSLY IN THE MINORS SINCE HIS BEANING, BUT HE HAS YET TO RETURN TO THE MAJORS -- MAKING HIM ONE OF ONLY TWO BIG LEAGUERS TO GET PLUNKED IN THEIR ONLY BIG LEAGUE PLATE APPEARANCE! THERE'S NO QUIT IN YOUNG ADAM, THOUGH, AND HE'S DETERMINED TO MAKE IT BACK TO THE SHOW! "I'M GOING TO ACCOMPLISH WHAT I SET OUT TO DO," ADAM SAID IN THE FALL OF 2008. "THEY'LL HAVE TO TEAR MY UNIFORM OFF BEFORE I QUIT." ADAM IS CURRENTLY PLAYING WITH THE BRIDGEPORT BLUEFISH, BUT, HOPEFULLY, HE'LL ONE DAY AGAIN WEAR THE UNIFORM OF A BIG LEAGUE BALLCLUB!
DON'T BET AGAINST ME!
THE SHOW

Jimmy DYKES

DESPITE HAVING YET DEMONSTRATED THE ABILITY TO HIT AT A BIG LEAGUE LEVEL, 21-YEAR-OLD GETTYSBURG SECOND BASEMAN JIMMY DYKES GOT HIS CHANCE TO GO TO THE SHOW WHEN THE PHILADELPHIA ATHLETICS LOST THEIR REGULAR SECOND SACKER TO THE ARMY DURING WORLD WAR I. JIMMY BARELY GOT HIS FEET WET BEFORE HE TOO WAS SNAPPED UP BY THE ARMY FOR A TOUR OF DUTY. UPON HIS RETURN, JIMMY BECAME A FULL-TIMER FOR THE A's AND IMMEDIATELY WENT ABOUT DEMONSTRATING THE PHENOMENAL FIELDING SKILLS THAT WOULD DEFINE HIS LONG CAREER. JIMMY PUT ON A PARTICULARLY IMPRESSIVE DISPLAY OF FIELDING ON AUGUST 17, 1921, WHEN HE FLAWLESSLY HANDLED 17 CHANCES AT SECOND BASE -- AN A.L. RECORD. A's MANAGER CONNIE MACK SOON REALIZED THAT JIMMY COULD PLAY ANYWHERE, SO HE STARTED USING DYKES ALL OVER THE BALLFIELD. HIS STRONG ARM ALSO ENTICED MR. MACK TO USE JIMMY ON THE MOUND FOR TWO RELIEF APPEARANCES IN 1927. IT WAS THAT SAME YEAR THAT DYKES' VERSATILITY TRULY BECAME LEGEND WHEN HE PLAYED SEVEN DIFFERENT POSITIONS IN ONE GAME!

WHILE JIMMY WAS BUSY DAZZLING THE FANS WITH HIS INCREDIBLE GLOVEWORK, HE HAD QUIETLY TURNED HIMSELF INTO A FORMIDABLE HITTER. HE BATTED .300 OR BETTER FIVE TIMES BETWEEN 1924 AND 1930, AND HIS HANDY STICKWORK WAS A KEY FACTOR IN THE RISING FORTUNES OF THE ATHLETICS -- CULMINATING IN THREE CONSECUTIVE A.L. FLAGS AND TWO WORLD SERIES TITLES. JIMMY'S .421 WORLD SERIES AVERAGE HELPED THE A's TO THE FIRST OF THEIR TWO BACK-TO-BACK SERIES TITLES, A FIVE-GAME TROUNCING OF THE CUBS IN 1929. DEPRESSION-ERA ECONOMICS FORCED MR. MACK TO SELL JIMMY'S CONTRACT FOLLOWING THE 1932 SEASON, SO JIMMY PLAYED THE LAST SEVEN YEARS OF HIS CAREER WITH THE WHITE SOX BEFORE TURNING HIS ATTENTION TO A LONG CAREER COACHING AND MANAGING. STARTING IN 1934, JIMMY WOULD SPEND 21 YEARS AS A BIG LEAGUE SKIPPER, MANAGING SIX DIFFERENT TEAMS -- A 20TH CENTURY RECORD. AS A MANAGER, JIMMY WAS KNOWN AS A FIRST-CLASS BENCH JOCKEY AND UMP BAITER, BUT THIS SHOULD NOT OBSCURE THE FACT THAT HE WAS A FINE LEADER. BOBBY SHANTZ ONCE SAID, "JIMMY GOT MORE OUT OF HIS PLAYERS THAN ANY MANAGER I HAD."

Don ZIMMER
THIRD BASE -- WASHINGTON SENATORS
DONALD WILLIAM ZIMMER WAS BORN ON JANUARY 17, 1931, IN CINCINNATI, OHIO! HE BEGAN HIS PROFESSIONAL BASEBALL CAREER IN 1949 WITH CAMBRIDGE OF THE EASTERN SHORE LEAGUE! DON PUT TOGETHER A GREAT SEASON THE FOLLOWING YEAR WHEN HE HIT .315 WITH 23 HOMERS AND 122 RBIs FOR HORNELL OF THE PONY LEAGUE! ZIM WAS LEADING THE AMERICAN ASSOCIATION WITH 23 HOMERS AND 63 RBIs WHEN HE WAS BEANED BY JIM KIRK ON JULY 7, 1953! UNCONSCIOUS AND NEAR DEATH FOR TWO WEEKS, DON BATTLED BACK AND WON A SPOT WITH THE 1954 DODGERS! DON HIT 15 LONG BALLS FOR THE 1955 WORLD CHAMPION DODGERS BEFORE MOVING ON TO STOPS WITH THE CUBS, METS, AND REDS! ON JUNE 24, 1963, THE SENATORS PURCHASED DON FROM THE DODGERS! DON THRIVED IN THE NATION'S CAPITAL HITTING 14 HOMERS IN 1963 AND 12 IN 1964! ZIM SAW ACTION IN 95 GAMES FOR THE 1965 SENATORS BEFORE MOVING ON TO A LONG CAREER COACHING AND MANAGING IN THE BIG LEAGUES!
ON AUGUST 16, 1951, WHILE WITH ELMIRA OF THE EASTERN LEAGUE, DON WED JEAN CAROL BAUERLE IN A CEREMONY AT HOME PLATE!
JOYNER ©2005
BASEBALL IS ME SPINACH!
DON'S TEAMMATES NICKNAMED HIM "POPEYE" BECAUSE OF HIS STRENGTH!
COULD YOU SPEED IT UP, ZIM? WE'RE READY TO START THE GAME!

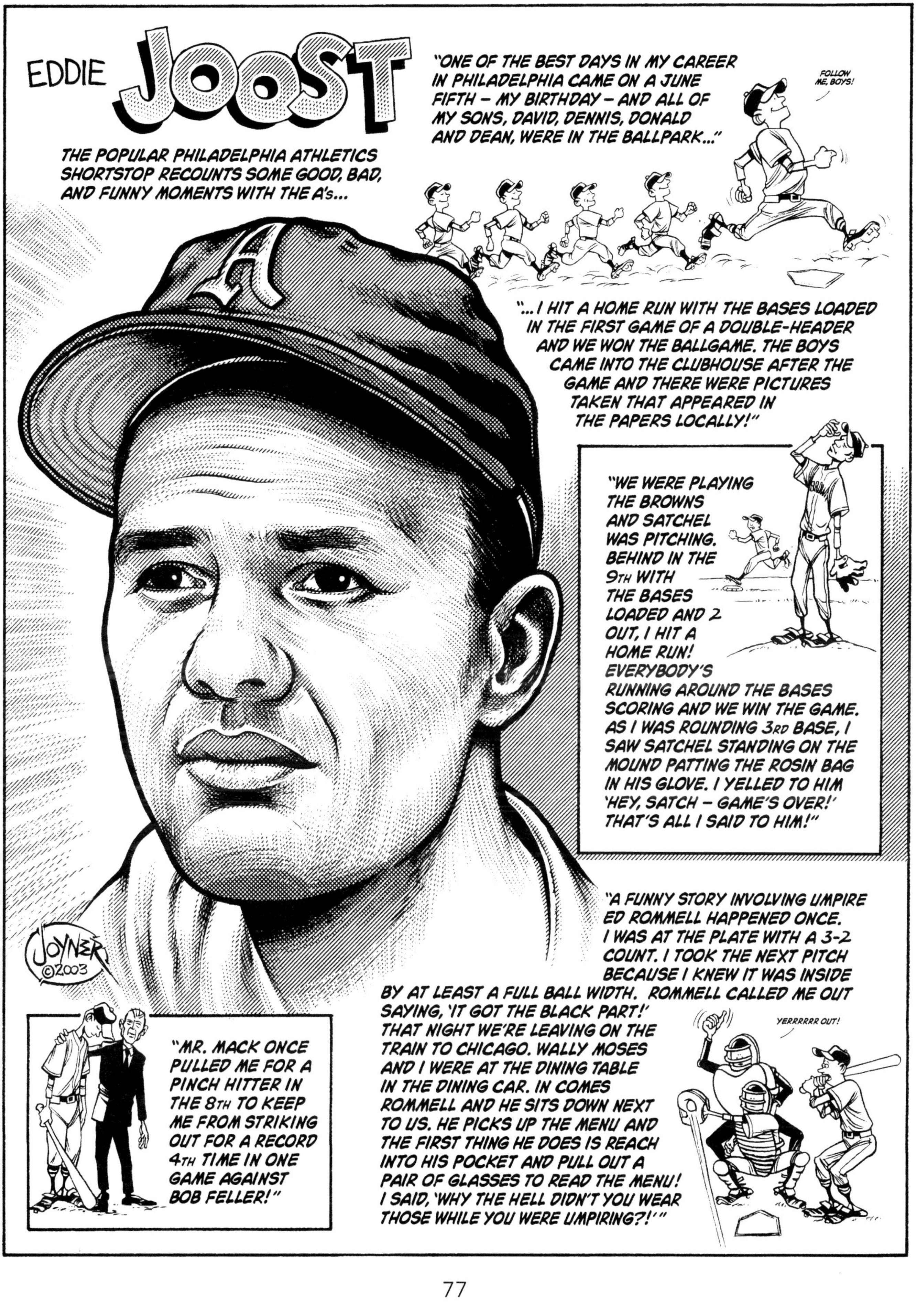
EDDIE JOOST
THE POPULAR PHILADELPHIA ATHLETICS SHORTSTOP RECOUNTS SOME GOOD, BAD, AND FUNNY MOMENTS WITH THE A's...
"ONE OF THE BEST DAYS IN MY CAREER IN PHILADELPHIA CAME ON A JUNE FIFTH – MY BIRTHDAY – AND ALL OF MY SONS, DAVID, DENNIS, DONALD AND DEAN, WERE IN THE BALLPARK..."
FOLLOW ME, BOYS!
"...I HIT A HOME RUN WITH THE BASES LOADED IN THE FIRST GAME OF A DOUBLE-HEADER AND WE WON THE BALLGAME. THE BOYS CAME INTO THE CLUBHOUSE AFTER THE GAME AND THERE WERE PICTURES TAKEN THAT APPEARED IN THE PAPERS LOCALLY!"
"WE WERE PLAYING THE BROWNS AND SATCHEL WAS PITCHING. BEHIND IN THE 9TH WITH THE BASES LOADED AND 2 OUT, I HIT A HOME RUN! EVERYBODY'S RUNNING AROUND THE BASES SCORING AND WE WIN THE GAME. AS I WAS ROUNDING 3RD BASE, I SAW SATCHEL STANDING ON THE MOUND PATTING THE ROSIN BAG IN HIS GLOVE. I YELLED TO HIM 'HEY, SATCH – GAME'S OVER!' THAT'S ALL I SAID TO HIM!"
"A FUNNY STORY INVOLVING UMPIRE ED ROMMELL HAPPENED ONCE. I WAS AT THE PLATE WITH A 3-2 COUNT. I TOOK THE NEXT PITCH BECAUSE I KNEW IT WAS INSIDE BY AT LEAST A FULL BALL WIDTH. ROMMELL CALLED ME OUT SAYING, 'IT GOT THE BLACK PART!' THAT NIGHT WE'RE LEAVING ON THE TRAIN TO CHICAGO. WALLY MOSES AND I WERE AT THE DINING TABLE IN THE DINING CAR. IN COMES ROMMELL AND HE SITS DOWN NEXT TO US. HE PICKS UP THE MENU AND THE FIRST THING HE DOES IS REACH INTO HIS POCKET AND PULL OUT A PAIR OF GLASSES TO READ THE MENU! I SAID, 'WHY THE HELL DIDN'T YOU WEAR THOSE WHILE YOU WERE UMPIRING?!'"
YERRRRRR OUT!
JOYNER ©2003
"MR. MACK ONCE PULLED ME FOR A PINCH HITTER IN THE 8TH TO KEEP ME FROM STRIKING OUT FOR A RECORD 4TH TIME IN ONE GAME AGAINST BOB FELLER!"

Clem
DREISEWERD
CLEM DREISEWERD WAS A LEFT-HANDED PITCHER WITH A HEATER COMPARABLE TO THAT OF BULLET BOB FELLER! AS A BOY, CLEM WOULD EXPERTLY NAIL TOGETHER BROKEN BATS FROM A LOCAL SEMI-PRO LEAGUE, FORESHADOWING HIS POST-BASEBALL CAREER AS AN ACCLAIMED NEW ORLEANS HOME-BUILDER!
I THINK YOU HAVE A BRIGHT FUTURE, CLEM!
IT WAS CLEM'S FASTBALL THAT GOT HIM SIGNED BY THE GIANTS ORGANIZATION IN 1934, BUT IT WAS HIS LATER MASTERY OF THE SCREWBALL THAT TRULY ELEVATED HIS GAME! ONCE, WHILE PITCHING FOR A CRACK NAVY TEAM IN 1945, CLEM STRUCK OUT NINE OPPOSITION BATTERS IN-A-ROW ON NOTHING BUT SCREWGIES! HIS CATCHER THAT DAY -- THE GREAT MICKEY OWEN!
ALRIGHT, MICKEY -- WHAT GIVES?!
CLEM WON 150 GAMES IN THE MINORS WITH A CAREER E.R.A. BELOW 3.00!
JOYNER ©2010
DESPITE POSSESSING GREAT TALENT, THE SOMETIMES-OPPRESSIVE CONTRACT SYSTEM OF THE 1930s AND '40s CAUSED CLEM TO SPEND THE BULK OF HIS 15-YEAR PRO CAREER IN THE MINORS! ALWAYS THERE TO HELP CLEM DEAL WITH THE HIGHS AND LOWS, HOWEVER, WAS HIS DEVOTED WIFE, EDNA! SHE WAS ULTRA-SUPPORTIVE -- WAY ABOVE AND BEYOND THAT OF THE AVERAGE BALLPLAYER'S WIFE! THROUGHOUT HIS CAREER, EDNA SERVED AS CLEM'S CATCHER, HELPING HIM STAY IN SHAPE DURING THE OFFSEASONS, AS WELL AS ASSISTING HIM IN REFINING HIS ARSENAL OF PITCHES! ALWAYS TOGETHER, THEY LOGGED THOUSANDS OF MILES TRAVELING FROM MINOR LEAGUE TOWN TO TOWN IN THEIR 21-FOOT CUSTOMIZED STEEL TRAILER! THEIR HARD WORK WAS FINALLY REWARDED WHEN CLEM MADE IT TO THE BIG LEAGUES WITH THE 1944 RED SOX! AFTER A YEAR IN THE NAVY, CLEM RETURNED TO THE SOX IN 1946 AND MADE AN APPEARANCE IN THE WORLD SERIES! CLEM OFTEN POINTED TO HIS SERIES WHIFF OF ENOS SLAUGHTER AS ONE OF THE HIGHLIGHTS OF HIS CAREER! IN "THE CATCHER WAS A LADY," EDNA'S MEMOIR OF THEIR ADVENTURES IN BASEBALL, SHE SUMMED UP THEIR FEELINGS BY SAYING, "IN SPITE OF ALL OUR DISAPPOINTMENTS AND ADVERSITIES, WE WOULDN'T TRADE THOSE MEMORIES OF BASEBALL FOR ANYTHING IN THE WORLD."

Jim King

JIM KING PLAYED THE ROLE OF HOME RUN KING ON JUNE 8, 1964, WHEN HE POLED THREE HOMERS AGAINST THE A'S. JIM HIT FOR THE CYCLE TWO WEEKS EARLIER AGAINST THE RED SOX -- SOMETHING ONLY HE WOULD ACHIEVE FOR THE NATS DURING THE 11-YEAR ERA (1961-71) OF THE EXPANSION SENATORS!

"JIM KING IS A MODEST FELLOW," WROTE SPORTSWRITER BOB ADDIE OF THE WASHINGTON POST, "WHO MERELY DOES HIS JOB AND DOESN'T GIVE ANYBODY ANY TROUBLE. HIS JOB IS PATROLING THE OUTFIELD AND SWINGING A BAT. ON OCCASION, HE IS SUPERB ON BOTH COUNTS." ADDIE'S WORDS PERFECTLY CAPTURED THE MOON-FACED, LEFT-HANDED SWINGING FLY-CHASER FROM ARKANSAS, AND SENATORS FANS BORE WITNESS TO THAT FOR SEVEN YEARS. JIM HAD ENJOYED A BIT OF SUCCESS DURING TIME WITH THE CUBS, CARDINALS, AND GIANTS FROM 1954-58, BUT HIS BIG BREAK CAME WHEN THE NATS MADE HIM THE 43RD PICK OF THE 1960 EXPANSION DRAFT. USED PRIMARILY AS A RIGHT-FIELDER BY THE NATS, JIM WAS A MORE THAN ADEQUATE BALL HAWK, AND ON OFFENSE BASHED 89 ROUND-TRIPPERS FROM 1961-67. FROM A POWER STANDPOINT, 1963 WAS JIM'S BEST SEASON AS HE SLAMMED 24 HOME RUNS -- A NEW TEAM RECORD FOR LEFT-HANDED HITTERS. JIM'S ROAD ROOMIE, CENTERFIELDER DON LOCK, ALSO POSTED EXCELLENT HOME RUN TOTALS IN '63! WHEN ONE D.C. WRITER COMPARED THEM TO THE FAMED M&M BOYS, JIM HUMBLY SAID, "WE'LL BE DOIN' REAL GOOD IF BOTH OF US COMBINED CAN BEAT ROGER MARIS' RECORD."

JIM POSSESSED ONE OF THE LEAGUE'S MOST RESPECTED ARMS -- A REAL HOSE! HIS REPUTATION FOR GUNNING DOWN BASERUNNERS MADE EVEN THE BRAVEST THIRD BASE COACHES A LITTLE MORE CONSERVATIVE. TIGERS THIRD BASE COACH TONY CUCCINELLO LIKED TO TELL THE STORY OF HOW HE ONCE HELD UP AL KALINE, THE TYING RUN, ON A FLY BALL TO JIM IN RIGHTFIELD. JIM, NONETHELESS, RIFLED A PERFECT ROPE TO THE PLATE. THE DETROIT CROWD GROANED WHEN THE CATCHER DROPPED JIM'S PEG, THINKING KALINE COULD HAVE SCORED. TONY REPORTED RECEIVING A LOT OF HATE MAIL FOR RESPECTING JIM'S ARM, ONE OF WHICH READ, "YOU'VE HELD UP MORE MEN THAN JESSE JAMES!"

Everette
JOYNER
BORN ON SEPTEMBER 9, 1926, IN MT. PLEASANT, MISSISSIPPI, EVERETTE J. JOYNER, JR. NEVER MADE IT TO THE BIG LEAGUES -- BUT HE SHOULD HAVE! HE IS SYMBOLIC OF AN ARMY OF BALLPLAYERS WHO, DESPITE PROVING THAT THEY HAD THE STUFF TO PLAY IN THE MAJORS, NEVER GOT THE SHOT THEY DESERVED! "EV" BEGAN HIS PRO CAREER IN 1949 WITH WEST FRANKFORT OF THE MISSISSIPPI-OHIO VALLEY LEAGUE! IT WAS THERE THAT HE DISPLAYED WHAT WOULD BE HIS LONG-RUNNING TRADEMARK -- A LETHAL LEFT-HANDED BAT! EV HIT .322 WITH 76 RBIs THAT SEASON, NUMBERS THAT WOULD PROVE TYPICAL FOR HIM IN YEARS TO COME! EV WAS WITH ALLENTOWN FROM 1950-51, THEN MOVED UP TO COLUMBUS (OHIO) IN 1952! HE WAS ONLY THERE BRIEFLY BEFORE BEING OPTIONED TO COLUMBUS (GEORGIA), BUT HE WAS THERE LONG ENOUGH TO BE FINED $21.20 FOR FISHING ON THE OLENTANGY RIVER WITHOUT A LICENSE -- A HEFTY SUM TO PAY WHEN TRYING TO MAKE ENDS MEET ON A MINOR LEAGUE SALARY! EV RESPONDED WELL TO THE CHANGE OF SCENERY IN GEORGIA AND BATTED .304 WITH ELEVEN HOMERS AND 82 RBIs IN 1952! HE SPENT THE BULK OF THE '53 SEASON BACK WITH COLUMBUS (GEORGIA), THIS TIME HITTING AT A .342-CLIP WITH 10 HOMERS AND 62 RBIs! THAT WAS GOOD ENOUGH TO EARN EV A NEW WRISTWATCH AFTER BEING NAMED THE BALLCLUB'S M.V.P.! EV SPENT 1954 THROUGH 1956 IN THE TEXAS LEAGUE WITH SHREVEPORT WHERE HE DID SOME OF HIS BEST STICKWORK! 1956 WAS PARTICULARLY GOOD FOR EV AS HE LED THE LEAGUE IN HITS WHILE BATTING .344 WITH 91 RBIs AND 13 LONG BALLS! THAT LED TO EV'S BEST CHANCE TO MAKE IT TO THE BIGS AS HE WAS INVITED TO SPRING TRAINING WITH THE MILWAUKEE BRAVES IN 1957, BUT THE 6'1" 180-LB FLYCHASER WAS OPTIONED TO WICHITA WHEN THE BRAVES HEADED NORTH! NOT TO BE DISCOURAGED, EV FORGED AHEAD AND POSTED MORE FINE SEASONS IN TOWNS LIKE ATLANTA, OMAHA, HOUSTON, DALLAS AND NASHVILLE! EV COULD DO IT ALL -- HIT, FIELD, AND RUN -- AND HE SHOULD'VE GOT A CHANCE TO PROVE IT ON THE BIG LEAGUE STAGE!
$21.20
TIME FOR ME TO GET A HIT!
S
EV STILL LIVES IN SHREVEPORT, THE SITE OF SOME OF HIS GREATEST EXPLOITS!
JOYNER ©2008

BIG BOPPERS

BIG STICKS
BABE
BLAZING A SLUGGING TRAIL NEVER SEEN BEFORE OR SINCE, BABE RUTH'S NAME IS NOW SYNONYMOUS WITH THE MIGHTY HOME RUN! 12 TIMES HE LED THE A.L. IN ROUND-TRIPPERS ON HIS WAY TO A CAREER TOTAL OF 714!
TED
TED WILLIAMS -- EXPERT PILOT, FISHERMAN AND HITTER -- WAS A LARGER-THAN-LIFE CHARACTER! TWO TRIPLE CROWNS, TWO MVPs, SIX BATTING TITLES, A .406 SEASON IN '41 AND 521 HOMERS MAKE HIM ONE OF THE BEST TO EVER WIELD THE LUMBER!
JOE D.
JOE DIMAGGIO CLOUTED 361 LONG BALLS IN HIS CAREER! HE'D HAVE HAD MANY MORE, TOO, HAD HE NOT BEEN A RIGHT-HANDED SWINGER PLAYING HALF HIS GAMES IN YANKEE STADIUM WITH ITS CAVERNOUS LEFT-CENTERFIELD DIMENSIONS! THE JOLTER'S .325 LIFETIME BATTING MARK PROVES HE COULD HIT FOR AVERAGE, TOO, AS DOES HIS MIND-BOGGLING 56-GAME HITTING STREAK OF '41!
JOYNER ©2008

BIG STICKS
HACK
HACK WILSON ROSE TO GREAT FAME DURING THE ROARING TWENTIES, AND HIS STYLE WAS PERFECTLY SUITED TO THAT DECADE -- HARD PLAYING AND EVEN HARDER LIVING! WHILE SMALL IN SIZE AT 5-FOOT-6, HACK WAS BIG ON POWER! A FOUR-TIME HOMER CHAMP, HACK DROVE IN 191 RBIs IN 1930!
HANK
HANK GREENBERG WAS A TRUE LEADER ON AND OFF THE FIELD! HIS PROLIFIC BAT POUNDED OUT 40 OR MORE HOMERS FOUR TIMES, AND HE WALLOPED A CAREER TOTAL OF 331!
STAN
STAN MUSIAL SPENT HIS ENTIRE 22-YEAR CAREER IN A CARDINALS UNIFORM AND TOTALED 475 HOMERS! MORE THAN JUST A SLUGGER, HOWEVER, "THE MAN" TOPPED THE .300-MARK 17 TIMES AND WON SEVEN BATTING CROWNS! STAN WAS A THREE-TIME MVP AND IS, AT THE TIME OF THIS WRITING, ARGUABLY THE GAME'S GREATEST LIVING HITTER!
JOYNER ©2008

GUS ZERNIAL
GUS EDWARD ZERNIAL WAS BORN ON JUNE 27, 1923, IN BEAUMONT, TEXAS! AT 6'3" 210 LBS, GUS CUT A POWERFUL PRESENCE AT THE PLATE WHEN HE ARRIVED IN THE BIG LEAGUES WITH THE WHITE SOX IN 1949! HE HAD ALREADY PROVED HIMSELF IN THE MINOR LEAGUES HITTING HOME RUNS WITH GREAT REGULARITY -- MOST RECENTLY 40 BOMBS WITH THE P.C.L. HOLLYWOOD STARS IN '48! GUS FINISHED FOURTH IN TOTAL A.L. HOME RUNS IN THE '50s, TRAILING ONLY HALL OF FAMERS MANTLE, BERRA, AND DOBY!
I'M IN GOOD COMPANY!
GUS' ABILITY ON THE BALLFIELD WAS NOT LIMITED TO HIS PRODIGIOUS BLASTS AT THE PLATE -- HE WAS ALSO FAST AND DID A FINE JOB IN THE OUTFIELD! IN 1951 HE LED A.L. OUTFIELDERS IN ASSISTS WITH 17! GUS' ALL-OUT STYLE OF PLAY WOULD OCCASIONALLY GET HIM IN TROUBLE, THOUGH, AS HE TWICE BROKE HIS COLLARBONE CHASING DOWN FLY BALLS!
WHO PUT THAT WALL THERE?
JOYNER ©2003
GUS PUT TOGETHER A HUGE DAY ON OCTOBER 1, 1950, WHILE STILL WITH THE WHITE SOX! HE HIT ONE HOME RUN IN THE FIRST GAME OF A TWIN BILL AND ADDED THREE MORE IN THE NIGHTCAP!
FRED HANEY, WHILE BROADCASTING GUS' HOLLYWOOD STARS GAMES, DUBBED THE TALL TEXAN "OZARK IKE" AFTER THE POPULAR COMIC STRIP CHARACTER OF THE SAME NAME!
DESPITE A BIG YEAR FOR CHICAGO IN 1950 THAT SAW GUS HIT 29 HOME RUNS AND 93 RBIs, HE WAS DEALT TO THE ATHLETICS EARLY IN THE 1951 SEASON! THE DEAL PAID IMMEDIATE DIVIDENDS FOR THE A's AS GUS WENT ON TO WIN THE HOME RUN AND RBI CROWN THAT YEAR! HE CONTINUED TO POST IMPRESSIVE NUMBERS FOR THE A's THROUGH THEIR FINAL SEASON IN PHILADELPHIA IN 1954, AND HE WENT WITH THE FRANCHISE WHEN THEY MOVED TO KANSAS CITY! GUS WOUND UP HIS CAREER IN 1959 WITH 237 CAREER HOMERS!

RON SANTO

RON SANTO WAS, UNQUESTIONABLY, THE MOST DOMINANT NATIONAL LEAGUE THIRD BASEMAN OF THE 1960s! HE DIDN'T BEGIN HIS CAREER AT THE HOT CORNER, HOWEVER -- HE, IN FACT, BEGAN HIS CAREER AS A CATCHER! A THREE-SPORT STAR AT SEATTLE'S FRANKLIN HIGH, RON WAS OFFERED BONUSES BY ALL 16 BIG LEAGUE TEAMS AFTER GRADUATING IN 1958! DESPITE THE FACT THAT THEY OFFERED LESS MONEY THAN ANY OTHER TEAM, RON SIGNED WITH THE CUBS BECAUSE HE FELT THEY PROVIDED HIM WITH THE QUICKEST ROUTE TO THE MAJORS! CONTRARY TO THE ADVICE OF THE MAN WHO SIGNED HIM, RON IMMEDIATELY RID HIMSELF OF HIS CATCHER'S GEAR AND MADE THE PERMANENT SWITCH TO THIRD BASE -- A MOVE THAT WAS THE FIRST STEP IN WHAT SURELY PROVED TO BE A HALL-OF-FAME-CALIBER CAREER!

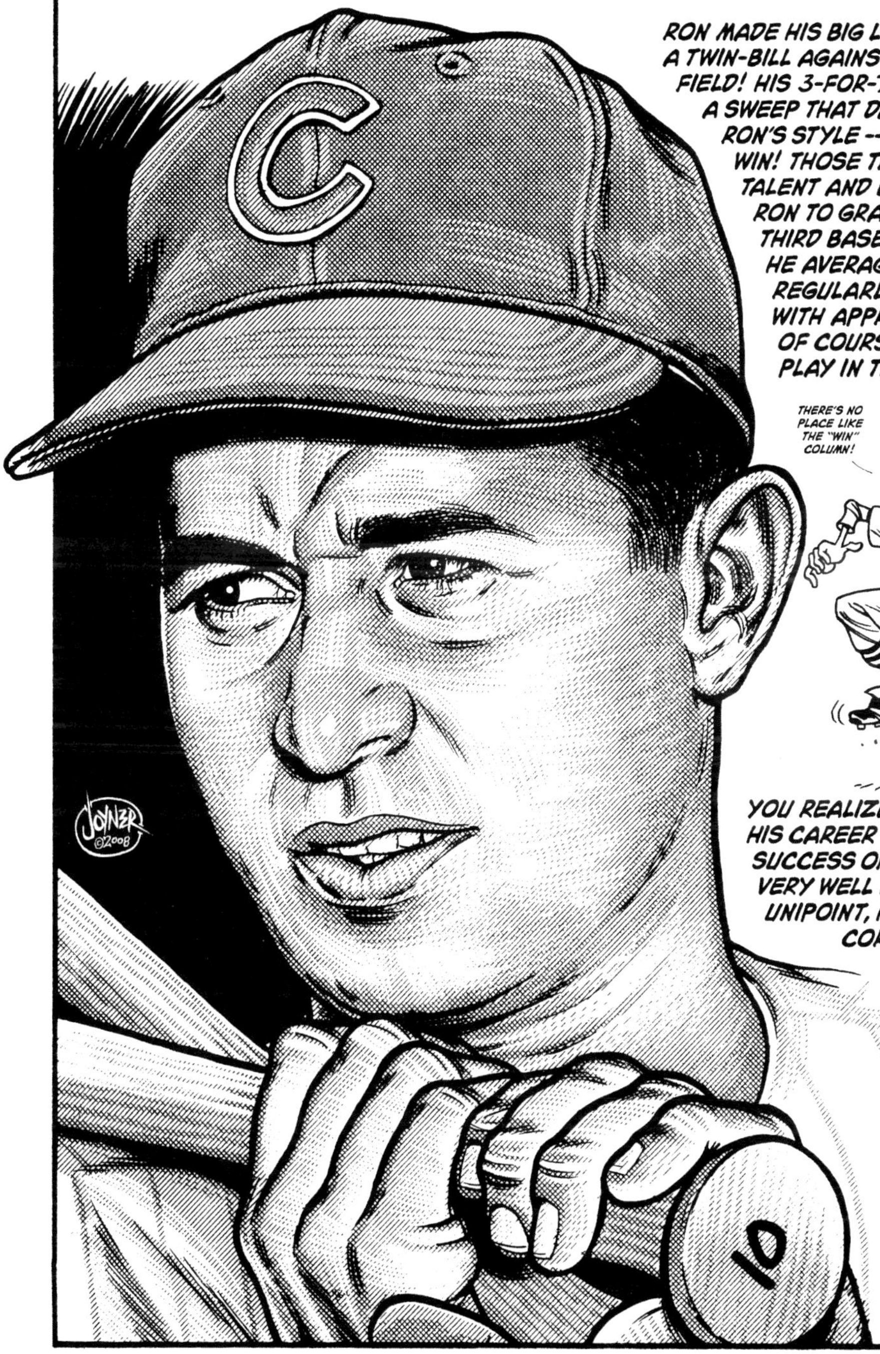

RON MADE HIS BIG LEAGUE DEBUT ON JUNE 26, 1960, IN A TWIN-BILL AGAINST THE 1st-PLACE PIRATES AT FORBES FIELD! HIS 3-FOR-7 WITH FIVE RBIs LED THE CUBS TO A SWEEP THAT DAY AND ESTABLISHED THE TONE FOR RON'S STYLE -- FIERY WITH AN INTENSE DESIRE TO WIN! THOSE TRAITS, COMBINED WITH HIS GOD-GIVEN TALENT AND BLUE-COLLAR WORK ETHIC, ALLOWED RON TO GRAB A STRANGLEHOLD ON THE CUBS' THIRD BASE POSITION THROUGH THE '73 SEASON! HE AVERAGED 159 GAMES PER CAMPAIGN WHILE REGULARLY SLAMMING 25 TO 30 LONG BALLS WITH APPROXIMATELY 100 RBIs -- ALL OF THIS, OF COURSE, IN CONJUNCTION WITH HIS SUPERB PLAY IN THE FIELD! RON'S ENTHUSIASM WAS ALWAYS ON DISPLAY, BUT IT HIT AN ALL-TIME HIGH IN '69 AS THE CUBS MADE THEIR NOW-LEGENDARY, AND ILL-FATED, RUN AT THE PENNANT! DURING THAT TIME RON CELEBRATED CUBBIE WINS WITH AN EXUBERANT CLICK OF HIS HEELS, SOMETHING SOME FELT WAS "SHOWY," BUT WAS REALLY JUST AN EXPRESSION OF JOY! RON'S CAREER IS ALL THE MORE AMAZING WHEN YOU REALIZE THAT HE PLAYED EVERY GAME OF HIS CAREER WITH DIABETES! RON PROVED TO BE A SUCCESS OFF THE FIELD AS WELL AS ON IT, DOING VERY WELL WITH KENTUCKY FRIED CHICKEN AND UNIPOINT, HIS TRUCK-STOP CORPORATION!

HARLOND B. Clift

WITH JUST TWO YEARS OF MINOR LEAGUE SERVICE UNDER HIS BELT, 21-YEAR-OLD HARLOND B. CLIFT JOINED THE LOWLY ST. LOUIS BROWNS IN 1934 WITH HOPES OF INJECTING SOME LIFE INTO THE MORIBUND FRANCHISE! EVEN WITH HARLOND ON THE ROSTER, THE BROWNIES WOULD CONTINUE TO LOSE, BUT HE DEVELOPED INTO THE MOST CONSISTENT POWER-HITTING 3RD BASEMAN OF HIS ERA! A RIGHT-HANDED SWINGER, HARLOND WAS A PULL HITTER IN SPITE OF HIS MANAGER'S ADVICE THAT HE SPRAY THE BALL TO ALL FIELDS! HIS MANAGER JUST HAPPENED TO BE THE GREATEST RIGHT-HANDED BATTER OF ALL TIME, ROGERS HORNSBY. BUT HARLOND'S DECISION TO PULL THE BALL SEEMED TO WORK OUT FOR THE BEST AS HE LED ALL AMERICAN LEAGUE 3RD BASEMEN IN HOMERS FOR FOUR STRAIGHT SEASONS FROM 1936-39! "I PLAYED MY BEST BALL FOR HIM," HARLOND SAID OF HORNSBY IN BASEBALL DIGEST BACK IN 1982, "BUT HE WAS MEAN. WE COULDN'T HAVE ANYTHING IN THE CLUBHOUSE EXCEPT BASEBALL. NO PAPERS, NO NOTHING. WHEN YOU WALKED IN THAT CLUBHOUSE IT WAS STRICTLY BASEBALL. EVERYONE HATED HIM." ONE OF HARLOND'S BEST DAYS AT THE PLATE CAME IN A TWIN-BILL SLUGFEST AGAINST THE NEW YORK YANKEES AT SPORTSMAN'S PARK IN ST. LOUIS ON JUNE 13, 1937! HARLOND DUELED THE GREAT JOE DIMAGGIO THAT DAY, EACH CLUBBING THREE HOMERS FOR HIS TEAM! THAT WAS QUITE A THRILL FOR HARLOND CONSIDERING HOW HE FELT ABOUT JOE D! "I THINK DIMAGGIO WAS THE GREATEST HITTER IN THE WHOLE WORLD," HARLOND SAID. "AND HE WAS A GENTLEMAN AT ALL TIMES, TOO. HE WOULD COME SLIDING INTO ME AT THIRD AND HE NEVER SPIKED ME OR NOTHING." NOT TO BE OVERLOOKED WAS HARLOND'S EXCELLENCE ON DEFENSE! HE WAS ONE OF THE BEST FIELDERS IN THE A.L.! IN '37 HE SET RECORDS FOR DOUBLE-PLAYS AND ASSISTS THAT STOOD UNTIL BROKEN BY GRAIG NETTLES IN 1971! IN A CRUEL TWIST OF IRONY, HARLOND LABORED THROUGH NEARLY A DECADE OF LOSING WITH ST. LOUIS ONLY TO BE DEALT TO THE SENATORS ONE YEAR BEFORE THE BROWNIES WON THEIR ONE AND ONLY PENNANT IN 1944!

DESPITE HIS TREMENDOUS HITTING AND FIELDING THROUGHOUT THE DECADE OF THE 1930s, HARLOND WAS MOSTLY OVERLOOKED BY BASEBALL FANS OF THE TIME! THE LOSING BROWNIES BARELY DREW 500 TO 1,000 FANS PER GAME -- UNLESS THE YANKEES WERE IN TOWN! AND IT WAS YANKS THIRD BASEMAN RED ROLFE WHO STOLE MOST OF THE ACCOLADES AND ALL-STAR APPEARANCES THAT SHOULD HAVE GONE TO HARLOND IN HIS PRIME -- EXCEPT IN 1937! THAT'S THE YEAR HARLOND BROKE THROUGH WITH HIS ONLY ALL-STAR SELECTION, ALTHOUGH HE DIDN'T PLAY IN THE GAME! "IN THOSE DAYS, THERE WAS NO RULE THAT YOU HAD TO CHANGE PLAYERS AND ROLFE PLAYED THE ENTIRE GAME," HARLOND SAID. "IN 1962, AT THE 25TH ANNIVERSARY OF THAT GAME, JOE McCARTHY CAME UP TO ME AND SAID, 'I'M SORRY I DIDN'T PLAY YOU, HARLOND. I RECEIVED ALMOST 10,000 LETTERS FROM ST. LOUIS FOR NOT PLAYING YOU!'"

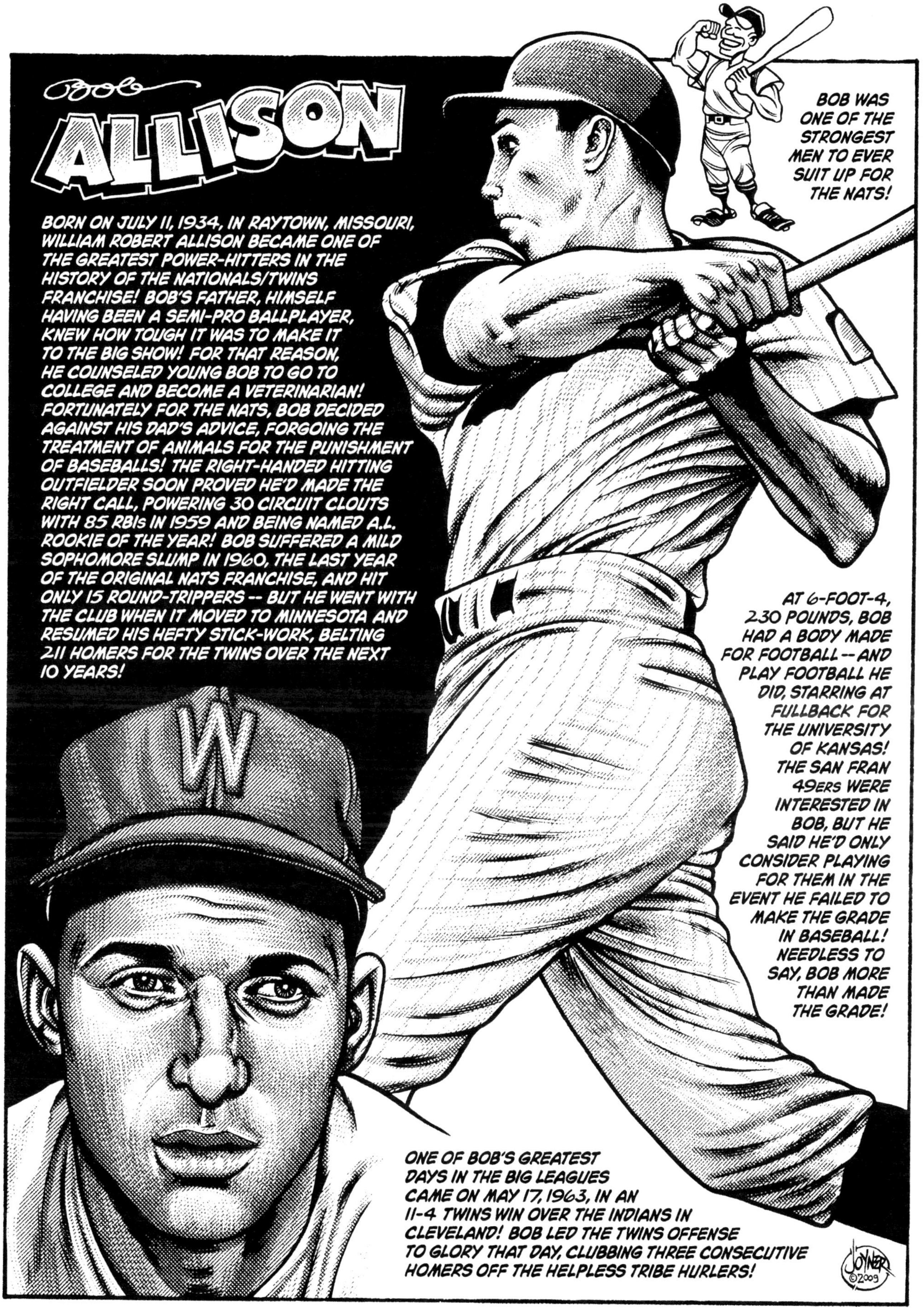
Bob
ALLISON
BORN ON JULY 11, 1934, IN RAYTOWN, MISSOURI, WILLIAM ROBERT ALLISON BECAME ONE OF THE GREATEST POWER-HITTERS IN THE HISTORY OF THE NATIONALS/TWINS FRANCHISE! BOB'S FATHER, HIMSELF HAVING BEEN A SEMI-PRO BALLPLAYER, KNEW HOW TOUGH IT WAS TO MAKE IT TO THE BIG SHOW! FOR THAT REASON, HE COUNSELED YOUNG BOB TO GO TO COLLEGE AND BECOME A VETERINARIAN! FORTUNATELY FOR THE NATS, BOB DECIDED AGAINST HIS DAD'S ADVICE, FORGOING THE TREATMENT OF ANIMALS FOR THE PUNISHMENT OF BASEBALLS! THE RIGHT-HANDED HITTING OUTFIELDER SOON PROVED HE'D MADE THE RIGHT CALL, POWERING 30 CIRCUIT CLOUTS WITH 85 RBIs IN 1959 AND BEING NAMED A.L. ROOKIE OF THE YEAR! BOB SUFFERED A MILD SOPHOMORE SLUMP IN 1960, THE LAST YEAR OF THE ORIGINAL NATS FRANCHISE, AND HIT ONLY 15 ROUND-TRIPPERS -- BUT HE WENT WITH THE CLUB WHEN IT MOVED TO MINNESOTA AND RESUMED HIS HEFTY STICK-WORK, BELTING 211 HOMERS FOR THE TWINS OVER THE NEXT 10 YEARS!
BOB WAS ONE OF THE STRONGEST MEN TO EVER SUIT UP FOR THE NATS!
AT 6-FOOT-4, 230 POUNDS, BOB HAD A BODY MADE FOR FOOTBALL -- AND PLAY FOOTBALL HE DID, STARRING AT FULLBACK FOR THE UNIVERSITY OF KANSAS! THE SAN FRAN 49ERS WERE INTERESTED IN BOB, BUT HE SAID HE'D ONLY CONSIDER PLAYING FOR THEM IN THE EVENT HE FAILED TO MAKE THE GRADE IN BASEBALL! NEEDLESS TO SAY, BOB MORE THAN MADE THE GRADE!
ONE OF BOB'S GREATEST DAYS IN THE BIG LEAGUES CAME ON MAY 17, 1963, IN AN 11-4 TWINS WIN OVER THE INDIANS IN CLEVELAND! BOB LED THE TWINS OFFENSE TO GLORY THAT DAY, CLUBBING THREE CONSECUTIVE HOMERS OFF THE HELPLESS TRIBE HURLERS!
JOYNER ©2009

SURE BEATS MY RUSTY OL' '34 FORD!
Mickey
Mantle
MICKEY, WHO HAILED FROM COMMERCE, OKLAHOMA, WAS KNOWN AS "THE COMMERCE COMET" BECAUSE OF HIS BLAZING SPEED!
THE BASEBALL LIFE OF MICKEY CHARLES MANTLE GOT OFF ON THE RIGHT FOOT WHEN HE WAS BORN ON OCTOBER 20, 1931 -- AND WAS THEN IMMEDIATELY NAMED AFTER THE IMMORTAL MICKEY COCHRANE! MANTLE MADE HIS BIG LEAGUE DEBUT ON APRIL 17, 1951, AND THEN PROCEEDED TO RIDE HIS INCREDIBLE ABILITY AND BOYISH GOOD LOOKS TO ICONIC STATUS! WHILE MICKEY WAS AN EXCELLENT FIELDER WITH A STRONG AND ACCURATE ARM, IT WAS HIS AWESOME POWER AT THE PLATE THAT BECAME HIS CALLING CARD! BY 1956 MICKEY HAD ASSERTED HIMSELF AS THE GREATEST SWITCH-HITTER IN THE GAME'S HISTORY, ELECTRIFYING FANS WITH HIS TREMENDOUS BLASTS FROM BOTH SIDES OF THE PLATE! MICKEY'S POPULARITY HIT AN ALL-TIME HIGH WHEN HE TEAMED WITH ROGER MARIS IN 1961 TO MAKE THEIR LEGENDARY RUN AT BABE RUTH'S SINGLE SEASON HOME RUN MARK!
JOYNER ©2005
61
54
HO...
...HUM!
WHY DO YOU KEEP FORGETTING THE LYRICS, MICKEY?
WHAT LYRICS?!
MICKEY MADE THE BILLBOARD POP CHARTS IN 1956 WHEN HE PAIRED WITH TERESA BREWER ON HER HIT RECORD "I LOVE MICKEY"! THE SONG PEAKED ON SEPTEMBER 29, 1956, THE SAME DAY THAT MICKEY HIT HIS 52ND HOMER OF THE YEAR!
MICKEY'S ACHIEVEMENTS ARE NUMEROUS: 20 ALL-STAR APPEARANCES, 4 HOME RUN TITLES, 3 M.V.P. AWARDS, A GOLD GLOVE, A TRIPLE CROWN, AND MUCH MORE! HE ALSO HELPED THE YANKEES WIN 12 PENNANTS AND 7 WORLD SERIES CHAMPIONSHIPS IN HIS FIRST 14 SEASONS! HE MADE THE MOST OF HIS WORLD SERIES APPEARANCES, TOO, ESTABLISHING MANY SERIES RECORDS, INCLUDING MOST HOME RUNS WITH 18! MICKEY RETIRED FOLLOWING THE 1968 SEASON, AND HIS TOTALS OF 536 ROUND-TRIPPERS, 2,415 HITS, AND .298 BATTING AVERAGE DEMANDED THAT HE BE A FIRST-BALLOT SELECTION TO THE HALL OF FAME IN 1974!

Roger Maris

THE NEW YORK YANKEES RETIRED ROGER'S NUMBER "9" IN 1984!

ROGER EUGENE MARIS SHOWED A FLAIR FOR DRAMA WHEN HE WAITED UNTIL THE LAST GAME OF THE 1961 CAMPAIGN TO POLE HIS RECORD SETTING 61ST LONG BALL OF THE SEASON! CAPTURING BASEBALL'S MOST COVETED SINGLE SEASON RECORD INSTANTLY ENSURED THAT ROGER'S NAME WOULD FOREVER BE MENTIONED ALONGSIDE OTHER GREATS OF THE GAME, BUT ROGER'S LEGACY WENT MUCH DEEPER THAN THE HOMER RECORD! ROGER, BORN ON SEPTEMBER 10, 1934, IN HIBBING, MINNESOTA, MOVED WITH HIS FAMILY TO FARGO, NORTH DAKOTA, AS A BOY, AND IT WAS THERE THAT HE GREW INTO A GREAT ALL-AROUND ATHLETE! A STANDOUT FOOTBALL PLAYER WHO ONCE SET A NATIONAL HIGH SCHOOL RECORD BY SCORING FOUR TOUCHDOWNS IN ONE GAME ON KICKOFF RETURNS, ROGER GAVE UP A SCHOLARSHIP TO PLAY FOOTBALL AT THE UNIVERSITY OF OKLAHOMA TO PURSUE A CAREER IN BASEBALL! ROGER QUICKLY ASCENDED THE MINOR LEAGUE LADDER THANKS IN PART TO HIS MANAGER AT KEOKUK, FORMER BIG LEAGUER JO-JO WHITE, WHO TAUGHT HIM TO PULL THE BALL -- SOMETHING THAT WOULD SERVE HIM WELL IN LATER YEARS AS A LEFT-HANDED POWER HITTER AT YANKEE STADIUM!

ROGER SPENT HIS EARLY YEARS WITH THE INDIANS AND ATHLETICS, BUT IT WAS WITH THE PINSTRIPERS THAT HE WOULD ESTABLISH HIMSELF AS ONE OF THE MOST DOMINANT PLAYERS OF THE FIRST HALF OF THE 1960s! AN ALL-STAR WHO WON TWO M.V.P. AWARDS, TWO RBI TITLES, ONE HOME RUN CROWN, AND A GOLD GLOVE, ROGER MARIS HELPED THE YANKEES KICK START A NEW DYNASTY THAT WON FIVE CONSECUTIVE A.L. PENNANTS FROM 1960-64! ROGER ENDED HIS CAREER IN ST. LOUIS WHERE HE HELPED THE CARDS TO PENNANTS IN 1967 AND '68!

ROGER HIT 275 HOME RUNS IN HIS CAREER, PLUS AN ADDITIONAL SIX IN WORLD SERIES PLAY! HIS FIRST CAREER CIRCUIT BLAST WAS A BIG ONE -- A GAME-WINNING GRAND SLAM IN THE 11TH INNING TO LEAD THE INDIANS TO VICTORY ON APRIL 18, 1957!

Jim Lemon

ON SEPTEMBER 6, 1959, SENATORS LONG-BALLER JIM LEMON WALLOPED TWO HOMERS IN ONE INNING TO LEAD HIS BALLCLUB IN A 14-2 WHIPPING OF THE RED SOX! THE FIRST DINGER, A 2-RUN SHOT OFF RIGHT-HANDER BILL MONBOUQUETTE, ERASED A 2-1 BOSTON LEAD! BY THE TIME JIM RETURNED TO THE PLATE LATER IN THE SAME FRAME, IT WAS EARL WILSON ON THE SLAB -- BUT THIS TIME THE SACKS WERE FULL! LEM GAVE WILSON THE SAME TREATMENT, DEPOSITING THE BALL INTO THE GRIFFITH STADIUM SEATS! JIM BECAME THE FIRST SENATOR TO SLAM TWO ROUND-TRIPPERS IN ONE INNING, AND HIS SIX RBIs IN ONE FRAME (A RECORD AT THAT TIME) PUT HIM IN AN ELITE GROUP CONSISTING OF JUST SIX OTHER BIG LEAGUERS! JIM LATER DOUBLED HOME A SEVENTH RUN AND ROBBED FRANK MALZONE OF A HOMER WITH A FINE CATCH AGAINST THE LEFT-FIELD BLEACHER FENCE! AS THE A.P. PUT IT, "IT WAS ONE OF THE BRIGHTEST AFTERNOONS IN THE CAREER IN THE 31-YEAR-OLD COVINGTON, VIRGINIA, NATIVE." AND IT WAS TRUE! JIM HAD WORKED HARD AND LONG TO REACH THIS POINT IN HIS CAREER, INCLUDING FAILED TRIALS WITH THE 1950 AND 1953 INDIANS, AS WELL AS TWO YEARS LOST TO SERVICE IN THE U.S. ARMY DURING THE KOREAN WAR! JIM HAD JOINED THE NATS BACK IN '54, BUT IT WASN'T UNTIL '56 THAT HE TRULY ESTABLISHED HIMSELF AS ONE OF THE GAME'S BONAFIDE HOME RUN THREATS AS HE SMASHED 27 BOMBS! JIM HIT ONLY 17 HOMERS IN 1957 AS PART OF AN EFFORT TO CUT DOWN ON HIS STRIKEOUTS, BUT THAT PLAN WAS SCRAPPED IN 1958 -- AND THE NEW, FREE-SWINGING LEM POLED 26 CIRCUITS! HE RAISED HIS HOMER TOTAL TO 33 IN 1959, THEN HAD HIS BEST POWER SEASON OF ALL IN 1960 WHEN HE CLUBBED 38 4-BAGGERS! THAT EARNED JIM HIS ONLY ALL-STAR APPEARANCE, AS INJURIES BEGAN TO SLOW HIM FROM 1961 THROUGH HIS LAST BIG LEAGUE SEASON IN 1963 -- BUT LEM HAD FOREVER SEALED HIS PLACE AMONG WASHINGTON D.C.'s BEST POWER BROKERS!

JIM'S POPULARITY WITH NATS FANS WAS REWARDED WHEN HE WAS NAMED TO MANAGE THEM IN 1968! IT WAS NOT, HOWEVER, ENOUGH TO SAVE HIS JOB WHEN THE HAPLESS NATS WON JUST 65 GAMES FOR HIM! NEW OWNER BOB SHORT, SOON TO BE REVILED IN D.C. FOR MOVING THE NATS TO TEXAS, FIRED JIM AS ONE OF HIS FIRST ACTS AS OWNER, AND REPLACED HIM WITH THE GREAT TED WILLIAMS! JIM STILL REMAINED A FAVORITE AROUND WASHINGTON, AND WAS OFTEN SEEN AROUND THE RESTAURANT HE WAS INVOLVED WITH, AS WELL AS HIS HYATTSVILLE, MARYLAND, GROCERY STORE! "THEY PAY ME TO HIT THE LONG BALL," JIM ONCE TOLD WASHINGTON POST WRITER BOB ADDIE, "AND THE ONLY WAY I CAN DO IT IS BY SWINGING FROM THE HEELS." GREAT ADVICE FOR BASEBALL... AND LIFE!

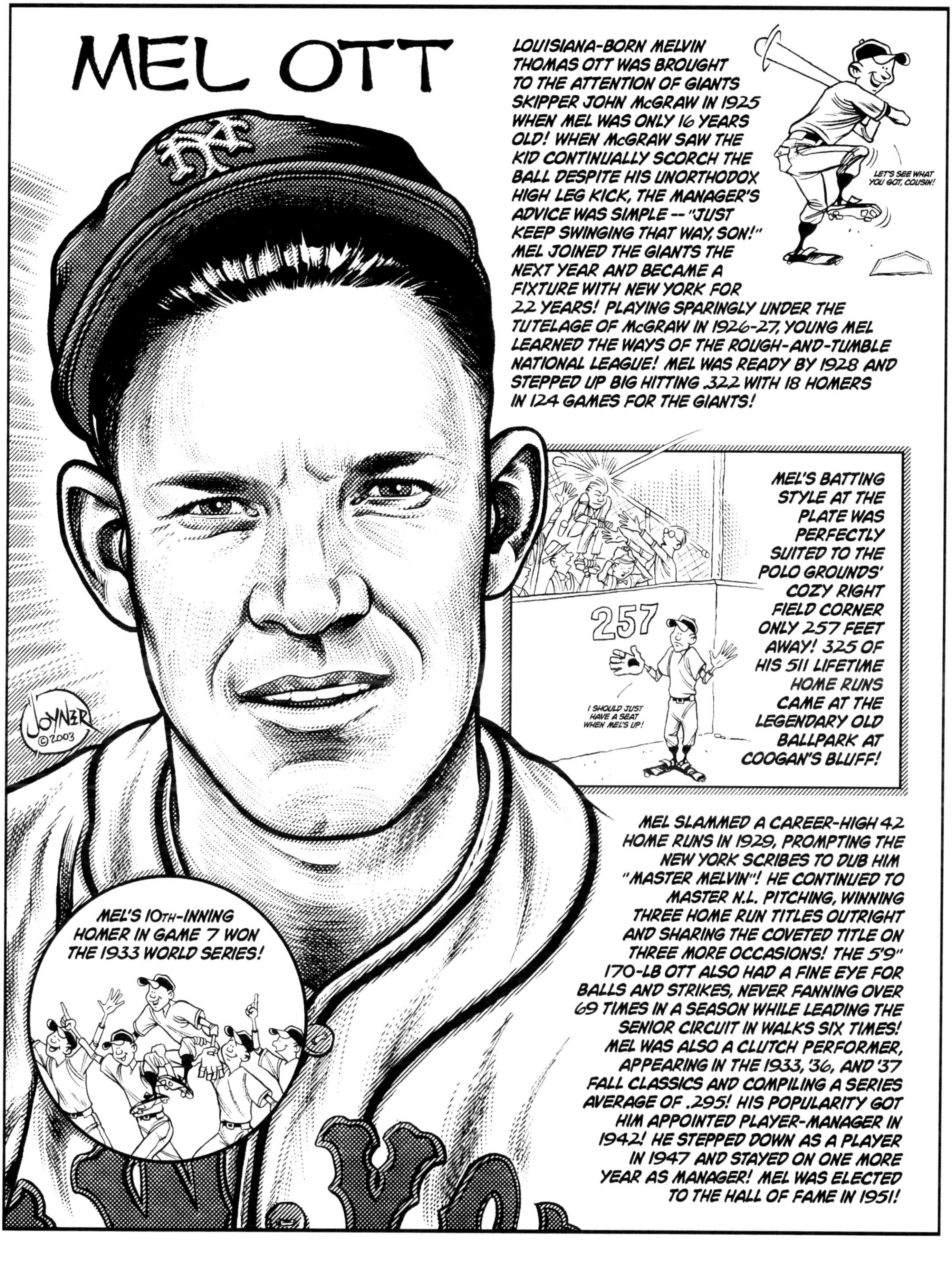
MEL OTT
LOUISIANA-BORN MELVIN THOMAS OTT WAS BROUGHT TO THE ATTENTION OF GIANTS SKIPPER JOHN McGRAW IN 1925 WHEN MEL WAS ONLY 16 YEARS OLD! WHEN McGRAW SAW THE KID CONTINUALLY SCORCH THE BALL DESPITE HIS UNORTHODOX HIGH LEG KICK, THE MANAGER'S ADVICE WAS SIMPLE -- "JUST KEEP SWINGING THAT WAY, SON!" MEL JOINED THE GIANTS THE NEXT YEAR AND BECAME A FIXTURE WITH NEW YORK FOR 22 YEARS! PLAYING SPARINGLY UNDER THE TUTELAGE OF McGRAW IN 1926-27, YOUNG MEL LEARNED THE WAYS OF THE ROUGH-AND-TUMBLE NATIONAL LEAGUE! MEL WAS READY BY 1928 AND STEPPED UP BIG HITTING .322 WITH 18 HOMERS IN 124 GAMES FOR THE GIANTS!
LET'S SEE WHAT YOU GOT, COUSIN!
MEL'S BATTING STYLE AT THE PLATE WAS PERFECTLY SUITED TO THE POLO GROUNDS' COZY RIGHT FIELD CORNER ONLY 257 FEET AWAY! 325 OF HIS 511 LIFETIME HOME RUNS CAME AT THE LEGENDARY OLD BALLPARK AT COOGAN'S BLUFF!
257
I SHOULD JUST HAVE A SEAT WHEN MEL'S UP!
JOYNER ©2003
MEL SLAMMED A CAREER-HIGH 42 HOME RUNS IN 1929, PROMPTING THE NEW YORK SCRIBES TO DUB HIM "MASTER MELVIN"! HE CONTINUED TO MASTER N.L. PITCHING, WINNING THREE HOME RUN TITLES OUTRIGHT AND SHARING THE COVETED TITLE ON THREE MORE OCCASIONS! THE 5'9" 170-LB OTT ALSO HAD A FINE EYE FOR BALLS AND STRIKES, NEVER FANNING OVER 69 TIMES IN A SEASON WHILE LEADING THE SENIOR CIRCUIT IN WALKS SIX TIMES! MEL WAS ALSO A CLUTCH PERFORMER, APPEARING IN THE 1933, '36, AND '37 FALL CLASSICS AND COMPILING A SERIES AVERAGE OF .295! HIS POPULARITY GOT HIM APPOINTED PLAYER-MANAGER IN 1942! HE STEPPED DOWN AS A PLAYER IN 1947 AND STAYED ON ONE MORE YEAR AS MANAGER! MEL WAS ELECTED TO THE HALL OF FAME IN 1951!
MEL'S 10TH-INNING HOMER IN GAME 7 WON THE 1933 WORLD SERIES!

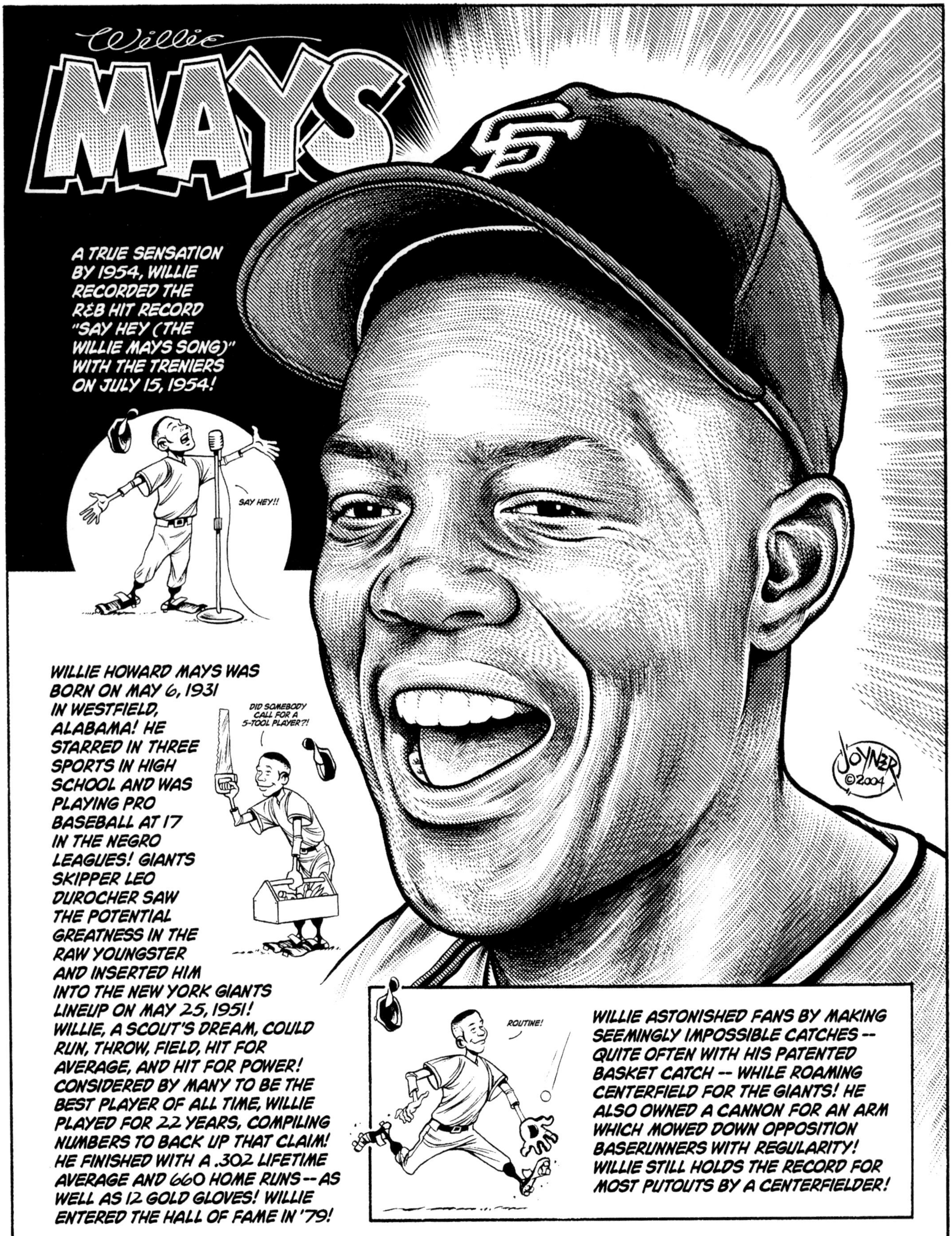
Willie
MAYS
A TRUE SENSATION BY 1954, WILLIE RECORDED THE R&B HIT RECORD "SAY HEY (THE WILLIE MAYS SONG)" WITH THE TRENIERS ON JULY 15, 1954!
SAY HEY!!
WILLIE HOWARD MAYS WAS BORN ON MAY 6, 1931 IN WESTFIELD, ALABAMA! HE STARRED IN THREE SPORTS IN HIGH SCHOOL AND WAS PLAYING PRO BASEBALL AT 17 IN THE NEGRO LEAGUES! GIANTS SKIPPER LEO DUROCHER SAW THE POTENTIAL GREATNESS IN THE RAW YOUNGSTER AND INSERTED HIM INTO THE NEW YORK GIANTS LINEUP ON MAY 25, 1951! WILLIE, A SCOUT'S DREAM, COULD RUN, THROW, FIELD, HIT FOR AVERAGE, AND HIT FOR POWER! CONSIDERED BY MANY TO BE THE BEST PLAYER OF ALL TIME, WILLIE PLAYED FOR 22 YEARS, COMPILING NUMBERS TO BACK UP THAT CLAIM! HE FINISHED WITH A .302 LIFETIME AVERAGE AND 660 HOME RUNS -- AS WELL AS 12 GOLD GLOVES! WILLIE ENTERED THE HALL OF FAME IN '79!
DID SOMEBODY CALL FOR A 5-TOOL PLAYER?!
JOYNER ©2004
ROUTINE!
WILLIE ASTONISHED FANS BY MAKING SEEMINGLY IMPOSSIBLE CATCHES -- QUITE OFTEN WITH HIS PATENTED BASKET CATCH -- WHILE ROAMING CENTERFIELD FOR THE GIANTS! HE ALSO OWNED A CANNON FOR AN ARM WHICH MOWED DOWN OPPOSITION BASERUNNERS WITH REGULARITY! WILLIE STILL HOLDS THE RECORD FOR MOST PUTOUTS BY A CENTERFIELDER!

DALE LONG ELECTRIFIED BASEBALL FANS ALL ACROSS THE U.S.A. WHEN HE WENT ON A RECORD-BREAKING HOME RUN STREAK 50 YEARS AGO! FROM MAY 19 THROUGH MAY 28, 1956, DALE HOMERED IN EIGHT CONSECUTIVE PIRATES GAMES! THE PREVIOUS BEST HAD BEEN SIX GAMES, A MARK SHARED BY FIVE PLAYERS UNTIL DALE SHATTERED THE OLD RECORD! DALE HELD SOLE POSSESSION OF THE RECORD FOR OVER 30 YEARS UNTIL THE MARK WAS FINALLY TIED IN 1987! THE RECORD WAS AGAIN EQUALED IN 1993 -- BUT IT'S NEVER BEEN ECLIPSED! IT WAS, AND STILL IS, A MONUMENTAL ACHIEVEMENT! WHEN GREAT BASEBALL RECORDS ARE DISCUSSED, DALE LONG'S EIGHT CONSECUTIVE GAME HOME RUN STREAK WILL ALWAYS BE REMEMBERED -- AS WILL DALE!
GAME 1: 2-RUN BOMB OFF CUBS' JIM DAVIS INTO THE UPPER DECK IN RIGHT AT FORBES FIELD! BUCS WIN, 7-4!
I GOT IT! I GOT IT! UH OH -- HE GOT IT!
BONK!
HOT DOGS
GAME 2: 3-RUN SMASH OFF BRAVES' RAY CRONE IN THE OPENER OF A TWIN-BILL AT FORBES FIELD! BUCS WIN AGAIN, 6-3!
THANKS FOR SETTIN' THE TABLE, FELLAS!
GAME 3: 2-RUN WALLOP OFF WARREN SPAHN IN THE NIGHTCAP! BUCS VICTORIOUS, 5-0!
I FEEL LIKE I'M BACK AT THE BULGE!
GAME 4: A BOOMING SOLO SHOT OFF CARDS' HERM WEHMEIER AT FORBES FIELD! PIRATES LOSE, 6-3, THE ONLY GAME THEY WOULD LOSE DURING DALE'S STREAK! DALE HIT .571 THROUGH THIS POINT IN THE STREAK!
I'M GETTIN' DEJA VU!
375
JOYNER ©2006
GAME 5: BASES-EMPTY BLAST OVER THE 436-FOOT SIGN IN CENTER AT FORBES OFF LINDY McDANIEL! BUCS TOP CARDS, 6-0!
WOW -- THAT'S GUS SUHR TERRITORY!
GAME 6: 2-RUN CIRCUIT-JOB OFF CURT SIMMONS AT PHILLY! BUCS WIN, 8-5!
MOVE OVER WILLIAMS, KELLY, GEHRIG, COOPER AND MAYS -- HERE I COME!
GAME 7: SET RECORD WITH SOLO JOLT OVER THE ROOF AT PHILLY OFF BEN FLOWERS! BALL LANDED ON PORCH ACROSS STREET AS PIRATES BEAT PHILS, 6-2!
LONG MUST BE UP!
GAME 8: SOLO KNOCK OFF CARL ERSKINE INTO RIGHTFIELD STANDS AT FORBES FIELD! BUCS EDGE BROOKS, 3-2!
ONE MORE FOR GOOD MEASURE!

Dick ALLEN

AS A SCHOOL KID AT WAMPUM HIGH IN RURAL PENNSYLVANIA, DICK ALLEN PUNISHED THE BASEBALL WITH A FEROCITY THAT HAD THE BIG LEAGUE SCOUTS DROOLING! THE PHILS GOT HIM, AND DICK BROUGHT HIS THRILLING GAME OF "CLOUT BALL" TO THE BIG SHOW WHERE HE WALLOPED 351 CAREER HOMERS!

A ROOKIE-OF-THE-YEAR AWARD, AN M.V.P. AWARD, AND NUMEROUS ALL-STAR GAME APPEARANCES ARE JUST A FEW OF THE HONORS THAT DEMONSTRATE WHAT A GIFTED PLAYER DICK WAS DURING HIS 15 YEARS IN THE MAJORS -- BUT HE IS ALSO REMEMBERED FOR BEING CONSTANTLY SURROUNDED BY TURBULENCE. TROUBLE WITH MANAGEMENT, FANS, SPORTSWRITERS, AND THE OCCASIONAL TEAMMATE ALL MARKED DICK'S CAREER IN PROPORTIONS ALMOST EQUAL TO HIS ON-FIELD HEROICS. WHILE DICK READILY ACCEPTED HIS PORTION OF THE RESPONSIBILITY FOR HIS DIFFICULTIES, IT'S SIMPLY TOO EASY TO DISMISS HIS TROUBLES AS MERELY THE ACTS OF A MALCONTENT. WHEN HE BROKE IN WITH THE PHILS IN 1963, DICK WAS FREE-SPIRITED KID -- SMART, CHARMING, CUTTING, ENIGMATIC, SENSITIVE, INDEPENDENT, OUTSPOKEN, COMPLEX... AND BLACK. THESE ELEMENTS DID NOT MIX WELL IN RACIALLY-CHARGED PHILADELPHIA AT THE PEAK OF THE CIVIL RIGHTS MOVEMENT, AND DICK'S RESOLVE TO BE HIS OWN MAN AT THAT TIME WAS AT THE ROOT OF HIS CONFLICTS WITH THE FANS, THE PRESS, AND THE FRONT OFFICE. STILL, HE ALWAYS PLAYED HARD WITH A BURNING DESIRE TO WIN!

"CRASH," DICK'S BRILLIANT AUTOBIOGRAPHY, WAS CRAMMED WITH WIT AND WISDOM THAT TURNED MANY OF THE MOST HARDCORE ALLEN HATERS INTO DEVOTED FANS! HERE ARE A FEW NUGGETS HE WROTE...

"ROBERTO CLEMENTE -- THERE WAS A CAT WHO COULD GIG. HE PLAYED THE RIGHT-FIELD WALL AT FORBES FIELD LIKE OSCAR PETERSON WORKING THE PIANO."

"PETE ROSE CAN TELL YOU ABOUT EVERY HIT HE EVER HAD, WHO HE HIT IT OFF, WHAT FIELD IT WAS HIT TO, AND THE KIND OF PITCH IT WAS. THAT KIND OF THING ALWAYS PUT ME TO SLEEP. ALL I WANTED TO DO WAS GRAB A BAT AND GO WIN US ONE."

"IT USE TO AMAZE ME THAT I COULD BE SO PRODUCTIVE IN MY ANGRY STATE OF MIND. I WOULD STAND IN AT THE PLATE AND GATHER ALL MY FRUSTRATION FOR ONE BIG SWING. JUDGING BY HOW FAR SOME OF THOSE BALLS WERE SAILING OUT OF THE PARK, I HAD A LOT OF FRUSTRATION."

"I WANT TO BE REMEMBERED AS THE COMPLETE BALLPLAYER. A GUY WHO PLAYED THE GAME HARD... VERY HARD."

Frank Thomas

DURING PRE-GAME BATTING PRACTICE ON JULY 3, 1965, A BRAWL BROKE OUT BETWEEN 36-YEAR-OLD PHILLIES RESERVE PLAYER FRANK THOMAS AND HIS TALENTED UP-AND-COMING YOUNG TEAMMATE RICHIE ALLEN. IT WAS A CLASSIC CASE OF "FRIENDLY" NEEDLING GONE TOO FAR. FEELINGS WERE HURT. RICHIE PUNCHED FRANK IN THE JAW. FRANK, WHO WAS BATTING AT THE TIME, RETALIATED BY SLAMMING HIS BAT INTO RICHIE'S SHOULDER. THE TWO CAME TOGETHER, BUT WERE QUICKLY SEPARATED BY TEAMMATES. THE INCIDENT WENT UNNOTICED BY THE EARLY BIRDS IN THE STANDS, AND THE GAME WENT ON AS USUAL. RICHIE AND FRANK TOOK THEIR FRUSTRATION OUT ON OPPOSITION PITCHING. RICHIE WAS 3-FOR-4 WITH TWO TRIPLES AND FOUR RBIs. FRANK CLOUTED AN 8TH-INNING GAME-TYING PINCH-HIT HOMER. "AS FAR AS I WAS CONCERNED, THE FIGHT WAS OVER," RICHIE LATER RECOUNTED IN HIS AUTOBIOGRAPHY. "AFTER THOMAS HIT THAT HOME RUN, I WALKED UP AND SHOOK HIS HAND. IN OUR OWN WAY, WE WERE GETTING OVER IT." BUT THE CITY OF PHILADELPHIA WOULDN'T LET THEM OFF THAT EASY. FRANK WAS WAIVED AFTER THE GAME, AND THE CITY, ALREADY REELING FROM THE HEATED EMOTIONS OF THE CIVIL RIGHTS MOVEMENT, WAS RACIALLY POLARIZED BY NEWPAPER ACCOUNTS OF THE FIGHT BETWEEN A BLACK AND WHITE TEAMMATE. IT WAS AN UGLY CHAPTER IN PHILLY RACE RELATIONS, AND IT LEFT PERMANENT SCARS ON FRANK AND RICHIE -- BUT THEY PATCHED THINGS UP AT A 1989 REUNION. "AS SOON AS I SAW HIM, I WENT UP TO HIM WITH FRIENDSHIP IN MY HEART," WROTE FRANK IN HIS AUTOBIOGRAPHY. "RICHIE GRABBED MY HAND AND SAID, 'I KNOW THIS HAS BEEN BOTHERING YOU FOR A LONG TIME, AND IT HAS BEEN BOTHERING ME TOO.' THEN HE GAVE ME A BIG BEAR HUG AND SAID, 'WE ARE BROTHERS.' THAT WAS VERY SPECIAL TO ME, AND A WONDERFUL WAY TO CLOSE THE WHOLE AFFAIR."

UNFORTUNATELY, "THE FIGHT" IS OFTEN THE FIRST THING MANY PEOPLE THINK OF WHEN THEY HEAR MENTION OF FRANK THOMAS -- AND THAT DOES A DISSERVICE TO HIS FINE CAREER. AFTER BRIEF TRIALS IN '51 AND '52, FRANK BROKE IN BIG WITH HIS HOMETOWN PITTSBURGH PIRATES BY SLAMMING 30 HOMERS IN 1953. HE SETTLED IN AS THE KEY RUN PRODUCER FOR THE BUCS, AVERAGING 24 HOMERS PER YEAR FOR THE NEXT FOUR SEASONS. FRANK POSTED A CAREER YEAR IN 1958 WHEN HE CLUBBED 35 HOME RUNS AND 109 RBIs -- NUMBERS THAT LANDED HIM ON THE COVER OF SPORTS ILLUSTRATED ON JULY 28, 1958. TRADED AWAY PRIOR TO THE '59 CAMPAIGN, FRANK LATER ENJOYED A REBIRTH WHEN HE HIT 34 ROUND-TRIPPERS FOR THE EXPANSION METS. A DEVOTED TO HUSBAND TO HIS WIFE DOLORES, FRANK RETIRED IN 1966 WITH 286 LONG BALLS -- AND EIGHT CHILDREN -- TO HIS CREDIT.

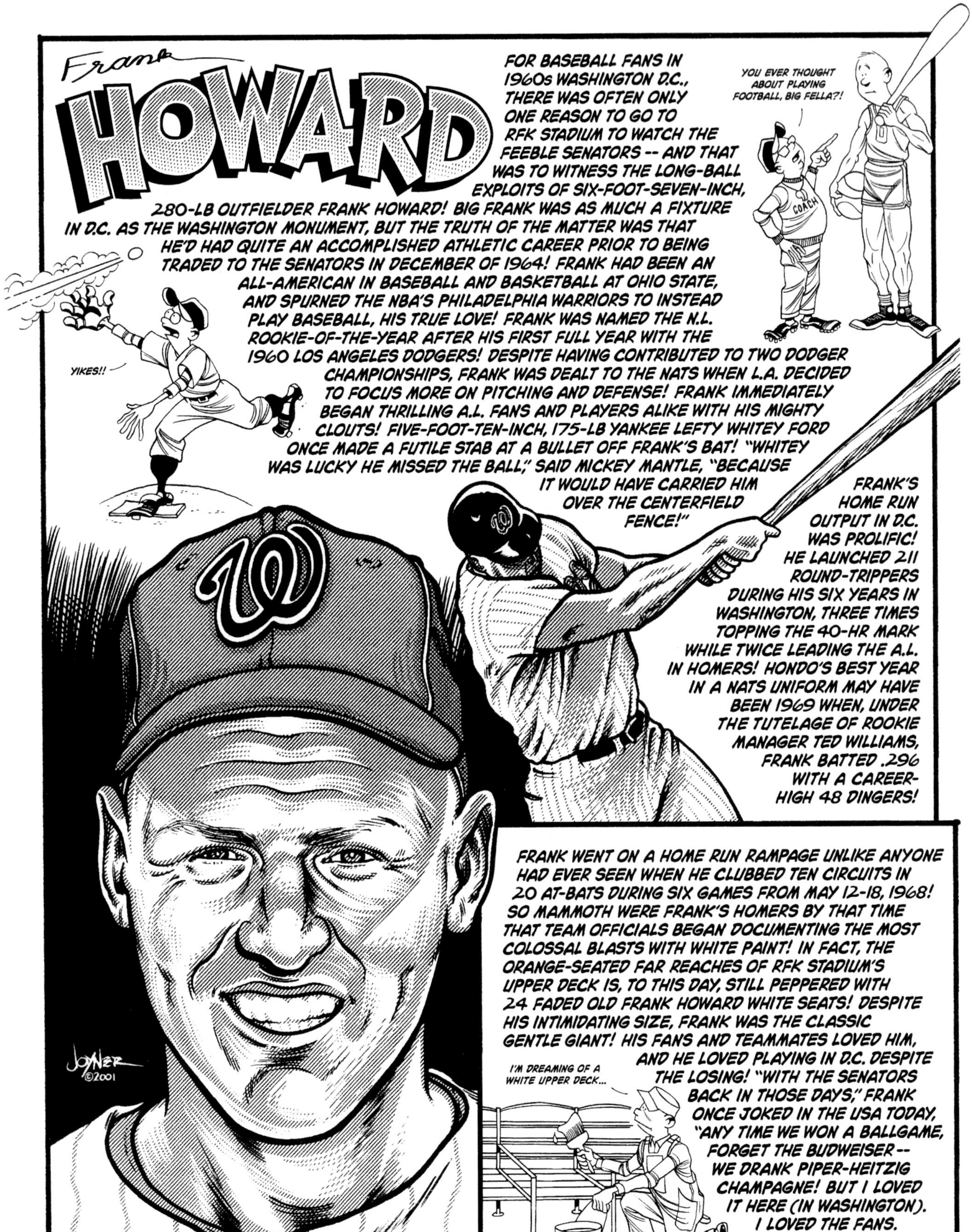
Frank
HOWARD
FOR BASEBALL FANS IN 1960s WASHINGTON D.C., THERE WAS OFTEN ONLY ONE REASON TO GO TO RFK STADIUM TO WATCH THE FEEBLE SENATORS -- AND THAT WAS TO WITNESS THE LONG-BALL EXPLOITS OF SIX-FOOT-SEVEN-INCH, 280-LB OUTFIELDER FRANK HOWARD! BIG FRANK WAS AS MUCH A FIXTURE IN D.C. AS THE WASHINGTON MONUMENT, BUT THE TRUTH OF THE MATTER WAS THAT HE'D HAD QUITE AN ACCOMPLISHED ATHLETIC CAREER PRIOR TO BEING TRADED TO THE SENATORS IN DECEMBER OF 1964! FRANK HAD BEEN AN ALL-AMERICAN IN BASEBALL AND BASKETBALL AT OHIO STATE, AND SPURNED THE NBA'S PHILADELPHIA WARRIORS TO INSTEAD PLAY BASEBALL, HIS TRUE LOVE! FRANK WAS NAMED THE N.L. ROOKIE-OF-THE-YEAR AFTER HIS FIRST FULL YEAR WITH THE 1960 LOS ANGELES DODGERS! DESPITE HAVING CONTRIBUTED TO TWO DODGER CHAMPIONSHIPS, FRANK WAS DEALT TO THE NATS WHEN L.A. DECIDED TO FOCUS MORE ON PITCHING AND DEFENSE! FRANK IMMEDIATELY BEGAN THRILLING A.L. FANS AND PLAYERS ALIKE WITH HIS MIGHTY CLOUTS! FIVE-FOOT-TEN-INCH, 175-LB YANKEE LEFTY WHITEY FORD ONCE MADE A FUTILE STAB AT A BULLET OFF FRANK'S BAT! "WHITEY WAS LUCKY HE MISSED THE BALL," SAID MICKEY MANTLE, "BECAUSE IT WOULD HAVE CARRIED HIM OVER THE CENTERFIELD FENCE!"
YOU EVER THOUGHT ABOUT PLAYING FOOTBALL, BIG FELLA?!
COACH
YIKES!!
FRANK'S HOME RUN OUTPUT IN D.C. WAS PROLIFIC! HE LAUNCHED 211 ROUND-TRIPPERS DURING HIS SIX YEARS IN WASHINGTON, THREE TIMES TOPPING THE 40-HR MARK WHILE TWICE LEADING THE A.L. IN HOMERS! HONDO'S BEST YEAR IN A NATS UNIFORM MAY HAVE BEEN 1969 WHEN, UNDER THE TUTELAGE OF ROOKIE MANAGER TED WILLIAMS, FRANK BATTED .296 WITH A CAREER-HIGH 48 DINGERS!
FRANK WENT ON A HOME RUN RAMPAGE UNLIKE ANYONE HAD EVER SEEN WHEN HE CLUBBED TEN CIRCUITS IN 20 AT-BATS DURING SIX GAMES FROM MAY 12-18, 1968! SO MAMMOTH WERE FRANK'S HOMERS BY THAT TIME THAT TEAM OFFICIALS BEGAN DOCUMENTING THE MOST COLOSSAL BLASTS WITH WHITE PAINT! IN FACT, THE ORANGE-SEATED FAR REACHES OF RFK STADIUM'S UPPER DECK IS, TO THIS DAY, STILL PEPPERED WITH 24 FADED OLD FRANK HOWARD WHITE SEATS! DESPITE HIS INTIMIDATING SIZE, FRANK WAS THE CLASSIC GENTLE GIANT! HIS FANS AND TEAMMATES LOVED HIM, AND HE LOVED PLAYING IN D.C. DESPITE THE LOSING! "WITH THE SENATORS BACK IN THOSE DAYS," FRANK ONCE JOKED IN THE USA TODAY, "ANY TIME WE WON A BALLGAME, FORGET THE BUDWEISER -- WE DRANK PIPER-HEITZIG CHAMPAGNE! BUT I LOVED IT HERE (IN WASHINGTON). I LOVED THE FANS. I HAD MY BEST YEARS HERE."
I'M DREAMING OF A WHITE UPPER DECK...
WHITE PAINT
JOYNER ©2001

LUKE
EASTER
FIRST BASE
CLEVELAND INDIANS
LUKE BURST ONTO THE SCENE AS A 34-YEAR-OLD ROOKIE IN 1950 WITH 28 HOME RUNS AND 107 RBIs!
BANG!
LUKE LUSCIOUS EASTER WAS BORN ON AUGUST 4, 1915, IN JONESTOWN, MISSISSIPPI!
THE 6'4" 240 POUND LUKE HIT A 477-FOOT HOME RUN IN 1950 AT CLEVELAND'S MUNICIPAL STADIUM -- STILL CONSIDERED THE LONGEST SHOT EVER HIT THERE!
MIND IF I SIT HERE? LUKE'S UP!
JOYNER ©2002
IF YOU ASK ME, THINK I'M EVEN BETTER, THAN BUCK LEONARD!
HISTORIAN BILL JAMES RANKED LUKE SECOND ONLY TO BUCK LEONARD AS THE NEGRO LEAGUES' BEST 1ST SACKER!
LUKE SPENT THE BULK OF HIS PLAYING DAYS IN THE NEGRO LEAGUES BEFORE THE GAME WAS INTEGRATED IN 1947! HE MADE THE MOST OF HIS LIMITED TIME HITTING 93 HOME RUNS WITH 340 RBIs WHILE HITTING .274 IN SIX YEARS IN THE BIG LEAGUES! LUKE'S CAREER YEAR WAS 1952 WHEN HE BLASTED 31 LONG BALLS AND 97 RBIs -- AT THE AGE OF 37!

Rocky COLAVITO

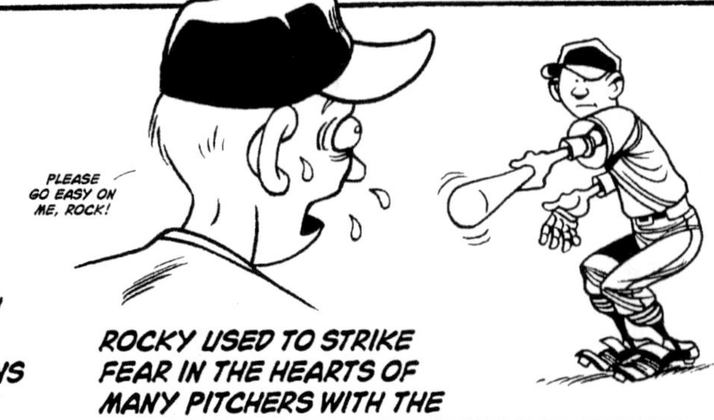

BORN IN THE BRONX, NEW YORK, ON AUGUST 10, 1933, ROCCO DOMENICO COLAVITO GREW UP IN THE SHADOW OF YANKEE STADIUM IDOLIZING THE GREAT JOE DIMAGGIO! ROCKY WAS A PROLIFIC BALLPLAYER AS A TEEN, BUT THE YANKEES PASSED ON THE LOCAL PHENOM -- SO THE INDIANS SIGNED HIM IN 1951! ROCKY HAD A FIVE-GAME TRIAL WITH CLEVELAND IN THE FALL OF '55, AND THE INDIANS LIKED WHAT THEY SAW, SO HE WAS UP IN THE BIGS FOR GOOD IN 1956! A STRONG-ARMED, POWER-HITTING FLYCHASER LIKE HIS HERO DIMAGGIO, ROCKY SMASHED 21 ROUND-TRIPPERS AS A ROOKIE, THUS BEGINNING AN ASTOUNDING 11-YEAR RUN WHERE HE HIT 20 OR MORE HOMERS! ROCKY ENJOYED TREMENDOUS POPULARITY AMONGST INDIANS FANS -- ESPECIALLY AFTER HIS BACK-TO-BACK 40-PLUS HOMER SEASONS OF 1958 AND 1959 -- YET HE WAS STILL SUBJECT TO CRITICISM FROM SOME OF CLEVELAND'S SPORTSWRITERS! THE FANS DEFENDED THEIR HERO WITH CHANTS OF "DON'T KNOCK THE ROCK," A PHRASE LIFTED FROM A '56 ROCK-N-ROLL B-MOVIE FEATURING BILL HALEY AND HIS COMETS! THE ROCK'S CAREER WAS STILL STREAKING LIKE A COMET WHEN HE WAS TRADED TO THE TIGERS PRIOR TO THE 1960 SEASON -- A DEAL THAT HAS GONE DOWN AS ONE OF CLEVELAND'S WORST EVER! SOME EVEN FEEL THE TRADE HAS CURSED THE INDIANS FROM EVER WINNING A WORLD SERIES! ROCKY WAS A DOMINANT FORCE FOR TEN YEARS, AND FINISHED WITH 374 HOMERS IN AN AGE WHEN THAT WAS A HALL-OF-FAME-WORTHY TOTAL! ROCKY ISN'T ALONE IN THE BELIEF THAT HE SHOULD BE IN THE H.O.F.! MAYBE IT'S TIME FOR A NEW CATCH-PHRASE, ONE AIMED AT THE H.O.F. VETERAN'S COMMITTEE -- "DON'T LOCK THE ROCK" -- OUT OF COOPERSTOWN, THAT IS!

ROCKY USED TO STRIKE FEAR IN THE HEARTS OF MANY PITCHERS WITH THE WAY HE USED TO POINT HIS BAT AT THEM PRIOR TO EACH PITCH -- A STYLE THAT WAS SOON COPIED BY COUNTLESS KIDS THROUGHOUT CLEVELAND!

HARMON KILLEBREW

IN MAYBE THE ONLY CASE OF A SENATOR SCOUTING A SENATOR, THE WASHINGTON "SENATORS" WERE FOREVER GRATEFUL TO IDAHO SENATOR HERMAN WELKER FOR TIPPING THEM OFF ABOUT A 17-YEAR-OLD WHO WAS WALLOPING TAPE-MEASURE HOME RUNS BACK HOME IN PAYETTE, IDAHO! TO HUMOR THE SENATOR, NATS OWNER CLARK GRIFFITH SENT FARM DIRECTOR OSSIE BLUEGE TO PAYETTE TO SEE THE KID PLAY IN HIS HOMETOWN BALLPARK! HARMON, RECOUNTING THE STORY TO BASEBALL DIGEST IN 1990, SAID, "I'D BEEN GOING TO THAT PARK SINCE I WAS A LITTLE KID AND I HAD NEVER SEEN ANYONE HIT ONE OVER THE LEFTFIELD FENCE, WHICH WAS 400 FEET AWAY. THAT NIGHT I HIT ONE OVER THAT FENCE AND IT LANDED IN A BEET FIELD. MR. BLUEGE WENT OUT THE NEXT MORNING AND STEPPED IT OFF AND SAID IT WAS 435 FEET. HE THOUGHT THAT WAS PRETTY GOOD FOR A 17-YEAR-OLD KID. SO HE CALLED MR. GRIFFITH AND SAID HE THOUGHT THEY SHOULD SIGN THIS KID, AND MR. GRIFFITH AGREED." THE YEAR WAS 1954, AND HARMON WAS GIVEN $50,000 TO SIGN! THE BONUS RULES OF THE TIME DEMANDED THAT THE NATS KEEP HARMON ON THE BIG LEAGUE ROSTER FOR TWO YEARS BEFORE THEY COULD SEND HIM TO THE MINORS FOR VALUABLE SEASONING! HE PLAYED SPARINGLY IN THAT TIME, STRUGGLING TO ESTABLISH HIMSELF! HARMON HEARD THE BOOS WHEN HE BOOTED A GROUNDER WHILE PLAYING THIRD BASE AGAINST THE TIGERS ON JUNE 24, 1955, BUT MINUTES LATER HE TURNED THE BOOS INTO CHEERS WHEN HE LAUNCHED HIS FIRST CAREER HOMER INTO THE GRIFFITH STADIUM SEATS! IT WASN'T UNTIL 1959 THAT HARMON PUT IT ALL TOGETHER WITH A LEAGUE-LEADING 42 LONG BALLS, BUT FROM THEN ON HE WOULD ALWAYS BE AMONG THE HOME RUN LEADERS, THRILLING FANS NOT ONLY WITH THE REGULARITY OF HIS CIRCUIT CLOUTS, BUT ALSO WITH THE HERETOFORE UNSEEN DISTANCE OF HIS MIGHTY BOMBS!

HARMON WENT WITH THE TEAM WHEN THE CLUB MOVED TO MINNESOTA WHERE HE CONTINUED TO FURIOUSLY ASSAULT THE BASEBALL! IN FACT, NO OTHER PLAYER HIT MORE HOME RUNS IN THE DECADE OF THE 1960s THAN HARMON! HIS 393 DINGERS PLACES HIM NUMBER ONE IN THE DECADE -- A DECADE THAT ALSO SAW HIM CLAIM FIVE MORE SINGLE SEASON HOME RUN CROWNS! AT THE TIME OF HIS RETIREMENT FOLLOWING THE 1975 SEASON, HARMON'S 573 HOMERS RANKED HIM AS THE AMERICAN LEAGUE'S ALL-TIME NUMBER ONE RIGHT-HANDED HOME RUN HITTER -- A FACT THE "KILLER" OFTEN CITES AS ONE OF HIS PROUDEST ACHIEVEMENTS!

Jimmie FOXX

JAMES EMORY FOXX WAS BORN ON THE FAMILY FARM IN SUDLERSVILLE, MARYLAND, ON OCTOBER 22, 1907! HE DEVELOPED INCREDIBLE STRENGTH FROM HIS FARM CHORES, AND THAT POWER ENABLED HIM TO BECOME A SUPERIOR HIGH SCHOOL ATHLETE! JIMMIE DISPLAYED A MIGHTY BAT IN HIGH SCHOOL, AND HIS PROLIFIC CLOUTS SOON NABBED THE ATTENTION OF FRANK "HOME RUN" BAKER WHO WAS MANAGING IN THE NEARBY EASTERN SHORE LEAGUE! BASED ON BAKER'S RECOMMENDATION, JIMMIE JOINED THE PHILADELPHIA A's IN 1925 AT THE AGE OF 17! JIMMIE WAS IN FULL SWING BY 1929, HITTING .354 WITH 33 HOMERS AND 118 RBIs! YEAR-IN AND YEAR-OUT, JIMMIE WOULD POST NUMBERS EQUAL TO OR BETTER THAN HIS BREAK-OUT SEASON OF '29, AND THAT HELPED PROPEL THE A's TO THREE PENNANTS AND TWO WORLD SERIES TITLES FROM 1929 THROUGH 1931! JIMMIE WAS A GOOD-NATURED, WELL-LIKED FELLOW, AND HIS BEST SEASON CAME IN 1932 WHEN HE CRACKED 58 ROUND-TRIPPERS! JIMMIE BECAME THE YOUNGEST PLAYER TO REACH 500 HOMERS WHEN HE, AT 32 YEARS AND 337 DAYS, HIT NUMBER 500 ON SEPTEMBER 24, 1940! LATE IN HIS CAREER JIMMIE TOOK TO THE MOUND IN NINE GAMES FOR THE 1945 PHILS WHERE HE WENT 1-AND-0 WITH A 1.59 ERA! WHEN HE RETIRED, JIMMIE'S 534 HOME RUNS WAS SECOND ONLY TO BABE RUTH!

MARYLAND PHARMACIST GIL DUNN CREATED A JIMMIE FOXX MUSEUM IN THE CORNER OF HIS DRUG STORE IN 1965 TO HONOR HIS BOYHOOD HERO! JIMMIE SHOCKED DUNN ONE YEAR LATER WHEN HE SHOWED UP UNANNOUNCED AND GAVE PRICELESS MEMORABILIA TO THE MAKESHIFT SHRINE!

JIMMIE MANAGED THE 1952 FT. WAYNE DAISIES OF THE ALL AMERICAN GIRLS PROFESSIONAL BASEBALL LEAGUE!

"WHEN NEIL ARMSTRONG FIRST SET FOOT ON THE MOON," LEFTY GOMEZ ONCE SAID, "HE AND ALL THE SPACE SCIENTISTS WERE PUZZLED BY AN UNIDENTIFIABLE WHITE OBJECT. I KNEW IMMEDIATELY WHAT IT WAS...

...IT WAS A HOME RUN BALL HIT OFF ME IN 1933 BY JIMMIE FOXX!"

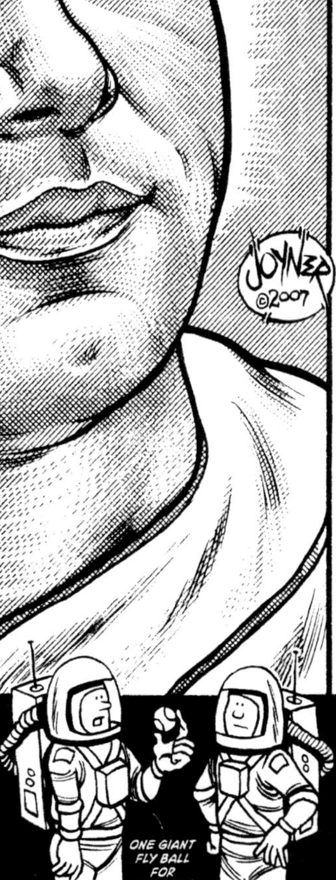

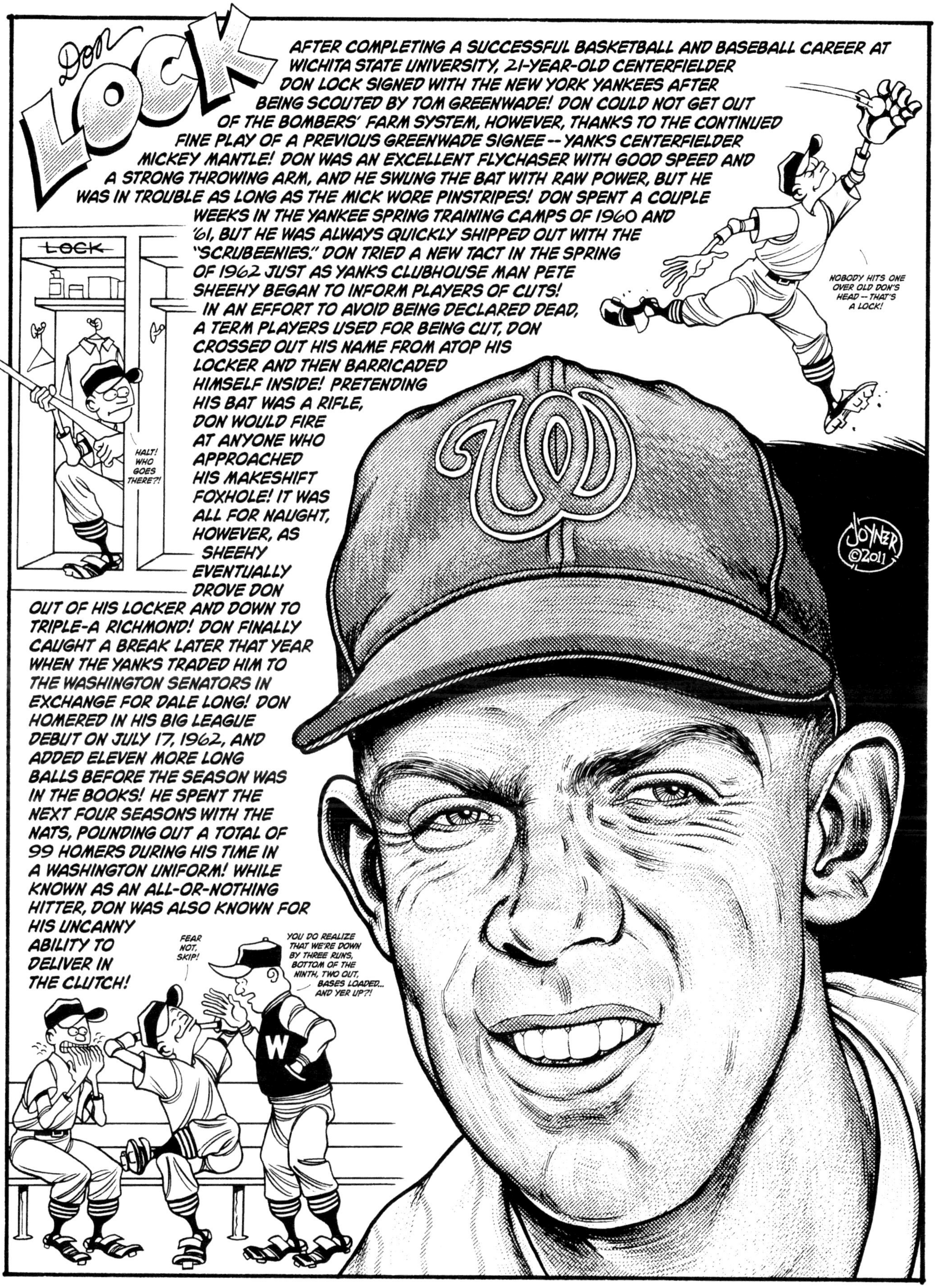
Don LOCK
AFTER COMPLETING A SUCCESSFUL BASKETBALL AND BASEBALL CAREER AT WICHITA STATE UNIVERSITY, 21-YEAR-OLD CENTERFIELDER DON LOCK SIGNED WITH THE NEW YORK YANKEES AFTER BEING SCOUTED BY TOM GREENWADE! DON COULD NOT GET OUT OF THE BOMBERS' FARM SYSTEM, HOWEVER, THANKS TO THE CONTINUED FINE PLAY OF A PREVIOUS GREENWADE SIGNEE -- YANKS CENTERFIELDER MICKEY MANTLE! DON WAS AN EXCELLENT FLYCHASER WITH GOOD SPEED AND A STRONG THROWING ARM, AND HE SWUNG THE BAT WITH RAW POWER, BUT HE WAS IN TROUBLE AS LONG AS THE MICK WORE PINSTRIPES! DON SPENT A COUPLE WEEKS IN THE YANKEE SPRING TRAINING CAMPS OF 1960 AND '61, BUT HE WAS ALWAYS QUICKLY SHIPPED OUT WITH THE "SCRUBEENIES." DON TRIED A NEW TACT IN THE SPRING OF 1962 JUST AS YANKS CLUBHOUSE MAN PETE SHEEHY BEGAN TO INFORM PLAYERS OF CUTS! IN AN EFFORT TO AVOID BEING DECLARED DEAD, A TERM PLAYERS USED FOR BEING CUT, DON CROSSED OUT HIS NAME FROM ATOP HIS LOCKER AND THEN BARRICADED HIMSELF INSIDE! PRETENDING HIS BAT WAS A RIFLE, DON WOULD FIRE AT ANYONE WHO APPROACHED HIS MAKESHIFT FOXHOLE! IT WAS ALL FOR NAUGHT, HOWEVER, AS SHEEHY EVENTUALLY DROVE DON OUT OF HIS LOCKER AND DOWN TO TRIPLE-A RICHMOND! DON FINALLY CAUGHT A BREAK LATER THAT YEAR WHEN THE YANKS TRADED HIM TO THE WASHINGTON SENATORS IN EXCHANGE FOR DALE LONG! DON HOMERED IN HIS BIG LEAGUE DEBUT ON JULY 17, 1962, AND ADDED ELEVEN MORE LONG BALLS BEFORE THE SEASON WAS IN THE BOOKS! HE SPENT THE NEXT FOUR SEASONS WITH THE NATS, POUNDING OUT A TOTAL OF 99 HOMERS DURING HIS TIME IN A WASHINGTON UNIFORM! WHILE KNOWN AS AN ALL-OR-NOTHING HITTER, DON WAS ALSO KNOWN FOR HIS UNCANNY ABILITY TO DELIVER IN THE CLUTCH!
NOBODY HITS ONE OVER OLD DON'S HEAD -- THAT'S A LOCK!
LOCK
HALT! WHO GOES THERE?!
JOYNER ©2011
FEAR NOT, SKIP!
YOU DO REALIZE THAT WE'RE DOWN BY THREE RUNS, BOTTOM OF THE NINTH, TWO OUT, BASES LOADED... AND YER UP?!

KING HENRY
AARON
HANK HIT THE FIRST OF HIS 755 HOME RUNS -- A SOLO SHOT -- OFF OF CARDINALS PITCHER VIC RASCHI ON APRIL 23, 1954, AT OLD SPORTSMAN'S PARK IN ST. LOUIS!
I THINK THIS FELLA'S GOIN' PLACES!
HENRY LOUIS "HANK" AARON WAS BORN ON FEBRUARY 5, 1934, IN MOBILE, ALABAMA! HANK WAS PLAYING SEMI-PRO BASEBALL AT THE AGE OF 15 BEFORE PLAYING TWO YEARS WITH THE INDIANAPOLIS CLOWNS OF THE NEGRO LEAGUES! IN 1952 THE MILWAUKEE BRAVES PAID THE CLOWNS A MERE $7,500 TO ACQUIRE HANK -- THE MAN WHO WOULD ONE DAY OWN THE ALL-TIME BIG LEAGUE HOME RUN RECORD!
HANK WORE NUMBER 5 IN HIS FIRST SEASON BEFORE SWITCHING TO HIS FAMOUS NUMBER 44! THAT NUMBER TURNED OUT TO BE A GOOD ONE FOR HANK AS HE LED THE LEAGUE IN HOME RUNS 4 TIMES -- WITH 44 HOMERS IN THREE OF THOSE YEARS! HANK WAS A CLUTCH PLAYER IN POST-SEASON PLAY! HE HIT A COMBINED .364 WITH 20 HITS AND 3 LONG BALLS IN THE '57 AND '58 WORLD SERIES! HE BATTED .357 WITH 3 ROUND-TRIPPERS IN THE 3-GAME 1969 LCS! HAMMERIN' HANK WAS REWARDED FOR HIS UNMATCHED PLAY BY BEING ELECTED TO EVERY ALL-STAR GAME DURING HIS ENTIRE CAREER SPANNING 1954-1976!
IT'S ALL YOURS, KID!
715
HANK BECAME "KING HENRY" WHEN HE HIT HOME RUN NUMBER 715 OFF OF AL DOWNING ON APRIL 8, 1974! THAT BLAST CROWNED HIM THE NEW CAREER HOME RUN KING DE-THRONING THE LEGENDARY BABE RUTH!

MIKE EPSTEIN
ALWAYS A KEEN STUDENT IN THE SCIENCE OF HITTING, MIKE EPSTEIN BECAME ONE OF THE MOST FEARED CLOUTERS OF HIS ERA!
I THINK I'VE DISCOVERED THE SECRET OF TORQUE FOR GENERATING BIG LEAGUE BAT SPEED AND POWER!
AFTER COMING UP THROUGH THE ORIOLES ORGANIZATION, MIKE WAS SENT TO THE SENATORS IN 1967! HE THRIVED IN THE CAPITOL CITY SETTING AND BASHED OUT 30 LONG BALLS FOR THE NATS WHILE HITTING AT A .278 CLIP IN 1969! 24 GAMES INTO THE 1971 SEASON MIKE WAS DEALT TO THE OAKLAND ATHLETICS! THE ADDED POWER OF HIS BAT HELPED THE A's REACH THE 1971 LEAGUE CHAMPIONSHIP SERIES! MIKE TURNED IN ANOTHER BIG SEASON FOR THE A's IN 1972 SMASHING 26 ROUND TRIPPERS, DRIVING IN 70 RBIs AND BATTING .270!
MIKE HAD PERHAPS THE BEST MENTOR OF ALL TIME FOR LEARNING THE SCIENCE OF HITTING -- THE GREAT TED WILLIAMS, WHO MANAGED MIKE FOR THREE YEARS WHILE WITH THE SENATORS! MIKE STUDIED TED, AND IS NOW A FINE HITTING INSTRUCTOR HIMSELF!
YOU DON'T KID AROUND WHEN YOU STUDY, MIKE!
THAT'S RIGHT, TED -- I'M FOLLOWING YOUR LEAD!
JOYNER ©2001
MIKE WAS AN ALL-AMERICAN PLAYER AT THE UNIV. OF CAL WHERE HIS LIFE-TIME AVERAGE OF .384 IS STILL A SCHOOL BEST!
A+
FIGHT ON GOLD AND BLUE... GRRR, RRRR, RRRRAH!
MIKE WAS A MEMBER OF THE USA'S FIRST OLYMPIC BASEBALL TEAM IN 1964--AND THEY WON THE COVETED GOLD MEDAL! HE WAS THE SPORTING NEWS MINOR LEAGUE PLAYER OF THE YEAR IN '66 AFTER HITTING .309 WITH 30 HOME RUNS AND 102 RBI -- AND BEING NAMED THE INTERNATIONAL LEAGUE'S M.V.P.! MIKE TIED A RARE RECORD IN 1971 WHEN HE HIT 4 HOME RUNS IN 4 CONSECUTIVE AT BATS! HE CONTRIBUTED WITH THE GLOVE, TOO, SETTING A RECORD FOR FIRST BASEMAN WITH 32 PUT-OUTS IN A 24-INNING GAME!

Andre DAWSON

MIAMI-BORN ANDRE DAWSON WAS A FIVE-TOOL OUTFIELDER WHOSE AMAZING CAREER FINALLY EARNED THE RESPECT IT DESERVED WHEN HE WAS ELECTED TO THE HALL OF FAME IN JANUARY OF 2010! HE WAS DESTINED TO SUCCEED THANKS TO UNWAVERING SUPPORT FROM HIS GRANDMOTHER, EUNICE, WHO INSISTED THAT ANDRE SPURN OFFERS TO TURN PRO OUT OF HIGH SCHOOL AND INSTEAD ATTEND COLLEGE! ANDRE WENT TO FLORIDA A&M WHERE HE WAS A BASEBALL STANDOUT UNDER LEGENDARY COACH COSTA "POP" KITTLES FROM 1973 TO '75 BEFORE BEING DRAFTED BY THE MONTREAL EXPOS! ANDRE STARRED FOR THE EXPOS FOR A DECADE, BEGINNING WITH HIS ROOKIE-OF-THE-YEAR SEASON OF 1977! BY THE END OF THE 1986 SEASON ANDRE HAD SLAMMED 225 LONG BALLS FOR MONTREAL WHILE DRIVING IN 838 RUNS! THE DOWNSIDE, HOWEVER, WAS THAT THE MANY YEARS OF PLAYING ON OLYMPIC STADIUM'S ROCK-HARD ARTIFICIAL TURF TOOK A TOLL ON ANDRE'S KNEES, LEAVING HIM CONTEMPLATING LIFE AS A CRIPPLE SHOULD HE STAY IN MONTREAL!

ANDRE LEFT MONTREAL FOR THE SOFT GRASS AND DAY GAMES OF WRIGLEY FIELD AS HE JOINED THE CUBS IN 1987! NEWLY REJUVENATED, ANDRE POSTED A MONSTER YEAR BY HITTING 49 HOMERS AND 137 RBIs -- NUMBERS THAT EARNED HIM AN M.V.P. AWARD DESPITE THE FACT THAT HIS CUBS FINISHED IN LAST PLACE! HE CONTINUED TO STAR FOR CHICAGO THROUGH THE 1992 SEASON BEFORE WINDING DOWN HIS CAREER WITH TWO-YEAR STINTS FOR THE RED SOX AND MARLINS! WHEN IT WAS ALL SAID AND DONE, ANDRE FINISHED WITH 2,774 HITS, 438 HOME RUNS AND 314 STOLEN BASES! THE HAWK'S POWER NUMBERS CAME PRIOR TO THE INFLATED NUMBERS OF THE STEROID ERA, AND IT'S SAFE TO SAY THAT HIS ELECTION TO THE HALL OF FAME WAS A BELATED STATEMENT IN SUPPORT OF THE GUYS, LIKE ANDRE, WHO DID IT CLEAN! ONE OF THE GAME'S TRUE GOOD GUYS, ANDRE PATIENTLY WAITED FOR HIS CALL TO THE HALL! NOW IN, HE SIMPLY SAYS, "IT WAS WORTH THE WAIT. I CAN'T REALLY DESCRIBE THE ELATION."

SIEVERS

NAMED THE A.L. ROOKIE OF THE YEAR AFTER HIS TREMENDOUS DEBUT SEASON WITH THE BROWNS IN 1949, ROY SIEVERS WAS ON THE FASTRACK TO SUPER-STARDOM UNTIL A SEVERELY SEPARATED SHOULDER THREATENED TO END HIS CAREER IN 1951! BROWNIE OWNER BILL VEECK SENT ROY TO A SPECIALIST AT JOHNS HOPKINS WHERE EXPERIMENTAL SURGERY GAVE THE SLUGGER A SECOND CHANCE! IT WOULDN'T BE THE BROWNS WHO WOULD REAP THE REWARDS OF ROY'S RENAISSANCE, HOWEVER -- IT WOULD BE THE WASHINGTON SENATORS! TRADED TO THE NATS PRIOR TO THE 1954 SEASON, ROY AVERAGED 30 LONG BALLS PER YEAR FOR THE NEXT SIX CAMPAIGNS, LEADING THE LEAGUE WITH A CAREER-HIGH 42 BOMBS IN 1957! ROY HAD TRULY JOINED THE SLUGGING ELITE THAT YEAR, A POINT HE HAMMERED HOME WITH AUTHORITY WHEN HE HOMERED IN SIX CONSECUTIVE GAMES TO TIE THE A.L. RECORD! "ON THE SEVENTH DAY I HIT A BALL I THOUGHT WAS GOING TO GO," ROY TOLD WRITER TODD NEWVILLE. "I THOUGHT I WOULD BREAK THE RECORD. IT WAS CAUGHT AGAINST THE LEFT-CENTERFIELD FENCE." ROY WENT ON TO HOMER 318 TIMES IN HIS 17-YEAR BIG LEAGUE CAREER -- 180 OF THEM DURING HIS EIGHT SEASONS IN WASHINGTON WHERE HE WAS A FAVORITE OF FUTURE PRESIDENT RICHARD NIXON! NO DOUBT, TRICKY DICK WAS SPEAKING THE WHOLE TRUTH WHEN HE DESCRIBED ROY AS A GUY WHO "SYMBOLIZES GREAT CHARACTER, SPORTSMANSHIP, AND GUTS."

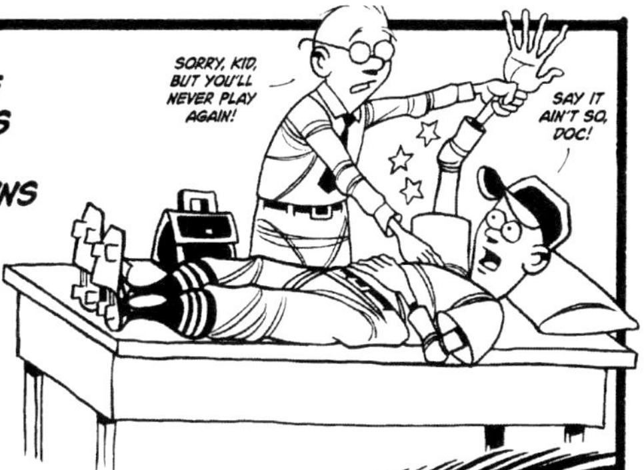

ROY WAS DUBBED "SQUIRREL" IN HIGH SCHOOL DUE TO THE "SQUIRRELLY" WAY HE HUNG AROUND THE BASKET WAITING TO SNATCH REBOUNDS! "WHEN I SIGNED MY FIRST LOUISVILLE SLUGGER BAT CONTRACT, THEY ASKED ME IF I HAD A NICKNAME I WANTED ON MY BATS," ROY RECOLLECTED. "I SAID 'SURE.' ON MY FIRST TRIP TO NEW YORK, ALL THE YANKEES WERE ON TOP OF THE BENCH YELLING, 'HEY, SQUIRREL, HOW'S YOUR NUTS TODAY?!' THAT'S ALL I HEARD FROM THEN ON." ALL ROY HEARS NOW ARE ACCOLADES FOR BEING ONE OF THE BEST SLUGGERS OF THE 1950s!

Dick MEANS

IN HIS 1981 "INSIDE SPORTS" ARTICLE ENTITLED "TWILIGHT OF THE LONGBALL GODS," ACCLAIMED SPORTSWRITER JOHN SCHULIAN PAID HOMAGE TO THE LEGACY OF THE MINOR LEAGUE SLUGGER -- THOSE BUSH LEAGUE CLOUTERS WHOSE TAPE-MEASURE HOME RUN HEROICS FILLED RICKETY STANDS DURING A GOLDEN AGE OF MINOR LEAGUE BALL... A GOLDEN AGE THAT WOULD LATER VANISH AS TELEVISION EVOLVED INTO AN ENTERTAINMENT JUGGERNAUT! A WEAKNESS FOR THE CURVE BALL WAS THE REASON MANY OF THESE MEN FAILED IN, OR NEVER MADE IT TO, THE BIG LEAGUES. BUT, AS SCHULIAN WROTE, "AS LONG AS THEY COULD GET AROUND ON THE FAST ONE, THEY KNEW THERE WOULD BE SOMEBODY WHO THOUGHT THEY COULD BRING A PENNANT TO BUSHVILLE AND A SMILE TO THE PAYING CUSTOMERS' FACES."

RICHARD B. MEANS, JR., BORN ON APRIL 9, 1936, DEFINITELY QUALIFIES AS A LONGBALL GOD! AS THE SON OF A SEMI-PRO PLAYER AND THE NEPHEW OF LONGTIME P.C.L. 1ST BASEMAN GEORGE McDONALD, DICK HAD HARDBALL IN HIS BONES! SIGNED BY THE WHITE SOX IN 1954, DICK NEVER GOT A CRACK AT THE BIG SHOW, BUT HE BASHED MORE THAN HIS SHARE OF CIRCUIT CLOUTS IN OUTPOSTS LIKE TOPEKA, WATERLOO, AND COLORADO SPRINGS! HE THRILLED SOUTH ATLANTIC LEAGUE FANS IN '62 AS HE WALLOPED A CAREER HIGH 36 TATERS WHILE SPLITTING THE SEASON BETWEEN CHARLOTTE AND ASHEVILLE!

DICK'S 36 BOMBS WON HIM THE LEAGUE HOME RUN CROWN IN 1962, BUT HE THEN SHOCKED HIS FANS BY RETIRING AT THE TOP OF HIS GAME TO PURSUE HIS OTHER PASSION -- SELLING CARS! WITH THAT, THE GAME BADE FAREWELL TO ANOTHER LONGBALL GOD!

NATURAL BORN HITTERS

TED WILLIAMS

THEODORE SAMUEL WILLIAMS WAS BORN ON AUGUST 30, 1918, IN SAN DIEGO, CALIFORNIA! THE KID'S BAT SOON MADE A NAME FOR TED AT NEARBY HERBERT HOOVER HIGH SCHOOL! TED SUBSEQUENTLY WENT PRO WHEN HE WAS SIGNED BY THE SAN DIEGO PADRES OF THE PACIFIC COAST LEAGUE!

TED WAS QUICKLY THROUGH WITH THE MINORS AFTER TEARING UP THE AMERICAN ASSOCIATION WITH THE MINNEAPOLIS MILLERS IN 1938! HE JOINED THE BOSTON RED SOX IN 1939 AND POSTED AN AMAZING ROOKIE SEASON THAT SAW HIM BAT .327 WITH 31 HOMERS! HE RAISED HIS AVERAGE TO .344 IN HIS SOPHOMORE YEAR, AND THEN CAPTIVATED AMERICA BY BATTING .406 IN 1941! HE TOPPED THE .400 MARK IN DRAMATIC FASHION BY GOING 6-FOR-8 IN A DOUBLEHEADER ON THE LAST DAY OF THE '41 CAMPAIGN!

"TEDDY BALLGAME" WAS NOT ONLY A HERO ON THE BALL FIELD-- HE WAS ALSO A HERO ON ON THE BATTLEFIELD! HE ENLISTED IN THE MARINES FOLLOWING THE 1942 SEASON TO SERVE AS A FIGHTER PILOT IN WORLD WAR II! THE WAR ENDED BEFORE TED WOULD GET THE CHANCE TO FLY ANY COMBAT MISSIONS, BUT HE WAS RECALLED TO DUTY IN THE KOREAN WAR WHERE HE FLEW MANY DANGEROUS MISSIONS! IN FACT, HIS JET WAS SHOT UP IN HIS FIRST COMBAT MISSION OVER KOREA, NECESSITATING A CRASH LANDING UPON HIS RETURN TO BASE!

TED'S BATTING STATISTICS ARE STAGGERING, THE MOST IMPRESSIVE BEING HIS .344 LIFETIME AVERAGE AND HIS 521 ROUND-TRIPPERS! HE WAS A FIRST-BALLOT HALL-OF-FAMER, AND EVEN HOMERED IN HIS LAST AT-BAT ON SEPTEMBER 28, 1960, AT FENWAY PARK!

THIRD BASE -- PHILADELPHIA ATHLETICS

GEORGE KELL

ARKANSAS-BORN GEORGE CLYDE KELL WAS ELECTED TO BASEBALL'S HALL OF FAME IN 1983 -- THE ULTIMATE TRIBUTE TO THE ALL-AROUND GREAT PLAYER THAT HE WAS! AFTER LEADING ALL MINOR LEAGUE HITTERS WITH A .396 AVERAGE AT LANCASTER IN 1942, THE 21-YEAR-OLD KELL CAME UP WITH THE PHILADELPHIA A's FOR 5 AT-BATS IN 1943! HE WAS BACK IN 1944 AS THE CLUB'S FULL-TIME THIRD-SACKER WHERE HE HIT .268 AND IMPROVING TO .272 IN 1945! WITH PLAYERS RETURNING FROM THE SERVICE IN 1946, KELL RATCHETED UP HIS PLAY EVEN MORE HITTING A ROBUST .322 FOLLOWING HIS TRADE TO THE TIGERS 26 GAMES INTO THE SEASON! THAT BEGAN A RUN OF EIGHT STRAIGHT YEARS THAT KELL WOULD TOP THE .300-MARK! THE FELLA COULD PICK IT, TOO, LEADING A.L. THIRD BASEMAN SEVEN TIMES IN FIELDING! STILL, IT'S KELL'S HOT BAT THAT HE IS REMEMBERED THE MOST FOR, AND HE TWICE LED THE LEAGUE IN HITS IN 1950 AND '51! 1956 WAS KELL'S LAST YEAR AS HE FINISHED UP WITH THE ORIOLES BATTING .297 AND OWNING A CAREER .306 AVERAGE!

KELL DENIED TED WILLIAMS A THIRD TRIPLE CROWN BY EDGING OUT THE SPLINTER FOR THE BATTING TITLE IN 1949 .34291 TO .34276! KELL STRUCK OUT ONLY 13 TIMES THAT SEASON -- THE LOWEST STRIKE OUT TOTAL FOR A BATTING CHAMP IN HISTORY!

Bill BUCKNER

WITH THE 25TH PICK OF THE 1968 DRAFT, THE DODGERS CHOSE NAPA HIGH SCHOOL BASEBALL STAR BILL BUCKNER. BILL HAD BATTED .667 FOR NAPA AS A JUNIOR, FOLLOWED BY A .529 CAMPAIGN AS A SENIOR. BY 1972 BILL WAS NOTCHING THE FIRST OF EIGHT BIG LEAGUE SEASONS IN WHICH HE WOULD TOP THE .300 MARK. HIS .314 AVERAGE IN 1974 HELPED THE DODGERS REACH THE WORLD SERIES, BUT THEY LOST TO A POWERFUL OAKLAND A'S TEAM. BILL TOOK HIS LETHAL BAT TO CHICAGO IN 1977 AND PROCEEDED TO HAVE SOME OF HIS FINEST SEASONS AT THE PLATE FOR THE CUBS, ONE OF WHICH WAS 1980 WHEN HE WON A BATTING CROWN. CHICAGO DEALT BILL TO BOSTON IN 1984 WHERE HIS CAREER-HIGH 18 ROUND-TRIPPERS AND 102 RBIs HELPED THE SOX REACH THE 1986 SERIES. SLOWED BY CHRONIC ANKLE TROUBLES, BILL SAW HIS PLAYING TIME BEGIN TO DIMINISH AS HE SPENT THE NEXT FEW YEARS PLAYING FOR THE ANGELS AND ROYALS AFTER LEAVING BOSTON IN JULY OF 1987. "BILLY BUCK" DID REJOIN THE RED SOX LONG ENOUGH TO RECORD THE LAST OF HIS 2,715 HITS, A SINGLE ON MAY 30, 1990, IN THE FINAL GAME OF HIS VERY DISTINGUISHED CAREER.

A DARK SIDEBAR TO BILL'S CAREER TOOK PLACE IN 1986 WHEN HIS GAME-ENDING ERROR CAUSED THE RED SOX TO LOSE GAME SIX OF THE WORLD SERIES vs. THE METS. WHEN THE RED SOX "TEAM" THEN LOST GAME SEVEN, MANY OF BOSTON'S ANGRY FANS AND MEDIA MADE BILL THE SINGULAR SCAPEGOAT FOR THE SOX'S FAILURE TO WIN THE SERIES. FROM THEN ON, BILL AND HIS FAMILY SUFFERED MEAN-SPIRITED AND UNFAIR PERSECUTION UNTIL 2004 WHEN THE SOX FINALLY WON THEIR FIRST WORLD SERIES TITLE SINCE 1918. HURT BY DECADES OF MISTREATMENT, BILL AT FIRST REJECTED INVITATIONS TO COME HOME TO BOSTON, BUT HE FINALLY MADE A TRIUMPHANT RETURN TO FENWAY PARK IN 2008 WHEN HE THREW OUT THE FIRST PITCH AT THE SOX'S HOME OPENER.

DOC CRAMER

ROGER MAXWELL CRAMER WAS BORN ON JULY 22, 1905, IN BEACH HAVEN, NEW JERSEY! YOUNG ROGER GREW UP ACROSS THE STREET FROM DOCTOR JOSHUA HILLIARD, A LOCAL LEGEND, AND ONE OF THE FEW DOCTORS IN TOWN! DR. HILLIARD ENJOYED TAKING ROGER WITH HIM AS HE DROVE AROUND TOWN MAKING HOUSE CALLS, AND SOON ROGER WAS NICKNAMED "DOC." THE NICKNAME TURNED OUT TO BE VERY APPROPRIATE FOR ROGER AS HE GREW UP -- NOT BECAUSE HE WENT INTO THE MEDICAL FIELD, BUT BECAUSE OF THE SURGICALLY PRECISE WAY HE COULD RAP THE OLD HORSEHIDE AROUND A BALLFIELD! DOC QUICKLY EXCELLED ON THE SANDLOTS OF BEACH HAVEN WHILE FACING TEAMS LIKE TOMS RIVER AND LAKEWOOD! PHILADELPHIA ATHLETICS SCOUT CY PERKINS EVENTUALLY DISCOVERED DOC PITCHING SEMI-PRO BALL, SO HE SIGNED HIM IN 1929 AND SENT HIM OFF FOR SEASONING AT MARTINSBURG OF THE BLUE RIDGE LEAGUE! LOCKED IN A TIGHT RACE WITH JOE VOSMIK FOR THAT YEAR'S BATTING TITLE, DOC PITCHED AGAINST VOSMIK'S TEAM ON THE LAST DAY OF THE SEASON! DOC WALKED HIS RIVAL FOUR TIMES AND WON THE HITTING CROWN WITH A .404 AVERAGE!

DOC WASN'T LONG FOR "SEASONING," HOWEVER, AND HE JOINED THE ATHLETICS LATE IN 1929, MAKING HIS BIG LEAGUE DEBUT ON SEPTEMBER 18! DOC HAD BECOME CONNIE MACK'S FULL-TIME CENTERFIELDER BY 1933, AND IT'S HARD TO SAY WHETHER IT WAS HIS INCREDIBLE BAT OR AMAZING GLOVE THAT TURNED HIM INTO A STAR! HE WAS FLEET-FOOTED AND AGILE WITH A RIFLE-ARM, AND SO GOOD AT JUDGING FLY BALLS THAT PHILLY SPORTSWRITER JIMMY ISAMINGER DUBBED DOC "FLIT" AFTER THE INSECTICIDE OF THE SAME NAME! WHY? BECAUSE DOC WAS DEATH TO FLY BALLS! AS A BATSMAN DOC WAS ALSO VERY SPECIAL! HE WAS A LEADOFF HITTER WHO SPECIALIZED IN SINGLES, AND HE'S THE ONLY BIG LEAGUER TO EVER NOTCH TWO 9-INNING 6-FOR-6 PERFORMANCES! OVER THE COURSE OF HIS 20-YEAR CAREER DOC LOGGED THREE 200-HIT SEASONS! DOC, AT THE AGE OF 40 IN 1945, KNOCKED OUT 11 HITS FOR A .379 AVERAGE IN THE TIGERS' WORLD SERIES WIN OVER THE CUBS! DOC'S 2,705 CAREER HITS ARE ALSO AN INCREDIBLE ACHIEVEMENT, AND IT IS HOPED BY MANY THAT HE WILL SOON TAKE A MUCH-DESERVED PLACE IN THE HALL OF FAME AT COOPERSTOWN!

DOC WAS AN EXCELLENT CARPENTER AND SPENT MANY OFFSEASONS WORKING IN THE TRADE! HE ALSO SPENT COUNTLESS HOURS WOOD-WORKING IN HIS GARAGE WORKSHOP AT THE FAMILY HOME IN NEW JERSEY!

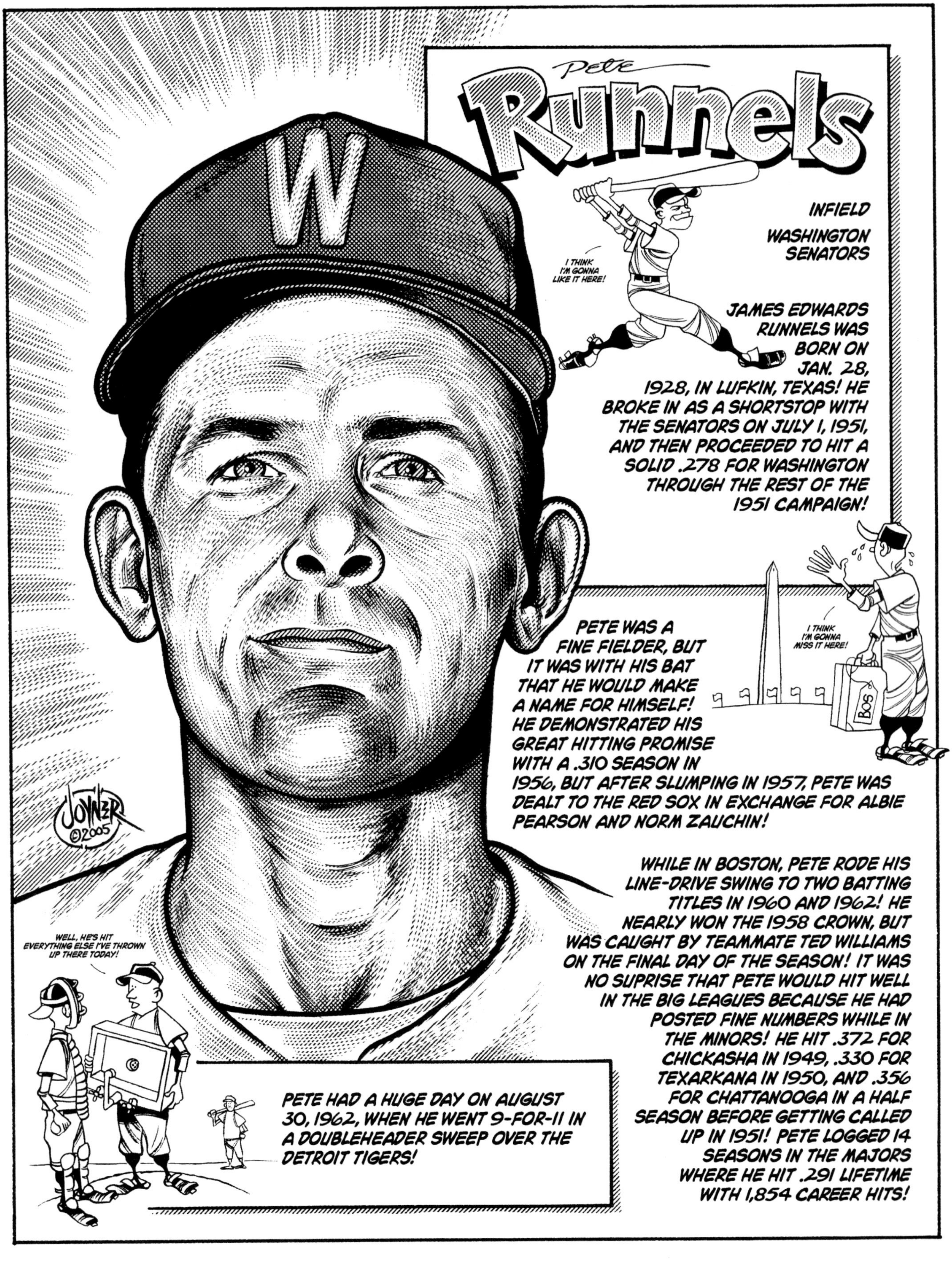
PETE
RUNNELS
INFIELD
WASHINGTON SENATORS
I THINK I'M GONNA LIKE IT HERE!
JAMES EDWARDS RUNNELS WAS BORN ON JAN. 28, 1928, IN LUFKIN, TEXAS! HE BROKE IN AS A SHORTSTOP WITH THE SENATORS ON JULY 1, 1951, AND THEN PROCEEDED TO HIT A SOLID .278 FOR WASHINGTON THROUGH THE REST OF THE 1951 CAMPAIGN!
I THINK I'M GONNA MISS IT HERE!
BOS
PETE WAS A FINE FIELDER, BUT IT WAS WITH HIS BAT THAT HE WOULD MAKE A NAME FOR HIMSELF! HE DEMONSTRATED HIS GREAT HITTING PROMISE WITH A .310 SEASON IN 1956, BUT AFTER SLUMPING IN 1957, PETE WAS DEALT TO THE RED SOX IN EXCHANGE FOR ALBIE PEARSON AND NORM ZAUCHIN!
JOYNER ©2005
WHILE IN BOSTON, PETE RODE HIS LINE-DRIVE SWING TO TWO BATTING TITLES IN 1960 AND 1962! HE NEARLY WON THE 1958 CROWN, BUT WAS CAUGHT BY TEAMMATE TED WILLIAMS ON THE FINAL DAY OF THE SEASON! IT WAS NO SUPRISE THAT PETE WOULD HIT WELL IN THE BIG LEAGUES BECAUSE HE HAD POSTED FINE NUMBERS WHILE IN THE MINORS! HE HIT .372 FOR CHICKASHA IN 1949, .330 FOR TEXARKANA IN 1950, AND .356 FOR CHATTANOOGA IN A HALF SEASON BEFORE GETTING CALLED UP IN 1951! PETE LOGGED 14 SEASONS IN THE MAJORS WHERE HE HIT .291 LIFETIME WITH 1,854 CAREER HITS!
WELL, HE'S HIT EVERYTHING ELSE I'VE THROWN UP THERE TODAY!
PETE HAD A HUGE DAY ON AUGUST 30, 1962, WHEN HE WENT 9-FOR-11 IN A DOUBLEHEADER SWEEP OVER THE DETROIT TIGERS!

NELLIE FOX
2ND BASEMAN
PHILADELPHIA A's
WHA -- YOU AGAIN?!
SCRAPPY AND TOUGH, NELLIE FOX LED THE LEAGUE IN AT-BATS 5 TIMES! NELLIE WAS BORN ON CHRISTMAS DAY IN 1925 AND PLAYED IN HIS FIRST BIG LEAGUE GAME AT THE AGE OF 19! AFTER PARTS OF 3 SEASONS WITH THE A's, HE WAS DEALT TO THE WHITE SOX ON OCTOBER 19, 1949!
NELLIE PLAYED WITH THE WHITE SOX FROM 1950-1963! HE SPENT HIS LAST 2 YEARS WITH THE HOUSTON COLT .45's! AFTER HIS PLAYING DAYS WERE THROUGH, HE BECAME A VALUABLE AND POPULAR BASE COACH FOR THE WASHINGTON SENATORS!
I KNOW YOU'RE TIRED OF GETTING STEPPED ON, AND PEOPLE WALKING ALL OVER YOU, BUT YOU'VE JUST GOTTA HANG IN THERE!
JOYNER ©2002
NELLIE WAS POSTHUMOUSLY ELECTED TO THE HALL OF FAME IN 1997!
BETTER LATE THAN NEVER!
NELLIE WAS A CATALYST FOR THE "GO-GO" WHITE SOX OF THE 1950s! THE 12-TIME ALL-STAR WAS THE A.L. M.V.P. IN 1959, LEADING THE SOX TO THEIR FIRST WORLD SERIES IN 40 YEARS! HE LED THE A.L. IN HITS FOUR TIMES AND IN FEWEST STRIKEOUTS 11 TIMES! HE COMPILED 2,663 HITS, WHILE STRIKING OUT JUST 216 TIMES IN 9,232 AT BATS! HE WAS A 3-TIME GOLD GLOVE WINNER AND SET THE RECORD FOR CONSECUTIVE GAMES PLAYED AT 2ND BASE AT 798!

Rogers Hornsby

AGREED BY MOST HISTORIANS TO BE THE GREATEST RIGHT-HANDED HITTER OF ALL TIME, IT'S A WONDER THAT THE NAME OF ROGERS HORNSBY IS NOT REMEMBERED BY THE GENERAL PUBLIC AS ARE THE NAMES OF RUTH AND COBB! ROGERS' BATTING RECORD IS STAGGERING: SEVEN BATTING TITLES (INCLUDING SIX IN-A-ROW); TOPPED THE .400-MARK THREE TIMES; HIS .424 AVERAGE IN '24 IS A 20TH CENTURY HIGH; HIS .359 CAREER AVERAGE IS THE BEST EVER IN THE N.L. (2ND OVERALL TO COBB'S .367); WON TWO TRIPLE CROWNS; AND WAS THE FIRST N.L. PLAYER TO AMASS 300 HOMERS! TED WILLIAMS LATER WROTE THAT ROGERS WAS THE MAJOR LEAGUE'S GREATEST HITTER -- EVER -- FOR POWER AND AVERAGE! ROGERS WAS MORE THAN JUST A GREAT HITTER -- HE WAS FAST AS BLAZES WHEN HE FIRST CAME UP! HALL OF FAMERS AL LOPEZ AND PIE TRAYNOR BOTH CLAIMED THAT ROGERS WAS ONE OF THE SPEEDIEST PLAYERS THE GAME HAD EVER SEEN! AND HE WAS A VERY WELL-RESPECTED 2ND BASEMAN, TOO, AS IS EVIDENCED BY HALL OF FAMER HUGHIE JENNING'S ASSERTION THAT ROGERS WAS ONE OF THE BEST-FIELDING 2ND SACKERS IN BASEBALL! HE COULD DO IT ALL, AND WAS REWARDED FOR HIS GREATNESS WITH TWO M.V.P. AWARDS -- WHICH WASN'T TOO SHABBY CONSIDERING THAT HE'D BEEN IN THE MAJORS FOR NINE YEARS BEFORE THE AWARD WAS CREATED! DESPITE ALL OF HIS INDIVIDUAL ACHIEVEMENTS, ROGERS WAS HAPPIEST WHEN HIS TEAM SUCCEEDED! WHENEVER ASKED, HE WOULD ALWAYS SAY HIS GREATEST CAREER HIGHLIGHT WAS TAGGING OUT BABE RUTH TO SEAL THE CARDINALS' 1926 WORLD SERIES CHAMPIONSHIP!

ROGERS CERTAINLY QUALIFIES AS "THE" NATIONAL LEAGUE PLAYER OF THE '20s, HAVING ENDED THE DECADE AS THE SENIOR CIRCUIT LEADER IN AVERAGE, HOMERS, AND RBIs! THAT MAKES HIM ONE OF ONLY FOUR MEN TO WIN THE SO-CALLED "DECADE TRIPLE CROWN"! ROGERS FELT HIS PEEPERS WERE THE KEY TO HIS GREAT SUCCESS AS A BATSMAN, SO HE WENT TO GREAT LENGTHS TO PREVENT ANY CHANCE OF EYE STRAIN -- LIKE REFUSING TO READ OR GO TO THE MOVIES!

ROGERS WAS A SOMEWHAT COMPLEX CHARACTER! CONSIDERED CONTENTIOUS, COLD, AND BRUTALLY FRANK, ROGERS ALIENATED MANY PLAYERS, WRITERS, AND TEAM EXECUTIVES! THIS PERSONAL SHORT-COMING OFTEN OVERSHADOWED HIS ON-FIELD GREATNESS AND LED TO HIM BE TRADED THREE TIMES IN FOUR YEARS WHILE STILL IN HIS PRIME! HIS DIFFICULT PERSONALITY ALSO LIMITED HIS SUCCESS AS A MANAGER, USUALLY LEADING TO HIM BEING FIRED EVEN IF HIS TEAM WAS PLAYING WELL! ALL THAT SAID, ROGERS WAS TRULY ONE OF THE GREATEST HITTERS EVER, AND DESERVES TO BE REMEMBERED AS SUCH!

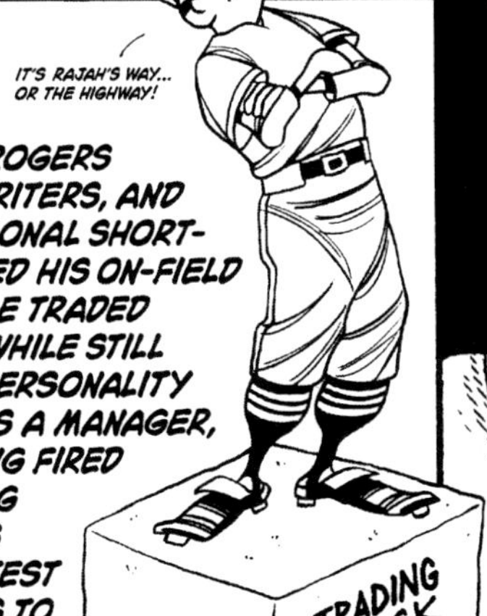

Albert PUJOLS
WHO SAYS I'M ALL HIT AND NO FIELD?!
ALBERT IS A GOLD GLOVE WINNER AT FIRST BASE!
HIS NUMBERS SPEAK FOR THEMSELVES! THEY SAY, "ALBERT PUJOLS IS, WITHOUT A DOUBT, THE BEST PLAYER IN BASEBALL!" IN HIS FIRST EIGHT SEASONS, ALBERT HAS NEVER BATTED LESS THAN .314, NEVER CLOUTED FEWER THAN 32 HOMERS, AND NEVER TOTALED FEWER THAN 103 RBIs! AT THIS PACE, HIS NUMBERS WILL ONE DAY DECLARE, "ALBERT PUJOLS IS, WITHOUT A DOUBT, ONE OF THE GREATEST PLAYERS OF ALL TIME!" AND HIS NUMBERS MAY BE RIGHT! ONLY TIME WILL TELL, BUT THE H.O.F. MAY WANT TO HOLD A SPOT FOR "EL HOMBRE"!
PUJOLS 5
I'D LIKE TO THANK GOD FOR MY ABILITY TO PULVERIZE A CURVE BALL!
PRINCE ALBERT IS TREATED LIKE ROYALTY IN ST. LOUIS, AND HE LOVES THE FANS BACK! BUT AS A DEVOUT CHRISTIAN HE GIVES ALL CREDIT TO THE LORD, SAYING, "GOD HAS GIVEN ME THE ABILITY TO DO SPECIAL THINGS!"
ALBERT IS NOT AFRAID OF BEING SUCH A PROLIFIC SLUGGER IN AN ERA SULLIED BY STEROIDS! HIS MESSAGE TO WARY FANS IS, "DON'T BE AFRAID TO BELIEVE IN ME -- I WON'T LET YOU DOWN." ALBERT SAYS THAT CHEATING DIRECTLY CONFLICTS WITH HIS FAITH, AND HE'D NEVER EVEN CONTEMPLATE IT! "I DON'T WANT TO BE REMEMBERED AS THE BEST EVER," HE TOLD SPORTS ILLUSTRATED, "I WANT TO BE REMEMBERED AS A GUY WHO LOVED THE LORD AND GAVE BACK TO THE COMMUNITY."
I THINK I'LL DONATE ANOTHER BASEBALL TO THE COMMUNITY IN THE BLEACHERS!
JOYNER ©2009

EDDIE COLLINS

EDWARD TROWBRIDGE COLLINS WAS BORN ON MAY 2, 1887, IN MILLERTON, NEW YORK! EDDIE BEGAN TO MAKE A NAME FOR HIMSELF AS THE STAR AND CAPTAIN OF THE COLUMBIA UNIVERSITY BASEBALL TEAM WHILE MOONLIGHTING IN THE BIG LEAGUES WITH THE 1906 PHILADELPHIA ATHLETICS UNDER THE PSUEDONYM "EDDIE SULLIVAN"! BY 1909, HIS FIRST FULL YEAR WITH THE A's, EDDIE'S CAREER HIT FULL STEAM AS HE BATTED A ROBUST .346 WHILE SWIPING 67 BAGS! HIS LEADERSHIP AND ALL-AROUND ABILITY HELPED ESTABLISH THE ATHLETICS AS ONE OF THE ALL-TIME GREAT DYNASTIES AS THEY WON FIVE PENNANTS AND THREE WORLD SERIES IN THE SIX YEARS FROM 1910 THROUGH 1915!

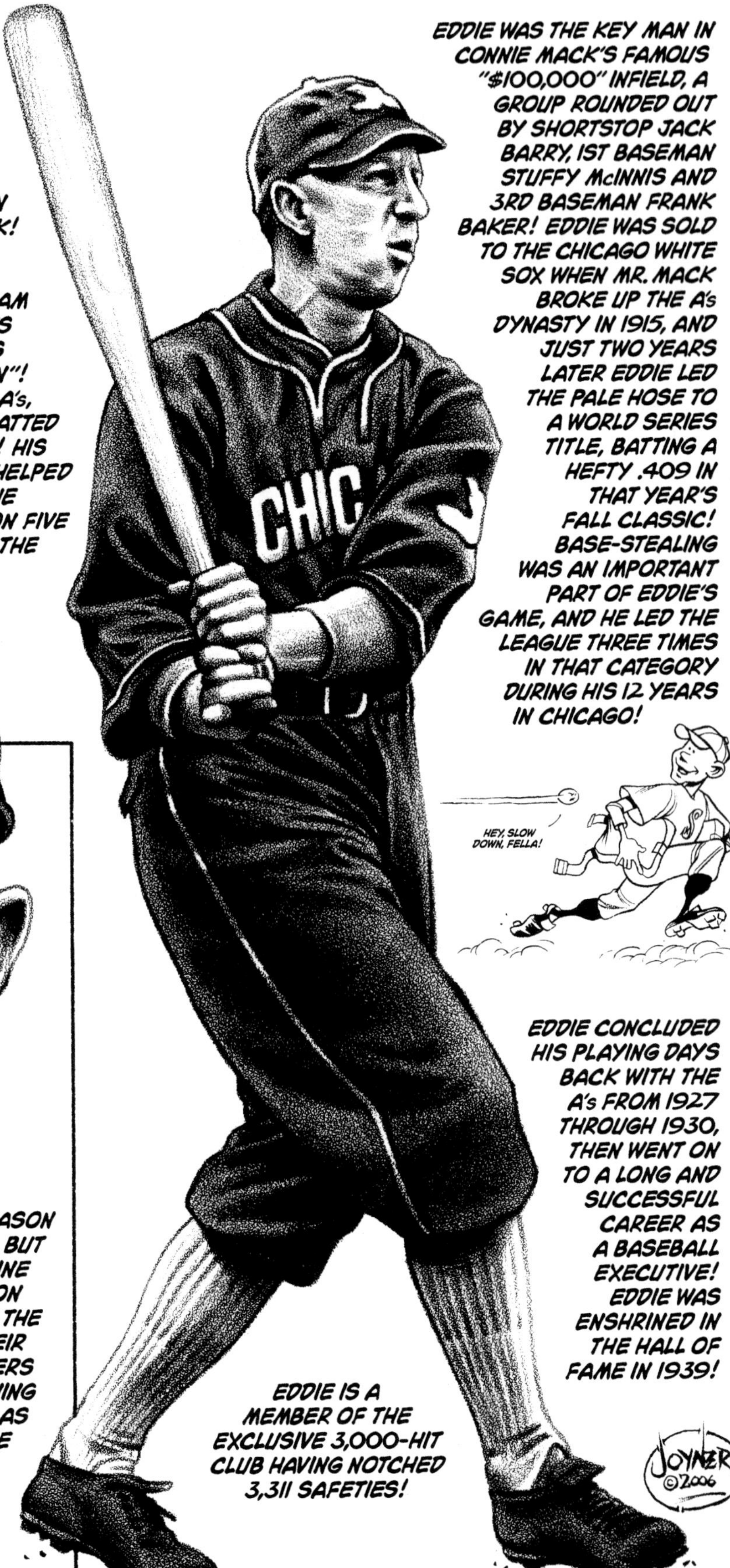

EDDIE WAS THE KEY MAN IN CONNIE MACK'S FAMOUS "$100,000" INFIELD, A GROUP ROUNDED OUT BY SHORTSTOP JACK BARRY, 1ST BASEMAN STUFFY McINNIS AND 3RD BASEMAN FRANK BAKER! EDDIE WAS SOLD TO THE CHICAGO WHITE SOX WHEN MR. MACK BROKE UP THE A's DYNASTY IN 1915, AND JUST TWO YEARS LATER EDDIE LED THE PALE HOSE TO A WORLD SERIES TITLE, BATTING A HEFTY .409 IN THAT YEAR'S FALL CLASSIC! BASE-STEALING WAS AN IMPORTANT PART OF EDDIE'S GAME, AND HE LED THE LEAGUE THREE TIMES IN THAT CATEGORY DURING HIS 12 YEARS IN CHICAGO!

EDDIE MISSED PART OF THE 1918 SEASON WHILE IN THE MARINES DURING WWI, BUT HE RETURNED TO POST ANOTHER FINE YEAR IN 1919 AS THE WHITE SOX WON ANOTHER PENNANT! CHICAGO LOST THE WORLD SERIES WHEN EIGHT OF THEIR PLAYERS CONSPIRED WITH GAMBLERS TO THROW THE CHAMPIONSHIP, EARNING THEM THE MONIKER "BLACK SOX" AS WELL AS A LIFETIME BAN FROM THE GAME! EDDIE, DESPITE ENDURING A RARE BAD SERIES AT THE PLATE, WAS DEEMED, WITHOUT QUESTION, TO BE ONE OF THE CLEAN SOX!

EDDIE CONCLUDED HIS PLAYING DAYS BACK WITH THE A's FROM 1927 THROUGH 1930, THEN WENT ON TO A LONG AND SUCCESSFUL CAREER AS A BASEBALL EXECUTIVE! EDDIE WAS ENSHRINED IN THE HALL OF FAME IN 1939!

EDDIE IS A MEMBER OF THE EXCLUSIVE 3,000-HIT CLUB HAVING NOTCHED 3,311 SAFETIES!

JOYNER ©2006

Heinie MANUSH

HENRY EMMETT MANUSH WAS BORN ON JULY 20, 1901, IN TUSCUMBIA, ALABAMA! "HEINIE," AS HE CAME TO BE KNOWN, WAS ONLY IN THE SECOND GRADE WHEN HIS OLDER BROTHER, FRANK, MADE IT TO THE BIG LEAGUES WITH THE PHILADELPHIA ATHLETICS! HEINIE SOON FOLLOWED IN FRANK'S FOOTSTEPS WHEN HE, TOO, SIGNED WITH THE A's, BUT IT WAS DETROIT WITH WHOM HE WOULD BREAK INTO THE BIG SHOW IN 1923! HEINIE SLIPPED INTO THE TIGER OUTFIELD ALONGSIDE TY COBB AND HARRY HEILMANN, AND EASILY HELD HIS OWN BY BATTING .334 IN 79 GAMES! HEINIE'S CAREER WAS IN FULL SWING BY 1926 WHEN HE CAPTURED THE A.L. BATTING CROWN WITH A ROBUST .378 AVERAGE! ALL IT TOOK FOR THE LEFTY-SWINGING MANUSH TO PULL IT OFF WAS A 6-FOR-9 PERFORMANCE ON THE LAST DAY OF THE SEASON TO OVERTAKE NONE OTHER THAN BABE RUTH! HEINIE MOVED TO THE BROWNS IN 1928 WHERE THE ST. LOUIS SURROUNDINGS SEEMED TO SUIT HIM AS HE AGAIN HIT .378 WHILE LEADING THE LOOP IN HITS WITH 241! HE CONTINUED TO PLAY WELL FOR THE BROWNS THROUGH JUNE OF 1930 WHEN HE WAS DEALT TO WASHINGTON IN EXCHANGE FOR GOOSE GOSLIN! HEINIE WAS A FIXTURE WITH THE NATIONALS THROUGH THE 1935 SEASON, WITH HIS BEST SEASON COMING IN 1933 WHEN HIS .336 AVERAGE, LEAGUE-LEADING 221 HITS, AND A.L.-BEST 17 TRIPLES HELPED LEAD THE NATS TO THE 1933 WORLD SERIES! HE ROUNDED OUT HIS PLAYING DAYS WITH STOPS IN BOSTON (A.L.), BROOKLYN AND PITTSBURGH IN 1939! HE CONTINUED TO PLAY AND MANAGE IN THE MINORS WELL INTO THE 1940s BEFORE EMBARKING ON A CAREER AS A SCOUT AND A COACH FOR THE SENATORS! HEINIE HIT .330 FOR HIS CAREER WITH 2,524 HITS, AND WAS ELECTED TO THE BASEBALL HALL OF FAME IN 1964!

HEINIE WAS THE FIRST PLAYER EVER EJECTED FROM A WORLD SERIES WHEN HE WAS TOSSED FROM GAME FOUR OF THE 1933 CLASSIC FOR SNAPPING THE ELASTIC BOW TIE OF UMPIRE CHARLEY MORAN!

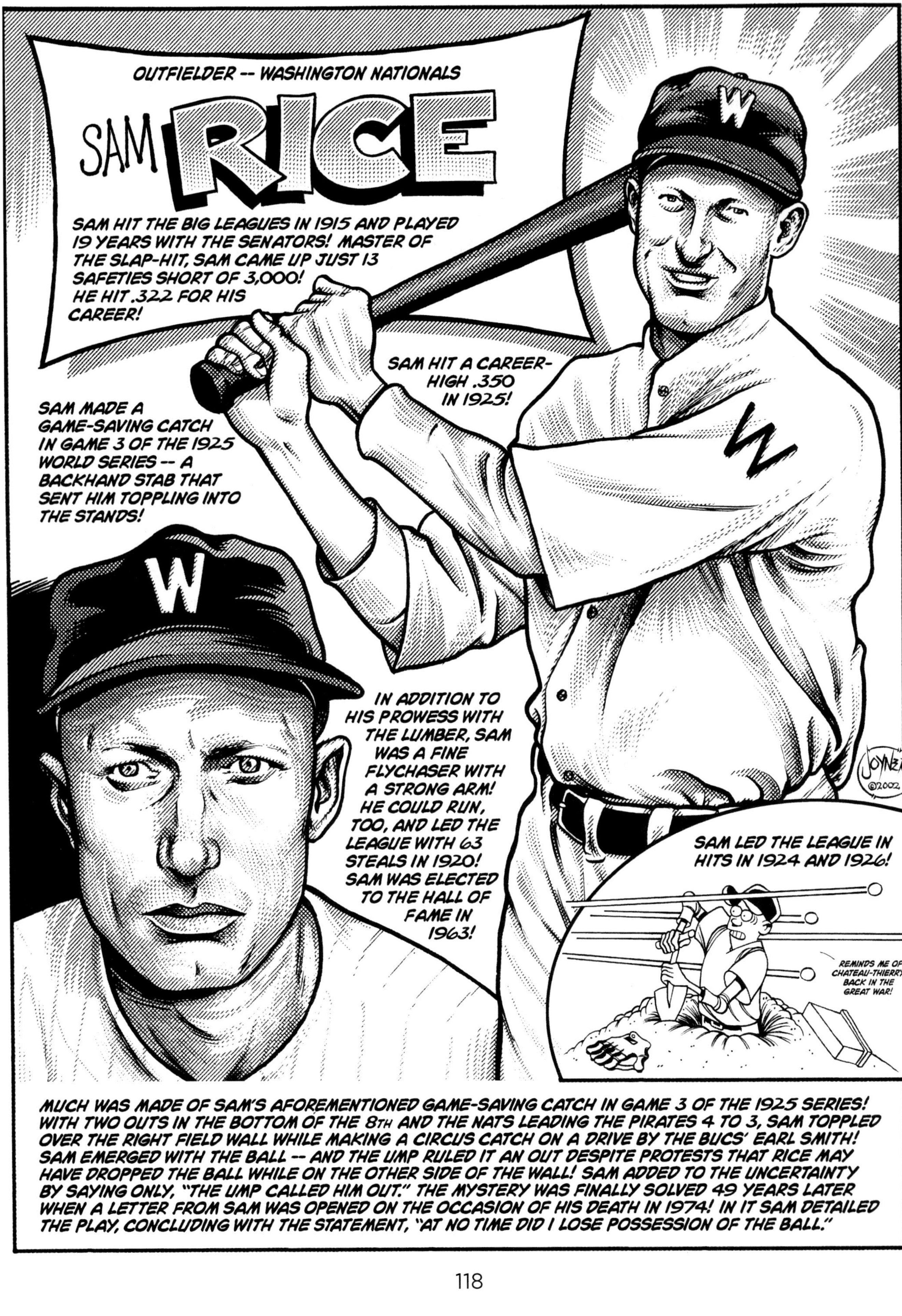
OUTFIELDER -- WASHINGTON NATIONALS
SAM RICE
SAM HIT THE BIG LEAGUES IN 1915 AND PLAYED 19 YEARS WITH THE SENATORS! MASTER OF THE SLAP-HIT, SAM CAME UP JUST 13 SAFETIES SHORT OF 3,000! HE HIT .322 FOR HIS CAREER!
SAM HIT A CAREER-HIGH .350 IN 1925!
SAM MADE A GAME-SAVING CATCH IN GAME 3 OF THE 1925 WORLD SERIES -- A BACKHAND STAB THAT SENT HIM TOPPLING INTO THE STANDS!
IN ADDITION TO HIS PROWESS WITH THE LUMBER, SAM WAS A FINE FLYCHASER WITH A STRONG ARM! HE COULD RUN, TOO, AND LED THE LEAGUE WITH 63 STEALS IN 1920! SAM WAS ELECTED TO THE HALL OF FAME IN 1963!
JOYNER ©2002
SAM LED THE LEAGUE IN HITS IN 1924 AND 1926!
REMINDS ME OF CHATEAU-THIERRY BACK IN THE GREAT WAR!
MUCH WAS MADE OF SAM'S AFOREMENTIONED GAME-SAVING CATCH IN GAME 3 OF THE 1925 SERIES! WITH TWO OUTS IN THE BOTTOM OF THE 8TH AND THE NATS LEADING THE PIRATES 4 TO 3, SAM TOPPLED OVER THE RIGHT FIELD WALL WHILE MAKING A CIRCUS CATCH ON A DRIVE BY THE BUCS' EARL SMITH! SAM EMERGED WITH THE BALL -- AND THE UMP RULED IT AN OUT DESPITE PROTESTS THAT RICE MAY HAVE DROPPED THE BALL WHILE ON THE OTHER SIDE OF THE WALL! SAM ADDED TO THE UNCERTAINTY BY SAYING ONLY, "THE UMP CALLED HIM OUT." THE MYSTERY WAS FINALLY SOLVED 49 YEARS LATER WHEN A LETTER FROM SAM WAS OPENED ON THE OCCASION OF HIS DEATH IN 1974! IN IT SAM DETAILED THE PLAY, CONCLUDING WITH THE STATEMENT, "AT NO TIME DID I LOSE POSSESSION OF THE BALL."

Al SIMMONS
CENTERFIELD -- PHILADELPHIA ATHLETICS
AL DID 3 TOURS OF DUTY WITH THE A's: 1924-32; 1940-41, AND 1944!
PLEASE, SKIP, DON'T MAKE ME PITCH TODAY -- BUCKETFOOT'S GOT MY NUMBER!
ALOIS SZYMANSKI WAS BORN ON MAY 22, 1902! HE EMBARKED ON HIS HALL OF FAME CAREER IN 1924 WHEN HE JOINED BILL LAMAR AND BING MILLER IN THE PHILADELPHIA A's OUTFIELD! THE 22-YEAR-OLD ROOKIE PUT TOGETHER A FINE DEBUT SEASON, HITTING .308 WITH 9 HOME RUNS AND 102 RBIs IN 594 AT-BATS! NOT A BELIEVER IN THE SOPHOMORE JINX, AL LED THE AMERICAN LEAGUE IN HITS THE NEXT YEAR WITH 253 WHILE BATTING AT A .384 CLIP! HE UPPED HIS RBI TOTALS, TOO, DRIVING IN 129 RUNNERS!
AL TORCHED OPPOSING PITCHERS HITTING .334 FOR HIS CAREER!
AL WAS DUBBED BUCKETFOOT FOR HIS PENCHANT FOR STEPPING "IN THE BUCKET," OR TOWARD 3RD BASE, ON HIS SWING! POISON FOR MOST BATSMEN, AL FLOURISHED WITH HIS TECHNIQUE, REGULARLY HITTING OVER .300 -- AND A CAREER HIGH .392 IN 1927!
DON'T TRY THIS AT HOME, KIDS!
JOYNER ©2002
AL WAS BORN IN MILWAUKEE, WISCONSIN!
I'M THE BIG CHEESE AROUND HERE!
AFTER LEADING THE LEAGUE IN AT-BATS AND HITS IN 1932, AL WAS SOLD TO THE CHICAGO WHITE SOX AT THE AGE OF 29! AL TURNED IN A COUPLE OF FINE YEARS IN CHICAGO BEFORE MOVING ON TO PLAY FOR THE TIGERS, SENATORS, BRAVES, REDS, AND RED SOX! HE FELL JUST 73 HITS SHY OF 3,000 FOR HIS CAREER, BUT STILL SLUGGED HIS WAY INTO THE HALL OF FAME IN 1953! CONNIE MACK ONCE DREAMED, "IF I COULD ONLY HAVE 9 PLAYERS NAMED SIMMONS!"

Paul WANER

42 YEARS AFTER HIS DEATH, AND 67 YEARS SINCE HE LAST PLAYED FOR THEM, THE PIRATES OF PITTSBURGH FINALLY HONORED ONE OF THEIR FRANCHISE'S GREATEST PLAYERS -- PAUL WANER! IN A CEREMONY BEFORE THE BUCS GAME AGAINST THE ASTROS ON JULY 21, 2007, THE PIRATES RETIRED "BIG POISON'S" NO. 11 JERSEY IN FRONT OF AN ENTHUSIASTIC PNC PARK CROWD! WITH FAMILY IN ATTENDANCE AND THE NUMBER 11 MOWED INTO THE RIGHTFIELD GRASS, WANER BECAME JUST THE NINTH PIRATE TO HAVE HIS NUMBER RETIRED, JOINING A SHORT LIST THAT INCLUDES HONUS WAGNER, PIE TRAYNOR, RALPH KINER, BILL MAZEROSKI, ROBERTO CLEMENTE, WILLIE STARGELL, AND MANAGERS BILLY MEYER AND DANNY MURTAUGH!

THE LITTLE BIT OF TEXT ON WANER'S HALL OF FAME PLAQUE GIVES A GLIMPSE INTO JUST HOW GOOD A PLAYER HE WAS... "LEFT-HANDED HITTING OUTFIELDER BATTED .300 OR BETTER 14 TIMES IN NATIONAL LEAGUE. ONE OF SEVEN PLAYERS TO COMPILE 3,000 OR MORE HITS. SET MODERN N.L. RECORD BY COLLECTING 200 OR MORE HITS EIGHT SEASONS. MOST VALUABLE PLAYER IN 1927 AND FOUR TIMES SELECTED FOR ALL STAR GAME." DESPITE CONTINUED SUCCESS AT THE PLATE, WANER BEGAN WEARING GLASSES LATE IN HIS CAREER! "HE HATED THEM," SPORTSWRITER RED SMITH REPORTED. "FOR THE FIRST TIME IN HIS LIFE, THAT THING THE PITCHERS WERE THROWING TURNED OUT TO BE A LITTLE THING, A SPINNING, SHARPLY DEFINED MISSLE NO BIGGER THAN A BASEBALL. HE HAD ALWAYS SEEN IT AS A FUZZY BLOB THE SIZE OF A GRAPEFRUIT. WANER HAD BEEN WHACKING THAT INDISTINCT MELON IN EXACT DEAD CENTER EVER SINCE HE LEFT THE TOWN TEAM IN HARRAH, OKLAHOMA." NOW, THE PRIDE OF HARRAH IS ONCE AGAIN THE PRIDE OF PITTSBURGH, HIS NAME AND NUMBER ETERNALLY ON DISPLAY ON THE PNC PARK THIRD BASE GRANDSTAND!

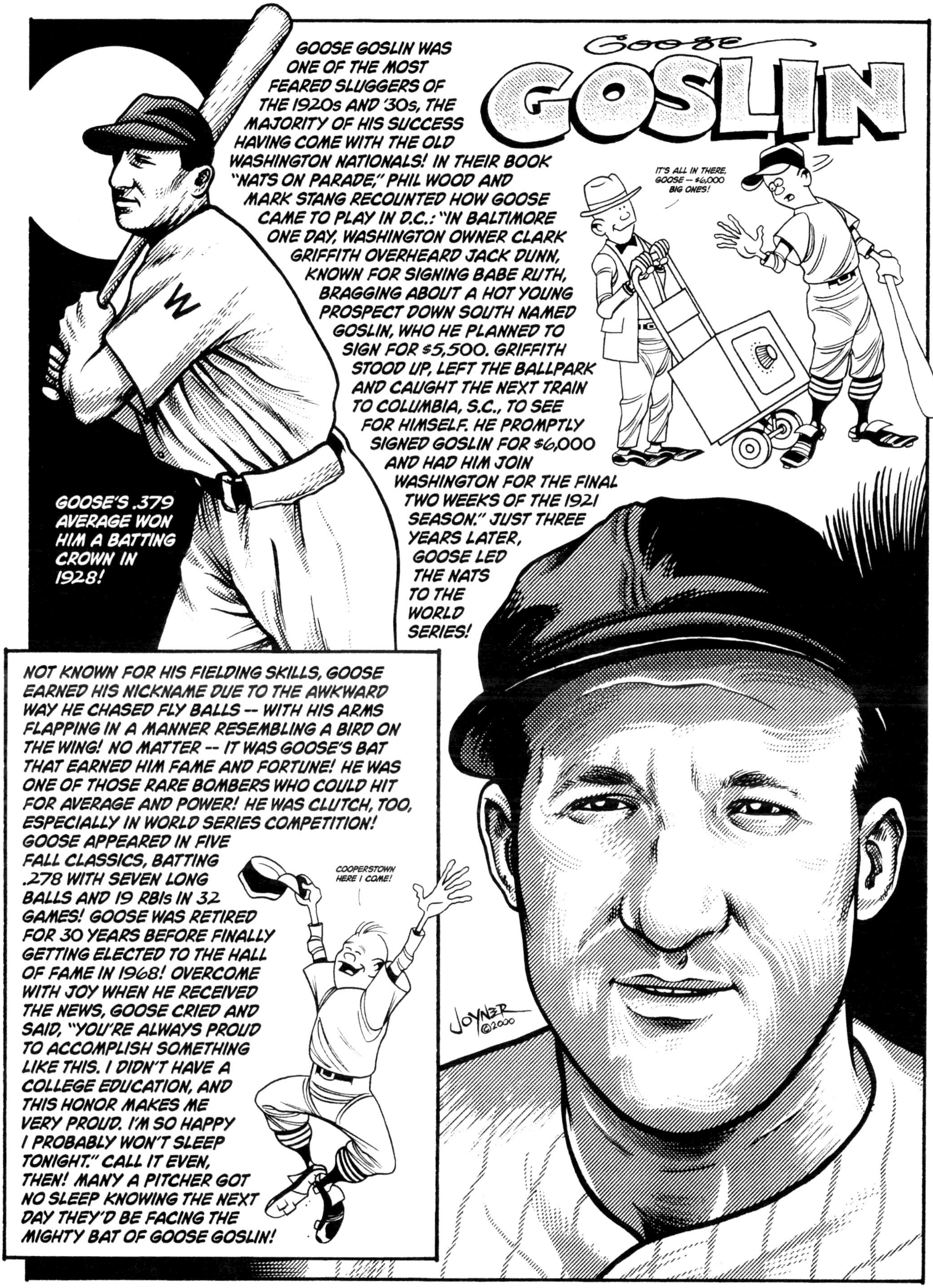
GOOSE GOSLIN
GOOSE GOSLIN WAS ONE OF THE MOST FEARED SLUGGERS OF THE 1920s AND '30s, THE MAJORITY OF HIS SUCCESS HAVING COME WITH THE OLD WASHINGTON NATIONALS! IN THEIR BOOK "NATS ON PARADE," PHIL WOOD AND MARK STANG RECOUNTED HOW GOOSE CAME TO PLAY IN D.C.: "IN BALTIMORE ONE DAY, WASHINGTON OWNER CLARK GRIFFITH OVERHEARD JACK DUNN, KNOWN FOR SIGNING BABE RUTH, BRAGGING ABOUT A HOT YOUNG PROSPECT DOWN SOUTH NAMED GOSLIN, WHO HE PLANNED TO SIGN FOR $5,500. GRIFFITH STOOD UP, LEFT THE BALLPARK AND CAUGHT THE NEXT TRAIN TO COLUMBIA, S.C., TO SEE FOR HIMSELF. HE PROMPTLY SIGNED GOSLIN FOR $6,000 AND HAD HIM JOIN WASHINGTON FOR THE FINAL TWO WEEKS OF THE 1921 SEASON." JUST THREE YEARS LATER, GOOSE LED THE NATS TO THE WORLD SERIES!
IT'S ALL IN THERE, GOOSE -- $6,000 BIG ONES!
W
GOOSE'S .379 AVERAGE WON HIM A BATTING CROWN IN 1928!
NOT KNOWN FOR HIS FIELDING SKILLS, GOOSE EARNED HIS NICKNAME DUE TO THE AWKWARD WAY HE CHASED FLY BALLS -- WITH HIS ARMS FLAPPING IN A MANNER RESEMBLING A BIRD ON THE WING! NO MATTER -- IT WAS GOOSE'S BAT THAT EARNED HIM FAME AND FORTUNE! HE WAS ONE OF THOSE RARE BOMBERS WHO COULD HIT FOR AVERAGE AND POWER! HE WAS CLUTCH, TOO, ESPECIALLY IN WORLD SERIES COMPETITION! GOOSE APPEARED IN FIVE FALL CLASSICS, BATTING .278 WITH SEVEN LONG BALLS AND 19 RBIs IN 32 GAMES! GOOSE WAS RETIRED FOR 30 YEARS BEFORE FINALLY GETTING ELECTED TO THE HALL OF FAME IN 1968! OVERCOME WITH JOY WHEN HE RECEIVED THE NEWS, GOOSE CRIED AND SAID, "YOU'RE ALWAYS PROUD TO ACCOMPLISH SOMETHING LIKE THIS. I DIDN'T HAVE A COLLEGE EDUCATION, AND THIS HONOR MAKES ME VERY PROUD. I'M SO HAPPY I PROBABLY WON'T SLEEP TONIGHT." CALL IT EVEN, THEN! MANY A PITCHER GOT NO SLEEP KNOWING THE NEXT DAY THEY'D BE FACING THE MIGHTY BAT OF GOOSE GOSLIN!
COOPERSTOWN HERE I COME!
JOYNER ©2000

Joe MEDWICK

JOE "DUCKY" MEDWICK, OR "MUSCLES," AS HE PREFERRED TO BE CALLED, WAS ELECTED INTO THE HALL OF FAME IN 1968 -- 20 YEARS AFTER HE PLAYED HIS LAST BIG LEAGUE GAME! NUMBERS INDICATE THAT HE SHOULD'VE BEEN ENSHRINED YEARS EARLIER -- MAYBE ON HIS FIRST BALLOT! JOE WAS, BY ALL ACCOUNTS, DIFFICULT TO GET ALONG WITH! HIS RELATIONSHIP WITH THE PRESS WAS BAD, TO SAY THE LEAST, AND IT WAS FOR THIS REASON THAT MANY BELIEVE JOE WAS SO LATE IN ENTERING THE HALL OF FAME! JOE WAS QUICK WITH THE FISTS, MANY TIMES EVEN SCRAPPING WITH HIS OWN TEAMMATES!

BORN JOSEPH MICHAEL MEDWICK ON NOVEMBER 24, 1911, IN CARTERET, NEW JERSEY, DUCKY FIRST ACHIEVED ATHLETIC GREATNESS AT CARTERET HIGH SCHOOL WHERE HE STARRED IN FOOTBALL, BASKETBALL AND BASEBALL! SO GREAT WERE HIS EXPLOITS ON THE GRIDIRON THAT HE WAS OFFERED MANY SCHOLARSHIPS, ONE TO NOTRE DAME! JOE OPTED, INSTEAD, TO PURSUE BASEBALL, AND HIS EXPLOITS WITH THE GAS HOUSE GANG ARE NOW LEGENDARY! HE BATTED OVER .300 IN ALL BUT THREE YEARS OF HIS 17-YEAR CAREER! HE LED THE LEAGUE IN RBIs AND DOUBLES FROM 1936-38, AND WAS A TRIPLE CROWN-WINNING M.V.P. IN 1937! JOE HIT .379 WITH A HOME RUN IN THE CARDINALS' 1934 WORLD SERIES WIN OVER THE TIGERS! POISED TO CHALLENGE THE ALL-TIME SERIES RECORD WITH 11 HITS, JOE NEVER GOT THE CHANCE AFTER BEING "REMOVED" IN THE 6TH INNING OF GAME SEVEN AFTER HIS HARD SLIDE INTO TIGERS 3RD BASEMAN MARV OWEN CAUSED A NEAR RIOT!

FOLLOWING HIS GAS HOUSE GANG DAYS, JOE WAS PART OF A U.S.O. TOUR FOR THE TROOPS IN 1944! UPON MEETING POPE PIUS XII, JOE TOLD THE PONTIFF, "I'M JOE MEDWICK. I, TOO, USED TO BE A CARDINAL."

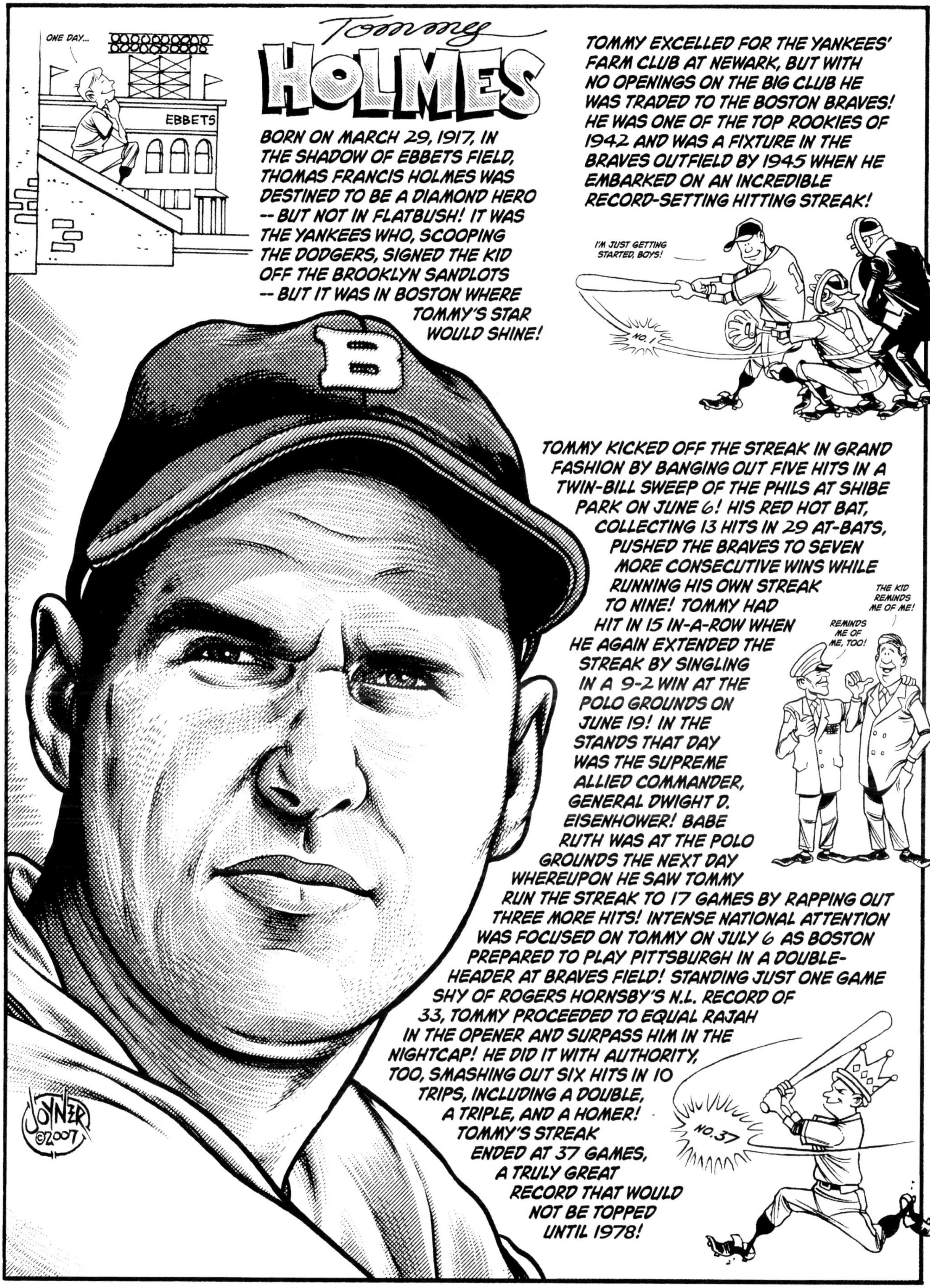
ONE DAY...
EBBETS
Tommy
HOLMES
BORN ON MARCH 29, 1917, IN THE SHADOW OF EBBETS FIELD, THOMAS FRANCIS HOLMES WAS DESTINED TO BE A DIAMOND HERO -- BUT NOT IN FLATBUSH! IT WAS THE YANKEES WHO, SCOOPING THE DODGERS, SIGNED THE KID OFF THE BROOKLYN SANDLOTS -- BUT IT WAS IN BOSTON WHERE TOMMY'S STAR WOULD SHINE!
TOMMY EXCELLED FOR THE YANKEES' FARM CLUB AT NEWARK, BUT WITH NO OPENINGS ON THE BIG CLUB HE WAS TRADED TO THE BOSTON BRAVES! HE WAS ONE OF THE TOP ROOKIES OF 1942 AND WAS A FIXTURE IN THE BRAVES OUTFIELD BY 1945 WHEN HE EMBARKED ON AN INCREDIBLE RECORD-SETTING HITTING STREAK!
I'M JUST GETTING STARTED, BOYS!
NO. 1
TOMMY KICKED OFF THE STREAK IN GRAND FASHION BY BANGING OUT FIVE HITS IN A TWIN-BILL SWEEP OF THE PHILS AT SHIBE PARK ON JUNE 6! HIS RED HOT BAT, COLLECTING 13 HITS IN 29 AT-BATS, PUSHED THE BRAVES TO SEVEN MORE CONSECUTIVE WINS WHILE RUNNING HIS OWN STREAK TO NINE! TOMMY HAD HIT IN 15 IN-A-ROW WHEN HE AGAIN EXTENDED THE STREAK BY SINGLING IN A 9-2 WIN AT THE POLO GROUNDS ON JUNE 19! IN THE STANDS THAT DAY WAS THE SUPREME ALLIED COMMANDER, GENERAL DWIGHT D. EISENHOWER! BABE RUTH WAS AT THE POLO GROUNDS THE NEXT DAY WHEREUPON HE SAW TOMMY RUN THE STREAK TO 17 GAMES BY RAPPING OUT THREE MORE HITS! INTENSE NATIONAL ATTENTION WAS FOCUSED ON TOMMY ON JULY 6 AS BOSTON PREPARED TO PLAY PITTSBURGH IN A DOUBLE-HEADER AT BRAVES FIELD! STANDING JUST ONE GAME SHY OF ROGERS HORNSBY'S N.L. RECORD OF 33, TOMMY PROCEEDED TO EQUAL RAJAH IN THE OPENER AND SURPASS HIM IN THE NIGHTCAP! HE DID IT WITH AUTHORITY, TOO, SMASHING OUT SIX HITS IN 10 TRIPS, INCLUDING A DOUBLE, A TRIPLE, AND A HOMER! TOMMY'S STREAK ENDED AT 37 GAMES, A TRULY GREAT RECORD THAT WOULD NOT BE TOPPED UNTIL 1978!
THE KID REMINDS ME OF ME!
REMINDS ME OF ME, TOO!
NO. 37
JOYNER ©2007

Lefty
O'DOUL
WHETHER IT WAS PITCHING, HITTING, OR MANAGING, FRANCIS JOSEPH "LEFTY" O'DOUL WAS GREAT AT IT! HE BEGAN HIS PRO CAREER AT THE AGE OF 20 AS A HARD-THROWING SOUTH-PAW FOR DES MOINES IN 1917! A 25-WIN CAMPAIGN WITH THE SAN FRANCISCO SEALS IN 1921 HAD LEFTY PEGGED FOR STARDOM, BUT ARM PROBLEMS CAUSED HIM TO ABANDON THE PITCHING PROFESSION AFTER SEEING LIMITED ACTION IN TRIALS WITH THE YANKS AND RED SOX IN 1919, '20, '22 AND '23! IT WAS THEN THAT LEFTY CHOSE TO CONVERT HIMSELF INTO AN OUTFIELDER AND ONE OF THE BEST HITTERS THE GAME HAS EVER SEEN! IN HIS HANDS, A BAT WAS A LETHAL WEAPON TO OPPOSITION PITCHERS! AFTER EVISCERATING MINOR LEAGUE PITCHING FOR THREE YEARS (.375 AND 24 HRs IN 1925; .338 AND 20 HRs IN 1926; .378 AND 33 HRs IN 1927), LEFTY RETURNED TO THE BIG LEAGUES AT THE AGE OF 31 WITH THE 1928 GIANTS! HIS NEXT FIVE YEARS IN THE MAJORS WAS DARN NEAR AS GOOD A 5-YEAR RUN AS ANYONE HAS EVER HAD! HE HIT AT A .361-CLIP IN THAT TIME SPAN, WHICH INCLUDED TWO BATTING TITLES (.398 IN 1929 AND .368 IN 1932)! LEFTY WRAPPED UP HIS TRIUMPHANT RETURN TO THE MAJORS WITH A .316 SEASON FOR THE 1934 GIANTS, THEN EMBARKED ON A LONG MANAGERIAL CAREER IN THE P.C.L. THAT SAW HIS CLUBS WIN 2,094 GAMES THROUGH THE 1957 SEASON! HANDSOME, IMMACULATELY ATTIRED, ARTICULATE, AND PERSONABLE, LEFTY WAS AN ICON IN HIS HOME CITY OF SAN FRANCISCO! EVEN NOW, DECADES AFTER HIS DEATH IN 1969, LEFTY IS STILL A LEGEND IN SAN FRANCISCO -- AND MAYBE ONE DAY IN COOPERSTOWN, NY!
THERE'S GOTTA BE A BETTER WAY TO MAKE A LIVIN'!
THIS LOOKS LIKE A GREAT TOOL WITH WHICH I CAN EVISCERATE PITCHERS!
JOYNER ©2002
A GROUP OF BALLPLAYERS INCLUDING LEFTY VISITED JAPAN IN 1931 IN AN EFFORT TO SPREAD THE GOSPEL OF BASEBALL! LEFTY RETURNED OFTEN THROUGHOUT THE '30s, TEACHING AND TRAINING THE JAPANESE PLAYERS IN THE FUNDAMENTALS OF THE GAME! WORLD WAR II TEMPORARILY ENDED HIS ACTIVITIES IN JAPAN, BUT LEFTY RETURNED IN 1949, AND HIS CONTINUED WORK THERE HELPED FOSTER RECONCILIATION BETWEEN THE U.S. AND JAPAN! LEFTY WAS AN IMPORTANT PLAYER IN THE ESTABLISHMENT OF THE JAPANESE PROFESSIONAL LEAGUE, AND HIS NAME IS SO REVERED THAT HE IS NOW ENSHRINED IN JAPANESE BASEBALL HALL OF FAME!
DOMO ARIGATO!

Mickey Vernon

KNOWN FOR HIS QUIET AND GENTLEMANLY DEMEANOR, MICKEY VERNON WAS A FAVORITE OF FANS AND PLAYERS ALIKE! HIS POPULARITY NEVER TRANSLATED TO BEING IN A WORLD SERIES, UNFORTUNATELY, DUE TO THE FACT HE PLAYED THE BULK OF HIS 20-YEAR CAREER WITH THE LOWLY SENATORS! HE RECEIVED AN UNLIKELY REWARD, HOWEVER, IN 1960 -- THE YEAR AFTER HE RETIRED AS A PLAYER! MICKEY WAS A COACH WITH THE PIRATES WHO WERE HEADED FOR A DATE WITH DESTINY IN THE WORLD SERIES! EVERYONE WANTED MICKEY TO BE A PART OF A PENNANT WINNER, SO THE BUCS ACTIVATED HIM ON SEPTEMBER 1, 1960! MICKEY MADE A FEW PINCH-HITTING APPEARANCES, AND PICKED UP WHAT WOULD BE HIS LAST BIG LEAGUE HIT -- NUMBER 2,495 -- ON SEPTEMBER 6! MICKEY WAS INELIGIBLE FOR THE WORLD SERIES ROSTER, BUT HE WAS OFFICIALLY A MEMBER OF THE WORLD CHAMPS WHEN THE PIRATES BEAT THE YANKEES TO TAKE THE TITLE! IN SPITE OF ALL OF HIS INDIVIDUAL ACCOMPLISHMENTS ON THE BALLFIELD, MICKEY OFTEN CITED THE CLIMAX OF THE 1960 SERIES AS HIS FAVORITE MEMORY. "THE BATTING TITLES WERE GREAT," MICKEY TOLD BASEBALL HISTORIAN JIM SARGENT, "BUT THE MOST EXCITING THING WAS MAZEROSKI HITTING THAT HOME RUN TO WIN THE 1960 WORLD SERIES."

MICKEY WAS ONE OF THE BEST HITTING FIRST BASEMEN OF HIS ERA, AND CAPTURED TWO BATTING TITLES (1946 AND 1953)! HIS HOME RUN TOTALS (172) WERE HELD DOWN BY PLAYING MOST OF HIS CAREER IN THE CAVERNOUS GRIFFITH STADIUM, BUT HE COMPENSATED BY SLAMMING DOUBLES, LEADING THE LEAGUE THREE TIMES IN THAT CATEGORY! MICKEY WAS ALSO A GREAT DEFENSIVE FIRST SACKER, AND RACKED UP COUNTLESS CAREER FIELDING MARKS! JACK DUNN, JR., MANAGER OF THE INTERNATIONAL LEAGUE'S BALTIMORE ORIOLES, PUT IT BEST WHEN HE SAID, "MICKEY WAS SO SMOOTH AROUND THE BAG THAT HE COULD HAVE PLAYED FIRST BASE WEARING A TUXEDO!" MICKEY COULD DO IT ALL ON THE DIAMOND, AND IT'S A MYSTERY WHY HE'S NOT IN THE HALL OF FAME -- AND THE PLAYERS AGREE! "MICKEY VERNON DESERVES TO BE IN THE HALL OF FAME," SAID GENE WOODLING. "MICKEY WAS A GREAT FIRST BASEMAN AND HE BELONGS IN THE HALL OF FAME," ADDED EDDIE YOST. SO LET'S GO, HALL -- OPEN YOUR DOORS TO THE GREAT MICKEY VERNON!

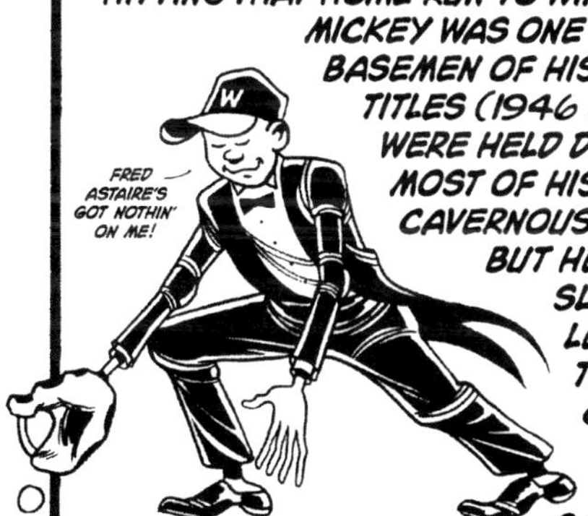

MICKEY VERNON, WHO SERVED TWO YEARS IN THE NAVY DURING WORLD WAR TWO, WAS A FAVORITE OF THE SUPREME COMMANDER, DWIGHT D. EISENHOWER, AND IT WAS EISENHOWER WHO PROVIDED MICKEY WITH ONE OF HIS FONDEST MEMORIES! "IN 1954, I HIT A HOME RUN IN EXTRA INNINGS TO BEAT THE YANKEES ON OPENING DAY," RECALLED MICKEY. "AS I ROUNDED THIRD, I SAW SOME OF THE PLAYERS WAITING AT HOME PLATE TO CONGRATULATE ME -- AND THERE WAS ONE CIVILIAN THERE. AS I CROSSED THE PLATE, HE GRABBED MY ARM. 'IT'S OKAY,' HE SAID, 'I'M A SECRET SERVICE MAN. THE PRESIDENT WANTS TO SEE YOU OVER AT HIS BOX.' MR. EISENHOWER WAS STANDING UP WITH A BIG GRIN AND HIS HAND OUT-STRETCHED. THAT WAS A BIG THRILL!"

al OLIVER

21-YEAR-OLD AL OLIVER JOINED THE PITTSBURGH PIRATES IN SEPTEMBER OF 1968, THEREBY BEGINNING AN 18-SEASON BIG LEAGUE CAREER THAT SAW THE SMOOTH-SWINGING LEFTY BATSMAN AMASS 2,743 HITS -- 219 OF WHICH WENT FOR THE CIRCUIT! A LIFETIME .303 HITTER, AL'S TICKET FOR THE HALL OF FAME IS CERTAINLY LONG OVERDUE, BUT HE STILL HAS FAITH THAT ONE DAY HE'LL BE JUSTLY ENSHRINED BY THE H.O.F.'S VETERANS COMMITTEE! "THE ONLY THING I CAN SAY," AL TOLD THE PITTSBURGH TRIBUNE-REVIEW IN 2006, "IS THAT THE NUMBERS ARE THERE. IF THEY LOOK VERY CLOSELY AT THE TOTAL PACKAGE, I LIKE TO THINK, IF THEY ARE FAIR, THERE'S A GOOD POSSIBILITY." THERE WERE COUNTLESS HIGHLIGHTS IN AL'S LONG CAREER, BUT ONE OF HIS FAVORITE MOMENTS WAS HIS 3-RUN HOMER IN THE PIRATES' GAME FOUR WIN OVER THE GIANTS IN THE '71 NATIONAL LEAGUE CHAMPIONSHIP SERIES! "I NEVER FELT MY FEET TOUCH THE GROUND AS I CIRCLED THE BASES," OLIVER TOLD AL DOYLE OF BASEBALL DIGEST. "I STILL HAVE THE PICTURE OF ME RUNNING THE BASES THAT DAY. THAT HOME RUN SOLIDIFIED OUR CHANCES TO WIN THE GAME AND GET INTO (AND WIN) THE WORLD SERIES. I'LL NEVER FORGET THAT HIT." TRADED TO THE TEXAS RANGERS IN 1978, AL PROCEEDED TO SHOW AMERICAN LEAGUE PITCHERS WHAT NATIONAL LEAGUE HURLERS ALREADY KNEW -- THAT HE WAS A TOUGH OUT! IT WAS WITH THE RANGERS ON AUGUST 17, 1980, THAT AL SET AN A.L. RECORD FOR TOTAL BASES IN A TWIN-BILL! "SCOOPS" RACKED UP 21 BAGS THAT DAY IN A SWEEP OF THE TIGERS IN DETROIT, HIS BIG BAT BOOMING OUT FOUR HOMERS, ONE DOUBLE, AND ONE TRIPLE! AL WON A BATTING TITLE WITH THE 1982 EXPOS, FURTHER CEMENTING HIS CREDENTIALS AS A HALL OF FAMER!

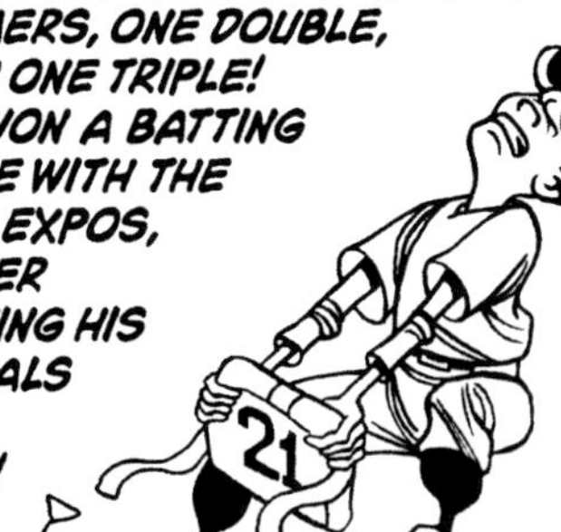

PETE ROSE

AFTER BEGINNING HIS CAREER IN AN 0-FOR-11 SLUMP, REDS 21-YEAR-OLD SWITCH-HITTING ROOKIE SECOND BASEMAN PETE ROSE TRIPLED OFF THE BUCS' BOB FRIEND ON APRIL 13, 1963, TO NOTCH HIS FIRST BIG LEAGUE HIT. NEARLY 23-1/2 YEARS LATER, PETE SLAPPED OUT HIS FINAL HIT -- A SINGLE OFF RIGHT-HANDED GIANTS PITCHER GREG MINTON. IT WAS THE 4,256TH HIT OF PETE'S ILLUSTRIOUS CAREER -- AN ALL-TIME RECORD THAT ALMOST SURELY WILL NEVER BE ECLIPSED. IN BETWEEN THOSE TWO HITS, PETE WON THE ROOKIE OF THE YEAR AWARD, AN M.V.P. AWARD, BATTING TITLES, WORLD SERIES RINGS AND GOLD GLOVE AWARDS, AS WELL AS 17 ALL-STAR GAME APPEARANCES. A HARD-NOSED HUSTLING GAMER, PETE GAVE EVERYTHING HE HAD EVERY TIME HE TOOK THE FIELD. WHEN HIS PLAYING DAYS WERE OVER, HE TRANSITIONED TO MANAGER, LEADING THE REDS TO A 412-373 RECORD FROM 1984 THROUGH '89. PETE WAS A SURE-FIRE FIRST-BALLOT HALL-OF-FAMER -- UNTIL IT WAS LEARNED THAT HE HAD A LONG HISTORY OF GAMBLING ON HIS TEAM WHILE HE WAS A PLAYER AND MANAGER. BANNED FROM THE GAME SINCE 1989, PETE HAS FINALLY ADMITTED HIS MISTAKE, HOPEFULLY CLEARING A PATH TO THE HALL OF FAME.

IN JULY OF 2009, HANK AARON WENT TO BAT FOR CHARLIE HUSTLE. "PETE ROSE DESERVES TO BE IN THE HALL OF FAME," HANK SAID. "HE NEEDS TO BE RIGHT THERE WITH ALL THE REST OF THE GUYS. HIS RECORD SPEAKS FOR ITSELF. IT SADDENS ME THAT PETE IS NOT IN THE HALL BECAUSE I KNOW WHAT KIND OF BALLPLAYER HE WAS. I PLAYED IN SEVERAL ALL-STAR GAMES WITH HIM. I GOT A CHANCE TO KNOW HIM VERY WELL. IT'S JUST TOO BAD. IF PETE WOULD HAVE ADMITTED THAT HE HAD BEEN INVOLVED IN GAMBLING YEARS AGO WHEN THIS FIRST CAME OUT, THEN I THINK THINGS WOULD HAVE BEEN A LOT DIFFERENT. BUT HE'S NOW ADMITTED THAT HE BET ON BASEBALL AND HE'S ASKED FOR FORGIVENESS -- AND THAT'S WHAT WE SHOULD LOOK AT. WE ALL HAVE DONE SOME WRONGS AT SOME TIME. ALL OF US. ALL OF US HAVE DONE SOMETHING THAT WE ARE ASHAMED OF. PETE MADE A MISTAKE, AND I THINK IT'S TIME FOR US TO WASH OUR HANDS OF THIS AND LET HIM IN THE HALL OF FAME WITH THE REST OF THE GUYS. HE'S GOT MORE HITS THAN ANYBODY ELSE IN BASEBALL, AND I DON'T THINK ANYBODY WILL EVER TOP THAT. PETE WAS A TERRIFIC BALLPLAYER, AND I WOULD LOVE TO SEE HIM IN THE HALL OF FAME."

ARMED AND DANGEROUS

WALTER
JOHNSON
FOR A $100 BONUS, TRAIN FARE, AND THE PROMISE OF $350 A MONTH, THE WASHINGTON SENATORS WERE ABLE TO SIGN A MAN WHO MANY BELIEVE TO BE THE GREATEST PITCHER OF ALL TIME -- WALTER JOHNSON! BORN ON NOVEMBER 6, 1887, IN HUMBOLDT, KANSAS, JOHNSON WAS JUST 19 WHEN THE NATS DISCOVERED HIM MOWING DOWN BATSMEN IN A SEMI-PRO LEAGUE IN IDAHO IN 1907! RUSHED TO THE NATION'S CAPITAL, THE KID WAS ABLE TO POST 5 WINS WITH A 1.87 E.R.A IN 14 STARTS FOR THE LAST-PLACE NATS DESPITE LITTLE OR NO RUN SUPPORT!
JOHNSON SPENT HIS ENTIRE 21 BIG LEAGUE SEASONS WITH THE PERENNIAL LAST-PLACE NATS! STILL, THE BIG TRAIN WAS ABLE TO LEAD THE LEAGUE IN WINS 5 TIMES! HIS PERSEVERANCE PAID OFF WHEN THE NATS FINALLY REACHED THE WORLD SERIES AND WON IT IN '24 WITH JOHNSON GETTING THE WIN IN A THRILLING GAME 7!
JOYNER ©2004
JOHNSON THREW WITH A SMOOTH SIDEARM MOTION! HIS BLAZING FASTBALL WAS SAID TO BE THE FASTEST IN THE GAME AND INVISIBLE TO BATTERS, STREAKING TO THE CATCHER WITH AN AUDIBLE "SWOOSH" AND SLAMMING INTO THE MITT WITH A LOUD "BOOM"!
WHAT WAS THAT SOUND, MUDDY?
UMMM, THAT WAS A STRIKE, BUB!
JOHNSON IS 2ND ALL-TIME IN WINS WITH 417; 1ST ALL-TIME IN SHUTOUTS WITH 110; AND 7TH ALL-TIME IN LIFETIME E.R.A AT 2.17! ADMIRED FOR HIS MILD, MODEST AND DECENT PERSONA, WALTER JOHNSON WAS A MEMBER OF THE 1939 INAUGURAL CLASS OF THE HALL OF FAME IN COOPERSTOWN!

Art DITMAR

RELYING ON FINESSE AND CONTROL, RIGHT-HANDER ART DITMAR SPENT NINE YEARS IN THE BIG LEAGUES WHERE HE WON 72 GAMES! A NATIVE OF SPRINGFIELD, MASSACHUSETTS, ART WAS PASSED ON BY THE NEARBY RED SOX, SO PHILADELPHIA ATHLETICS SCOUT DUTCH BRENNAN POUNCED AND SIGNED THE PITTSFIELD HIGH SCHOOL GRADUATE! "THE RED SOX COULD HAVE SIGNED ME FOR NOTHING," ART RECALLED, "THAT'S HOW MUCH MY DAD LOVED THE TEAM." THE RED SOX'S LOSS WAS PHILADELPHIA'S GAIN, HOWEVER, AND AFTER FOUR YEARS IN THE A'S FARM SYSTEM AND TWO YEARS IN THE ARMY DURING THE KOREAN WAR, ART FINALLY MADE IT TO THE MAJORS IN 1954! HE BEGAN THAT SEASON WITH THE BIG CLUB, BUT WAS SENT BACK DOWN TO OTTAWA BEFORE GETTING CALLED UP FOR GOOD LATER IN THE CAMPAIGN! 1954 WAS THE LAST SEASON IN THE STORIED HISTORY OF THE PHILADELPHIA ATHLETICS, AND ART MADE HIS MARK BY STARTING THE LAST GAME THE BALLCLUB PLAYED AT SHIBE PARK, THEIR HOME FIELD! HE ALSO STARTED AND WON THE TEAM'S 1954 REGULAR SEASON FINALE -- AN 8-6 VICTORY OVER THE NEW YORK YANKS IN THE BRONX! 1955 SAW ART BID FAREWELL TO PHILLY AS HE MOVED WITH THE CLUB TO THEIR NEW DIGS IN KANSAS CITY!

ART OFTEN PITCHED WELL AGAINST THE YANKEES, SO THEY ACQUIRED THE SINKERBALLER PRIOR TO THE 1957 SEASON! HE PITCHED WELL FOR THE THEM FOR THREE-PLUS YEARS, EVEN LEADING THE '60 STAFF IN WINS WITH 15! ART ALLOWED NO RUNS IN ANY OF HIS SERIES APPEARANCES OF 1957 AND '58, BUT HE HAD A ROUGH SERIES vs. THE BUCS IN '60, ABSORBING THE LOSS IN GAMES ONE AND FIVE! TO ADD INSULT TO INJURY, LEGENDARY ANNOUNCER CHUCK THOMPSON MISTAKENLY NAMED ART AS THE PITCHER WHO SURRENDERED THE SERIES-ENDING HOMER TO MAZEROSKI! WHEN BUDWEISER USED THE FAULTY AUDIO IN AN '85 T.V. AD, ART SUED! HIS CASE WENT ALL THE WAY TO THE SUPREME COURT, BUT WAS EVENTUALLY KICKED BACK TO THE DISTRICT LEVEL WHERE ART RECEIVED NO SYMPATHY FROM A FEMALE JUDGE WHO FAILED TO UNDERSTAND WHY A HOME RUN SHOULD BE SO IMPORTANT!

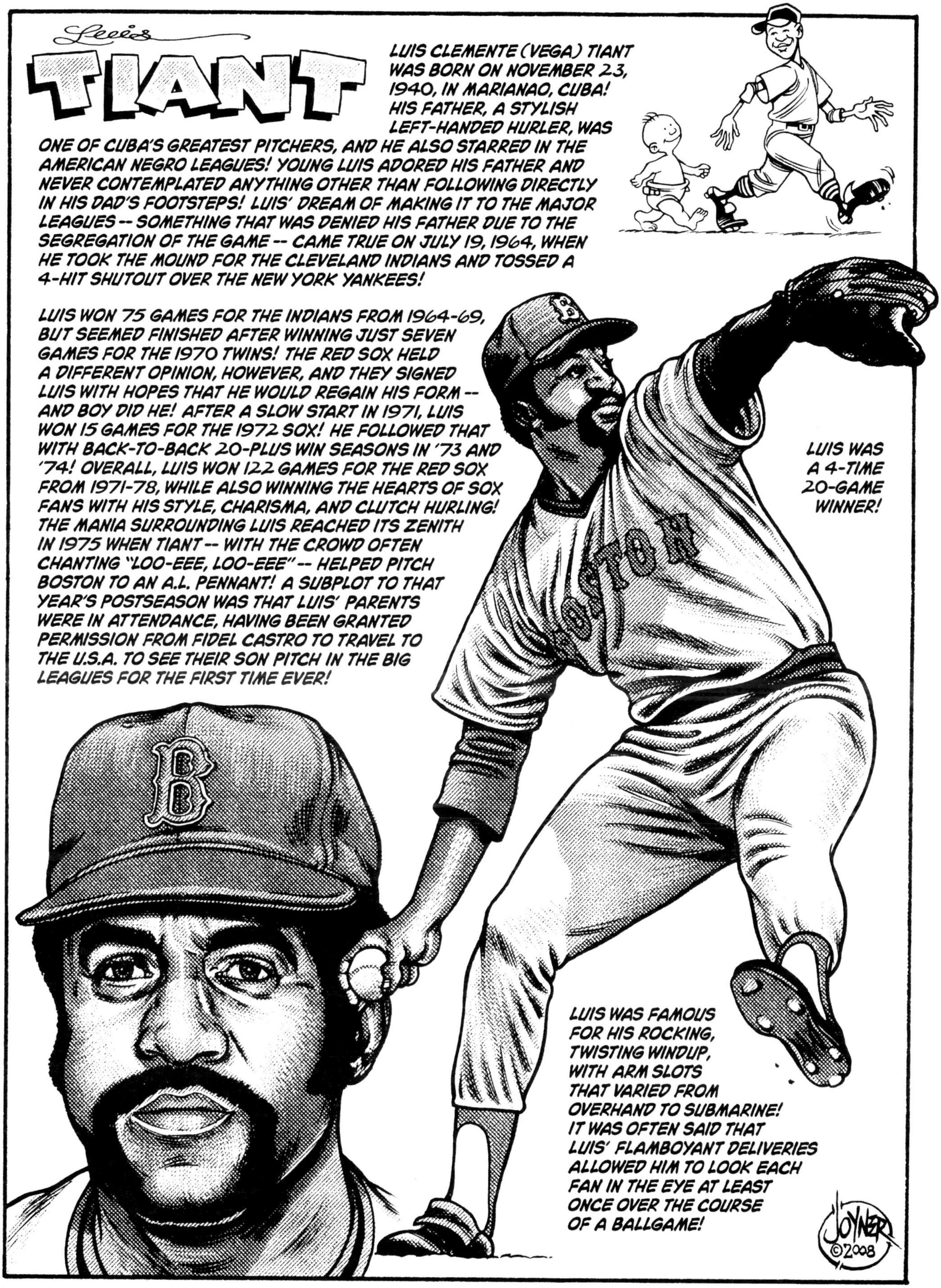
TIANT
LUIS CLEMENTE (VEGA) TIANT WAS BORN ON NOVEMBER 23, 1940, IN MARIANAO, CUBA! HIS FATHER, A STYLISH LEFT-HANDED HURLER, WAS ONE OF CUBA'S GREATEST PITCHERS, AND HE ALSO STARRED IN THE AMERICAN NEGRO LEAGUES! YOUNG LUIS ADORED HIS FATHER AND NEVER CONTEMPLATED ANYTHING OTHER THAN FOLLOWING DIRECTLY IN HIS DAD'S FOOTSTEPS! LUIS' DREAM OF MAKING IT TO THE MAJOR LEAGUES -- SOMETHING THAT WAS DENIED HIS FATHER DUE TO THE SEGREGATION OF THE GAME -- CAME TRUE ON JULY 19, 1964, WHEN HE TOOK THE MOUND FOR THE CLEVELAND INDIANS AND TOSSED A 4-HIT SHUTOUT OVER THE NEW YORK YANKEES!
LUIS WON 75 GAMES FOR THE INDIANS FROM 1964-69, BUT SEEMED FINISHED AFTER WINNING JUST SEVEN GAMES FOR THE 1970 TWINS! THE RED SOX HELD A DIFFERENT OPINION, HOWEVER, AND THEY SIGNED LUIS WITH HOPES THAT HE WOULD REGAIN HIS FORM -- AND BOY DID HE! AFTER A SLOW START IN 1971, LUIS WON 15 GAMES FOR THE 1972 SOX! HE FOLLOWED THAT WITH BACK-TO-BACK 20-PLUS WIN SEASONS IN '73 AND '74! OVERALL, LUIS WON 122 GAMES FOR THE RED SOX FROM 1971-78, WHILE ALSO WINNING THE HEARTS OF SOX FANS WITH HIS STYLE, CHARISMA, AND CLUTCH HURLING! THE MANIA SURROUNDING LUIS REACHED ITS ZENITH IN 1975 WHEN TIANT -- WITH THE CROWD OFTEN CHANTING "LOO-EEE, LOO-EEE" -- HELPED PITCH BOSTON TO AN A.L. PENNANT! A SUBPLOT TO THAT YEAR'S POSTSEASON WAS THAT LUIS' PARENTS WERE IN ATTENDANCE, HAVING BEEN GRANTED PERMISSION FROM FIDEL CASTRO TO TRAVEL TO THE U.S.A. TO SEE THEIR SON PITCH IN THE BIG LEAGUES FOR THE FIRST TIME EVER!
LUIS WAS A 4-TIME 20-GAME WINNER!
LUIS WAS FAMOUS FOR HIS ROCKING, TWISTING WINDUP, WITH ARM SLOTS THAT VARIED FROM OVERHAND TO SUBMARINE! IT WAS OFTEN SAID THAT LUIS' FLAMBOYANT DELIVERIES ALLOWED HIM TO LOOK EACH FAN IN THE EYE AT LEAST ONCE OVER THE COURSE OF A BALLGAME!
JOYNER ©2008

Dutch LEONARD

IT'S NOT OFTEN THAT AN ARM INJURY TURNS OUT TO BE A BLESSING FOR A BUDDING PITCHER, BUT THAT APPEARS TO HAVE BEEN THE CASE WITH KNUCKLEBALL MASTER EMIL "DUTCH" LEONARD! A PROMISING YOUNG FASTBALLER, DUTCH HURT HIS GOLDEN RIGHT ARM WHILE PLAYING HIGH SCHOOL BASKETBALL IN 1927! ROBBED OF A FEW CRITICAL MILES-PER-HOUR, DUTCH IMMEDIATELY BEGAN FOOLING AROUND WITH THE KNUCKLER TO COMPENSATE! THE DODGERS LIKED DUTCH AND HIS FLOATER, SO THEY SIGNED HIM AND GAVE HIM 35 STARTS FROM 1933-36! WHILE HE WAS ABLE TO POST 18 WINS IN THAT TIME, BROOKLYN FELT DUTCH NEEDED MORE SEASONING -- SO IT WAS BACK TO THE MINORS! DUTCH RETURNED TO THE MAJORS IN 1938, THIS TIME WEARING A WASHINGTON UNIFORM! "I WAS WITH THE SENATORS NINE YEARS," DUTCH SAID, "AND I GUESS YOU COULD CALL THOSE MY BEST SEASONS." AND HOW! DESPITE PLAYING ON SOME TERRIBLE NATS TEAMS, DUTCH KNUCKLED HIS WAY TO 118 WINS AND AN IMPRESSIVE 3.27 E.R.A. DURING HIS YEARS IN D.C.! DUTCH WAS A SERIOUS COMPETITOR ON THE MOUND, BUT ONE OF THE MORE COMICAL PLAYS OF ALL TIME HAPPENED ONE DAY WHILE HE WAS ON THE HILL! A PHILADELPHIA ATHLETICS BATTER DROVE A BLISTERING LINE-DRIVE RIGHT AT DUTCH, WHEREUPON THE BALL DISAPPEARED INTO THE MISTAKENLY-OPEN FLY OF LEONARD'S PANTS! BY THE TIME HE FISHED OUT THE BALL, THE BATTER WAS SAFE ON FIRST!

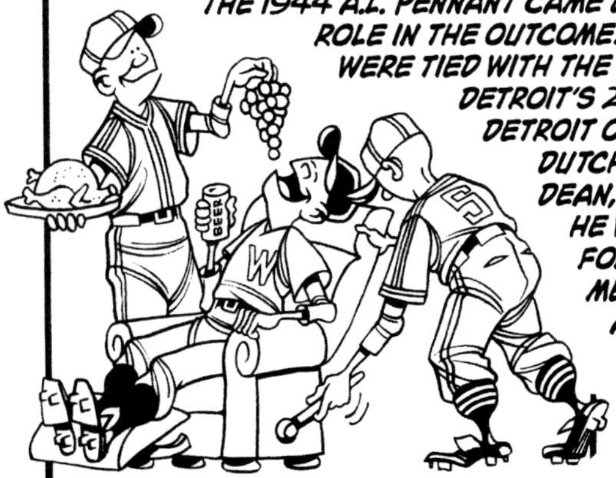

THE 1944 A.L. PENNANT CAME DOWN TO THE LAST GAME OF THE SEASON, AND DUTCH PLAYED A KEY ROLE IN THE OUTCOME! HIS NATS WERE IN DETROIT TO PLAY THE TIGERS -- AND THE TIGERS WERE TIED WITH THE BROWNS FOR FIRST PLACE! DUTCH WENT THE DISTANCE AGAINST DETROIT'S 27-GAME WINNER DIZZY TROUT AND BEAT THE TIGERS 4-1! "I KNOCKED DETROIT OUT OF THE PENNANT THAT DAY AND GAVE IT TO THE ST. LOUIS BROWNS," DUTCH RECALLED YEARS LATER. "I HADN'T LEFT THE HOTEL YET WHEN DIZZY DEAN, WHO WAS BROADCASTING FOR THE BROWNS, CALLED ME FROM ST. LOUIS. HE WOULDN'T LET ME OFF THE PHONE UNTIL I PROMISED TO GO TO ST. LOUIS FOR A BIG PARTY THEY WERE GOING TO HAVE. WHEN I GOT THERE THEY PUT ME IN A BIG EASY CHAIR AND TOLD ME TO SIT BACK AND RELAX AND HAVE ANYTHING I WANTED TO EAT OR DRINK." WHILE GREATLY APPRECIATED IN ST. LOUIS, DUTCH MAY HAVE BEEN A LITTLE UNDERAPPRECIATED BACK HOME IN D.C.! THE SENATORS JUST BARELY MISSED A PENNANT IN 1945, AND NATS OWNER CLARK GRIFFITH BLAMED DUTCH, CITING HIS "REDUCED" PRODUCTION -- 17-AND-7 WITH A 2.13 E.R.A.!

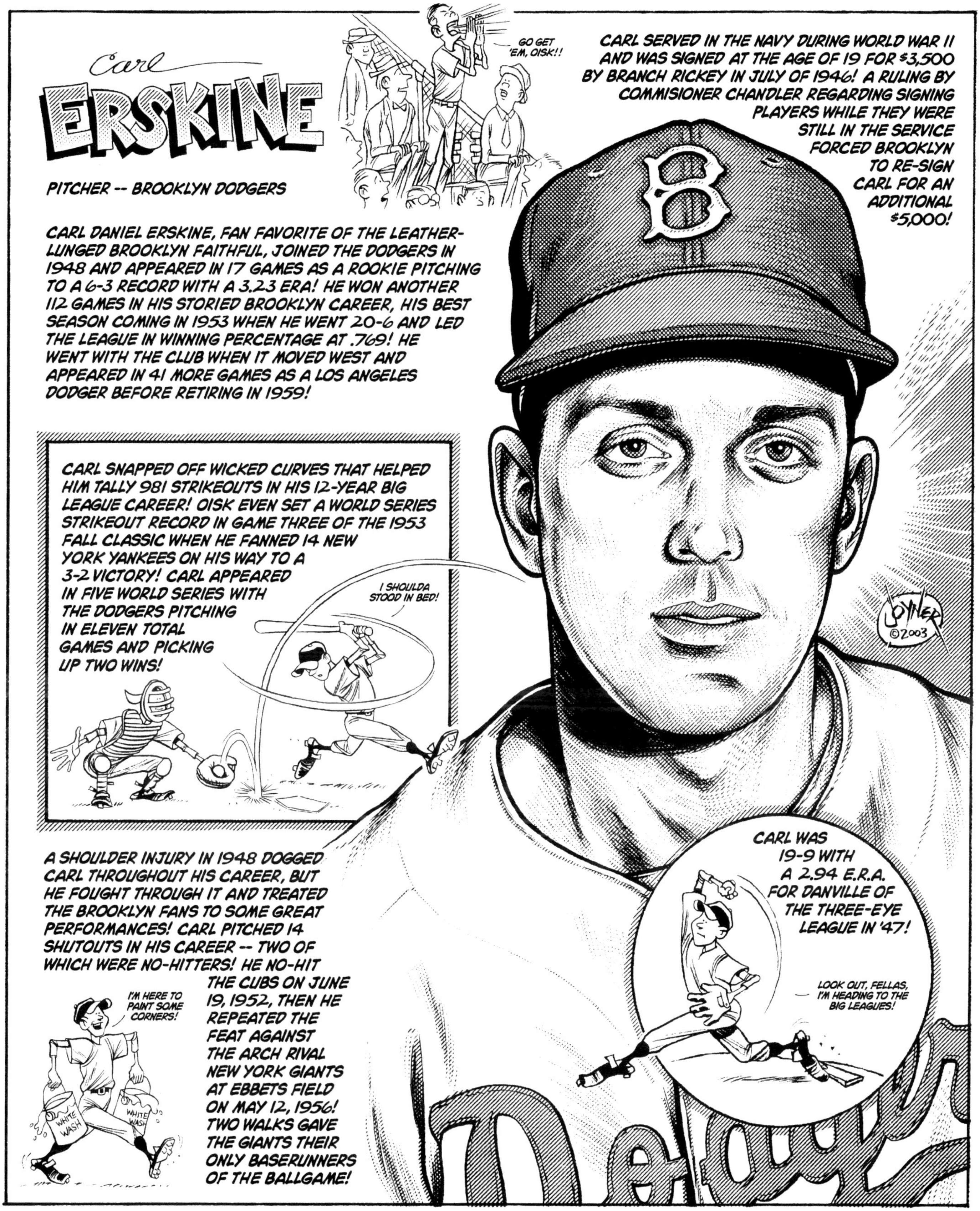
Carl
ERSKINE
PITCHER -- BROOKLYN DODGERS
GO GET 'EM, OISK!!
CARL SERVED IN THE NAVY DURING WORLD WAR II AND WAS SIGNED AT THE AGE OF 19 FOR $3,500 BY BRANCH RICKEY IN JULY OF 1946! A RULING BY COMMISIONER CHANDLER REGARDING SIGNING PLAYERS WHILE THEY WERE STILL IN THE SERVICE FORCED BROOKLYN TO RE-SIGN CARL FOR AN ADDITIONAL $5,000!
CARL DANIEL ERSKINE, FAN FAVORITE OF THE LEATHER-LUNGED BROOKLYN FAITHFUL, JOINED THE DODGERS IN 1948 AND APPEARED IN 17 GAMES AS A ROOKIE PITCHING TO A 6-3 RECORD WITH A 3.23 ERA! HE WON ANOTHER 112 GAMES IN HIS STORIED BROOKLYN CAREER, HIS BEST SEASON COMING IN 1953 WHEN HE WENT 20-6 AND LED THE LEAGUE IN WINNING PERCENTAGE AT .769! HE WENT WITH THE CLUB WHEN IT MOVED WEST AND APPEARED IN 41 MORE GAMES AS A LOS ANGELES DODGER BEFORE RETIRING IN 1959!
CARL SNAPPED OFF WICKED CURVES THAT HELPED HIM TALLY 981 STRIKEOUTS IN HIS 12-YEAR BIG LEAGUE CAREER! OISK EVEN SET A WORLD SERIES STRIKEOUT RECORD IN GAME THREE OF THE 1953 FALL CLASSIC WHEN HE FANNED 14 NEW YORK YANKEES ON HIS WAY TO A 3-2 VICTORY! CARL APPEARED IN FIVE WORLD SERIES WITH THE DODGERS PITCHING IN ELEVEN TOTAL GAMES AND PICKING UP TWO WINS!
I SHOULDA STOOD IN BED!
JOYNER ©2003
A SHOULDER INJURY IN 1948 DOGGED CARL THROUGHOUT HIS CAREER, BUT HE FOUGHT THROUGH IT AND TREATED THE BROOKLYN FANS TO SOME GREAT PERFORMANCES! CARL PITCHED 14 SHUTOUTS IN HIS CAREER -- TWO OF WHICH WERE NO-HITTERS! HE NO-HIT THE CUBS ON JUNE 19, 1952, THEN HE REPEATED THE FEAT AGAINST THE ARCH RIVAL NEW YORK GIANTS AT EBBETS FIELD ON MAY 12, 1956! TWO WALKS GAVE THE GIANTS THEIR ONLY BASERUNNERS OF THE BALLGAME!
I'M HERE TO PAINT SOME CORNERS!
WHITE WASH
WHITE WASH
CARL WAS 19-9 WITH A 2.94 E.R.A. FOR DANVILLE OF THE THREE-EYE LEAGUE IN '47!
LOOK OUT, FELLAS, I'M HEADING TO THE BIG LEAGUES!

Greg MADDUX

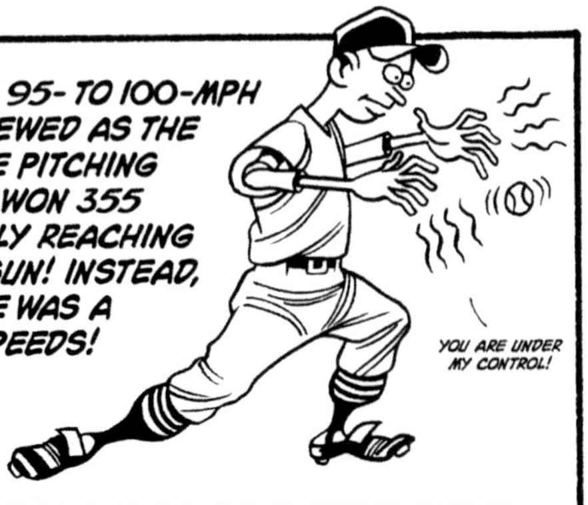

IN A MODERN AGE WHERE 95- TO 100-MPH FASTBALLS ARE OFTEN VIEWED AS THE ONLY PATH TO BIG LEAGUE PITCHING SUCCESS, GREG MADDUX WON 355 GAMES WHILE ONLY RARELY REACHING 90 MPH ON THE JUGGS GUN! INSTEAD, GREG'S SUCCESS ON THE MOUND CAN BE ATTRIBUTED TO THE FACT THAT HE WAS A MASTER OF CONTROL, RELYING ON PINPOINT ACCURACY AND CHANGE OF SPEEDS! IN OTHER WORDS, COMPLETE COMMAND OF EVERY PITCH HE THREW! IN THE WAKE OF HIS MASTERY WERE COUNTLESS FRUSTRATED BATSMEN WHO SPENT THE BULK OF THE LATE-1980s AND 1990s TAPPING OUT, POPPING UP, AND WHIFFING AT GREG'S OFFERINGS! SUCCESS WAS NOT IMMEDIATE FOR GREG! HE CAME UP WITH THE CHICAGO CUBS AND STRUGGLED IN HIS FIRST TWO SEASONS THERE, BUT IT ALL CLICKED FOR HIM IN HIS THIRD SEASON AS HE BROKE THROUGH WITH AN 18-WIN SEASON! GREG CONTINUED TO PITCH WELL FOR THE CUBS FOR FOUR MORE SEASONS, THE FINAL YEAR OF THAT RUN BEING THE FIRST OF BACK-TO-BACK 20-WIN SEASONS IN 1992 AND '93!

NOT CONTENT TO FOCUS ON SIMPLY MAKING GREAT PITCHES, GREG KNEW THAT ANOTHER KEY TO WINNING WAS TO BE THE VERY BEST HE COULD POSSIBLY BE AT FIELDING HIS POSITION! HE WORKED HARD AT IT, AND IT'S DIFFICULT TO ARGUE WITH THE RESULTS -- A RECORD 18 GOLD GLOVE AWARDS! IT'S IMPOSSIBLE TO SAY EXACTLY HOW MANY OF GREG'S 355 WINS CAN BE ATTRIBUTED TO A GREAT PLAY HE MADE OFF THE MOUND, BUT IT SUFFICES TO SAY THAT IT'S MORE THAN A FEW! WHEN YOU COMBINE HIS PITCHING AND FIELDING SKILLS WITH THE FACT THAT GREG WAS A GOOD HITTING PITCHER AND A FIERY COMPETITOR, IT'S NO MYSTERY WHY HE'S HEADED FOR FUTURE ENSHRINEMENT IN THE HALL OF FAME!

DURING HIS PRIME, GREG REGULARLY TURNED IN E.R.A.s THAT LOOKED RIGHT OUT OF THE DEADBALL PERIOD -- ESPECIALLY HIS 1994 E.R.A. OF 1.56, THE THIRD BEST IN BASEBALL SINCE 1919!

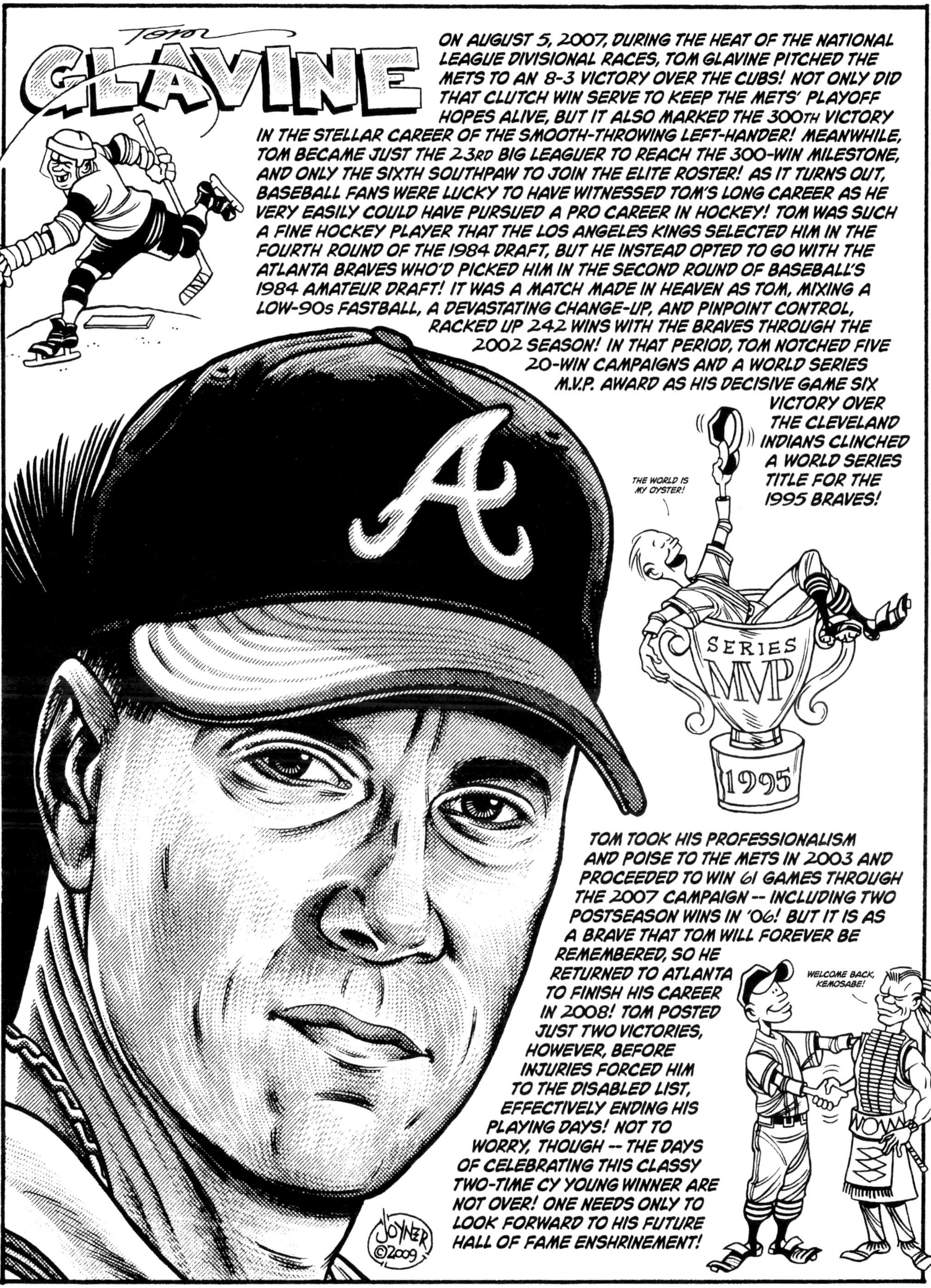
Tom
GLAVINE
ON AUGUST 5, 2007, DURING THE HEAT OF THE NATIONAL LEAGUE DIVISIONAL RACES, TOM GLAVINE PITCHED THE METS TO AN 8-3 VICTORY OVER THE CUBS! NOT ONLY DID THAT CLUTCH WIN SERVE TO KEEP THE METS' PLAYOFF HOPES ALIVE, BUT IT ALSO MARKED THE 300TH VICTORY IN THE STELLAR CAREER OF THE SMOOTH-THROWING LEFT-HANDER! MEANWHILE, TOM BECAME JUST THE 23RD BIG LEAGUER TO REACH THE 300-WIN MILESTONE, AND ONLY THE SIXTH SOUTHPAW TO JOIN THE ELITE ROSTER! AS IT TURNS OUT, BASEBALL FANS WERE LUCKY TO HAVE WITNESSED TOM'S LONG CAREER AS HE VERY EASILY COULD HAVE PURSUED A PRO CAREER IN HOCKEY! TOM WAS SUCH A FINE HOCKEY PLAYER THAT THE LOS ANGELES KINGS SELECTED HIM IN THE FOURTH ROUND OF THE 1984 DRAFT, BUT HE INSTEAD OPTED TO GO WITH THE ATLANTA BRAVES WHO'D PICKED HIM IN THE SECOND ROUND OF BASEBALL'S 1984 AMATEUR DRAFT! IT WAS A MATCH MADE IN HEAVEN AS TOM, MIXING A LOW-90s FASTBALL, A DEVASTATING CHANGE-UP, AND PINPOINT CONTROL, RACKED UP 242 WINS WITH THE BRAVES THROUGH THE 2002 SEASON! IN THAT PERIOD, TOM NOTCHED FIVE 20-WIN CAMPAIGNS AND A WORLD SERIES M.V.P. AWARD AS HIS DECISIVE GAME SIX VICTORY OVER THE CLEVELAND INDIANS CLINCHED A WORLD SERIES TITLE FOR THE 1995 BRAVES!
THE WORLD IS MY OYSTER!
SERIES MVP
1995
TOM TOOK HIS PROFESSIONALISM AND POISE TO THE METS IN 2003 AND PROCEEDED TO WIN 61 GAMES THROUGH THE 2007 CAMPAIGN -- INCLUDING TWO POSTSEASON WINS IN '06! BUT IT IS AS A BRAVE THAT TOM WILL FOREVER BE REMEMBERED, SO HE RETURNED TO ATLANTA TO FINISH HIS CAREER IN 2008! TOM POSTED JUST TWO VICTORIES, HOWEVER, BEFORE INJURIES FORCED HIM TO THE DISABLED LIST, EFFECTIVELY ENDING HIS PLAYING DAYS! NOT TO WORRY, THOUGH -- THE DAYS OF CELEBRATING THIS CLASSY TWO-TIME CY YOUNG WINNER ARE NOT OVER! ONE NEEDS ONLY TO LOOK FORWARD TO HIS FUTURE HALL OF FAME ENSHRINEMENT!
WELCOME BACK, KEMOSABE!
JOYNER ©2009

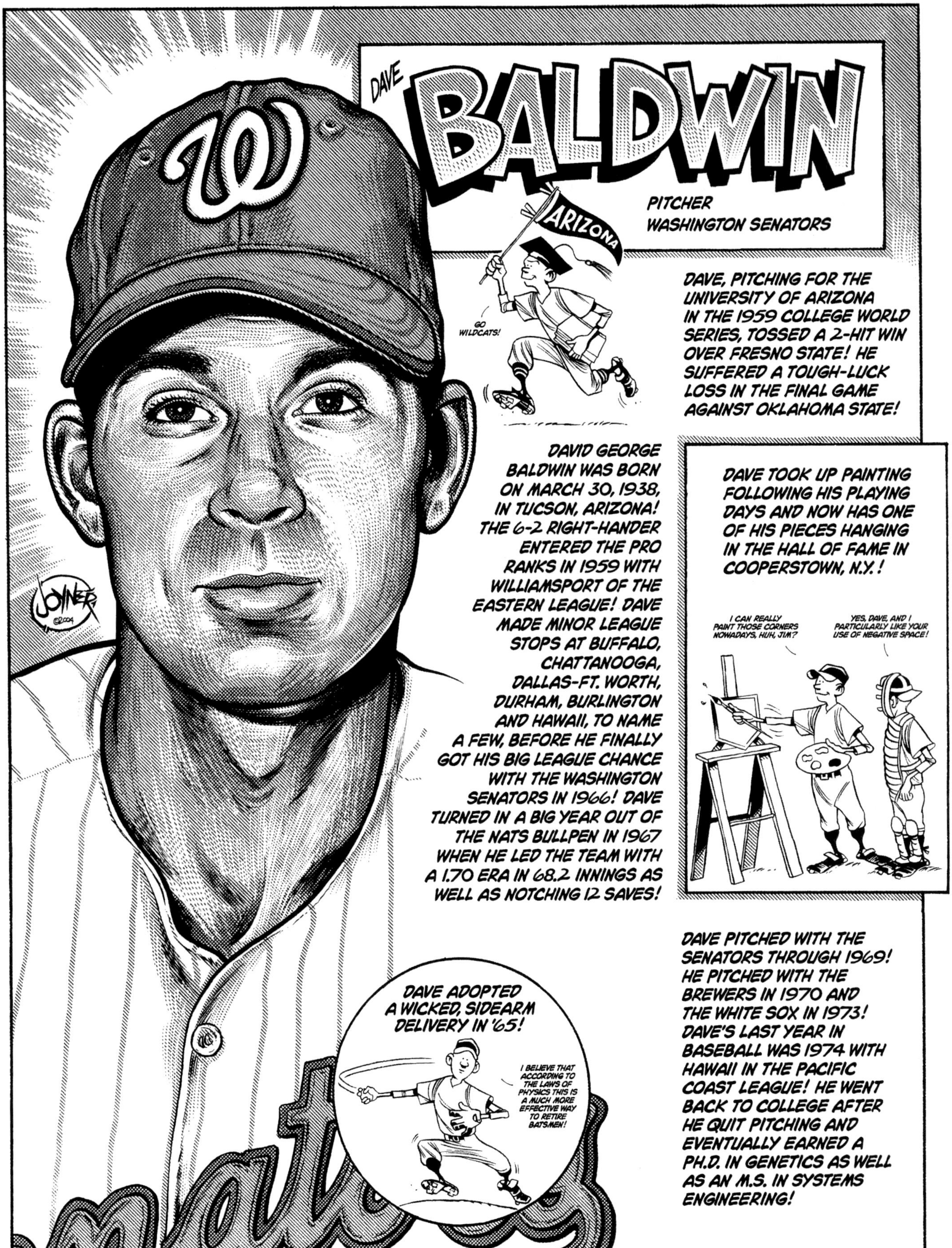
DAVE
BALDWIN
PITCHER
WASHINGTON SENATORS
ARIZONA
GO WILDCATS!
DAVE, PITCHING FOR THE UNIVERSITY OF ARIZONA IN THE 1959 COLLEGE WORLD SERIES, TOSSED A 2-HIT WIN OVER FRESNO STATE! HE SUFFERED A TOUGH-LUCK LOSS IN THE FINAL GAME AGAINST OKLAHOMA STATE!
DAVID GEORGE BALDWIN WAS BORN ON MARCH 30, 1938, IN TUCSON, ARIZONA! THE 6-2 RIGHT-HANDER ENTERED THE PRO RANKS IN 1959 WITH WILLIAMSPORT OF THE EASTERN LEAGUE! DAVE MADE MINOR LEAGUE STOPS AT BUFFALO, CHATTANOOGA, DALLAS-FT. WORTH, DURHAM, BURLINGTON AND HAWAII, TO NAME A FEW, BEFORE HE FINALLY GOT HIS BIG LEAGUE CHANCE WITH THE WASHINGTON SENATORS IN 1966! DAVE TURNED IN A BIG YEAR OUT OF THE NATS BULLPEN IN 1967 WHEN HE LED THE TEAM WITH A 1.70 ERA IN 68.2 INNINGS AS WELL AS NOTCHING 12 SAVES!
DAVE TOOK UP PAINTING FOLLOWING HIS PLAYING DAYS AND NOW HAS ONE OF HIS PIECES HANGING IN THE HALL OF FAME IN COOPERSTOWN, N.Y.!
I CAN REALLY PAINT THOSE CORNERS NOWADAYS, HUH, JIM?
YES, DAVE, AND I PARTICULARLY LIKE YOUR USE OF NEGATIVE SPACE!
DAVE ADOPTED A WICKED, SIDEARM DELIVERY IN '65!
I BELIEVE THAT ACCORDING TO THE LAWS OF PHYSICS THIS IS A MUCH MORE EFFECTIVE WAY TO RETIRE BATSMEN!
DAVE PITCHED WITH THE SENATORS THROUGH 1969! HE PITCHED WITH THE BREWERS IN 1970 AND THE WHITE SOX IN 1973! DAVE'S LAST YEAR IN BASEBALL WAS 1974 WITH HAWAII IN THE PACIFIC COAST LEAGUE! HE WENT BACK TO COLLEGE AFTER HE QUIT PITCHING AND EVENTUALLY EARNED A PH.D. IN GENETICS AS WELL AS AN M.S. IN SYSTEMS ENGINEERING!

Jim
BROSNAN
I LOVE THE MOUNTAIN AIR!
PITCHER -- CINCINNATI REDS
IN HIS 1947 SEASON WITH ELIZABETHTON IN THE APPALACHIAN LEAGUE, JIM BROSNAN WON 17 AND LOST ONLY 8 WHILE STRIKING OUT 171!
BORN ON OCTOBER 29, 1929 IN CINCINNATI, OHIO, JAMES PATRICK BROSNAN MADE IT TO THE BIG LEAGUES IN 1954 WITH THE CHICAGO CUBS! THE 6' 4" RIGHT-HANDER SAW ACTION IN 18 GAMES FOR THE CUBBIES THAT YEAR AND WAS BACK IN THE MINORS IN 1955 FOR MORE SEASONING! BY 1956 "THE PROFESSOR" WAS IN THE MAJORS TO STAY! USED MOSTLY THROUGHOUT HIS CAREER AS A RELIEVER, BROSNAN WAS ALWAYS CONSISTENT AND RELIABLE DURING HIS 9-YEAR CAREER! AFTER HIS ROOKIE SEASON OF 1954 HE NEVER PITCHED TO AN ERA OVER 3.79! AFTER SPENDING 1954-57 WITH THE CUBS, BROSNAN WAS DEALT TO THE ST. LOUIS CARDINALS DURING THE 1958 CAMPAIGN! BROSNAN WAS AGAIN DEALT IN MID-SEASON OF 1959 -- THIS TIME TO HIS HOMETOWN CINCINNATI REDS! HE DID SOME OF HIS FINEST WORK ON THE MOUND FOR THE REDS FROM '59-63! IN 1961 BROSNAN HELPED THE REDS REACH THE WORLD SERIES BY PITCHING TO A 10-4 RECORD OUT OF THE BULLPEN WITH A STELLAR 3.04 ERA!
THE PROFESSOR APPEARED IN 57 GAMES FOR THE 1960 REDS PITCHING TO 2.36 ERA!
BROSNAN PITCHED FOR NINE YEARS IN THE MAJOR LEAGUES COMPILING A RECORD OF 55 WINS AND 47 LOSSES WITH A LIFETIME ERA OF 3.54! JIM BLAZED THE WAY FOR TODAY'S RELIEF SPECIALISTS ACHIEVING THE BULK OF HIS SUCCESS FROM THE PEN!
YOU'RE NOT PUTTING ANYTHING IN THERE ABOUT THAT NIGHT AT THE EMPRESS BURLESQUE THEATER, ARE YOU JIM?
JIM BROSNAN AUTHORED MANY BOOKS ON BASEBALL INCLUDING "THE LONG SEASON"
JOYNER ©2001

Fergie JENKINS

FROM THE UNLIKELY LOCATION OF SOUTH CHATHAM, ONTARIO, CANADA, CAME A SEVEN-TIME 20-GAME WINNER -- THE GREAT FERGUSON JENKINS! FERGIE WAS A TREMENDOUS ALL-AROUND ATHLETE, AND HAD A LEGITIMATE OPPORTUNITY TO BE THE NHL's SECOND BLACK PLAYER, BUT HE CHOSE BASEBALL -- MUCH TO THE DISMAY OF BIG LEAGUE HITTERS! FERGIE CAME UP AS A RELIEVER FOR THE PHILLIES IN 1965, BUT IT WAS HIS TRADE TO THE CUBS THAT CLEARED THE WAY TO SUPERSTARDOM! CONVERTED TO A STARTER BY MANAGER LEO DUROCHER, FERGIE WON 20 GAMES FOR THE CUBBIES IN HIS FIRST FULL SEASON IN CHI-TOWN -- THEN WON 20 OR MORE FOR THE NEXT FIVE YEARS! THE TALL, HARD-THROWING RIGHT-HANDER DEFIED THE NOTION THAT WRIGLEY FIELD WAS A HITTER'S PARK, WINNING 167 GAMES FOR THE CUBS DURING HIS YEARS WITH THEM! ACTUALLY, THE KEYS TO FERGIE'S SUCCESS WOULD WORK IN ANY BALLPARK! COACH JOE BECKER SAID, "I BELIEVE THE REASON FERGIE'S SO SUCCESSFUL AT WRIGLEY IS THAT HE KEEPS THE BALL DOWN. HIS CONTROL IS GOOD, AND HE'S A LOT FASTER THAN HE LOOKS. HE'S LOOSE AND LIMBER AND REALLY WHIPS THAT BALL. IT'S ON TOP OF THE HITTER BEFORE HE REALIZES IT." AN ATHLETE THROUGH AND THROUGH, FERGIE WAS AN EXCELLENT BASKETBALL PLAYER IN HIGH SCHOOL! SO GOOD WAS HE, IN FACT, THAT HE SPENT A FEW OFFSEASONS EARLY IN HIS CAREER AS A MEMBER OF THE HARLEM GLOBETROTTERS! FURTHER PROOF THAT FERGIE WAS AN ALL-AROUND ATHLETE COULD BE FOUND IN THE FACT THAT HE COULD HIT! HIS BEST SEASON WITH THE LUMBER WAS 1971 WHEN HE BATTED .243 WITH SIX HOMERS AND 20 RBIs!

FERGUSON JENKINS RACKED UP 284 WINS BY THE TIME HIS BIG LEAGUE CAREER ENDED FOLLOWING THE 1983 SEASON! IT TOOK THE BASEBALL WRITERS A FEW MORE YEARS THAN IT SHOULD HAVE TO REALIZE THAT FERGIE WAS A SLAM DUNK HALL OF FAMER! BUT FINALLY, IN 1991, THE BASEBALL WRITERS DID THEIR DUTY AND ENSHRINED FERGIE IN COOPERSTOWN!

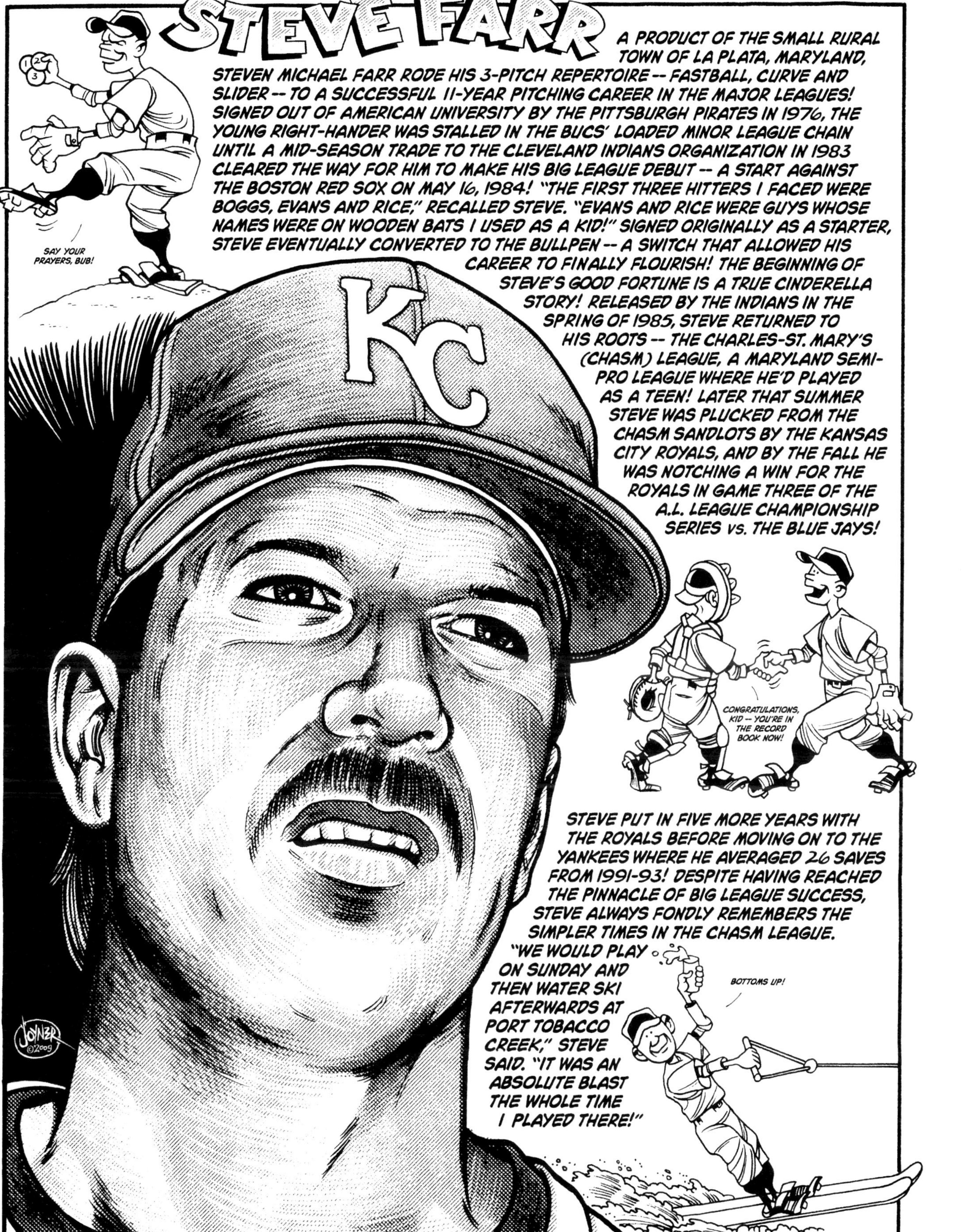
STEVE FARR
A PRODUCT OF THE SMALL RURAL TOWN OF LA PLATA, MARYLAND, STEVEN MICHAEL FARR RODE HIS 3-PITCH REPERTOIRE -- FASTBALL, CURVE AND SLIDER -- TO A SUCCESSFUL 11-YEAR PITCHING CAREER IN THE MAJOR LEAGUES! SIGNED OUT OF AMERICAN UNIVERSITY BY THE PITTSBURGH PIRATES IN 1976, THE YOUNG RIGHT-HANDER WAS STALLED IN THE BUCS' LOADED MINOR LEAGUE CHAIN UNTIL A MID-SEASON TRADE TO THE CLEVELAND INDIANS ORGANIZATION IN 1983 CLEARED THE WAY FOR HIM TO MAKE HIS BIG LEAGUE DEBUT -- A START AGAINST THE BOSTON RED SOX ON MAY 16, 1984! "THE FIRST THREE HITTERS I FACED WERE BOGGS, EVANS AND RICE," RECALLED STEVE. "EVANS AND RICE WERE GUYS WHOSE NAMES WERE ON WOODEN BATS I USED AS A KID!" SIGNED ORIGINALLY AS A STARTER, STEVE EVENTUALLY CONVERTED TO THE BULLPEN -- A SWITCH THAT ALLOWED HIS CAREER TO FINALLY FLOURISH! THE BEGINNING OF STEVE'S GOOD FORTUNE IS A TRUE CINDERELLA STORY! RELEASED BY THE INDIANS IN THE SPRING OF 1985, STEVE RETURNED TO HIS ROOTS -- THE CHARLES-ST. MARY'S (CHASM) LEAGUE, A MARYLAND SEMI-PRO LEAGUE WHERE HE'D PLAYED AS A TEEN! LATER THAT SUMMER STEVE WAS PLUCKED FROM THE CHASM SANDLOTS BY THE KANSAS CITY ROYALS, AND BY THE FALL HE WAS NOTCHING A WIN FOR THE ROYALS IN GAME THREE OF THE A.L. LEAGUE CHAMPIONSHIP SERIES vs. THE BLUE JAYS!
SAY YOUR PRAYERS, BUB!
KC
CONGRATULATIONS, KID -- YOU'RE IN THE RECORD BOOK NOW!
STEVE PUT IN FIVE MORE YEARS WITH THE ROYALS BEFORE MOVING ON TO THE YANKEES WHERE HE AVERAGED 26 SAVES FROM 1991-93! DESPITE HAVING REACHED THE PINNACLE OF BIG LEAGUE SUCCESS, STEVE ALWAYS FONDLY REMEMBERS THE SIMPLER TIMES IN THE CHASM LEAGUE. "WE WOULD PLAY ON SUNDAY AND THEN WATER SKI AFTERWARDS AT PORT TOBACCO CREEK," STEVE SAID. "IT WAS AN ABSOLUTE BLAST THE WHOLE TIME I PLAYED THERE!"
BOTTOMS UP!
JOYNER ©2009

Tim Drummond

BORN IN LA PLATA, MARYLAND, ON CHRISTMAS EVE OF 1964, TIMOTHY DARNELL DRUMMOND WOULD MAKE HIS SMALL HOMETOWN PROUD WHEN HE BEAT THE ODDS AND MADE IT ALL THE WAY TO THE MAJOR LEAGUES! THE HARD-THROWING RIGHT-HANDER WAS SIGNED OUT OF THOMAS STONE HIGH SCHOOL BY LEGENDARY PITTSBURGH PIRATES SCOUT JOE CONSOLI AFTER BEING TAKEN IN THE 12TH ROUND OF THE 1983 AMATEUR DRAFT!

TIM WAS CONVERTED TO A RELIEVER WHILE DOWN ON THE PIRATES FARM IN 1986--AND HE RESPONDED BY POSTING FINE SEASONS IN 1986 AND '87! THAT EARNED TIM AN END-OF-SEASON CALL-UP TO THE BUCS THAT SAW HIM PITCH IN SIX GAMES! HIS DEBUT CAME ON SEPTEMBER 12, 1987 VS. THE PHILLIES, AND THE FIRST MAN TIM FACED WAS THE GREAT MIKE SCHMIDT! "I WAS SO NERVOUS I DIDN'T EVEN SEE A BATTER -- JUST A CATCHER'S MITT THE SIZE OF A TRASH CAN," TIM RECALLED! TIM RETIRED SCHMIDT AND THE OTHER FIVE PHILS HE FACED THAT DAY TO START HIS BIG LEAGUE CAREER OFF RIGHT! HE WAS WITH THE TWINS IN 1990 WHEN HE LOGGED HIS CAREER-BEST MAJOR LEAGUE CAMPAIGN WHILE APPEARING IN 35 GAMES! EDGED OFF THE '91 TWINS ROSTER BY THE ARRIVAL OF HIGH-PRICED FREE AGENT STEVE BEDROSIAN, TIM RETURNED TO THE MINORS WHICH INCLUDED STOPS AT ROCHESTER AND HAGERSTOWN -- TWO CLUBS IN THE FARM SYSTEM OF TIM'S HOMETOWN TEAM, THE BALTIMORE ORIOLES!

RELEASED BY BALTIMORE PRIOR TO THE 1993 SEASON, TIM RETURNED HOME TO PLAY BALL WHERE IT ALL BEGAN FOR HIM A DECADE EARLIER -- THE SEMI-PRO CHARLES-ST. MARY'S (CHASM) LEAGUE IN MARYLAND! HOWEVER, THREE GAMES INTO HIS SEMI-PRO RETURN, TIM SUFFERED A CAREER-ENDING ELBOW INJURY! BECAUSE OF THAT, TIM PLAYED IN VERY FEW GAMES AT THE CHASM LEAGUE'S HISTORIC LEGION FIELD, BUT HE RECALLS THE PARK AS "A GREAT SETTING!" TIM WAS A HARD WORKER AND LEFT IT ALL ON THE FIELD -- SOMETHING TO WHICH ALL BALLPLAYERS SHOULD STRIVE!

Randy GUMPERT
ON JANUARY 23, 1918, ON A SEVEN-ACRE FARM IN MONOCACY, PENNSYLVANIA, RANDALL PENNINGTON GUMPERT WAS BORN! BY THE AGE OF 16 RANDY HAD GROWN TO 6-FOOT-3 AND 185 LBS -- PLUS HE'D DEVELOPED A MIGHTY FINE PITCHING WING! A LETTER FROM HIS FATHER TO CONNIE MACK PROMPTED THE ATHLETICS MANAGER TO TAKE A LOOK AT THE TEENAGE CHUCKER! IMPRESSED WITH WHAT HE SAW, MACK LET THE KID PITCH BATTING PRACTICE FOR TWO SEASONS WHILE HE FURTHER DEVELOPED! MACK SIGNED RANDY IN 1936 FOR $300 A MONTH, THEN IMMEDIATELY THREW THE YOUNG RIGHTY INTO THE BIG LEAGUE FIRE WITHOUT EVER PITCHING AN INNING IN THE MINOR LEAGUES! RANDY APPEARED IN 22 GAMES FOR THE 1936 ATHLETICS, ALL IN RELIEF, WITH THE EXCEPTION OF THREE STARTS IN LATE AUGUST AND EARLY SEPTEMBER!
RANDY, WHILE PITCHING FOR THE CHISOX IN 1951, GAVE UP THE FIRST HOME RUN HIT BY FUTURE HALL OF FAMER MICKEY MANTLE! "HE HIT A SCREWBALL THAT DIDN'T SCREW AS MUCH AS IT SHOULD HAVE," SAID RANDY. "HE HIT IT INTO THE CENTERFIELD BULLPEN AT COMISKEY PARK WHERE YANKEE BACKUP CATCHER CHARLIE SILVERA CAUGHT IT."
WHAT'S THIS – MANTLE'S FIRST HOME RUN BALL? I'D SAVE IT IF I THOUGHT IT'D BE WORTH SOMETHING ONE DAY, BUT THERE'S NO FUTURE IN BASEBALL MEMORABILIA!
PLOP!
RANDY PITCHED FOR TEN SEASONS IN THE BIGS, MISSING 1943 THROUGH 1945 TO SERVE OUR COUNTRY IN WORLD WAR II! RANDY'S BEST CAMPAIGN WAS WITH THE 1946 YANKS WHEN HE WON ELEVEN WHILE LOSING ONLY THREE WITH A MAGNIFICENT 2.31 ERA!
ONE OF 18-YEAR-OLD RANDY'S 1936 STARTS WAS AGAINST 17-YEAR-OLD BOB FELLER! NEVER BEFORE OR SINCE HAD A BIG LEAGUE GAME FEATURED SUCH A YOUNG MATCH-UP OF STARTING HURLERS! RANDY WENT THE FULL NINE, BUT LOST AS THE FIREBALLER FROM IOWA STRUCK OUT 17 A's BATSMEN! RANDY'S LUCK WASN'T ALL BAD IN 1936, HOWEVER, AND ON AUGUST 27TH HE REELED OFF A SPECTACULAR 2-HIT WIN OVER THE CHICAGO WHITE SOX AT SHIBE PARK!
JOYNER ©2006

ELI GRBA

BORN IN CHICAGO ON AUGUST 9, 1934, RIGHT-HANDED HURLER ELI GRBA HIT THE BIG LEAGUES WITH THE 1959 YANKEES! HE RETIRED THE RED SOX 1-2-3 IN HIS FIRST APPEARANCE -- THE THIRD OUT COMING ON A CALLED STRIKE THREE TO THE GREAT TED WILLIAMS! "GRBA," IN THE WORDS OF SPORTSWRITER BOB ADDIE, SOUNDED LIKE THE "STENGELESE" OFTEN SPOKEN BY THE YANKEE SKIPPER, BUT ELI'S NAME WAS GOLDEN TO CASEY IN 1960 AS GRBA TURNED IN A FINE SEASON FOR THE A.L. PENNANT WINNERS! ELI WAS LEFT UNPROTECTED FOR THE 1961 EXPANSION DRAFT -- SO THE ANGELS SCOOPED HIM UP WITH THE FIRST PICK! ELI QUICKLY NOTCHED THE FRANCHISE'S FIRST WIN, THEN PROCEEDED TO REEL OFF TEN MORE WINS ON THE SEASON! ELI WAS KNOWN AS MUCH FOR HIS TEMPER AS HIS HEATER, AND HE SHOWED IT ON APRIL 20, 1961, IN HIS FIRST GAME AGAINST HIS FORMER TEAMMATES! HOPING FOR AN EASY DAY WITH YANK SLUGGER MICKEY MANTLE AFTER HEARING THAT THE MICK HAD A BAD HANGOVER, ELI INSTEAD SURRENDERED TWO LONG HOMERS TO THE COMMERCE COMET! "ELI CHASED MICKEY AROUND THE BASES, SHOUTING OBSCENITIES AT HIM ALL THE WAY," RECALLED ANGELS OUTFIELDER KEN HUNT. "MANTLE HIT HOME PLATE, WITH ELI RIGHT BEHIND HIM, STUMBLED INTO THE DUGOUT AND FELL DOWN LAUGHING. I'VE NEVER SEEN ELI SO ANGRY."

AT 6-FOOT-2 205-LBS, ELI WAS AN IMPOSING SIGHT ON THE MOUND! FEARLESS AGAINST ENEMY BATSMEN, ELI WAS NOT SO STRONG WHEN IT CAME TO BOOZE. AFTER DECADES AS AN ALCOHOLIC -- AN ADDICTION THAT SURELY SHORTENED HIS CAREER -- ELI FINALLY WON HIS BATTLE WITH WITH THE BOTTLE AND HAS BEEN SOBER SINCE 1981!

DESPITE HIS SETBACK AT THE HANDS OF THE MICK, GRBA HAS GREAT FONDNESS FOR HIS TIME WITH NEW YORK! "HOW MANY GUYS CALLED 'ELI GRBA' CAN SAY THEY PLAYED WITH THE YANKEES?" LAUGHED GRBA. "NOT TOO MANY!"

Bob FELLER
AN IOWA FARMER PLOWS UP PART OF HIS LAND TO BUILD A BALLFIELD FOR HIS YOUNG SON! STUNNED BY THE YOUNGSTER'S GOLDEN ARM, THE CLEVELAND INDIANS SIGN THE KID BY GIVING HIM A BONUS CONSISTING OF ONE DOLLAR AND A TEAM-SIGNED BASEBALL! THE KID BECOMES A MAJOR LEAGUE SENSATION, SETTING STRIKEOUT RECORDS WHILE STILL IN HIGH SCHOOL! THE KID QUITS THE GAME AT HIS PEAK TO FIGHT FOR HIS COUNTRY IN WORLD WAR II! HE RETURNS FROM THE WAR A HIGHLY-DECORATED COMBAT VETERAN, THEN, DESPITE THE ODDS, RECLAIMS HIS PLACE AS ONE OF BASEBALL'S BEST PITCHERS! COUNTLESS AWARDS, A WORLD SERIES RING, FINANCIAL SUCCESS, AND THE HALL OF FAME FOLLOW! IT MAY SOUND LIKE FICTION -- BUT IT'S NOT! IT'S THE STORY OF ROBERT WILLIAM ANDREW FELLER -- ONE OF THE GAME'S GREATEST EVER!
DON'T LET THE MONEY BURN A HOLE IN YOUR POCKET, KID!
HERE COMES A HEATER FROM VAN METER!
JOYNER ©2010
BOB HAD A ROCKET LAUNCHER FOR A RIGHT ARM! USING PRIMITIVE SPEED MEASURING TECHNOLOGIES OF THE TIME, BOB WAS CLOCKED THROWING 98.6 M.P.H. -- BUT MOST FOLKS THINK HE THREW WELL OVER 100 M.P.H.! BOB ALSO POSSESSED A WICKED CURVE BALL THAT MADE HIS "HEATER FROM VAN METER" ALL THE MORE DEVASTATING! BOB HAD JUST COMPLETED HIS THIRD STRAIGHT 20-PLUS-WIN SEASON WHEN HE BECAME THE FIRST MAJOR LEAGUER TO ENLIST FOLLOWING THE JAPANESE ATTACK ON PEARL HARBOR! BOB LOST NEARLY FOUR FULL SEASONS WHILE SERVING ABOARD THE USS ALABAMA -- BUT HE DIDN'T REGRET A MINUTE OF IT! INSTEAD, HE CONSIDERED HIS NAVY SERVICE HIS PROUDEST ACHIEVEMENT! THAT SAID, BOB'S MAJOR LEAGUE RECORD WAS SOMETHING TO BE PROUD OF, TOO -- 266 WINS AGAINST JUST 162 LOSSES AND 2,581 STRIKEOUTS! WHEN BOB FELLER PASSED AWAY ON DECEMBER 15, 2010, AT THE AGE OF 92, BASEBALL LOST A TRUE ICON OF THE GAME -- AND AMERICA LOST A PATRIOT FROM THE GREATEST GENERATION!
SO LONG FOLKS! IT'S BEEN A GREAT RIDE!
FELLER
19

Al Worthington

AL WORTHINGTON WAS A MULTI-SPORT ATHLETE AT THE UNIVERSITY OF ALABAMA, BUT IT WAS IN BASEBALL, WHICH WASN'T EVEN HIS FAVORITE SPORT, WHERE HE'D LEAVE A FINE LEGACY! AFTER JUST 2-1/2 YEARS IN THE BUSHES, AL WAS BROUGHT UP BY THE NEW YORK GIANTS WHERE HE PROCEEDED TO MAKE QUITE A SPLASH BY CHUCKING BACK-TO-BACK SHUTOUTS IN HIS FIRST TWO APPEARANCES! THE 6-FOOT-2-INCH 195-LB RIGHT-HANDER FIRST WHITEWASHED THE PHILLIES 6-0 IN HIS MAJOR LEAGUE DEBUT ON JULY 6, 1953, THEN BLANKED THE DODGERS BY THE SAME SCORE IN HIS SECOND GAME JUST FIVE DAYS LATER! THINGS SLOWED TO A MORTAL PACE FOR AL AFTER THAT, BUT HE WENT ON TO RACK UP 32 WINS FOR THE GIANTS FROM 1953 THROUGH 1959!

AL DENIED THE GREAT ROBIN ROBERTS A 20-WIN SEASON BY DEFEATING PHILADELPHIA IN THE FINAL GAME OF THE 1956 SEASON! NOT KNOWN FOR HIS BAT, AL SURPRISED EVERYONE WHEN HE CLOUTED A ROBERTS OFFERING INTO THE SEATS IN LEFT FIELD FOR THE ONLY HOME RUN OF HIS 14-YEAR BIG LEAGUE CAREER! "I KNEW SOMEWHAT HOW ROBIN FELT WHEN I HIT THAT HOME RUN," AL HUMBLY SAID. "DURING MY FEW YEARS IN BASEBALL UP TO THAT TIME, I HAD MY SHARE OF HOME RUNS HIT OFF ME."

AL'S LIFE CHANGED FOREVER WHEN HE WAS "SAVED" IN 1958 AFTER HEARING BILLY GRAHAM SPEAK AT THE COW PALACE IN SAN FRANCISCO! SINCE THEN, AL HAS BEEN A DEDICATED SERVANT OF GOD, DOING HIS BEST TO SPREAD THE WORD TO AS MANY FOLKS AS POSSIBLE!

MEANWHILE, AL'S BASEBALL CAREER TOOK A DRAMATIC TURN UPWARD WHEN HE JOINED THE TWINS IN 1964 AT THE AGE OF 35! USED STRICTLY IN RELIEF, AL PITCHED BRILLIANTLY TO THE TUNE OF A 1.37 E.R.A. IN 41 APPEARANCES! HE WAS EVEN BETTER IN 1965 WHERE HIS 10-AND-7 RECORD WITH 21 SAVES AND 2.13 E.R.A. HELPED THE TWINS WIN THE A.L. PENNANT! AL CONTINUED HIS AMAZING WORK OUT OF THE MINNESOTA PEN, AVERAGING OVER 50 APPEARANCES PER SEASON UNTIL HIS RETIREMENT AFTER THE 1969 CAMPAIGN! AL JOINED JERRY FALWELL'S LIBERTY UNIVERSITY IN 1974 AND BUILT THEM, FROM SCRATCH, A TOP-FLIGHT BASEBALL PROGRAM! HE RETIRED FROM LIBERTY IN '86, AT WHICH POINT THEIR BALLPARK WAS RENAMED WORTHINGTON FIELD!

Johnny
JAMES
BORN IN BONNER'S FERRY, IDAHO, ON JULY 23, 1933, JOHN PHILLIP JAMES REFINED HIS BASEBALL ABILITY ON THE SANDLOTS OF SOUTHERN CALIFORNIA AFTER HIS FAMILY MOVED THERE WHEN HE WAS 12 YEARS OLD! JOHNNY WAS SPOTTED BY A YANKEE SCOUT IN 1952 WHILE PITCHING FOR THE U. OF SOUTHERN CALIFORNIA, WHEREUPON HE WAS QUICKLY SIGNED AND DISPATCHED TO BOISE OF THE PIONEER LEAGUE!
JUST SIGN ON THE DOTTED LINE, MY BOY!
USC
UTILIZING A LIVE SINKING FASTBALL, A NASTY SLIDER, AND GOOD CONTROL, JOHNNY WORKED HIS WAY UP THE YANKEE FARM SYSTEM AND WAS CALLED UP IN TIME TO APPEAR IN ONE GAME ON SEPTEMBER 6, 1958! IT WAS THE NATIONALLY TELEVISED "GAME OF THE WEEK," CALLED BY DIZZY DEAN AND SEEN BY MILLIONS! JOHNNY THREW 3 SCORELESS INNINGS AGAINST THE SENATORS, BUT IT WAS THE 9TH THAT PROVED PARTICULARLY AMAZING! WITH TWO ON AND NONE OUT, CLINT COURTNEY LINED INTO A TRIPLE PLAY TO END THE GAME -- McDOUGALD TO KUBEK TO SKOWRON! "IT HAPPENED SO QUICK," RECALLED JOHNNY, "THAT ALL I COULD DO WAS TURN AND WALK OFF THE FIELD WHILE DIZ WAS SAYING WHAT A GREAT PLAY I HAD MADE, 'FORCING' COURTNEY TO HIT INTO THAT TRIPLE PLAY!"
JOYNER ©2007
WOW! THIS KID REMINDS ME OF... ME!
JOHNNY WAS TRADED TO THE ANGELS AFTER APPEARING IN JUST ONE GAME FOR THE '61 YANKS! ON JUNE 12TH HE GAVE UP A HOMER TO HIS EX-TEAMMATE ROGER MARIS, NUMBER 20 ON ROGER'S WAY TO 61!
AN ARM INJURY FORCED JOHNNY FROM THE GAME PREMATURELY! BUT HE WENT ON TO BECOME A SUCCESSFUL BUSINESSMAN WHO ENJOYS FLY FISHING AND PHOTOGRAPHY! "I WAS FORTUNATE," SAYS JOHNNY, "TO HAVE TAKEN THE MOUND AND PITCHED FOR THE YANKEES."
SAY CHEESE!

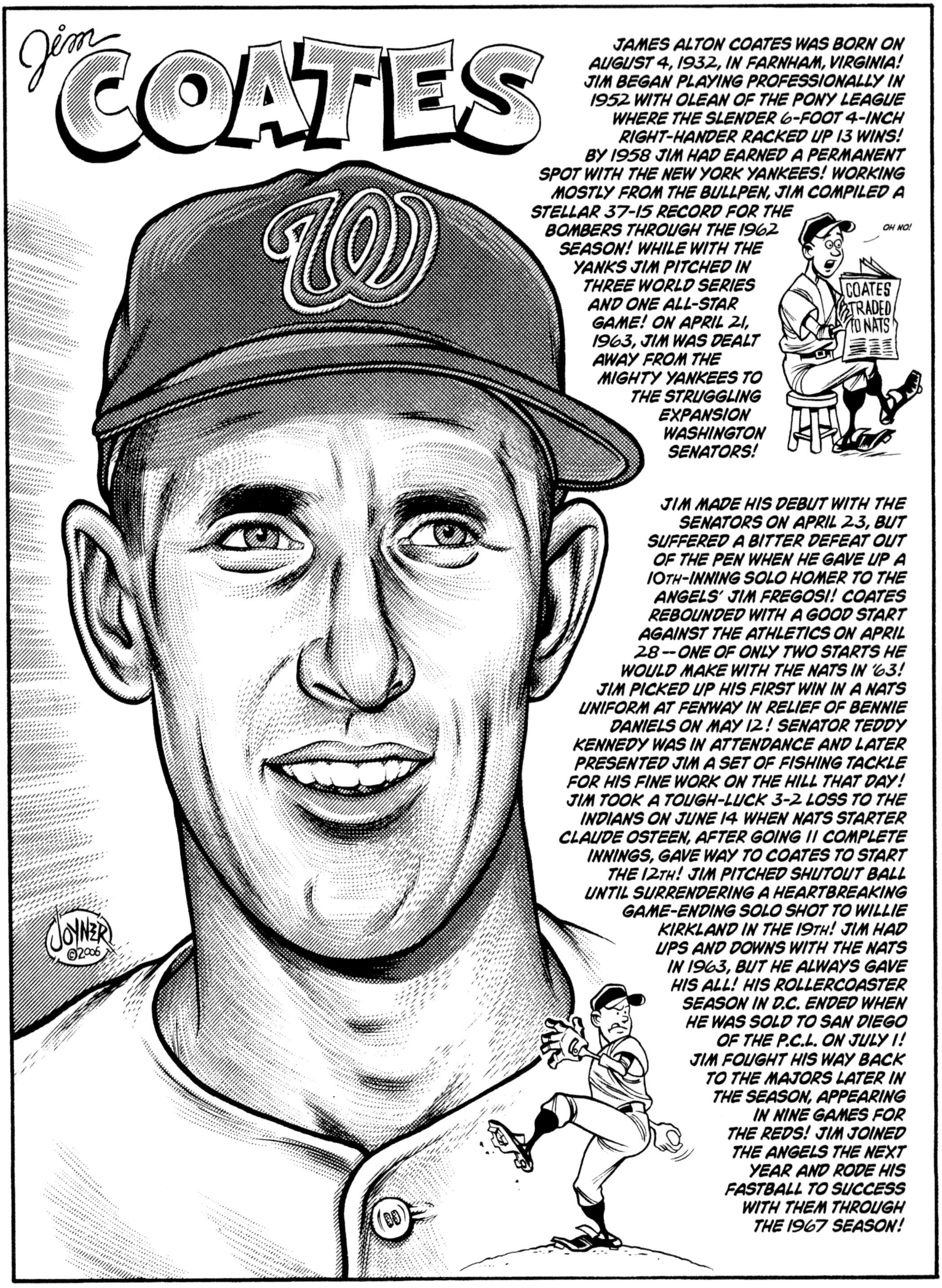
Jim COATES
JAMES ALTON COATES WAS BORN ON AUGUST 4, 1932, IN FARNHAM, VIRGINIA! JIM BEGAN PLAYING PROFESSIONALLY IN 1952 WITH OLEAN OF THE PONY LEAGUE WHERE THE SLENDER 6-FOOT 4-INCH RIGHT-HANDER RACKED UP 13 WINS! BY 1958 JIM HAD EARNED A PERMANENT SPOT WITH THE NEW YORK YANKEES! WORKING MOSTLY FROM THE BULLPEN, JIM COMPILED A STELLAR 37-15 RECORD FOR THE BOMBERS THROUGH THE 1962 SEASON! WHILE WITH THE YANKS JIM PITCHED IN THREE WORLD SERIES AND ONE ALL-STAR GAME! ON APRIL 21, 1963, JIM WAS DEALT AWAY FROM THE MIGHTY YANKEES TO THE STRUGGLING EXPANSION WASHINGTON SENATORS!
OH NO!
COATES TRADED TO NATS
JIM MADE HIS DEBUT WITH THE SENATORS ON APRIL 23, BUT SUFFERED A BITTER DEFEAT OUT OF THE PEN WHEN HE GAVE UP A 10TH-INNING SOLO HOMER TO THE ANGELS' JIM FREGOSI! COATES REBOUNDED WITH A GOOD START AGAINST THE ATHLETICS ON APRIL 28 -- ONE OF ONLY TWO STARTS HE WOULD MAKE WITH THE NATS IN '63! JIM PICKED UP HIS FIRST WIN IN A NATS UNIFORM AT FENWAY IN RELIEF OF BENNIE DANIELS ON MAY 12! SENATOR TEDDY KENNEDY WAS IN ATTENDANCE AND LATER PRESENTED JIM A SET OF FISHING TACKLE FOR HIS FINE WORK ON THE HILL THAT DAY! JIM TOOK A TOUGH-LUCK 3-2 LOSS TO THE INDIANS ON JUNE 14 WHEN NATS STARTER CLAUDE OSTEEN, AFTER GOING 11 COMPLETE INNINGS, GAVE WAY TO COATES TO START THE 12TH! JIM PITCHED SHUTOUT BALL UNTIL SURRENDERING A HEARTBREAKING GAME-ENDING SOLO SHOT TO WILLIE KIRKLAND IN THE 19TH! JIM HAD UPS AND DOWNS WITH THE NATS IN 1963, BUT HE ALWAYS GAVE HIS ALL! HIS ROLLERCOASTER SEASON IN D.C. ENDED WHEN HE WAS SOLD TO SAN DIEGO OF THE P.C.L. ON JULY 1! JIM FOUGHT HIS WAY BACK TO THE MAJORS LATER IN THE SEASON, APPEARING IN NINE GAMES FOR THE REDS! JIM JOINED THE ANGELS THE NEXT YEAR AND RODE HIS FASTBALL TO SUCCESS WITH THEM THROUGH THE 1967 SEASON!
JOYNER ©2006

DAVE "BOO" FERRIS

THE SON OF COTTON FARMERS W.D. AND LELLIE FERRIS, DAVID MEADOW FERRIS WAS BORN ON DECEMBER 5, 1921, IN SHAW, MISSISSIPPI! DAVID, AS A TODDLER, LIKED TO ADDRESS HIS OLDER BROTHER WILL D. AS "BROTHER," BUT HE ALWAYS MISPRONOUNCED IT AS "BOO!" THAT SOON BECAME THE YOUNG BOY'S NICKNAME, AND IT STUCK WITH HIM FOREVER! BASEBALL FANS, HOWEVER, WOULD HAVE NO PROBLEM WITH BOO'S NAME, AS IT WAS ALWAYS ON THE TIPS OF THEIR TONGUES WHILE HE DOMINATED THE AMERICAN LEAGUE FROM 1945-46!

BOO'S FATHER PLAYED, COACHED, AND UMPIRED BASEBALL, AND HE PASSED HIS LOVE OF THE GAME ON TO HIS SON! BOO QUICKLY DEVELOPED INTO QUITE A PLAYER, AND AT THE AGE OF 13 HE WAS PULLED OUT OF THE STANDS AND ASKED TO PLAY SECOND BASE FOR THE HIGH SCHOOL TEAM! BOO, A RIGHT-HANDED THROWER, BROKE HIS RIGHT WRIST IN THAT GAME AFTER BEING BOWLED OVER BY AN OPPOSING PLAYER! HE SPENT THE REST OF THE SUMMER LEARNING HOW TO THROW SOUTHPAW, EVENTUALLY BECOMING PROFICIENT ENOUGH TO PLAY 1st BASE LEFT-HANDED AS WELL AS PITCHING AN OCCASIONAL B.P. SESSION FROM THE LEFT SIDE!

BOO WAS ON TRACK FOR ANOTHER FINE YEAR IN 1947 WHEN A SHOULDER INJURY SLOWED HIM! HE PITCHED THROUGH THE PAIN, BUT THE ARM WAS NEVER RIGHT AGAIN, CUTTING SHORT WHAT HAD BEEN A VERY PROMISING BIG LEAGUE CAREER!

BOO GOT HIS FEET WET IN THE PRO RANKS WHEN HE PITCHED FOR GREENSBORO IN 1942! FROM 1943-44 BOO WAS IN THE ARMY AIR FORCE UNTIL A RECURRENCE OF AN OLD ASTHMA CONDITION FORCED HIS MEDICAL DISCHARGE IN FEBRUARY OF 1945! HE THEN STORMED ONTO THE BIG LEAGUE SCENE BY WINNING 21 GAMES AS A ROOKIE WITH THE '45 RED SOX! THE STRAPPING 6-FOOT 2-INCH 210-POUND FERRIS WAS EVEN BETTER IN 1946, COPPING 25 WINS AND HELPING THE SOX TO THEIR FIRST A.L. PENNANT SINCE 1918! BOO PITCHED A 4-0 SHUTOUT TO WIN GAME THREE OF THE '46 SERIES, OVERPOWERING THE CARDINALS HITTERS WHILE ALLOWING JUST SIX HITS!

IN 1959 BOO ACCEPTED A JOB AT DELTA STATE AS THEIR BASEBALL COACH AND ATHLETIC DIRECTOR! IN 26 SEASONS THERE HE COACHED HIS TEAMS TO A RECORD OF 639 WINS AGAINST 387 LOSSES! IN 2004 DELTA STATE WON THE NCAA D-II NATIONAL TITLE!

JOYNER ©2006

Tex CLEVENGER

TRUMAN "TEX" CLEVENGER WAS NOT FROM TEXAS. "I WAS WITH THE RED SOX ORGANIZATION IN THE EARLY 1950s," TEX TOLD MAURY ALLEN IN 2004. "I WAS TALL AND PRETTY LANKY AND HAD SORT OF A SIDEARM MOTION. JOHNNY PESKY, AN INFIELDER WITH THE CLUB, SAW ME PITCH AND SAID THAT I PITCHED LIKE ONE OF HIS GREAT OLD TEAMMATES, TEX HUGHSON. HE BEGAN CALLING ME TEX, AND IT STUCK. WHEN I TOLD GUYS I WAS FROM CALIFORNIA AND HAD NEVER BEEN TO TEXAS, THEY LOOKED AT ME KIND OF FUNNY. IT WAS ALWAYS GOOD FOR A LAUGH. I USED TO SAY THAT IT WAS BETTER THAN BEING FROM LOUISIANA. THEN THE PLAYERS WOULD HAVE CALLED ME LOUISE." TEX MOVED FROM THE RED SOX TO THE SENATORS FOR A FIVE-YEAR STINT THAT RAN FROM 1956 THROUGH 1959. THOSE WERE TOUGH YEARS FOR THE NATS, BUT TEX STILL MANAGED TO COMPILE A NEAR-500 RECORD OF 29-AND-31 DURING THAT SPAN. "WASHINGTON WAS A BAD BALLCLUB," TEX SAID, "AND I DIDN'T GET A LOT OF SUPPORT THERE. I COULDN'T MAKE MUCH MONEY PITCHING FOR THE SENATORS, BUT AT LEAST I WAS IN THE BIG LEAGUES." THE NATS LEFT TEX UNPROTECTED FOR THE 1961 EXPANSION DRAFT, AND HE WAS TAKEN BY THE ANGELS. TEX PITCHED IN JUST 12 GAMES FOR THE '61 HALOS, BUT HE WAS SO SHARP THAT THE YANKEES TRADED FOR HIM IN MAY. TEX, PITCHING STRICTLY IN RELIEF, HELPED THE YANKS TO WORLD SERIES TITLES IN '61 AND '62. "IT WAS EXCITING TO BE PART OF THAT YANKEES TEAM," TEX SAID. "I'LL NEVER FORGET THE DAY ROGER HIT THE HOME RUN TO BREAK THE RUTH RECORD."

AUGUST 14, 1959: TEX GOT HIS FIRST START AFTER 33 RELIEF APPEARANCES. HIS MISSION -- TO BREAK THE NATS' MISERABLE 18-GAME LOSING STREAK. HIS FIRST PITCH OF THE GAME HIT INDIANS LEADOFF-MAN BILLY MARTIN IN THE FACE, CAUSING MULTIPLE FRACTURES AND KNOCKING HIM OUT FOR THE SEASON... THEN TEX WENT ON TO SHUT OUT THE TRIBE ON JUST SEVEN HITS.

GENE CONLEY

DONALD EUGENE CONLEY'S BIG LEAGUE CAREER HAD A RATHER QUIET BEGINNING WHEN THE ROOKIE RIGHT-HANDER WENT 0-AND-3 IN FOUR GAMES FOR THE 1952 BOSTON BRAVES, BUT BY THE TIME HE RETIRED FROM PRO SPORTS IN 1964, MANY CONSIDERED HIM ONE OF THE GREATEST ATHLETES OF ALL TIME! WHY? BECAUSE GENE ACCOMPLISHED SOMETHING NO ONE ELSE HAS EVER DONE... HE WON CHAMPIONSHIP RINGS IN TWO MAJOR PROFESSIONAL SPORTS -- BASEBALL AND BASKETBALL! BORN ON NOVEMBER 10, 1930, IN MUSKOGEE, OKLAHOMA, GENE AND HIS FAMILY MOVED TO RICHLAND, WASHINGTON, WHEN HE WAS 12 YEARS OF AGE! A FEW SHORT YEARS LATER, GENE GRADUATED AS RICHLAND HIGH'S MOST PRODIGIOUS ATHLETE, HAVING EXCELLED IN BOTH BASEBALL AND BASKETBALL! GENE CONTINUED HIS TWO-SPORT DOMINANCE IN 1950 AS HE PITCHED WASHINGTON STATE INTO THE COLLEGE WORLD SERIES, AND THEN FOLLOWED THAT PERFORMANCE BY LEADING ALL PAC-8 HOOPSTERS IN SCORING! AN OFFER FROM BOSTON PROVED TOO GOOD TO REFUSE, SO GENE LEFT SCHOOL AND JOINED THE BRAVES' HARTFORD FARM CLUB WHERE HE WAS A 20-GAME WINNER IN 1951! NOW OUT OF SCHOOL, GENE WAS A PRIME CANDIDATE TO BE DRAFTED INTO THE KOREAN WAR, BUT WHEN THE ARMY GOT A LOOK AT HIS 6-FOOT-9 INCH FRAME, HE WAS INSTANTLY DEFERRED!

GENE WAS THE WINNING PITCHER IN THE 1955 ALL-STAR GAME!

GENE DOUBLE-DIPPED AND PLAYED IN 39 GAMES FOR THE 1952-53 CELTICS! HIS BASEBALL POTENTIAL WAS SO HIGH, HOWEVER, THAT THE BRAVES SOON BEGAN PAYING GENE NOT TO PLAY BASKETBALL IN THE OFFSEASON! GENE PROVED THE BRAVES RIGHT, TOO, BECOMING A THREE-TIME NATIONAL LEAGUE ALL-STAR, AS WELL AS CONTRIBUTING TO THE BRAVES' 1957 WORLD SERIES TITLE! AFTER A ROUGH 0-6 SEASON IN 1958, GENE RESUMED HIS OFFSEASON ACTIVITIES WITH THE CELTICS! HE PLAYED WITH THEM THROUGH 1964, HELPING THEM TO THREE CHAMPIONSHIPS! AN ARM INJURY ENDED GENE'S BASEBALL CAREER IN 1964, AND HE WAS QUITE DISTRAUGHT! SEEING CONLEY SOBBING IN A BACK PEW, A CHURCH DEACON ASKED GENE IF HE'D LOST HIS MOTHER. "NO," GENE REPLIED, "I LOST MY FASTBALL!"

Bobo HOLLOMAN

ALVA LEE HOLLOMAN, JR., WAS BORN ON MARCH 7, 1923, AT A LITTLE SPOT ON THE ROAD NEAR THOMASTON, GEORGIA, CALLED "THE ROCK"! HE WAS RAISED ON THE FAMILY FARM WHERE A STEADY DIET OF HIS MOTHER'S SOUTHERN-STYLE GREEN BEANS, TURNIP SALAD, HOECAKES, BISCUITS, AND CORN PONES GAVE HIM ALL HE NEEDED TO GROW INTO A 6-FOOT-2, 210-POUND HOSS WHO COULD FIRE A BASEBALL THROUGH A BRICK WALL! FARM LIFE SAW TO IT THAT HE WAS STRONG AS AN OX, TOO, AND BY THE AGE OF 15 HE COULD LIFT TWO BUSHELS OF SWEET POTATOES OVER HIS HEAD! ALTHOUGH STILL "GREEN AS GRASS" AFTER SERVING IN THE NAVY DURING WORLD WAR II, BOBO EMBARKED ON HIS PRO BASEBALL CAREER IN 1946! HE HAD RAW TALENT BUT WAS SOMETIMES UNDONE BY HIS TEMPER, THE WORST INCIDENT COMING IN 1950 WHEN BOBO TOOK A BAT TO THE BEAUTIFUL MAHOGANY DESK OF SALTY PARKER, HIS MANAGER AT SHREVEPORT!

WITH HIS TEMPER UNDER CONTROL, AS WELL AS HIS FASTBALL, BOBO WAS READY FOR THE MAJORS! DESPITE A SORE ARM HE'D DEVELOPED WHILE PITCHING SANTURCE TO A CHAMPIONSHIP IN THE PUERTO RICAN WINTER LEAGUE, BOBO MADE THE '53 BROWNS! HE SAW LIMITED ACTION AS A RELIEVER AND WAS FACING BEING CUT WHEN HE "PESTERED" MANAGER MARTY MARION INTO GIVING HIM A START! IT WAS MAY 6, 1953, AND BOBO RESPONDED BY TOSSING A NO-HITTER AGAINST THE A'S! WITH THAT, BOBO BECAME THE ONLY PITCHER OF THE 20TH CENTURY TO PITCH A NO-NO IN HIS FIRST BIG LEAGUE START! SADLY, BOBO'S FAIRY TALE SOON ENDED AS CONTINUED ARM MISERIES SAW HIM SENT DOWN BEFORE THE SEASON WAS OVER -- AND HE WAS OUT OF BASEBALL BY '55! HOWEVER, SOLID FAITH AND A STRONG FAMILY ALLOWED BOBO TO EVENTUALLY ACCEPT HIS PREMATURE DEPARTURE FROM THE GAME HE LOVED WITH ALL HIS HEART!

Roger CLEMENS

NICKNAMED "THE ROCKET" FOR THE BLAZING NATURE OF HIS FASTBALL, ROGER CLEMENS ENJOYED A METEORIC RISE TO THE HEIGHTS OF BASEBALL STARDOM WHEN HE WON BACK-TO-BACK CY YOUNG AWARDS IN HIS FIRST TWO FULL SEASONS IN THE BIGS -- 1986 AND 1987! SUCCESS ON THE MAJOR LEAGUE LEVEL SEEMED A CERTAINTY TO SCOUTS WHO SAW ROGER TWICE NAMED ALL-AMERICAN AT THE UNIVERSITY OF TEXAS, THEN PITCH THE LONGHORNS TO A COLLEGE WORLD SERIES CROWN IN 1983! ROGER PROVED HIS COLLEGIATE SUCCESS WAS NO FLUKE AS HE RACKED UP 192 WINS, THREE CY YOUNGS, AND AN M.V.P. AWARD WHILE WITH THE RED SOX FROM 1984 THROUGH 1996! TWICE DURING THAT SPAN -- ONCE IN 1986 AND THEN AGAIN IN 1996 -- ROGER STRUCK OUT A RECORD 20 BATTERS IN A 9-INNING GAME! IN SPITE OF THE ROCKET'S MANY ACHIEVEMENTS, SOX G.M. DAN DUQUETTE STATED THAT HE FELT ROGER WAS IN THE "TWILIGHT OF HIS CAREER" -- SO HE CHOSE NOT TO RE-SIGN THE BIG RIGHT-HANDER! ROGER RESPONDED TO THE SLIGHT BY SIGNING WITH DIVISION RIVAL TORONTO, AND THEN PUTTING TOGETHER TWO INCREDIBLE BACK-TO-BACK CAMPAIGNS THAT SAW HIM COLLECT TWO MORE CY YOUNG AWARDS! DURING THOSE TWO YEARS ROGER ALSO WON THE ELUSIVE PITCHER'S TRIPLE CROWN BY LEADING THE LEAGUE IN WINS, E.R.A., AND STRIKEOUTS! ROGER WENT ON TO HAVE MORE SUCCESS WITH THE YANKEES AND ASTROS, INCLUDING TWO WORLD SERIES TITLES WHILE WITH NEW YORK! ALREADY A SURE-BET HALL OF FAMER, ROGER SEALED THE DEAL WHEN HE JOINED THE 300-WIN CLUB WITH HIS JUNE 13, 2003 VICTORY OVER THE CARDS AT YANKEE STADIUM! CHEERING HIM ON TO GREATNESS ALL THE WHILE HAVE BEEN HIS FOUR SONS -- KOBY, KORY, KACY, AND KODY! THEIR NAMES ALL BEGIN WITH THE LETTER "K" AS A NOD TO THE WELL-KNOWN SCOREKEEPER'S SYMBOL FOR THE STRIKEOUT -- THE ROCKET'S SPECIALTY!

Ray HERBERT

RAYMOND ERNEST HERBERT WAS BORN ON DECEMBER 15, 1929, IN DETROIT, MICHIGAN! AFTER JUST TWO YEARS AT TOLEDO, RAY MADE HIS MAJOR LEAGUE DEBUT WHEN HE STARTED FOR THE TIGERS AGAINST THE ATHLETICS AT SHIBE PARK ON AUGUST 27, 1950!

RAY PUT TOGETHER AN INCREDIBLE STREAK OF FOUR CONSECUTIVE WHITEWASHES IN 1963, FINISHING WITH A LEAGUE-LEADING SEVEN!

RAY SAW ACTION IN 8 GAMES THROUGH THE LAST MONTH OF THE 1950 SEASON, AND THE PROMISING YOUNG RIGHT-HANDER WAS 4-0 OUT OF THE TIGER BULLPEN IN EARLY 1951 WHEN HE WAS DRAFTED INTO THE U.S. ARMY FOR TWO YEARS! UPON HIS RETURN TO THE BENGALS IN 1953, RAY LED THE CLUB IN APPEARANCES WITH 43, AND FOLLOWED THAT WITH 42 IN 1954! DEALT TO KANSAS CITY PRIOR TO THE '55 SEASON AND CONVERTED TO A FULLTIME STARTER BY A's SKIPPER LOU BOUDREAU, RAY GOT BETTER IN EACH OF HIS FIRST FOUR SEASONS WITH THE ATHLETICS, FINISHING THE 1960 CAMPAIGN WITH 14 WINS! ON JULY 14 OF THAT SEASON RAY SHOWED HIS FULL POTENTIAL WHEN HE SHUTOUT THE ORIOLES, 1-0, ON 4 HITS! RAY JOINED THE WHITE SOX IN MID-1961, AND IT WAS THERE THAT HE WENT ON TO DO HIS FINEST PITCHING!

WITH HELP FROM SOX PITCHING COACH RAY BERRES, HERBERT FOUND THE MAGICAL FORMULA THAT ENABLED HIM TO WIN A CAREER-HIGH 20 GAMES IN '62! NUMBER 20 OF THAT SEASON CAME IN VERY DRAMATIC FASHION ON THE LAST DAY OF THE CAMPAIGN WHEN WHITE SOX ROOKIE BRIAN McCALL HIT TWO HOMERS TO HELP RAY BEAT THE YANKEES, 8-4, AT YANKEE STADIUM! INCIDENTALLY -- THOSE WERE THE ONLY HOME RUNS McCALL EVER HIT IN THE BIG LEAGUES!

RAY'S LAST YEAR IN THE BIGS WAS 1966, BUT HE STAYED IN THE GAME AS A TIGERS BATTING PRACTICE PITCHER FROM 1967-92!

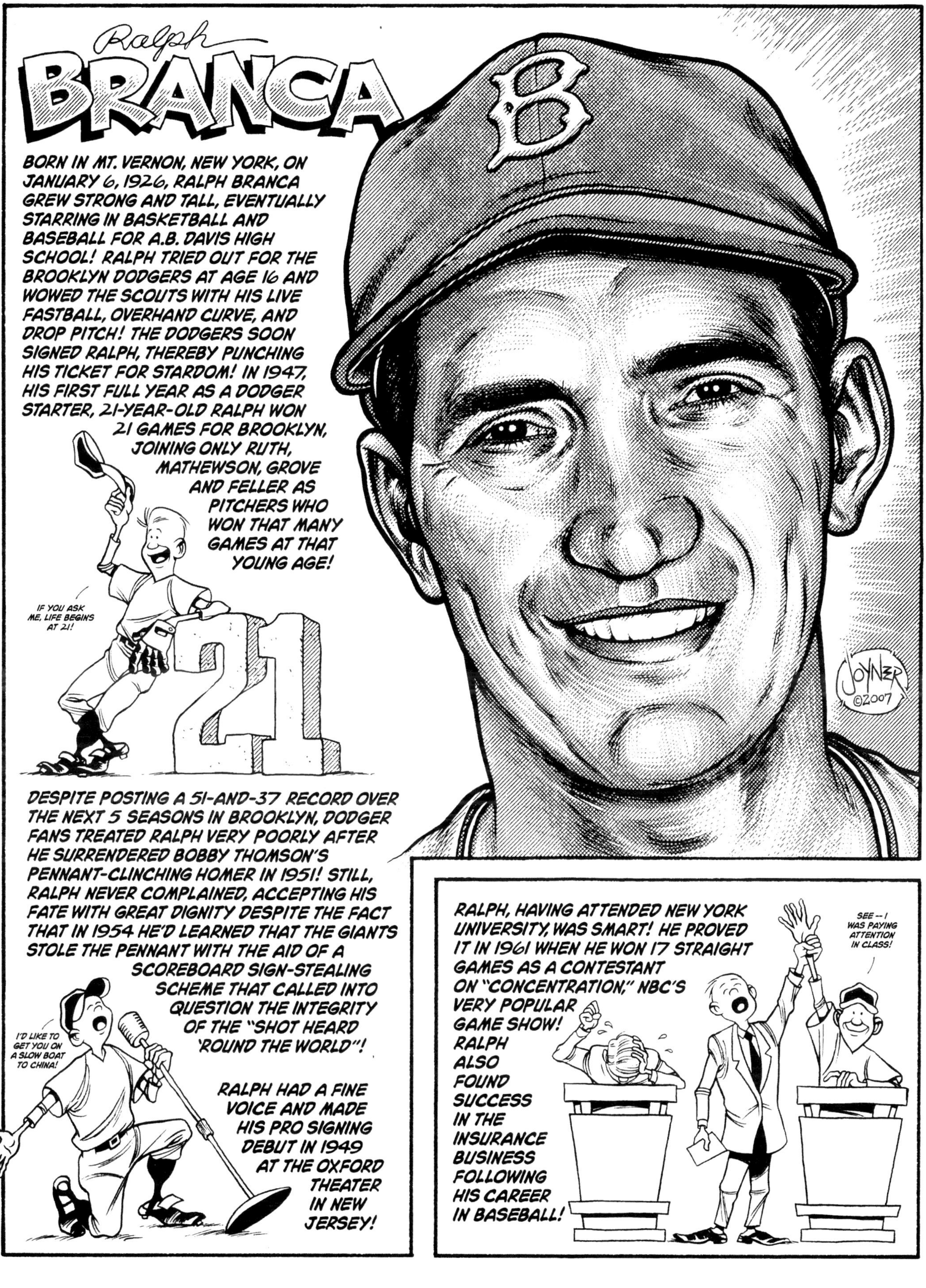
Ralph
BRANCA
BORN IN MT. VERNON, NEW YORK, ON JANUARY 6, 1926, RALPH BRANCA GREW STRONG AND TALL, EVENTUALLY STARRING IN BASKETBALL AND BASEBALL FOR A.B. DAVIS HIGH SCHOOL! RALPH TRIED OUT FOR THE BROOKLYN DODGERS AT AGE 16 AND WOWED THE SCOUTS WITH HIS LIVE FASTBALL, OVERHAND CURVE, AND DROP PITCH! THE DODGERS SOON SIGNED RALPH, THEREBY PUNCHING HIS TICKET FOR STARDOM! IN 1947, HIS FIRST FULL YEAR AS A DODGER STARTER, 21-YEAR-OLD RALPH WON 21 GAMES FOR BROOKLYN, JOINING ONLY RUTH, MATHEWSON, GROVE AND FELLER AS PITCHERS WHO WON THAT MANY GAMES AT THAT YOUNG AGE!
IF YOU ASK ME, LIFE BEGINS AT 21!
21
JOYNER ©2007
DESPITE POSTING A 51-AND-37 RECORD OVER THE NEXT 5 SEASONS IN BROOKLYN, DODGER FANS TREATED RALPH VERY POORLY AFTER HE SURRENDERED BOBBY THOMSON'S PENNANT-CLINCHING HOMER IN 1951! STILL, RALPH NEVER COMPLAINED, ACCEPTING HIS FATE WITH GREAT DIGNITY DESPITE THE FACT THAT IN 1954 HE'D LEARNED THAT THE GIANTS STOLE THE PENNANT WITH THE AID OF A SCOREBOARD SIGN-STEALING SCHEME THAT CALLED INTO QUESTION THE INTEGRITY OF THE "SHOT HEARD 'ROUND THE WORLD"!
I'D LIKE TO GET YOU ON A SLOW BOAT TO CHINA!
RALPH HAD A FINE VOICE AND MADE HIS PRO SIGNING DEBUT IN 1949 AT THE OXFORD THEATER IN NEW JERSEY!
RALPH, HAVING ATTENDED NEW YORK UNIVERSITY, WAS SMART! HE PROVED IT IN 1961 WHEN HE WON 17 STRAIGHT GAMES AS A CONTESTANT ON "CONCENTRATION," NBC'S VERY POPULAR GAME SHOW! RALPH ALSO FOUND SUCCESS IN THE INSURANCE BUSINESS FOLLOWING HIS CAREER IN BASEBALL!
SEE -- I WAS PAYING ATTENTION IN CLASS!

Casey COX
RIGHT-HAND PITCHER
WASHINGTON SENATORS
CASEY'S BEST PITCHES WERE HIS SLIDER AND A DEVASTATING SINKER THAT REALLY DROPPED OFF THE TABLE!
SURF'S UP, DUDE!
JOSEPH CASEY COX WAS BORN ON JULY 3, 1941, IN LONG BEACH, CALIFORNIA! AFTER PLAYING COLLEGE BALL AT LOS ANGELES STATE COLLEGE WHERE HE ONCE STRUCK OUT 17 BATTERS IN A SINGLE GAME, CASEY SPENT 1962-65 WORKING HIS WAY UP THE REDS AND INDIANS MINOR LEAGUE SYSTEMS! THE SENATORS ACQUIRED THE 6-FOOT 5-INCH HURLER IN '63, AND BY 1966 CASEY WAS A MAINSTAY OF THE NATS BULLPEN WHERE HE MADE 66 RELIEF APPEARANCES AND PICKED UP FOUR WINS AND SEVEN SAVES WITH A 3.50 ERA!
BULL PEN
GO GET 'EM, CASE!
JOYNER ©2005
NICE JOB, BUSH! YOU MAY JUST YET CHANGE MY OPINION OF PITCHERS!
CASEY WAS KEY IN THE 1969 EXPANSION SENATORS FINISHING WITH THE ONLY WINNING SEASON IN THEIR HISTORY AS HE SAW HIS EFFECTIVENESS REACH ITS ZENITH UNDER THE TUTELAGE OF ROOKIE MANAGER TED WILLIAMS! IN SPITE OF WILLIAMS' WELL-KNOWN DISLIKE FOR PITCHERS, HE PROVIDED INSIGHTS THAT SET COX ON A COURSE FOR SUCCESS THAT SET SAIL WITH A CLASSIC 8-2/3-INNING SHUTOUT RELIEF APPEARANCE IN AN APRIL 6 WIN OVER CLEVELAND! BY MID-SEASON COX HAD BECOME AN EXCELLENT SPOT-STARTER, WINDING UP THE 1969 CAMPAIGN WITH A 12-7 RECORD AND A TIDY 2.78 ERA!

STEVE CARLTON
ON SEPTEMBER 23, 1983, PHILLIES SOUTHPAW STEVE CARLTON EMBLAZONED HIS NAME INTO THE RECORD BOOKS BY BECOMING JUST THE 16TH PITCHER TO WIN 300 BALLGAMES! THE MILESTONE VICTORY CAME AGAINST HIS FORMER CLUB, THE ST. LOUIS CARDINALS! EMPLOYING HIS SMOOTH, MECHANICALLY-SOUND DELIVERY THAT FEATURED A HIGH KNEE KICK, STEVE WORKED EIGHT INNINGS AND STRUCK OUT 12 REDBIRDS ON HIS WAY TO A 6-2 WIN! HIS CAREER HAD LONG BEEN STREAKING TO A FINAL DESTINATION AT COOPERSTOWN'S HALL OF FAME, BUT JOINING THE 300-WIN-CLUB SEALED THE DEAL AND LEFTY WAS ENSHRINED IN 1994! DURING HIS ACCEPTANCE SPEECH STEVE REMINDED FOLKS THAT HE'D FIRST MADE HIS MARK AT THE HALL OF FAME BACK IN 1966 WHEN HE WAS RECALLED FROM TULSA TO PITCH FOR THE CARDS AGAINST THE TWINS IN THE H.O.F.'S ANNUAL MID-SUMMER EXHIBITION GAME! IN THAT GAME STEVE WENT THE DISTANCE WHILE STRIKING OUT TEN TWINS TO EARN THE VICTORY -- AND SERVE NOTICE THAT HE HOPED TO ONE DAY RETURN UNDER A DIFFERENT SET OF CIRCUMSTANCES!
300 DOWN, 29 MORE TO GO!
DOUBLEDAY FIELD
I'LL BE BACK... IN 28 YEARS!
RELYING ON A HARD FASTBALL, A GOOD CURVE, AND A DEVASTATING SLIDER, STEVE IS SECOND TO ONLY WARREN SPAHN ON THE LIST OF WINNINGEST LEFTHANDERS! HE IS ALSO FOURTH IN CAREER WHIFFS, TRAILING ONLY NOLAN RYAN, ROGER CLEMENS, AND RANDY JOHNSON! STEVE WAS DOMINANT IN THE N.L. FROM THE LATE-60s THROUGH THE EARLY-80s, RACKING UP FOUR CY YOUNGS AND SIX 20-WIN SEASONS! ASIDE FROM HIS GREAT ABILITY ON THE MOUND, STEVE ALSO BROUGHT A VIBRANT, QUIRKY PERSONALITY TO THE GAME! HOWEVER, FEELING INCREASINGLY MISREPRESENTED BY THE SPORTSWRITERS, STEVE EMBARKED ON A SELF-IMPOSED "NO TALK" POLICY IN 1978 THAT HE MAINTAINED UNTIL NEARLY THE END OF HIS CAREER!
STEVE -- CARE TO COMMENT ON YOUR 300TH WIN?
MMMNNNRRRMMTH!
JOYNER ©2009

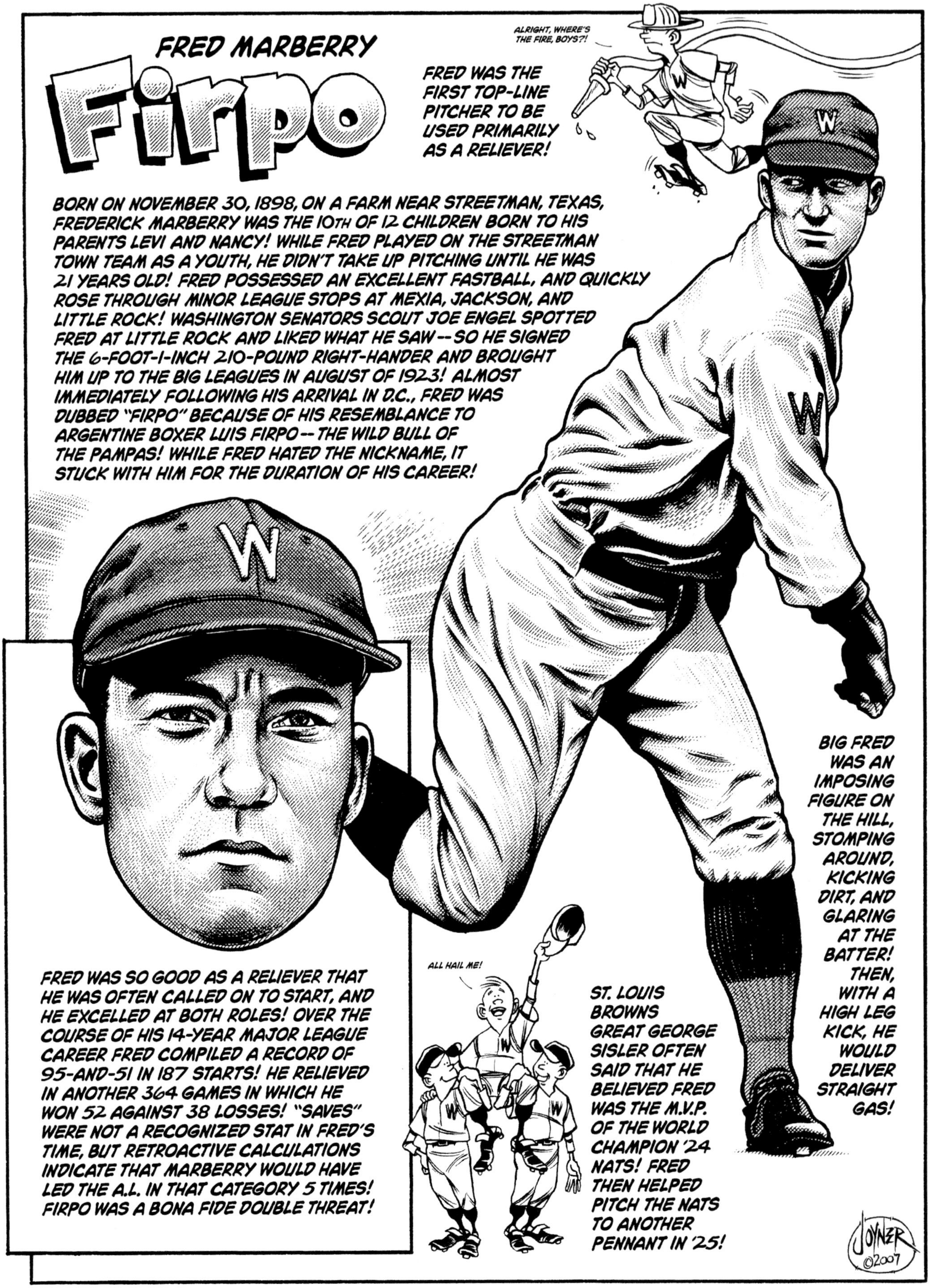
FRED MARBERRY
Firpo
FRED WAS THE FIRST TOP-LINE PITCHER TO BE USED PRIMARILY AS A RELIEVER!
ALRIGHT, WHERE'S THE FIRE, BOYS?!
BORN ON NOVEMBER 30, 1898, ON A FARM NEAR STREETMAN, TEXAS, FREDERICK MARBERRY WAS THE 10TH OF 12 CHILDREN BORN TO HIS PARENTS LEVI AND NANCY! WHILE FRED PLAYED ON THE STREETMAN TOWN TEAM AS A YOUTH, HE DIDN'T TAKE UP PITCHING UNTIL HE WAS 21 YEARS OLD! FRED POSSESSED AN EXCELLENT FASTBALL, AND QUICKLY ROSE THROUGH MINOR LEAGUE STOPS AT MEXIA, JACKSON, AND LITTLE ROCK! WASHINGTON SENATORS SCOUT JOE ENGEL SPOTTED FRED AT LITTLE ROCK AND LIKED WHAT HE SAW--SO HE SIGNED THE 6-FOOT-1-INCH 210-POUND RIGHT-HANDER AND BROUGHT HIM UP TO THE BIG LEAGUES IN AUGUST OF 1923! ALMOST IMMEDIATELY FOLLOWING HIS ARRIVAL IN D.C., FRED WAS DUBBED "FIRPO" BECAUSE OF HIS RESEMBLANCE TO ARGENTINE BOXER LUIS FIRPO--THE WILD BULL OF THE PAMPAS! WHILE FRED HATED THE NICKNAME, IT STUCK WITH HIM FOR THE DURATION OF HIS CAREER!
BIG FRED WAS AN IMPOSING FIGURE ON THE HILL, STOMPING AROUND, KICKING DIRT, AND GLARING AT THE BATTER! THEN, WITH A HIGH LEG KICK, HE WOULD DELIVER STRAIGHT GAS!
FRED WAS SO GOOD AS A RELIEVER THAT HE WAS OFTEN CALLED ON TO START, AND HE EXCELLED AT BOTH ROLES! OVER THE COURSE OF HIS 14-YEAR MAJOR LEAGUE CAREER FRED COMPILED A RECORD OF 95-AND-51 IN 187 STARTS! HE RELIEVED IN ANOTHER 364 GAMES IN WHICH HE WON 52 AGAINST 38 LOSSES! "SAVES" WERE NOT A RECOGNIZED STAT IN FRED'S TIME, BUT RETROACTIVE CALCULATIONS INDICATE THAT MARBERRY WOULD HAVE LED THE A.L. IN THAT CATEGORY 5 TIMES! FIRPO WAS A BONA FIDE DOUBLE THREAT!
ALL HAIL ME!
ST. LOUIS BROWNS GREAT GEORGE SISLER OFTEN SAID THAT HE BELIEVED FRED WAS THE M.V.P. OF THE WORLD CHAMPION '24 NATS! FRED THEN HELPED PITCH THE NATS TO ANOTHER PENNANT IN '25!
JOYNER ©2007

NED GARVER
THE BIG LEAGUES -- SURE BEATS THE HECK OUT OF PITCHING CORN COBS BACK ON THE FARM!
THE BROWNS FIRST BROUGHT UP NED GARVER IN 1948 AT AGE 23! NED NEVER PITCHED TO AN E.R.A. OVER 3.98 IN HIS 4-1/2 SEASONS IN ST. LOUIS, AND TWICE LED IN COMPLETE GAMES!
IN 1951 NED PITCHED TO A BRILLIANT 20-AND-12 RECORD! WITH THAT HE BECAME THE ONLY PITCHER IN THE 20TH CENTURY TO WIN 20 GAMES ON A TEAM THAT LOST 100 GAMES!
NED WAS BORN ON CHRISTMAS DAY IN NEY, OHIO! HE HAD BASE-BALL IN HIS BLOOD, BUT HE ALSO HAD POLITICS IN HIM! NED BECAME THE MAYOR OF NEY AFTER HIS PLAYING DAYS!
NED FOR MAYOR
A VOTE FOR NED IS A VOTE FOR CHANGE... UPS!
JOYNER ©2001
DON'T FORGET TO ALSO GIVE ME A DOZEN OF YOUR CUSTOM SPORTSHIRTS, MR. VEECK!
NED SIGNED A FAT $25,000 CONTRACT WITH THE BROWNS IN 1952!
IN 14 BIG LEAGUE SEASONS, NED GARVER WON 129 GAMES AGAINST 157 DEFEATS WITH A SOLID LIFETIME E.R.A. OF 3.73! AFTER HIS TENURE IN ST. LOUIS, HE PLAYED WITH THE TIGERS, THE ATHLETICS, AND THE ANGELS! NED WAS QUITE AN ADEQUATE HITTER, TOO! HE PUNISHED OHIO STATE LEAGUE PITCHERS WITH A .407 AVERAGE IN 1944, AND HE WAS A .218 HITTER IN THE MAJORS WITH 7 HOME RUNS!

Darold KNOWLES

TWO DAYS AFTER THE JAPANESE ATTACK ON PEARL HARBOR, DAROLD DUANE KNOWLES WAS BORN IN BRUNSWICK, MISSOURI! HE WOULD LATER ATTACK BIG LEAGUE HITTERS BY EFFECTIVELY MIXING HIS SINKER, SLIDER, AND CURVE!

DAROLD WAS A MULTI-SPORT STAR IN HIGH SCHOOL, LETTERING IN BASEBALL, BASKETBALL, AND TRACK! HIS ATHLETICISM SERVED HIM WELL, AND DAROLD HAD HIS TICKET TO THE MAJORS PUNCHED IN 1965 WHEN HE MADE HIS BIG LEAGUE DEBUT BY APPEARING IN FIVE GAMES FOR THE BALTIMORE ORIOLES! DAROLD FOUND HIMSELF PITCHING FOR THE PHILLIES THE NEXT SEASON, AND PITCHING A LOT, APPEARING IN 69 GAMES, ALL IN RELIEF! FEARING THAT HE HAD "WORN OUT" THE YOUNG SOUTHPAW, PHILS MANAGER GENE MAUCH HAD DAROLD DEALT TO THE WASHINGTON SENATORS PRIOR TO THE '67 CAMPAIGN! DAROLD WAS WITH THE NATS UNTIL MAY OF 1971, AND HE THRIVED IN THE NATION'S CAPITAL! ONE OF HIS BEST SEASONS CAME IN 1969 WHEN DAROLD RACKED UP A 9-AND-2 RECORD WITH 13 SAVES AND A 2.24 E.R.A. WHILE RELIEVING IN 53 GAMES! SENATORS MANAGER TED WILLIAMS CALLED HIM "THE BEST RELIEF PITCHER IN BASEBALL," AND DAROLD'S FINE

HURLING EARNED HIM A SPOT ON THE 1969 ALL-STAR SQUAD! WHILE OLD TEDDY BALLGAME MAY HAVE BEEN HIGH ON DAROLD, ANOTHER A.L. SKIPPER HATED THE SIGHT OF NUMBER 32 ENTERING THE GAME -- THE WHITE SOX'S DON GUTTERIDGE! IN JUNE OF 1970, DAROLD SLAMMED THE DOOR ON GUTTERIDGE'S PITIFUL SOX FOR THREE SAVES IN THREE DAYS! DAROLD MOVED ON TO OAKLAND IN 1971 AND CONTINUED TO EXCEL ON THE MOUND! IN FACT, HIS TORTURE OF GUTTERIDGE PALED IN COMPARISON TO HIS TREATMENT OF THE METS IN THE 1973 WORLD SERIES, WHERE HE PITCHED IN ALL SEVEN GAMES! THAT WAS, AND STILL IS, A SERIES RECORD!

Lou SLEATER

LOUIS MORTIMER SLEATER WAS BORN ON SEPTEMBER 8, 1926, IN ST. LOUIS, MISSOURI! THE SON OF A LOCAL SOCCER STAR, YOUNG LOU FOLLOWED IN HIS FATHER'S ATHLETIC FOOTSTEPS, BUT IT WAS IN BASEBALL WHERE THE YOUNGSTER WOULD MAKE HIS NAME! THE SLEATER FAMILY MOVED TO BALTIMORE WHEN LOU WAS 14, AND IT WAS THERE THAT PEOPLE BEGAN TO NOTICE THE STYLISH LEFT-HANDER! LOU SIGNED WITH THE BRAVES FOLLOWING HIS GRADUATION FROM HIGH SCHOOL, BUT A 2-YEAR HITCH IN THE U.S. NAVY POSTPONED HIS ENTRY INTO THE PRO RANKS UNTIL HIS DISCHARGE IN 1946! HE PITCHED HIS WAY UP THE MINOR LEAGUE RANKS FROM 1946-49 WHILE OWNERSHIP OF HIS RIGHTS WAS PASSED FROM THE BRAVES TO THE CUBS AND THEN TO THE GIANTS! FINALLY, IN 1950 AS A MEMBER OF THE ST. LOUIS BROWNS, LOU MADE HIS BIG LEAGUE DEBUT IN A SCORELESS RELIEF APPEARANCE ON APRIL 25TH! IN ADDITION TO MORE TIME IN THE MINORS, LOU DID STINTS WITH THE SENATORS IN 1952 AND THE ATHLETICS IN 1955! HE SPENT THE ENTIRE 1956 SEASON WITH THE BRAVES WHERE HE WAS WITNESS TO HIS CLUB LOSING THE PENNANT TO BROOKLYN IN THE LAST GAME OF THE SEASON, AN OCCURENCE HE CALLS "THE SADDEST DAY OF MY CAREER."

BRIGHTER DAYS LAY AHEAD FOR LOU, AND HE HAD PERHAPS HIS BEST YEAR WITH THE '57 TIGERS! NOT ONLY WAS HE STRONG OUT OF THE BULLPEN IN 41 APPEARANCES, HE SWUNG A MIGHTY STICK, TOO, HOMERING THREE TIMES! "I WAS ALWAYS A PRETTY GOOD HITTER," LOU SAID. "I WENT TO BAT 20 TIMES IN '57 AND HIT THREE HOMERS. THEN I HIT A HOME RUN OFF RAY NARLESKI IN MY FIRST AT-BAT OF 1958, SO I HIT 4 HOMERS IN 21 AT-BATS." ALL SET FOR CONTINUED SUCCESS IN 1958, LOU INSTEAD SAW THE SEASON WRECKED BY INJURIES! THERE WAS FRUSTRATION AS HE RETIRED PRIOR TO THE 1959 CAMPAIGN, BUT LOU WILL ALWAYS BE PART OF AN ELITE GROUP -- GOOD HITTIN' PITCHERS!

PITCHER
PHILADELPHIA ATHLETICS
Carl
Scheib
BORN: JANUARY 1, 1927
WHERE: GRATZ, PA
THROWS: RIGHT
BATS: RIGHT
CARL HELPED HIMSELF TO A WIN ON MAY 8, 1948, WHEN HE CLOUTED A GRAND SLAM!
THAT'S THE SPIRIT!
WHEN CARL ALVIN SCHEIB NAILED DOWN HIS 45TH AND FINAL BIG LEAGUE CAREER WIN WITH THE 1953 PHILADELPHIA ATHLETICS, HE HAD COME A LONG WAY! ONLY 11 YEARS EARLIER HE HAD LED HIS GRATZ HIGH SCHOOL TEAM TO A LEAGUE TITLE! JUST ONE YEAR LATER, AT THE TENDER AGE OF 16, CARL BECAME THE YOUNGEST PLAYER IN A.L. HISTORY WHEN HE TOOK THE MOUND FOR THE A's ON SEPTEMBER 5, 1943! HARD-THROWING CARL WENT ON TO APPEAR IN FIVE MORE GAMES FOR THE '43 MACKMEN AND 15 GAMES FOR THE '44 CLUB BEFORE MARCHING OFF TO MILITARY SERVICE IN WORLD WAR II! UPON HIS RETURN HE BECAME A KEY MAN IN THE ATHLETICS ROTATION, MOST NOTABLY IN 1948 WHEN HE NOTCHED A 14-8 MARK AS THE A's MADE A RARE RUN AT A PENNANT! ALWAYS A GOOD HITTING PITCHER, CARL HIT .298 WITH TWO ROUND-TRIPPERS FOR THE '48 SQUAD! THE PEOPLE OF GRATZ HONORED THEIR NATIVE SON IN 2005 BY REFURBISHING THE BALLFIELD WHERE CARL CUT HIS TEETH AND RENAMING IT "SCHEIB PARK" -- WITH A BRONZE MONUMENT!
ARE YOU SERIOUS -- YOU'RE REALLY SUPPOSED TO BE HOME BEFORE DARK?!
JOYNER ©2005

PASCUAL

ONE OF THE GREATEST BIG LEAGUE PLAYERS TO EMERGE FROM PRE-CASTRO CUBA WAS RIGHT-HANDED PITCHER CAMILO PASCUAL, BORN IN HAVANA ON JANUARY 20, 1934. AN ESTABLISHED MAJOR LEAGUER BY 1954, CAMILO STILL HAD CUBA AS HIS BASE OF OPERATIONS UNTIL 1961 WHEN HE LOST ALL OF HIS MONEY AND PROPERTY WHEN HE, WITH HIS FATHER IN TOW, LEFT THE COUNTRY FOR GOOD IN THE WAKE OF FIDEL CASTRO'S EVER-GROWING ALLIANCE WITH THE SOVIET UNION. TWO YEARS LATER, ANTI-CASTRO PROTESTERS RUSHED THE FIELD AT YANKEE STADIUM AS CAMILO, PITCHING FOR THE TWINS, WAGED BATTLE WITH THE MIGHTY BRONX BOMBERS. CAMILO STOOD DUMBFOUNDED AS THE EIGHT DEMONSTRATORS DRAPED HIM WITH A CUBAN FLAG, THEN DANCED AROUND THE MOUND WHILE DISPLAYING A BANNER THAT READ "UNITED TO LIBERATE CUBA." WHILE HE WAS EMBARRASSED BY THE EVENT, CAMILO WAS CHOSEN BY THE PROTESTERS BECAUSE HE WAS A TRUE ICON TO CUBANS EVERYWHERE. THE PIPELINE OF CUBAN-BORN BASEBALL TALENT WAS CUT WHEN CASTRO CLOSED CUBAN EMIGRATION IN 1966, BUT IT WAS CAMILO WHO WAS RESPONSIBLE FOR DISCOVERING ONE OF THE LAST CUBAN-BORN SUPERSTARS WHEN HE SIGNED JOSE CANSECO TO THE OAKLAND ATHLETICS IN JUNE OF 1982.

KNOWN FOR HIS MENACING SCOWL ON THE MOUND, CAMILO HAD A PLEASANT DISPOSITION OFF THE FIELD! JUST DON'T TELL THAT TO ALL THE G.M.'s WHO CAMILO TORTURED IN CONTRACT SQUABBLES AND HOLD-OUTS!

ON APRIL 27, 1965, CAMILO HELPED LEAD HIS TWINS TO VICTORY WHEN HE LAUNCHED A GRAND SLAM HOMER OFF INDIANS RIGHTY STAN WILLIAMS. IT WASN'T THE FIRST TIME CAMILO HAD HELPED HIS OWN PITCHING CAUSE BY CLUBBING A GRANNY! ON AUGUST 14, 1960, HE TATTOOED ONE OFF YANKEE FLAMETHROWER BULLET BOB TURLEY TO LEAD THE NATS TO A 5-4 VICTORY. DRIVING IN HIS OWN RUNS WAS PROBABLY CAMILO'S BEST BET FOR WINNING WITH THE LOWLY NATS OF THE 1950s, AS THEY OFTEN SEEMED CHALLENGED TO SCORE WHEN HE PITCHED -- AND THAT IS PARTLY TO BLAME FOR HIS LIMITED SUCCESS DURING HIS TIME WITH WASHINGTON. WHILE HE WAS CONSIDERED TO HAVE SOME OF THE BEST "STUFF" IN THE MAJORS, PARTICULARLY HIS BIG ROUNDHOUSE CURVE, CAMILO ONLY WON 57 GAMES FOR THE SENATORS FROM 1954-60. BUT THE TEAM'S MOVE TO MINNESOTA BROUGHT OUT THE BEST IN CAMILO, AND HE WON 88 GAMES FOR THEM FROM '61-66, INCLUDING TWO 20-WIN CAMPAIGNS. ARM INJURIES HAD REDUCED HIS EFFECTIVENESS BY 1966, SO THE TWINS DEALT CAMILO BACK TO WASHINGTON, THIS TIME TO SERVE WITH THE EXPANSION SENATORS WHO'D COME INTO THE LEAGUE IN 1961. THESE NEW NATS WERE AS BAD AS THE OLD NATS, BUT CAMILO DID WELL FOR THEM BY WINNING 25 GAMES OVER THE COURSE OF THE 1967 AND 1968 SEASONS. A COLORFUL CHARACTER AND TALENTED HURLER, CAMILO, A 3-TIME STRIKEOUT LEADER, IS DEFINITLEY A MAN UPON WHOM THE CUBAN PEOPLE CAN STILL HANG THEIR PRIDE.

BULLET BOB
TURLEY
ROBERT LEE TURLEY WAS BORN ON SEPTEMBER 19, 1930, IN TROY, ILLINOIS! HE ACHIEVED HIS GREATEST PITCHING FEATS WITH THE NEW YORK YANKEES, BUT HE WAS ORIGINALLY A MEMBER OF THE A.L. ST. LOUIS BROWNS! BOB BROKE IN WITH THE BROWNS IN 1951, AND ALSO PITCHED FOR THEM IN 1953!
I LOOK GOOD IN BROWN!
Browns
THAT'S A SPICY MEATBALL!
BOB WAS ACQUIRED BY NEW YORK AFTER THE 1954 SEASON, AND USED HIS BLAZING FASTBALL TO WIN 17 GAMES WITH A 3.06 E.R.A. FOR THE YANKEES IN 1955!
POP!
BOB WENT WITH THE BROWNS WHEN THEY MOVED TO BALTIMORE AND BECAME THE ORIOLES' BEST PITCHER IN THEIR FIRST YEAR, WINNING 14 GAMES AND LEADING THE LEAGUE IN STRIKEOUTS!
JOYNER ©2003
21 WINS
MY CUP RUNNETH OVER!
BOB ENJOYED HIS GREATEST SEASON IN 1958 WHEN HE WENT 21-AND-7 FOR THE YANKS AND WON THE A.L. CY YOUNG AWARD! HIS SUCCESS CONTINUED INTO THE '58 WORLD SERIES AGAINST MILWAUKEE WHERE HIS TWO VICTORIES HELPED LEAD THE BOMBERS TO ANOTHER TITLE! FACING ELIMINATION IN GAME FIVE, BOB SHUT OUT THE BRAVES ON A FIVE-HITTER! GAME SIX SAW BOB ENTER THE GAME IN THE 10TH INNING WITH TWO OUTS AND THE TYING RUN ON THIRD-- BOB RETIRED FRANK TORRE TO NAIL DOWN THE WIN! HIS HEROICS CULMINATED IN GAME SEVEN WHEN HE RELIEVED DON LARSEN IN THE THIRD INNING, GIVING UP JUST TWO HITS THE REST OF THE WAY IN THE YANKS' 6-2 WIN! FOR HIS EFFORTS, BOB EARNED THE SERIES MOST VALUABLE PLAYER AWARD!

Bobby Shantz

FRIDAY, MAY 6, 1949: PHILADELPHIA ATHLETICS AT DETROIT TIGERS! A 3-RUN TIGER UPRISING IN THE BOTTOM OF THE 4TH LEFT A's OWNER/MANAGER CONNIE MACK SCANNING HIS BULLPEN FOR A REPLACEMENT FOR ATHLETICS STARTER CARL SCHEIB! AT THE END OF THE BENCH SAT AN EAGER LOOKING KID -- 24-YEAR-OLD LEFT-HANDER BOBBY SHANTZ! ACTUALLY, BOBBY SHOULDN'T HAVE EVEN BEEN THERE! HE'D MADE HIS BIG LEAGUE DEBUT JUST FIVE DAYS EARLIER, PITCHING TWO-THIRDS OF AN INNING IN RELIEF, AND THEN WAS FARMED OUT TO BUFFALO OF THE INTERNATIONAL LEAGUE THE VERY NEXT DAY! WHEN A COUPLE OF A's HURLERS CAME UP LAME LESS THAN 24 HOURS LATER, BOBBY WAS IMMEDIATELY RECALLED! HE HADN'T PITCHED SINCE HIS RECALL, BUT THAT WASN'T THE MAIN REASON FOR MR. MACK'S RELUCTANCE TO USE BOBBY! REALLY, IT WAS MR. MACK'S PREJUDICE AGAINST LITTLE GUYS THAT MADE HIM DOUBT WHETHER BOBBY WOULD EVER MAKE IT IN THE BIG LEAGUES! AND IF EVER ANYONE QUALIFIED AS A LITTLE GUY, BOBBY SHANTZ, AT 5-FOOT-SIX AND 139-LBS, COULD BE CONSIDERED OVER-QUALIFIED! WITH FEW OPTIONS, MR. MACK SENT BOBBY TO THE HILL -- AND THE REST IS HISTORY! TRAILING 3-TO-1 WITH NO OUTS, BOBBY PROCEEDED TO PITCH NINE HITLESS INNINGS! THE MOST SERIOUS TROUBLE HE ENCOUNTERED WAS DUE TO THE SEVEN WALKS HE ISSUED -- BUT HE SHOWED HIS GRIT AND DETERMINATION BY STRIKING OUT SEVEN TO WRIGGLE OUT OF EACH TIGHT SPOT! IN ADDITION TO HIS BRILLIANT PITCHING, BOBBY DEMONSTRATED EXCELLENT DEFENSIVE ABILITY WHEN HE POUNCED ON A FAILED BUNT ATTEMPT AND TURNED IT INTO A KEY DOUBLE-PLAY! BOBBY ALSO CHIPPED IN HIS FIRST MAJOR LEAGUE HIT! THE A's CAME BACK TO WIN IT, GIVING BOBBY HIS FIRST BIG LEAGUE WIN! IT WAS AN AMAZING BEGINNING TO WHAT WOULD PROVE TO BE AN EXCELLENT CAREER!

BOBBY WENT ON TO WIN SIX GAMES IN '49, THEN POSTED EIGHT WINS IN 1950, BUT HIS CAREER TOOK OFF WHEN MR. MACK RETIRED PRIOR TO THE 1951 CAMPAIGN! WITH NEW SKIPPER JIMMIE DYKES NOW CALLING THE SHOTS, BOBBY WON 18 GAMES IN '51, FOLLOWED BY A SEASON FOR THE AGES IN 1952 THAT SAW HIM LEAD THE LEAGUE WITH 24 VICTORIES WHILE NABBING THE M.V.P. AWARD IN A LANDSLIDE! ARM INJURIES SLOWED BOBBY FROM 1953-56, BUT HE MADE A STARTLING COMEBACK WITH THE 1957 YANKEES WHERE HE WENT 11-AND-5 WITH A LEAGUE-LEADING 2.45 E.R.A.! WORKING AS A STARTER AND OUT OF THE BULLPEN, BOBBY CONTINUED TO PITCH WELL FOR THE BOMBERS THROUGH THE 1960 SEASON, EARNING HIMSELF A WORLD SERIES RING IN 1958! HE WOUND DOWN A FINE 16-YEAR CAREER IN '64 WITH A CAREER MARK OF 119-AND-99 WITH A 3.38 E.R.A.!

Mel PARNELL

BORN ON JUNE 13, 1922, IN HOT AND SULTRY NEW ORLEANS, MELVIN LLOYD PARNELL WENT NORTH TO BOSTON IN 1947, BRINGING WITH HIM AN ARRAY OF CRAFTY LEFT-HANDED OFFERINGS THAT WOULD MAKE HIM ONE OF THE RED SOX'S BEST PITCHERS OF ALL TIME!

MEL BROKE INTO PRO BALL IN 1941 WITH CENTREVILLE, THEN MOVED UP TO CANTON IN '42 BEFORE SPENDING 1943-45 IN THE ARMY AIR COPRS! HE RETURNED TO BASEBALL WITH A BRILLIANT YEAR AT SCRANTON IN 1946 WHICH EARNED HIM A TRIAL WITH THE RED SOX IN THE SPRING OF '47! MEL WAS SOON FARMED OUT TO LOUISVILLE FOR ADDITIONAL SEASONING, AND WHILE THERE HE BROKE A FINGER AS HE TRIED TO MAKE A BARE-HANDED STOP ON A LINE DRIVE! THE FINGER HEALED CROOKED, RESULTING IN, AMAZINGLY ENOUGH, INCREASED EFFECTIVENESS ON SOME OF MEL'S PITCHES!

MEL WAS A WORKHORSE FOR THE SOX, PITCHING WELL OVER 200 INNINGS PER YEAR FROM 1948-53 WHILE AVERAGING 18 WINS ANNUALLY IN THAT SPAN! MEL WAS FINALLY SLOWED WHEN HIS THROWING ARM WAS BROKEN BY A MICKEY McDERMOTT PITCH IN 1954! PLAYING IN PAIN, MEL WON ONLY 12 GAMES FROM 1954 THROUGH 1956, BUT FINISHED AT A PHENOMENAL 123-75!

ON JULY 14, 1956, MEL REMINDED BOSTON FANS OF HIS GREATNESS WHEN HE TOSSED A NO-HITTER AGAINST THE WHITE SOX! HE BECAME THE ONLY PITCHER IN HISTORY TO END A NO-HITTER WITH AN UNASSISTED PUTOUT WHEN HE GLOVED A WALT DROPO COME-BACKER AND TOOK IT TO THE BAG HIMSELF!

TRAGEDIES AND NEAR TRAGEDIES

Roberto
CLEMENTE
ON AUGUST 18, 1934, IN A WOODEN HOUSE ON KILOMETER SEVEN OF ROAD 887 IN CAROLINA, PUERTO RICO, MELCHOR AND LUISA CLEMENTE'S FAMILY OF EIGHT GREW BY ONE WITH THE BIRTH OF ROBERTO WALKER CLEMENTE. MOTHER AND FATHER HAD HIGH HOPES FOR THEIR NEW BABY BOY, BUT THEY COULD NEVER HAVE DREAMED THAT LITTLE ROBERTO WOULD FIRST RISE TO THE TOP OF THE SPORTS WORLD, THEN BECOME A MYTHOLOGICAL SYMBOL FOR ALL HUMANITY.
ROBERTO SPENT ALL 18 YEARS OF HIS CAREER WITH THE PITTSBURGH PIRATES. HE WAS AN EXTRAORDINARY OUTFIELDER WITH AN ARM UNSURPASSED BY ANY OF HIS PEERS. ROBERTO WAS ALSO A BRILLIANT HITTER, WINNING FOUR BATTING TITLES AND CLUBBING 240 HOME RUNS. WHILE HE WAS A PERENNIAL ALL-STAR AND THE 1966 N.L. M.V.P., TRUE NATIONAL RECOGNITION OF HIS GREATNESS DID NOT COME UNTIL HIS M.V.P. PERFORMANCE IN THE '71 WORLD SERIES.
CLEMENTE'S PLACE AMONGST BASEBALL'S ALL-TIME GREATS WAS ALREADY SECURED BY 1972, HIS LAST YEAR IN THE MAJORS. HE ONLY ADDED TO HIS RICH LEGACY WHEN HE RAPPED OUT HIS 3,000TH CAREER HIT ON SEPTEMBER 30 -- A DOUBLE OFF METS HURLER JOHN MATLACK. AS HE STOOD ON SECOND BASE, ROBERTO TIPPED HIS CAP TO THE FANS AT THREE RIVERS STADIUM. THAT AT-BAT TURNED OUT TO BE ROBERTO'S LAST EVER, FOR THREE MONTHS LATER HE WAS GONE -- KILLED IN A PLANE CRASH. HE WAS ON A SELF-ORGANIZED HUMANITARIAN MISSION TO FLY MUCH-NEEDED MATERIALS TO VICTIMS OF A HUGE EARTHQUAKE IN NICARAGUA.
"IF YOU HAVE A CHANCE TO HELP OTHERS AND FAIL TO DO SO," HE OFTEN SAID, "THEN YOU ARE WASTING YOUR TIME ON THIS EARTH." ROBERTO CLEMENTE'S TIME HERE WAS TOO BRIEF, BUT HIS HEROIC LEGACY WILL NEVER BE FORGOTTEN.
JOYNER ©2008
PIRATES
21

"Harvard" Eddie GRANT

EDWARD LESLIE GRANT DEFIED THE STEREOTYPICAL ROWDY BALLPLAYER OF HIS TIMES! INSTEAD OF DRINKING AND FIGHTING, SLICK-FIELDING EDDIE ATTENDED HARVARD AND STUDIED FOR A POST-BASEBALL CAREER IN LAW! EDDIE'S FIRST BIG LEAGUE ACTION CAME WITH THE INDIANS VS. THE RED SOX ON AUGUST 4, 1905, WHEN HE FILLED IN FOR AN AILING NAP LAJOIE -- AND COLLECTED THREE HITS! THE BULK OF HIS CAREER, HOWEVER, WAS SPENT WITH THE PHILLIES WITH WHOM HE FINISHED SECOND IN HITS IN 1909! WHILE EDDIE WAS QUITE A SPEEDY LEADOFF MAN, IT WAS ON DEFENSE WHERE HE TRULY SPARKLED! "HE COULD LAY BACK NEAR THIRD BASE AND STILL THROW OUT THE FASTEST RUNNERS AFTER THEY'D BUNTED," SAID LONG-TIME NATIONAL LEAGUER TURKEY MIKE DONLIN! A GENUINE DOUBLE THREAT, EDDIE WAS OFTEN ASKED BY OTHER PLAYERS FOR LEGAL ADVICE ON THEIR CONTRACTS! AFTER A 2-1/2 YEAR STINT WITH THE REDS, EDDIE JOINED JOHN McGRAW'S 1913 GIANTS -- A CLUB THAT WON THE N.L. PENNANT, BUT LOST TO THE ATHLETICS IN THE WORLD SERIES!

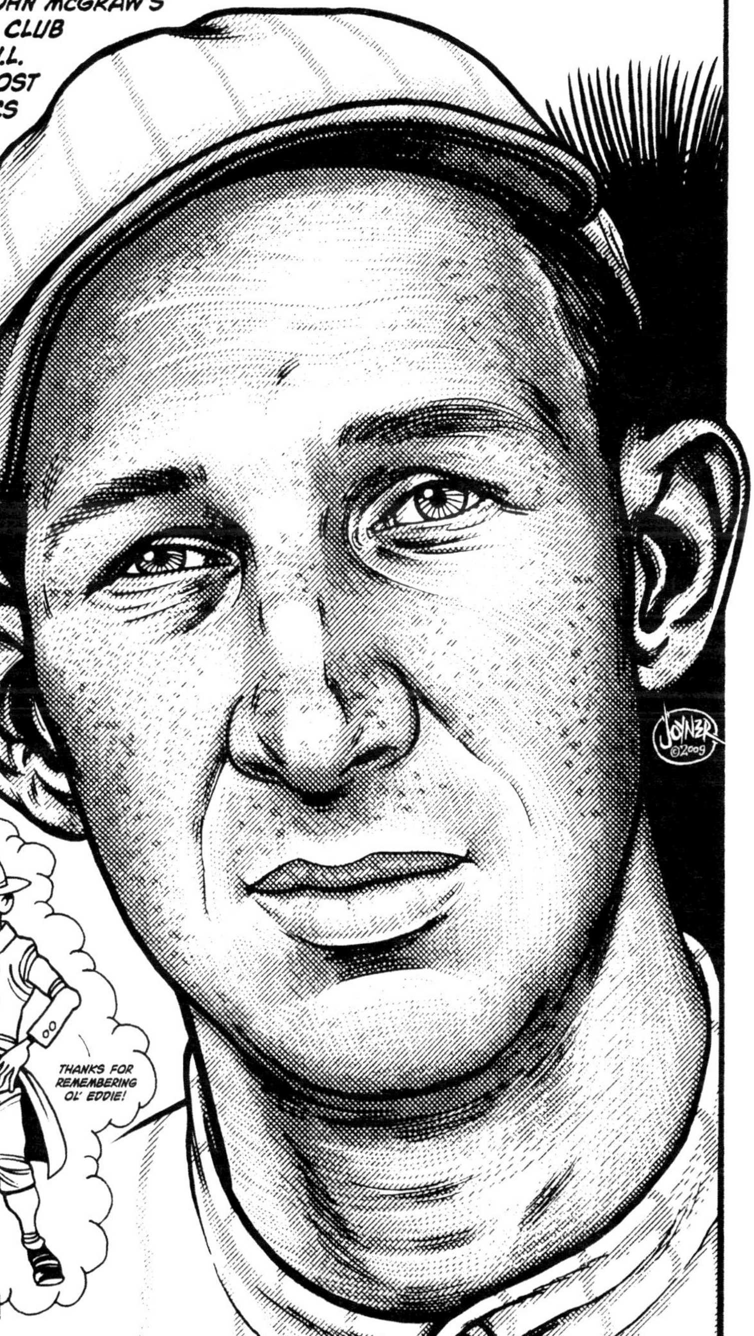

1915 WAS EDDIE'S LAST YEAR IN BALL, THEN HE TURNED HIS ATTENTION TO FULL-TIME LAWYERING. HE'D BARELY HAD TIME TO BUILD A CLIENT BASE BEFORE THE U.S. ENTERED WORLD WAR I AND EDDIE, DESPITE BEING AGE-EXEMPT, ENLISTED. "I AM GOING TO TRY TO BE AN OFFICER," EDDIE TOLD A FRIEND. "IF I AM NOT SUCCESSFUL, I SHALL BE A PRIVATE, FOR THERE IS NO GREATER DUTY THAT I OWE FOR BEING WHAT I AM -- AN AMERICAN CITIZEN." EDDIE MADE GOOD AS AN OFFICER, BUT HE DIED IN ACTION ON OCTOBER 5, 1918, WHILE LEADING HIS MEN IN BATTLE IN THE ARGONNE FOREST. EDDIE WAS THE ONLY MAJOR LEAGUER TO GIVE HIS LIFE IN THE WAR. MEMORIAL DAY OF '21 SAW A MONUMENT TO EDDIE UNVEILED IN DEEP CENTERFIELD OF THE POLO GROUNDS. A WREATH-LAYING CEREMONY TOOK PLACE EACH SUBSEQUENT MEMORIAL DAY UNTIL THE GIANTS LEFT FOR SAN FRANCISCO FOLLOWING THE 1957 SEASON. EDDIE'S PLAQUE WAS STOLEN DURING THE MELEE THAT FOLLOWED THE GIANTS' LAST GAME AT THE POLO GROUNDS -- AND IT'S NEVER BEEN FOUND. THE GIANTS FINALLY MADE A REPLICA AND INSTALLED IT AT PAC BELL PARK PRIOR TO THE 2006 SEASON.

CARL MAYS

"NOBODY, IT SEEMS, EVER REMEMBERS ANYTHING ABOUT ME EXCEPT ONE THING -- THAT A PITCH I THREW CAUSED A MAN TO DIE." THOSE WERE THE WORDS OF RIGHT-HANDED SUBMARINE PITCHER CARL MAYS SHORTLY BEFORE HIS DEATH AT AGE 79 IN 1971. CARL'S 207-126 RECORD AND 2.92 CAREER E.R.A. ARE IMPRESSIVE, AS ARE HIS FIVE 20-WIN SEASONS AND APPEARANCES IN THE 1916, 1918, 1921 AND 1922 WORLD SERIES. BUT IN THE LONG RUN, NOTHING WOULD EVER ALLOW CARL TO ESCAPE THE SHADOW CAST BY HIS TRAGIC PITCH. DISLIKED BY MANY FOR BEING A "LONER," CARL'S DEADLY PITCH STRUCK RAY CHAPMAN, A MAN LOVED BY ALL FOR HIS CHEERFULNESS -- AND THAT FURTHER GUARANTEED ETERNAL SCORN FOR CARL.

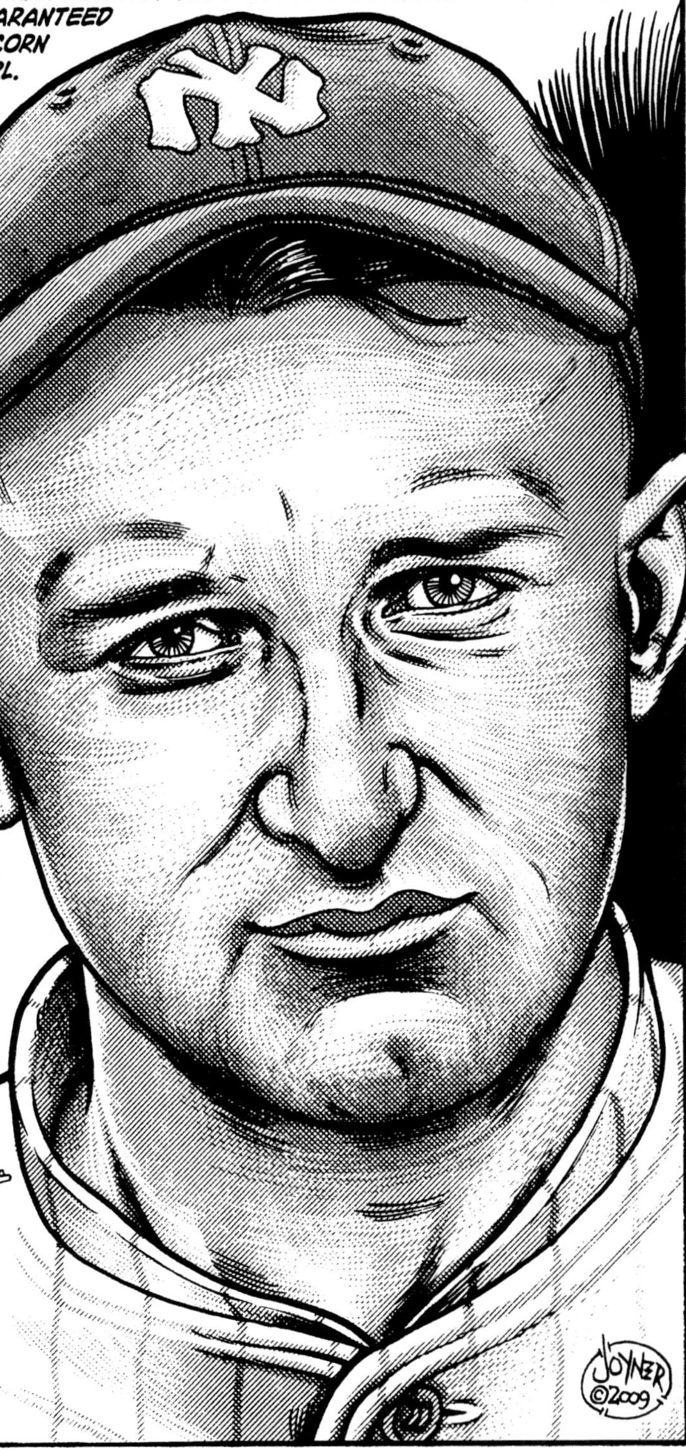

PERHAPS HIS OWN WORDS ABOUT THE TRAGEDY OFFER THE BEST WAY FOR FOLKS TO DECIDE HOW BEST TO JUDGE CARL. "IT WAS AN ACCIDENT, NOTHING ELSE," CARL TOLD SPORTSWRITER BOB McGARIGLE IN 1971. "THE MAN I HIT WAS A RIGHT-HANDED BATTER WHO DRAPED HIMSELF OVER THE PLATE, SO I ALWAYS DREADED PITCHING TO HIM. THE COUNT WENT TO ONE-AND-ONE AND MY NEXT PITCH WAS TO HAVE BEEN A LOW FASTBALL IN THE STRIKE ZONE. BUT JUST AS MY ARM REACHED THE FURTHEST POINT OF MY BACKSWING, I SAW RAY SHIFT HIS BACK FOOT INTO THE POSITION HE TOOK FOR A RUNNING BUNT -- A PUSH BUNT. SO AT THE LAST SPLIT SECOND, I CHANGED TO A HIGH-AND-TIGHT STRIKE PITCH SO AS TO MAKE HIM FOUL OFF THE PITCH OR MISS IT. IT WAS THE ONLY DEFENSE A PITCHER HAD WHEN FACED WITH THIS SITUATION. AND THAT'S THE WAY, AND WHY, I PITCHED THAT BALL. USUALLY A BATTER WOULD FALL AWAY FROM SUCH A PITCH, BUT CHAPMAN DIDN'T. I HAD THE GREATEST ADMIRATION FOR RAY CHAPMAN. HE WAS ONE OF THE GAMEST PLAYERS IN THE LEAGUE. I DIDN'T MEAN TO HIT HIM, OF COURSE, BUT I HAD TO PITCH TO THE STRIKE ZONE. THAT'S WHAT I WAS PAID TO DO. GET THE BALL OVER THE PLATE."

CARL SPENT THE LATTER YEARS OF HIS LIFE HAPPILY HUNTING AROUND HIS REMOTE HOME IN DAYVILLE, OREGON. IN SPITE OF BEING UNFAIRLY CAST AS A VILLAIN BY BASEBALL, CARL LOVED THE GAME UNTIL THE DAY HE DIED, SHARING HIS KNOWLEDGE BY COACHING KIDS.

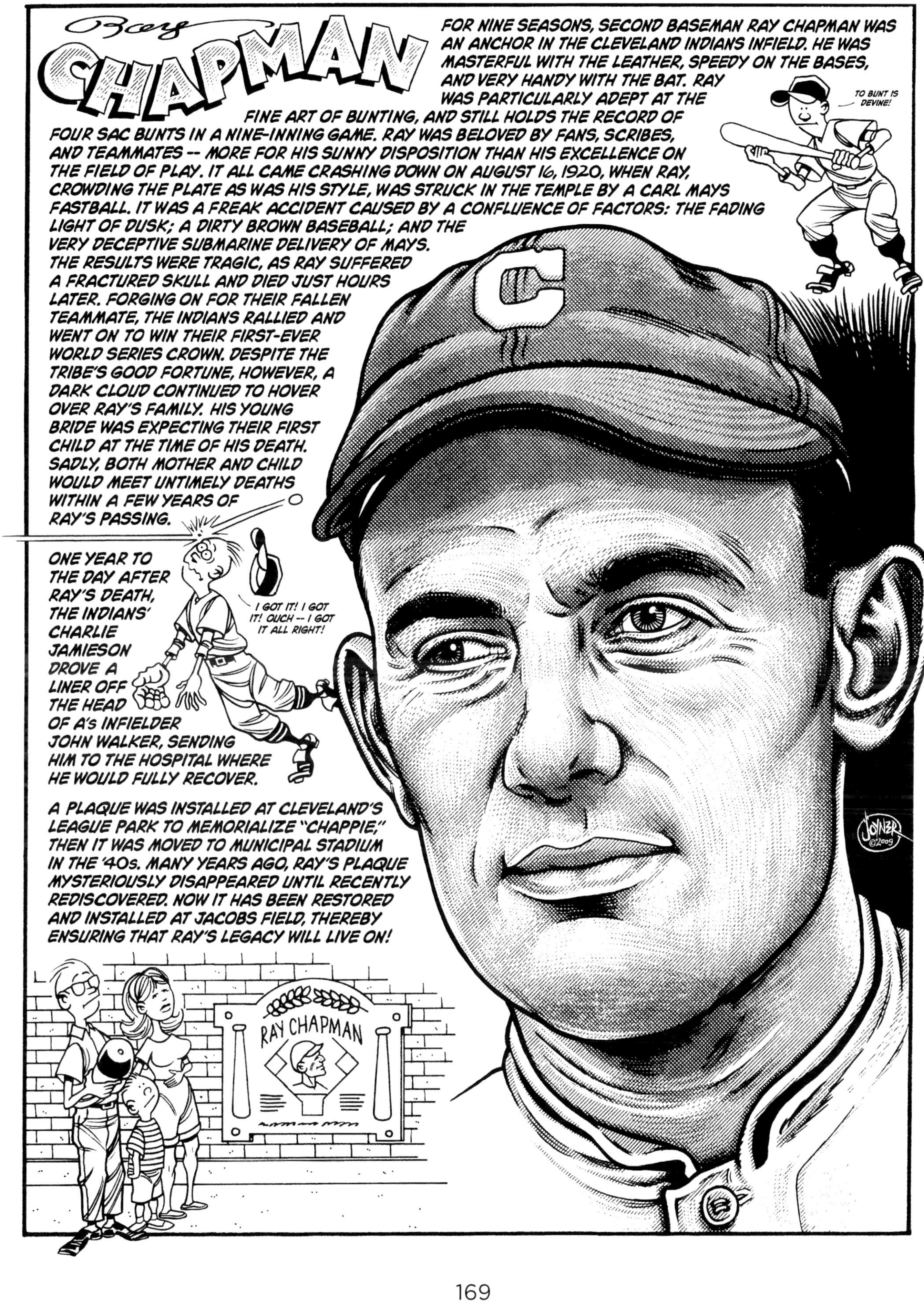
Ray CHAPMAN
FOR NINE SEASONS, SECOND BASEMAN RAY CHAPMAN WAS AN ANCHOR IN THE CLEVELAND INDIANS INFIELD. HE WAS MASTERFUL WITH THE LEATHER, SPEEDY ON THE BASES, AND VERY HANDY WITH THE BAT. RAY WAS PARTICULARLY ADEPT AT THE FINE ART OF BUNTING, AND STILL HOLDS THE RECORD OF FOUR SAC BUNTS IN A NINE-INNING GAME. RAY WAS BELOVED BY FANS, SCRIBES, AND TEAMMATES -- MORE FOR HIS SUNNY DISPOSITION THAN HIS EXCELLENCE ON THE FIELD OF PLAY. IT ALL CAME CRASHING DOWN ON AUGUST 16, 1920, WHEN RAY, CROWDING THE PLATE AS WAS HIS STYLE, WAS STRUCK IN THE TEMPLE BY A CARL MAYS FASTBALL. IT WAS A FREAK ACCIDENT CAUSED BY A CONFLUENCE OF FACTORS: THE FADING LIGHT OF DUSK; A DIRTY BROWN BASEBALL; AND THE VERY DECEPTIVE SUBMARINE DELIVERY OF MAYS. THE RESULTS WERE TRAGIC, AS RAY SUFFERED A FRACTURED SKULL AND DIED JUST HOURS LATER. FORGING ON FOR THEIR FALLEN TEAMMATE, THE INDIANS RALLIED AND WENT ON TO WIN THEIR FIRST-EVER WORLD SERIES CROWN. DESPITE THE TRIBE'S GOOD FORTUNE, HOWEVER, A DARK CLOUD CONTINUED TO HOVER OVER RAY'S FAMILY. HIS YOUNG BRIDE WAS EXPECTING THEIR FIRST CHILD AT THE TIME OF HIS DEATH. SADLY, BOTH MOTHER AND CHILD WOULD MEET UNTIMELY DEATHS WITHIN A FEW YEARS OF RAY'S PASSING.
TO BUNT IS DEVINE!
ONE YEAR TO THE DAY AFTER RAY'S DEATH, THE INDIANS' CHARLIE JAMIESON DROVE A LINER OFF THE HEAD OF A's INFIELDER JOHN WALKER, SENDING HIM TO THE HOSPITAL WHERE HE WOULD FULLY RECOVER.
I GOT IT! I GOT IT! OUCH -- I GOT IT ALL RIGHT!
A PLAQUE WAS INSTALLED AT CLEVELAND'S LEAGUE PARK TO MEMORIALIZE "CHAPPIE," THEN IT WAS MOVED TO MUNICIPAL STADIUM IN THE '40s. MANY YEARS AGO, RAY'S PLAQUE MYSTERIOUSLY DISAPPEARED UNTIL RECENTLY REDISCOVERED. NOW IT HAS BEEN RESTORED AND INSTALLED AT JACOBS FIELD, THEREBY ENSURING THAT RAY'S LEGACY WILL LIVE ON!
RAY CHAPMAN
JOYNER ©2009

Tony HORTON

AT THE CONCLUSION OF THE 1969 SEASON, TONY HORTON, THE INDIANS' 24-YEAR OLD SLUGGING FIRST BASEMAN, WAS LOOKING BACK UPON A BREAKOUT YEAR -- A .278 AVERAGE WITH 27 HOME RUNS AND 93 RBIs. ELEVEN MONTHS LATER, TONY SAT IN HIS CAR JUST OUTSIDE OF THE CLEVELAND HOTEL ROOM HE RENTED, BLEEDING TO DEATH FROM SELF-INFLICTED SLASHES TO BOTH WRISTS.

TONY WAS THE SON OF TROY HORTON, A FOOTBALL AND BASKETBALL STAR AT UCLA. FOLLOWING IN HIS FATHER'S FOOTSTEPS, TONY ALSO EXCELLED IN ATHLETICS, STARRING IN THREE SPORTS AT LOS ANGELES' UNIVERSITY HIGH SCHOOL. REJECTING THE OFFER OF A BASKETBALL SCHOLARSHIP FROM USC, TONY INSTEAD OPTED TO GO PRO IN BASEBALL. AFTER THRILLING RED SOX EXECS WITH A PROLIFIC LONGBALL DISPLAY IN A TRYOUT AT FENWAY PARK, THE 6-FOOT-THREE-INCH 210-POUND FENCE-BUSTER SIGNED WITH THE RED SOX FOR A HUGE BONUS. TONY DELIVERED PLENTY OF HOMERS DOWN ON THE SOX FARM, AND HE ALSO SHOWED REAL PROMISE IN TRIALS WITH THE BIG CLUB IN 1964, '65 AND '66. IT WAS A TRADE TO THE POWER-STARVED INDIANS ON JUNE 4, 1967, HOWEVER, THAT REALLY OPENED THE DOOR FOR TONY. GIVEN THE OPPORTUNITY TO PLAY MORE REGULARLY, HE HIT .284 WITH 10 BOMBS IN 1967; UPPED HIS ROUND-TRIPPER OUTPUT TO 14 IN 1968; THEN PUT IT ALL TOGETHER DURING HIS BREAKOUT SEASON OF 1969.

TONY WAS ALWAYS INTENSE. DESPITE HIS SUCCESS, HE RARELY SMILED AND WAS NEVER SATISFIED WITH HIS PRODUCTION. TONY AND INDIANS MANAGEMENT WERE AT ODDS OVER HIS 1970 SALARY, SO TONY HELD OUT AND MISSED THREE WEEKS OF SPRING TRAINING. AS A RESULT, HE STARTED SLOWLY AND QUICKLY DREW BOOS FROM ANGRY INDIANS FANS. THE '70 SEASON REALLY PROVED TO BE A ROLLERCOASTER RIDE FOR TONY. THE UPS FEATURED INCREDIBLE PERFORMANCES LIKE HIS 3-HOMER GAME AGAINST THE YANKS IN MAY AND HIS JULY CYCLE VERSUS THE ORIOLES. THE DOWNS WERE AN EARLY SEASON BACK INJURY; MYSTERIOUS HEADACHES; AN EMBARRASSING INCIDENT THAT SAW TONY HUMILIATED BY STEVE HAMILTON'S "FOLLY FLOATER" EEPHUS PITCH... AND THE BOOS. "I REALIZE THAT PEOPLE PAY GOOD MONEY TO SEE US PLAY AND THAT GIVES THEM, I SUPPOSE, A RIGHT TO BOO," TONY TOLD THE CLEVELAND PAPERS, "BUT IT'S HARD TO DO THE JOB AND WORRY ABOUT THE FANS, TOO." TONY'S SUICIDE ATTEMPT CAME SHORTLY AFTER THOSE COMMENTS. FORTUNATELY, TONY SURVIVED AND RECEIVED TREATMENT FOR HIS MENTAL ILLNESS. WITH HIS SKILLS, THE SKY WAS THE LIMIT FOR TONY ON THE BALLFIELD -- IF IT DIDN'T KILL HIM FIRST. A COMPLETE AND PERMANENT BREAK FROM BASEBALL WAS WHAT TONY CHOSE TO DO TO SAVE HIMSELF -- AND HE'S STAYED TRUE TO HIS DECISION. BASEBALL LOST OUT, BUT THE DECISION PROVED TO BE THE RIGHT ONE FOR TONY AS HE'S ALIVE AND WELL AND A SUCCESSFUL BUSINESSMAN.

Johnny MOSTIL

CENTERFIELDER JOHNNY MOSTIL FIRST SAW ACTION IN THE BIG LEAGUES DURING A TEN-GAME TRIAL WITH THE 1918 WHITE SOX. HE RETURNED TO THE MINORS WHILE THE "BLACK SOX" ROLLED TO INFAMY IN 1919 AND '20, THEN REJOINED THE SOX FULL-TIME IN 1921 WITH THE UNENVIABLE TASK OF TRYING TO MAKE THE COMISKEY PARK FANS FORGET ABOUT POPULAR -- YET BANNED -- OUTFIELDERS JOE JACKSON AND HAPPY FELSCH. FLEET-FOOTED JOHNNY TURNED OUT TO BE THE PERFECT MAN FOR THE JOB, DAZZLING CHISOX FANS WITH CIRCUS CATCHES AND STOLEN BASES. HE PLAYED HIS ENTIRE CAREER WITH THE SOX, AND BY THE TIME HE WAS DONE FOLLOWING THE '29 CAMPAIGN, MANY CONSIDERED JOHNNY ONE OF THE GREATEST CENTERFIELDERS OF ALL TIME. "HE COULD GO GET 'EM -- IT WAS LIKE TURNING A RABBIT LOOSE WHEN A BALL WAS HIT TO CENTER," SAID TEAMMATE TED LYONS. EDDIE COLLINS, ANOTHER LEGENDARY TEAMMATE, SAID, "FOR COVERING GROUND, MOSTIL WAS IN A CLASS BY HIMSELF. I NEVER SAW HIS EQUAL." EVEN BABE RUTH HAD HIGH PRAISE FOR MOSTIL IN 1928 WHEN HE CALLED JOHNNY "ONE OF THE GREATEST OUTFIELDERS THE GAME HAS KNOWN."

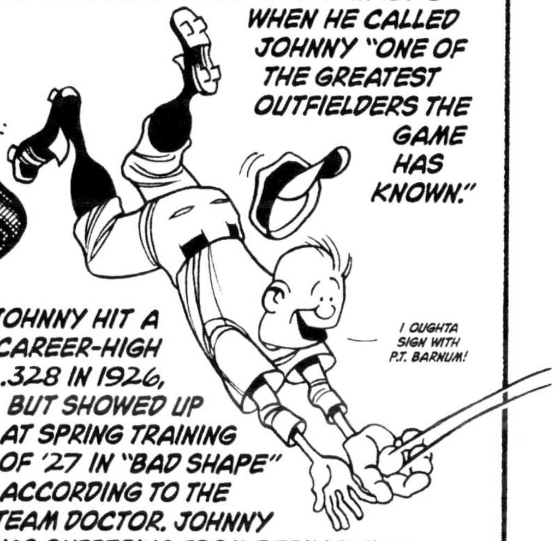

JOHNNY HIT A CAREER-HIGH .328 IN 1926, BUT SHOWED UP AT SPRING TRAINING OF '27 IN "BAD SHAPE" ACCORDING TO THE TEAM DOCTOR. JOHNNY WAS SUFFERING FROM DEBILITATING DENTAL ISSUES, AS WELL AS A PAINFUL NERVE CONDITION IN HIS LEFT SHOULDER. MAYBE IT WAS HIS ILL HEALTH -- NO ONE KNOWS FOR SURE -- BUT ON MARCH 9, 1927, JOHNNY TRIED TO END HIS LIFE BY SLASHING HIS THROAT, WRISTS AND ANKLES, WHILE ALSO STABBING HIMSELF IN THE CHEST. FOUND NEAR DEATH IN A HOTEL ROOM, HE WAS ADMINISTERED LAST RITES AND GIVEN LITTLE CHANCE TO RECOVER. MIRACULOUSLY, HE DID RECOVER, BUT HE WAS NEVER THE SAME PLAYER. REFUSING TO BELIEVE THAT SEVERE PAIN COULD HAVE DRIVEN JOHNNY TO ATTEMPT SUCH A DESPERATE ACT, WILD RUMORS BEGAN TO CIRCULATE. ONE THEORY HAD TEAMMATE RED FABER THREATENING TO KILL JOHNNY OVER AN AFFAIR WITH THE SPITBALLER'S WIFE. ANOTHER CLAIMED JOHNNY WAS DESPONDENT AFTER LEARNING THAT HIS GIRLFRIEND, MARGARET CARROLL, HAD LEFT HIM FOR BILL BARRETT, HIS SOX ROOMMATE. WHILE BARRETT AND CARROLL WOULD ONE DAY MARRY, NONE OF THE PARTIES INVOLVED EVER GAVE CREEDENCE TO THE STORY. JOHNNY WENT ON TO A LONG CAREER AS A MINOR LEAGUE MANAGER AND SCOUT, TAKING HIS SECRET -- IF THERE WAS ONE -- WITH HIM TO HIS GRAVE AT AGE 74.

Hank THOMPSON

JUST THE THIRD BLACK MAN TO PLAY IN THE MAJOR LEAGUES, 21-YEAR-OLD HANK THOMPSON JOINED THE ST. LOUIS BROWNS ON JULY 17, 1947. HANK HAD PROVEN HIMSELF AS A PLAYER IN THE NEGRO LEAGUES, AND HE'D PROVEN HIS TOUGHNESS AS A MACHINE GUNNER WITH THE 1695TH COMBAT ENGINEERS DURING THE BATTLE OF THE BULGE, SO HE APPEARED TO BE UP TO THE CHALLENGES HE KNEW HE WOULD FACE AS ONE OF THE FEW BLACKS IN THE BIGS. STILL, AFTER HITTING JUST .256 IN 27 GAMES, THE BROWNS RELEASED HIM, STATING THAT HANK'S PRODUCTION HAD "FAILED TO REACH MAJOR LEAGUE STANDARDS." DESPITE THE FACT THAT THE HAPLESS BROWNIE ROSTER WAS LOADED WITH WHITE PLAYERS WHO MANY FELT WERE NOT BIG LEAGUE CALIBER, IT WAS HANK, NOT THEM, WHO WAS AXED. HANK WOULD LATER MAKE GOOD, THOUGH, WITH THE NEW YORK GIANTS. THREE TIMES HE WOULD TOP 20 HOMERS, AND HIS .364 WORLD SERIES AVERAGE HELPED THE GIANTS TO A DOMINATING SWEEP OF THE HEAVILY-FAVORED INDIANS IN THE 1954 FALL CLASSIC.

ON THE FIELD, HANK WAS ALL BASEBALL. OFF THE FIELD, HE STRUGGLED. HE SPENT PART OF HIS YOUTH IN REFORM SCHOOL, AND HIS TROUBLES CONTINUED INTO ADULTHOOD. HE SHOT A MAN TO DEATH IN 1948; STOLE A CAR IN 1958; BEAT A WOMAN IN 1959; AND ROBBED A BAR AT GUNPOINT IN 1961. ANOTHER ARMED ROBBERY FINALLY LANDED HANK IN JAIL FOR A LONG HITCH IN 1963. PAROLED FOUR YEARS LATER, HANK SEEMED TO BE TURNING HIS LIFE AROUND WHEN HE DIED SUDDENLY IN 1969. HANK THOMPSON WAS JUST 43 YEARS OLD.

Len Koenecke

BORN ON JANUARY 18, 1904, IN BARABOO, WISCONSIN, LEONARD GEORGE KOENECKE'S LIFE FOLLOWED A BIZARRE ARC NEVER BEFORE -- OR SINCE -- SEEN IN A MAJOR LEAGUER! KOENECKE JOINED THE NEW YORK GIANTS IN 1932 AFTER A FINE YEAR WITH INDIANAPOLIS, BUT HE FAILED MAKE THE GRADE, BATTING JUST .255 WITH FOUR HOMERS IN 42 GAMES UNDER MANAGER JOHN McGRAW! BROOKLYN TOOK A CHANCE AND SIGNED THE TALENTED KOENECKE WITH DODGER MANAGER CASEY STENGEL PERSONALLY HELPING THE 5-FOOT 10-INCH CENTERFIELDER WORK ON HIS HITTING! IT PAID OFF IN SPADES AS KOENECKE BATTED .320 WITH 14 HOMERS AND 73 RBIs FOR THE BUMS OF 1935! HIS WORK IN THE GARDEN WAS SPECTACULAR, TOO, AS HE SET A NEW RECORD FOR NATIONAL LEAGUE FLYCHASERS WITH A FIELDING AVERAGE OF .994!

IT WAS DOWNHILL FROM THERE, HOWEVER! KOENECKE SLUMPED TO .283 IN 1936, AND HIS POWER LEFT HIM AS HE BELTED JUST FOUR ROUND-TRIPPERS! THE CLUB LET HIM GO IN MID-SEPTEMBER, AND A DISTRAUGHT KOENECKE DID NOT TAKE THE NEWS WELL! APPEARING DRUNK AND AGITATED, HE CHARTERED A PLANE TO FLY HIM HOME, THEN GOT INTO A HARROWING 15-MINUTE MID-AIR FIGHT WITH THE TWO-MAN CREW OF THE PLANE! FEARING THAT THE CRAZED BALLPLAYER WAS ABOUT TO CAUSE THE PLANE TO CRASH, THE PILOT KILLED KOENECKE BY BASHING HIM OVER THE HEAD WITH A FIRE EXTINGUISHER, THEN LANDED THE CRIPPLED PLANE IN A FIELD! IT WAS A HORRIFIC SCENE THE COPS WITNESSED WHEN THEY ARRIVED, AND DESPITE INITIAL CHARGES OF MANSLAUGHTER, THE PILOT AND HIS CREWMATE WERE QUICKLY EXONERATED!

THE BASEBALL WORLD WAS STUNNED BY THIS STORY, BUT LESS SO LATER AS TID-BITS TRICKLED OUT ABOUT PREVIOUS INCIDENTS OF DRINKING AND ERRATIC BEHAVIOR ON THE PART OF KOENECKE! IN HIS BOOK "STENGEL," ROBERT W. CREAMER REPORTED VETERAN SCRIBES AS SAYING THAT KOENECKE CAUSED THE BRAWL BY MAKING HOMOSEXUAL ADVANCES TO THE PLANE'S CREW! WHATEVER THE CASE, IT'S A TRAGIC STORY! BETTER TO REMEMBER THE GOOD TIMES -- CHASING DOWN FLY BALLS IN SUN-DRENCHED EBBETS FIELD!

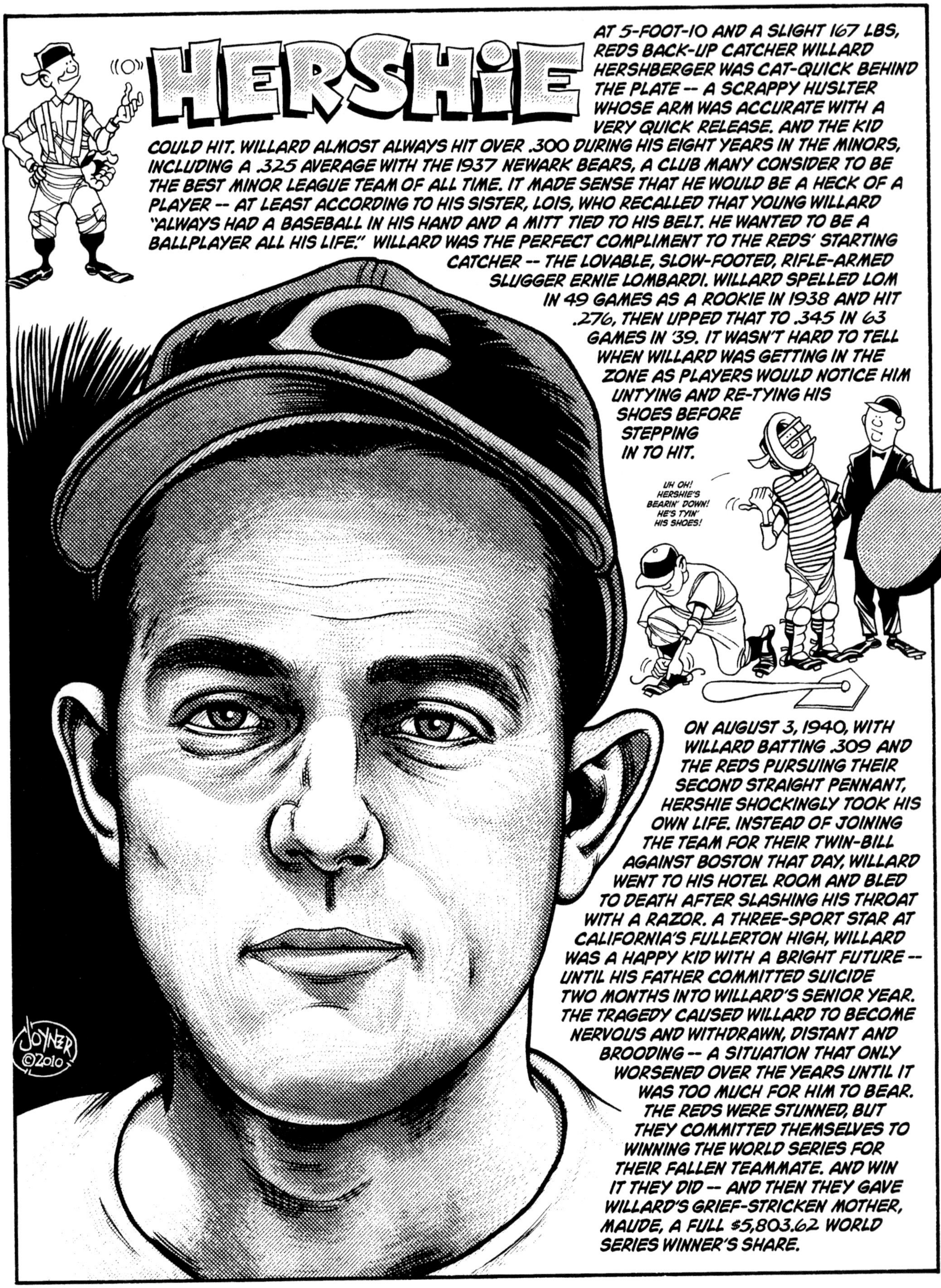
HERSHiE
AT 5-FOOT-10 AND A SLIGHT 167 LBS, REDS BACK-UP CATCHER WILLARD HERSHBERGER WAS CAT-QUICK BEHIND THE PLATE -- A SCRAPPY HUSLTER WHOSE ARM WAS ACCURATE WITH A VERY QUICK RELEASE. AND THE KID COULD HIT. WILLARD ALMOST ALWAYS HIT OVER .300 DURING HIS EIGHT YEARS IN THE MINORS, INCLUDING A .325 AVERAGE WITH THE 1937 NEWARK BEARS, A CLUB MANY CONSIDER TO BE THE BEST MINOR LEAGUE TEAM OF ALL TIME. IT MADE SENSE THAT HE WOULD BE A HECK OF A PLAYER -- AT LEAST ACCORDING TO HIS SISTER, LOIS, WHO RECALLED THAT YOUNG WILLARD "ALWAYS HAD A BASEBALL IN HIS HAND AND A MITT TIED TO HIS BELT. HE WANTED TO BE A BALLPLAYER ALL HIS LIFE." WILLARD WAS THE PERFECT COMPLIMENT TO THE REDS' STARTING CATCHER -- THE LOVABLE, SLOW-FOOTED, RIFLE-ARMED SLUGGER ERNIE LOMBARDI. WILLARD SPELLED LOM IN 49 GAMES AS A ROOKIE IN 1938 AND HIT .276, THEN UPPED THAT TO .345 IN 63 GAMES IN '39. IT WASN'T HARD TO TELL WHEN WILLARD WAS GETTING IN THE ZONE AS PLAYERS WOULD NOTICE HIM UNTYING AND RE-TYING HIS SHOES BEFORE STEPPING IN TO HIT.
UH OH! HERSHIE'S BEARIN' DOWN! HE'S TYIN' HIS SHOES!
ON AUGUST 3, 1940, WITH WILLARD BATTING .309 AND THE REDS PURSUING THEIR SECOND STRAIGHT PENNANT, HERSHIE SHOCKINGLY TOOK HIS OWN LIFE. INSTEAD OF JOINING THE TEAM FOR THEIR TWIN-BILL AGAINST BOSTON THAT DAY, WILLARD WENT TO HIS HOTEL ROOM AND BLED TO DEATH AFTER SLASHING HIS THROAT WITH A RAZOR. A THREE-SPORT STAR AT CALIFORNIA'S FULLERTON HIGH, WILLARD WAS A HAPPY KID WITH A BRIGHT FUTURE -- UNTIL HIS FATHER COMMITTED SUICIDE TWO MONTHS INTO WILLARD'S SENIOR YEAR. THE TRAGEDY CAUSED WILLARD TO BECOME NERVOUS AND WITHDRAWN, DISTANT AND BROODING -- A SITUATION THAT ONLY WORSENED OVER THE YEARS UNTIL IT WAS TOO MUCH FOR HIM TO BEAR. THE REDS WERE STUNNED, BUT THEY COMMITTED THEMSELVES TO WINNING THE WORLD SERIES FOR THEIR FALLEN TEAMMATE. AND WIN IT THEY DID -- AND THEN THEY GAVE WILLARD'S GRIEF-STRICKEN MOTHER, MAUDE, A FULL $5,803.62 WORLD SERIES WINNER'S SHARE.
JOYNER ©2010

Jake POWELL

ON A CLUB FEATURING NAMES LIKE DIMAGGIO, LAZZERI, AND GEHRIG, IT WAS LITTLE-KNOWN YANK JAKE POWELL WHO STOLE THE SHOW IN THE 1936 WORLD SERIES AS HE BANGED OUT TEN HITS IN 22 AT-BATS DURING THE BRONX BOMBERS' SIX-GAME VICTORY OVER THE N.Y. GIANTS!

THE MARYLAND-BORN OUTFIELDER HAD COME TO THE YANKS JUST FOUR MONTHS EARLIER IN A STRAIGHT-UP SWAP FOR BEN CHAPMAN, A KNOWN RACIST WHO HAD ALIENATED THE YANKEE FAITHFUL BY TAUNTING THEIR DEVOTED JEWISH FANS WITH NAZI SALUTES AND DISPARAGING ETHNIC REMARKS. UNFORTUNATELY, POWELL HAD DEMONS THAT MADE CHAPMAN LOOK LIKE AN ALTAR BOY. FUELED BY ANTI-SEMITISM, POWELL PLOWED OVER HANK GREENBERG IN A DIRTY PLAY AT FIRST BASE ON APRIL 29, 1936. THE COLLISION RESULTED IN A BROKEN WRIST FOR HAMMERIN' HANK, ABRUPTLY ENDING HIS SEASON. THE NATS WERE HAPPY TO PART COMPANY WITH POWELL SHORTLY THEREAFTER. NOT ONLY WAS HIS RACISM AN EMBARRASSMENT, BUT HE ALSO HAD A WILD REPUTATION OFF THE FIELD. POWELL WASN'T VERY GOOD AT MANAGING HIS FINANCES, EITHER, AND HIS CREDITORS WERE THREATENING TO SUE THE NATIONALS TO COLLECT ON JAKE'S DEBTS. POWELL KEPT HIS NOSE CLEAN FOR TWO YEARS AFTER JOINING THE YANKEES, BUT HE CAUSED AN UPROAR ON JULY 29, 1938, WHEN HE UNLEASHED A RACIST QUIP THAT GOT HIM IN DEEP TROUBLE. IN A LIVE IMPROMPTU PRE-GAME RADIO INTERVIEW WITH WGN'S BOB ELSON, POWELL, USING A DEROGATORY RACIAL EPITHET, CLAIMED HE KEPT FIT IN THE OFFSEASON BY WORKING AS A COP AND CRACKING BLACKS OVER THE HEAD WITH HIS NIGHTSTICK. THE COMMENT CAUSED AN IMMEDIATE UPROAR AND PROMPTED A 10-DAY SUSPENSION FOR POWELL. MANY FOUND THE SUSPENSION HYPOCRITICAL CONSIDERING BASEBALL'S OWN RACIST "UNWRITTEN" POLICY THAT FORBADE BLACKS FROM PLAYING IN THE MAJORS. POWELL'S CAREER NEVER FULLY RECOVERED FROM THE INCIDENT, AND BY 1948 HE WAS TRYING TO HANG ON DOWN IN THE CLASS-D FLORIDA LEAGUE! A MONTH AFTER THE SEASON ENDED, POWELL WAS ARRESTED IN WASHINGTON ON A CHARGE OF PASSING BAD CHECKS. THE TROUBLED FLYCHASER THEN SHOCKED EVERYONE AT THE POLICE STATION WHEN HE PULLED OUT A .28-CALIBER HANDGUN AND SAID, "TO HELL WITH ALL THIS -- I'M GOING TO END IT ALL!" WITH THAT, JAKE POWELL SHOT HIMSELF ONCE IN THE CHEST AND ONCE IN THE TEMPLE, THUS ENDING ONE OF THE DARKEST CHAPTERS IN THE ANNALS OF MAJOR LEAGUE BASEBALL.

THAT LOOKS LIKE THE BEGINNING OF A BEAUTIFUL FRIENDSHIP!
Billy
JURGES
BORN IN THE BRONX ON MAY 9, 1908, AND RAISED IN BROOKLYN, SHORTSTOP BILLY JURGES JOINED THE CUBS IN 1931! TEAMING WITH FELLOW ROOKIE BILLY HERMAN, THEY FORMED THE N.L.'S PREMIER DOUBLE-PLAY COMBINATION AND HELPED LEAD THE CUBS TO THREE WORLD SERIES APPEARANCES! JURGES' CAREER WAS NEARLY ENDED DURING HIS SECOND YEAR, HOWEVER, WHEN HE WAS SHOT BY HIS PSYCHOTIC EX-GIRLFRIEND, BURLESQUE DANCER VIOLET VALLI! UPSET OVER BILLY'S ATTEMPT TO BREAK OFF THEIR ROMANCE, VIOLET WROTE A NOTE SAYING SHE NO LONGER WANTED TO LIVE-- AND SHE INTENDED TO "TAKE BILLY WITH ME." SHE THEN WENT TO HIS ROOM AT THE CARLOS HOTEL IN CHICAGO AND AIMED A HEATER AT HIM AFTER HE LET HER IN! SHOCKED AT THE TURN OF EVENTS, BILLY WRESTLED AWAY HER PISTOL, BUT WAS SHOT TWICE IN THE PROCESS WHILE THE CRAZED SHOWGIRL WAS SHOT ONCE! BOTH SURVIVED THE SHOOTING, AND BILLY REFUSED TO PRESS CHARGES! THE INCIDENT RESULTED IN A CAREER BOOST FOR VIOLET, HER BOOKINGS JUMPING WHILE SHE BILLED HERSELF AS "VIOLET, WHAT I DID FOR LOVE, VALLI, THE MOST TALKED ABOUT GIRL IN CHICAGO," BUT SHE THEN DISAPPEARED INTO OBSCURITY! MANY BELIEVE THAT THIS SCANDAL SPARKED "THE NATURAL," BERNARD MALAMUD'S CLASSIC NOVEL!
REALLY, BILLY, I JUST WANT TO "TALK" TO YOU!
JOYNER ©2007
I SAVED THE BEST FOR LAST!
BILLY REBOUNDED FROM HIS SHOOTING TO PLAY 15 MORE YEARS IN THE BIG LEAGUES, THEN A LONG CAREER COACHING, MANAGING, AND SCOUTING! NOT KNOWN AS A POWER HITTER, BILLY MADE THE LAST OF HIS 43 CAREER HOMERS A MEMORABLE ONE! SHIFTED FROM COACH BACK TO PLAYER IN A DESPERATION MOVE BY THE CUBS ON AUGUST 23RD, 1947, BILLY REWARDED THEIR FAITH TWO DAYS LATER WITH A GAME-WINNING HOME RUN!

Ronnie WILLIAMSON

RONALD KEITH WILLIAMSON WAS AN OUTFIELDER WITH ALL THE TOOLS REQUIRED TO MAKE IT BIG IN THE MAJOR LEAGUES. HE HAD SIZE, SPEED, A SOLID GLOVE, POWER AT THE PLATE, AND A RIFLE FOR A RIGHT ARM. AFTER AN ALL-STATE SENIOR YEAR AT OKLAHOMA'S ASHER HIGH SCHOOL, THE NATION'S ALL-TIME WINNINGEST HIGH SCHOOL BASEBALL PROGRAM, THE OAKLAND ATHLETICS MADE RONNIE THEIR SECOND PICK IN THE 1971 AMATEUR DRAFT. HE WAS THE 41st OF 800 PLAYERS DRAFTED. BY SEPTEMBER 19, 1994, RONNIE SAT ON OKLAHOMA'S DEATH ROW, JUST FIVE DAYS AWAY FROM EXECUTION BY LETHAL INJECTION.

BORN ON FEBRUARY 3, 1953, RONNIE THOUGHT HE WAS FOLLOWING IN THE FOOTSTEPS OF HIS CHILDHOOD IDOL, FELLOW OKLAHOMAN MICKEY MANTLE, WHEN HE WAS DRAFTED BY OAKLAND. RONNIE SIGNED FOR A $50,000 BONUS, THEN HIT THE MINOR LEAGUES WITH THE CLASS-A COOS BAY-NORTH BEND A'S. HE STRUGGLED TO FIND HIS FORM, HOWEVER, AND FARED EVEN WORSE IN HIS SECOND SEASON DOWN ON THE FARM. THE A'S CUT RONNIE AFTER A '74 SPRING TRAINING ELBOW INJURY -- AND WITH THAT HE WAS OUT OF THE GAME HE LOVED. RONNIE STRUGGLED TO ADJUST, AND SPIRALED INTO A PATTERN OF ALCOHOL AND DRUG ABUSE. HIS ELBOW HEALED, SO RONNIE SWITCHED TO PITCHING AND ATTEMPTED A COMEBACK WITH THE 1976 ONEONTA YANKEES AND THE '77 FT. LAUDERDALE YANKEES, BUT A SHOULDER INJURY FORCED HIM TO HANG UP HIS BASEBALL DREAM FOR GOOD IN 1978. DISTRAUGHT OVER HIS FAILURE, RONNIE BECAME MORE INVOLVED WITH DRUGS AND ALCOHOL -- AND EVEN SUFFERED BOUTS OF MENTAL ILLNESS. IT ALL CAME CRASHING DOWN ON RONNIE ON MAY 8, 1987, WHEN HE WAS ARRESTED FOR A 1982 RAPE AND MURDER. WITH NO EVIDENCE OTHER THAN THE FALSE TESTIMONY OF SHADY WITNESS, RONNIE WAS CONVICTED AND SENTENCED TO DIE. FOR ELEVEN TORTUROUS YEARS, RONNIE SAT ON DEATH ROW, PROCLAIMING HIS INNOCENCE WHILE SLIPPING DEEPER INTO MENTAL ILLNESS. DNA EVIDENCE FULLY EXONERATED HIM IN 1998 AND HE WAS FREED, BUT THE MENTAL AND PHYSICAL TRAUMA OF HIS INCARCERATION HAD TAKEN ITS TOLL, AND RON DIED IN 2004 AT 51. "ALL I EVER WANTED TO DO WAS PLAY BALL," RONNIE SAID PRIOR TO HIS DEATH, "IT'S THE ONLY FUN I EVER HAD." TO LEARN MORE ABOUT RONNIE, READ JOHN GRISHAM'S BOOK "THE INNOCENT MAN."

WORLD WAR II

Harry O'NEILL

BORN IN PHILADELPHIA, PENNSYLVANIA, ON MAY 8, 1917 -- A TIME WHEN SO MANY AMERICAN MEN WERE DYING IN THE GREAT WAR -- HARRY O'NEILL WOULD HIMSELF MAKE THE ULTIMATE SACRIFICE IN THE NEXT WORLD WAR. HE WAS A MULTI-SPORT STAR AT DARBY HIGH SCHOOL BEFORE MOVING ON TO GETTYSBURG COLLEGE WHERE HE AGAIN EXCELLED AT ATHLETICS. WHILE MAJORING IN HISTORY AT G.C., HARRY PLAYED CENTER ON THE FOOTBALL TEAM, CENTER ON THE BASKETBALL TEAM, AND CATCHER FOR THE BASEBALL NINE. HARRY'S ACCOMPLISHMENTS FOR THE G.C. BULLETS LED TO HIS 1980 INDUCTION IN THE SCHOOL'S PRESTIGIOUS HALL OF ATHLETIC HONOR.

HARRY'S ABILITY ON THE BASEBALL DIAMOND DID NOT GO UNNOTICED BY CONNIE MACK, MANAGER OF THE PHILADELPHIA A's, SO HE SIGNED THE KID AS SOON AS HE FINISHED AT GETTYSBURG AND PROMPTLY HAD HIM JOIN THE BALLCLUB. THAT WAS JUNE 5, 1939, AND WHILE HARRY SPENT THE REST OF THE SEASON WITH THE CLUB, HE NEEDED SEASONING AND THEREFORE APPEARED IN JUST ONE GAME. HARRY ENTERED AS A LATE-INNING DEFENSIVE REPLACEMENT IN A 16-3 A's LOSS ON JULY 23, 1939.

HARRY NEVER EVEN GOT A CHANCE TO BAT THAT DAY, BUT NO ONE THOUGHT TWICE ABOUT IT AT THE TIME -- SURELY THERE WOULD BE MANY MORE OPPORTUNITIES FOR THE YOUNGSTER FROM PHILLY. BUT FATE HAD OTHER PLANS, AND HARRY WAS KILLED IN ACTION ON MARCH 6, 1945, AS HE FOUGHT HIS WAY INLAND ON THE ISLAND OF IWO JIMA. IT WAS A TRAGIC LOSS, BUT FIRST LIEUTENANT HARRY O'NEILL DIED DOING WHAT HE WANTED TO DO -- FIGHTING FOR AMERICA AS A PROUD FOURTH DIVISION MARINE.

Elmer GEDEON

ON SEPTEMBER 19, 1939, ELMER JOHN GEDEON, THE WASHINGTON SENATORS' LEAN, FLEET-FOOTED, 6-FOOT-4-INCH ROOKIE CENTERFIELDER, RAPPED OUT THREE HITS IN FOUR AT-BATS IN THE NATS' 10-9 WIN OVER THE CLEVELAND INDIANS. ELMER HAD MADE HIS MAJOR LEAGUE DEBUT THE DAY BEFORE, AND HAD A BRIGHT FUTURE AHEAD OF HIM, BUT HE WOULD PLAY IN JUST THREE MORE BIG LEAGUE GAMES. HE SPENT 1940 EARNING MORE EXPERIENCE WITH CHARLOTTE, THEN HAD HIS SIGHTS SET ON WINNING A FULL-TIME JOB WITH THE NATS WHEN UNCLE SAM CAME CALLING IN EARLY 1941. ELMER JOINED THE AIR FORCE AND WAS FLYING BOMBING MISSIONS OVER EUROPE BY THE SPRING OF 1944. IT WAS HAZARDOUS DUTY, BUT ELMER HAD LONG AGO PROVED HIS COURAGE. ELMER WAS A NAVIGATOR ABOARD A B-25 THAT CRASHED ON TAKE-OFF AT RALEIGH, NORTH CAROLINA, IN 1942. TWO OF THE SEVEN CREW MEMBERS WERE KILLED IN THE FIERY WRECKAGE. ELMER ESCAPED WITH THREE BROKEN RIBS AND SEVERE BURNS, BUT HE RE-ENTERED THE BURNING PLANE TO RESCUE CORPORAL JOHN BARRAT WHO HAD SUFFERED A BROKEN NECK AND TWO BROKEN LEGS. FOR THAT, ELMER WAS PROMOTED TO 1st LIEUTENANT AND DECORATED WITH THE SOLDIERS' MEDAL. A FULL-FLEDGED CAPTAIN AND PILOT BY 1944, ELMER WAS FLYING A B-26 MARAUDER WHEN HIS BOMBER WAS HIT BY NAZI FLAK OVER FRANCE. ELMER WAS KILLED INSTANTLY, AND ONLY ONE CREW MEMBER -- CO-PILOT JAMES TAAFFE -- MANAGED TO BAIL OUT AND SURVIVE. ELMER DIED YOUNG, BUT LIVED A VERY FULL LIFE IN HIS 27 YEARS. A 3-SPORT STAR AT THE UNIVERSITY OF MICHIGAN, A BIG LEAGUE BALLPLAYER, AND A COMBAT PILOT -- ELMER GEDEON WAS A TRUE AMERICAN HERO!

Billy SOUTHWORTH "Junior"

BILLY BROOKS SOUTHWORTH -- OR "JUNIOR" AS HE WAS OFTEN CALLED -- WAS BORN ON JUNE 10, 1916, IN PORTLAND, OREGON, WHILE HIS POP WAS BUSY ROAMING THE OUTFIELD FOR THE PCL'S PORTLAND BEAVERS! DAD CARVED OUT A FINE CAREER AS A BIG LEAGUE PLAYER, BUT IT WAS HIS MANAGERIAL ACUMEN THAT WOULD LEAD TO HIS EVENTUAL ENSHRINEMENT IN THE HALL OF FAME! YOUNG BILLY, TOO, WOULD GAIN IMMORTALITY, BUT AS A HERO OF A DIFFERENT KIND! LIKE HIS FATHER, BILLY LOVED BASEBALL AND EXCELLED AT IT, BEGINNING HIS MINOR LEAGUE CAREER WITH ASHEVILLE IN 1936! ACCORDING TO LEGENDARY SPORTSWRITER ARTHUR DALEY, BILLY WAS A "HARD-HITTING OUTFIELDER WHO HAD A WHIP-LIKE ARM AND COULD RUN LIKE A DEER," AND JUNIOR RODE THOSE SKILLS TO AN M.V.P. SEASON IN 1938 WITH ROME OF THE CANADIAN-AMERICAN LEAGUE! POISED TO MAKE IT TO THE BIG LEAGUES IN 1941, BILLY PUT ASIDE HIS BASEBALL AMBITIONS AND ENLISTED IN THE ARMY AIR CORPS TO BE READY FOR THE IMPENDING WAR WITH GERMANY! IN DOING SO, BILLY BECAME THE FIRST PRO BALLPLAYER TO JOIN THE WAR EFFORT! BILLY EARNED HIS PILOT'S WINGS AND JOINED THE 427TH BOMB SQUADRON, 303RD BOMB GROUP, IN MOLESWORTH, ENGLAND, WHERE HE WOULD PILOT DANGEROUS MISSIONS IN A B-17 FLYING FORTRESS!

BILLY COMPLETED 25 MISSIONS, A FULL TOUR OF DUTY, THEN RETURNED TO THE STATES WHERE HE TRAINED PILOTS TO FLY THE NEW B-29 SUPER-FORTRESS! ON FEBRUARY 15, 1945, WHILE FLYING A B-29 OUT OF NEW YORK, ENGINE TROUBLE CAUSED THE PLANE TO CRASH, KILLING BILLY AND FOUR OTHER CREW MEMBERS! FIVE CREW MEMBERS DID, HOWEVER, SURVIVE, A MIRACLE THAT CAN ONLY BE ATTRIBUTED TO BILLY'S HEROIC EFFORT TO TO LAND THE HUGE, STRICKEN PLANE! THE TRAGEDY ENDED A BRIGHT FUTURE FOR BILLY AND LEFT HIS DAD DEVASTATED, BUT THE LEGEND OF THE "FLYING OUTFIELDER" WILL NEVER DIE!

Buck
COMPTON
BORN ON NEW YEAR'S EVE, 1921, IN LOS ANGELES, CALIFORNIA, LYNN DAVIS COMPTON -- UNHAPPY WITH HAVING A "GIRL'S" FIRST NAME -- TOOK TO CALLING HIMSELF "BUCK" BECAUSE IT SOUNDED LIKE "TRUCK," WHICH WAS THE NAME OF TRUCK HANNAH, THE STAR CATCHER FOR THE P.C.L. LOS ANGELES ANGELS! LIKE HIS NAMESAKE, BUCK ALSO BECAME A CATCHER! HE PLAYED FOR THE U.C.L.A. BRUINS WHERE HE EARNED ALL-LEAGUE HONORS AND WAS A TEAMMATE OF JACKIE ROBINSON! BUCK WAS ALSO ON THE U.C.L.A. FOOTBALL TEAM -- A TEAM THAT PLAYED IN THE ROSE BOWL ON JANUARY 1, 1943! EIGHTEEN MONTHS LATER, DURING THE EARLY HOURS OF JUNE 6, 1944, BUCK PARACHUTED IN BEHIND THE GERMAN LINE AT NORMANDY AS PART OF THE ALLIED D-DAY INVASION! SERVING WITH THE NOW-FAMOUS "EASY" COMPANY OF THE 506TH PARACHUTE INFANTRY REGIMENT, BUCK DISTINGUISHED HIMSELF IN COMBAT FROM FRANCE TO HOLLAND TO BELGIUM -- SERVICE FOR WHICH HE RECEIVED A SILVER STAR AND A PURPLE HEART! BUCK WILL FOREVER BE REMEMBERED BY NEW GENERATIONS THANKS TO NEAL McDONOUGH'S FINE PORTRAYAL OF HIM IN HBO'S CLASSIC SERIES "BAND OF BROTHERS." DESPITE HIS LOVE OF THE GAME, BUCK TURNED DOWN OFFERS TO PLAY MINOR LEAGUE BALL AFTER THE WAR, INSTEAD OPTING TO ATTEND LAW SCHOOL! BUCK ROSE TO THE POSITION OF DEPUTY DISTRICT ATTORNEY OF L.A. COUNTY WHERE HE PROSECUTED MANY MAJOR FELONY CASES, INCLUDING THE TRIAL OF SIRHAN SIRHAN FOR THE 1968 MURDER OF ROBERT F. KENNEDY!
BUCK WAS AN L.A.P.D. COP EARLY IN HIS CAREER; LATER BECOMING A PLAINCLOTHES DETECTIVE! FOLLOWING HIS 19 YEARS OF WORK IN THE D.A.'S OFFICE, BUCK BECAME A JUDGE FOR CALIFORNIA'S COURT OF APPEALS!
JOYNER ©2008

Cecil TRAVIS

THE LAST OF JAMES AND ADA TRAVIS' TEN CHILDREN, CECIL HOWELL TRAVIS WAS BORN ON AUGUST 8, 1913, ON THE FAMILY FARM IN RIVERDALE, GEORGIA! IT WAS ON THAT FARM THAT CECIL CULTIVATED THE FLUID LEFT-HANDED SWING THAT WOULD SEND HIM TO THE BIG LEAGUES! "INSTEAD OF CHOPPING COTTON," HE OFTEN SAID, "I'D PICK UP ROCKS AND WHACK 'EM WITH MY HOE." CECIL'S ABILITY TO "WHACK 'EM" ALLOWED HIM TO REACH THE MAJORS AT THE AGE OF ONLY 19! HIS DEBUT WITH THE WASHINGTON SENATORS ON MAY 19, 1933, WAS A SPECTACULAR ONE, TOO, AS CECIL, HAVING ARRIVED AT GRIFFITH STADIUM JUST 30 MINUTES PRIOR TO THE GAME, COLLECTED FIVE HITS IN HIS FIRST FIVE AT-BATS!

CECIL QUICKLY DEVELOPED INTO A FULL-FLEDGED SUPERSTAR, HIS GREATNESS REACHING ITS PEAK IN 1941! WHILE PLAYING TYPICALLY SOLID AT SHORTSTOP, HIS BAT WAS ANYTHING BUT TYPICAL AS HE HIT .359 WITH A LEAGUE-LEADING 218 HITS! ON A SURE PATH TO THE HALL OF FAME, CECIL'S BASEBALL CAREER WAS PUT ON HIATUS AS HE SPENT 1942-45 AS A MEMBER OF THE SPECIAL FORCES IN THE 76TH "ONAWAY" INFANTRY DIVISION! THE 76TH PURSUED AS HITLER'S FORCES RETREATED FROM THE BATTLE OF THE BULGE, AND IT WAS DURING THAT TIME THAT CECIL EARNED A BRONZE STAR WHILE ALSO SUFFERING FROSTBITE ON HIS LEFT FOOT! CECIL RETURNED TO THE BIGS FOR TWO FULL SEASONS, BUT THE FROSTBITE AND TIME AWAY HAD ERODED HIS SKILLS, SO HE RETIRED AT 33 FOLLOWING THE '47 CAMPAIGN! ALWAYS ULTRA-CLASSY, CECIL REFUSED TO BLAME THE WAR, INSTEAD SAYING, "WE HAD A JOB TO DO, AN OBLIGATION, AND WE DID IT. I WAS HARDLY THE ONLY ONE."

A TRUE SOUTHERN GENTLEMAN, EVERYONE LOVED CECIL -- EVEN THE UMPS! LEGENDARY UMPIRE BILL McGOWAN ONCE SAID, "CECIL'S THE ONLY BALLPLAYER I EVER FELT SORRY ABOUT CALLING OUT!"

Lou BRISSIE
PITCHER -- PHILADELPHIA A's
YOUNG LOU'S BASEBALL CAREER WAS ALMOST ENDED BEFORE IT BEGAN WHEN HIS LEFT LEG WAS SHATTERED BY A GERMAN SHELL IN BATTLE WHILE HE WAS SERVING IN THE 351st INFANTRY IN THE APPENNINE MOUNTAINS IN ITALY IN DECEMBER OF 1944! LOU EARNED TWO PURPLE HEARTS AND A BRONZE STAR FOR HIS VALOR ON THE BATTLEFIELD, BUT THE INJURIES HE SUSTAINED WOULD PLAGUE HIM THROUGHOUT HIS BASEBALL CAREER. AFTER BEING WOUNDED HE EMBARKED ON A LONG, PAINFUL RECOVERY WHICH REQUIRED OVER 20 OPERATIONS TO RECONSTRUCT HIS LEG WITH WIRE AND PLATES!
BORN ON JUNE 5, 1924, IN ANDERSON, SOUTH CAROLINA, THE 6-FOOT 4-1/2-INCH TALL LELAND "LOU" BRISSIE WAS SIGNED BY CONNIE MACK RIGHT OUT OF HIGH SCHOOL IN 1941! PART OF THE DEAL WAS THAT MR. MACK WOULD SEND LOU TO COLLEGE, AFTER WHICH THE YOUNGSTER WOULD BEGIN HIS PITCHING CAREER! THAT PLAN WAS IN EFFECT UNTIL WORLD WAR II INTERVENED AND LOU ENTERED THE U.S. ARMY!
I'LL BE BACK! NO LOUSY GERMAN MORTAR CAN STOP ME!
AFTER A LONG REHABILITATION LOU RETURNED TO BASEBALL IN 1947 WHEN HE PLAYED FOR THE SAVANNAH INDIANS IN THE SALLY LEAGUE! LOU PUT TOGETHER A MAGICAL SEASON THAT SAW HIM GO 23-5 WITH A 1.91 ERA WHILE SETTING A NEW SINGLE-SEASON LEAGUE STRIKEOUT RECORD WITH 278! THE INDIANS WON THE SALLY LEAGUE CHAMPIONSHIP, AND LOU EARNED HIS FIRST BIG LEAGUE CALL-UP! HE STARTED HIS FIRST GAME ON SEPTEMBER 28, 1947! HE LOST THAT GAME BUT HE WON HIS BATTLE AGAINST THE ODDS!
LOU TURNED IN A SOLID ROOKIE SEASON WITH THE ATHLETICS IN 1948 GOING 14-10 WITH 127 STRIKEOUTS! HE TURNED IN ANOTHER FINE SEASON IN 1949 WHEN HE PITCHED TO A 16-11 RECORD! LOU MAY HAVE PITCHED HIS BEST BALL IN 1950, BUT A WEAK HITTING A's TEAM HURT HIM IN THE WIN COLUMN AS HE FELL TO 7-19!
LOU WENT OVER TO THE CLEVELAND INDIANS FOR THE 1952 AND 1953 SEASONS WHERE HE WORKED MOSTLY OUT OF THE PEN! LOU'S BIG LEAGUE RECORD AS A PITCHER IS 44-48 WITH A 4.07 ERA! LOU'S RECORD AS A MAN READS SIMPLER -- AMERICAN HERO!
JOYNER ©2004

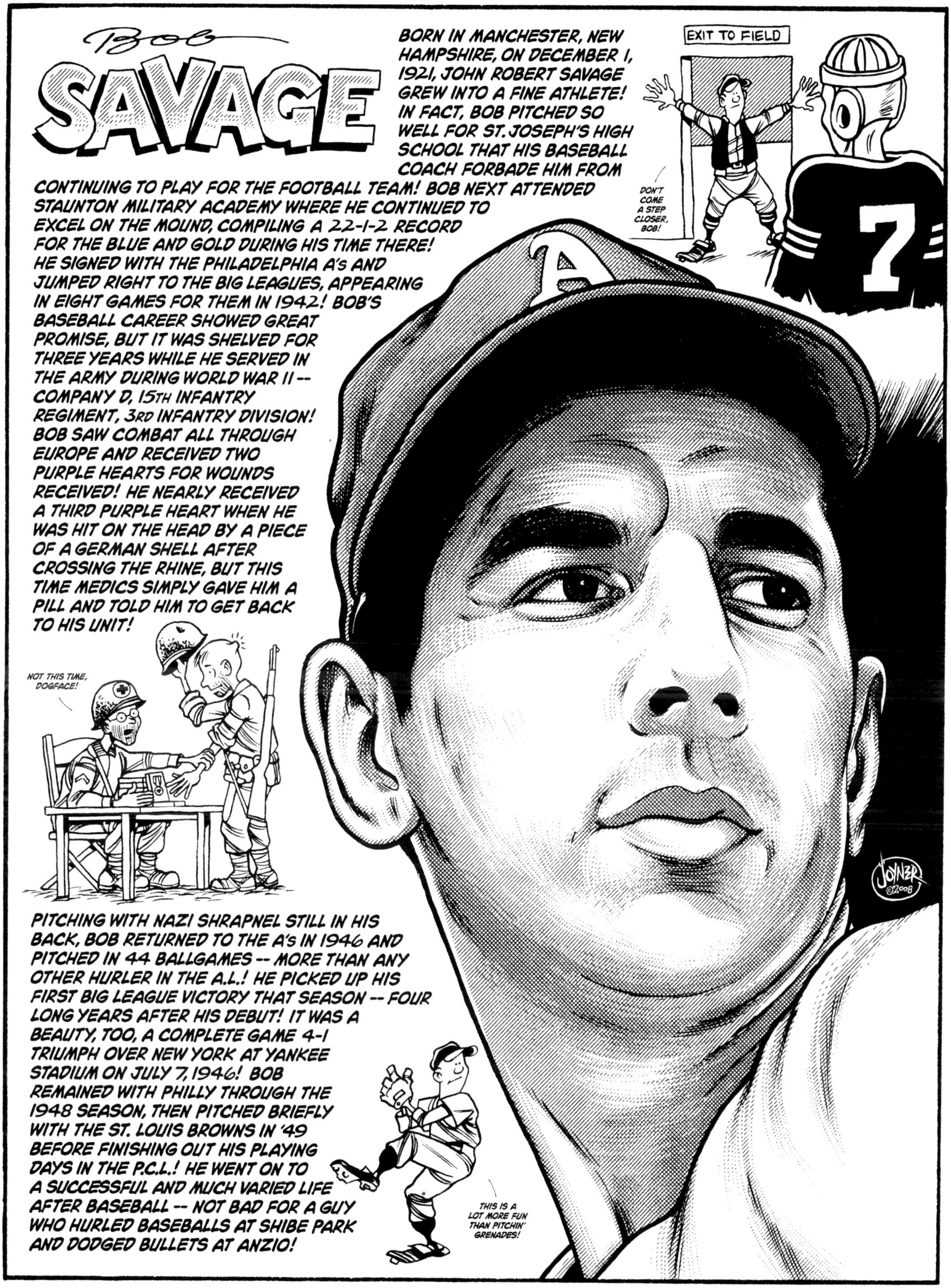
Bob
SAVAGE
BORN IN MANCHESTER, NEW HAMPSHIRE, ON DECEMBER 1, 1921, JOHN ROBERT SAVAGE GREW INTO A FINE ATHLETE! IN FACT, BOB PITCHED SO WELL FOR ST. JOSEPH'S HIGH SCHOOL THAT HIS BASEBALL COACH FORBADE HIM FROM CONTINUING TO PLAY FOR THE FOOTBALL TEAM! BOB NEXT ATTENDED STAUNTON MILITARY ACADEMY WHERE HE CONTINUED TO EXCEL ON THE MOUND, COMPILING A 22-1-2 RECORD FOR THE BLUE AND GOLD DURING HIS TIME THERE! HE SIGNED WITH THE PHILADELPHIA A'S AND JUMPED RIGHT TO THE BIG LEAGUES, APPEARING IN EIGHT GAMES FOR THEM IN 1942! BOB'S BASEBALL CAREER SHOWED GREAT PROMISE, BUT IT WAS SHELVED FOR THREE YEARS WHILE HE SERVED IN THE ARMY DURING WORLD WAR II -- COMPANY D, 15TH INFANTRY REGIMENT, 3RD INFANTRY DIVISION! BOB SAW COMBAT ALL THROUGH EUROPE AND RECEIVED TWO PURPLE HEARTS FOR WOUNDS RECEIVED! HE NEARLY RECEIVED A THIRD PURPLE HEART WHEN HE WAS HIT ON THE HEAD BY A PIECE OF A GERMAN SHELL AFTER CROSSING THE RHINE, BUT THIS TIME MEDICS SIMPLY GAVE HIM A PILL AND TOLD HIM TO GET BACK TO HIS UNIT!
EXIT TO FIELD
DON'T COME A STEP CLOSER, BOB!
7
NOT THIS TIME, DOGFACE!
PITCHING WITH NAZI SHRAPNEL STILL IN HIS BACK, BOB RETURNED TO THE A's IN 1946 AND PITCHED IN 44 BALLGAMES -- MORE THAN ANY OTHER HURLER IN THE A.L.! HE PICKED UP HIS FIRST BIG LEAGUE VICTORY THAT SEASON -- FOUR LONG YEARS AFTER HIS DEBUT! IT WAS A BEAUTY, TOO, A COMPLETE GAME 4-1 TRIUMPH OVER NEW YORK AT YANKEE STADIUM ON JULY 7, 1946! BOB REMAINED WITH PHILLY THROUGH THE 1948 SEASON, THEN PITCHED BRIEFLY WITH THE ST. LOUIS BROWNS IN '49 BEFORE FINISHING OUT HIS PLAYING DAYS IN THE P.C.L.! HE WENT ON TO A SUCCESSFUL AND MUCH VARIED LIFE AFTER BASEBALL -- NOT BAD FOR A GUY WHO HURLED BASEBALLS AT SHIBE PARK AND DODGED BULLETS AT ANZIO!
THIS IS A LOT MORE FUN THAN PITCHIN' GRENADES!
JOYNER ©2008

Ralph HOUK

PLAYING IN HIS FIRST-EVER BIG LEAGUE GAME ON MAY 26, 1947, YANKEE CATCHER RALPH HOUK WENT THREE-FOR-THREE AT THE PLATE IN A 3-1 WIN OVER THE SENATORS! JUST TWO SHORT YEARS EARLIER, RALPH WAS IN A FAR DIFFERENT PLACE -- GERMANY -- WHERE HE FACED NAZIS INSTEAD OF NATS! RALPH WAS WITH THE 9TH ARMORED DIVISION -- COMPANY I, 89TH CAVALRY RECONNAISSANCE SQUADRON -- AS THEY PUSHED ONTO GERMAN SOIL DURING THE LAST MONTHS OF WORLD WAR II!

RALPH WAS QUITE A SOLDIER, GRADUATING FROM OFFICERS CANDIDATE SCHOOL AS A SECOND LIEUTENANT, AND LATER BEING PROMOTED TO CAPTAIN WHERE HE LED PLATOONS INTO MANY HOT SPOTS! BY THE TIME HE LEFT THE ARMY, RALPH HAD RISEN ALL THE WAY UP TO MAJOR! YOU NEED LOOK NO FURTHER THAN HIS COMMANDING OFFICER FOR PROOF OF RALPH'S TENACITY AS A SOLDIER. "I SENT HIM ON THREE MISSIONS IN APRIL OF 1945," RECALLED THE C.O., "AND ONE DAY HE RETURNED WITH NINE PRISONERS OF WAR." BY WAR'S END, RALPH HAD BEEN AWARDED THE PURPLE HEART, SILVER STAR, BRONZE STAR WITH OAK LEAF CLUSTER, FOUR CAMPAIGN STARS AND CLUSTERS!

DESPITE HAVING SKILLS THAT MAY HAVE ALLOWED HIM TO START ELSEWHERE, RALPH STAYED WITH THE YANKS AS A BACKUP TO YOGI BERRA FROM 1947-54! HE MADE THE MOST OF HIS LIMITED WORLD SERIES AT-BATS, HOWEVER, GOING 1-FOR-2 -- HIS LONE HIT BEING A PINCH-SINGLE IN GAME SIX OF THE '47 FALL CLASSIC! RALPH BECAME THE YANKEE MANAGER IN 1961 AND LED THE BOMBERS TO A WORLD SERIES CHAMPIONSHIP, THEN REPEATED THE FEAT IN 1962! RALPH WON ANOTHER PENNANT IN 1963, THEN MOVED INTO THE YANKEE FRONT OFFICE! HE WOULD DO ANOTHER STINT AS YANKEE SKIPPER, THEN MOVE ON TO MANAGE THE TIGERS AND RED SOX! RIVAL MANAGER EARL WEAVER ONCE JOKED THAT "WHAT HOUK DID BEST WAS KICK HIS CAP. IN A MOMENT OF ANGER, I ONCE SAW HIM KICK IT FROM HOME PLATE ALL THE WAY OUT TO SECOND. THAT'S THE RECORD!"

Murry
DICKSON
THE YOUNGEST OF FIVE CHILDREN, MURRY MONROE DICKSON WAS BORN ON AUGUST 21, 1916, IN TRACY, MISSOURI! MURRY CAUGHT THE EYE OF ST. LOUIS CARDINALS SCOUT JACK RYAN IN 1936 AND WAS QUICKLY SIGNED AND SENT TO GRAND ISLAND OF THE NEBRASKA STATE LEAGUE! A 22-GAME WINNER WITH HOUSTON IN '39, MURRY WAS BROUGHT UP TO THE CARDINALS IN SEPTEMBER! HE GOT INTO JUST ONE GAME IN RELIEF, BUT SHOWED GOOD STUFF WHILE HURLING 3-2/3 SCORELESS INNINGS! IN FACT, IT WAS MURRY'S "STUFF" THAT SEPARATED HIM FROM THE PACK! EDDIE DYER, MURRY'S MANAGER AT HOUSTON, NICKNAMED HIM "TOM EDISON, JR." BECAUSE THE LITTLE RIGHTHANDER ALWAYS SEEMED TO BE EXPERIMENTING ON THE MOUND IN AN EFFORT TO DEVELOP MORE STUFF! HIS EFFORTS WERE REWARDED IN 1942 WHEN THE CARDS BROUGHT HIM UP FOR GOOD, AND MURRY ANSWERED WITH TWO FINE YEARS OUT OF THE PEN! HE WAS DRAFTED INTO THE ARMY BEFORE THE '43 SEASON ENDED, BUT, IN AN UNPRECEDENTED MOVE, JUDGE LANDIS HELPED ARRANGE A FURLOUGH FOR MURRY THAT ENABLED HIM TO PITCH IN THE WORLD SERIES! HE SPENT 1944-45 FIGHTING THROUGH FRANCE, BELGIUM LUXEMBOURG AND GERMANY WITH THE 35TH DIVISION, EARNING FOUR BATTLE STARS ALONG THE WAY! MURRY ONCE HAD ESTEEMED COMPANY IN HIS FOXHOLE WHEN GEORGE S. PATTON PILED IN ON TOP OF HIM! THE GENERAL HAD COME DOWN FROM AN OBSERVATION POST FOR A CLOSER LOOK AT THE GERMAN ARTILLERY WHEN AN EXPLODING SHELL FORCED HIM TO SEEK COVER WITH MURRY! PATTON LATER WANTED MURRY TO BE HIS DRIVER, BUT MURRY GOT OUT OF IT DUE TO HIS FEAR THAT PATTON WAS "CRAZY AND WOULD GET ME KILLED!"
HMMM, WHAT HAVE WE HERE?!
HEADS UP, SOLDIER... AND SHAVE THOSE WHISKERS!
MURRY DID IT ALL IN HIS 18 BIG LEAGUE SEASONS, PITCHING FOR PENNANT-WINNERS AND CELLAR-DWELLERS! HE WAS TWICE A 20-GAME LOSER, BUT WAS ALSO ONCE A 20-GAME WINNER ON HIS WAY TO 172 CAREER WINS! IN FACT, MURRY'S 20-WIN SEASON MAY HAVE BEEN HIS BEST FOR IT CAME WITH THE 1951 PIRATES, A TEAM THAT WON A TOTAL OF ONLY 64 GAMES!
I SURE COULD USE A LITTLE HELP AROUND HERE!
ICE
JOYNER ©2007

Kirby
HIGBE
WALTER KIRBY HIGBE, GRANDSON OF A CONFEDERATE SOLDIER, WAS BORN ON APRIL 8, 1915, IN COLUMBIA, SOUTH CAROLINA! KIRBY QUIT SCHOOL AND WENT TO WORK AFTER THE SEVENTH GRADE TO HELP HIS FAMILY GET THROUGH THE DEPRESSION! IN THE MEANTIME, HE PITCHED FOR LOCAL BASEBALL TEAMS! KIRBY WAS RAW BUT COULD REALLY BRING THE HEAT, SO HE WAS SOON SIGNED BY THE PIRATES AND DESIGNATED FOR ASSIGNMENT AT TULSA IN THE TEXAS LEAGUE! ONLY 17 AT THE TIME, KIRBY WAS OFTEN PLAGUED BY HOMESICKNESS, WHICH OCCASIONALLY CAUSED HIM TO SKIP OUT ON HIS TEAMS TO RETURN HOME! WILDNESS ON THE MOUND HELD UP KIRBY'S ENTRY INTO THE BIG LEAGUES, BUT HE FINALLY MADE IT WHEN HE BROKE IN WITH THE CUBS IN 1937! HE WAS TRADED TO THE LOWLY PHILS IN '39 WHERE HE LOST REGULARLY UNTIL SOLD TO THE DODGERS PRIOR TO THE 1941 SEASON! HIS NEW SURROUNDINGS SERVED HIM WELL AS HE WON A LEAGUE-LEADING 22 GAMES WHILE HIS BALLCLUB TOOK THE PENNANT! KIRBY WAS VERY POPULAR IN BROOKLYN AND WON 29 GAMES OVER THE NEXT TWO YEARS, THEN ENTERED THE ARMY WHERE HE SAW FIERCE COMBAT IN GERMANY AS A RIFLEMAN IN THE 342ND INFANTRY! KIRBY RETURNED TO THE BROOKS IN '46 AND POSTED A FINE CAMPAIGN, WINNING 17 GAMES! HE MADE A SERIOUS ERROR IN JUDGMENT WHEN HE SIDED WITH FOUR OTHER DODGERS WHO REFUSED TO PLAY ALONGSIDE JACKIE ROBINSON IN '47, AND HE WAS QUICKLY DISPATCHED TO THE PITTSBURGH PIRATES!
I DON'T WANNA GO! PLEASE DON'T MAKE ME!
A SORE ARM FORCED KIRBY OUT OF THE GAME BY 1951, AND LIFE AFTER BASEBALL WAS TOUGH ON HIM! STRUGGLING TO EKE OUT A LIVING, KIRBY EVENTUALLY LANDED IN JAIL AFTER WRITING BAD CHECKS! UPON HIS RELEASE HE BEGAN WORKING AT THE PRISON AS A GUARD, BUT SOON FOUND HIMSELF ONCE AGAIN AN INMATE AFTER BEING CONVICTED OF SMUGGLING SLEEPING PILLS IN TO THE PRISONERS!
KIRBY EVENTUALLY GOT HIS LIFE TOGETHER AND BECAME A PRODUCTIVE MEMBER OF SOCIETY! HE REGRETTED THE POOR DECISIONS HE'D MADE AND ACCEPTED COMPLETE RESPONSIBILITY FOR HIS MISSTEPS! HE FELT IT WAS HIS LACK OF EDUCATION THAT STEERED HIM WRONG, AND HE OFFERED SOME SAGE ADVICE FOR BASEBALL LOVING BOYS LIKE HIM! "I WOULD LIKE FOR ALL THE BOYS TO BE BIG LEAGUE BALLPLAYERS," HE SAID IN HIS 1967 AUTOBIOGRAPHY, "FOR IT IS THE GREATEST GAME IN THE WORLD. BUT FIRST I WANT THEM TO GO TO COLLEGE."
JOYNER ©2007

TWIG

WILLARD WAYNE "TWIG" TERWILLIGER WAS BORN ON JUNE 27, 1925, IN CLARE, MICHIGAN! THE FOUNDATION OF TWIG'S BASEBALL ABILITY CAME IN HIS YARD WHERE HE'D BOUNCE A BALL OFF THE STEPS, PLAYING THE REBOUND WHILE IMAGINING TO BE PLAYERS FROM HIS BELOVED DETROIT TIGERS! DESPITE BEING SMALL, TWIG'S DETERMINATION ENABLED HIM TO PLAY BASEBALL, FOOTBALL, AND BASKETBALL AT CHARLOTTE HIGH SCHOOL IN MICHIGAN, AND THEN AT WESTERN MICHIGAN UNIVERSITY!

TWIG HAD DREAMS OF PLAYING BIG LEAGUE BASEBALL, BUT HE PUT THAT DREAM ON HOLD WHILE HE SERVED IN WORLD WAR II! ADMITTEDLY A "GUNG-HO MARINE," TWIG WAS PART OF THE 2ND ARMORED AMPHIBIAN BATTALION AND SAW ACTION ON SAIPAN, TINIAN, AND IWO JIMA! UPON HIS RETURN TO THE STATES, TWIG ENTERED THE MINORS WHERE HE PLAYED WITH DES MOINES AND LOS ANGELES BEFORE JOINING THE '49 CUBS FOR 36 GAMES! HE MADE THE MOST OF HIS CALL-UP, TYING A ROOKIE MARK BY RAPPING 8 CONSECUTIVE HITS! 1950, HIS FIRST FULL SEASON, WAS A GOOD ONE FOR TWIG AS HE HIT .242 WITH 10 LONG BALLS FOR CHICAGO WHILE DISPLAYING TOP-NOTCH GLOVEWORK AT SECOND BASE! ON JUNE 15, 1951, JUST PRIOR TO A SERIES AGAINST BROOKLYN, THE CUBS TRADED TWIG TO THE DODGERS WHERE HE WOULD BE WITNESS TO BOBBY THOMSON'S "SHOT HEARD 'ROUND THE WORLD!" TWIG'S BEST YEAR AS A PLAYER WOULD COME TWO YEARS LATER WITH THE 1953 SENATORS!

AT THE CONCLUSION OF HIS BIG LEAGUE PLAYING CAREER IN 1961, TWIG EMBARKED ON A LONG CAREER IN COACHING AND MANAGING! HE'S STILL AT IT, TOO, CURRENTLY COACHING WITH THE FT. WORTH CATS! AT 81 YEARS OF AGE, TWIG'S POSITIVE OUTLOOK AND BOUNDLESS ENERGY IS A TRUE MARVEL TO ALL WHO KNOW HIM!

Al Rosen

BORN ON FEBRUARY 29, 1924, IN SPARTANBURG, SOUTH CAROLINA, ALBERT LEONARD ROSEN WAS A SICKLY KID, HIS ASTHMATIC CONDITION FORCING HIS FAMILY TO MOVE TO THE MORE SUITABLE CLIMATE OF MIAMI! THE CHANGE IN SCENERY SEEMED TO SUIT AL PERFECTLY AS HE GREW INTO A STRAPPING SLUGGER WHOSE RIPPLING BICEPS EXPLODED MENACINGLY OUT OF HIS CUT-OFF JERSEY SLEEVES! AL HAD SPENT JUST ONE YEAR IN ORGANIZED BALL BEFORE JOINING THE NAVY IN 1943! IN THE SPRING OF 1945, AL NAVIGATED AN ASSAULT BOAT IN THE INITIAL LANDING FOR THE BITTER BATTLE OF OKINAWA! AL RETURNED TO THE MINORS IN 1946, SERVING NOTICE WITH HIS MIGHTY BAT BY POSTING A .323 AVERAGE AND 15 CIRCUIT BLASTS FOR PITTSFIELD! FOLLOWING THREE BRIEF TRIALS IN THE LATE 1940s, AL WAS IN THE MAJORS FOR GOOD BY 1950, WHERE HE POUNDED OUT 192 HOME RUNS BEFORE INJURIES FORCED HIM TO PREMATURELY RETIRE AT AGE 32! AL IS A HERO TO ALL BASEBALL FANS, BUT HIS JEWISH HERITAGE MAKES HIM A PARTICULAR HERO TO PEOPLE OF THE JEWISH FAITH, AND THEY CONSIDER HIM TO BE ONE OF THE GREATEST OF ALL TIME!

"FLIP," AS HE WAS OFTEN CALLED, TURNED IN ONE OF THE FINEST SEASONS EVER IN 1953 WHEN HE NEARLY COPPED THE ELUSIVE TRIPLE CROWN! WITH THE HOME RUN AND RBI TITLES ALREADY IN THE BAG, AL, WITH HIS .333 AVERAGE, HAD HIS EYE ON MICKEY VERNON'S LEAGUE-LEADING .336 MARK AS EACH PLAYER'S TEAM ENTERED THE LAST GAME OF THE SEASON! AL'S INDIANS PLAYED THE TIGERS IN CLEVELAND, WHILE VERNON'S NATS PLAYED THE A's IN WASHINGTON! THE GAMES WERE PLAYED CONCURRENTLY, WITH ONGOING RESULTS WIRED TO EACH OTHERS' PRESSBOXES, THEN RELAYED TO THE FANS OVER THE P.A. SYSTEM! AL WOULD'VE WON THE BATTING CROWN OUTRIGHT HAD HE HIT SAFELY IN HIS LAST AT-BAT, BUT HE MISSED FIRST BASE AS HE TRIED TO BEAT OUT AN INFIELD HIT, FINISHING AT .336 -- A CLOSE SECOND TO VERNON'S LEAGUE-BEST .337!

Phil MARCHILDON
YOU'RE COMING WITH ME, KID!
A LATE-COMER TO THE GAME OF BASEBALL, CANADIAN-BORN PHIL MARCHILDON DIDN'T BEGIN PLAYING UNTIL HE WAS IN HIGH SCHOOL! IT WAS QUICKLY LEARNED THAT HE HAD A RIFLE FOR A RIGHT ARM, SO PHIL WAS SOON PITCHING FOR A SEMI-PRO CLUB WHILE WORKING IN THE LOCAL NICKEL MINES! PHIL EARNED A TRYOUT WITH THE TORONTO MAPLE LEAFS, AND LEAFS SCOUT DAN HOWLEY WAS IMPRESSED WITH WHAT HE SAW! PHIL WASN'T SO SURE, HOWEVER, SO HE SLIPPED AWAY AND RETURNED TO THE MINES WITHOUT SPEAKING TO HOWLEY! "HOWLING" DAN SPED TO THE MINES AND LITERALLY PLUCKED PHIL OFF A LIFT THAT WAS CARRYING THE YOUNGSTER DOWN INTO THE GROUND! "I PUT A HALF-NELSON ON HIM AND FORCED A PEN INTO HIS HAND AND TOLD HIM TO WRITE HIS SIGNATURE," SAID HOWLEY. "I SAVED HIM FROM BEING A MOLE." PHIL SPENT 1939 AND MOST OF 1940 DOWN ON THE ATHLETICS FARM WORKING ON HIS GAME, AND WAS CALLED UP IN SEPTEMBER OF 1940 FOR A BRIEF TWO-GAME TRIAL! WITH HELP ON HIS MECHANICS FROM A's PITCHING COACH EARLE BRUCKER, PHIL WON 10 GAMES IN 1941, FOLLOWED BY 17 VICTORIES IN 1942! "LATER ON IT WAS ESTIMATED THAT MY FASTBALL TRAVELED ABOUT 95 MILES PER HOUR," PHIL SAID. "THE MOVEMENT ON IT WAS SO DISTINCTIVE THAT IT BECAME KNOWN AROUND THE AMERICAN LEAGUE AS 'JOHNNY JUMP-UP.'" PHIL SPENT 1943-45 IN THE ROYAL CANADIAN AIR FORCE BEFORE HIS RETURN TO THE MAJORS! HE WON 13 GAMES IN 1946, THEN BAGGED 19 WINS IN 1947! PHIL CLAIMED HIS BIGGEST THRILL WAS A NEAR PERFECT GAME HE PITCHED AGAINST THE INDIANS ON JULY 10, 1947 -- A GAME HE EVENTUALLY WON WITH A 12TH-INNING RBI DOUBLE!
JOYNER ©1999
PHIL'S MILITARY SERVICE IS THE STUFF OF LEGEND. A TAIL-GUNNER ON A HALIFAX BOMBER, PHIL'S CREW HAD COMPLETED 25 MISSIONS OVER GERMANY AND NEEDED TO COMPLETE JUST FIVE MORE IN ORDER TO BE SENT HOME. THEY WERE SHOT DOWN, HOWEVER, ON THEIR 26TH MISSION. PHIL AND A CREWMATE SURVIVED BY BAILING OUT INTO THE ICY SEA OF DENMARK, BUT THE REST OF THE CREW PERISHED. PHIL SPENT NINE MONTHS IN THE NOTORIOUS GERMAN P.O.W. CAMP STALAG LUFT III -- THE PRISON MADE FAMOUS BY THE MOVIE "THE GREAT ESCAPE." PHIL ENDURED GREAT MENTAL AND PHYSICAL SUFFERING DURING HIS IMPRISONMENT, AND THE EXPERIENCE DARKENED HIS DEMEANOR FOR THE REST OF HIS LIFE. HE TYPIFIED THE STRENGTH OF HIS GENERATION, THOUGH, AND PERSEVERED, FORGING AHEAD THROUGH TOUGH MEMORIES TO CONTINUE HIS BASEBALL CAREER AND RAISE A WONDERFUL FAMILY.
HANG IN THERE, A'S FANS -- I'LL BE BACK WHEN I'M FINISHED KICKING SOME NAZI BUTT!

Dick FOWLER
AFTER SHOWING SOME REAL POTENTIAL WITH THE '41 TORONTO MAPLE LEAFS, CONNIE MACK ACQUIRED THE CONTRACT OF 20-YEAR-OLD RIGHT-HANDED HURLER DICK FOWLER FOR HIS WOEFUL PHILADELPHIA ATHLETICS! YOUNG DICK MADE HIS DEBUT A FEW DAYS LATER AND WHIPPED THE WHITE SOX, 3-1, ON SEPTEMBER 13, 1941! THE ONTARIO-BORN KID STRUGGLED A BIT IN 1942, AND WAS SOON OFF TO SERVE IN WORLD WAR II WITH THE 48TH HIGHLANDERS OF THE CANADIAN ARMY! DICK PITCHED QUITE A BIT WHILE SERVING FROM 1943-45, AND IT WAS IN THAT TIME THAT HE REALLY DEVELOPED INTO A FINE MOUNDSMAN! "THAT IS WHERE I REALLY LEARNED TO PITCH," DICK ONCE SAID, "BECAUSE TOO MUCH WASN'T AT STAKE. IT WAS ONLY ABOUT CLASS-C BALL -- AND MY JOB DIDN'T DEPEND ON WINNING!" HE FINE-TUNED HIS CURVE AND CHANGE-UP TO COMPLEMENT HIS FASTBALL, AND THEN UNLEASHED HIS NEW REPERTOIRE ON BIG LEAGUE HITTERS WHEN HE WAS DISCHARGED FROM THE ARMY IN AUGUST OF 1945! DICK WON 52 GAMES FROM THE TIME OF HIS RETURN THROUGH THE 1949 SEASON BEFORE FALLING VICTIM TO SHOULDER PROBLEMS! A TRUE GENTLEMAN WHO WAS LIKED BY ALL, DICK LEFT THE MAJORS AFTER THE 1952 SEASON!
THIS WAR HAS REALLY ARMED ME!
FOR PROOF THAT DICK'S PITCHING SKILLS HAD PROGRESSED BEYOND BELIEF WHILE HE WAS IN THE ARMY, ONE NEED LOOK NO FURTHER THAN HIS FIRST START ON SEPTEMBER 9, 1945 -- JUST THREE WEEKS AFTER HIS DISCHARGE! IN THAT GAME, DICK THREW A NO-HITTER AGAINST THE ST. LOUIS BROWNS -- THE FIRST NO-HIT BALLGAME IN THE AMERICAN LEAGUE SINCE BOB FELLER'S OPENING DAY NO-NO IN 1940! IT WAS AN AMAZING PERFORMANCE IN WHICH DICK ALLOWED JUST FIVE BALLS TO BE HIT OUT OF THE INFIELD! TRYING AGAIN TO TAP INTO DICK'S HOT HAND, MR. MACK SENT DICK IN TO PINCH HIT IN THE 9TH INNING OF THE NEXT DAY'S GAME! DICK BLASTED A TRIPLE OFF BROWNIE CHUCKER JACK KRAMER, BUT THE A'S CAME UP SHORT, LOSING 3-2!
WHAT GIVES, BUDDY? CAN'T ANYBODY HIT ANYMORE?
JOYNER ©2000

CHAPMAN
SAMUEL BLAKE CHAPMAN WAS BORN ON APRIL 11, 1916, IN TIBURON, CALIFORNIA! YOUNG SAM DEVELOPED INTO A FINE ATHLETE, EVENTUALLY ATTENDING TAMALPAIS HIGH SCHOOL IN MILL VALLEY WHERE HE LETTERED IN FIVE SPORTS! MANY STILL CONSIDER SAM THE BEST ATHLETE EVER TO EMERGE FROM MARIN COUNTY!
TAM HIGH FOREVER!
SAM HUNG UP HIS SPIKES FROM 1942-45 TO AID THE WAR EFFORT AS A NAVY PILOT AND FLIGHT INSTRUCTOR!
FEAR NOT, A's FAITHFUL — I'LL BE BACK!
CHAPMAN
SAM ATTENDED COLLEGE AT THE UNIVERSITY OF CALIFORNIA WHERE HE WAS AN ALL-AMERICAN AT FOOTBALL, STARRING ON THE CAL "THUNDER TEAMS" OF 1935, 1936, AND 1937! HE WAS ALSO A POWER-HITTER AND FLEET FIELDER FOR THE CAL BASEBALL SQUAD! UPON GRADUATION, SAM TURNED DOWN A CONTRACT TO PLAY FOOTBALL FOR THE WASHINGTON REDSKINS, INSTEAD SIGNING TO PLAY BASEBALL WITH THE PHILADELPHIA ATHLETICS! SAM WENT RIGHT INTO THE BIG LEAGUES AND BELTED 17 ROUND-TRIPPERS FOR THE 1938 A's! THE STRONG-ARMED FLYCHASER FOLLOWED WITH HOMER TOTALS OF 24 IN 1939, AND 26 IN 1940! SAM HIT .322 WITH 29 CIRCUITS AND 106 RBIS IN '41, HIS LAST FULL SEASON BEFORE ENLISTING IN THE NAVY TO SERVE IN WORLD WAR II!
JOYNER ©2005
THAT'S PAYBACK FOR OL' "WRONG WAY" RIEGELS!
ON MAY 5, 1939, SAM HIT FOR THE CYCLE IN A 10-5 WIN OVER THE BROWNS! THE NEXT DAY HE HOMERED IN HIS FIRST TWO AT-BATS! SAM COMPLETED HIS BIG LEAGUE CAREER IN 1951 WITH A LIFETIME AVERAGE OF .266 WITH 180 FOUR-BAGGERS!
I'M SWINGIN' LIKE BENNY GOODMAN!

SAMMY
WEST
OUTFIELD -- WASHINGTON SENATORS
BORN ON OCTOBER 5, 1904, SAMUEL FILMORE WEST MADE IT TO THE BIG LEAGUES 23 YEARS LATER WHEN HE SAW ACTION IN 18 GAMES FOR THE SENATORS! THIS BEGAN WHAT WOULD BE A SOLID 16-YEAR CAREER IN THE MAJOR LEAGUES THAT SAW SAMMY AMASS 1,838 HITS WHILE BATTING .300 OR BETTER IN 8 OF HIS 12 SEASONS!
SAMMY'S GREAT PRODUCTION THROUGH THE LATE '20s AND EARLY '30s EARNED HIM RESPECT AROUND THE LEAGUE -- AND IT ALSO EARNED HIM A SPOT ON THE FIRST ALL-STAR TEAM IN 1933! HE MADE THE SQUAD TWICE MORE IN 1934 AND '37! SAMMY DID TWO STINTS IN THE NATION'S CAPITAL! HE PLAYED WITH THE NATS FROM 1927-32, BUT WAS TRADED TO THE BROWNS FOLLOWING THE SEASON! HE SPENT 5-1/2 SEASONS IN ST. LOUIS BEFORE RETURNING TO THE SENATORS IN A MID-SEASON TRADE IN 1938! SAMMY REMAINED WITH THE NATS THROUGH THE '41 SEASON, FINISHING UP WITH THE WHITE SOX IN 1942! HE THEN SERVED IN THE AIR FORCE UNTIL THE END OF WORLD WAR II WHEN HE REJOINED THE SENATORS AS A COACH! NAT'S TEAM-MATE OSSIE BLUEGE HAD HIGH PRAISE FOR SAMMY, SAYING THAT WEST WAS "THE BEST OUTFIELDER TO EVER PICK UP A GLOVE!"
ZAT ALL YA GOT ?
1
2
3
4
5
6
7
8
SAMMY'S BAT WAS PROLIFIC, BUT HE WAS SOMETHING SPECIAL ON DEFENSE, TOO! 1927 WAS TRIS SPEAKER'S ONLY SEASON IN A NAT'S UNIFORM, BUT IT COINCIDED WITH SAMMY'S ROOKIE YEAR! THE VETERAN FLYCHASER TUTORED THE KID AND TURNED HIM INTO ONE OF THE BEST IN THE LEAGUE! SAMMY THEN SET A SINCE-BROKEN A.L. FIELDING RECORD OF .996 IN 1928!
TEXAS-BORN SAMMY WEST SLUGGED HIS WAY INTO THE RECORD BOOKS WHEN HE STRUNG TOGETHER EIGHT CONSECUTIVE HITS IN 1933 WHILE HE WAS WITH THE ST. LOUIS BROWNS! SIX OF THOSE HITS CAME IN ONE GAME ON APRIL 13 -- AN 11-INNING VICTORY OVER THE CHICAGO WHITE SOX! IN THAT GAME SAMMY COLLECTED FIVE SINGLES AND A DOUBLE OFF HALL OF FAMER TED LYONS!
JOYNER ©2003

Virgil TRUCKS

ONE OF THIRTEEN CHILDREN BORN TO OLIVER AND LULA BELLE TRUCKS, VIRGIL WOULD BRING HONOR TO THE FAMILY NAME BY BECOMING A BONA FIDE BIG LEAGUE PITCHING STAR! VIRGIL'S PITCHING FOUNDATION CAME FROM HIS FATHER WHO WAS A FINE ALABAMA SANDLOT PITCHER! VIRGIL MADE QUITE A SPLASH IN 1938 -- HIS FIRST SEASON IN PRO BALL! THAT YEAR THE HARD-THROWING RIGHT-HANDER FANNED 420 ALABAMA-FLORIDA LEAGUE BATSMEN -- A NEW RECORD FOR ANY LEVEL OF PROFESSIONAL BASEBALL! VIRGIL ARRIVED IN THE MAJORS WITH HIGH EXPECTATIONS, AND HE DELIVERED THE GOODS, POSTING A 30-AND-18 RECORD WITH A 2.80 E.R.A. FOR THE TIGERS IN HIS FIRST TWO FULL SEASONS (1942 AND '43)! POSITIONED FOR EVEN GREATER SUCCESS IN 1944, VIRGIL INSTEAD FOUND HIMSELF IN THE U.S. NAVY! HE WAS SOON PITCHING FOR UNCLE SAM, AND HIS HURLING HELPED THE NAVY DEFEAT THE ARMY IN THE HIGHLY-PUBLICIZED ARMY-NAVY WORLD SERIES IN HAWAII! DISCHARGED IN LATE-SEPTEMBER OF 1945, VIRGIL WAS PITCHING IN THE "REAL" WORLD SERIES A FEW SHORT DAYS LATER -- AND HIS COMPLETE-GAME VICTORY IN GAME TWO HELPED THE TIGERS DEFEAT THE CUBS FOR THE SERIES TITLE! WITH A NEAR-100 M.P.H. HEATER, VIRGIL WAS ALWAYS A THREAT TO TOSS A NO-HITTER! IN 1952 HE BECAME JUST THE THIRD BIG LEAGUER TO THROW TWO NO-NOs IN THE SAME SEASON WHEN HE NO-HIT THE NATS ON MAY 15, FOLLOWED BY THE YANKS ON AUGUST 25! VIRGIL WAS NO STRANGER TO NO-HITTERS, HAVING PITCHED FOUR WHILE IN THE MINORS! BUT, AMAZINGLY, HIS TWO NO-HITTERS OF '52 CAME IN A RARE DOWN SEASON -- A SEASON IN WHICH VIRGIL NOTCHED ONLY FIVE WINS IN 25 STARTS FOR A BAD DETROIT BALLCLUB!

NICKNAMED "FIRE" TRUCKS BECAUSE OF HIS RED HOT HEATER, VIRGIL BLAZED HIS WAY TO 108 WINS AND ONE SERIES RING FOR DETROIT FROM 1941-52! HE DIVIDED THE REST OF HIS CAREER BETWEEN THE BROWNS, WHITE SOX, TIGERS (AGAIN IN '56), AND ATHLETICS (KANSAS CITY)! HE WRAPPED UP HIS CAREER WITH THE YANKS IN 1958, AND PICKED UP HIS SECOND SERIES RING FOR HIS WORK THERE THAT SEASON! VIRGIL NABBED ONE MORE SERIES RING AS A BATTING PRACTICE PITCHER FOR THE 1960 PIRATES! "THEY WERE A VERY CHEAP CLUB," SAID VIRGIL. "THEY PAID ME ONLY $750 PER MONTH, SO I SUPPLEMENTED MY PAY BY WINNING ABOUT $1,000 A YEAR FROM FIRST BASEMAN DICK STUART IN GOLF. DICK WAS A GREAT GUY, BUT HE THOUGHT HE WAS A BETTER GOLFER THAN HE WAS. THEY TRADED HIM AFTER 1961, SO I WENT IN AND AND ASKED GENERAL MANAGER JOE BROWN FOR A $1,000 RAISE. HE SAID NO. WHEN I EXPLAINED TO HIM THAT HIS TRADE OF STUART WAS COSTING ME $1,000, JOE AGREED TO THE RAISE! I NEVER REALLY THOUGHT IT WOULD WORK, BUT I WALKED OUT WITH A RAISE."

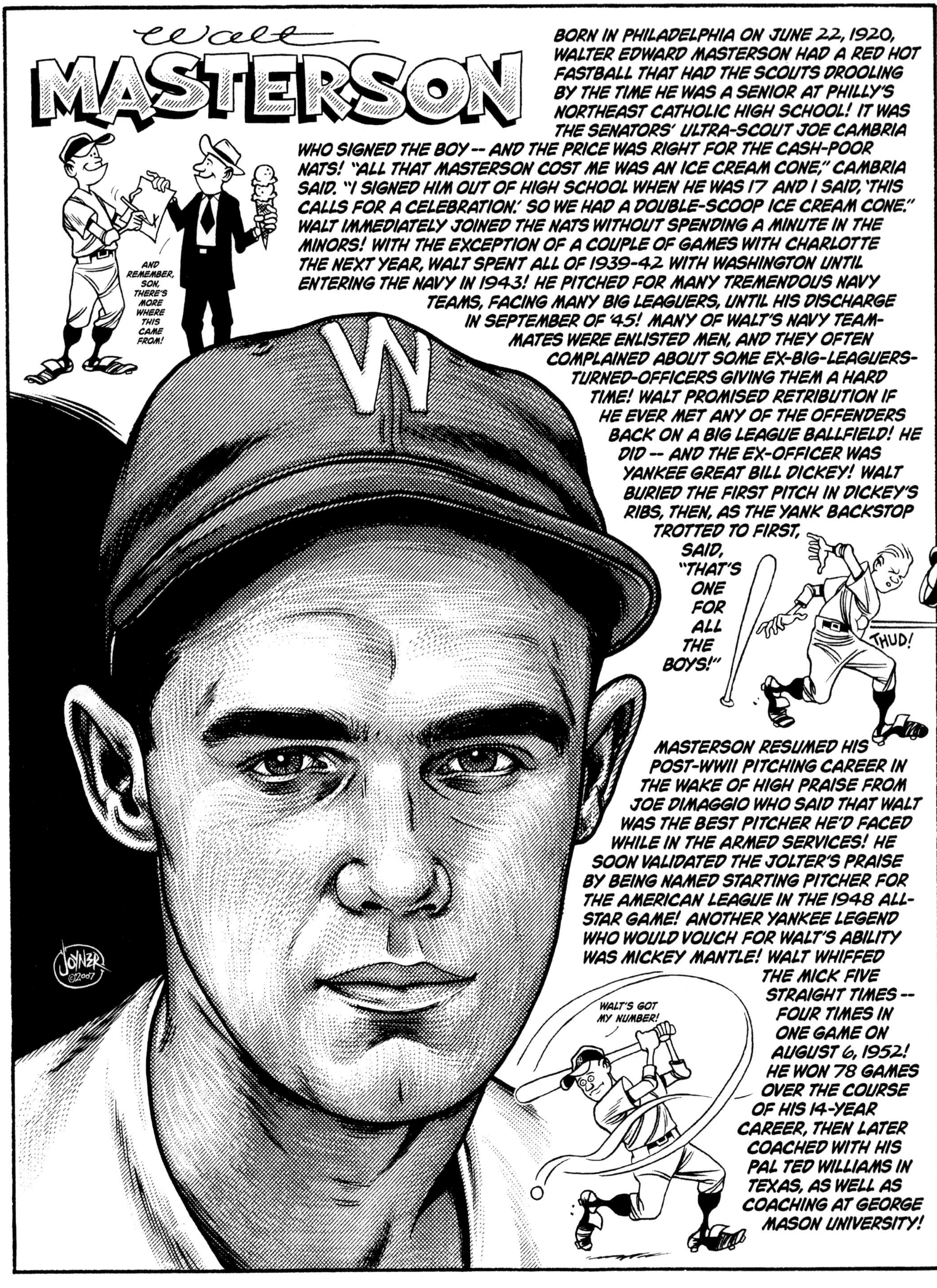
Walt
MASTERSON
BORN IN PHILADELPHIA ON JUNE 22, 1920, WALTER EDWARD MASTERSON HAD A RED HOT FASTBALL THAT HAD THE SCOUTS DROOLING BY THE TIME HE WAS A SENIOR AT PHILLY'S NORTHEAST CATHOLIC HIGH SCHOOL! IT WAS THE SENATORS' ULTRA-SCOUT JOE CAMBRIA WHO SIGNED THE BOY -- AND THE PRICE WAS RIGHT FOR THE CASH-POOR NATS! "ALL THAT MASTERSON COST ME WAS AN ICE CREAM CONE," CAMBRIA SAID. "I SIGNED HIM OUT OF HIGH SCHOOL WHEN HE WAS 17 AND I SAID, 'THIS CALLS FOR A CELEBRATION.' SO WE HAD A DOUBLE-SCOOP ICE CREAM CONE." WALT IMMEDIATELY JOINED THE NATS WITHOUT SPENDING A MINUTE IN THE MINORS! WITH THE EXCEPTION OF A COUPLE OF GAMES WITH CHARLOTTE THE NEXT YEAR, WALT SPENT ALL OF 1939-42 WITH WASHINGTON UNTIL ENTERING THE NAVY IN 1943! HE PITCHED FOR MANY TREMENDOUS NAVY TEAMS, FACING MANY BIG LEAGUERS, UNTIL HIS DISCHARGE IN SEPTEMBER OF '45! MANY OF WALT'S NAVY TEAM-MATES WERE ENLISTED MEN, AND THEY OFTEN COMPLAINED ABOUT SOME EX-BIG-LEAGUERS-TURNED-OFFICERS GIVING THEM A HARD TIME! WALT PROMISED RETRIBUTION IF HE EVER MET ANY OF THE OFFENDERS BACK ON A BIG LEAGUE BALLFIELD! HE DID -- AND THE EX-OFFICER WAS YANKEE GREAT BILL DICKEY! WALT BURIED THE FIRST PITCH IN DICKEY'S RIBS, THEN, AS THE YANK BACKSTOP TROTTED TO FIRST, SAID, "THAT'S ONE FOR ALL THE BOYS!"
AND REMEMBER, SON, THERE'S MORE WHERE THIS CAME FROM!
THUD!
MASTERSON RESUMED HIS POST-WWII PITCHING CAREER IN THE WAKE OF HIGH PRAISE FROM JOE DIMAGGIO WHO SAID THAT WALT WAS THE BEST PITCHER HE'D FACED WHILE IN THE ARMED SERVICES! HE SOON VALIDATED THE JOLTER'S PRAISE BY BEING NAMED STARTING PITCHER FOR THE AMERICAN LEAGUE IN THE 1948 ALL-STAR GAME! ANOTHER YANKEE LEGEND WHO WOULD VOUCH FOR WALT'S ABILITY WAS MICKEY MANTLE! WALT WHIFFED THE MICK FIVE STRAIGHT TIMES -- FOUR TIMES IN ONE GAME ON AUGUST 6, 1952! HE WON 78 GAMES OVER THE COURSE OF HIS 14-YEAR CAREER, THEN LATER COACHED WITH HIS PAL TED WILLIAMS IN TEXAS, AS WELL AS COACHING AT GEORGE MASON UNIVERSITY!
WALT'S GOT MY NUMBER!
JOYNER ©2007

AL BRANCATO

ALBERT "BRONK" BRANCATO WAS BORN IN SOUTH PHILADELPHIA ON MAY 29, 1919! ONE OF SEVEN CHILDREN OF ITALIAN IMMIGRANTS, AL PLAYED SPORTS EVERY MINUTE THAT HE WAS NOT WORKING AT THE FAMILY GROCERY STORE! AL GREW INTO A FINE ATHLETE AT PHILLY'S SOUTHERN HIGH SCHOOL WHERE HE PLAYED BASEBALL, FOOTBALL, BASKETBALL AND GYMNASTICS! IT WAS BASEBALL WHERE THE KID REALLY SHINED, EVENTUALLY GARNERING THE ATTENTION OF CONNIE MACK, OWNER OF THE PHILADELPHIA ATHLETICS! "MR. MACK SIGNED ME WHILE I WAS STILL A SENIOR AT SOUTHERN," SAYS AL, "SO I LEFT SCHOOL AT THE AGE OF 17 AND HEADED OFF TO SPRING TRAINING. I WAS ON CLOUD NINE!"

AL MADE HIS BIG LEAGUE DEBUT WITH THE A's AT THE END OF THE 1939 SEASON AFTER LEADING THE EASTERN LEAGUE IN RBIs WHILE WITH WILLIAMSPORT! THE STEEL-ARMED ROOKIE THIRD-SACKER BANGED OUT HIS FIRST TWO BIG LEAGUE HITS IN A 9-1 ROMP OVER THE BROWNS AT SHIBE PARK! TWO WEEKS LATER, AL UNLOADED HIS FIRST CAREER HOMER OFF SENATORS RIGHT-HANDER JOE HAYNES! "I HIT THE BALL HARD," SAYS AL, "BUT I WASN'T REALLY A POWER GUY. I WAS MORE OF A DOUBLES AND TRIPLES TYPE." AL SPENT THE ENTIRE 1940 AND '41 SEASONS WITH THE ATHLETICS WHERE HE BANGED OUT 31 DOUBLES, 11 TRIPLES, 3 HOMERS AND 72 RBIs OVER 251 GAMES! AL BECAME SO POPULAR WITH THE KIDS IN SOUTH PHILLY THAT HE OPENED A SPORTING GOODS STORE TO GIVE THEM ACCESS TO EQUIPMENT THAT WAS PREVIOUSLY UNAVAILABLE!

AL SPENT 1942-45 IN THE SERVICE WHERE HE PLAYED ON MANY FINE NAVY TEAMS, BUT HIS TIME IN THE SERVICE ENDED ANY REAL HOPES HE HAD OF MAKING IT BACK TO THE BIGS! AL DID PLAY IN A FEW MORE GAMES WITH THE A's LATE IN 1945 BEFORE MOVING ON TO PLAY EIGHT MORE YEARS IN THE MINORS -- EVEN WHILE ALSO MANAGING AT ELMIRA IN 1953!

Ray
COLEMAN
OUTFIELD -- ST. LOUIS BROWNS
23 HRS
RAY HIT .295 WITH 23 HOME RUNS AND 113 RBIs WITH THE BUFFALO BISON OF THE INTERNATIONAL LEAGUE IN 1949!
RAYMOND LeROY COLEMAN WAS BORN ON JUNE 4, 1922, IN DUNSMUIR, CALIFORNIA! HE PATROLLED THE OUTFIELD DURING HIS PLAYING DAYS -- AFTER HE PATROLLED THE DECKS OF THE U.S.S. McCULLOUGH IN WWII!
RAY BROKE IN WITH THE ST. LOUIS BROWNS IN 1947 AND DELIVERED A SOLID ROOKIE YEAR HITTING .259! STILL, THE BROWNS DEALT HIM TO THE ATHLETICS IN EXCHANGE FOR GEORGE "BINGO" BINKS IN 1948!
HELLO, RAY!
HIYA, GEORGE!
PHIL.
STL.
JOYNER ©2001
SPORTSMAN'S PARK
I'LL BE BACK!
RAY WAS TRADED 5 TIMES -- EACH INVOLVING THE BROWNIES!
RAY HAD A FINE SEASON IN 1950 WHEN HE HIT .271 WITH 8 DINGERS FOR ST. LOUIS! RAY'S BEST SEASON CAME IN 1951 -- A YEAR HE SPLIT BETWEEN THE BROWNS AND THE WHITE SOX! HE HIT .280 WITH 8 HOME RUNS AND 76 RBIs! RAY ENDED UP A .258 LIFETIME HITTER WITH TOTALS OF 446 HITS, 20 HOMERS AND 199 RBIs!

BAMA WAS A GREAT ATHLETE WHO ATTENDED LSU ON A FOOTBALL SCHOLARSHIP!
WHO WANTS TO GET HIT?!
BAMA
ROWELL
OUTFIELD -- BOSTON BRAVES
CARVEL WILLIAM "BAMA" ROWELL WAS BORN ON JANUARY 13, 1916, IN CITRONELLE, ALABAMA! IN SIX BIG LEAGUE SEASONS, WITH FOUR MISSED WHILE HE SERVED IN THE ARMY IN WORLD WAR II, BAMA HIT .275 WITH 19 HOME RUNS AND 217 RBIs IN 1,901 AT-BATS!
IN A GAME AGAINST THE DODGERS AT EBBETS FIELD ON MAY 30, 1946, BAMA SLAMMED A LONG FLY BALL OFF THE BULOVA CLOCK HIGH ATOP THE RIGHT-FIELD WALL! THE BLAST SHATTERED THE FACE OF THE CLOCK, RAINING GLASS DOWN UPON DODGERS RIGHTFIELDER DIXIE WALKER! THE BULOVA CLOCK CONTINUED TO RUN, ALBEIT BRIEFLY, BUT AT 5:25 PM, EXACTLY ONE HOUR AFTER BAMA'S PRODIGIOUS WALLOP, THE CLOCK STOPPED DEAD! THE BRAVES RALLY WAS VERY MUCH ALIVE, HOWEVER, AND WITH THE HELP OF BAMA'S DOUBLE OFF THE CLOCK, THE BRAVES WENT ON TO WIN 10-8! THE INCIDENT THAT DAY SO IMPRESSED NOVELIST BERNARD MALAMUD THAT IT INSPIRED HIM TO WRITE A SIMILAR SCENE IN HIS 1952 CLASSIC "THE NATURAL"! IN IT SLUGGER ROY HOBBS DRIVES A MAMMOTH CLOUT OFF A LIGHT TOWER, SHATTERING GLASS WHICH SUBSEQUENTLY RAINED DOWN ON THE FIELD! INCIDENTALLY, BULOVA ALWAYS PROMISED A FREE WATCH TO ANY PLAYER WHO HIT THE CLOCK, BUT BAMA, FOR SOME REASON, NEVER RECEIVED ONE! TOLD OF THE ANCIENT GAFFE, BULOVA FINALLY MADE GOOD WHEN THEY PRESENTED BAMA WITH HIS WATCH IN 1987!
BALLS
R H E
3 0 1
7 2 0
5 P O
2 P O
TE
CH
PH
PIT
ST.
EL CHEAPO AIN'T GONNA LIKE THIS!
JOYNER ©2005

Rugger ARDIZOIA
BORN IN OLEGGIO, ITALY, ON NOVEMBER 20, 1919, RINALDO JOSEPH ARDIZOIA IMMIGRATED TO SAN FRANCISCO WHEN HE WAS JUST A TODDLER! RUGGER, AS HE WAS NICKNAMED, QUICKLY FELL IN LOVE WITH BASEBALL WHILE DEVELOPING INTO A FINE RIGHT-HANDED PITCHER IN HIGH SCHOOL AND AMERICAN LEGION! HE SIGNED WITH THE MISSION REDS OF THE PACIFIC COAST LEAGUE IN 1937, THUS BEGINNING A LONG AND VERY SUCCESSFUL PRO CAREER, MOST OF WHICH WAS SPENT IN THE P.C.L.! ONE OF THE HIGHLIGHTS OF RUGGER'S CAREER OCCURRED IN 1941 WHEN, AT THE URGING OF YANKS SUPER-SCOUT JOE DEVINE, ARDIZOIA WAS SIGNED BY THE MIGHTY BRONX BOMBERS! RUGGER'S BEST CHANCE TO MAKE IT WITH THE YANKS ENDED, HOWEVER, WHEN HE SERVED IN THE ARMY FROM 1943-45, BUT HE DID MANAGE TO MAKE ONE BIG LEAGUE APPEARANCE FOR NEW YORK ON APRIL 30, 1947! ANOTHER TOP MOMENT FOR RUGGER CAME IN '49 WHEN HE WAS PITCHING FOR SEATTLE AGAINST THE HOLLYWOOD STARS, HIS FORMER TEAM! RUGGER TOSSED NINE SHUTOUT INNINGS, AND THEN WON THE BALLGAME, 1-0, WITH A LAST-INNING RBI-SINGLE!
WELCOME TO THE BIG TIME, MY BOY!
YOU DIDN'T THINK RUGGER HAD IT IN HIM, DID'YA?!
JOYNER ©2007
RUGGER PITCHED FOR THE 7TH A.A.F. BASEBALL CLUB WHILE STATIONED IN HONOLULU, BUT ONE OF HIS WORK DUTIES WAS TOW-TARGET OPERATOR! IT COULD BE DANGEROUS WORK -- SO DANGEROUS, IN FACT, THAT RUGGER'S COMMANDING OFFICER ONCE HAD HIM REMOVED FROM THE CREW PRIOR TO A BIG GAME! IN AN INCREDIBLE TWIST OF FATE, IT WAS ON THAT DAY THAT THE PLANE WHICH WOULD HAVE CARRIED RUGGER CRASHED! RUGGER PITCHED FOR ARMY TEAMS ALL OVER THE PACIFIC, PROVIDING A VALUABLE MORALE BOOST FOR MANY SOLDIERS! "WATCHING US PLAY BALL KEPT THEM OCCUPIED," SAYS RUGGER, "AND BOY DID THEY ENJOY IT!"
I HOPE THE FELLAS GOT PLENTY OF SHUT-EYE LAST NIGHT!

Barney
McCOSKY
IF YOU HAPPENED TO BE BUYING A CAR FROM LES STANFORD CHEVROLET IN DEARBORN, MICHIGAN, IN THE EARLY 1980s, YOU MIGHT HAVE BOUGHT IT FROM THE 1940 AMERICAN LEAGUE HITS LEADER -- TIGERS OUTFIELDER BARNEY McCOSKY! "I SOLD CARS FOR ABOUT 17 YEARS," BARNEY TOLD AUTHOR RICHARD BAK IN 1990. "I LIKED IT. I MET A LOT OF PEOPLE. WE TALKED BASEBALL A LOT." ABOUT 50 YEARS PRIOR THAT, BARNEY WAS TEARING UP THE MAJORS WITH A SCORCHING BAT THAT TOPPED THE .300-MARK IN SIX OF THE ELEVEN SEASONS IN WHICH HE PLAYED! BARNEY EXPERTLY PLAYED THE ROLE OF LOCAL-BOY-MAKES-GOOD WHEN HE GRADUATED FROM DETROIT'S SOUTHWESTERN HIGH AND THEN WENT ON TO STAR FOR THE TIGERS! HIS .340 AVERAGE AND LEAGUE LEADING 200 HITS HELPED PROPEL DETROIT TO A PENNANT IN 1940, BUT DESPITE BARNEY'S .304 SERIES AVERAGE, THE TIGERS LOST TO THE REDS IN A 7-GAME CLASSIC! BARNEY LOST THREE PRIME YEARS TO SERVICE IN WORLD WAR II, THEN GOT TRADED TO THE LOWLY ATHLETICS 25 GAMES INTO THE 1946 SEASON! DESPITE HIS DEJECTION OVER THE TRADE, BARNEY TURNED IT ON FOR THE A's AND BATTED .354 FOR THEM IN 92 GAMES! HE WAS BACK AT IT IN '47, HIS .328 AVERAGE GOOD ENOUGH FOR A 2ND-PLACE FINISH TO A.L. BATTING CHAMP TED WILLIAMS!
THIS IS GONNA MAKE A GREAT STORY FOR SOME LUCKY CAR BUYER ONE DAY!
200 HITS
1948 WAS BARNEY'S LAST GREAT SEASON! HE HIT .326 FOR THE ATHLETICS THAT YEAR, BUT A SERIOUS BACK INJURY SUFFERED IN A COLLISION WITH THE OUTFIELD WALL AT TIGER STADIUM PLAGUED HIM IN SUBSEQUENT SEASONS! BARNEY HUNG AROUND UNTIL '53, SLAPPING OUT HITS FOR THE REDS AND INDIANS, UNTIL HE WALKED AWAY TO BEGIN LIFE AFTER BASEBALL AS A STORE OWNER, AND THEN AS A CHEVY SALESMAN -- WHERE HE COULD TALK LOTS OF BASEBALL! "PLAYING IN DETROIT," HE SAID IN 1990, "I COULDN'T GET ENOUGH BASEBALL. AFTER THE GAME I'D LEAVE THE BALLPARK, DRIVE HOME, AND GO OUT BEHIND THE SCHOOL WHERE THE KIDS WERE PLAYING. I'D BRING PLENTY OF BALLS. THE KIDS LOVED IT. INSTEAD OF TAPED BALLS, THEY HAD BALLS WITH COVERS. I'D STAY OUT THERE FOR HOURS AND NEVER THINK ANYTHING ABOUT IT. I JUST LOVED IT. I COULDN'T GET ENOUGH BASEBALL."
BASEBALLS COURTESY OF THE DETROIT TIGERS... JUST DON'T LET THEM KNOW!
PROPERTY OF DETROIT TIGERS
JOYNER ©2000

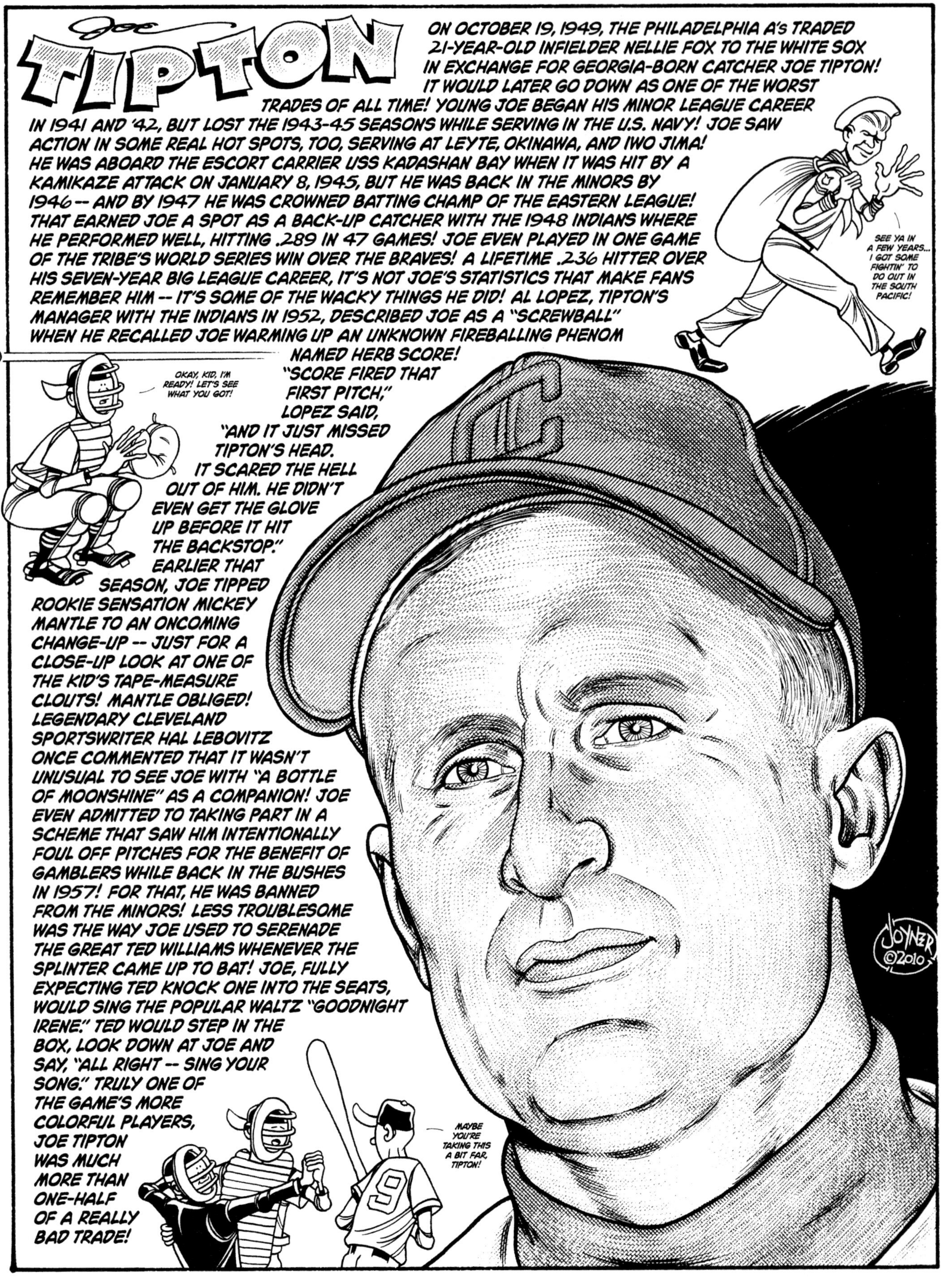
JOE TIPTON
ON OCTOBER 19, 1949, THE PHILADELPHIA A'S TRADED 21-YEAR-OLD INFIELDER NELLIE FOX TO THE WHITE SOX IN EXCHANGE FOR GEORGIA-BORN CATCHER JOE TIPTON! IT WOULD LATER GO DOWN AS ONE OF THE WORST TRADES OF ALL TIME! YOUNG JOE BEGAN HIS MINOR LEAGUE CAREER IN 1941 AND '42, BUT LOST THE 1943-45 SEASONS WHILE SERVING IN THE U.S. NAVY! JOE SAW ACTION IN SOME REAL HOT SPOTS, TOO, SERVING AT LEYTE, OKINAWA, AND IWO JIMA! HE WAS ABOARD THE ESCORT CARRIER USS KADASHAN BAY WHEN IT WAS HIT BY A KAMIKAZE ATTACK ON JANUARY 8, 1945, BUT HE WAS BACK IN THE MINORS BY 1946 -- AND BY 1947 HE WAS CROWNED BATTING CHAMP OF THE EASTERN LEAGUE! THAT EARNED JOE A SPOT AS A BACK-UP CATCHER WITH THE 1948 INDIANS WHERE HE PERFORMED WELL, HITTING .289 IN 47 GAMES! JOE EVEN PLAYED IN ONE GAME OF THE TRIBE'S WORLD SERIES WIN OVER THE BRAVES! A LIFETIME .236 HITTER OVER HIS SEVEN-YEAR BIG LEAGUE CAREER, IT'S NOT JOE'S STATISTICS THAT MAKE FANS REMEMBER HIM -- IT'S SOME OF THE WACKY THINGS HE DID! AL LOPEZ, TIPTON'S MANAGER WITH THE INDIANS IN 1952, DESCRIBED JOE AS A "SCREWBALL" WHEN HE RECALLED JOE WARMING UP AN UNKNOWN FIREBALLING PHENOM NAMED HERB SCORE! "SCORE FIRED THAT FIRST PITCH," LOPEZ SAID, "AND IT JUST MISSED TIPTON'S HEAD. IT SCARED THE HELL OUT OF HIM. HE DIDN'T EVEN GET THE GLOVE UP BEFORE IT HIT THE BACKSTOP." EARLIER THAT SEASON, JOE TIPPED ROOKIE SENSATION MICKEY MANTLE TO AN ONCOMING CHANGE-UP -- JUST FOR A CLOSE-UP LOOK AT ONE OF THE KID'S TAPE-MEASURE CLOUTS! MANTLE OBLIGED! LEGENDARY CLEVELAND SPORTSWRITER HAL LEBOVITZ ONCE COMMENTED THAT IT WASN'T UNUSUAL TO SEE JOE WITH "A BOTTLE OF MOONSHINE" AS A COMPANION! JOE EVEN ADMITTED TO TAKING PART IN A SCHEME THAT SAW HIM INTENTIONALLY FOUL OFF PITCHES FOR THE BENEFIT OF GAMBLERS WHILE BACK IN THE BUSHES IN 1957! FOR THAT, HE WAS BANNED FROM THE MINORS! LESS TROUBLESOME WAS THE WAY JOE USED TO SERENADE THE GREAT TED WILLIAMS WHENEVER THE SPLINTER CAME UP TO BAT! JOE, FULLY EXPECTING TED KNOCK ONE INTO THE SEATS, WOULD SING THE POPULAR WALTZ "GOODNIGHT IRENE." TED WOULD STEP IN THE BOX, LOOK DOWN AT JOE AND SAY, "ALL RIGHT -- SING YOUR SONG." TRULY ONE OF THE GAME'S MORE COLORFUL PLAYERS, JOE TIPTON WAS MUCH MORE THAN ONE-HALF OF A REALLY BAD TRADE!
SEE YA IN A FEW YEARS... I GOT SOME FIGHTIN' TO DO OUT IN THE SOUTH PACIFIC!
OKAY, KID, I'M READY! LET'S SEE WHAT YOU GOT!
MAYBE YOU'RE TAKING THIS A BIT FAR, TIPTON!
JOYNER ©2010

JOE ASTROTH

CATCHER -- PHILADELPHIA ATHLETICS

JOSEPH HENRY ASTROTH WAS BORN IN EAST ALTON, ILLINOIS, ON SEPTEMBER 1, 1922! JOE'S ATHLETIC PURSUITS WERE NEARLY ENDED WHEN HE LOST THE TIPS OF TWO FINGERS AT AGE 17! HE OVERCAME THAT, THOUGH, AND WENT ON TO CATCH FOR 10 YEARS IN THE MAJOR LEAGUES! AFTER SERVING IN THE COAST GUARD IN WORLD WAR II, JOE SIGNED WITH THE A's BUT SAW ONLY LIMITED ACTION IN 1945 AND 1946! DISPATCHED TO THE MINORS, JOE POSTED NICE YEARS FOR LANCASTER IN 1946, SAVANNAH IN 1947, AND MEMPHIS IN 1948! BACK WITH THE A's IN 1949, JOE HIT .243 IN 55 GAMES FOLLOWED BY A .327 AVERAGE IN 39 GAMES IN 1950! WHILE ONLY SEEING LIMITED DUTY AGAIN IN 1951, JOE MADE THE BEST OF THE SITUATION BY BECOMING THE FAVORITE CATCHER OF A's ACE PITCHER BOBBY SHANTZ! JOE CAUGHT ALMOST EVERY PITCH THROWN BY SHANTZ IN THEIR 8 YEARS TOGETHER! SHANTZ THOUGHT A LOT OF HIS BATTERY-MATE! FOLLOWING BOBBY'S APPEARANCE IN THE 1952 ALL-STAR GAME HE WAS ASKED HOW IT FELT TO PITCH TO THE BEST CATCHER IN BASEBALL -- YOGI BERRA! BOBBY SAID, "I DO EVERYDAY!" HE WAS, OF COURSE, SPEAKING OF JOE ASTROTH!

JOE, AT ONLY 5'-9", WAS STILL A THREE-SPORT STAR AT THE UNIVERSITY OF ILLINOIS!

JOE DROVE IN 6 RBIs IN ONE INNING AGAINST THE WASHINGTON SENATORS WITH A GRAND SLAM AND A 2-RUN SINGLE ON SEPTEMBER 23, 1950!

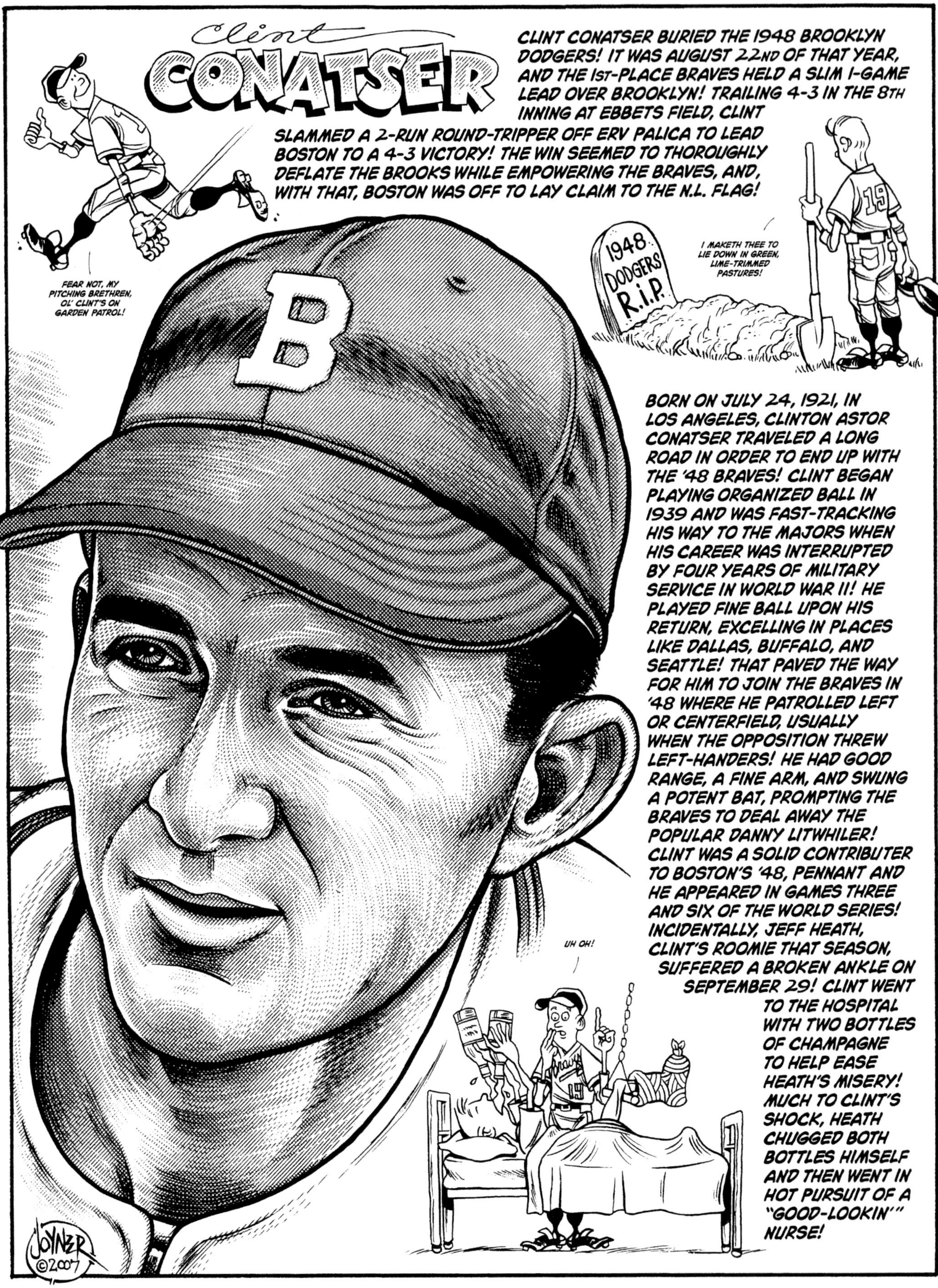
Clint
CONATSER
CLINT CONATSER BURIED THE 1948 BROOKLYN DODGERS! IT WAS AUGUST 22ND OF THAT YEAR, AND THE 1ST-PLACE BRAVES HELD A SLIM 1-GAME LEAD OVER BROOKLYN! TRAILING 4-3 IN THE 8TH INNING AT EBBETS FIELD, CLINT SLAMMED A 2-RUN ROUND-TRIPPER OFF ERV PALICA TO LEAD BOSTON TO A 4-3 VICTORY! THE WIN SEEMED TO THOROUGHLY DEFLATE THE BROOKS WHILE EMPOWERING THE BRAVES, AND, WITH THAT, BOSTON WAS OFF TO LAY CLAIM TO THE N.L. FLAG!
FEAR NOT, MY PITCHING BRETHREN, OL' CLINT'S ON GARDEN PATROL!
1948 DODGERS R.I.P.
I MAKETH THEE TO LIE DOWN IN GREEN, LIME-TRIMMED PASTURES!
19
B
BORN ON JULY 24, 1921, IN LOS ANGELES, CLINTON ASTOR CONATSER TRAVELED A LONG ROAD IN ORDER TO END UP WITH THE '48 BRAVES! CLINT BEGAN PLAYING ORGANIZED BALL IN 1939 AND WAS FAST-TRACKING HIS WAY TO THE MAJORS WHEN HIS CAREER WAS INTERRUPTED BY FOUR YEARS OF MILITARY SERVICE IN WORLD WAR II! HE PLAYED FINE BALL UPON HIS RETURN, EXCELLING IN PLACES LIKE DALLAS, BUFFALO, AND SEATTLE! THAT PAVED THE WAY FOR HIM TO JOIN THE BRAVES IN '48 WHERE HE PATROLLED LEFT OR CENTERFIELD, USUALLY WHEN THE OPPOSITION THREW LEFT-HANDERS! HE HAD GOOD RANGE, A FINE ARM, AND SWUNG A POTENT BAT, PROMPTING THE BRAVES TO DEAL AWAY THE POPULAR DANNY LITWHILER! CLINT WAS A SOLID CONTRIBUTER TO BOSTON'S '48, PENNANT AND HE APPEARED IN GAMES THREE AND SIX OF THE WORLD SERIES! INCIDENTALLY, JEFF HEATH, CLINT'S ROOMIE THAT SEASON, SUFFERED A BROKEN ANKLE ON SEPTEMBER 29! CLINT WENT TO THE HOSPITAL WITH TWO BOTTLES OF CHAMPAGNE TO HELP EASE HEATH'S MISERY! MUCH TO CLINT'S SHOCK, HEATH CHUGGED BOTH BOTTLES HIMSELF AND THEN WENT IN HOT PURSUIT OF A "GOOD-LOOKIN'" NURSE!
UH OH!
JOYNER ©2007

Walt
JUDNICH
SAN FRANCISCO HAD A WELL-DESERVED REPUTATION FOR PRODUCING SOME FINE BALLPLAYERS IN THE EARLY-1900s, ONE OF WHOM WAS OUTFIELDER WALT JUDNICH -- BORN IN THE CITY BY THE BAY ON JANUARY 24, 1917! THE YANKS SIGNED WALT IN 1935 AND WERE SO IMPRESSED WITH HIM BY '37 THAT THEY RATED HIM A BETTER BIG LEAGUE PROSPECT THAN ANOTHER WEST COAST YOUNGSTER THEY WERE WERE SCOUTING -- TED WILLIAMS! YANKEE SCOUT JOE DEVINE SUMMED UP HIS REPORT BY SIMPLY STATING, "I LIKE JUDNICH BETTER BETTER THAN WILLIAMS."
DON'T WORRY, BOSS, I WON'T LET THIS ONE GET AWAY!
THE YANKEES OF THE LATE 30s WERE SO OVERSTOCKED WITH TALENT, HOWEVER, THAT THEY HAD NO ROOM ON THE BIG LEAGUE ROSTER FOR WALT -- SO THEY SOLD HIM TO THE LOWLY ST. LOUIS BROWNS ON JANUARY 30, 1940! ON OPENING DAY THREE MONTHS LATER, WALT MADE HIS BIG LEAGUE DEBUT AND COLLECTED HIS FIRST HIT -- A HOME RUN OFF DETROIT TIGER BOBO NEWSOM! IT WAS OFF TO THE RACES FROM THERE AS WALT PUT TOGETHER A TREMENDOUS ROOKIE CAMPAIGN THAT SAW HIM WALLOP 24 LONG BALLS WHILE DRIVING IN 89 WITH A .303 AVERAGE! HE POSTED SIMILAR NUMBERS IN 1941 AND '42, BUT THEN WAS OFF TO THE ARMY WHERE WALT SERVED FROM 1943-45! WALT PLAYED BALL ON SOME GREAT ARMY TEAMS IN THOSE YEARS -- TEAMS THAT FEATURED MAJOR LEAGUERS LIKE JOE DIMAGGIO, BOB DILLINGER, FERRIS FAIN, AND DARIO LODIGIANI TO NAME A FEW -- BUT IT MAY HAVE TAKEN ITS TOLL ON HIM FOR HE WAS NEVER ABLE TO REGAIN HIS PRE-WAR FORM UPON HIS RETURN TO THE BROWNIES IN '46! WALT STILL BANGED OUT 15 HOMERS FOR ST. LOUIS IN 1946, FOLLOWED BY 18 CIRCUITS IN 1947, BUT IT WAS OBVIOUS HE WAS SLOWING DOWN, SO THE BROWNIES TRADED HIM TO THE INDIANS ON NOVEMBER 20, 1947! WALT WAS UNFORTUNATE TO HAVE MISSED THE BROWNS' ONE-AND-ONLY PENNANT THAT THEY WON IN 1944 WHILE HE WAS IN THE ARMY, BUT HE DID HIS OLD BALLCLUB ONE BETTER BY WINNING A WORLD SERIES RING AS A PLATOON PLAYER WITH THE '48 TRIBE!
M-1 GARAND, LOUISVILLE SLUGGER -- IT DON'T MATTER TO ME -- I'M AN EXPERT MARKSMAN WITH BOTH!
JOYNER 2004
WHILE LEAVING THE YANKS MUST HAVE BEEN BITTER-SWEET, JOINING THE BROWNIES WAS GOOD FOR WALT BECAUSE HE IMMEDIATELY BECAME A VALUED EVERYDAY PLAYER! IT'S HUMAN NATURE, HOWEVER, TO DRAW A LITTLE EXTRA ADRENALINE WHEN FACING YOUR FORMER TEAM, AND THAT SEEMS TO HAVE BEEN THE CASE WITH WALT IN 1940! HE PUNISHED THE YANKS WITH HIS BAT, ESPECIALLY DURING A 3-GAME SERIES IN ST. LOUIS IN JULY! WALT LED THE BROWNIES TO VICTORY IN THE OPENER WITH A PAIR OF HOMERS; HE WON THE NEXT AFTERNOON'S BATTLE WITH A 9TH-INNING GAME-ENDING 2-RUN SHOT; THEN TRIPLED IN THE SERIES FINALE!
I TOLD YOU STIFFS YOU SHOULDN'T HAVE TRADED ME!
YOU TELL 'EM, KID!

BOB "DUCKY"
DETWEILER
ROBERT STERLING DETWEILER WAS BORN ON FEBRUARY 15, 1919, IN TRUMBAUERSVILLE, PENNSYLVANIA! AFTER STARRING IN FOUR SPORTS FOR QUAKERTOWN HIGH SCHOOL, DUCKY WAS INVITED TO TRY OUT FOR THE PHILADELPHIA ATHLETICS IN 1938! CONNIE MACK, A's OWNER-MANAGER, WAS SO IMPRESSED THAT HE IMMEDIATELY SIGNED DUCKY FOR $75 A MONTH AND DISPATCHED HIM TO FEDERALSBURG OF THE EASTERN SHORE LEAGUE FOR THE 1939 SEASON!
DUCKY PLAYED WELL IN '39, BATTING .292 WITH 10 HOMERS AND 49 RUNS BATTED IN! THIS PROMPTED MACK TO BRING THE YOUNGSTER IN TO HIS OFFICE AT SHIBE PARK WHERE HE AWARDED DUCKY A $400 BONUS! "I WAS A HAPPY MAN WHEN I WALKED OUT OF THAT OFFICE," DUCKY RECALLED! HIS MOST MEMORABLE MOMENT ON THE FIELD THAT SEASON CAME WHEN HE HOMERED 3 TIMES IN ONE GAME! DUCKY POSTED FINE SEASONS AT OTHER STOPS IN WILMINGTON, BRIDGEPORT, AND BRADFORD! A HUGE YEAR AT EVANSVILLE IN '42 PROMPTED AN END-OF-YEAR CALL-UP TO THE BOSTON BRAVES!
DUCKY DETWEILER AT YOUR SERVICE!
ARMY
DUCKY MADE THE MOST OF HIS LATE-SEASON TRIAL WITH CASEY STENGEL'S 1942 BRAVES! PLAYING THIRD BASE AND BATTING 8TH, DUCKY MADE HIS BIG LEAGUE DEBUT ON SEPTEMBER 12 AND SINGLED IN HIS FIRST AT-BAT OFF BUCS RIGHT-HANDER HANK GORNICKI! IT TURNED OUT THAT DUCKY WAS JUST WARMING UP! PLAYING IN THE BRAVES' LAST 12 GAMES, HE HIT SAFELY IN TEN OF THOSE CONTESTS -- RECORDING MULTI-HIT GAMES IN THREE OF THE FIRST FOUR! IN ONE OF THOSE TILTS, AN 11-6 VICTORY OVER THE CUBS ON SEPTEMBER 13, DUCKY POWERED THE BRAVES WITH A TWO-BAGGER, A THREE-BAGGER, AND 3 RBIs! DUCKY CLOSED THE 1942 SEASON WITH HITS IN BOTH ENDS OF A TWIN BILL AT THE POLO GROUNDS! THE FINAL TALLY ON HIS '42 TRIAL WAS AN IMPRESSIVE .318!
POISED FOR A BREAKOUT YEAR WITH THE 1943 BRAVES, DUCKY WAS INSTEAD DRAFTED INTO THE U.S. ARMY! HE SACRIFICED THREE PRIME YEARS TO THE WORLD WAR II EFFORT, BECOMING A SPECIAL SERVICES OFFICER IN THE MEDICAL CORPS WHILE ALSO PLAYING BALL FOR MANY CRACK ARMY TEAMS! BACK FROM THE WAR, DUCKY HIT OVER .400 IN SPRING TRAINING FOR THE 1946 BRAVES -- AND MADE THE TEAM, BUT IN MAY, AFTER JUST ONE AT-BAT, HE WAS SENT DOWN TO TRIPLE-A! DUCKY RETIRED FROM THE GAME IN 1952, EVENTUALLY EMBARKING ON A LONG CAREER WITH THE U.S. POSTAL SERVICE! HE IS PROUD TO HAVE PLAYED, OFTEN SAYING, "I MADE IT TO THE BIG TIME FOR A CUP OF COFFEE!"
JOYNER ©2006

Bobby Bragan
I BELIEVE, FINE SIR, THAT YOU HAVE ERRED IN YOUR ASSESSMENT OF THE SITUATION!
CATCHER -- BROOKLYN DODGERS
LONG BEFORE HE BECAME FAMOUS FOR HIS EPIC BATTLES WITH UMPIRES AS MANAGER FOR THE PIRATES, INDIANS, AND BRAVES, BOBBY BRAGAN BEGAN HIS BIG LEAGUE CAREER AS THE FULL-TIME SHORTSTOP FOR THE PHILADELPHIA PHILLIES IN 1940! HE TOOK UP CATCHING AS A WAY OF PROLONGING HIS PLAYING CAREER, AND WAS ACQUIRED BY THE BROOKLYN DODGERS ON MARCH 24, 1943! AFTER A STINT IN THE ARMY DURING WORLD WAR II, BOBBY RETURNED TO THE DODGERS IN 1947! WITH ONLY 36 AT-BATS ALL SEASON, BOBBY DELIVERED A CLUTCH, SIXTH-INNING PINCH-HIT DOUBLE OFF YANKEE RELIEF ACE JOE PAGE THAT TIED GAME SIX OF THE 1947 WORLD SERIES! THE DODGERS WON THAT GAME, FORCING A GAME SEVEN! BRAGAN STILL CALLS THAT MOMENT "MY MOST PRICELESS BASEBALL MEMORY." HE BECAME PLAYER-MANAGER FOR THE FT. WORTH CATS OF THE TEXAS LEAGUE IN 1948 AND LED THEM TO A FIRST-PLACE FINISH! THEY REPEATED AS LEAGUE CHAMPIONS IN 1949 AND NEVER FINISHED BELOW .500 WITH BRAGAN AT THE HELM! THE KID FROM BIRMINGHAM'S #10 JERSEY IS NOW RETIRED BY THE CATS AND HANGS PROUDLY OVER LaGRAVE FIELD!
WHAT NERVES?!
BOBBY BRAGAN WAS A FINE PIANO PLAYER AND OFTEN ENTERTAINED PLAYERS AND FRIENDS WHEN A PIANO WAS AVAILABLE! THE WHOLE DODGER TEAM GATHERED AROUND THE PIANO TO CELEBRATE THE 1947 PENNANT WITH A ROUSING VERSION OF "BEAUTIFUL DAY FOR A BALL GAME"!
JOYNER ©2003

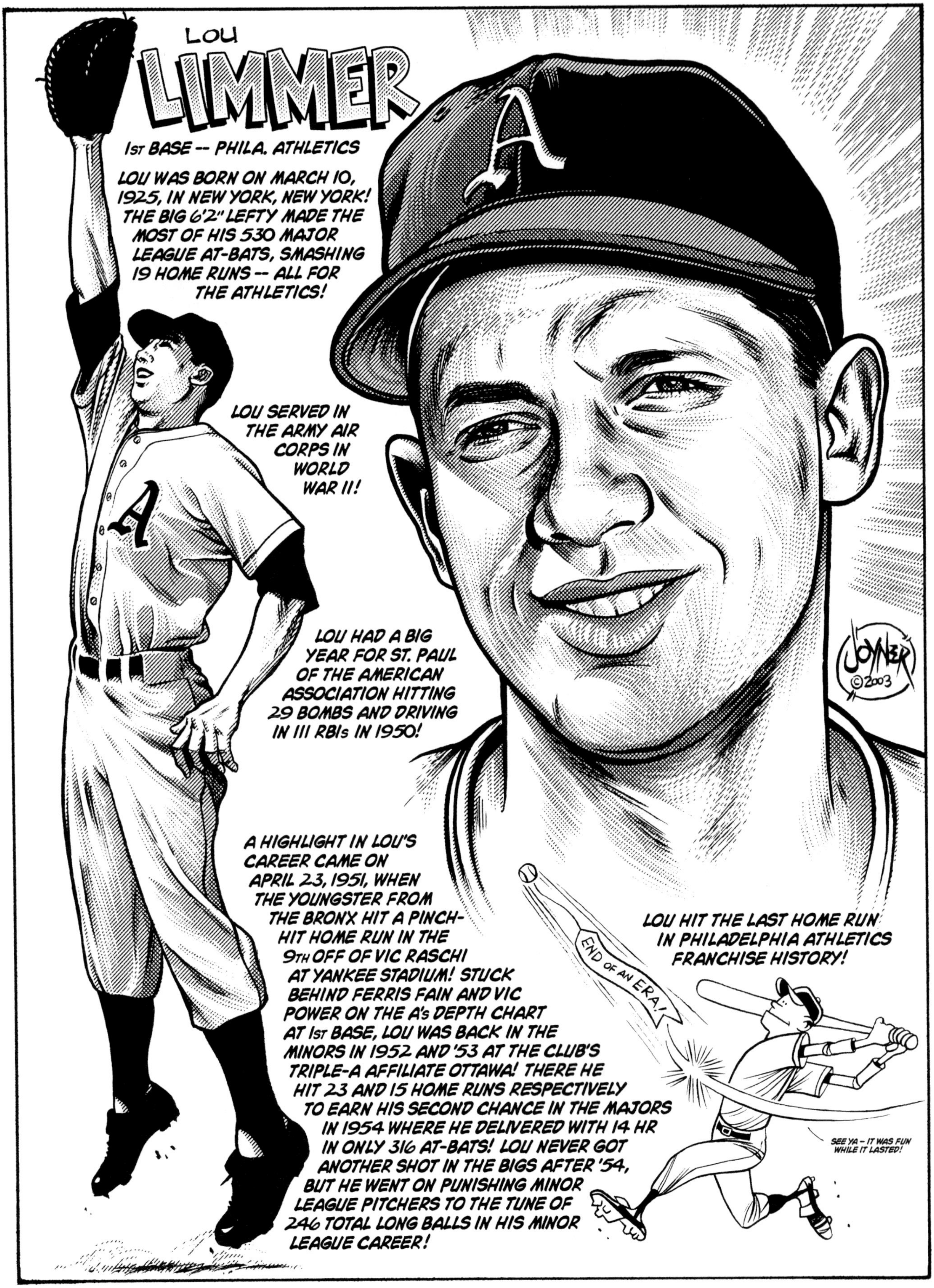

LOU
LIMMER
1st BASE -- PHILA. ATHLETICS
LOU WAS BORN ON MARCH 10, 1925, IN NEW YORK, NEW YORK! THE BIG 6'2" LEFTY MADE THE MOST OF HIS 530 MAJOR LEAGUE AT-BATS, SMASHING 19 HOME RUNS -- ALL FOR THE ATHLETICS!
LOU SERVED IN THE ARMY AIR CORPS IN WORLD WAR II!
LOU HAD A BIG YEAR FOR ST. PAUL OF THE AMERICAN ASSOCIATION HITTING 29 BOMBS AND DRIVING IN 111 RBIs IN 1950!
JOYNER ©2003
A HIGHLIGHT IN LOU'S CAREER CAME ON APRIL 23, 1951, WHEN THE YOUNGSTER FROM THE BRONX HIT A PINCH-HIT HOME RUN IN THE 9th OFF OF VIC RASCHI AT YANKEE STADIUM! STUCK BEHIND FERRIS FAIN AND VIC POWER ON THE A's DEPTH CHART AT 1st BASE, LOU WAS BACK IN THE MINORS IN 1952 AND '53 AT THE CLUB'S TRIPLE-A AFFILIATE OTTAWA! THERE HE HIT 23 AND 15 HOME RUNS RESPECTIVELY TO EARN HIS SECOND CHANCE IN THE MAJORS IN 1954 WHERE HE DELIVERED WITH 14 HR IN ONLY 316 AT-BATS! LOU NEVER GOT ANOTHER SHOT IN THE BIGS AFTER '54, BUT HE WENT ON PUNISHING MINOR LEAGUE PITCHERS TO THE TUNE OF 246 TOTAL LONG BALLS IN HIS MINOR LEAGUE CAREER!
LOU HIT THE LAST HOME RUN IN PHILADELPHIA ATHLETICS FRANCHISE HISTORY!
END OF AN ERA!
SEE YA – IT WAS FUN WHILE IT LASTED!

KOREA AND VIETNAM

Bobby
NEIGHBORS
SHORTSTOP -- ST. LOUIS BROWNS
ROBERT OTIS NEIGHBORS WAS BORN ON NOVEMBER 9, 1917, IN THE TOWN OF TALAHINA, OKLAHOMA! BOBBY WAS A GREAT YOUTH ATHLETE, EXCELLING IN BASEBALL AND BASKETBALL! FOLLOWING HIS GRADUATION FROM HIGH SCHOOL, BOBBY PLAYED ON AN ALL-STAR HOOPS TEAM LED BY CARL HUBBELL! IT WAS IN BASEBALL, THOUGH, THAT BOBBY WAS MEANT TO SHINE, AND HIS SLICK FIELDING, RIFLE-ARM, AND SOLID HITTING IMPRESSED THE ST. LOUIS BROWNS SO MUCH THAT THEY SIGNED HIM IN 1936! HE TURNED IN A FINE ROOKIE SEASON AT SILOAM SPRINGS IN '36, FLASHING FANCY GLOVEWORK AT SHORT WHILE HITTING .278 WITH 16 LONG BALLS! BY 1939 BOBBY HAD EARNED AN END-OF-SEASON CALL-UP! HE SAW ACTION IN ONLY 7 GAMES, PICKING UP JUST 2 HITS IN 11 AT-BATS, BUT ONE OF THOSE HITS WAS OF THE BIG FLY VARIETY -- A SOLO HOME RUN OFF OF VETERAN DENNY GALEHOUSE ON SEPTEMBER 21 INTO THE FENWAY PARK STANDS! BOBBY SPENT THE NEXT FEW YEARS IN THE MINORS FOR ADDITIONAL SEASONING, BUT HE SHELVED HIS BASEBALL CAREER IN 1941 WHEN HE ENLISTED IN THE ARMY AIR CORPS TO SERVE IN WORLD WAR II WHERE HE FLEW MANY DANGEROUS MISSIONS IN EUROPE!
POW
I AIN'T AFRAID OF NO GREEN MONSTER!
INSTEAD OF RETURNING TO BASEBALL WHEN WWII ENDED, BOB DECIDED TO BE A CAREER AIR FORCE MAN! HE FLEW MORE DANGEROUS MISSIONS IN KOREA AND WAS SADLY KILLED IN ACTION WHEN SHOT DOWN IN 1952! HE WAS AN AMERICAN HERO, THOUGH -- THE ONLY BIG LEAGUE BALLPLAYER TO DIE IN THE KOREAN WAR -- AND BOB WAS HONORED BY MAJOR LEAGUE BASEBALL AT ARLINGTON CEMETERY ON JUNE 14, 2000!
JOYNER ©2004

Jerry COLEMAN

GERALD FRANCIS COLEMAN WAS BORN ON SEPTEMBER 14, 1924, IN SAN JOSE, CALIFORNIA! AFTER A FINE YEAR WITH THE KANSAS CITY BLUES IN 1947, "JERRY" LOOKED LIKE A SURE THING TO MAKE THE YANKEES IN SPRING TRAINING OF 1948! INSTEAD, HE WAS THE LAST MAN CUT, AN ACT THAT ONLY SERVED TO INCREASE HIS DESIRE TO MAKE THE CLUB IN 1949! NOT ONLY DID THE YOUNG SECOND BASEMAN MAKE THE 1949 YANKS, HE ENDED UP BEING NAMED THE ASSOCIATED PRESS ROOKIE OF THE YEAR!

JERRY HAS BEEN THE VOICE OF THE SAN DIEGO PADRES SINCE 1972!

IT WAS JERRY'S 8TH-INNING 3-RUN DOUBLE AGAINST BOSTON IN THE LAST GAME OF THE 1949 SEASON THAT SECURED A.L. PENNANT FOR THE YANKEES, AND HIS FIVE HITS AND FOUR RBIs IN THE WORLD SERIES HELPED NEW YORK BEAT THE DODGERS IN FIVE GAMES! JERRY FOLLOWED HIS ROOKIE SEASON WITH AN EVEN BETTER CAMPAIGN IN 1950, BATTING A CAREER-HIGH .287 WHILE TURNING 137 TWIN-KILLINGS -- A YANKEE TEAM RECORD! HE CAPPED THE YEAR BY WINNING THE WORLD SERIES M.V.P. AWARD AS THE BOMBERS SWEPT THE PHILLIES IN FOUR HARD-FOUGHT CONTESTS! WHILE HIS .286 SERIES AVERAGE MAY LOOK RATHER PEDESTRIAN, THE TIMELY NATURE OF HIS HITS IS WHAT LIFTED HIM ABOVE THE REST AS TWO OF HIS FOUR HITS DROVE IN GAME-WINNING RUNS! INJURIES MAY HAVE PREVENTED JERRY FROM ACHIEVING HIS FULL POTENTIAL, BUT HE BATTLED FIERCELY TO CARVE OUT A FINE 9-YEAR CAREER -- ALL WITH THE YANKEES! "'HE ONLY GOES 1-FOR-4,'" JERRY RECALLED FOLKS SAYING ABOUT HIM, "'BUT THAT ONE HIT WILL BEAT YOU.' I WAS PROUD OF THAT."

JERRY ANSWERED HIS COUNTRY'S WWII CALL BY ENLISTING IN THE NAVY'S V-5 PREFLIGHT PROGRAM IN SEPTEMBER OF 1942! BY THE FALL OF '44 JERRY WAS A MARINE PILOT FLYING A DAUNTLESS DIVE-BOMBER AGAINST THE JAPANESE IN THE SOLOMONS, AND LATER IN THE PHILIPPINES! JERRY WENT BACK INTO ACTION IN THE KOREAN WAR WHERE HE FLEW 63 MISSIONS IN A CORSAIR ATTACK PLANE! WHILE HIGHLY DECORATED, JERRY SUMS UP HIS SERVICE IN A MOST HUMBLE WAY, SAYING, "I SIMPLY DID MY DUTY."

GLEASON

DODGERS ROOKIE ROY GLEASON WAS AS PROUD AS A KID COULD BE AS HE STOOD ON SECOND FOLLOWING HIS PINCH-HIT DOUBLE OFF PHILLIES LEFTY DENNIS BENNETT ON SEPTEMBER 28, 1963! WHILE IT APPEARED THAT ROY'S FUTURE IN BASEBALL WOULD BE LONG, THAT AT-BAT TURNED OUT TO BE THE ONLY ONE OF HIS BIG LEAGUE CAREER. ROY WAS A FIVE-TOOL PLAYER IN HIGH SCHOOL WITH A HOWITZER FOR A THROWING ARM! THE DODGERS SIGNED HIM FOR A BIG BONUS WITH HOPES THAT HE WOULD HELP FILL L.A.'S OUTFIELD NEEDS FOR YEARS TO COME! ROY SPENT THE 1964-66 SEASONS BACK IN THE MINORS FOR ADDITIONAL SEASONING, AND WAS SLATED TO RETURN TO THE DODGERS IN 1967 WHEN HE WAS DRAFTED INTO THE U.S. ARMY. ROY WAS SENT TO VIETNAM IN DECEMBER OF THAT YEAR, AND SOON FOUND HIMSELF ON THE FRONT LINES. HE FOUGHT BRAVELY, EARNING A BRONZE STAR, AS WELL AS BEING NAMED "SOLDIER OF THE MONTH" IN JUNE OF 1968. MEANWHILE, ROY'S NUMBER ONE HOPE WAS THAT HE WOULD MAKE IT HOME IN ONE PIECE SO HE COULD RETURN TO THE MAJORS. THAT DREAM CAME TO A CRASHING HALT WHEN HE WAS SEVERELY WOUNDED DURING A PATROL ON JULY 24TH OF '68. ROY EVENTUALLY MADE A FULL RECOVERY, BUT THE STARS NEVER QUITE ALIGNED FOR HIM TO BE ABLE TO MAKE A RETURN TO THE BIGS. AS IT STANDS, ROY GLEASON AND CHUCK GOGGIN ARE THE ONLY TWO MAJOR LEAGUERS WOUNDED IN VIETNAM -- AN EXCLUSIVE GROUP TO SAY THE LEAST! ROY'S SACRIFICE WAS LOST TO THE AGES, BUT LONG-OVERDUE RECOGNITION FINALLY CAME WHEN HE WAS HONORED AT DODGER STADIUM ON SEPTEMBER 20, 2003! "I AM INDEBTED TO ALL WHO'VE RECOGNIZED NOT WHAT 'I'VE' DONE," SAYS ROY, "BUT TO WHAT 'WE' DID. WHAT 'WE' SACRIFICED IN THOSE JUNGLES. IT WAS A PLACE WHERE NO ONE WANTED TO GO -- AND A PLACE FROM WHERE MANY NEVER RETURNED."

ROY SPENT MUCH OF HIS YOUTH IN A SMALL HOME IN LaGRANGE, ILLINOIS! THE LITTLE HOUSE WAS LOCATED IN A FOREST PRESERVE -- MEANING IT WAS ILLEGAL TO CHOP DOWN ANY TREES! BUT THAT DIDN'T STOP YOUNG ROY FROM CHOPPING DOWN A CHERRY TREE THAT STOOD IN THE MIDDLE OF A BALLFIELD HE'D HAND-CRAFTED IN THE BACK YARD! HE CAUGHT HELL FOR THE ACT, BUT ROY WOULD DO ANYTHING TO PLAY THE ONLY GAME HE TRULY LOVED!

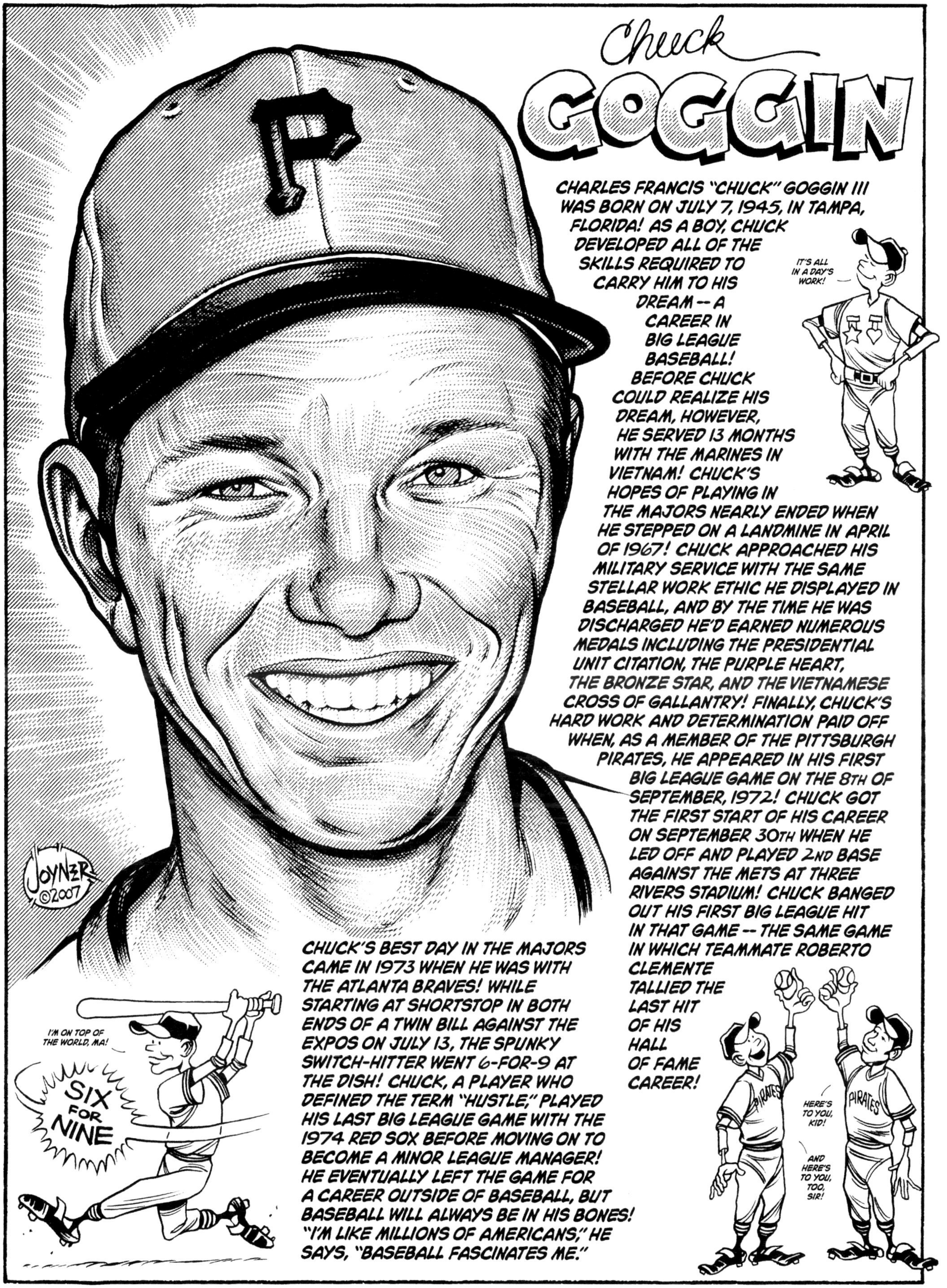
Chuck
GOGGIN
CHARLES FRANCIS "CHUCK" GOGGIN III WAS BORN ON JULY 7, 1945, IN TAMPA, FLORIDA! AS A BOY, CHUCK DEVELOPED ALL OF THE SKILLS REQUIRED TO CARRY HIM TO HIS DREAM -- A CAREER IN BIG LEAGUE BASEBALL! BEFORE CHUCK COULD REALIZE HIS DREAM, HOWEVER, HE SERVED 13 MONTHS WITH THE MARINES IN VIETNAM! CHUCK'S HOPES OF PLAYING IN THE MAJORS NEARLY ENDED WHEN HE STEPPED ON A LANDMINE IN APRIL OF 1967! CHUCK APPROACHED HIS MILITARY SERVICE WITH THE SAME STELLAR WORK ETHIC HE DISPLAYED IN BASEBALL, AND BY THE TIME HE WAS DISCHARGED HE'D EARNED NUMEROUS MEDALS INCLUDING THE PRESIDENTIAL UNIT CITATION, THE PURPLE HEART, THE BRONZE STAR, AND THE VIETNAMESE CROSS OF GALLANTRY! FINALLY, CHUCK'S HARD WORK AND DETERMINATION PAID OFF WHEN, AS A MEMBER OF THE PITTSBURGH PIRATES, HE APPEARED IN HIS FIRST BIG LEAGUE GAME ON THE 8TH OF SEPTEMBER, 1972! CHUCK GOT THE FIRST START OF HIS CAREER ON SEPTEMBER 30TH WHEN HE LED OFF AND PLAYED 2ND BASE AGAINST THE METS AT THREE RIVERS STADIUM! CHUCK BANGED OUT HIS FIRST BIG LEAGUE HIT IN THAT GAME -- THE SAME GAME IN WHICH TEAMMATE ROBERTO CLEMENTE TALLIED THE LAST HIT OF HIS HALL OF FAME CAREER!
IT'S ALL IN A DAY'S WORK!
JOYNER ©2007
CHUCK'S BEST DAY IN THE MAJORS CAME IN 1973 WHEN HE WAS WITH THE ATLANTA BRAVES! WHILE STARTING AT SHORTSTOP IN BOTH ENDS OF A TWIN BILL AGAINST THE EXPOS ON JULY 13, THE SPUNKY SWITCH-HITTER WENT 6-FOR-9 AT THE DISH! CHUCK, A PLAYER WHO DEFINED THE TERM "HUSTLE," PLAYED HIS LAST BIG LEAGUE GAME WITH THE 1974 RED SOX BEFORE MOVING ON TO BECOME A MINOR LEAGUE MANAGER! HE EVENTUALLY LEFT THE GAME FOR A CAREER OUTSIDE OF BASEBALL, BUT BASEBALL WILL ALWAYS BE IN HIS BONES! "I'M LIKE MILLIONS OF AMERICANS," HE SAYS, "BASEBALL FASCINATES ME."
I'M ON TOP OF THE WORLD, MA!
SIX FOR NINE
HERE'S TO YOU, KID!
AND HERE'S TO YOU, TOO, SIR!
PIRATES
PIRATES

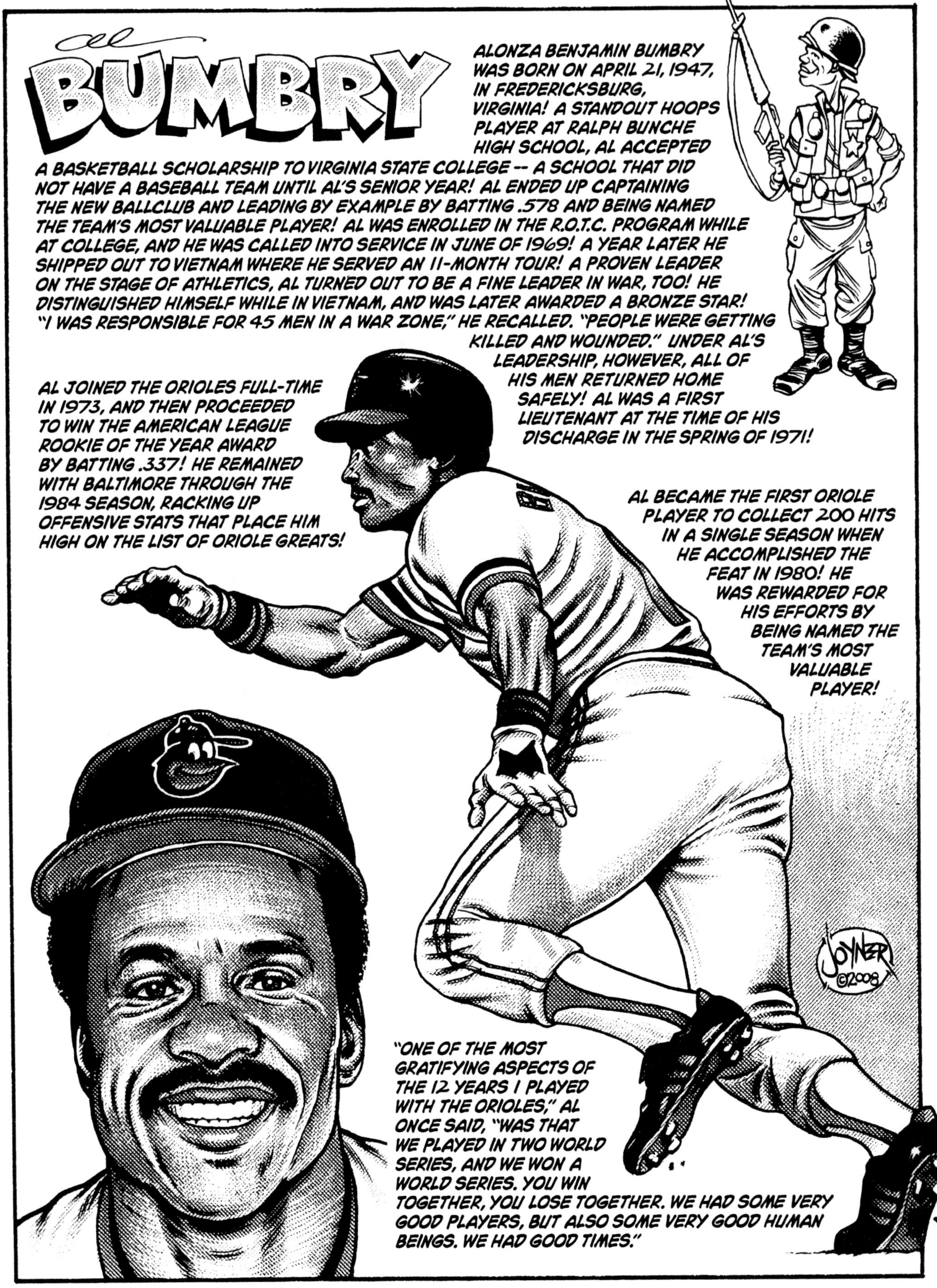
BUMBRY
ALONZA BENJAMIN BUMBRY WAS BORN ON APRIL 21, 1947, IN FREDERICKSBURG, VIRGINIA! A STANDOUT HOOPS PLAYER AT RALPH BUNCHE HIGH SCHOOL, AL ACCEPTED A BASKETBALL SCHOLARSHIP TO VIRGINIA STATE COLLEGE -- A SCHOOL THAT DID NOT HAVE A BASEBALL TEAM UNTIL AL'S SENIOR YEAR! AL ENDED UP CAPTAINING THE NEW BALLCLUB AND LEADING BY EXAMPLE BY BATTING .578 AND BEING NAMED THE TEAM'S MOST VALUABLE PLAYER! AL WAS ENROLLED IN THE R.O.T.C. PROGRAM WHILE AT COLLEGE, AND HE WAS CALLED INTO SERVICE IN JUNE OF 1969! A YEAR LATER HE SHIPPED OUT TO VIETNAM WHERE HE SERVED AN 11-MONTH TOUR! A PROVEN LEADER ON THE STAGE OF ATHLETICS, AL TURNED OUT TO BE A FINE LEADER IN WAR, TOO! HE DISTINGUISHED HIMSELF WHILE IN VIETNAM, AND WAS LATER AWARDED A BRONZE STAR! "I WAS RESPONSIBLE FOR 45 MEN IN A WAR ZONE," HE RECALLED. "PEOPLE WERE GETTING KILLED AND WOUNDED." UNDER AL'S LEADERSHIP, HOWEVER, ALL OF HIS MEN RETURNED HOME SAFELY! AL WAS A FIRST LIEUTENANT AT THE TIME OF HIS DISCHARGE IN THE SPRING OF 1971!
AL JOINED THE ORIOLES FULL-TIME IN 1973, AND THEN PROCEEDED TO WIN THE AMERICAN LEAGUE ROOKIE OF THE YEAR AWARD BY BATTING .337! HE REMAINED WITH BALTIMORE THROUGH THE 1984 SEASON, RACKING UP OFFENSIVE STATS THAT PLACE HIM HIGH ON THE LIST OF ORIOLE GREATS!
AL BECAME THE FIRST ORIOLE PLAYER TO COLLECT 200 HITS IN A SINGLE SEASON WHEN HE ACCOMPLISHED THE FEAT IN 1980! HE WAS REWARDED FOR HIS EFFORTS BY BEING NAMED THE TEAM'S MOST VALUABLE PLAYER!
JOYNER ©2008
"ONE OF THE MOST GRATIFYING ASPECTS OF THE 12 YEARS I PLAYED WITH THE ORIOLES," AL ONCE SAID, "WAS THAT WE PLAYED IN TWO WORLD SERIES, AND WE WON A WORLD SERIES. YOU WIN TOGETHER, YOU LOSE TOGETHER. WE HAD SOME VERY GOOD PLAYERS, BUT ALSO SOME VERY GOOD HUMAN BEINGS. WE HAD GOOD TIMES."

MEN OF DESEGREGATION

JACKIE
ROBINSON
JACKIE STOLE HOME 19 TIMES IN HIS CAREER, THE MOST FAMOUS BEING HIS SWIPE OF THE DISH IN GAME ONE OF THE 1955 WORLD SERIES AGAINST THE YANKEES!
STOP! THIEF!
A BIG MAN ON CAMPUS, JACKIE WAS THE BRUINS' FIRST-EVER 4-LETTER MAN!
UCLA
I GET GOOD GRADES, TOO!
JACK ROOSEVELT ROBINSON DIDN'T JUST CHANGE MAJOR LEAGUE BASEBALL WHEN HE BECAME THE FIRST BLACK MAN IN THE 20TH CENTURY TO PLAY IN THE BIG LEAGUES ON APRIL 15, 1947-- HE CHANGED AMERICA! LONG BEFORE JACKIE MADE HISTORY THAT DAY WITH THE BROOKLYN DODGERS, HE SET COLLEGIATE ATHLETICS ON ITS EAR BY EXCELLING IN FOOTBALL, BASEBALL, BASKETBALL, AND TRACK AT UCLA! JACKIE DEMONSTRATED AN EARLY PASSION FOR CIVIL RIGHTS WHILE SERVING IN THE U.S. ARMY DURING WORLD WAR II WHEN HE REFUSED TO MOVE TO THE BACK OF A BUS AND FACED A COURT-MARTIAL! VICTORIOUS AGAINST HIS ACCUSERS IN THAT CASE, HE THEN MOVED ON TO VICTORY ON THE NATION'S BALLFIELDS! SPOTTED BY DODGER SCOUT CLYDE SUKEFORTH WHILE PLAYING FOR THE NEGRO LEAGUE KANSAS CITY MONARCHS, JACKIE WAS THEN PEGGED BY BROOKLYN G.M. BRANCH RICKEY AS THE MAN WHO WOULD BREAK BASEBALL'S COLOR LINE IN WHAT CAME TO BE CALLED "THE GREAT EXPERIMENT"!
I'M ON QUITE A RUN!
JOYNER ©2005
THE JACKIE ROBINSON STORY
Dodgers
MOVE OVER OSCAR!
JACKIE PROVED TO BE THE PERFECT MAN TO MAKE RICKEY'S EXPERIMENT A PURE SUCCESS WHEN IN THE FACE OF EXTREME RACISM HE TURNED IN AN INCREDIBLE DEBUT SEASON THAT SAW HIM NAMED ROOKIE OF THE YEAR -- ALL WHILE MAINTAINING AMAZING RESTRAINT! A BATTING TITLE, AN M.V.P. AWARD, ALL-STAR GAMES, A MOVIE OF HIS LIFE STARRING HIMSELF, A WORLD CHAMPIONSHIP, AND ELECTION TO THE HALL OF FAME FOLLOWED, BUT NONE WAS BIGGER THAN WHAT HE DID FOR HUMANITY!

Bobby
ESTALELLA
MANY BASEBALL HISTORIANS BELIEVE THAT BASEBALL'S MODERN ERA "COLOR LINE" WAS CROSSED YEARS BEFORE THE BIG LEAGUE DEBUT OF JACKIE ROBINSON IN 1947! SOME, IN FACT, BELIEVE THAT IT FIRST HAPPENED ON SEPTEMBER 7, 1935, WHEN CUBAN ROBERTO "BOBBY" ESTALELLA MADE HIS BIG LEAGUE DEBUT WITH THE WASHINGTON SENATORS! BOBBY WENT ON TO PLAY NINE YEARS IN THE MAJORS, HIS BEST SEASONS COMING WITH THE PHILADELPHIA A's FROM 1943-45! BOBBY COULD REALLY HANDLE THE LUMBER, BUT HIS DEFENSIVE DEFICIENCIES PREVENTED HIM FROM ACHIEVING THE STARDOM THAT MANY PREDICTED FOR HIM! A DOZEN OR SO CUBANS HAD PRECEDED BOBBY'S ENTRY TO THE MAJORS, BUT THEY WERE LIGHT-SKINNED AND EASILY PASSED FOR CAUCASIANS! BOBBY'S COMPLEXION WAS DARKER, HIS HAIR KINKY, AND SOME OF HIS FACIAL FEATURES MORE AFRICAN, SO HIS ARRIVAL IN THE BIGS RAISED MANY AN EYEBROW! BOBBY FACED INTENSE RACISM AS HE TRIED TO GAIN A FOOTHOLD ON THE BALLFIELD, HIS HEAD BEING THE TARGET OF MANY BIGOTED MOUNDSMEN! STILL, HE PERSEVERED AND CHALKED UP A VERY RESPECTABLE CAREER! HIS MINOR LEAGUE CAREER, WHICH SPANNED FROM 1934-51, IS PARTICULARLY IMPRESSIVE! BOBBY PLAYED DOWN HIS ROLE IN BASEBALL'S INTEGRATION, HUMBLY SAYING IT WAS "ABSURD," BUT IT CANNOT BE DENIED THAT HE WAS A PIONEER IN THE DESEGREGATION OF THE GAME!
BOBBY WAS A POWERFULLY BUILT 5-FOOT-6 AND 185-LBS WHEN HE BROKE IN, AND HIS MUSCULATURE QUICKLY EARNED HIM THE NICKNAME "TARZAN!"
JOHNNY WEISSMULLER'S GOT NOTHIN' ON ME!
BOBBY WON THE PIEDMONT LEAGUE'S TRIPLE CROWN IN 1938 AND LED HIS CHARLOTTE HORNETS TO THE LEAGUE CHAMPIONSHIP! HIS BIG SEASON EARNED HIM THE M.V.P. AWARD, BEATING OUT PHIL RIZZUTO BY ONE VOTE!
JOYNER ©2007

Satchel PAIGE

LEROY "SATCHEL" PAIGE WAS ALREADY A NEGRO LEAGUES LEGEND BY THE TIME HE, AT THE AGE OF 42, MADE HIS MAJOR LEAGUE DEBUT WITH BILL VEECK'S 1948 CLEVELAND INDIANS! SATCHEL'S FINE SEASON HELPED THE TRIBE WIN THE WORLD SERIES THAT YEAR, BUT HE FOUND HIMSELF OUT OF THE BIG LEAGUES WHEN HIS PAL VEECK SOLD THE INDIANS FOLLOWING THE '49 CAMPAIGN! VEECK PROMISED THAT HE'D BRING SATCHEL BACK TO THE MAJORS AS SOON AS HE ACQUIRED A NEW FRANCHISE -- AND HE DELIVERED ON HIS PROMISE AFTER BUYING THE ST. LOUIS BROWNS IN 1951! HERE ARE A FEW OF SATCHEL'S MEMORIES OF PLAYING WITH THE BROWNIES FROM 1951 THROUGH 1953...

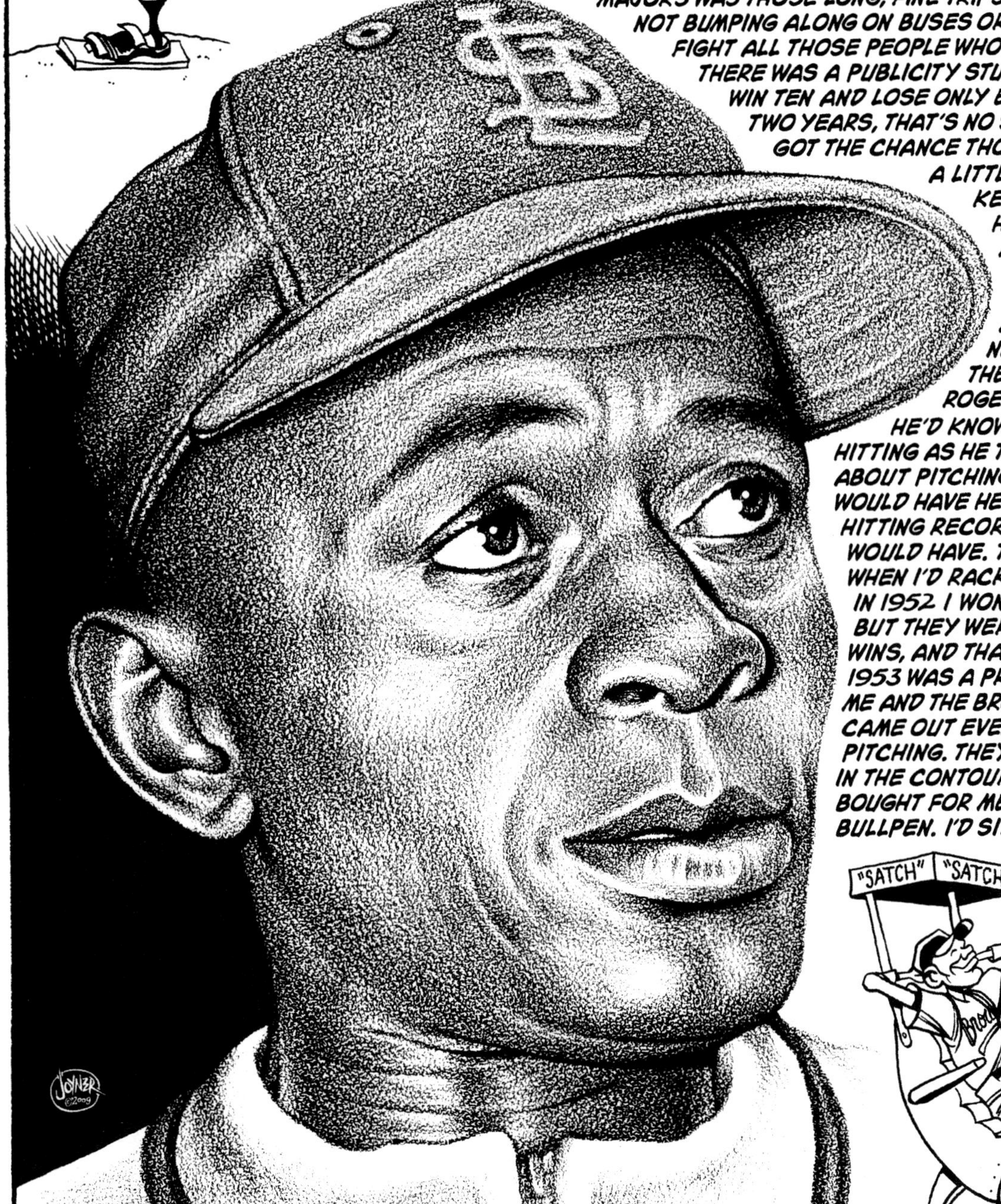

"EVERYBODY ASKED ME WHEN I WAS GONNA QUIT. AS LONG AS I COULD FOG 'EM PAST THOSE BATTERS, I WANTED TO BE IN THERE. IN THE TWO MONTHS I PITCHED FOR THE BROWNS IN 1951, I WON THREE AND LOST ONLY FOUR WITH THAT BAD, LAST-PLACE BALL CLUB. I GOT ALONG WITH THE BROWNS REAL GOOD. THEY WERE A FINE BUNCH, EVEN IF THEY WERE LAST-PLACERS. THE BEST THING ABOUT BEING BACK IN THE MAJORS WAS THOSE LONG, FINE TRIPS ON THE TRAINS -- NOT BUMPING ALONG ON BUSES OR IN A CAR. I HAD TO FIGHT ALL THOSE PEOPLE WHO SAID MY BEING UP THERE WAS A PUBLICITY STUNT, BUT WHEN YOU WIN TEN AND LOSE ONLY EIGHT IN YOUR FIRST TWO YEARS, THAT'S NO STUNT. WHENEVER I GOT THE CHANCE THOSE DAYS, I'D CLOWN A LITTLE. THE CLOWNING KEPT A LOT OF FOLKS HAPPY, BUT IT WAS MAINLY MY PITCHING THAT KEPT THE BROWNS HAPPY. MR. VEECK GOT A NEW MANAGER FOR THE BROWNS IN 1952 -- ROGERS HORNSBY. IF HE'D KNOWN AS MUCH ABOUT HITTING AS HE THOUGHT HE KNEW ABOUT PITCHING, TY COBB NEVER WOULD HAVE HELD ALL THOSE HITTING RECORDS -- HORNSBY WOULD HAVE. THERE'D BEEN YEARS WHEN I'D RACKED UP 70 WINS, BUT IN 1952 I WON ONLY A HANDFUL. BUT THEY WERE MAJOR LEAGUE WINS, AND THAT'S THE DIFFERENCE. 1953 WAS A PRETTY BAD YEAR FOR ME AND THE BROWNS. BUT THE FANS CAME OUT EVEN WHEN I WASN'T PITCHING. THEY WANTED TO SEE ME IN THE CONTOUR CHAIR MR. VEECK'D BOUGHT FOR ME TO SIT IN OUT IN THE BULLPEN. I'D SIT THERE AND DOZE UNTIL MR. MARION SIGNALED ME IN. BUT WHEN I GOT THERE, I WASN'T LOAFING ANY."

OUTFIELD/1ST BASE -- PHILADELPHIA A's
VIC POWER
VICTOR PELLOT POWER WAS BORN ON NOVEMBER 1, 1931 IN ARECIBO, PUERTO RICO! VIC, ALONG WITH TEAMMATE ELSTON HOWARD, BECAME THE FIRST BLACK PLAYERS ON THE YANKEES ROSTER IN 1954, BUT VIC WAS DEALT TO THE ATHLETICS BEFORE THE SEASON BEGAN!
VIC WAS A SLICK-FIELDING 1ST BASEMAN THAT MADE IT LOOK, EASY WINNING SEVEN GOLD GLOVE AWARDS!
THWAP!
C'MON, BOYS, YOU CAN DO BETTER THAN THAT!
AFTER BREAKING IN WITH THE PHILADELPHIA A's IN 1954, VIC WENT ON TO PLAY FOR KANSAS CITY, CLEVELAND, MINNESOTA, THE PHILLIES, AND THE ANGELS IN HIS 12-YEAR CAREER! VIC HIT FOR A LIFETIME AVERAGE OF .284 -- 3 TIMES HITTING OVER .300 -- WITH 1,716 HITS AND 126 HOME RUNS!
VIC STOLE HOME TWICE IN ONE GAME IN 1958!
YOU KIDDIN' ME?!
VIC HIT .349 IN THE A.A. IN 1953!
.349
JOYNER 2002

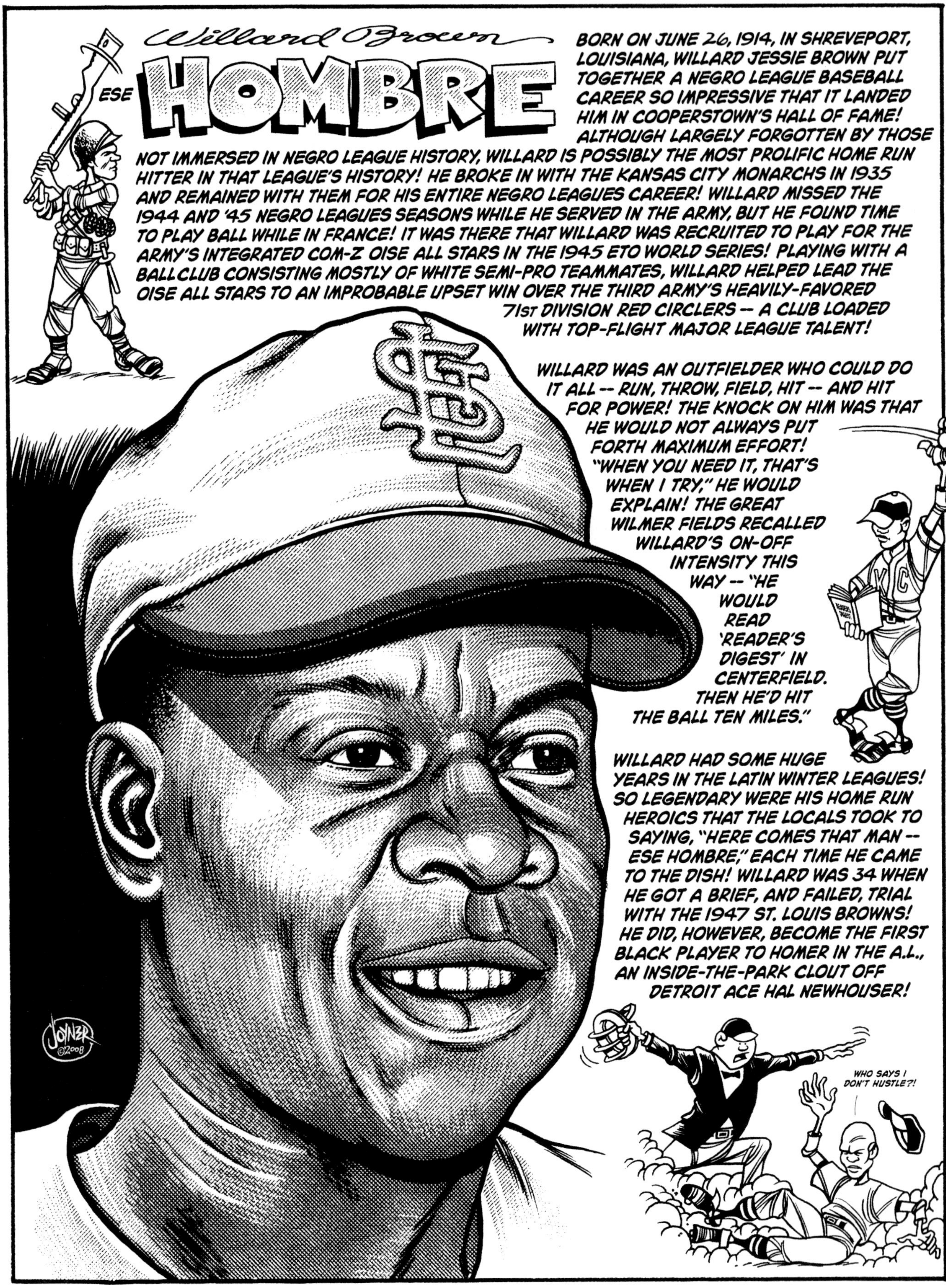
Willard Brown
ESE HOMBRE
BORN ON JUNE 26, 1914, IN SHREVEPORT, LOUISIANA, WILLARD JESSIE BROWN PUT TOGETHER A NEGRO LEAGUE BASEBALL CAREER SO IMPRESSIVE THAT IT LANDED HIM IN COOPERSTOWN'S HALL OF FAME! ALTHOUGH LARGELY FORGOTTEN BY THOSE NOT IMMERSED IN NEGRO LEAGUE HISTORY, WILLARD IS POSSIBLY THE MOST PROLIFIC HOME RUN HITTER IN THAT LEAGUE'S HISTORY! HE BROKE IN WITH THE KANSAS CITY MONARCHS IN 1935 AND REMAINED WITH THEM FOR HIS ENTIRE NEGRO LEAGUES CAREER! WILLARD MISSED THE 1944 AND '45 NEGRO LEAGUES SEASONS WHILE HE SERVED IN THE ARMY, BUT HE FOUND TIME TO PLAY BALL WHILE IN FRANCE! IT WAS THERE THAT WILLARD WAS RECRUITED TO PLAY FOR THE ARMY'S INTEGRATED COM-Z OISE ALL STARS IN THE 1945 ETO WORLD SERIES! PLAYING WITH A BALLCLUB CONSISTING MOSTLY OF WHITE SEMI-PRO TEAMMATES, WILLARD HELPED LEAD THE OISE ALL STARS TO AN IMPROBABLE UPSET WIN OVER THE THIRD ARMY'S HEAVILY-FAVORED 71st DIVISION RED CIRCLERS -- A CLUB LOADED WITH TOP-FLIGHT MAJOR LEAGUE TALENT!
WILLARD WAS AN OUTFIELDER WHO COULD DO IT ALL -- RUN, THROW, FIELD, HIT -- AND HIT FOR POWER! THE KNOCK ON HIM WAS THAT HE WOULD NOT ALWAYS PUT FORTH MAXIMUM EFFORT! "WHEN YOU NEED IT, THAT'S WHEN I TRY," HE WOULD EXPLAIN! THE GREAT WILMER FIELDS RECALLED WILLARD'S ON-OFF INTENSITY THIS WAY -- "HE WOULD READ 'READER'S DIGEST' IN CENTERFIELD. THEN HE'D HIT THE BALL TEN MILES."
WILLARD HAD SOME HUGE YEARS IN THE LATIN WINTER LEAGUES! SO LEGENDARY WERE HIS HOME RUN HEROICS THAT THE LOCALS TOOK TO SAYING, "HERE COMES THAT MAN -- ESE HOMBRE," EACH TIME HE CAME TO THE DISH! WILLARD WAS 34 WHEN HE GOT A BRIEF, AND FAILED, TRIAL WITH THE 1947 ST. LOUIS BROWNS! HE DID, HOWEVER, BECOME THE FIRST BLACK PLAYER TO HOMER IN THE A.L., AN INSIDE-THE-PARK CLOUT OFF DETROIT ACE HAL NEWHOUSER!
WHO SAYS I DON'T HUSTLE?!
JOYNER ©2008

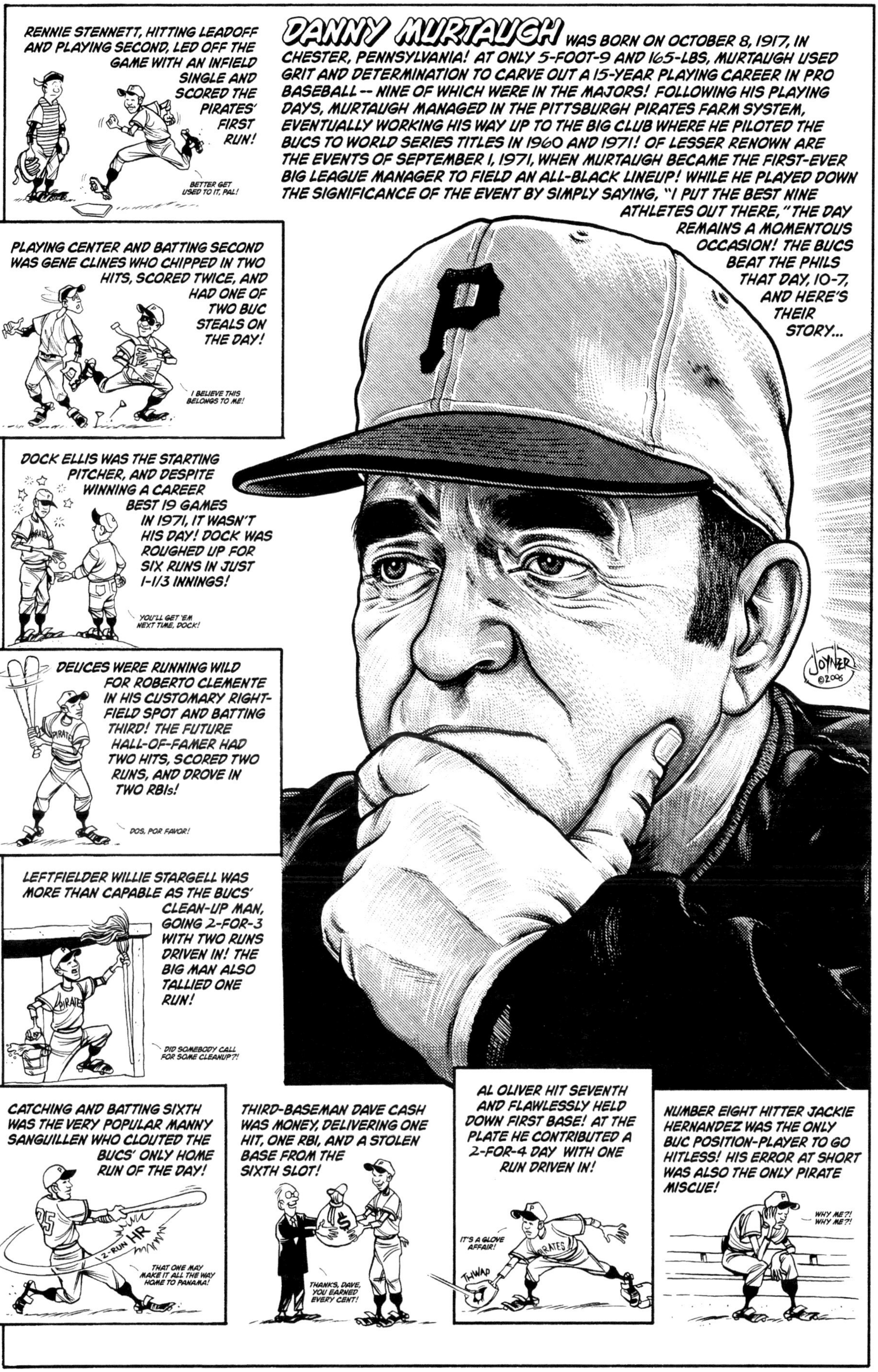
DANNY MURTAUGH WAS BORN ON OCTOBER 8, 1917, IN CHESTER, PENNSYLVANIA! AT ONLY 5-FOOT-9 AND 165-LBS, MURTAUGH USED GRIT AND DETERMINATION TO CARVE OUT A 15-YEAR PLAYING CAREER IN PRO BASEBALL -- NINE OF WHICH WERE IN THE MAJORS! FOLLOWING HIS PLAYING DAYS, MURTAUGH MANAGED IN THE PITTSBURGH PIRATES FARM SYSTEM, EVENTUALLY WORKING HIS WAY UP TO THE BIG CLUB WHERE HE PILOTED THE BUCS TO WORLD SERIES TITLES IN 1960 AND 1971! OF LESSER RENOWN ARE THE EVENTS OF SEPTEMBER 1, 1971, WHEN MURTAUGH BECAME THE FIRST-EVER BIG LEAGUE MANAGER TO FIELD AN ALL-BLACK LINEUP! WHILE HE PLAYED DOWN THE SIGNIFICANCE OF THE EVENT BY SIMPLY SAYING, "I PUT THE BEST NINE ATHLETES OUT THERE," THE DAY REMAINS A MOMENTOUS OCCASION! THE BUCS BEAT THE PHILS THAT DAY, 10-7, AND HERE'S THEIR STORY...
RENNIE STENNETT, HITTING LEADOFF AND PLAYING SECOND, LED OFF THE GAME WITH AN INFIELD SINGLE AND SCORED THE PIRATES' FIRST RUN!
BETTER GET USED TO IT, PAL!
PLAYING CENTER AND BATTING SECOND WAS GENE CLINES WHO CHIPPED IN TWO HITS, SCORED TWICE, AND HAD ONE OF TWO BUC STEALS ON THE DAY!
I BELIEVE THIS BELONGS TO ME!
DOCK ELLIS WAS THE STARTING PITCHER, AND DESPITE WINNING A CAREER BEST 19 GAMES IN 1971, IT WASN'T HIS DAY! DOCK WAS ROUGHED UP FOR SIX RUNS IN JUST 1-1/3 INNINGS!
YOU'LL GET 'EM NEXT TIME, DOCK!
DEUCES WERE RUNNING WILD FOR ROBERTO CLEMENTE IN HIS CUSTOMARY RIGHT-FIELD SPOT AND BATTING THIRD! THE FUTURE HALL-OF-FAMER HAD TWO HITS, SCORED TWO RUNS, AND DROVE IN TWO RBIs!
DOS, POR FAVOR!
LEFTFIELDER WILLIE STARGELL WAS MORE THAN CAPABLE AS THE BUCS' CLEAN-UP MAN, GOING 2-FOR-3 WITH TWO RUNS DRIVEN IN! THE BIG MAN ALSO TALLIED ONE RUN!
DID SOMEBODY CALL FOR SOME CLEANUP?!
CATCHING AND BATTING SIXTH WAS THE VERY POPULAR MANNY SANGUILLEN WHO CLOUTED THE BUCS' ONLY HOME RUN OF THE DAY!
2-RUN HR
THAT ONE MAY MAKE IT ALL THE WAY HOME TO PANAMA!
THIRD-BASEMAN DAVE CASH WAS MONEY, DELIVERING ONE HIT, ONE RBI, AND A STOLEN BASE FROM THE SIXTH SLOT!
THANKS, DAVE. YOU EARNED EVERY CENT!
AL OLIVER HIT SEVENTH AND FLAWLESSLY HELD DOWN FIRST BASE! AT THE PLATE HE CONTRIBUTED A 2-FOR-4 DAY WITH ONE RUN DRIVEN IN!
IT'S A GLOVE AFFAIR!
THWAP
NUMBER EIGHT HITTER JACKIE HERNANDEZ WAS THE ONLY BUC POSITION-PLAYER TO GO HITLESS! HIS ERROR AT SHORT WAS ALSO THE ONLY PIRATE MISCUE!
WHY ME?! WHY ME?!

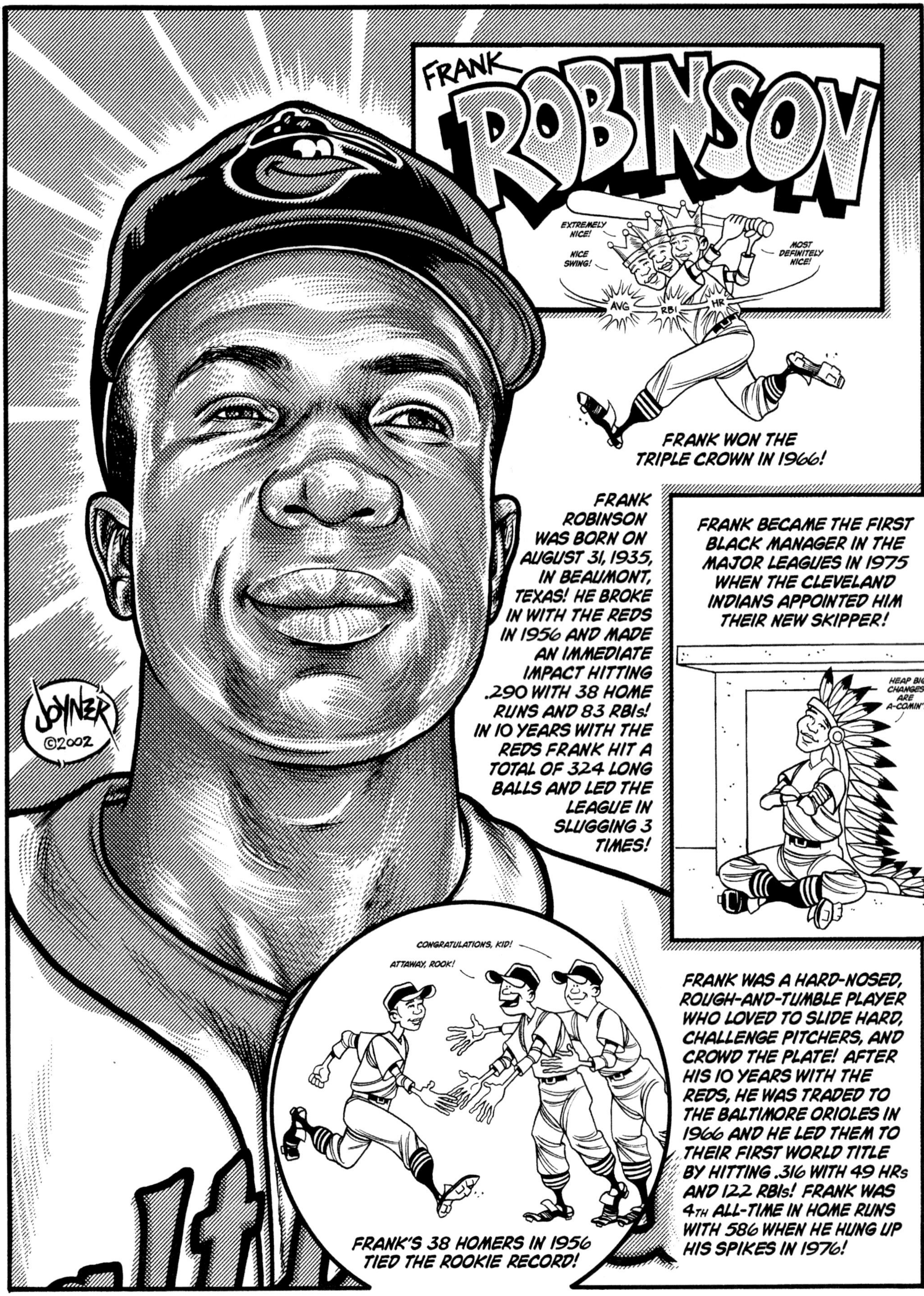

FRANK ROBINSON
EXTREMELY NICE!
NICE SWING!
MOST DEFINITELY NICE!
AVG
RBI
HR
FRANK WON THE TRIPLE CROWN IN 1966!
FRANK ROBINSON WAS BORN ON AUGUST 31, 1935, IN BEAUMONT, TEXAS! HE BROKE IN WITH THE REDS IN 1956 AND MADE AN IMMEDIATE IMPACT HITTING .290 WITH 38 HOME RUNS AND 83 RBIs! IN 10 YEARS WITH THE REDS FRANK HIT A TOTAL OF 324 LONG BALLS AND LED THE LEAGUE IN SLUGGING 3 TIMES!
FRANK BECAME THE FIRST BLACK MANAGER IN THE MAJOR LEAGUES IN 1975 WHEN THE CLEVELAND INDIANS APPOINTED HIM THEIR NEW SKIPPER!
HEAP BIG CHANGES ARE A-COMIN'!
JOYNER ©2002
CONGRATULATIONS, KID!
ATTAWAY, ROOK!
FRANK'S 38 HOMERS IN 1956 TIED THE ROOKIE RECORD!
FRANK WAS A HARD-NOSED, ROUGH-AND-TUMBLE PLAYER WHO LOVED TO SLIDE HARD, CHALLENGE PITCHERS, AND CROWD THE PLATE! AFTER HIS 10 YEARS WITH THE REDS, HE WAS TRADED TO THE BALTIMORE ORIOLES IN 1966 AND HE LED THEM TO THEIR FIRST WORLD TITLE BY HITTING .316 WITH 49 HRs AND 122 RBIs! FRANK WAS 4TH ALL-TIME IN HOME RUNS WITH 586 WHEN HE HUNG UP HIS SPIKES IN 1976!

Bill WHITE

NEW YORK GIANTS 1st BASEMAN BILL WHITE WAS A RAW-BONED, UNKNOWN, 23-YEAR-OLD ROOKIE WHEN HE CLUBBED A HOME RUN IN HIS FIRST BIG LEAGUE AT-BAT ON MAY 7, 1956. THE CLOUT, A SOLO SHOT OFF CARDINALS RIGHT-HANDER BEN FLOWERS, LANDED ON THE ROOF OF SPORTSMAN'S PARK. BY THE TIME BILL WALLOPED THREE HOMERS IN ONE GAME AGAINST THE DODGERS ON JULY 5, 1961, HE WAS KNOWN LEAGUE-WIDE AS ONE OF THE MOST FEARED SLUGGERS IN THE MAJORS. BILL TURNED IN A FINE ROOKIE SEASON WITH THE GIANTS, BUT WAS THEN LOST FOR NEARLY TWO YEARS TO THE ARMY. HE RETURNED TO THE GIANTS ONLY TO FIND HIS POSITION IN THE FIRM GRASP OF ROOKIE PHENOM ORLANDO CEPEDA. DEALT TO THE CARDS PRIOR TO THE 1959 SEASON, BILL SPENT THE NEXT SEVEN YEARS IN ST. LOUIS, REGULARLY HITTING 20 OR MORE HOME RUNS WHILE TOPPING THE 100-RBI MARK THREE TIMES. BILL WAS A SLICK-FIELDER AT 1st BASE, TOO, HELPING HIS TEAMS ON DEFENSE AS WELL AS OFFENSE. BILL WAS A KEY ELEMENT OF THE CARDINALS' 1964 WORLD CHAMPIONSHIP, BATTING .303 WITH 21 HOMERS AND 102 RUNS BATTED IN. BILL SPENT THREE SEASONS WITH THE PHILLIES BEFORE RETURNING TO ST. LOUIS TO FINISH HIS PLAYING CAREER IN '69. HE THEN BEGAN A LONG CAREER AS A BROADCASTER, AND LATER SERVED AS PRESIDENT OF THE NATIONAL LEAGUE -- A POSITION THAT MADE HIM THE HIGHEST-RANKING BLACK EXECUTIVE IN THE HISTORY OF SPORTS. BILL, LIKE MOST BLACK PLAYERS, SUFFERED MANY RACIAL INJUSTICES, AND HE BECAME KNOWN FOR HIS EFFORTS TO COMBAT THOSE ISSUES -- BUT HE HAS NO SOUR GRAPES. "BASEBALL HAS TREATED ME REAL GOOD," BILL ONCE SAID. "IT'S JUST THAT IT WOULD BE NICE IF INDUSTRY AND PEOPLE HAD THE SAME ATTITUDE TO BLACK PEOPLE OFF THE FIELD AS THEY HAVE TOWARD BLACK BALLPLAYERS ON THE FIELD."

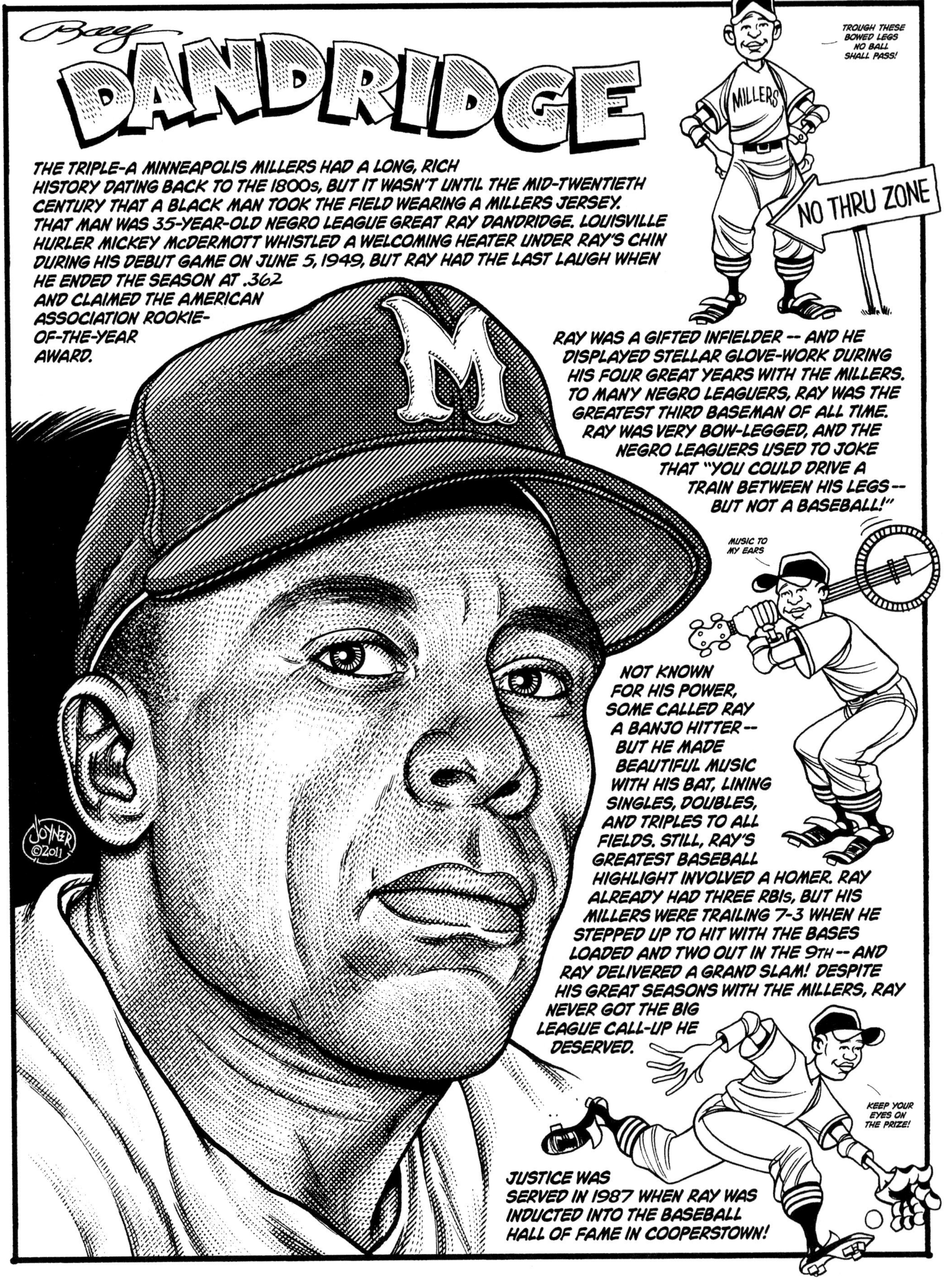

DANDRIDGE
THE TRIPLE-A MINNEAPOLIS MILLERS HAD A LONG, RICH HISTORY DATING BACK TO THE 1800s, BUT IT WASN'T UNTIL THE MID-TWENTIETH CENTURY THAT A BLACK MAN TOOK THE FIELD WEARING A MILLERS JERSEY. THAT MAN WAS 35-YEAR-OLD NEGRO LEAGUE GREAT RAY DANDRIDGE. LOUISVILLE HURLER MICKEY McDERMOTT WHISTLED A WELCOMING HEATER UNDER RAY'S CHIN DURING HIS DEBUT GAME ON JUNE 5, 1949, BUT RAY HAD THE LAST LAUGH WHEN HE ENDED THE SEASON AT .362 AND CLAIMED THE AMERICAN ASSOCIATION ROOKIE-OF-THE-YEAR AWARD.
TROUGH THESE BOWED LEGS NO BALL SHALL PASS!
MILLERS
NO THRU ZONE
RAY WAS A GIFTED INFIELDER -- AND HE DISPLAYED STELLAR GLOVE-WORK DURING HIS FOUR GREAT YEARS WITH THE MILLERS. TO MANY NEGRO LEAGUERS, RAY WAS THE GREATEST THIRD BASEMAN OF ALL TIME. RAY WAS VERY BOW-LEGGED, AND THE NEGRO LEAGUERS USED TO JOKE THAT "YOU COULD DRIVE A TRAIN BETWEEN HIS LEGS -- BUT NOT A BASEBALL!"
M
MUSIC TO MY EARS
NOT KNOWN FOR HIS POWER, SOME CALLED RAY A BANJO HITTER -- BUT HE MADE BEAUTIFUL MUSIC WITH HIS BAT, LINING SINGLES, DOUBLES, AND TRIPLES TO ALL FIELDS. STILL, RAY'S GREATEST BASEBALL HIGHLIGHT INVOLVED A HOMER. RAY ALREADY HAD THREE RBIs, BUT HIS MILLERS WERE TRAILING 7-3 WHEN HE STEPPED UP TO HIT WITH THE BASES LOADED AND TWO OUT IN THE 9TH -- AND RAY DELIVERED A GRAND SLAM! DESPITE HIS GREAT SEASONS WITH THE MILLERS, RAY NEVER GOT THE BIG LEAGUE CALL-UP HE DESERVED.
JOYNER ©2011
KEEP YOUR EYES ON THE PRIZE!
JUSTICE WAS SERVED IN 1987 WHEN RAY WAS INDUCTED INTO THE BASEBALL HALL OF FAME IN COOPERSTOWN!

MUSIC, MOVIES, AND TV

Lee Maye

"I FEEL THAT I AM THE BEST SINGING ATHLETE THAT EVER LIVED," LEE MAYE ONCE TOLD MUSIC HISTORIAN PHIL MILSTEIN. "I'M NOT BRAGGING, IT'S JUST A FACT." AND ONE WOULD BE HARD PRESSED TO PROVE HIM WRONG WERE ONE INCLINED TO TRY! AS A BALLPLAYER, LEE WAS A SOLID 13-YEAR BIG LEAGUER THAT SPENT HIS BEST SEASONS (1959-65) IN THE BRAVES OUTFIELD ALONGSIDE THE GREAT HANK AARON! LEE WAS A FINE PLAYER IN HIGH SCHOOL! ALTHOUGH HE HAD ONLY AN AVERAGE ARM, LEE WAS A GOOD FIELDER AND AN EXCELLENT LINE DRIVE HITTER! IT WAS LEE'S BLAZING SPEED, HOWEVER, THAT MADE BRAVES SCOUT JOHNNY MOORE INK HIM TO A MINOR LEAGUE CONTRACT IN 1954! DESPITE BEING A HIGHLY PRODUCTIVE EVERYDAY PLAYER IN THE BUSHES, LEE WAS PLATOONED FROM HIS FIRST CALL-UP IN 1959 THROUGH THE 1963 SEASON! HE ALWAYS POSTED GOOD NUMBERS, TOO, SO THE BRAVES FINALLY MADE HIM AN EVERYDAY PLAYER IN 1964 -- AND LEE RESPONDED WITH A CAREER YEAR IN WHICH HE HIT .304 WITH 10 HOMERS, 96 RUNS SCORED, AND A LEAGUE-LEADING 44 TWO-BAGGERS! POSITIONED FOR ANOTHER BIG SEASON IN 1965, LEE WAS SLOWED BY A SERIOUS ANKLE INJURY WHICH LED HIM TO BE TRADED TO HOUSTON!

AFTER MOVING TO THE ASTROS IN 1965, LEE WENT ON TO PLAY FOR THE INDIANS, SENATORS, AND WHITE SOX THROUGH 1971 -- HIS LAST YEAR IN THE MAJORS! LEE HIT .274 OVER HIS FINE CAREER, WITH 1,109 HITS AND 94 HOME RUNS!

LEE'S ASSERTION THAT HE WAS THE "BEST SINGING ATHLETE EVER" WAS NOT A STATEMENT ON THE GREATNESS OF HIS SINGING VOICE! THERE WERE PROBABLY PLAYERS ALL AROUND THE LEAGUE WHO HAD GREAT SINGING VOICES! LEE'S CLAIM WENT TO THE FACT THAT, WHILE UNKNOWN TO THE PUBLIC AT LARGE, HE WAS A SEMINAL VOICE IN THE EARLY YEARS OF ROCK-N-ROLL! LEE GRADUATED IN 1954 FROM JEFFERSON HIGH IN SOUTH CENTRAL L.A.-- A HOTBED OF MUSICAL TALENT WHOSE ALUMNI WOULD PLACE A STAMP ON THE FOUNDATION OF ROCK-N-ROLL IN GROUPS LIKE THE PENGUINS, THE PLATTERS, AND THE COASTERS, TO NAME A FEW! LEE WAS IN THE THICK OF THE WEST COAST DOO-WOP MOVEMENT, TOO, EITHER AS A SOLO ACT, OR AS THE FRONT-MAN FOR GROUPS LIKE THE "5" HEARTS, THE RAMS, AND THE CROWNS! WHILE LEE NEVER ACHIEVED THE FAME OF SOME OF HIS PEERS, THE SONGS HE WAXED WERE EVERY BIT AS GOOD AND INFLUENTIAL ON THE NASCENT ROCK-N-ROLL SCENE! IN FACT, IT WAS PROBABLY LEE'S COMMITMENT TO HIS BASEBALL CAREER THAT PREVENTED HIM FROM HITTING THE CHARTS! HE WOULD BURN UP THE MINORS IN THE SPRINGS AND SUMMERS OF 1954-60, THEN RECORD IN THE WINTERS AND FALLS! WHILE THIS PART-TIME ACTIVITY MIGHT HAVE HINDERED LEE FROM ACHIEVING FAME AND FORTUNE, IT CERTAINLY DIDN'T REDUCE THE QUALITY OF THE SONGS THAT HE LAID DOWN! WHILE RECORDING FOR LEGENDARY LABELS LIKE FLAIR, MODERN, RPM, AND SPECIALTY, LEE CREATED A BODY OF WORK TO RIVAL ANY DOO-WOPPER, INCLUDING CLASSICS LIKE "LOVE ME ALWAYS," "TRULY," "I WANNA LOVE," "GLORIA," "LOOP DE LOOP DE LOOP," AND "A FOOL'S PRAYER," TO LIST A SMALL SAMPLING! LEE EVEN SANG BACK-UP VOCALS ON THE ORIGINAL "LOUIE LOUIE," WRITTEN AND RECORDED BY HIS BEST FRIEND, THE LEGENDARY RICHARD BERRY! LEE MAYE WAS TRULY A ONE-OF-A-KIND ROCK-N-ROLL/BASEBALL DOUBLE-THREAT -- A CREDIT TO TWO OF AMERICA'S GREATEST CREATIONS!

Charley PRIDE

LONG BEFORE HE RULED THE COUNTRY CHARTS WITH SONGS LIKE "KISS AN ANGEL GOOD MORNING," CHARLEY PRIDE WAS AN ASPIRING RIGHT-HANDED PITCHER AND OUTFIELDER WHO GOT HIS PRO START WITH THE 1953 MEMPHIS RED SOX OF THE NEGRO LEAGUES! HIS BASEBALL DREAM CAME TO AN END EIGHT YEARS LATER, HOWEVER, WHEN HE WAS LET GO BY THE EXPANSION CALIFORNIA ANGELS! TOMMY "FERGIE" FERGUSON, THE ANGELS EQUIPMENT MANAGER, TOLD THE STORY TO BASEBALL DIGEST IN 1981. "IN 1960, THE ANGELS HAD A CAMP PRIOR TO SPRING TRAINING. THEY SIGN A BLACK PITCHER NAMED MORRIS CIGAR. FRED HANEY, THE MANAGER, INTRODUCES ME TO THIS OTHER YOUNG BLACK GUY AND SAYS, 'GET HIM A UNIFORM.' HE WAS GOING TO BE A ROOMATE FOR MORRIS CIGAR. TWO OR THREE WEEKS GO BY, AND THE KID COMES AND TELLS ME HE'S BEEN RELEASED. I GOT HIM A COUPLA TUNA FISH SANDWICHES AND A COUPLE ORANGES OUT OF THE PRESS ROOM, AND WISHED HIM LUCK. I REMEMBER HIM LEAVING FOR MISSOULA, MONTANA, WITH A GUITAR ON HIS BACK. NOW IT'S 1972, AND I'M TRAVELING SECRETARY WITH THE BREWERS. WE'RE IN ARIZONA, AND DAVE BRISTOL, THE MANAGER, CALLS ME ON THE PHONE AND SAYS A FELLA NAMED CHARLEY PRIDE, THE COUNTRY-WESTERN SINGER, SAYS HE KNOWS ME AND WOULD I COME DOWN AND SAY HELLO. WELL, I DIDN'T KNOW CHARLEY PRIDE, BUT I WENT DOWN. THEN BRISTOL SAYS, 'SAY HELLO TO CHARLEY PRIDE.' SO THIS HANDSOME BLACK GUY SAYS, 'I KNOW YOU FERGIE. YOU DON'T REMEMBER ME, DO YOU?' I SAID, 'YOU OWE ME ANY MONEY?' HE SAID, 'NO. BUT I OWE YOU TWO TUNA SANDWICHES AND A COUPLE OF ORANGES.' I SAID, 'HOLY ----! MORRIS CIGAR'S ROOMMATE!' AND NOW HE'S A MILLIONAIRE."

CHARLEY HAD A CURVE AND KNUCKLER TO GO WITH HIS LOW-90s HEATER, AND HE HAD A LITTLE POP IN HIS BAT, TOO! STILL, CHARLEY IS HUMBLE ABOUT HIS ABILITY, OFTEN OPTING TO TELL FOLKS THE FUNNY BUT TRUE STORY OF HOW HE AND HIS LOUISVILLE CLIPPERS TEAMMATE, JESSIE MITCHELL, WERE TRADED TO THE BIRMINGHAM BLACK BARONS IN EXCHANGE FOR A NEW TEAM BUS!

Bobby MURCER

THE COMPARISONS TO MICKEY MANTLE WERE OBVIOUS: HIGH SCHOOL PHENOM SHORTSTOP FROM OKLAHOMA; LEFT-HANDED POWER STROKE; SPEED ON THE BASEPATHS; AND SIGNED TO THE YANKS BY TOM GREENWADE -- THE SAME SCOUT WHO'D SIGNED THE MICK! BOBBY RAY MURCER WAS THRILLED AT THE COMPARISON -- HECK, HE GREW UP IDOLIZING MANTLE, AND DREAMED OF ONE DAY WEARING PINSTRIPES! BOBBY'S DREAM CAME TRUE WHEN HE MADE HIS YANKEE DEBUT ON SEPTEMBER 8, 1965, IN A GAME AGAINST THE SENATORS AT YANKEE STADIUM! IN HIS SECOND GAME A WEEK LATER, WITH HIS IDOL AND TEAMMATE MANTLE RESTING ON THE BENCH, BOBBY GOT HIS FIRST MAJOR LEAGUE HIT-- A 2-OUT, 2-RUN HOMER OFF WASHINGTON'S JIM DUCKWORTH! HE WOULD HAVE TO WAIT A BIT, HOWEVER, BEFORE THE MANTLE TORCH WAS TRULY PASSED TO HIM BECAUSE UNCLE SAM CAME CALLING AND BOBBY LOST ALL OF 1967 AND '68 TO THE U.S. ARMY! HE MADE THE YANKS IN 1969 AND SHOWED HIS POWER BY CLUBBING 26 HOMERS, WHILE PLAYING MOST OF THE SEASON AT THIRD BASE AND RIGHTFIELD! BY SEPTEMBER, HOWEVER, HE WAS PERMANENTLY MOVED TO CENTERFIELD, THEREBY FULFILLING THE MEDIA'S PREDICTIONS FOR BOBBY AS HEIR-APPARENT TO THE MICK WHO'D RETIRED PRIOR TO THE '69 CAMPAIGN! BOBBY PROVED TO BE HUGELY POPULAR AND PRODUCTIVE FOR THE YANKS, SMASHING 140 LONG BALLS AND EARNING FOUR ALL-STAR SELECTIONS PRIOR TO HIS TRADE TO SAN FRANCISCO AFTER THE 1974 SEASON! BOBBY WAS HEARTBROKEN TO LEAVE NEW YORK, BUT HE STILL MANAGED TO DELIVER SOME FINE STICKWORK FOR THE GIANTS AND CUBS FROM 1975 THROUGH JUNE OF '79 WHEN HE RETURNED TO HIS BELOVED YANKEES FOR A SECOND AND FINAL STINT! WHILE NO LONGER THE PLAYER HE WAS IN HIS YOUNGER DAYS, BOBBY STILL HAD SOME BIG MOMENTS LEFT, AND HIS PART-TIME PLAY HELPED THE YANKEES TO TWO DIVISION TITLES AND AN AMERICAN LEAGUE PENNANT IN 1981!

BOBBY VENTURED INTO COUNTRY MUSIC IN '83 WHEN HE RECORDED A WELL-RECEIVED SINGLE ENTITLED "SKOAL DIPPIN' MAN," BACKED WITH "BAD WHISKEY," FOR COLUMBIA RECORDS! WHILE IT WAS GOOD FUN, NOTHING WOULD EVER MAKE YANKEE FANS FORGET SOME OF BOBBY'S GREATEST ON-FIELD ACHIEVEMENTS, LIKE HIS FOUR STRAIGHT HOMERS IN A 1970 TWIN BILL; HIS CYCLE AGAINST THE RANGERS IN 1972; OR THE DAY IN 1979 WHEN HE EULOGIZED TEAMMATE THURMAN MUNSON AT HIS FUNERAL AND THEN DROVE IN ALL FIVE YANKEE RUNS THAT EVENING AS NEW YORK DEFEATED THE ORIOLES! BOBBY RETIRED DURING THE 1983 SEASON, BUT MOVED UPSTAIRS TO BECOME A LONGTIME YANKS BROADCASTER! MANTLE OBLIGED BOBBY'S GOOD SENSE OF HUMOR IN '92 WHEN HE PRESENTED MURCER FOR INDUCTION INTO THE OKLAHOMA SPORTS HALL OF FAME! "THE FIRST TIME I EVER HEARD OF BOBBY MURCER," DEADPANNED THE MICK, "THEY SAID A KID FROM OKLAHOMA WAS GONNA BE THE NEXT MICKEY MANTLE. THEY WERE RIGHT. SURE ENOUGH, HE COULDN'T PLAY SHORTSTOP EITHER."

PITCHER -- MILWAUKEE BRAVES
LEW BURDETTE
WEST VIRGINIAN SELVA LEWIS BURDETTE WAS BORN ON NOVEMBER 22, 1926! HE SPENT MOST OF HIS 18-YEAR BIG LEAGUE CAREER PITCHING FOR THE BRAVES! LEW RACKED UP 203 VICTORIES WITH A 3.66 ERA -- AND 12 HOME RUNS!
LEW WAS A TWO-TIME 20-GAME WINNER WITH 20 IN '58 AND A LEAGUE-LEADING 21 IN 1959!
HERE COMES ME BREAD-N-BUTTER!
LEW WON 19 GAMES IN 1956, AND HIS 2.70 ERA WAS TOPS IN THE NATIONAL LEAGUE!
JOYNER ©2002
LEW PITCHED IN TWO ALL-STAR GAMES AND ALLOWED ONLY ONE RUN IN SEVEN TOTAL INNINGS!
LEW RECORDED THE ROCKABILLY RECORD "MARY LOU" IN 1957!
MOVE OVER, PRESLEY!
LEW WAS MVP OF THE '57 SERIES WITH HIS 3-0 RECORD AND 0.67 ERA!
I LIVE FOR PRESSURE!
MVP
LEW TOSSED A NO-HITTER AGAINST THE PHILLIES ON AUGUST 18, 1960!

Lon WARNEKE

IN AN ERA DOMINATED BY THE LARGER THAN LIFE PERSONA OF DIZZY DEAN, FELLOW ARKANSAN LONNIE WARNEKE IS VIEWED BY MANY TO HAVE BEEN, IN THE LONG RUN, THE GREATER OF THE TWO HURLERS -- AND MAYBE JUST AS COLORFUL! LONNIE, IN JUST HIS SECOND FULL SEASON IN 1932, WON 22 GAMES FOR THE N.L. CHAMPION CUBS! HE LOGGED TWO MORE 20-WIN CAMPAIGNS FOR CHICAGO IN 1934 AND 1935, TOPPING OFF THE '35 SEASON BY WINNING TWO GAMES IN THE CUBS' WORLD SERIES LOSS TO THE TIGERS! LONNIE WAS DEALT TO THE ST. LOUIS CARDINALS FOLLOWING A 16-WIN EFFORT IN 1936! THE CARDS WERE HAPPY TO HAVE LONNIE, NOT ONLY FOR HIS ABILITY ON THE MOUND, BUT ALSO FOR HIS TALENT AS A HILLBILLY SINGER AND GUITAR PLAYER! HE WAS IMMEDIATELY PUT TO WORK AS A FEATURED PART OF PEPPER MARTIN'S MUDCAT BAND ALONG WITH TEAMMATES FIDDLER McGEE, LEFTY WEILAND, AND FRENCHY BORDAGARAY! LON'S HEATER WASN'T WHAT IT HAD ONCE BEEN DURING HIS PRIME IN CHICAGO, BUT HE ADJUSTED AND NOTCHED 83 VICTORIES FOR THE CARDS FROM 1937 THROUGH JULY OF 1942 WHEN HE REJOINED THE CUBS! LONNIE PITCHED WELL FOR CHICAGO AFTER HIS RETURN, BUT WAS SOON GONE AGAIN AS HE JOINED THE WAR EFFORT BY SERVING IN THE ARMY IN 1944 AND '45! THE LONG AND LEAN RIGHT-HANDER WAS A REAL FIGHTER ON THE SLAB, BUT OFF THE FIELD HE ENJOYED SPINNING HIS DOWN-HOME WIT AND WISDOM, AS WELL AS PLAYING THE ROLE OF PRANKSTER! ONE TIME DURING A TOUR OF NOTORIOUS SING SING PRISON WITH A FEW OF HIS GAS HOUSE GANG TEAMMATES IN TOW, LON TALKED HIS ROOMIE, DON GUTTERIDGE, INTO TAKING A SEAT IN THE ELECTRIC CHAIR! AS SOON AS DON SAT DOWN, LON SECRETLY SWITCHED OFF THE LIGHTS IN THE ROOM! "I JUMPED OUT OF THAT CHAIR SO FAST I THINK I HIT THE CEILING!" DON WROTE IN HIS 1999 MEMOIR. "LON WAS TRULY A FUNNY GUY."

WITH 192 WINS UNDER HIS BELT, LONNIE PASSED ON THE TEMPTATION TO CHASE THE 200-WIN MARK, INSTEAD OPTING TO BECOME AN UMPIRE IN 1946! AFTER THREE YEARS IN THE P.C.L., LONNIE SPENT A DECADE AS A NATIONAL LEAGUE UMP! MOST FELT HE WAS GOOD AT IT -- WITH THE EXCEPTION OF LON'S FORMER TEAMMATE, THE OUTSPOKEN LEO DUROCHER! "HE'D JUST STAND THERE WITH THAT LITTLE SMILE," WROTE THE LIP, "AND SAY, VERY TIMIDLY, 'WELL, THAT'S THE WAY I SAW IT.'"

Eddie ROBINSON

ON OCTOBER 11, 1948, INDIANS FIRST BASEMAN EDDIE ROBINSON RAPPED OUT A RUN-SCORING SINGLE IN THE EIGHTH INNING OFF BRAVES LEFT-HANDER WARREN SPAHN! IT TURNED OUT TO BE THE DECISIVE RUN OF THE WORLD SERIES AS THE INDIANS WON THE GAME, 4-3, AND THE SERIES, FOUR GAMES TO TWO! WHILE NEAR THE TOP ON EDDIE'S HIGHLIGHTS LIST, IT STILL RANKS BEHIND WHAT HE CONSIDERS A GREATER ACHIEVEMENT FROM EARLIER THAT YEAR! "I HIT THREE HOME RUNS IN A DOUBLEHEADER IN CLEVELAND IN FRONT OF ABOUT 80,000 FANS," EDDIE TOLD BASEBALL WRITER RICH MARAZZI. "IT WAS A GREAT SWEEP FOR US THAT DAY. THE YANKEES WERE EXPECTED TO WIN THE PENNANT." EDDIE SOON FOUND HIMSELF PLAYING FOR THE YANKEES, BUT NOT BEFORE STINTS WITH THE NATS, CHISOX, AND ATHLETICS! HANDSOME EDDIE ENJOYED THE BRIGHT LIGHTS OF NEW YORK WHILE WITH THE YANKEES, AND EVEN DATED ONE OF THE HIT PARADE'S BIGGEST STARS OF THE ERA -- PATTI PAGE!

EDDIE GOT HIS FIRST TASTE OF THE BIGS WITH THE TRIBE IN 1942, BUT THEN SWAPPED HIS FLANNELS FOR NAVY DENIM FOR THE DURATION OF WWII! BACK IN THE MAJORS FULL TIME IN '47, EDDIE SPENT THE NEXT 12 YEARS POUNDING BIG LEAGUE PITCHERS TO THE TUNE OF 172 CAREER HOMERS! FOLLOWING THE '57 SEASON HE MOVED FROM THE FIELD TO A LONG AND SUCCESSFUL CAREER AS A COACH, SCOUT, AND FRONT OFFICE EXEC!

EDDIE HAS DONE IT ALL IN BASEBALL -- AND IN 2011, AT THE AGE OF 90, EDDIE BECAME AN AUTHOR WHEN HE WROTE "LUCKY ME," A MEMOIR OF HIS COLORFUL LIFE! "I BEGAN PLAYING PRO BASEBALL IN 1939 AND RETIRED FROM MY LAST BASEBALL JOB IN 2004," WROTE EDDIE. "IT GOES WITHOUT SAYING THAT I OWE ALL OF MY GOOD FORTUNE TO OUR NATIONAL PASTIME."

JOHNNY Berardino

JOHNNY PLAYED DR. STEVE HARDY ON TV'S GENERAL HOSPITAL FOR 33 YEARS! HE HAS A STAR ON THE HOLLYWOOD WALK OF FAME IN HONOR OF HIS CONTRIBUTION TO TELEVISION!

WHEN A GUY PASSES AWAY AT AGE 79 AFTER HAVING BEEN A FULL-TIME ACTOR FOR THE LAST 43 YEARS OF HIS LIFE, THAT'S HOW HE'S REMEMBERED BY THE MAJORITY OF THE GENERAL PUBLIC -- AS AN ACTOR! THAT SCENARIO PRETTY WELL DESCRIBES THE WAY JOHNNY BERARDINO IS RECALLED BY THE PUBLIC AT LARGE -- ESPECIALLY FANS OF DAYTIME SOAP OPERAS! BUT THAT DOES A GREAT DISSERVICE TO JOHNNY, WHO FOR ELEVEN SEASONS (MINUS FOUR PRIME YEARS OF SERVICE IN THE ARMY DURING WORLD WAR II) WAS A VERSATILE, TOUGH-AS-NAILS, MAJOR LEAGUE INFIELDER! PART OF THE REASON FOR THE PEOPLE'S FORGETFULNESS OF JOHNNY'S BASEBALL DAYS IS THE FACT THAT HIS BEST YEARS WERE SPENT TOILING FOR THE HAPLESS ST. LOUIS BROWNS! ACKNOWLEDGING THE FRUSTRATION OF PLAYING FOR THE BROWNIES, JOHNNY TOLD BASEBALL DIGEST, "IT'S NO FUN TO PLAY WITH JUST A FEW HUNDRED PEOPLE IN THE STANDS." NONETHELESS, JOHNNY PLAYED HARD AS THE BROWNS' EVERYDAY 2ND BASEMAN IN HIS ROOKIE YEAR OF 1939, THEN MOVED OVER TO BECOME THE REGULAR SHORTSTOP FROM 1940-41! ONE OF JOHNNY'S FAVORITE BASEBALL MOMENTS CAME FROM THAT '41 SEASON -- WITH JOE DIMAGGIO'S 56-GAME HITTING STREAK SITTING AT NO. 37! HITLESS ON THE DAY AGAINST BROWNIE HURLER ELDON AUKER, THE JOLTER STEPPED UP TO THE PLATE IN THE BOTTOM OF THE 8TH, MAN ON 2ND, AND THE YANKS DOWN BY TWO. "LOGIC SAYS YOU WALK HIM," SAID JOHNNY. "I WALKED OVER TO ELDON AND SAID, 'IF YOU WALK THIS GUY, 30,000 PEOPLE ARE GOING TO COME OUT OF THE STANDS AND BREAK BOTH OF YOUR LEGS.' ON THE FIRST PITCH DIMAG HIT A LINE DRIVE OVER MY HEAD TO KEEP HIS STREAK INTACT AT 38 GAMES." JOHNNY PLAYED BRIEFLY IN 1942 BEFORE MARCHING OFF TO WAR, THEN RETURNED IN 1946 TO PLAY HIS LAST SEASON AS A REGULAR! JOHNNY SPENT THE LAST FIVE YEARS OF HIS CAREER AS A VALUABLE UTILITY MAN! "IT REALLY WASN'T MY CUP OF TEA TO BE A UTILITY MAN," HE RECALLED, "BUT IT WAS FUN PLAYING FOR BILL VEECK WHO WAS A GREAT GUY. HE ALSO DOUBLED MY SALARY."

THE BROWNS DEALT JOHNNY TO THE INDIANS IN 1948, AND IT WAS THERE THAT HE CAME TO KNOW VEECK! THE COLORFUL INDIANS OWNER WAS ALREADY MAKING A NAME FOR HIMSELF AS A PUBLICITY INNOVATOR, AND HE SAW IN JOHNNY A GOLDEN OPPORTUNITY. "AS ONE OF HIS PUBLICITY STUNTS," RECALLED JOHNNY, "BILL INSURED MY FACE FOR A MILLION DOLLARS BECAUSE I WAS ALSO ACTING." JOHNNY EARNED A WORLD SERIES RING WITH THE TRIBE IN 1948, BUT HAD TO RELUCTANTLY HOCK IT IN 1952 AS HE STRUGGLED TO TRANSITION INTO A FULL-TIME ACTOR! IT ALL WORKED OUT, THOUGH, AS JOHNNY EVENTUALLY WENT ON TO ACT IN COUNTLESS MOVIES AND TV SHOWS!

Chuck Connors

KEVIN JOSEPH ALOYSIUS CONNORS WAS BORN ON APRIL 10, 1921, IN BROOKLYN, NEW YORK! THE FAIR-HAIRED LAD GREW TO 6-1/2 FEET TALL AND EXCELLED AT BASEBALL AND BASKETBALL! NICKNAMED "CHUCK" FOR HOW HE IMPLORED TEAMMATES TO "CHUCK IT TO ME, BABY, CHUCK IT TO ME!", CONNORS' ATHLETIC ABILITY EARNED HIM A SCHOLARSHIP TO SETON HALL COLLEGE WHERE HE PLAYED BOTH SPORTS FOR THREE YEARS UNTIL HE ENLISTED IN THE ARMY IN 1942! DESPITE CHUCK'S DESIRE TO SEE COMBAT, ARMY BRASS FELT HIS IMPOSING SIZE AND OUTGOING DEMEANOR WAS BETTER SUITED AS A TRAINER OF MEN! HE WAS ASSIGNED TO WEST POINT AS A TANK INSTRUCTOR WHICH ALLOWED HIM TO SQUEEZE IN SOME WEEKEND SEMI-PRO BASEBALL FOR THE WAR'S DURATION!

CHUCK HIT 3 HOMERS IN ONE GAME WITH THE 1951 L.A. ANGELS OF THE P.C.L.!

FOLLOWING HIS DISCHARGE IN 1946, CHUCK SPLIT TIME BETWEEN BASEBALL AND BASKETBALL! IN THE VERY FIRST GAME FOR THE FLEDGLING BOSTON CELTICS ON NOV. 2, 1946, CHUCK WAS THEIR STARTING CENTER! HIS TRUE PASSION, HOWEVER, WAS BASEBALL, SO BY THE SPRING OF '46 HE FOCUSED ALL HIS EFFORTS AT MAKING IT TO THE BIG LEAGUES! A GOOD FIELDING FIRST-BASEMAN WITH POP IN HIS BAT, CHUCK HIT 106 MINOR LEAGUE HOMERS FROM 1946-52 -- NUMBERS THAT GOT HIM A SHORT CALL-UP WITH BROOKLYN IN '49! HE GOT A LONGER TRIAL WITH THE CUBS IN 1951 AFTER HITTING .321 WITH 22 HOMERS AND 71 RBIs THROUGH 98 GAMES OF THE 168-GAME SCHEDULE OF THE CUBS' P.C.L. AFFILIATE LOS ANGELES ANGELS! HIS SLUGGING SOON GOT NOTICED -- BY HOLLYWOOD -- AND WITH HIM FUTURE BASEBALL STARDOM A REAL POSSIBILITY, CHUCK HUNG UP HIS SPIKES IN FAVOR OF A CAREER IN TV AND MOVIES! HE HIT IT BIG, MOST NOTABLY AS LUCAS McCAIN IN "THE RIFLEMAN," BUT BASEBALL ALWAYS REMAINED HIS TRUE LOVE! "I OWE ALL THAT I HAVE TO BASEBALL," CHUCK LIKED TO SAY, "AND TO THE GREATEST GAME IN THE WORLD I SHALL BE ETERNALLY IN DEBT!"

CHUCK WAS FAMOUS FOR HIS RECITATIONS OF "CASEY AT THE BAT"! ROOKIE WILLIE MAYS ONCE DUPED CHUCK INTO A MID-GAME PERFORMANCE, THEN PROMPTLY STOLE 2ND BASE WHEN CHUCK -- COMPLETELY ENGROSSED IN HIS SOLILOQUY -- FAILED TO SEE THE PITCHER'S PICKOFF ATTEMPT! THE THROW HIT THE FUTURE EMMY-WINNER IN THE CHEST -- A BASEBALL MOMENT HE CLASSIFIED AS HIS MOST EMBARASSING EVER!

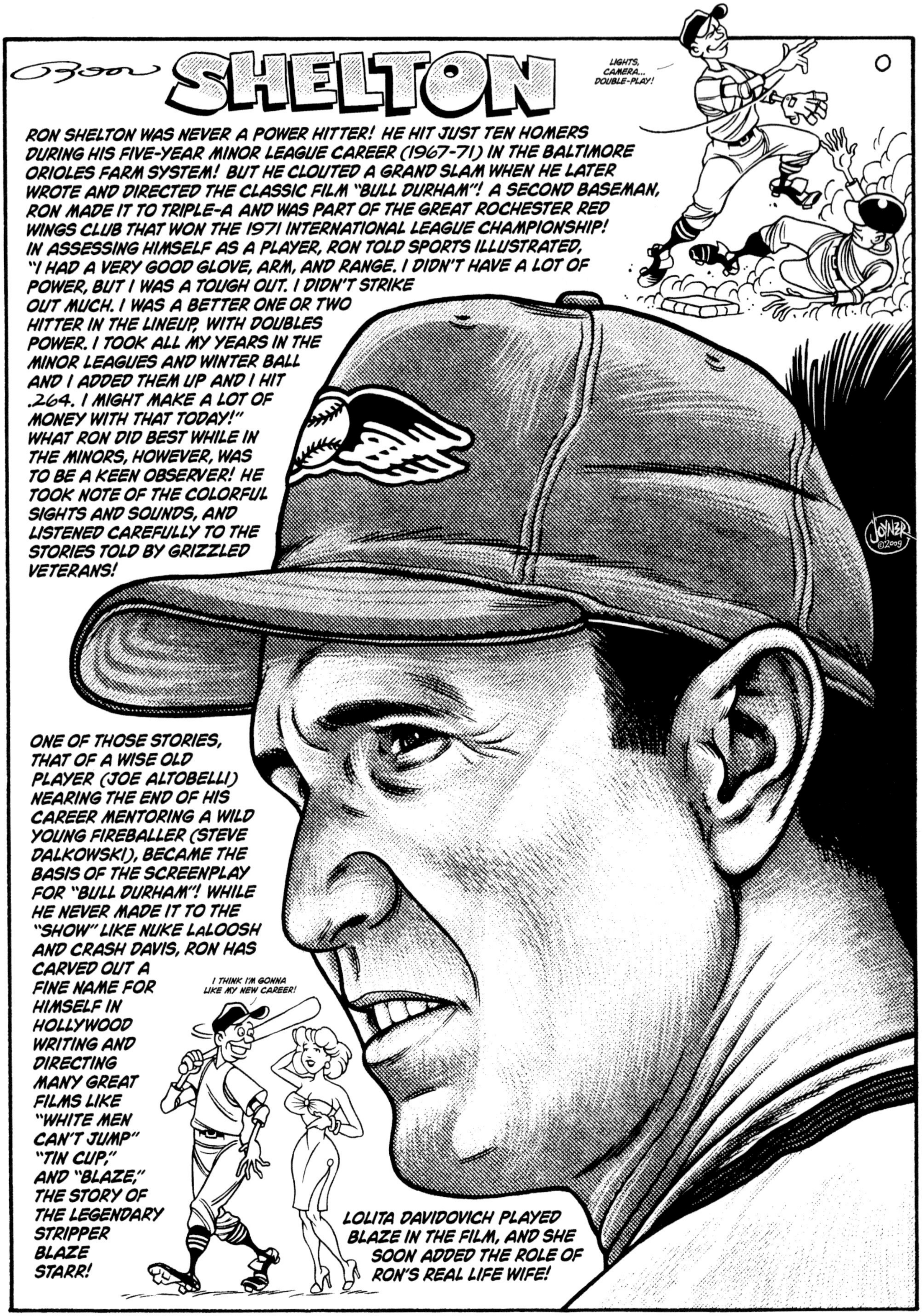
SHELTON
LIGHTS, CAMERA... DOUBLE-PLAY!
RON SHELTON WAS NEVER A POWER HITTER! HE HIT JUST TEN HOMERS DURING HIS FIVE-YEAR MINOR LEAGUE CAREER (1967-71) IN THE BALTIMORE ORIOLES FARM SYSTEM! BUT HE CLOUTED A GRAND SLAM WHEN HE LATER WROTE AND DIRECTED THE CLASSIC FILM "BULL DURHAM"! A SECOND BASEMAN, RON MADE IT TO TRIPLE-A AND WAS PART OF THE GREAT ROCHESTER RED WINGS CLUB THAT WON THE 1971 INTERNATIONAL LEAGUE CHAMPIONSHIP! IN ASSESSING HIMSELF AS A PLAYER, RON TOLD SPORTS ILLUSTRATED, "I HAD A VERY GOOD GLOVE, ARM, AND RANGE. I DIDN'T HAVE A LOT OF POWER, BUT I WAS A TOUGH OUT. I DIDN'T STRIKE OUT MUCH. I WAS A BETTER ONE OR TWO HITTER IN THE LINEUP, WITH DOUBLES POWER. I TOOK ALL MY YEARS IN THE MINOR LEAGUES AND WINTER BALL AND I ADDED THEM UP AND I HIT .264. I MIGHT MAKE A LOT OF MONEY WITH THAT TODAY!" WHAT RON DID BEST WHILE IN THE MINORS, HOWEVER, WAS TO BE A KEEN OBSERVER! HE TOOK NOTE OF THE COLORFUL SIGHTS AND SOUNDS, AND LISTENED CAREFULLY TO THE STORIES TOLD BY GRIZZLED VETERANS!
JOYNER ©2009
ONE OF THOSE STORIES, THAT OF A WISE OLD PLAYER (JOE ALTOBELLI) NEARING THE END OF HIS CAREER MENTORING A WILD YOUNG FIREBALLER (STEVE DALKOWSKI), BECAME THE BASIS OF THE SCREENPLAY FOR "BULL DURHAM"! WHILE HE NEVER MADE IT TO THE "SHOW" LIKE NUKE LaLOOSH AND CRASH DAVIS, RON HAS CARVED OUT A FINE NAME FOR HIMSELF IN HOLLYWOOD WRITING AND DIRECTING MANY GREAT FILMS LIKE "WHITE MEN CAN'T JUMP" "TIN CUP," AND "BLAZE," THE STORY OF THE LEGENDARY STRIPPER BLAZE STARR!
I THINK I'M GONNA LIKE MY NEW CAREER!
LOLITA DAVIDOVICH PLAYED BLAZE IN THE FILM, AND SHE SOON ADDED THE ROLE OF RON'S REAL LIFE WIFE!

CRASH DAVIS

LAWRENCE COLUMBUS DAVIS WAS BORN ON JULY 14, 1919, IN CANON, GEORGIA! "CRASH," ON THE OTHER HAND, WAS BORN YEARS LATER IN HIGH SCHOOL FOLLOWING A COLLISION WITH A TEAMMATE! DAVIS, PLAYING SHORTSTOP, SLAMMED INTO THE LEFTFIELDER WHILE CHASING A POP-UP, AND WAS SOON RE-CHRISTENED AS CRASH DAVIS! "I'VE BEEN THAT ALL MY LIFE," CRASH USED TO SAY! "IT FOLLOWED ME THROUGH MY SCHOOL DAYS, MY PROFESSIONAL CAREER, RIGHT UP TO THE MOVIE "BULL DURHAM."

NEARLY 50 YEARS LATER, AN UNKNOWN MOVIE DIRECTOR NAMED RON SHELTON FLIPPED THROUGH AN OLD CAROLINA LEAGUE RECORD BOOK LOOKING FOR AN UNKNOWN "SOMETHING" TO ADD COLOR TO A BASEBALL MOVIE HE WAS WORKING ON! HE FOUND IT WHEN HE READ THE NAME OF THE DURHAM BULLS PLAYER WHO'D HIT .315 IN '48 WHILE LEADING THE CAROLINA LEAGUE IN DOUBLES -- CRASH DAVIS! SHELTON DECIDED TO SET HIS FILM AROUND THE BULLS WHILE ALSO NAMING HIS LEAD CHARACTER CRASH DAVIS! IT WAS PURE MOVIE MAGIC, LAUNCHING THE CAREERS OF SHELTON AND LEAD ACTOR KEVIN COSTNER INTO THE STRATOSPHERE! THE "REAL" CRASH DAVIS DIDN'T DO TOO BAD, EITHER! HE BECAME KNOWN WORLD-WIDE, AND LOVED EVERY MINUTE OF IT! "ANYWHERE I GO IN AMERICA, THEY KNOW MY NAME," CRASH SAID! "IT'S BEEN FUN!"

AFTER GRADUATING FROM DUKE, CRASH DAVIS WAS A MIDDLE INFIELDER FOR CONNIE MACK'S PHILADELPHIA ATHLETICS FROM 1940-42! HE THEN SERVED IN THE NAVY DURING WORLD WAR II BEFORE RETURNING TO BASEBALL IN 1946! CRASH PLAYED MINOR LEAUE BALL FROM 1946-52 BEFORE MOVING ON TO TEACHING, COACHING AND, ULTIMATELY, A LONG CAREER WITH BURLINGTON INDUSTRIES! "I WASN'T ALWAYS THE BEST PLAYER ON MY TEAM," CRASH WOULD HUMBLY SAY, "BUT I ALWAYS GOT A HIT WHEN IT COUNTED -- AND I COULD TURN THE DOUBLE-PLAY AS GOOD AS ANYONE!" CRASH DAVIS DIED IN 2001, BUT HIS NAME WILL LIVE ON FOREVER, AS FATE WOULD HAVE IT, THANKS TO A FORTUITOUS COLLISION IN SHALLOW LEFT!

Steve DALKOWSKI

IN THE MINDS OF MANY WELL-RESPECTED CAREER BASEBALL MEN, STEVE DALKOWSKI THREW A BASEBALL HARDER THAN ANYONE EVER! UNFORTUNATELY, STEVE WAS NOT ABLE TO CONTROL HIS WORLD-CLASS HEATER, AND THAT FACT LEFT MOST OF THE BATTERS HE FACED QUAKING IN THEIR SPIKES!

STEVE WAS AN ORIOLES FARMHAND, SO MOST OF THE STORIES OF HIS LEGENDARY FASTBALL COME COURTESY OF EX-ORIOLES! HE TOILED IN THE MINORS FROM 1957-65, AN ERA BEFORE VIDEO CAMERAS AND RADAR GUNS, AND THIS HAS HELPED CONTRIBUTE TO THE EVER-INCREASING LEGEND OF DALKO! IN OTHER WORDS, THERE IS NO WAY TO EVER PROVE THAT STEVE WAS THE FASTEST EVER -- BUT THERE'LL NEVER BE A WAY TO DISPROVE IT, EITHER! EARL WEAVER, STEVE'S MANAGER AT ELMIRA, HAD SEEN ALL THE HARDEST THROWERS OF THE 1960s -- RYAN, KOUFAX, McDOWELL, RADATZ, ETC. "DALKO THREW HARDER THAN ALL OF THEM," WEAVER SAID WITH CONFIDENCE. BUT STEVE WAS ALSO WILDER THAN ALL OF THEM. HALL-OF-FAMER BOB LEMON RECALLED THAT STEVE ONCE BEANED A FAN BUYING A HOT DOG!

STEVE'S SPEED DIDN'T COME FROM HIS SIZE -- HE WAS JUST 5-FOOT-11 AND 175-LBS! THE LEFTY'S VELOCITY, GUESSED BY MANY TO HAVE BEEN 110-MPH, SEEMS TO HAVE BEEN A GIFT FROM THE BASEBALL GODS! STEVE STRUGGLED IN VAIN TO HARNESS THE POWER OF HIS FASTBALL, BUT TUTELAGE FROM EARL WEAVER FINALLY HAD THE KID TICKETED FOR THE BIGS IN THE SPRING OF '63! STEVE WAS PHOTOGRAPHED BY TOPPS (HE APPEARS ON 1963 TOPPS #496), THEN FITTED FOR HIS O'S UNIFORM ON MARCH 23! LATER THAT DAY IN A CRUEL TWIST OF FATE, STEVE INJURED AN ELBOW LIGAMENT PITCHING IN AN EXHIBITION GAME! HE NEVER FULLY RECOVERED AND WAS OUT OF BASEBALL BY 1966 -- WITHOUT EVER GETTING HIS SHOT IN THE MAJORS! IT WAS A TOUGH BREAK -- AND IT ALMOST BROKE STEVE -- BUT HE EVENTUALLY CAME TO PEACE WITH IT! "I'M A BIG FAN," STEVE SAYS. "SOMETIMES, PEOPLE STILL ASK ME FOR MY AUTOGRAPH. I WISH THINGS HAD BEEN DIFFERENT FOR ME, BUT I STILL LOVE BASEBALL." INCIDENTALLY, RON SHELTON, ONE-TIME ORIOLES FARMHAND AND WRITER OF "BULL DURHAM," BASED THE CHARACTER "NUKE LaLOOSH" ON STEVE DALKOWSKI!

MOONLIGHT Graham

ARCHIBALD WRIGHT GRAHAM WAS BORN ON NOVEMBER 10, 1879, IN FAYETTEVILLE, NORTH CAROLINA. YOUNG ARCHIE DREAMED OF TWO THINGS -- PLAYING MAJOR LEAGUE BASEBALL AND BECOMING A DOCTOR. WHILE THEY APPEARED TO BE INCONGRUOUS GOALS, ARCHIE WAS DETERMINED -- SO HE STUDIED HARD WHILE PLAYING COLLEGE BALL AT THE UNIVERSITY OF NORTH CAROLINA. SOON HE BEGAN PLAYING MINOR LEAGUE BALL WHILE CONTINUING TO "MOONLIGHT" AS A MED STUDENT AT THE UNIVERSITY OF MARYLAND. THAT, PLUS THE FACT THAT ARCHIE WAS AS "QUICK AS A FLASH OF MOONLIGHT," MEANT THAT A GREAT NICKNAME WAS BORN. AGAINST ALL ODDS, ARCHIE WAS CALLED UP TO THE NEW YORK GIANTS IN EARLY JUNE OF 1905. HE SAT ON THE BENCH UNTIL SENT OUT TO RIGHT FIELD FOR THE EIGHTH AND NINTH INNINGS OF A GAME ON JUNE 29. LEFT STANDING ON DECK WHEN THE LAST OUT WAS MADE, ARCHIE DID NOT BAT IN THE GAME. IN FACT, HE NEVER PLAYED IN THE BIG LEAGUES AGAIN. SHIPPED BACK TO THE MINORS A WEEK AFTER HIS MOMENT IN THE SHOW, ARCHIE NEVER RECEIVED ANOTHER CALL-UP. HE CERTAINLY DESERVED A SECOND CHANCE AFTER THE 1906 SEASON AT SCRANTON WHERE HE LED HIS CLUB TO A TITLE AND WAS CROWNED THE LEAGUE'S BATTING CHAMP. BUT ARCHIE, NOW GRADUATED FROM MED SCHOOL AND RE-NICKNAMED "DOC," NEVER GOT ANOTHER SHOT AT THE MAJORS. 1908 WAS HIS LAST YEAR IN THE MINORS, AT WHICH POINT HE BEGAN THE SECOND OF HIS CHILDHOOD DREAMS -- A LIFETIME OF SERVICE AS A DOCTOR.

DOC GRAHAM SERVED THE PEOPLE OF CHISHOLM, MINNESOTA, FROM '09 UNTIL HIS DEATH IN 1965. DOC WAS REBORN AND IMMORTALIZED WHEN HIS NAME AND STORY WERE INCLUDED IN W.P. KINSELLA'S 1982 NOVEL "SHOELESS JOE." DOC WAS LATER ELEVATED TO ICONIC STATUS WHEN HOLLYWOOD TURNED KINSELLA'S BOOK INTO THE CLASSIC FILM "FIELD OF DREAMS." W.P. CAPTURED THE "REAL" DOC'S SPIRIT WHEN HE WROTE THE PERFECT LINES FOR THE "FICTITIOUS" DOC TO ADDRESS THE NOTION THAT HIS FIVE MINUTES IN THE MAJORS WAS A TRAGEDY. "IF I'D ONLY GOT TO BE A DOCTOR FOR FIVE MINUTES, NOW THAT WOULD HAVE BEEN A TRAGEDY."

Sibby SISTI
SEBASTIAN DANIEL SISTI WAS BORN ON JULY 26, 1920, IN BUFFALO, NEW YORK! YOUNG "SIBBY" QUICKLY DEVELOPED INTO SUCH A FINE BALLPLAYER THAT THE RED SOX GAVE HIM A TRYOUT AT AGE 15 -- BUT IT WAS THE BRAVES WHO WOULD ULTIMATELY SIGN HIM, COMMITTING TO THE LAD BEFORE HE GRADUATED HIGH SCHOOL IN 1938! THE BRAVES SENT SIBBY TO HARTFORD IN 1939, BUT BY JULY HE HAD JOINED THE BIG CLUB -- AND AT AGE 18 HE WAS THE YOUNGEST PLAYER IN THE BIG LEAGUES!
SIBBY WAS SUCH A VALUABLE UTILITY MAN THAT HE BECAME KNOWN AS "SUPER SUB"!
THIS BEATS THE HECK OUT OF DOIN' HOMEWORK!
SIBBY WAS THE BRAVES' FULL-TIME 3RD BASEMAN FROM 1940-42 BEFORE JOINING THE COAST GUARD WHERE HE SERVED FROM 1943-45! BOSTON SENT SIBBY TO INDIANAPOLIS IN 1946 SO HE COULD TRAIN TO BE THEIR SHORTSTOP OF THE FUTURE! WHILE THERE HE HIT .343, LEADING THE AMERICAN ASSOCIATION IN BATTING, HITS, AND TRIPLES! HIS BIG YEAR EARNED HIM THE SPORTING NEWS' MINOR LEAGUE PLAYER OF THE YEAR AWARD -- AND A RETURN TO THE BIGS IN '47! A MID-'47 SEASON SHOULDER INJURY REDUCED SIBBY TO A ROLE PLAYER, BUT HE HANDLED IT WELL AND WAS A KEY CONTRIBUTOR TO THE BRAVES THROUGH HIS RETIREMENT IN 1954!
JOYNER ©2006
SIBBY PLAYED THE MANAGER OF THE PIRATES IN THE 1983 FILM "THE NATURAL"! IT WAS SIBBY WHO SIGNALED THE BULLPEN FOR THE SOUTHPAW YOUNGBERRY IN THE CLIMACTIC SCENE, ONLY TO HAVE ROY HOBBS, PLAYED BY ROBERT REDFORD, HOMER INTO THE LIGHT TOWER TO WIN THE PENNANT FOR THE KNIGHTS! AFTER YEARS OF RELIVING HIS MANAGERIAL ERROR ON TV RERUNS OF THE MOVIE, SIBBY JOKINGLY VOWED "IF THEY EVER MAKE A 'NATURAL 2,' I'M GOING OUT THERE AGAIN. BUT THIS TIME, ON THE FIRST PITCH, REDFORD'S GOING RIGHT DOWN ON HIS ASS!"
HEY -- THAT WASN'T IN THE SCRIPT!

Joe Judge

IN THE LATE 1940s, A YOUNG JOURNALIST NAMED DOUGLASS WALLOP WOULD VISIT HIS GIRLFRIEND AT HER HOME IN CHEVY CHASE, MARYLAND. DOUGLASS WOULD CAREFULLY OBSERVE DOROTHY'S FIFTY-SOMETHING-YEAR-OLD FATHER AS HE WATCHED HIS HOME TEAM, THE WASHINGTON SENATORS, ON TELEVISION. THE NATS OF THAT TIME WERE WOEFUL, AND DOROTHY'S FATHER WOULD BE IN AGONY AS HE WATCHED THE TEAM FIND NEVER-ENDING WAYS TO LOSE BALLGAMES. THE OLD MAN WOULD TALK TO THE TV SET -- GIVING ADVICE, ARGUING BOTCHED PLAYS, AND CURSING BAD CALLS -- WHILE DOUGLASS TOOK IT ALL IN. A FEW YEARS LATER, DOUGLASS PUBLISHED A NOVEL CALLED "THE YEAR THE YANKEES LOST THE PENNANT," AND THE MAIN CHARACTER, JOE BOYD, WAS BASED ON DOROTHY'S FRUSTRATED FATHER. THE NOVEL WAS SOON ADAPTED INTO THE BROADWAY PLAY "DAMN YANKEES," A HUGE HIT THAT TOLD THE STORY OF MIDDLE-AGED JOE BOYD, A FRUSTRATED NATS FAN WHO SOLD HIS SOUL TO THE DEVIL TO BECOME JOE HARDY, A SUPERSTAR SLUGGER WHO WOULD LEAD WASHINGTON TO UNLIKELY PENNANT GLORY OVER THE HATED YANKS. IRONICALLY, DOROTHY'S FATHER REALLY HAD, IN FACT, HELPED THE NATS STEAL A PENNANT FROM THE YANKS. THE YEAR WAS 1924, THE ONLY YEAR A WASHINGTON BASEBALL CLUB HAS EVER WON THE WORLD SERIES, AND DOROTHY'S FATHER WAS THE CLUB'S FIRST BASEMAN. DRUMROLL PLEASE... DOROTHY'S FATHER WAS THE GREAT JOE JUDGE, ONE OF BASEBALL'S ALL-TIME FINEST FIRST SACKERS!

LEST YOU THINK LITTLE JOE UNWORTHY OF SUCH LOFTY PRAISE, CONSIDER THIS: JOE LED OR TIED A.L. 1st BASEMEN IN FIELDING SIX TIMES; COMPILED A .993 LIFETIME FIELDING MARK; BATTED ABOVE .300 IN NINE FULL SEASONS; COLLECTED 2,352 CAREER HITS; AND HIT .385 IN THE SENATORS' THRILLING 7-GAME WORLD SERIES WIN OVER THE GIANTS IN '24. JOE JUDGE, WHILE JUST 5-FOOT-8 AND 185-LBS, WAS TRULY A GIANT DURING HIS ERA OF THE GAME!

INDIRECTLY, JOE MAY HAVE CONTRIBUTED TO THE BLACK SOX SCANDAL OF 1919! CONFIDENT THAT IN JOE THEY HAD FOUND THEIR 1st BASEMAN OF THE FUTURE, THE NATS SHIPPED CHICK GANDIL OFF TO CLEVELAND PRIOR TO THE 1916 SEASON. CHICK HAD SPENT FOUR FINE YEARS IN WASHINGTON, BUT JOE'S UNLIMITED POTENTIAL MADE IT EASY FOR THE NATS TO UNLOAD THE SURLY GANDIL. THE INDIANS SENT CHICK TO THE WHITE SOX AFTER ONE SEASON, AND JUST FOUR YEARS AFTER LEAVING D.C., CHICK BECAME THE RINGLEADER OF CHICAGO'S INFAMOUS EIGHT MEN OUT!

JIMMY PIERSALL

FOR WELL OVER A DECADE, CENTERFIELDER JIMMY PIERSALL DAZZLED BASEBALL FANS WITH TOP-NOTCH DEFENSIVE SKILLS! PLAYING VERY SHALLOW, JIMMY WAS VERY ADEPT AT GOING BACK ON THE BALL, AND HIS STYLE OF PLAY MADE HIM THE MASTER OF THE CIRCUS CATCH! JIMMY ESTABLISHED HIMSELF AS A GREAT FLYCHASER DURING HIS YEARS WITH THE BOSTON RED SOX ('50,'52-58), BUT IT WAS CASEY STENGEL, JIMMY'S MANAGER WITH THE METS IN 1963, WHO PAID HIM THE ULTIMATE COMPLIMENT! "I THOUGHT JOE DIMAGGIO WAS THE GREATEST DEFENSIVE OUTFIELDER I EVER SAW," CASEY SAID, "BUT I HAVE TO RATE PIERSALL BETTER." SADLY, IT WASN'T JUST HIS GLOVE THAT DAZZLED! JIMMY ALSO DAZZLED PLAYERS, FANS, AND SPORTSWRITERS WITH VERY ERRATIC BEHAVIOR! SOON AFTER HIS ARRIVAL IN THE MAJORS, JIMMY BEGAN ANTAGONIZING FANS, UMPIRES, AND PLAYERS! HIS ANTICS WERE SO BAD BY JULY OF 1952 THAT HE WAS COMMITTED TO A PSYCHIATRIC HOSPITAL, WHERE HIS TREATMENT INCLUDED SHOCK THERAPY! HE WAS BACK WITH THE RED SOX IN '53, THUS BEGINNING A FOUR-YEAR PERIOD WITH FEWER OUTBURSTS AND EXCELLENT PLAY -- CULMINATING IN PERHAPS HIS FINEST SEASON IN WHICH HE BATTED .293 WITH 14 HOMERS AND 87 RBIs IN 1956! JIMMY PLAYED THROUGH THE 1967 SEASON, AND WHILE HIS BEHAVIOR WAS LESS ERRATIC, HIS OCCASIONAL "CRAZY" MOMENTS STILL OVERSHADOWED HIS FINE PLAY ON THE FIELD -- LIKE THE TIME THAT JIMMY BELTED HIS 100TH HOME RUN, THEN CIRCLED THE BASES BACKWARDS, ALBEIT IN THE PROPER ORDER!

JIMMY WAS DIAGNOSED AS BIPOLAR AND MANIC DEPRESSIVE! HIS MOTHER ALSO SUFFERED FROM MENTAL ILLNESS THROUGHOUT HIS CHILDHOOD! HE WROTE ABOUT HIS STRUGGLES IN THE BOOK "FEAR STRIKES OUT," WHICH WAS MADE INTO A MOVIE IN 1957! JIMMY WASN'T A BIG FAN OF THE FILM BECAUSE HE SAID IT DISTORTED FACTS -- AND HE WAS ALSO UNHAPPY WITH THE BALLPLAYING SKILL OF ANTHONY PERKINS, THE ACTOR WHO PORTRAYED HIM! DESCRIBING PERKINS' ABILITIES ON THE FIELD, JIMMY SAID, "HE THREW A BASEBALL LIKE A GIRL, AND DANCED AROUND IN THE OUTFIELD LIKE A BALLERINA." JIMMY TAKES HIS LEGACY IN STRIDE, ONCE SAYING, "PROBABLY THE BEST THING THAT EVER HAPPENED TO ME WAS GOING NUTS. WHO EVER HEARD OF JIMMY PIERSALL UNTIL THAT HAPPENED?"

Ken HUNT

KEN HUNT WAS A BLUE-CHIP YANKEE PROSPECT FROM THE DAY THEY SIGNED HIM IN 1952 AND SENT HIM OFF TO PLAY WITH THE JOPLIN MINERS OF THE CLASS-C WESTERN ASSOCIATION! HIS FINE SHOWING ON THE FARM WOULD HAVE WARRANTED A QUICK DEBUT IN THE BIG LEAGUES WITH MOST ANY OTHER CLUB, BUT OPPORTUNITIES WERE FEW FOR A FLYCHASER IN THE TALENT-RICH YANKEE ORGANIZATION! KEN WAS THRILLED TO BE A YANKEE, BUT HE GOT JUST TWO BRIEF CALL-UPS IN 1959 AND 1960! HIS BIG BREAK CAME WHEN HE WAS DRAFTED BY THE LOS ANGELES ANGELS FOR THEIR EXPANSION SEASON OF 1961! "THERE WERE AN AWFUL LOT OF GUYS SITTING IN TRIPLE-A WITH NO SPOTS FOR THEM IN AN EIGHT-TEAM LEAGUE," KEN SAID. "EXPANSION OPENED UP SPOTS. I WAS 25. I WASN'T GOING TO GET ANOTHER CHANCE." KEN CASHED IN ON HIS SHOT BY PLAYING GREAT DEFENSE WHILE BELTING 25 LONG-BALLS FOR THE '61 HALOS!

KEN, WHO WAS OFTEN KIDDED ABOUT HIS LARGE HAT SIZE, EARNED THE GOOD-NATURED NICKNAME "BUCKET HEAD" FROM ANGELS INFIELDER JOE KOPPE! ONCE UNABLE TO FIND HIS HELMET WHEN CALLED UPON TO PINCH-HIT, KOPPE TOSSED A BUCKET AND SAID, "HEY HUNT -- WEAR THIS!"

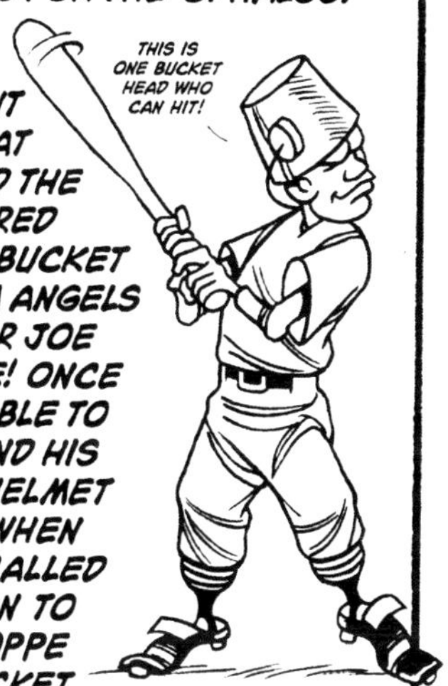

KEN'S 1962 SEASON WAS LOST WHEN HE SUFFERED A FREAK SHOULDER INJURY WHILE LOOSENING UP IN THE ON-DECK CIRCLE! UNABLE TO REGAIN HIS FORM, KEN SOON FOUND HIMSELF IN WASHINGTON WHERE HE FINISHED HIS CAREER AS A PART-TIMER FOR THE 1963-64 SENATORS! KEN STAYED IN TOUCH WITH HIS LOS ANGELES FRIENDS AND FANS AS THE LONG-TIME OWNER OF THE VERY POPULAR LEI ALOHA BAR!

WHILE IN LOS ANGELES, KEN FELL IN LOVE WITH AND MARRIED PATTI LILLEY, THE MOTHER OF PATRICK LILLEY, ALSO KNOWN AS BUTCH PATRICK -- OR "EDDIE MUNSTER" AS HE WAS KNOWN ON TV! KEN WAS OFTEN KIDDED THAT HE EARNED LESS MONEY PLAYING BALL THAN BUTCH MADE PLAYING EDDIE! KEN ONCE PORTRAYED A BALLPLAYER IN A MUNSTERS EPISODE THAT SAW "HERMAN" TRY OUT FOR THE MAJOR LEAGUES!

David
ECKSTEIN
DESPITE BEING A TWO-TIME ALL-STATE HIGH SCHOOL PLAYER, DAVID DID NOT WIN ANY BASEBALL SCHOLARSHIPS! INSTEAD, HE WAS A WALK-ON AT THE UNIVERSITY OF FLORIDA WHERE HE TWICE BECAME AN ALL-SEC SELECTION!
WHICH WAY TO SHORTSTOP, BUB?
HEY, THAT'S MY POSITION!
FLORIDA
DAVID'S HUSTLE AND TENACITY WERE KEY TO THE WORLD SERIES TITLE HE WON WITH THE ANGELS IN 2002! HE LATER BROUGHT THOSE SAME QUALITIES TO THE CARDINALS, AND THEY QUICKLY REAPED THE BENEFITS -- A WORLD SERIES CROWN IN 2006! HIS HITTING SPARKED THE CLUB TO VICTORY, EARNING DAVID THE HIGHLY COVETED M.V.P. AWARD!
M.V.P.
I'M GONNA NEED A BIGGER TROPHY CASE!
JOYNER ©2009
THAT'S MY LITTLE ASHLEY!
DAVID IS MARRIED TO ACTRESS ASHLEY DRANE, STAR OF COUNTLESS TV AND FILM ROLES! THEY MARRIED ON NOVEMBER 26, 2005, IN A FAIRY TALE WEDDING AT THE WALT DISNEY RESORT IN ORLANDO! "HE'S AWESOME," ASHLEY SAYS, "AND I LOVE BASEBALL!"
SMALL IN STATURE, DAVID'S SUCCESS IS AN INSPIRATION TO UNDERDOGS EVERYWHERE! HE RECENTLY WROTE ABOUT HIS LIFE IN A BOOK TITLED "HAVE HEART." AIMED AT KIDS, THE BOOK STRIVES TO TEACH THEM TO ALWAYS DO THEIR BEST AND NEVER LOSE HOPE -- JUST LIKE DAVID!
"THEN, ON JAN. 20, 1976, I TURNED ONE YEAR OLD..."

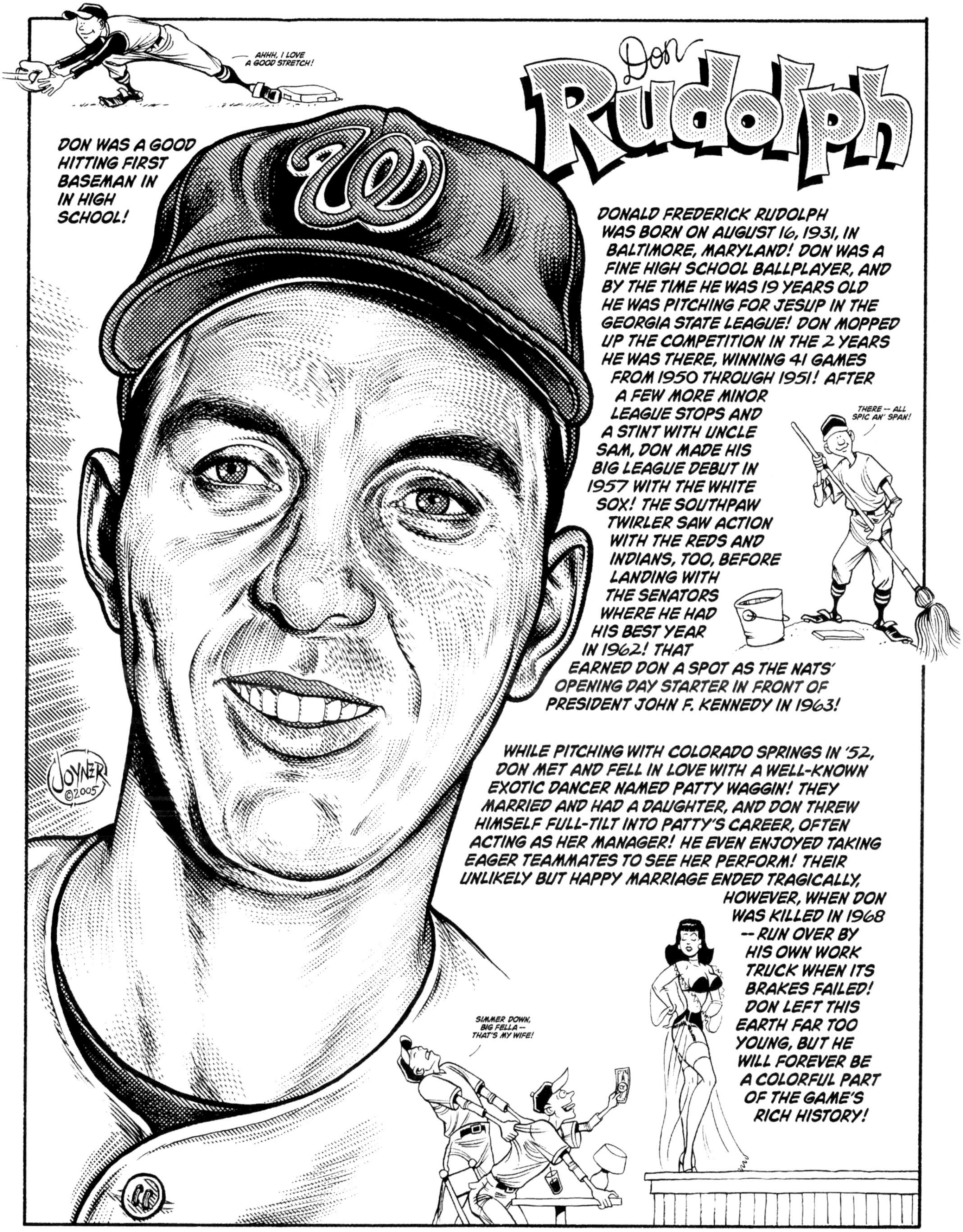
AHHH, I LOVE A GOOD STRETCH!
Don Rudolph
DON WAS A GOOD HITTING FIRST BASEMAN IN IN HIGH SCHOOL!
DONALD FREDERICK RUDOLPH WAS BORN ON AUGUST 16, 1931, IN BALTIMORE, MARYLAND! DON WAS A FINE HIGH SCHOOL BALLPLAYER, AND BY THE TIME HE WAS 19 YEARS OLD HE WAS PITCHING FOR JESUP IN THE GEORGIA STATE LEAGUE! DON MOPPED UP THE COMPETITION IN THE 2 YEARS HE WAS THERE, WINNING 41 GAMES FROM 1950 THROUGH 1951! AFTER A FEW MORE MINOR LEAGUE STOPS AND A STINT WITH UNCLE SAM, DON MADE HIS BIG LEAGUE DEBUT IN 1957 WITH THE WHITE SOX! THE SOUTHPAW TWIRLER SAW ACTION WITH THE REDS AND INDIANS, TOO, BEFORE LANDING WITH THE SENATORS WHERE HE HAD HIS BEST YEAR IN 1962! THAT EARNED DON A SPOT AS THE NATS' OPENING DAY STARTER IN FRONT OF PRESIDENT JOHN F. KENNEDY IN 1963!
THERE -- ALL SPIC AN' SPAN!
JOYNER ©2005
WHILE PITCHING WITH COLORADO SPRINGS IN '52, DON MET AND FELL IN LOVE WITH A WELL-KNOWN EXOTIC DANCER NAMED PATTY WAGGIN! THEY MARRIED AND HAD A DAUGHTER, AND DON THREW HIMSELF FULL-TILT INTO PATTY'S CAREER, OFTEN ACTING AS HER MANAGER! HE EVEN ENJOYED TAKING EAGER TEAMMATES TO SEE HER PERFORM! THEIR UNLIKELY BUT HAPPY MARRIAGE ENDED TRAGICALLY, HOWEVER, WHEN DON WAS KILLED IN 1968 -- RUN OVER BY HIS OWN WORK TRUCK WHEN ITS BRAKES FAILED! DON LEFT THIS EARTH FAR TOO YOUNG, BUT HE WILL FOREVER BE A COLORFUL PART OF THE GAME'S RICH HISTORY!
SIMMER DOWN, BIG FELLA — THAT'S MY WIFE!

Ernie ORSATTI

WHEN TALES OF THE LEGENDARY GAS HOUSE GANG ARE RECALLED, IT'S NAMES LIKE FRISCH, DEAN, DUROCHER, MARTIN AND MEDWICK THAT DOMINATE THE CONVERSATION! BUT THERE'S ANOTHER NAME THAT DESERVES TO BE INCLUDED IN ANY CONVERSATION ABOUT THE GAS HOUSERS, AND THAT'S THE NAME OF OUTFIELDER ERNIE ORSATTI! ERNIE WAS WITH THE CARDINALS FOR HIS ENTIRE CAREER, 1927 THROUGH '35, AND HIS SEVEN HITS IN THE 1934 FALL CLASSIC HELPED ST. LOUIS CLAIM THE FRANCHISE'S THIRD WORLD SERIES TITLE! MANY BELIEVE THAT 1934 WAS THE YEAR THAT THE NAME "GAS HOUSE GANG" WAS COINED, AND ERNIE FIT RIGHT IN WITH THE TRAITS THAT CAME TO DEFINE THE GANG! WEARING A UNIFORM THAT WAS USUALLY FILTHY, ERNIE WAS A DAREDEVIL IN THE OUTFIELD, TRACKING DOWN FLY BALLS WITH ACROBATIC AND RECKLESS ABANDON! HE WAS QUICK OF FOOT, TOO, AND HELPED BUILD THE GAS HOUSE TRADITION OF RUNNING AND SLIDING ON THE BASEPATHS! WHILE SMALL (ERNIE STOOD JUST 5-FOOT-7 AND WEIGHED BUT 155 LBS), THE LOS ANGELES-BORN ORSATTI HIT THE BALL HARD AND ENDED WITH A CAREER .306 AVERAGE! ERNIE WAS USUALLY A PART-TIME PLAYER, SOMETHING HE EXPLAINED BY SAYING, "EVERY YEAR I'D GO TO CAMP THINKING I FINALLY HAD A REGULAR JOB WRAPPED UP WHEN SOME PHENOM WOULD COME ALONG -- LIKE JOE MEDWICK!" ERNIE WAS A SNAZZY DRESSER, RIVALING TEAMMATE LEO DUROCHER FOR THE TITLE OF BEST DRESSED! ERNIE ONCE WALKED PAST A GROUP OF STUNNED TEAMMATES WEARING HIS FINEST BRIGHT GREEN SWEATER, WHITE KNICKERS AND GOLD SOCKS! SUNNY JIM BOTTOMLEY BROKE THE GANG UP WITH LAUGHTER WHEN HE STOPPED ERNIE AND SAID, "YOU'RE JUST TOO BEAUTIFUL TO LET YOU GET AWAY -- I WANT TO KISS YOU GOODBYE!" ERNIE DEVELOPED MUCH OF HIS FLAIR BY GROWING UP AROUND HOLLYWOOD BACK LOTS, WHERE HE WOULD EVENTUALLY BECOME A STUNT-MAN! ONE OF HIS MORE CELEBRATED JOBS WAS AS PROP-MAN AND STAND-IN FOR SILENT FILM LEGEND BUSTER KEATON! ON ONE OCCASION ERNIE EVEN ACTED AS LIFE-SAVER FOR BUSTER! "I WAS ALMOST STRANGLED WHILE EXPERIMENTING WITH A DEEP-SEA DIVER'S SUIT," KEATON ONCE RECALLED. "THE GAG CALLED FOR ME TO BE SMOKING A CIGARETTE WHEN A GIRL PUT MY HELMET ON. ACCIDENTALLY, SHE GAVE IT A TWIST, LOCKING IT. ERNIE ORSATTI, THE CARDINALS BALLPLAYER, NOTICED THE TROUBLE AND TWISTED OFF THE HELMET IN THE NICK OF TIME." ERNIE LATER RAN THE ORSATTI TALENT AGENCY, WHILE HIS SON WENT ON TO ACHIEVE FAME AS THE STUNT-MAN WHO PLUNGED THROUGH A STAINED-GLASS CEILING IN 1972's "THE POSEIDON ADVENTURE"!

Clyde McCullough

BORN ON MARCH 4, 1917, IN NASHVILLE, TENNESSEE, CLYDE McCULLOUGH ENJOYED A 15-YEAR BIG LEAGUE CAREER. THE 5-FOOT-11-INCH 180-LB CATCHER SPENT HIS FIRST SEVEN YEARS WITH THE CUBS, MISSING 1944 AND 1945 WHILE SERVING IN THE NAVY DURING WORLD WAR II. ACTUALLY, CLYDE RETURNED TO THE CUBBIES JUST IN TIME TO MAKE ONE PINCH-HITTING APPEARANCE IN THE FINAL GAME OF THE '45 WORLD SERIES. WHILE NOT KNOWN AS A HOME RUN HITTER, CLYDE ONCE CLUBBED THREE CIRCUITS IN ONE GAME -- THIS IN A SEASON THAT SAW HIM TOTAL JUST FIVE! CLYDE SPENT 1949-52 WITH THE PIRATES BEFORE RETURNING TO THE CUBS FOR THE FINAL FOUR YEARS OF HIS PLAYING DAYS. HE WAS LATER A MINOR LEAGUE MANAGER AND BIG LEAGUE COACH UNTIL HIS UNTIMELY DEATH IN 1982.

WITH THE 1952 SEASON IN THE BOOKS, CLYDE TOOK OFF IN HIS BEAT-UP OLD NASH STATION WAGON FOR AN EXHIBITION GAME IN IOWA. AFTER THAT HE WAS TO JOIN A FEW BUDDIES FOR A HUNTING TRIP. CLYDE SAW A DESPERATE-LOOKING TRIO OF HITCH-HIKERS AT THE END OF THE PENNSYLVANIA TURNPIKE, SO HE PICKED THEM UP. THE THREE YOUNGSTERS WERE UNKNOWNS AT THE TIME, BUT ALL WOULD LATER ACHIEVE SUCCESS IN SHOWBIZ. BILL BAST WOULD BECOME AN ACCLAIMED SCREENWRITER; LIZ SHERIDAN WOULD GAIN FAME IN TV SITCOMS LIKE "SEINFELD"; AND JAMES DEAN WOULD BECOME A SILVER SCREEN LEGEND! DEAN HAD PLAYED BASEBALL IN HIGH SCHOOL, SO HE WAS THRILLED WHEN HE LEARNED THAT THEIR DRIVER WAS NONE OTHER THAN BUCS CATCHER CLYDE McCULLOUGH! THE KIDS WERE HITCHHIKING FROM NEW YORK TO DEAN'S FAMILY FARM IN INDIANA, AND THEY RODE WITH CLYDE FOR NEARLY TWO DAYS. THEY TALKED, SANG, AND ATE TOGETHER -- WITH CLYDE PICKING UP ALL THE TABS FOR THE YOUNG STARVING ARTISTS. THEY BECAME FAST FRIENDS DURING THAT TRIP, BUT THEY'D NEVER SEE EACH OTHER AGAIN -- AND CLYDE NEVER FOUND OUT ABOUT THE JAMES DEAN CONNECTION. "A HUG FOR EACH OF US AND HE WAS GONE," WROTE LIZ IN 2000, "HIS POWERFUL HAND WAVING A LAST GOODBYE."

JAMES DEAN

A TRUE AMERICAN CULTURAL ICON, JAMES DEAN WILL FOREVER BE REMEMBERED FOR THE ELECTRIC STYLE HE BROUGHT TO MOVIE SCREENS IN THE SPRING OF 1955 -- ONLY TO DIE TRAGICALLY BY THE TIME THE CALENDAR TURNED TO FALL. A FEW YEARS BEFORE HE BECAME FAMOUS PLAYING TROUBLED BUT SENSITIVE OUTCASTS, JAMES WAS PLAYING BASEBALL -- AND LETTERING -- FOR THE FAIRMOUNT HIGH SCHOOL QUAKERS. WHILE SMALL IN STATURE AT JUST 5-FOOT-8, JAMES WAS, IN FACT, QUITE A GOOD ATHLETE, ALSO MAKING A NAME FOR HIMSELF IN BASKETBALL AND TRACK-AND-FIELD WHILE AT INDIANA'S FAIRMOUNT HIGH. AND WHILE FILM BUFFS DEBATE WHICH MOVIE-RELATED PHOTOS OF JAMES ARE THE BEST, THERE IS BUT ONE PHOTOGRAPH THAT BRINGS A KNOWING SMILE TO THE FACES OF THE MOST ARDENT BASEBALL FANS. IT'S A TEAM PHOTO IN WHICH JAMES IS FRONT-AND-CENTER ON ONE KNEE, LEANING ON A BAT, ARMS STILL WELL-MUSCLED FROM FARM WORK. AND HE'S WEARING THE GLASSES THAT WERE ABSENT IN HIS LATER FILMS, GLASSES OF WHICH HIS UNCLE MARCUS (WITH WHOM HE LIVED) SAID, "HE SMASHED FIFTEEN PAIR OF 'EM TRYIN' TO BE AN ATHLETE. BREAKIN' 'EM AS FAST AS I COULD GET 'EM." ONE OF THE HIGHLIGHTS OF JAMES' SHORT LIFE RELATED TO BASEBALL. WHILE HITCHHIKING HOME TO FAIRMOUNT FROM NEW YORK IN 1952 WITH SHOW BIZ PALS BILL BAST AND LIZ SHERIDAN, THE THREE WERE PICKED UP BY A RIFLE-TOTING MAN IN AN OLD NASH RAMBLER! AS FATE WOULD HAVE IT, THE DRIVER TURNED OUT TO BE PIRATES CATCHER CLYDE McCULLOUGH ON HIS WAY TO A POST-SEASON EXHIBITION GAME AND HUNTING TRIP. JAMES WAS THRILLED TO TALK BASEBALL WITH CLYDE, AND HE WAS JUST AS EXCITED TO LEARN ABOUT THEIR BURGEONING SHOW BIZ CAREERS. CLYDE DROVE THEM ALL THE WAY TO FAIRMOUNT, NEVER KNOWING THAT ONE OF HIS RIDERS WOULD SOON LIGHT UP THE SILVER SCREEN. AND JAMES WOULD NEVER FORGET HIS "RIDE WITH CLYDE."

Charlie
SHEEN
YEAH, I GOT GAME!
CHARLIE SHEEN WAS ALREADY AN A-LIST HOLLYWOOD STAR BY THE TIME HE SIGNED TO PLAY RICK "WILD THING" VAUGHN IN THE 1989 MOVIE "MAJOR LEAGUE," AND HE'D EVEN GIVEN A SMALL PEEK AT HIS BASEBALL SKILLS THE PREVIOUS YEAR WHEN HE PLAYED HAP FELSCH IN THE FILM "EIGHT MEN OUT," BUT PORTRAYING A FLAME-THROWING RELIEF PITCHER IN "MAJOR LEAGUE" WOULD BE A TRUE TEST OF HIS BALLPLAYING ABILITY!
THE CRITICS WOULD HAVE EATEN HIM ALIVE HAD HE NOT BEEN CONVINCING AS A HARD-THROWING CLOSER! THE MINUTE CHARLIE DELIVERED HIS FIRST PITCH AS RICK VAUGHN, HOWEVER, HE EARNED THE RESPECT OF EVERYONE WHO KNEW THE GAME! THIS WAS NO ANTHONY PERKINS "THROWING LIKE A GIRL" IN THE JIMMY PIERSALL BIO-PIC "FEAR STRIKES OUT!" CHARLIE, INSTEAD, DISPLAYED PERFECT MECHANICS AND A LEGITIMATE MID-80s HEATER! STEVE YEAGER, A FORMER BIG LEAGUE CATCHER AND TECHNICAL ADVISOR ON THE FILM, TOLD THE USA TODAY THAT "CHARLIE COULD BE A PRO PLAYER IF HE WANTED TO." THIS CAME AS NO SURPRISE TO THOSE WHO KNEW CHARLIE WELL -- HE'D BEEN A STAR PITCHER AND SHORTSTOP IN HIGH SCHOOL WITH THE SANTA MONICA VIKINGS!
IN FACT, CHARLIE'S POTENTIAL AS A BALLPLAYER HAD EVEN EARNED HIM SCHOLARSHIP OFFERS TO A FEW COLLEGES, THE UNIVERSITY OF KANSAS BEING ONE OF HIS SUITORS!
PLEEEEEASE COME PLAY FOR US AT KANSAS!
SORRY, SIR, BUT HOLLYWOOD'S CALLIN'!
HOLLYWOOD
AS CHARLIE'S HOLLYWOOD CAREER CONTINUED TO FLOURISH IN THE '90s, SO DID HIS BASEBALL ACTIVITIES -- MOST NOTABLY IN THE FORM OF COLLECTING HIGH-END BASEBALL MEMORABILIA! HIS COLLECTION INCLUDED MANY PRICELESS ARTIFACTS, INCLUDING THE INFAMOUS BALL THAT ROLLED THROUGH BILL BUCKNER'S LEGS IN GAME SIX OF THE 1986 WORLD SERIES! NOW, THROUGH ALL THESE YEARS, CHARLIE HAS GONE TO GREAT LENGTHS TO MAINTAIN HIS BASEBALL SKILLS BY PLAYING REGULARLY WITH CLOSE FRIENDS! A NATURAL RIGHT-HANDED HITTER, CHARLIE TAUGHT HIMSELF TO HIT LEFTY AND WAS FILMED PULLING A BALL OVER THE RIGHTFIELD WALL AT DODGER STADIUM DURING A 2007 BATTING PRACTICE SESSION!
NOT BAD FOR A 41-YEAR-OLD 155-POUNDER!
"I DON'T REGRET NOT CONTINUING WITH BASEBALL, BUT I'LL ALWAYS WONDER," CHARLIE ONCE SAID! DESPITE THE INCREDIBLE CAREER HE'S HAD IN SHOW BUSINESS, A CLOSE FRIEND SAYS CHARLIE "WOULD TRADE IT ALL FOR ONE MAJOR LEAGUE AT-BAT," AND THAT'S AS FINE A TRIBUTE AS YOU WILL EVER HEAR TO THE GREAT GAME OF BASEBALL!
JOYNER ©2011

TONY TODD
TO QUOTE SAM AND DAVE-- HOLD ON, I'M COMIN'!
FANS OF THE 1994 MOVIE "LITTLE BIG LEAGUE" WILL ALWAYS REMEMBER THE CLIMACTIC SCENE WHERE LIGHT-HITTING TWINS SECOND BASEMAN MICKEY SCALES CLOUTED A SEASON-SAVING HOME RUN! PORTRAYING SCALES WAS TONY TODD -- A RARE ACTOR WHO KNEW HIS WAY AROUND A BALLFIELD! AND WHY NOT -- TONY PLAYED COLLEGIATE BASEBALL AT THE UNIVERSITY OF NEW MEXICO! TONY LEARNED ABOUT THE TRYOUTS FOR "LITTLE BIG LEAGUE" AT THE LAST MOMENT! HE RACED HOME, GOT HIS GEAR, RACED BACK TO THE TRYOUTS, THEN BEAT OUT 250 OTHER ACTORS TO WIN THE COVETED ROLE!
TONY HAS MADE THE HIGHLIGHT REEL MORE THAN A FEW TIMES PLAYING IN THE ANNUAL MAJOR LEAGUE BASEBALL CELEBRITY ALL-STAR SOFTBALL GAME!
Dodgers 42
THE GREAT JACKIE ROBINSON-- AWESOME!
TONY HAS SINCE PLAYED MANY VARIED ROLES, BUT HE AGAIN USED HIS BASEBALL SKILLS WHILE PLAYING JACKIE ROBINSON IN A 2005 EPISODE OF "COLD CASE" ON CBS! TONY WAS ALL SET TO PLAY RUNNING BACK AT USC UNTIL SUFFERING A SERIOUS ANKLE INJURY DURING HIS SENIOR YEAR AT SANTA MONICA HIGH (SAMOHI)!
GO VIKINGS!
SAMOHI
TONY STARRED IN BASEBALL AT SAMOHI WHERE ONE OF HIS TEAMMATES WAS CHARLIE SHEEN! CHARLIE AND TONY HAVE BEEN THE BEST OF FRIENDS SINCE THEY WERE EIGHT YEARS OF AGE!
JOYNER ©2011

SPEEDSTERS

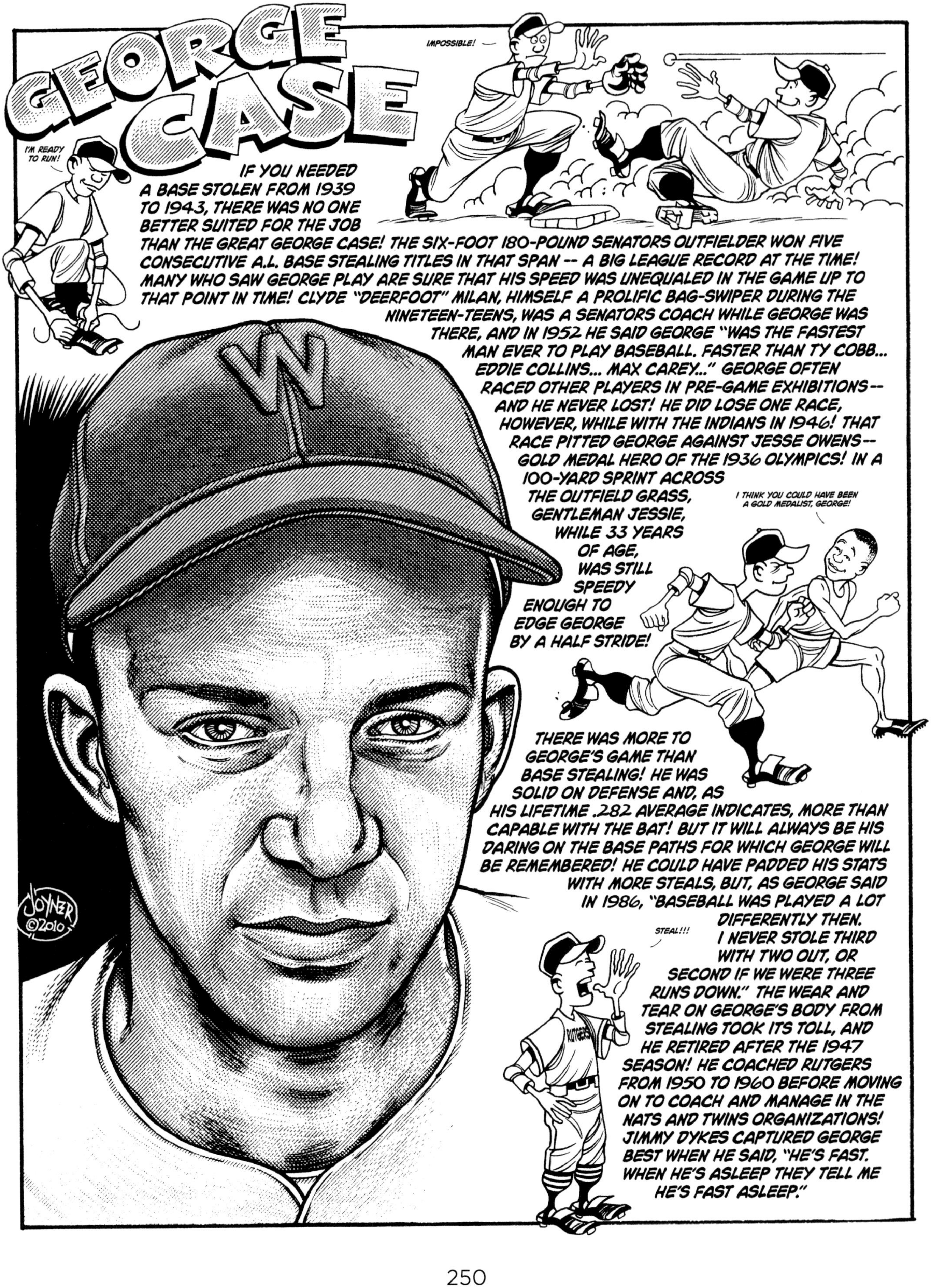
GEORGE CASE
I'M READY TO RUN!
IMPOSSIBLE!
IF YOU NEEDED A BASE STOLEN FROM 1939 TO 1943, THERE WAS NO ONE BETTER SUITED FOR THE JOB THAN THE GREAT GEORGE CASE! THE SIX-FOOT 180-POUND SENATORS OUTFIELDER WON FIVE CONSECUTIVE A.L. BASE STEALING TITLES IN THAT SPAN -- A BIG LEAGUE RECORD AT THE TIME! MANY WHO SAW GEORGE PLAY ARE SURE THAT HIS SPEED WAS UNEQUALED IN THE GAME UP TO THAT POINT IN TIME! CLYDE "DEERFOOT" MILAN, HIMSELF A PROLIFIC BAG-SWIPER DURING THE NINETEEN-TEENS, WAS A SENATORS COACH WHILE GEORGE WAS THERE, AND IN 1952 HE SAID GEORGE "WAS THE FASTEST MAN EVER TO PLAY BASEBALL. FASTER THAN TY COBB... EDDIE COLLINS... MAX CAREY..." GEORGE OFTEN RACED OTHER PLAYERS IN PRE-GAME EXHIBITIONS -- AND HE NEVER LOST! HE DID LOSE ONE RACE, HOWEVER, WHILE WITH THE INDIANS IN 1946! THAT RACE PITTED GEORGE AGAINST JESSE OWENS -- GOLD MEDAL HERO OF THE 1936 OLYMPICS! IN A 100-YARD SPRINT ACROSS THE OUTFIELD GRASS, GENTLEMAN JESSIE, WHILE 33 YEARS OF AGE, WAS STILL SPEEDY ENOUGH TO EDGE GEORGE BY A HALF STRIDE!
I THINK YOU COULD HAVE BEEN A GOLD MEDALIST, GEORGE!
THERE WAS MORE TO GEORGE'S GAME THAN BASE STEALING! HE WAS SOLID ON DEFENSE AND, AS HIS LIFETIME .282 AVERAGE INDICATES, MORE THAN CAPABLE WITH THE BAT! BUT IT WILL ALWAYS BE HIS DARING ON THE BASE PATHS FOR WHICH GEORGE WILL BE REMEMBERED! HE COULD HAVE PADDED HIS STATS WITH MORE STEALS, BUT, AS GEORGE SAID IN 1986, "BASEBALL WAS PLAYED A LOT DIFFERENTLY THEN. I NEVER STOLE THIRD WITH TWO OUT, OR SECOND IF WE WERE THREE RUNS DOWN." THE WEAR AND TEAR ON GEORGE'S BODY FROM STEALING TOOK ITS TOLL, AND HE RETIRED AFTER THE 1947 SEASON! HE COACHED RUTGERS FROM 1950 TO 1960 BEFORE MOVING ON TO COACH AND MANAGE IN THE NATS AND TWINS ORGANIZATIONS! JIMMY DYKES CAPTURED GEORGE BEST WHEN HE SAID, "HE'S FAST. WHEN HE'S ASLEEP THEY TELL ME HE'S FAST ASLEEP."
STEAL!!!
RUTGERS
JOYNER ©2010

MAURY WILLS

ON SEPTEMBER 23, 1962, MAURY WILLS BROKE TY COBB'S 47-YEAR-OLD SINGLE-SEASON RECORD OF 97 STOLEN BASES! BY SEASON'S END HE WOULD TOTAL AN ASTOUNDING 104 STEALS -- IN ADDITION TO COPPING THE N.L. M.V.P. AWARD! MAURY WENT ON TO LEAD THE NATIONAL LEAGUE IN STOLEN BASES FOR SIX STRAIGHT SEASONS, FROM 1960-1965, AND ENDED HIS CAREER WITH A TOTAL OF 585 SWIPES! MAURY WAS A KEY FACTOR WITH THE L.A. DODGERS FOR FOURTEEN YEARS, AND HELPED LEAD THEM TO THREE WORLD SERIES TITLES IN 1959, 1963, AND 1965! IT BEGAN FOR MAURY ON OCTOBER 2, 1932, WHEN HE WAS BORN IN WASHINGTON, D.C.! ONE OF THIRTEEN KIDS BORN TO A BAPTIST PREACHER, MAURY WENT ON TO A TREMENDOUS FOOTBALL AND BASEBALL CAREER AT D.C.'s CARDOZO HIGH SCHOOL! HE SIGNED WITH THE BROOKLYN DODGERS FOR $500 AFTER IMPRESSING THE SCOUTS AT AN OPEN TRYOUT AT GRIFFITH STADIUM! A FEW YEARS LATER, MAURY WAS OFF AND RUNNING IN THE BIGS, REVOLUTIONIZING THE FINE ART OF BASE STEALING! IT CAME FULL CIRCLE FOR HIM ON MARCH 25, 2009, WHEN CARDOZO HIGH RECHRISTENED THEIR PARK IN HIS HONOR BY CHANGING ITS NAME TO "MAURY WILLS FIELD." IN FACT, THE ENTIRE CITY OF WASHINGTON CELEBRATED MAURY'S LEGACY AS D.C. MAYOR ADRIAN M. FENTY OFFICIALLY DECLARED THE DATE TO BE "MAURY WILLS DAY." MAURY WAS THERE, AND HE WAS OBVIOUSLY MOVED BY THE CEREMONY! "WHEN I THINK OF THIS," SAID MAURY, "I THINK OF THE FACT THAT I CAME FROM NO SHOES IN PARKSIDE IN THE PROJECTS ALL THE WAY TO WHERE WE ARE TODAY. THAT'S A LOT OF PROGRESS. I'M KIND OF EMOTIONAL RIGHT NOW. I REALLY APPRECIATE THIS. I'VE BEEN ASKED SO MANY TIMES, 'WHAT'S YOUR GREATEST THRILL IN THE GAME, MAURY?' I'M EXPERIENCING IT TODAY."

Bob DILLINGER

ROBERT BERNARD DILLINGER WAS BORN ON SEPTEMBER 17, 1918, IN GLENDALE, CALIFORNIA! GIFTED WITH BLAZING SPEED, BOB SPED TO SUCCESS AS A THREE-SPORT STAR ATHLETE AT GLENDALE HIGH SCHOOL! BOB ACCEPTED A FOOTBALL SCHOLARSHIP TO THE UNIVERSITY OF IDAHO, BUT A TWICE-BROKEN COLLARBONE MADE THE SLENDER SPEEDSTER TURN HIS ATTENTION TO BASEBALL! BOB'S DECISION TO FOCUS ON BASEBALL QUICKLY PROVED TO BE A GOOD ONE WHEN HE WAS SIGNED BY THE ST. LOUIS BROWNS IN 1939! SADDLED WITH GLASSES FOR AS LONG AS HE COULD REMEMBER, BOB OVERCAME THE HANDICAP AND DEVELOPED A GREAT BATTING EYE! HE HIT .314 IN HIS FIRST YEAR OF PRO BALL WITH LINCOLN IN '39 AND STOLE AN ASTOUNDING 67 BAGS! BOB HIT .312 WITH YOUNGSTOWN IN 1940 AND AGAIN SWIPED 67 PILLOWS!

BOB POSTED SOLID YEARS AT SAN ANTONIO AND TOLEDO IN 1941 AND '42! ALL SET TO BREAK INTO THE MAJORS IN 1943, BOB INSTEAD SPENT 1943-45 IN THE ARMY AIR FORCE! WHILE IN THE SERVICE BOB PLAYED BASEBALL ALL OVER THE SOUTH PACIFIC ON SOME OF THE BEST A.A.F. TEAMS EVER PUT TOGETHER! BOB OUTPLAYED COUNTLESS BIG LEAGUERS, JOE DIMAGGIO INCLUDED, AND WAS ULTIMATELY NAMED "THE PLAYER OF THE PACIFIC"! BOB JOINED THE BIG LEAGUE BROWNS IN 1946 AND HIT A RESPECTABLE .280, BUT HE REALLY HIT HIS STRIDE THE NEXT SEASON WHEN HE BATTED .294 WHILE LEADING THE LEAGUE IN STEALS WITH 34! HE WAS EVEN BETTER IN '48 WHEN HE HIT .321 WITH A LEAGUE LEADING 207 HITS AND 28 STEALS! 1949 SAW BOB CONTINUE HIS GREAT PLAY AS HE LEAD THE LOOP IN STEALS FOR THE THIRD STRAIGHT SEASON WHILE BATTING .324 AND BEING NAMED TO THE ALL-STAR TEAM! BOB WAS DEALT TO THE ATHLETICS IN 1950, AND EVENTUALLY PLAYED FOR THE PIRATES AND WHITE SOX THROUGH THE CONCLUSION OF THE 1951 CAMPAIGN!

BOB WAS WITH THE SACRAMENTO SOLONS OF THE PCL FROM 1952-55, BUT HE PROVED HE STILL HAD A BIG LEAGUE STICK WHEN HE LED THE COAST IN HITTING WITH A .366 AVERAGE IN 1953!

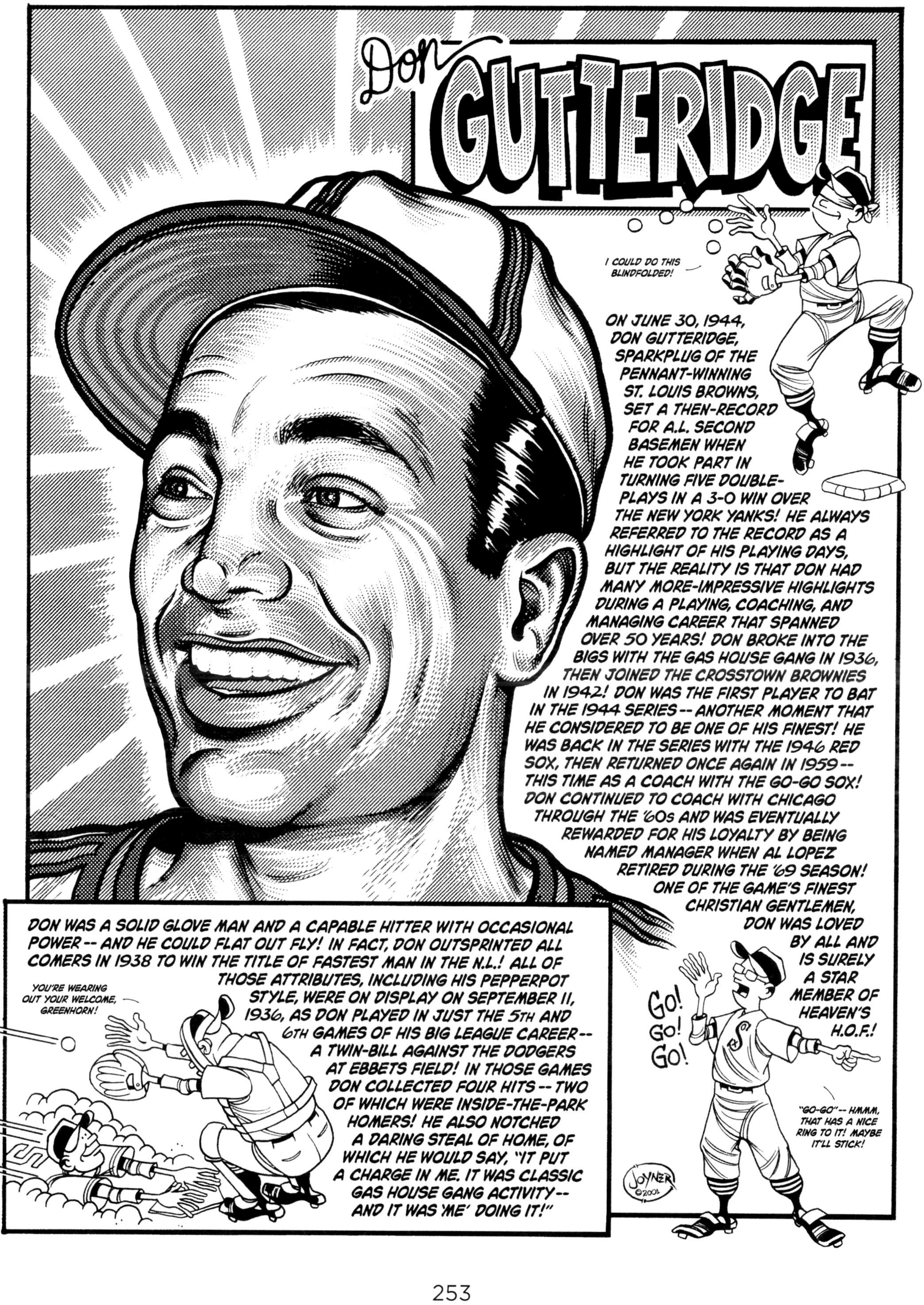
Don
GUTTERIDGE
I COULD DO THIS BLINDFOLDED!
ON JUNE 30, 1944, DON GUTTERIDGE, SPARKPLUG OF THE PENNANT-WINNING ST. LOUIS BROWNS, SET A THEN-RECORD FOR A.L. SECOND BASEMEN WHEN HE TOOK PART IN TURNING FIVE DOUBLE-PLAYS IN A 3-0 WIN OVER THE NEW YORK YANKS! HE ALWAYS REFERRED TO THE RECORD AS A HIGHLIGHT OF HIS PLAYING DAYS, BUT THE REALITY IS THAT DON HAD MANY MORE-IMPRESSIVE HIGHLIGHTS DURING A PLAYING, COACHING, AND MANAGING CAREER THAT SPANNED OVER 50 YEARS! DON BROKE INTO THE BIGS WITH THE GAS HOUSE GANG IN 1936, THEN JOINED THE CROSSTOWN BROWNIES IN 1942! DON WAS THE FIRST PLAYER TO BAT IN THE 1944 SERIES -- ANOTHER MOMENT THAT HE CONSIDERED TO BE ONE OF HIS FINEST! HE WAS BACK IN THE SERIES WITH THE 1946 RED SOX, THEN RETURNED ONCE AGAIN IN 1959 -- THIS TIME AS A COACH WITH THE GO-GO SOX! DON CONTINUED TO COACH WITH CHICAGO THROUGH THE '60s AND WAS EVENTUALLY REWARDED FOR HIS LOYALTY BY BEING NAMED MANAGER WHEN AL LOPEZ RETIRED DURING THE '69 SEASON! ONE OF THE GAME'S FINEST CHRISTIAN GENTLEMEN, DON WAS LOVED BY ALL AND IS SURELY A STAR MEMBER OF HEAVEN'S H.O.F.!
DON WAS A SOLID GLOVE MAN AND A CAPABLE HITTER WITH OCCASIONAL POWER -- AND HE COULD FLAT OUT FLY! IN FACT, DON OUTSPRINTED ALL COMERS IN 1938 TO WIN THE TITLE OF FASTEST MAN IN THE N.L.! ALL OF THOSE ATTRIBUTES, INCLUDING HIS PEPPERPOT STYLE, WERE ON DISPLAY ON SEPTEMBER 11, 1936, AS DON PLAYED IN JUST THE 5TH AND 6TH GAMES OF HIS BIG LEAGUE CAREER -- A TWIN-BILL AGAINST THE DODGERS AT EBBETS FIELD! IN THOSE GAMES DON COLLECTED FOUR HITS -- TWO OF WHICH WERE INSIDE-THE-PARK HOMERS! HE ALSO NOTCHED A DARING STEAL OF HOME, OF WHICH HE WOULD SAY, "IT PUT A CHARGE IN ME. IT WAS CLASSIC GAS HOUSE GANG ACTIVITY -- AND IT WAS 'ME' DOING IT!"
YOU'RE WEARING OUT YOUR WELCOME, GREENHORN!
GO! GO! GO!
"GO-GO" -- HMMM, THAT HAS A NICE RING TO IT! MAYBE IT'LL STICK!
JOYNER ©2001

Ralph GARR

BORN ON DECEMBER 12, 1945, RALPH ALLEN GARR WAS ONE OF THE LEGITIMATE HITTING STARS OF THE 1970s! NICKNAMED "THE ROADRUNNER" BECAUSE OF HIS BLAZING SPEED, RALPH BUSTED OUT WITH A MONSTER YEAR IN HIS FIRST SEASON AS A REGULAR WHEN HE HIT .343 WITH 219 HITS IN 1971! "I'VE ALWAYS BEEN ABLE TO HIT A LITTLE BIT WHEREVER I WAS," RALPH UNDERSTATEDLY TOLD JACK WILKINSON IN HIS 2007 BOOK, "GAME OF MY LIFE: ATLANTA BRAVES." CONTINUING, RALPH SAID, "I WON BATTING TITLES IN THE DOMINICAN REPUBLIC, TOO, IN 1969 AND '70 WHEN I PLAYED WINTER BALL THERE. I HIT .400 ONE YEAR." ONCE A GRAMBLING UNIVERSITY FOOTBALL STAR, RALPH'S GRIDIRON SPEED WAS KEY TO HIS ABILITY LEG OUT INFIELD HITS THAT WOULD BE EASY OUTS FOR MERE MORTALS! ALSO KEY, HOWEVER, WAS THE PIECE OF LUMBER WIELDED BY THE 5-FOOT-ELEVEN-INCH, 197-POUND, LEFT-HANDED SWINGER FROM MONROE, LOUISIANA! "I USED A BIG BAT," RALPH RECALLED. WAVING HIS 36-INCH 38-OUNCE CLUB, RALPH WOULD SIMPLY "MAKE CONTACT, THEN JUST USE MY SPEED."

RALPH BLISTERED NATIONAL LEAGUE PITCHING THROUGH THE 1975 SEASON, THEN GAVE THE SAME TREATMENT TO THE AMERICAN LEAGUE HURLERS WHEN THE BRAVES DEALT HIM TO THE WHITE SOX PRIOR TO THE 1976 CAMPAIGN! WHILE KNOWN MAINLY FOR HIS ABILITY TO HIT SINGLES, DOUBLES AND TRIPLES TO ALL FIELDS, RALPH COULD OCCASIONALLY MUSCLE-UP AND GO DEEP! IN FACT, THE LONG-BALL IS RESPONSIBLE FOR ONE OF RALPH'S ALL-TIME HIGHLIGHTS! "I HIT A COUPLE OF HOME RUNS AGAINST THE METS AT FULTON COUNTY STADIUM. I HIT A HOMER OFF TOM SEAVER IN THE 8TH OR 9TH INNING TO TIE THE GAME, AND THEN I HIT ONE IN THE 13TH INNING OFF RON TAYLOR TO WIN IT. THAT WAS JUST SOMETHING THAT MADE ME PROUD." ANOTHER THING RALPH SHOULD BE PROUD OF IS HIS FINE WORK AS A SCOUT FOR THE BRAVES. HE WAS RECENTLY HONORED WITH THE BUCK O'NEIL PROFESSIONAL SCOUTS AND COACHES ASSOCIATION MAN OF THE YEAR AWARD!

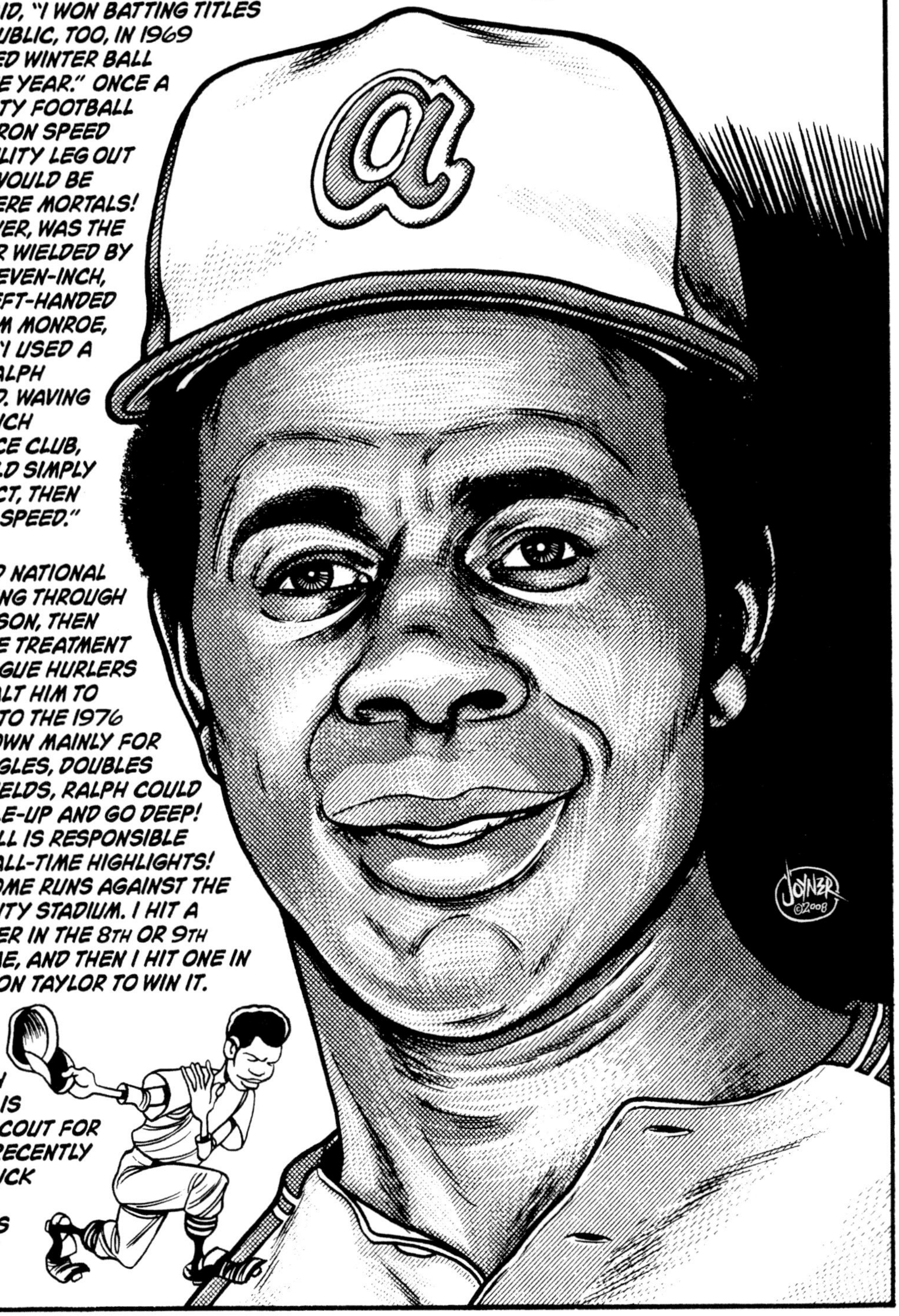

AMOS OTIS

AMOS HAD FOUR HITS AND FIVE STOLEN BASES IN A 4-3 ROYALS WIN OVER THE BREWERS ON SEPTEMBER 7, 1971!

BORN AND RAISED IN MOBILE, ALABAMA, 10-YEAR-OLD AMOS JOSEPH OTIS WAS A BALLPLAYER AHEAD OF HIS YEARS AS HE PLAYED ON TEAMS WITH 18-YEAR-OLDS! HE HAD LEGIONS OF SCOUTS FOLLOWING HIS EVERY MOVE BY THE TIME HE WAS IN HIGH SCHOOL, SO HE SIGNED WITH THE RED SOX IN 1965! LEFT UNPROTECTED, THE METS DRAFTED AMOS AWAY FROM THE SOX, AND HE SAW SOME LIMITED ACTION WITH THE AMAZINS IN '67 AND '69! THEN ON DECEMBER 3, 1969, WHILE WATCHING THE 'TODAY SHOW,' AMOS HEARD JOE GARAGIOLA ANNOUNCE THAT HE HAD BEEN TRADED TO THE KANSAS CITY ROYALS FOR JOEY FOY! "I WENT FROM THE TEAM THAT HAD WON THE WORLD SERIES TO AN EXPANSION TEAM THAT HAD JUST FINISHED ITS FIRST SEASON." THE DEAL TURNED OUT TO BE ONE OF THE BEST IN ROYALS HISTORY, AND ONE OF THE WORST THE METS EVER MADE! FOY WAS QUICKLY OUT OF THE GAME, AND AMOS WENT ON TO STAR IN THE KANSAS CITY OUTFIELD FOR 14 YEARS! AMOS WAS A LEGIT 5-TOOL PLAYER --VERY STYLISH WITH AN ENIGMATIC PERSONALITY THAT SOMETIMES LEFT HIM MISUNDERSTOOD BY THE MEDIA! ROYALS FANS LOVED HIM, THOUGH, CHEERING HIM ON WITH CHANTS OF "A-O, A-O!" AMOS WAS JUST THE SECOND ROYALS ALL-STAR, AND IT WAS HIS PERFECT STRIKE TO RAY FOSSE THAT SET THE STAGE FOR THE INFAMOUS 12TH-INNING HOME PLATE COLLISION BETWEEN FOSSE AND A HARD-CHARGING PETE ROSE! AMOS WAS TWICE A .300-HITTER, WHILE CLOUTING 193 CAREER LONG BALLS! HE WAS A MAINSTAY OF FOUR ROYALS DIVISION WINNERS, AND LED ALL HITTERS IN THE 1980 WORLD SERIES WITH ELEVEN SAFETIES!

"I TOOK THE MOST PRIDE IN MY BASE STEALING," AMOS OFTEN SAYS. "I MADE BETS WITH MY TEAMMATES THAT I COULD STEAL SECOND STANDING UP. WE'D BET DINNER WITH ALL THE TRIMMINGS. THEN I'D STEAL A BASE AND WIPE THE DUST OFF MY SHOES. I USUALLY COULD DO THAT WHEN I WANTED TO."

Buddy
BLAIR
2008 MARKED THE 75TH ANNIVERSARY OF LOUISIANA STATE UNIVERSITY'S FIRST NATIONAL CHAMPIONSHIP IN TRACK AND FIELD! THE 1933 TITLE HELPED LAY THE FOUNDATION FOR LSU TO BECOME ONE OF THE ELITE COLLEGIATE TRACK AND FIELD PROGRAMS-- A DISTINCTION THAT CONTINUES TO THIS DAY! IN WINNING THE '33 TITLE, THE 5-MAN LSU SQUAD HAD TO UPSET THE MUCH LARGER AND HEAVILY-FAVORED TEAM FROM USC! A KEY MAN MAN FOR THE TIGERS WAS LOUIS NATHAN "BUDDY" BLAIR, A GREAT ALL-AROUND TRACK STAR WHOSE JAVELIN THROWS HELPED SECURE GLORY FOR LSU! BY 1936 BUDDY WAS TRAINING FOR THE OLYMPICS IN GERMANY WHERE HE WAS TO COMPETE IN THE DECATHALON, BUT HE ENDED HIS TRACK CAREER BY SIGNING TO PLAY BASEBALL WITH THE YANKEES!
PARDON MY DUST, LITTLE FELLER!
THE YANKS WERE EXCITED BY BUDDY'S SPEED, SLICK FIELDING, AND POTENT BAT, SO HE WAS SENT TO THE MINORS WHERE HE WOULD BE GROOMED TO ONE DAY REPLACE FRANKIE CROSETTI!
AFTER FINE SEASONS WITH NORFOLK, OAKLAND, AND BINGHAMPTON IN 1936-37, BUDDY WAS PROMOTED TO NEWARK IN 1938! HE WAS OFF TO A FAST START WHEN HE SUFFERED A DEVASTATING KNEE INJURY IN A COLLISION WITH BEARS TEAMMATE JIMMY GLEESON! THE INJURY ROBBED BUDDY OF HIS SPEED -- BUT NOT HIS DREAM OF MAKING IT TO THE BIGS! HE BATTLED THROUGH SURGERIES, PAIN, AND TOUGH TIMES, BUT HE FINALLY MADE IT TO THE MAJORS WITH THE 1942 PHILADELPHIA ATHLETICS! BUDDY WAS MOVED TO THIRD BASE TO HELP COMPENSATE FOR HIS DAMAGED KNEE, AND HE DELIVERED A FINE SEASON FOR THE A's, BATTING .279 WITH FIVE HOMERS AND 66 RUNS DRIVEN IN! 1943 HELD EVEN MORE PROMISE, BUT BUDDY OPTED TO THROW IN WITH THE WORLD WAR II EFFORT BY JOINING THE AIR FORCE! BUDDY KNEW HE WAS FINISHED AS A BIG LEAGUER UPON HIS DISCHARGE FROM THE SERVICE IN 1945, BUT BASEBALL WAS STILL IN HIS BONES, SO HE RETURNED TO THE MINORS AS A PLAYER-MANAGER FOR MANY YEARS! HE THEN BEGAN A SUCCESSFUL 18-YEAR CAREER IN THE SPORTING GOODS BUSINESS -- ALL WHILE BEING A DEVOTED HUSBAND AND FATHER!
BUDDY IS A SPORTS LEGEND DOWN IN LOUISIANA, AND WAS ENSHRINED IN THE STATE'S SPORTS HALL OF FAME IN 1981! ASIDE FROM HIS TRACK AND BASEBALL EXPLOITS, BUDDY WAS A TREMENDOUS BASKETBALL PLAYER, LEADING LSU TO A NATIONAL TITLE IN 1935! BUDDY'S LEGEND REMAINS RELEVANT TODAY THANKS TO A YEARLY ATHLETIC SCHOLARSHIP BEARING HIS NAME!
BUDDY BLAIR
LOUISIANA SPORTS HALL OF FAME
JOYNER ©2008

SPOOK
Jacobs
I ALWAYS WANTED TO BE A STEAL WORKER!
DESIPITE FINISHING FOURTH IN THE A.L. IN STOLEN BASES AS A ROOKIE IN 1954, FORREST VANDERGRIFT JACOBS WAS MUCH MORE THAN A BAG-SWIPING SPECIALIST! TRAPPED IN THE BROOKLYN DODGERS' TALENT-LOADED MINOR LEAGUE SYSTEM, FORREST PROVED HE BELONGED IN THE BIG LEAGUES BY PILING UP YEAR AFTER YEAR OF TREMENDOUS HITTING, FIELDING, AND BASE-STEALING ACCOMPLISHMENTS -- BUT STILL HE NEVER GOT CALLED TO BROOKLYN! NOTING THAT FORREST HAD A "SPOOKY" ABILITY TO FLARE HITS JUST OVER THE OUTSTRETCHED GLOVES OF OPPOSITION INFIELDERS, ONE CLEVER SCRIBE NICKNAMED HIM "SPOOK" IN '47! THE NAME STUCK, AND HAS SINCE BEEN A SOURCE OF ENDLESS SPECULATION BY CURIOUS FANS! SPOOK MORE THAN MADE UP FOR HIS LACK OF SIZE (5'-8" 150-LBS) BY PLAYING WITH A TENACITY THAT OCCASIONALLY LED TO BRAWLS -- LIKE THE LEGENDARY 1957 DONNYBROOK THAT SAW SPOOK TAKE ON THE ENTIRE LOS ANGELES ANGELS INFIELD AFTER BEING BEANED BY ANGELS LEFT-HANDER TOMMY LASORDA! NOT ONLY WAS SPOOK A STAR AT EVERY LEVEL OF THE MINORS, HE WAS ALSO A SENSATION DURING NINE SEASONS OF LATIN AND CARIBBEAN WINTER BALL, AND IS NOW ENSHRINED IN THE CUBAN BASEBALL HALL OF FAME! SPOOK'S BIG LEAGUE CAREER MAY HAVE BEEN BRIEF (1954-56), BUT HE PLAYED EVERY INNING OF A 14-SEASON PRO CAREER, NO MATTER WHAT LEVEL, WITH MAJOR LEAGUE HUSTLE AND INTENSITY! NOW THAT'S SPOOKY!
EASY, SPOOK, I JUST ATE A BIG DISH OF LINGUINI AND CLAM SAUCE BEFORE THE GAME!
JOYNER ©2001
SPOOK IS A PILLAR OF HIS DELAWARE COMMUNITY! HE AND HIS WIFE, BOBBIE, OWNED THE MILFORD BUS CENTER FOR 17 YEARS, AND THEN OWNED A MR. DONUT SHOP FOR 25 YEARS! BOTH PLACES WERE TREASURED GATHERING PLACES FOR THE FOLKS OF MILFORD, AND SPOOK AND BOBBIE WERE FRIENDS TO ALL!
HMMMM... I THINK I HAVE A GOOD IDEA!
DONUT

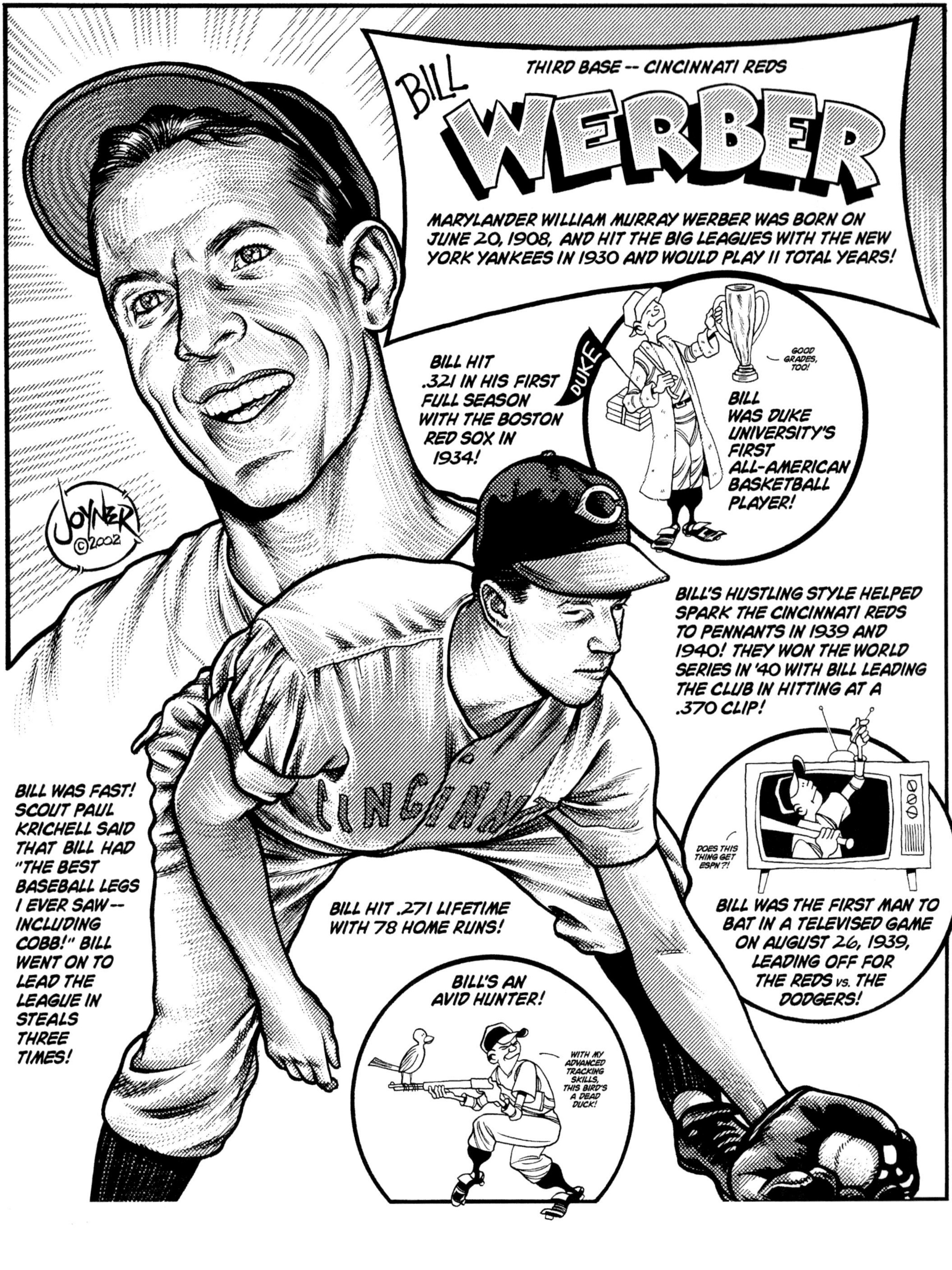
THIRD BASE -- CINCINNATI REDS
BILL WERBER
MARYLANDER WILLIAM MURRAY WERBER WAS BORN ON JUNE 20, 1908, AND HIT THE BIG LEAGUES WITH THE NEW YORK YANKEES IN 1930 AND WOULD PLAY 11 TOTAL YEARS!
BILL HIT .321 IN HIS FIRST FULL SEASON WITH THE BOSTON RED SOX IN 1934!
DUKE
GOOD GRADES, TOO!
BILL WAS DUKE UNIVERSITY'S FIRST ALL-AMERICAN BASKETBALL PLAYER!
JOYNER ©2002
BILL'S HUSTLING STYLE HELPED SPARK THE CINCINNATI REDS TO PENNANTS IN 1939 AND 1940! THEY WON THE WORLD SERIES IN '40 WITH BILL LEADING THE CLUB IN HITTING AT A .370 CLIP!
BILL WAS FAST! SCOUT PAUL KRICHELL SAID THAT BILL HAD "THE BEST BASEBALL LEGS I EVER SAW -- INCLUDING COBB!" BILL WENT ON TO LEAD THE LEAGUE IN STEALS THREE TIMES!
DOES THIS THING GET ESPN?!
BILL HIT .271 LIFETIME WITH 78 HOME RUNS!
BILL WAS THE FIRST MAN TO BAT IN A TELEVISED GAME ON AUGUST 26, 1939, LEADING OFF FOR THE REDS vs. THE DODGERS!
BILL'S AN AVID HUNTER!
WITH MY ADVANCED TRACKING SKILLS, THIS BIRD'S A DEAD DUCK!

Burt Shotton

LONG BEFORE HIS NAME BECAME FOREVER LINKED WITH THE ICONIC BRANCH RICKEY, BURT SHOTTON CARVED OUT A FINE CAREER AS A SPEEDY, BASE-STEALING OUTFIELDER, SPANNING THE YEARS 1909 THROUGH 1923! BURT DIVIDED HIS PLAYING DAYS BETWEEN ST. LOUIS' TWO BIG LEAGUE CLUBS -- THE BROWNS AND THE CARDINALS -- SANDWICHED AROUND ONE SEASON WITH THE SENATORS IN 1918! BURT PLAYED IN 1,387 GAMES AND HIT A RESPECTABLE .271 FOR HIS CAREER, BUT HE WAS REALISTIC ABOUT HIS ABILITY! "I WAS A LEATHER MAN AND LEG HITTER," BURT USED TO SAY, MEANING IT WAS HIS EXCELLENT FIELDING AND SPEED ON THE BASES FOR WHICH HE WAS PAID! BRANCH RICKEY, IN HIS FIRST YEAR MANAGING THE CARDINALS IN 1919, RECOGNIZED BURT'S SKILL ON THE BALLFIELD, BUT HE ALSO SAW SHOTTON'S FUTURE POTENTIAL AS A MANAGER -- SO HE BROUGHT BURT TO THE CARDS THAT SEASON! RICKEY IMMEDIATELY NAMED BURT THE TEAM'S CAPTAIN, THEN ASSIGNED HIM THE DUTY OF MANAGING THE BALLCLUB ON SUNDAYS SINCE RICKEY HAD LONG AGO MADE A RELIGIOUS COMMITMENT NOT TO ATTEND SUNDAY GAMES! "THEY CALLED ME A SUNDAY MANAGER," BURT SAID, "BUT THAT'S NOT AN ACCURATE DESCRIPTION. RICK WAS STILL THE MANAGER. I MERELY FOLLOWED HIS INSTRUCTIONS." AFTER YEARS OF MANAGERIAL DUES-PAYING IN THE MINORS, AS WELL AS DEAD-END BIG LEAGUE PLACES LIKE PHILLY (N.L.), BURT'S LIFE CHANGED FOREVER WHEN, ON THE EVE OF THE 1947 OPENER, HE RECEIVED A CRYPTIC TELEGRAM FROM HIS OLD PAL BRANCH RICKEY -- THEN THE GENERAL MANAGER OF THE BROOKLYN DODGERS! "BE IN BROOKLYN IN THE MORNING," STATED THE WIRE. "CALL NOBODY, SEE NO ONE." AS IT TURNED OUT, POPULAR DODGERS MANAGER LEO DUROCHER WAS TO BE SUSPENDED FOR A YEAR, AND RICKEY WANTED BURT TO STEP IN FOR HIM -- WHICH BURT DID! IT WAS A TUMULTUOUS YEAR FOR THE DODGERS DUE THE ADDED RACIAL TENSION OF IT BEING JACKIE ROBINSON'S ROOKIE SEASON, BUT BURT'S MELLOW DEMEANOR WAS A CALMING INFLUENCE, AND BEHIND HIS LEADERSHIP THE DODGERS WENT ON TO WIN THE NATIONAL LEAGUE PENNANT! BURT GLADLY STEPPED DOWN THE NEXT YEAR WHEN "THE LIP" RETURNED TO BROOKLYN, BUT SHOTTON STEPPED RIGHT BACK INTO THE HOT SEAT LATER THAT SEASON WHEN LEO WAS SENT ACROSS THE HARLEM RIVER TO MANAGE THE GIANTS! BURT LED THE BROOKS TO ONE MORE PENNANT, BUT WAS FORCED OUT AS SKIPPER FOLLOWING THE '50 SEASON WHEN WALTER O'MALLEY TOOK OVER THE DODGERS!

ON MAY 15, 1918, THE SENATORS NEEDED 18 INNINGS TO BEAT THE WHITE SOX 1-0! BURT, PLAYING RIGHTFIELD THAT DAY, DID NOT HAVE A SINGLE FIELDING CHANCE -- TRULY AN AMAZING FEAT! "FIFTEEN YEARS AS A BIG LEAGUER, AND THE BEST I COULD DO WAS STRICTLY A NEGATIVE," LAMENTED BURT! "WHAT A FEELING OF FRUSTRATION COMES OVER ME WHEN I THINK OF THAT."

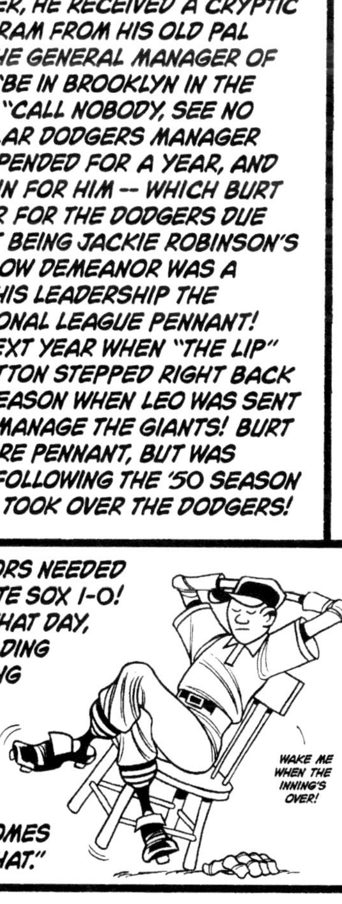

COOL COUPLINGS

George ALTMAN

AFTER FLYING SOMEWHAT UNDER THE NATIONAL RADAR DURING 1959 AND 1960 -- HIS FIRST TWO SEASONS IN THE MAJORS -- CUBBIE CENTERFIELDER GEORGE ALTMAN BECAME KNOWN COAST TO COAST WITH AN ALL-STAR SEASON IN 1961 THAT SAW HIM SMASH 27 HOMERS WITH 97 RBIs AND A .303 AVERAGE! FORMERLY A HOOPS STAR AT TENNESSEE A&I, GEORGE USED HIS ATHLETICISM TO TRANSITION INTO A FINE BIG LEAGUE BALLHAWK AND BATSMAN! HIS "PARALLEL SWING, KNOWLEDGE OF THE STRIKE ZONE, ABILITY TO HIT TO ALL FIELDS, AND POWER" LED TY COBB TO CALL GEORGE "A NATURAL HITTER" AFTER SEEING HIM PLAY AS A ROOKIE IN THE SPRING OF 1959! NEGRO LEAGUE LEGEND BUCK O'NEIL WAS MANAGING THE KANSAS CITY MONARCHS IN 1955 AND GAVE GEORGE HIS FIRST BIG BREAK BY SIGNING THE KID TO PLAY FOR HIM! O'NEIL JOINED THE CUBS ORGANIZATION THE NEXT YEAR, AND ONE OF THE FIRST THINGS HE DID WAS RECOMMEND THAT CHICAGO SIGN GEORGE! "BUCK MADE AN IMPACT ON ME," SAID GEORGE. "WITH THAT BIG VOICE, HE WAS QUITE AN INSPIRATIONAL GUY."

Buck O'NEIL

BORN ON NOVEMBER 13, 1911, IN RURAL CURRABELLE, FLORIDA, JOHN JORDAN "BUCK" O'NEIL ENJOYED A LIFE-LONG LOVE AFFAIR WITH BASEBALL THAT HE BEGAN AS A CLUTCH-HITTING, SMOOTH-FIELDING FIRST BASEMAN WITH THE NEGRO LEAGUE KANSAS CITY MONARCHS FROM THE LATE-'30s THROUGH THE MID-'50s! BUCK BECAME THE FIRST BLACK COACH IN THE BIG LEAGUES WHEN HE JOINED THE STAFF OF THE 1962 CUBS! DESPITE THE FACT THAT HE WAS DENIED THE CHANCE TO PLAY IN THE MAJORS DUE TO THE SEGREGATION OF THE GAME DURING HIS PRIME, BUCK WAS NEVER BITTER! HE SUMMED UP HIS LOVE OF THE GAME BY SAYING, "IT'S A RELIGION FOR ME. IT TAUGHT ME TO ABIDE BY THE RULES. IT CAN BRING YOU UP, BUT IT CAN BRING YOU DOWN, TOO. BUT ONE THING -- THERE ALWAYS WILL BE A TOMORROW. YOU GOT ME TODAY, BUT I'M COMING BACK."

Al LaMacchia

AL SERVED IN THE U.S. ARMY DURING WORLD WAR II!

ALFRED ANTHONY LaMACCHIA WAS BORN ON JULY 22, 1921, IN ST. LOUIS! NEARLY 22 YEARS LATER, AL, BY THEN A HIGHLY REGARDED RIGHT-HANDED PITCHING PROSPECT, MADE HIS BIG LEAGUE DEBUT WITH HIS HOMETOWN AMERICAN LEAGUE TEAM -- THE 1943 ST. LOUIS BROWNS! AL SPENT MUCH OF 1944 WITH BROWNIE FARM TEAM TOLEDO! HE TURNED IN A FINE SEASON FOR THE MUD HENS, WINNING 12 AND LOSING JUST 3, BUT ST. LOUIS HAD A SOLID PITCHING STAFF IN '44, SO DESPITE BEING WITH THE BROWNIES AT THE BEGINNING AND END OF THE CAMPAIGN, AL NEVER GOT A SHOT TO PITCH WITH THE A.L. PENNANT WINNERS -- BUT HE'LL PROUDLY TELL YOU THAT HE THREW BATTING PRACTICE DURING THE WORLD SERIES! OVERALL, AL APPEARED IN JUST 16 MAJOR LEAGUE GAMES, BUT HE RECORDED A FINE CAREER IN THE MINORS THAT RAN FROM 1939 THROUGH 1954, INCLUDING A 20-WIN SEASON AT WICHITA FALLS IN 1952! AL BEGAN SCOUTING FOR THE PHILLIES IN 1956, THUS BEGINNING A LONG AND SUCCESSFUL CAREER THAT CONTINUES TO THIS DAY WITH THE DODGERS! AL'S EYE FOR TALENT IS AS SHARP AS EVER, TOO, HAVING RECENTLY DELIVERED A PLUM PRODUCT IN OUTFIELDER ANDRE ETHIER!

Andre Ethier

BORN ON APRIL 10, 1982, ANDRE ETHIER HAS BEEN A STAR FOR THE DODGERS SINCE HE BROKE IN WITH THEM IN 2006! HE PLAYED HIS COLLEGE BALL AT ARIZONA STATE AND WAS DRAFTED BY THE ATHLETICS IN 2003, BUT WAS STUCK IN THE OAKLAND FARM SYSTEM WHEN AL LaMACCHIA CONVINCED THE DODGER BRASS TO TRADE FOR ANDRE! ACCORDING TO BILL PLASCHKE OF THE L.A. TIMES, AL LOGGED "THOUSANDS OF MILES IN HIS OLD FORD, AND PAGES OF SCRIBBLING IN HIS LITTLE BLACK DATE BOOK" TO WATCH ANDRE! 84-YEAR-OLD AL WAS SO TAKEN WITH ANDRE'S RAW ABILITY THAT THE OLD SCOUT BEGAN TO SHOUT COACHING TIPS TO A MYSTIFIED YOUNG ETHIER. "I THOUGHT HE WAS JUST SOME CRAZY OLD MAN YELLING AT ME FROM THE STANDS," SAID ANDRE, "BUT I REALLY CAME TO RESPECT HIM AND LISTEN TO HIM. IN THE END, I'M A DODGER BECAUSE OF THAT CRAZY OLD MAN. I CAN'T THANK HIM ENOUGH." FOR AL, MORE SUCCESS FOR ANDRE IS THANKS ENOUGH!

Eddie BRINKMAN

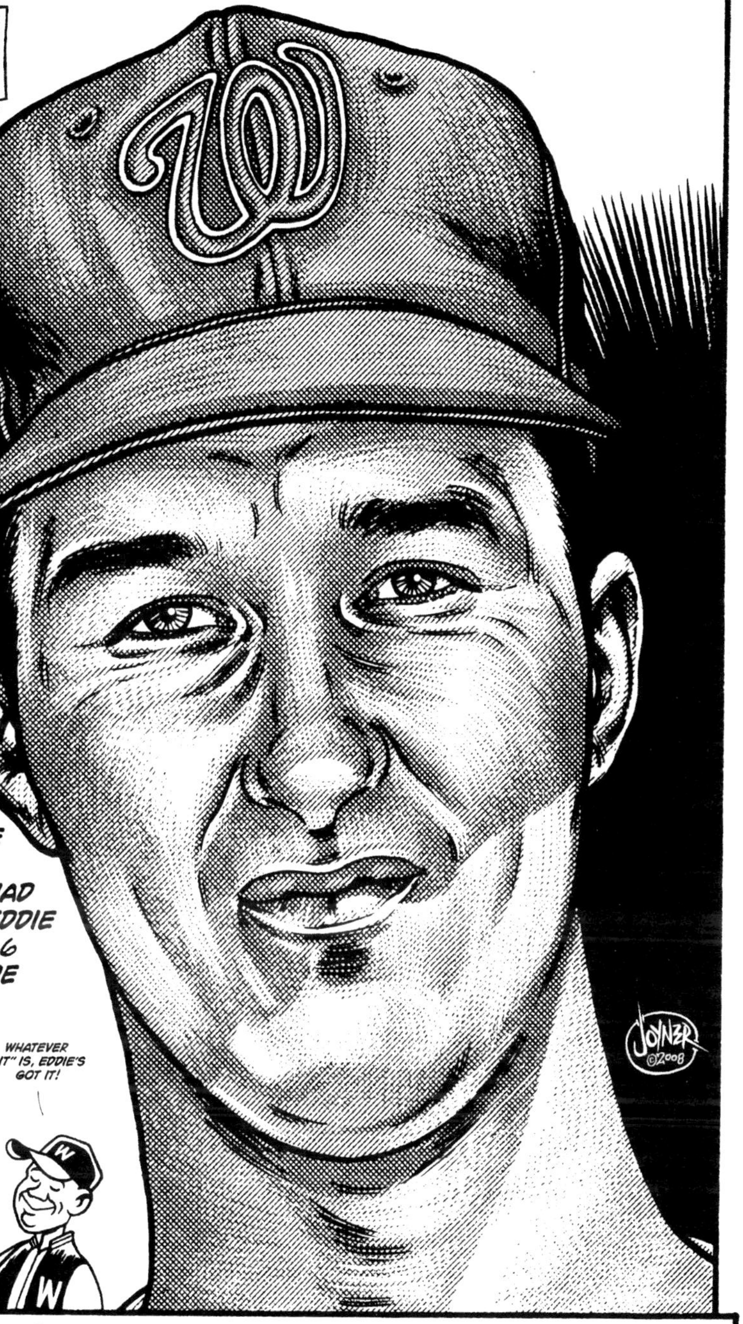

BY SEPTEMBER OF 1961, WITH THEIR INFIELD PERFORMING POORLY, THE EXPANSION WASHINGTON SENATORS PROMOTED THEIR $60,000 BONUS BABY THIRD-SACKER TO SOLIDIFY THE DEFENSE! BORN EDWIN ALBERT BRINKMAN ON DECEMBER 8, 1941, IN CINCINNATI, OHIO, EDDIE HAD BEEN A HIGH SCHOOL PHENOM PRIOR TO GOING PRO, EVEN OUTSHINING TEAMMATE PETE ROSE! EDDIE'S ARRIVAL IN D.C. DEFINITELY HELPED LESSEN THE NATS' INFIELD WOES, ESPECIALLY AFTER HE WAS PERMANENTLY SHIFTED TO SHORTSTOP DURING THE 1962 CAMPAIGN! EDDIE STRUGGLED MIGHTILY AT THE PLATE IN THOSE EARLY YEARS, BUT NATS MANAGER MICKEY VERNON NEVER LOST FAITH IN THE KID! "HE'S A BIG LEAGUE SHORTSTOP RIGHT NOW," MICKEY SAID IN APRIL OF '63, "ONE OF THE GOOD ONES. THE MORE HE SEES OF PITCHING, THE MORE HE'LL HIT." WHILE EDDIE'S GLOVE NEVER FALTERED, HIS BAT NEVER DEVELOPED! "HE'D HIT A LOT OF HOME RUNS IN HIGH SCHOOL AND SAW HIMSELF AS A POWER HITTER," REFLECTED MICKEY YEARS LATER. "I WANTED HIM TO CHOKE UP ON THE BAT AND SPRAY IT AROUND A LITTLE BIT." TED WILLIAMS, THE NATS' 1969 MANAGER, HAD THE SAME ADVICE FOR EDDIE -- AND THIS TIME EDDIE LISTENED! THE RESULT WAS A CAREER-HIGH .266 AVERAGE! EDDIE WOULD OFTEN LAUGH AND CHIDE HIMSELF FOR BEING "TOO DUMB" TO LISTEN TO MICKEY'S EARLIER ADVICE!

Mickey VERNON

JAMES BARTON "MICKEY" VERNON WAS ALREADY A LEGEND IN WASHINGTON BY THE TIME HE WAS TABBED TO MANAGE THE 1961 EXPANSION WASHINGTON SENATORS! THE TWO-TIME AMERICAN LEAGUE BATTING CHAMP HAD HIS WORK CUT OUT FOR HIM, HOWEVER, IN TRYING TO GET THE "NEW" NATS TO PLAY WELL! UNFORTUNATELY, THEY PLAYED A LOT LIKE THE OLD NATS, AND MICKEY WAS RELIEVED JUST 40 GAMES INTO THE 1963 SEASON! EDDIE BRINKMAN TRIED TO GIVE PERSPECTIVE TO MICKEY'S BRIEF STINT AS MANAGER, SAYING, "MICKEY WAS A LAID-BACK GUY BECAUSE HE HAD A LOT OF VETERAN PLAYERS. I ALWAYS LIKED HIM, AND I THOUGHT HE WAS A TERRIFIC INDIVIDUAL. WE REALLY DIDN'T HAVE A GOOD CLUB -- AN EXPANSION CLUB. I THINK HE DID AS WELL AS COULD BE EXPECTED."

FAYE Throneberry
LABELED A "CAN'T MISS" PROSPECT, SCOUTS WERE THRILLED BY THE SKILLS OF FAYE THRONEBERRY, A TENNESSEE-BORN LEFT-HANDED HITTING FLYCHASER! SO THRILLED, IN FACT, THAT THE LITTLE ROCK TRAVELERS, A DETROIT TIGERS FARM CLUB, SIGNED FAYE WHILE HE WAS STILL A HIGH SCHOOL STUDENT! A CLEAR VIOLATION, BASEBALL COMMISSIONER HAPPY CHANDLER VOIDED THE DEAL, AND FAYE EVENTUALLY ENDED UP AS PROPERTY OF THE BOSTON RED SOX! IT LOOKED LIKE A PERFECT FIT, TOO, AS FAYE CONNECTED FOR GRAND SLAMS ON HIS FIRST TWO HOMERS AS A ROOKIE EARLY IN THE 1952 SEASON!
WHAT FUN! I'M ON PACE TO HIT 23,672 GRAND SLAMS BY 1961!
GRANNY NO. 2
IN SPITE OF THE LONGBALL FIREWORKS THAT KICKED OFF FAYE'S BIG LEAGUE CAREER, POWER WASN'T REALLY HIS GAME! AS SOX MANAGER JOE CRONIN PUT IT, THORNY WAS A "CUT-AND-SLASH TYPE OF PLAYER, LIKE ENOS SLAUGHTER -- ALL BUSINESS ONCE HE'S ON THE BALLFIELD." FAYE NEVER HIT AS WELL AS OL' COUNTRY SLAUGHTER, HOWEVER, AND BY 1957 HE FOUND HIMSELF TOILING FOR THE SENATORS IN WASHINGTON! THERE HE SERVED AS A BACK-UP OUTFIELDER THROUGH 1960, NEVER PLAYING IN MORE THAN 85 GAMES -- EXCEPT FOR 1959! THAT YEAR FAYE PLAYED IN 117 GAMES FOR THE NATS AND HIT TEN HOME RUNS WHILE DRIVING IN 42! LEFT UNPROTECTED BY THE TWINS AFTER THE FRANCHISE MOVED TO MINNESOTA, FAYE WAS THE 22ND SELECTION OF THE EXPANSION LOS ANGELES ANGELS, AND HE PLAYED HIS LAST BIG LEAGUE GAMES WITH THE 1961 HALOS!
JOYNER ©2010
MARV Throneberry
IN A NOW-LEGENDARY 1976 LITE BEER COMMERCIAL, "MARVELOUS" MARV THRONEBERRY SELF-DEPRECATINGLY SAID, "YOU KNOW, IT USED TO TAKE 43 MARV THRONEBERRY CARDS TO GET ONE CARL FURILLO." WITH THAT, THE LONG-FORGOTTEN SLUGGER OF THE '62 METS RE-ENTERED THE CONSCIOUSNESS OF AMERICA'S BASEBALL FANS, AND NOW HAS ACHIEVED ETERNAL CULT STATUS AS THE SYMBOL OF THE EXPANSION METS' FUTILITY! MARV WOULD THRILL THE FANS WITH A LONG HOMER, BUT THEN FRUSTRATE THEM WITH SUBSEQUENT BLUNDERS IN THE FIELD AND ON THE BASES! BUT MARV HANDLED IT WITH HUMOR, AND IS THEREFORE FOREVER BELOVED!

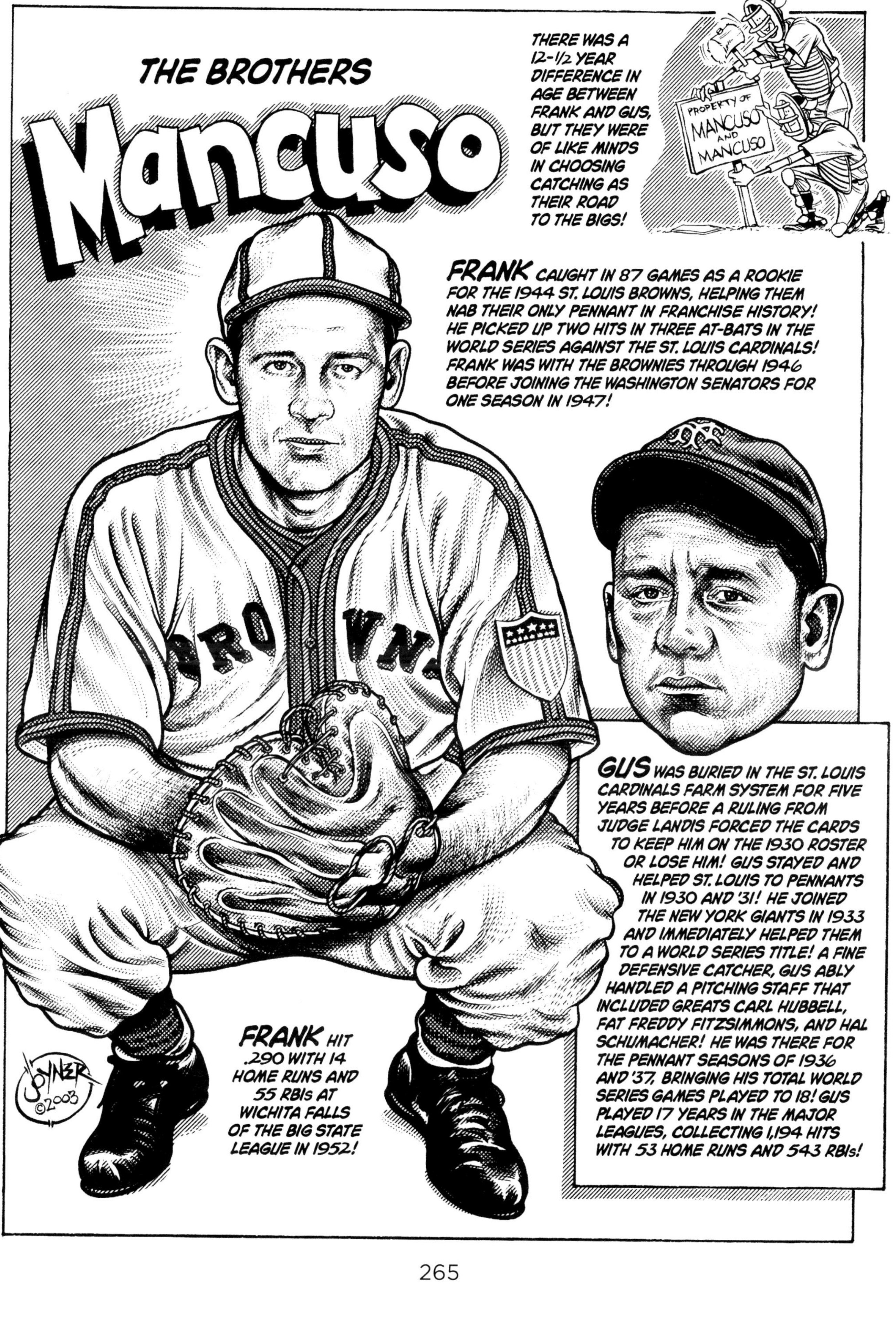
THE BROTHERS
MANCUSO
THERE WAS A 12-1/2 YEAR DIFFERENCE IN AGE BETWEEN FRANK AND GUS, BUT THEY WERE OF LIKE MINDS IN CHOOSING CATCHING AS THEIR ROAD TO THE BIGS!
PROPERTY OF MANCUSO AND MANCUSO
FRANK CAUGHT IN 87 GAMES AS A ROOKIE FOR THE 1944 ST. LOUIS BROWNS, HELPING THEM NAB THEIR ONLY PENNANT IN FRANCHISE HISTORY! HE PICKED UP TWO HITS IN THREE AT-BATS IN THE WORLD SERIES AGAINST THE ST. LOUIS CARDINALS! FRANK WAS WITH THE BROWNIES THROUGH 1946 BEFORE JOINING THE WASHINGTON SENATORS FOR ONE SEASON IN 1947!
GUS WAS BURIED IN THE ST. LOUIS CARDINALS FARM SYSTEM FOR FIVE YEARS BEFORE A RULING FROM JUDGE LANDIS FORCED THE CARDS TO KEEP HIM ON THE 1930 ROSTER OR LOSE HIM! GUS STAYED AND HELPED ST. LOUIS TO PENNANTS IN 1930 AND '31! HE JOINED THE NEW YORK GIANTS IN 1933 AND IMMEDIATELY HELPED THEM TO A WORLD SERIES TITLE! A FINE DEFENSIVE CATCHER, GUS ABLY HANDLED A PITCHING STAFF THAT INCLUDED GREATS CARL HUBBELL, FAT FREDDY FITZSIMMONS, AND HAL SCHUMACHER! HE WAS THERE FOR THE PENNANT SEASONS OF 1936 AND '37, BRINGING HIS TOTAL WORLD SERIES GAMES PLAYED TO 18! GUS PLAYED 17 YEARS IN THE MAJOR LEAGUES, COLLECTING 1,194 HITS WITH 53 HOME RUNS AND 543 RBIs!
FRANK HIT .290 WITH 14 HOME RUNS AND 55 RBIs AT WICHITA FALLS OF THE BIG STATE LEAGUE IN 1952!
JOYNER ©2003

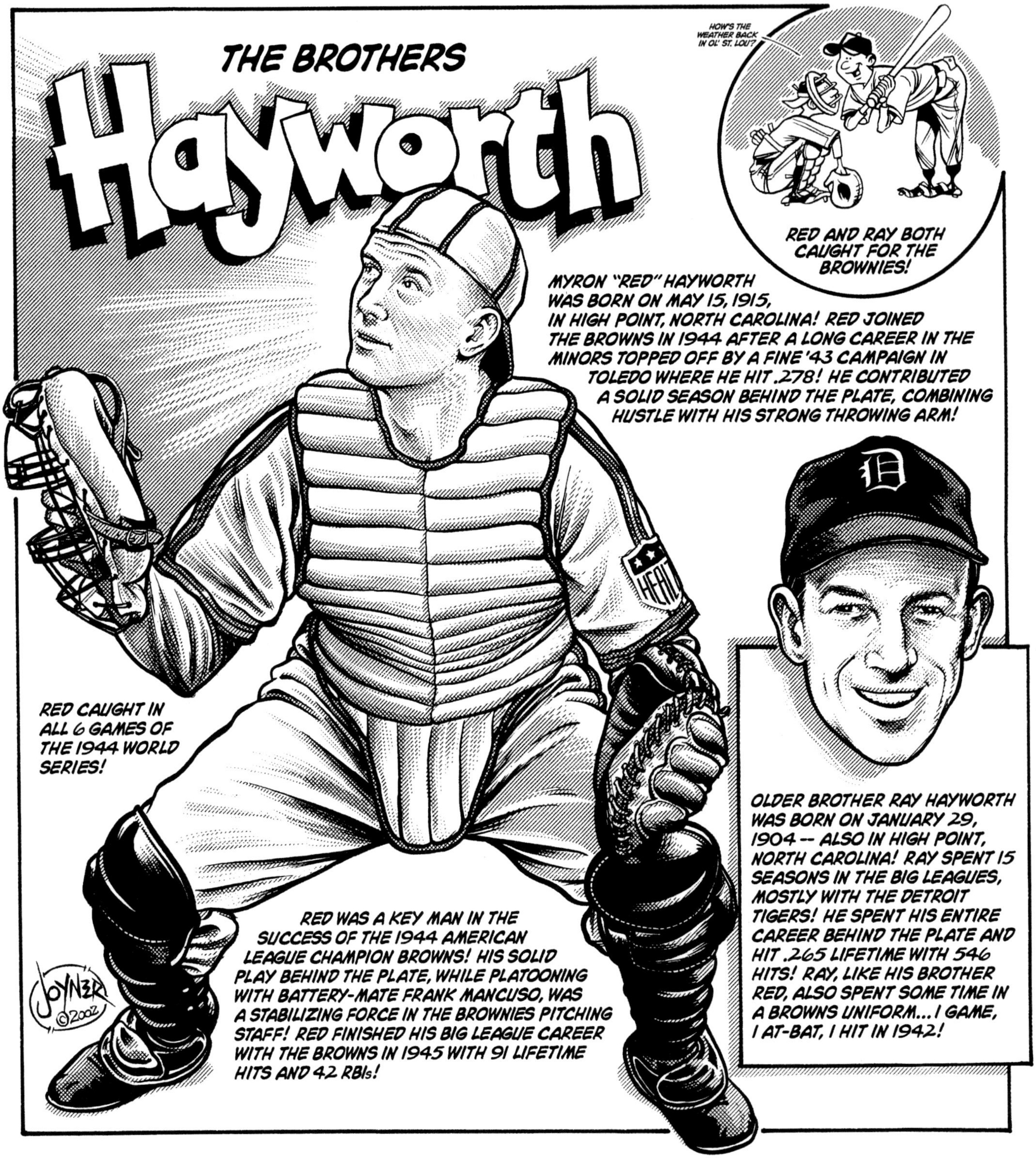
THE BROTHERS
Hayworth
HOW'S THE WEATHER BACK IN OL' ST. LOU?
RED AND RAY BOTH CAUGHT FOR THE BROWNIES!
MYRON "RED" HAYWORTH WAS BORN ON MAY 15, 1915, IN HIGH POINT, NORTH CAROLINA! RED JOINED THE BROWNS IN 1944 AFTER A LONG CAREER IN THE MINORS TOPPED OFF BY A FINE '43 CAMPAIGN IN TOLEDO WHERE HE HIT .278! HE CONTRIBUTED A SOLID SEASON BEHIND THE PLATE, COMBINING HUSTLE WITH HIS STRONG THROWING ARM!
RED CAUGHT IN ALL 6 GAMES OF THE 1944 WORLD SERIES!
OLDER BROTHER RAY HAYWORTH WAS BORN ON JANUARY 29, 1904 -- ALSO IN HIGH POINT, NORTH CAROLINA! RAY SPENT 15 SEASONS IN THE BIG LEAGUES, MOSTLY WITH THE DETROIT TIGERS! HE SPENT HIS ENTIRE CAREER BEHIND THE PLATE AND HIT .265 LIFETIME WITH 546 HITS! RAY, LIKE HIS BROTHER RED, ALSO SPENT SOME TIME IN A BROWNS UNIFORM... 1 GAME, 1 AT-BAT, 1 HIT IN 1942!
RED WAS A KEY MAN IN THE SUCCESS OF THE 1944 AMERICAN LEAGUE CHAMPION BROWNS! HIS SOLID PLAY BEHIND THE PLATE, WHILE PLATOONING WITH BATTERY-MATE FRANK MANCUSO, WAS A STABILIZING FORCE IN THE BROWNIES PITCHING STAFF! RED FINISHED HIS BIG LEAGUE CAREER WITH THE BROWNS IN 1945 WITH 91 LIFETIME HITS AND 42 RBIs!
JOYNER ©2002

JOOST AND SUDER INC.

THEY MAY NOT HAVE THE NAME RECOGNITION OF TINKERS AND EVERS, BUT ASK ANY 1940s/50s PHILADELPHIA A's FAN WHO MADE UP THE GREATEST DOUBLE-PLAY PIVOT OF ALL TIME AND THEY'LL UNDOUBTEDLY TELL YOU IT WAS EDDIE JOOST AND PETE SUDER -- OR JOOST AND SUDER, INC., AS THEY CAME TO BE KNOWN! WITH EDDIE AT SHORT AND PETE AT SECOND, THE A's PROVED TO BE UNEQUALED AT EXECUTING TWIN-KILLINGS, BECOMING THE FIRST BALLCLUB TO TURN MORE THAN 200 DOUBLE-PLAYS THREE YEARS IN A ROW! PETE ATTRIBUTED A GREAT DEAL OF THEIR SUCCESS TO CHEATING, SAYING, "I WAS THE BIGGEST CHEAT YOU EVER WANT TO SEE! I TOUCHED THE BAG, BUT WAS ACROSS IT BEFORE I GOT THE BALL. THAT WAY I GOT THE BALL AWAY QUICKER." PETE ALSO CREDITED THE BRILLIANT ARMS OF JOOST AND THIRD BASEMAN HANK MAJESKI. "BOY, COULD THEY THROW IT STRAIGHT. PERFECT THROWS, RIGHT IN THE CHEST ON A LINE. NO RAINBOWS." NOT TO BE LEFT OUT, PETE INCLUDED YOUNG NELLIE FOX AND FIRST BASEMAN FERRIS FAIN AS KEY PARTS OF THE TEAM'S DOUBLE-PLAY SUCCESS. "YOU TRY TO BUNT A MAN OVER FROM FIRST, FAIN WOULD GET HIM AT SECOND. TRY TO MOVE A MAN FROM SECOND TO THIRD, HE'D FIELD THAT BALL ON THE BASE LINE AND GET THAT GUY AT THIRD." IT WAS AN ERA WHEN FANS APPRECIATED THE BEAUTY OF A SMOOTH TWIN-KILLING AS MUCH OR MORE THAN THEY ADMIRED THE LONG BALL -- AND NO DUO DID IT BETTER THAN JOOST AND SUDER!

THE BROTHERS
DiMaggio
SONS OF SICILIAN IMMIGRANTS GIUSEPPE AND ROSALIE DIMAGGIO, JOSEPH, DOMINIC AND VINCENT CAPTURED THE AMERICAN DREAM WHEN THEY ROSE TO THE HEIGHTS OF SUCCESS AS MAJOR LEAGUE BALLPLAYERS! ALL THREE BOYS PLAYED AT LEAST TEN SEASONS IN THE BIG LEAGUES, LEAVING A MARK ON THE GAME THAT WILL BE REMEMBERED AS LONG AS KIDS PLAY BALL!
JOE PLAYED 13 YEARS WITH THE NEW YORK YANKEES, CARVING OUT A CAREER THAT LANDED HIM IN THE HALL OF FAME! HIS INCREDIBLE 56-GAME HITTING STREAK IN 1941 CAPTIVATED THE COUNTRY AND EVEN SPAWNED THE HIT RECORD "JOLTIN' JOE DIMAGGIO" BY BAND-LEADER LES BROWN!
SHUCKS, WHY'D THEY HAVE TO HAVE TO PUT THAT "GOODBYE STREAK, DIMAGGIO" VERSE IN THERE?!
TODAY, RUBBER! TOMORROW, THE WORLD!
DOM SPENT HIS ENTIRE BIG LEAGUE CAREER WITH THE RED SOX, SETTING A HIGH EXAMPLE FOR HOW TO PLAY CENTERFIELD! AFTER HE HUNG UP HIS SPIKES HE BECAME A SUCCESSFUL BUSINESSMAN IN THE FIELD OF FOAM RUBBER AND SYNTHETIC FIBERS!
VINCE PACKED A WALLOP INTO HIS 5'-11 1/2" FRAME, BELTING 125 HOME RUNS IN HIS 10-YEAR CAREER! HE COULD ALSO BELT OUT A TUNE WITH HIS FINE SINGING VOICE, PARTICULARLY EXCELLING IN OPERA!
I GOT IT, I GOT IT
I'M GONNA LEAD THE LEAGUE IN ARIAS!
JOYNER © 2003
BOSTON

Fritz
Mike
PETERSON & KEKICH
LEFT-HANDED HURLER FRITZ PETERSON USED EXCELLENT COMMAND AND FINESSE TO WIN 109 GAMES FOR THE YANKEES FROM 1966 THROUGH APRIL OF '74 -- INCLUDNG A 20-WIN SEASON IN 1970! MIKE KEKICH, A HARD THROWING SOUTHPAW, BROKE IN WITH THE '65 DODGERS, BUT LATER JOINED THE YANKEES VIA A TRADE! MIKE, USED BOTH AS A STARTER AND RELIEVER, APPEARED IN 155 GAMES FOR THE BOMBERS FROM 1969 THROUGH JUNE OF '73, WINNING 33 GAMES IN THAT SPAN!
FRITZ AND MIKE TOOK PART IN PERHAPS THE WILDEST TRADE IN BASEBALL HISTORY WHEN THEY SWAPPED WIVES IN THE SUMMER OF '72! THE TWO HAD BEEN GREAT FRIENDS AND ROAD ROOMMATES WITH THE YANKEES SINCE 1969! THIER WIVES AND CHILDREN ALSO SOON BECAME VERY CLOSE -- TOO CLOSE, PERHAPS! SOME TIME DURING THE 1972 SEASON, MIKE KEKICH FELL FOR MARILYN PETERSON, WHILE FRITZ PETERSON WAS BUSY FALLING IN LOVE WITH SUZANNE KEKICH! AFTER SOME SUPPOSEDLY LIGHT-HEARTED JOKING ABOUT WIFE-SWAPPING, A HOT NEW FAD WITH SOME OF THE MORE ADVENTUROUS COUPLES OF THE SWINGING '70s, THE JOKE BECAME REALITY WHEN THE FIRST SWAP TOOK PLACE AFTER A JULY PARTY AT THE HOME OF NEW YORK WRITER MAURY ALLEN! BY OCTOBER, THE PLAYERS HAD NOT JUST SWAPPED WIVES, THEY'D "SWAPPED LIVES," ACCORDING TO MIKE! FRITZ AND SUZANNE EVENTUALLY MARRIED AND ARE STILL TOGETHER, BUT MIKE AND MARILYN DID NOT FARE SO WELL, AND THEY BROKE UP AFTER A COUPLE MONTHS! ALL PARTIES DEFENDED THE ARRANGEMENT AS "NOTHING SORDID," BUT THERE WAS NEGATIVE REACTION AROUND THE LEAGUE, AND BOTH PITCHERS STRUGGLED AFTER THE SWAP! "NEITHER FRITZ NOR I WILL EVER MAKE THE HALL OF FAME," MIKE SAID, "BUT OUR NAMES KEEP POPPING UP IN THE HALL OF SHAME. I DON'T LOSE SLEEP, BUT I DON'T THINK IT'S FAIR."
JOYNER ©2009
I BET MICKEY AND ROGER WISH THEY'D HAVE THOUGHT OF THIS!

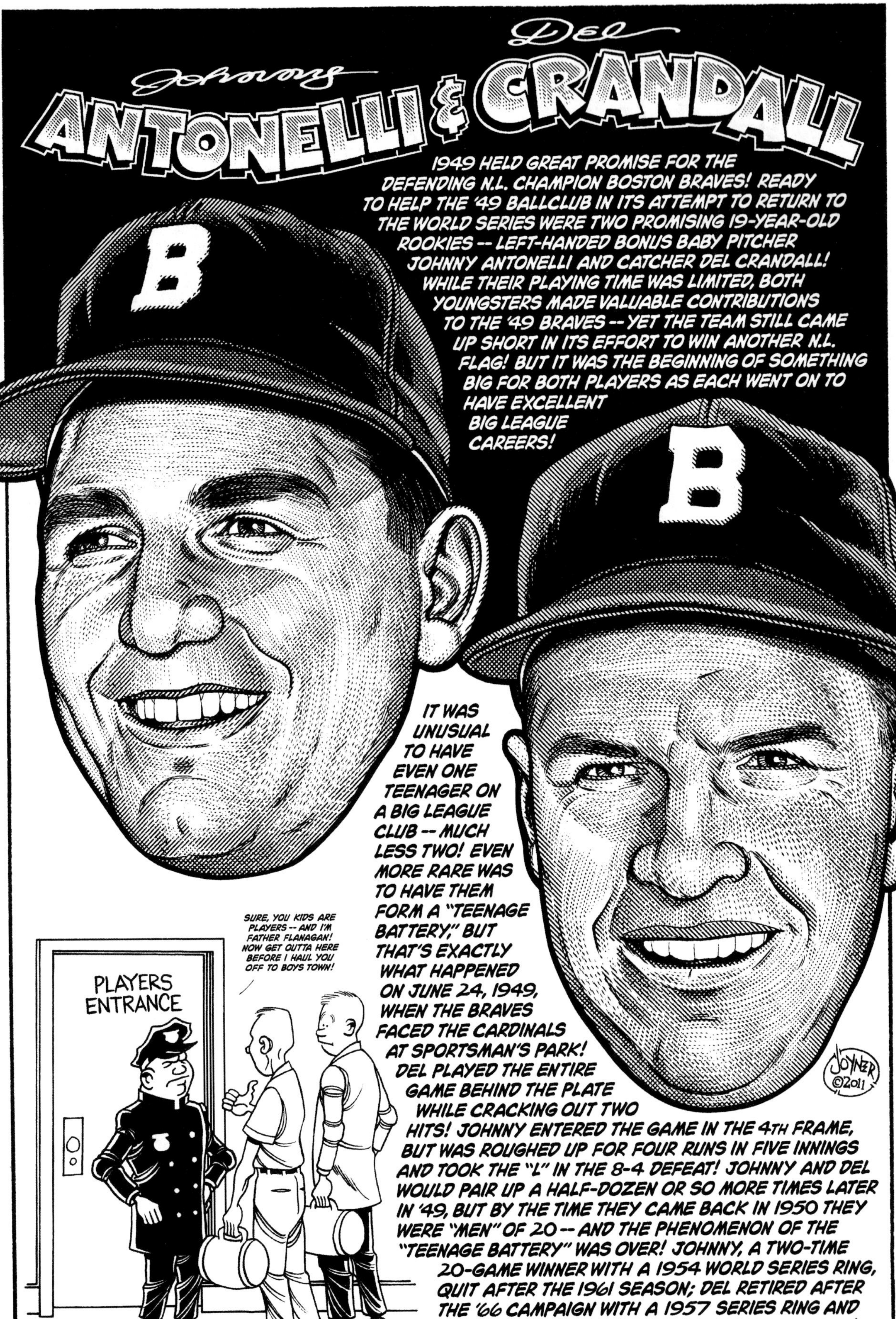
Johnny
ANTONELLI &
Del
CRANDALL
1949 HELD GREAT PROMISE FOR THE DEFENDING N.L. CHAMPION BOSTON BRAVES! READY TO HELP THE '49 BALLCLUB IN ITS ATTEMPT TO RETURN TO THE WORLD SERIES WERE TWO PROMISING 19-YEAR-OLD ROOKIES -- LEFT-HANDED BONUS BABY PITCHER JOHNNY ANTONELLI AND CATCHER DEL CRANDALL! WHILE THEIR PLAYING TIME WAS LIMITED, BOTH YOUNGSTERS MADE VALUABLE CONTRIBUTIONS TO THE '49 BRAVES -- YET THE TEAM STILL CAME UP SHORT IN ITS EFFORT TO WIN ANOTHER N.L. FLAG! BUT IT WAS THE BEGINNING OF SOMETHING BIG FOR BOTH PLAYERS AS EACH WENT ON TO HAVE EXCELLENT BIG LEAGUE CAREERS!
B
B
IT WAS UNUSUAL TO HAVE EVEN ONE TEENAGER ON A BIG LEAGUE CLUB -- MUCH LESS TWO! EVEN MORE RARE WAS TO HAVE THEM FORM A "TEENAGE BATTERY," BUT THAT'S EXACTLY WHAT HAPPENED ON JUNE 24, 1949, WHEN THE BRAVES FACED THE CARDINALS AT SPORTSMAN'S PARK! DEL PLAYED THE ENTIRE GAME BEHIND THE PLATE WHILE CRACKING OUT TWO HITS! JOHNNY ENTERED THE GAME IN THE 4TH FRAME, BUT WAS ROUGHED UP FOR FOUR RUNS IN FIVE INNINGS AND TOOK THE "L" IN THE 8-4 DEFEAT! JOHNNY AND DEL WOULD PAIR UP A HALF-DOZEN OR SO MORE TIMES LATER IN '49, BUT BY THE TIME THEY CAME BACK IN 1950 THEY WERE "MEN" OF 20 -- AND THE PHENOMENON OF THE "TEENAGE BATTERY" WAS OVER! JOHNNY, A TWO-TIME 20-GAME WINNER WITH A 1954 WORLD SERIES RING, QUIT AFTER THE 1961 SEASON; DEL RETIRED AFTER THE '66 CAMPAIGN WITH A 1957 SERIES RING AND 1,276 HITS ... NOT BAD FOR A COUPLE TEENAGERS!
SURE, YOU KIDS ARE PLAYERS -- AND I'M FATHER FLANAGAN! NOW GET OUTTA HERE BEFORE I HAUL YOU OFF TO BOYS TOWN!
PLAYERS ENTRANCE
JOYNER ©2011

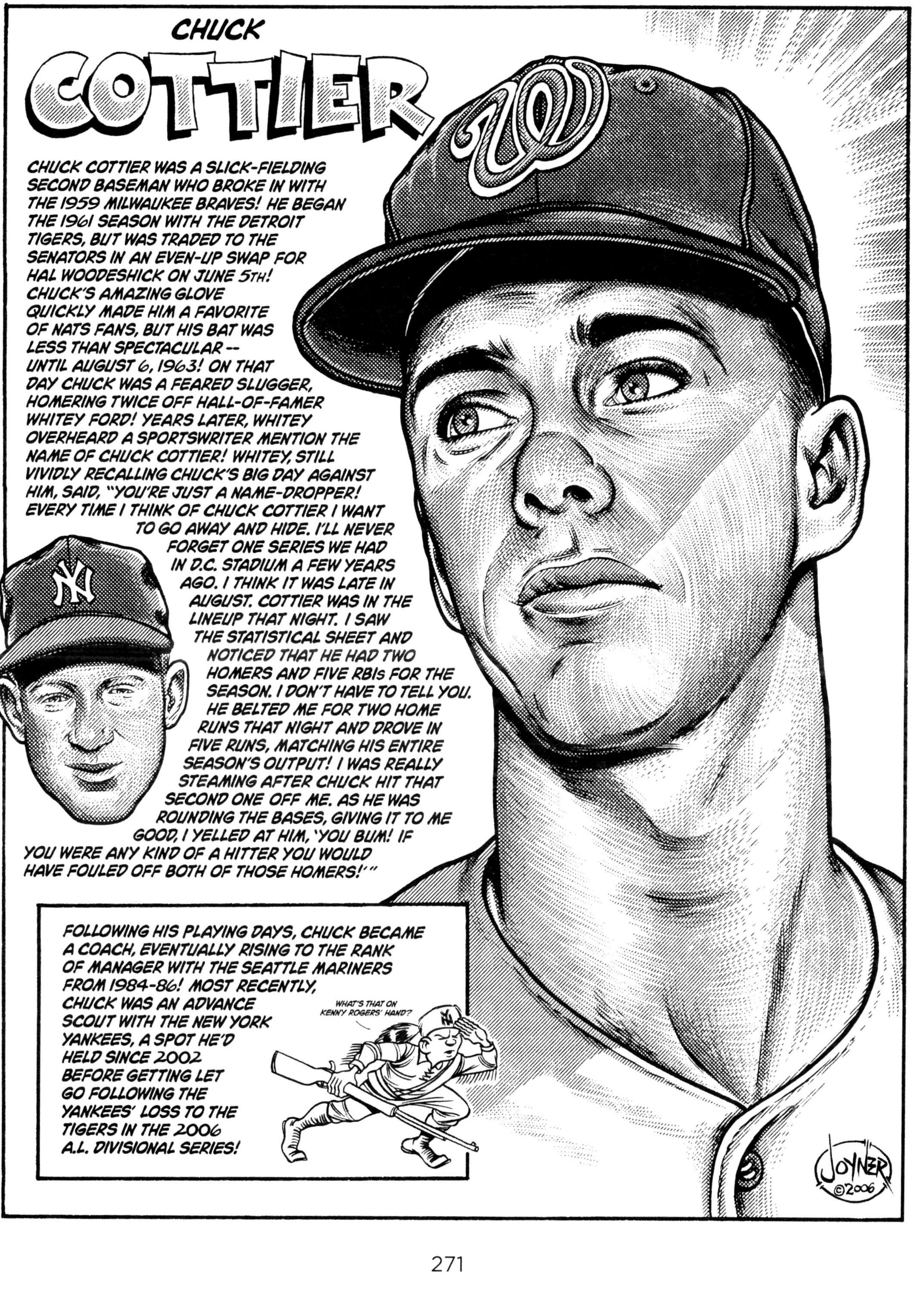
CHUCK
COTTIER
CHUCK COTTIER WAS A SLICK-FIELDING SECOND BASEMAN WHO BROKE IN WITH THE 1959 MILWAUKEE BRAVES! HE BEGAN THE 1961 SEASON WITH THE DETROIT TIGERS, BUT WAS TRADED TO THE SENATORS IN AN EVEN-UP SWAP FOR HAL WOODESHICK ON JUNE 5TH! CHUCK'S AMAZING GLOVE QUICKLY MADE HIM A FAVORITE OF NATS FANS, BUT HIS BAT WAS LESS THAN SPECTACULAR -- UNTIL AUGUST 6, 1963! ON THAT DAY CHUCK WAS A FEARED SLUGGER, HOMERING TWICE OFF HALL-OF-FAMER WHITEY FORD! YEARS LATER, WHITEY OVERHEARD A SPORTSWRITER MENTION THE NAME OF CHUCK COTTIER! WHITEY, STILL VIVIDLY RECALLING CHUCK'S BIG DAY AGAINST HIM, SAID, "YOU'RE JUST A NAME-DROPPER! EVERY TIME I THINK OF CHUCK COTTIER I WANT TO GO AWAY AND HIDE. I'LL NEVER FORGET ONE SERIES WE HAD IN D.C. STADIUM A FEW YEARS AGO. I THINK IT WAS LATE IN AUGUST. COTTIER WAS IN THE LINEUP THAT NIGHT. I SAW THE STATISTICAL SHEET AND NOTICED THAT HE HAD TWO HOMERS AND FIVE RBIs FOR THE SEASON. I DON'T HAVE TO TELL YOU. HE BELTED ME FOR TWO HOME RUNS THAT NIGHT AND DROVE IN FIVE RUNS, MATCHING HIS ENTIRE SEASON'S OUTPUT! I WAS REALLY STEAMING AFTER CHUCK HIT THAT SECOND ONE OFF ME. AS HE WAS ROUNDING THE BASES, GIVING IT TO ME GOOD, I YELLED AT HIM, 'YOU BUM! IF YOU WERE ANY KIND OF A HITTER YOU WOULD HAVE FOULED OFF BOTH OF THOSE HOMERS!'"
FOLLOWING HIS PLAYING DAYS, CHUCK BECAME A COACH, EVENTUALLY RISING TO THE RANK OF MANAGER WITH THE SEATTLE MARINERS FROM 1984-86! MOST RECENTLY, CHUCK WAS AN ADVANCE SCOUT WITH THE NEW YORK YANKEES, A SPOT HE'D HELD SINCE 2002 BEFORE GETTING LET GO FOLLOWING THE YANKEES' LOSS TO THE TIGERS IN THE 2006 A.L. DIVISIONAL SERIES!
WHAT'S THAT ON KENNY ROGERS' HAND?
JOYNER
©2006

WHOLLY-WORTHY HALF-PAGERS

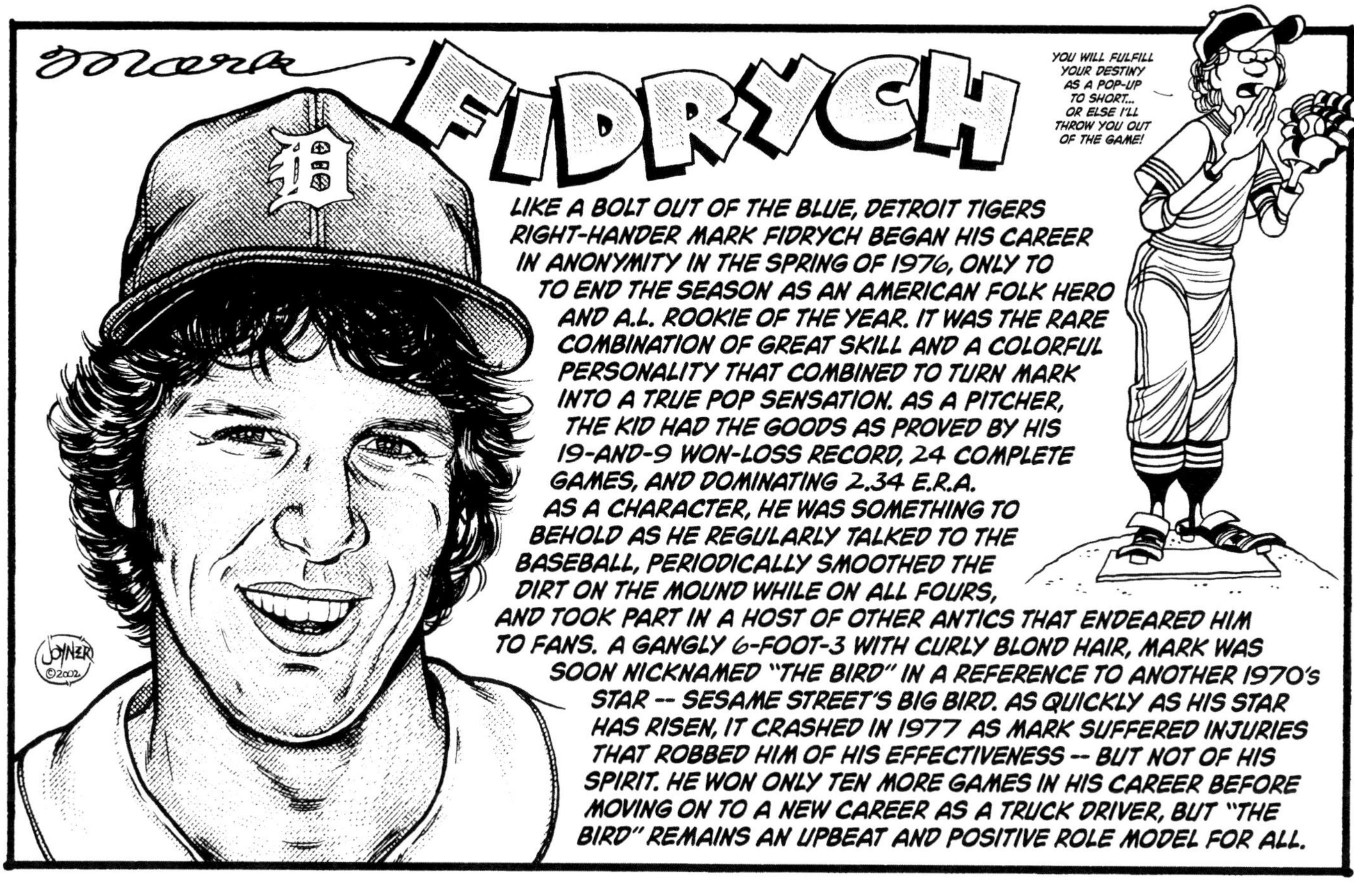
Mark
FIDRYCH
YOU WILL FULFILL YOUR DESTINY AS A POP-UP TO SHORT... OR ELSE I'LL THROW YOU OUT OF THE GAME!
LIKE A BOLT OUT OF THE BLUE, DETROIT TIGERS RIGHT-HANDER MARK FIDRYCH BEGAN HIS CAREER IN ANONYMITY IN THE SPRING OF 1976, ONLY TO TO END THE SEASON AS AN AMERICAN FOLK HERO AND A.L. ROOKIE OF THE YEAR. IT WAS THE RARE COMBINATION OF GREAT SKILL AND A COLORFUL PERSONALITY THAT COMBINED TO TURN MARK INTO A TRUE POP SENSATION. AS A PITCHER, THE KID HAD THE GOODS AS PROVED BY HIS 19-AND-9 WON-LOSS RECORD, 24 COMPLETE GAMES, AND DOMINATING 2.34 E.R.A. AS A CHARACTER, HE WAS SOMETHING TO BEHOLD AS HE REGULARLY TALKED TO THE BASEBALL, PERIODICALLY SMOOTHED THE DIRT ON THE MOUND WHILE ON ALL FOURS, AND TOOK PART IN A HOST OF OTHER ANTICS THAT ENDEARED HIM TO FANS. A GANGLY 6-FOOT-3 WITH CURLY BLOND HAIR, MARK WAS SOON NICKNAMED "THE BIRD" IN A REFERENCE TO ANOTHER 1970's STAR -- SESAME STREET'S BIG BIRD. AS QUICKLY AS HIS STAR HAS RISEN, IT CRASHED IN 1977 AS MARK SUFFERED INJURIES THAT ROBBED HIM OF HIS EFFECTIVENESS -- BUT NOT OF HIS SPIRIT. HE WON ONLY TEN MORE GAMES IN HIS CAREER BEFORE MOVING ON TO A NEW CAREER AS A TRUCK DRIVER, BUT "THE BIRD" REMAINS AN UPBEAT AND POSITIVE ROLE MODEL FOR ALL.
JOYNER ©2002

Fernando
VALENZUELA
FOUR SEASONS HAD PASSED SINCE "THE BIRD" CRAZE OF 1976, AND BASEBALL WAS DUE FOR SOMETHING FRESH BY 1981 -- AND THAT "SOMETHING" CAME IN THE FORM OF A ROUND-SHAPED MEXICAN SCREWBALL-TOSSING ROOKIE LEFT-HANDER NAMED FERNANDO VALENZUELA. FERNANDO GOT HIS FIRST BIG LEAGUE START AS A LAST-MINUTE REPLACEMENT ON OPENING DAY OF 1981 AND PROCEEDED TO THROW A SHUTOUT. HE THEN CONVINCINGLY WON HIS NEXT SEVEN STARTS -- AND WITH THAT, "FERNANDO MANIA" WAS OFFICIALLY BORN. FERNANDO MANIA WAS ONLY FURTHER ENHANCED BY HIS STYLISH WIND-UP, A DELIVERY THAT SAW FERNANDO CAST HIS EYES SKYWARD JUST PRIOR TO HIS DRIVE TOWARD THE DISH. DODGER STADIUM WAS A FESTIVE SCENE WHENEVER FERNANDO PITCHED THAT SEASON AS THE MEXICAN COMMUNITY CAME OUT IN FORCE TO CHEER ON THEIR NEW HERO. WHEN THE CURTAIN CAME DOWN ON THE 1981 CAMPAIGN, FERNANDO HAD WON A CY YOUNG AWARD, THE N.L. ROOKIE-OF-THE-YEAR AWARD, AND A WORLD SERIES RING AS HIS DODGERS DEFEATED THE YANKEES IN THE FALL CLASSIC. FERNANDO WENT ON TO HAVE A VERY GOOD CAREER -- INCLUDING A 21-WIN SEASON IN 1986 -- BUT HE'LL ALWAYS BE FONDLY REMEMBERED FOR THE FUN THE FERNANDO MANIA CRAZE BROUGHT TO BASEBALL IN 1981.
JOYNER ©2002

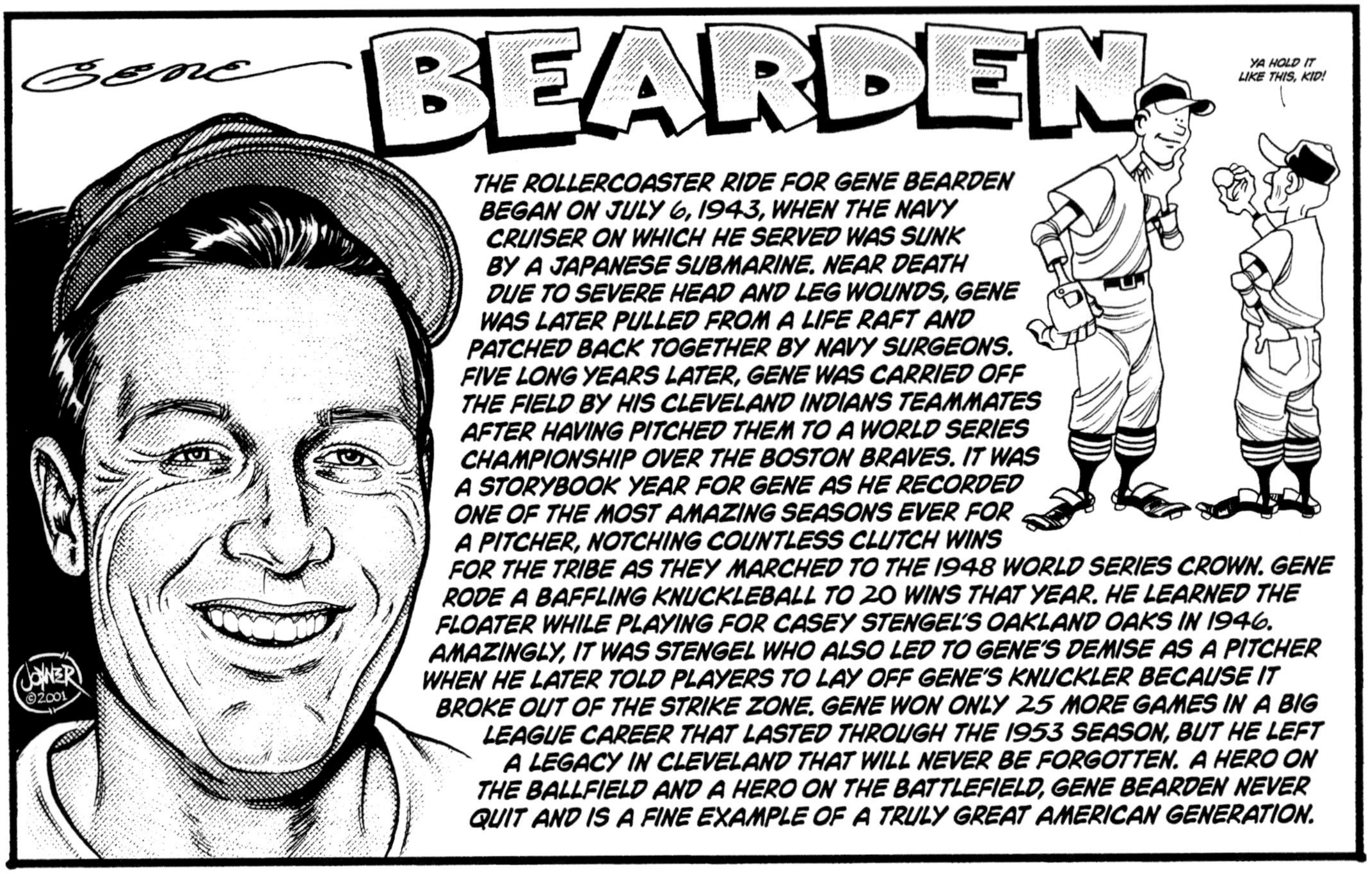
Gene
BEARDEN
YA HOLD IT LIKE THIS, KID!
THE ROLLERCOASTER RIDE FOR GENE BEARDEN BEGAN ON JULY 6, 1943, WHEN THE NAVY CRUISER ON WHICH HE SERVED WAS SUNK BY A JAPANESE SUBMARINE. NEAR DEATH DUE TO SEVERE HEAD AND LEG WOUNDS, GENE WAS LATER PULLED FROM A LIFE RAFT AND PATCHED BACK TOGETHER BY NAVY SURGEONS. FIVE LONG YEARS LATER, GENE WAS CARRIED OFF THE FIELD BY HIS CLEVELAND INDIANS TEAMMATES AFTER HAVING PITCHED THEM TO A WORLD SERIES CHAMPIONSHIP OVER THE BOSTON BRAVES. IT WAS A STORYBOOK YEAR FOR GENE AS HE RECORDED ONE OF THE MOST AMAZING SEASONS EVER FOR A PITCHER, NOTCHING COUNTLESS CLUTCH WINS FOR THE TRIBE AS THEY MARCHED TO THE 1948 WORLD SERIES CROWN. GENE RODE A BAFFLING KNUCKLEBALL TO 20 WINS THAT YEAR. HE LEARNED THE FLOATER WHILE PLAYING FOR CASEY STENGEL'S OAKLAND OAKS IN 1946. AMAZINGLY, IT WAS STENGEL WHO ALSO LED TO GENE'S DEMISE AS A PITCHER WHEN HE LATER TOLD PLAYERS TO LAY OFF GENE'S KNUCKLER BECAUSE IT BROKE OUT OF THE STRIKE ZONE. GENE WON ONLY 25 MORE GAMES IN A BIG LEAGUE CAREER THAT LASTED THROUGH THE 1953 SEASON, BUT HE LEFT A LEGACY IN CLEVELAND THAT WILL NEVER BE FORGOTTEN. A HERO ON THE BALLFIELD AND A HERO ON THE BATTLEFIELD, GENE BEARDEN NEVER QUIT AND IS A FINE EXAMPLE OF A TRULY GREAT AMERICAN GENERATION.

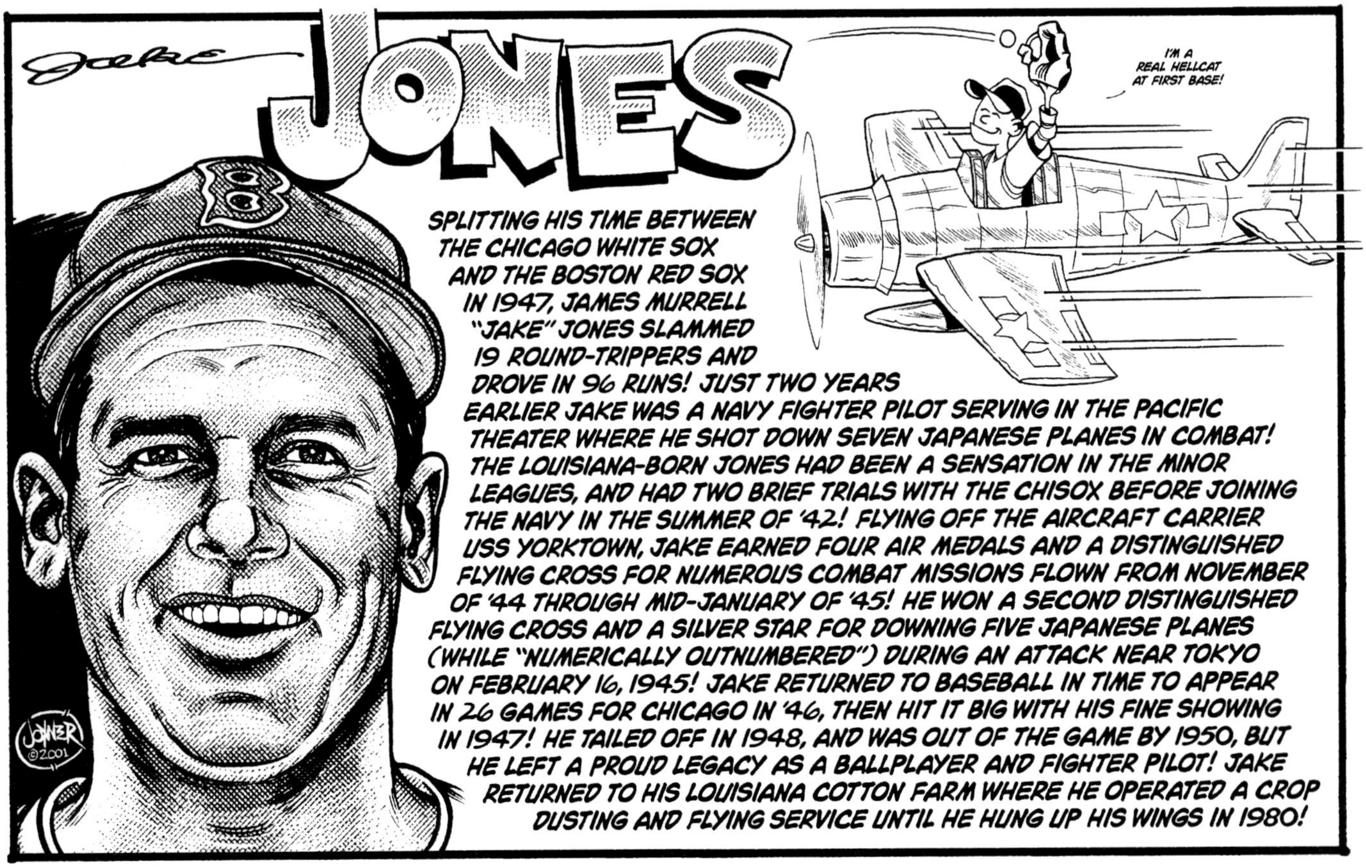
Jake
JONES
I'M A REAL HELLCAT AT FIRST BASE!
SPLITTING HIS TIME BETWEEN THE CHICAGO WHITE SOX AND THE BOSTON RED SOX IN 1947, JAMES MURRELL "JAKE" JONES SLAMMED 19 ROUND-TRIPPERS AND DROVE IN 96 RUNS! JUST TWO YEARS EARLIER JAKE WAS A NAVY FIGHTER PILOT SERVING IN THE PACIFIC THEATER WHERE HE SHOT DOWN SEVEN JAPANESE PLANES IN COMBAT! THE LOUISIANA-BORN JONES HAD BEEN A SENSATION IN THE MINOR LEAGUES, AND HAD TWO BRIEF TRIALS WITH THE CHISOX BEFORE JOINING THE NAVY IN THE SUMMER OF '42! FLYING OFF THE AIRCRAFT CARRIER USS YORKTOWN, JAKE EARNED FOUR AIR MEDALS AND A DISTINGUISHED FLYING CROSS FOR NUMEROUS COMBAT MISSIONS FLOWN FROM NOVEMBER OF '44 THROUGH MID-JANUARY OF '45! HE WON A SECOND DISTINGUISHED FLYING CROSS AND A SILVER STAR FOR DOWNING FIVE JAPANESE PLANES (WHILE "NUMERICALLY OUTNUMBERED") DURING AN ATTACK NEAR TOKYO ON FEBRUARY 16, 1945! JAKE RETURNED TO BASEBALL IN TIME TO APPEAR IN 26 GAMES FOR CHICAGO IN '46, THEN HIT IT BIG WITH HIS FINE SHOWING IN 1947! HE TAILED OFF IN 1948, AND WAS OUT OF THE GAME BY 1950, BUT HE LEFT A PROUD LEGACY AS A BALLPLAYER AND FIGHTER PILOT! JAKE RETURNED TO HIS LOUISIANA COTTON FARM WHERE HE OPERATED A CROP DUSTING AND FLYING SERVICE UNTIL HE HUNG UP HIS WINGS IN 1980!

Russ Christopher

WHEN IT CAME TIME FOR THE YANKEES TO SIGN SLUGGING OUTFIELDER LLOYD CHRISTOPHER, HE HAD ONLY ONE DEMAND -- THAT THEY ALSO SIGN HIS OLDER BROTHER, RIGHT-HAND PITCHER RUSS CHRISTOPHER. LLOYD KNEW IT MIGHT BE THE ONLY WAY TO GET HIS BROTHER A CONTRACT DUE TO THE FACT THAT RUSS WAS PLAYING WITH A HEART WEAKENED BY A CHILDHOOD BOUT OF RHEUMATIC FEVER. THE YANKS SIGNED THEM BOTH, BUT LET RUSS GO TO THE ATHLETICS ORGANIZATION VIA THE RULE 5 DRAFT IN 1941. RUSS' TICKER MIGHT HAVE BEEN WEAK, BUT THAT NEVER STOPPED HIM FROM PITCHING WITH AS MUCH OR MORE HEART THAN ANYONE WHO EVER TOED THE SLAB. SPLITTING HIS APPEARANCES AS A STARTER AND RELIEVER, RUSS WON 51 GAMES WHILE LOSING ONLY 62 FOR SOME NOT-SO-GOOD A'S TEAMS FROM 1942 TO 1947. PLAYING ON "BORROWED TIME" DUE TO HIS WORSENING HEART CONDITION, RUSS JOINED THE INDIANS IN 1948 AND CHIPPED IN A LEAGUE-LEADING 17 SAVES AS THE TRIBE WON A WORLD SERIES CHAMPIONSHIP. THAT TURNED OUT TO BE RUSS' LAST SEASON AS HIS HEART CONDITION FORCED HIM TO RETIRE AT THE AGE OF 30. LATE IN THE EVENING OF DECEMBER 5, 1954, RUSS' TIRED HEART FINALLY GAVE OUT ON HIM AND HE PASSED AWAY, LEAVING BEHIND A WIFE AND THREE CHILDREN -- AND A LEGACY AS A FEARLESS MOUND WARRIOR.

Ford Garrison

FORD GARRISON WAS A VERY GOOD MINOR LEAGUE BALLPLAYER, AVERAGING .298 AT THE PLATE OVER HIS SIXTEEN YEARS IN THE BUSHES! AND FOR TWO WEEKS IN THE SPRING OF 1944, FORD WAS AN ABSOLUTE GREAT MAJOR LEAGUE BALLPLAYER -- MAYBE THE BEST IN THAT SPAN! THE RED SOX TRADED FORD TO THE PHILADELPHIA ATHLETICS ON MAY 7, 1944, IN AN EVEN-UP SWAP FOR HAL WAGNER! A's OWNER CONNIE MACK KNEW THAT FORD WAS HAVING SOME FINANCIAL TROUBLES, SO HE SLIPPED THE SOUTH CAROLINA BORN OUTFIELDER AN ENVELOPE CONTAINING $1,500! FORD WAS ALREADY KNOWN AS A WORLD-CLASS HUSTLER, EASILY ON THE SAME LEVEL AS LEGENDARY HUSTLER ENOS SLAUGHTER! INSPIRED BY MR. MACK'S GENEROSITY, FORD TOOK TO THE FIELD WITH A VENGEANCE, HITTING SAFELY IN HIS FIRST TWELVE GAMES WITH THE A's! WHETHER IT BE BUNT SINGLES OR HOME RUNS, AND EVERYTHING IN BETWEEN, FORD DID IT! HE BATTED .429 WITH A .595 SLUGGING PERCENTAGE IN THOSE TWO WEEKS, AND THE A's WON SEVEN OF THE FIRST NINE GAMES IN WHICH HE PLAYED! FORD WAS THE TALK OF THE TOWN, AND FANS CAME IN DROVES TO WATCH HIM PLAY! IT'S ESTIMATED THAT FORD'S HOT STREAK BROUGHT 100,000 FANS TO SHIBE PARK -- NOT A BAD RETURN ON MR. MACK'S $1,500 INVESTMENT! FORD ENDED AT .269 FOR THE SEASON, AND WAS AT .304 WHEN HE ENTERED THE NAVY IN THE SPRING OF '45!

PETE Gray

PETE GOT FIVE HITS IN A TWIN-BILL vs. THE YANKEES ON MAY 20, 1945!

NANTICOKE, PENNSYLVANIA'S PETE GRAY MADE HIS MAJOR LEAGUE DEBUT ON APRIL 17, 1945. PLAYING LEFTFIELD FOR THE ST. LOUIS BROWNS THAT DAY, PETE WENT 1-FOR-4 AT THE PLATE, PICKING UP HIS FIRST BIG LEAGUE HIT OFF DETROIT ACE HAL NEWHOUSER. SURELY A MOMENTOUS OCCASION FOR ANY ROOKIE, IT WAS ALL THE MORE AMAZING DUE TO THE FACT THAT PETE GRAY HAD ONLY ONE ARM AFTER LOSING HIS RIGHT ARM IN A CHILDHOOD ACCIDENT. PETE POSSESSED GREAT SPEED, A VERY STRONG THROWING ARM, AND AN INCREDIBLY ATHLETIC TECHNIQUE FOR FIELDING A BATTED BALL. WEARING A FLOPPY GLOVE ON HIS LEFT HAND, PETE WOULD FIELD THE BALL, FLIP IT IN THE AIR WHILE PULLING THE GLOVE OFF HIS HAND WITH THE STUMP OF HIS RIGHT ARM, SNATCH THE BALL OUT OF THE AIR WITH HIS NOW-BARE HAND, AND FIRE IT INTO THE INFIELD -- ALL IN ONE QUICK, FLUID MOTION. SWINGING FROM THE LEFT SIDE OF THE PLATE, PETE WHIPPED HIS BAT THROUGH THE ZONE QUICKLY, AND COULD GET AROUND ON THE BEST FASTBALLS IN THE LEAGUE. WHEN PITCHERS LEARNED THIS, THEY RESORTED TO OFFSPEED PITCHES WHICH WERE MORE DIFFICULT FOR PETE. STILL, HE BATTED .218 IN 234 CAREER AT-BATS -- ALL IN 1945. WHILE PETE WAS AN INSPIRATION TO MANY, THERE WAS RESENTMENT AMONG SOME BROWNS WHO FELT THAT PETE'S SPOT ON THEIR ROSTER COST THEM A CHANCE TO WIN A SECOND STRAIGHT A.L. PENNANT. WHATEVER THE CASE MAY BE, THE STORY OF PETE GRAY IS ONE OF TRIUMPH, AND THE SAGA OF THE "ONE-ARMED WONDER" WILL LIVE FOREVER.

Junior STEPHENS

VERN STEPHENS WON ONE HOME RUN TITLE AND THREE RBI CROWNS DURING HIS 15-YEAR BIG LEAGUE CAREER!

THE ST. LOUIS BROWNS WON ONLY ONE PENNANT IN THEIR 51-YEAR HISTORY, AND NO ONE WAS MORE KEY TO THAT TITLE THAN THEIR 23-YEAR-OLD SHORTSTOP VERNON "JUNIOR" STEPHENS! NOT ONLY WAS VERN ROCK SOLID ON DEFENSE WITH A CANNON FOR AN ARM, HE WAS ALSO A FORCE TO BE RECKONED WITH AT THE PLATE! IN JUST HIS SECOND FULL SEASON, VERN HIT .293 WITH 20 HOMERS AND A LEAGUE-LEADING 109 RBIs FOR THE '44 A.L. CHAMPS! FRUSTRATED WITH THE CASH-POOR OWNERSHIP OF THE BROWNS, VERN JUMPED TO THE HIGH-PAYING OUTLAW MEXICAN LEAGUE IN THE SPRING OF 1946 -- BUT WISELY RETURNED WHEN COMMISSIONER CHANDLER THREATENED A 5-YEAR BAN TO ANY PLAYER WHO STAYED IN MEXICO! VERN LATER CASHED IN WHEN HE JOINED THE RED SOX IN 1948! HE AVERAGED 33 ROUND-TRIPPERS PER YEAR IN HIS FIRST THREE YEARS IN BOSTON BEFORE INJURIES BEGAN TO SLOW HIM! HE WAS AHEAD OF HIS TIME AS A POWER-HITTING SHORTSTOP, AND FINISHED WITH 247 CAREER LONG BALLS! NOW FORGOTTEN EXCEPT TO THE TRUE BASEBALL HISTORIANS, MANY OF VERN'S PEERS CONSIDERED HIM TO BE A HALL OF FAMER!

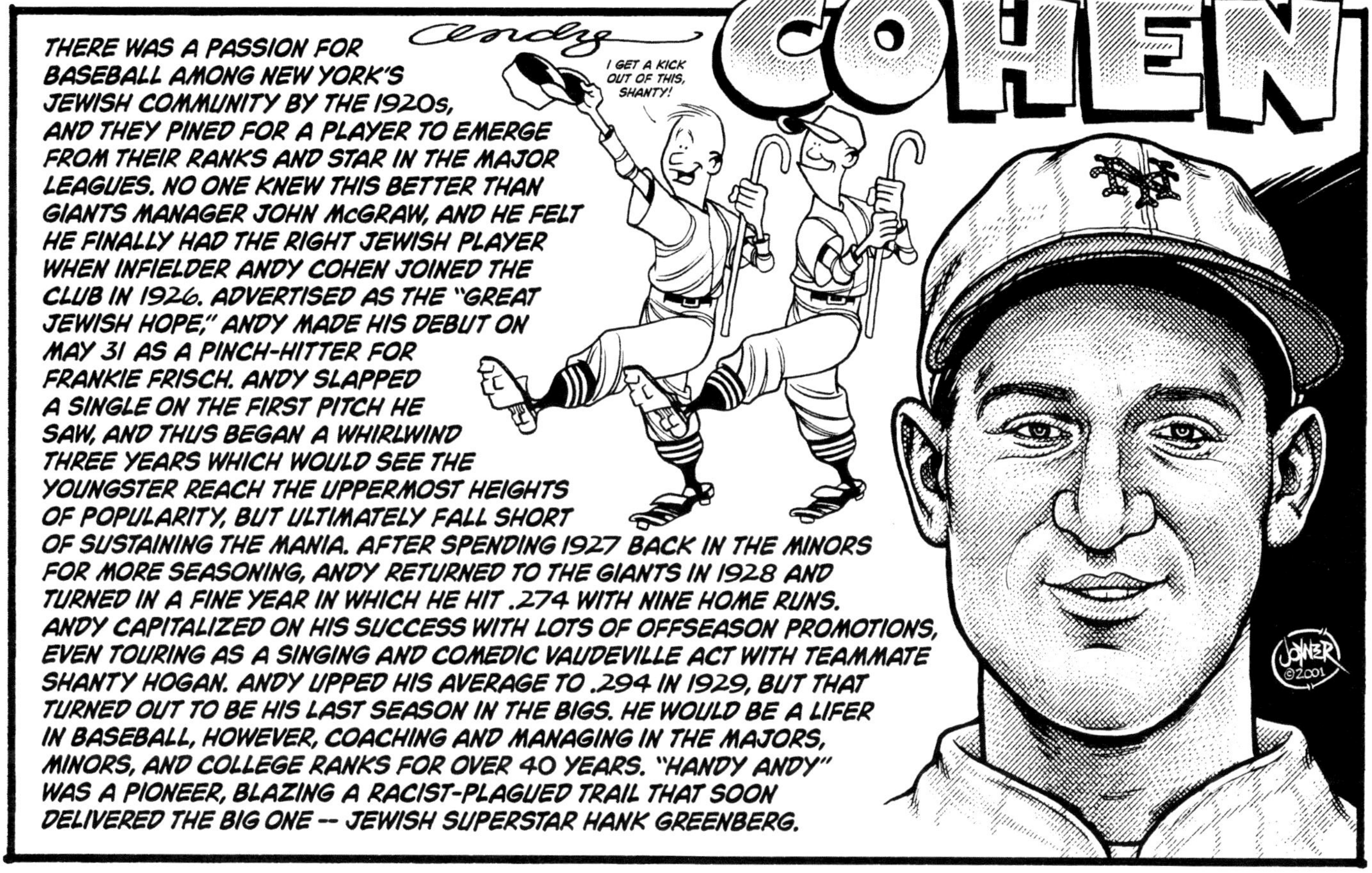
Andy
COHEN
I GET A KICK OUT OF THIS, SHANTY!
THERE WAS A PASSION FOR BASEBALL AMONG NEW YORK'S JEWISH COMMUNITY BY THE 1920s, AND THEY PINED FOR A PLAYER TO EMERGE FROM THEIR RANKS AND STAR IN THE MAJOR LEAGUES. NO ONE KNEW THIS BETTER THAN GIANTS MANAGER JOHN McGRAW, AND HE FELT HE FINALLY HAD THE RIGHT JEWISH PLAYER WHEN INFIELDER ANDY COHEN JOINED THE CLUB IN 1926. ADVERTISED AS THE "GREAT JEWISH HOPE," ANDY MADE HIS DEBUT ON MAY 31 AS A PINCH-HITTER FOR FRANKIE FRISCH. ANDY SLAPPED A SINGLE ON THE FIRST PITCH HE SAW, AND THUS BEGAN A WHIRLWIND THREE YEARS WHICH WOULD SEE THE YOUNGSTER REACH THE UPPERMOST HEIGHTS OF POPULARITY, BUT ULTIMATELY FALL SHORT OF SUSTAINING THE MANIA. AFTER SPENDING 1927 BACK IN THE MINORS FOR MORE SEASONING, ANDY RETURNED TO THE GIANTS IN 1928 AND TURNED IN A FINE YEAR IN WHICH HE HIT .274 WITH NINE HOME RUNS. ANDY CAPITALIZED ON HIS SUCCESS WITH LOTS OF OFFSEASON PROMOTIONS, EVEN TOURING AS A SINGING AND COMEDIC VAUDEVILLE ACT WITH TEAMMATE SHANTY HOGAN. ANDY UPPED HIS AVERAGE TO .294 IN 1929, BUT THAT TURNED OUT TO BE HIS LAST SEASON IN THE BIGS. HE WOULD BE A LIFER IN BASEBALL, HOWEVER, COACHING AND MANAGING IN THE MAJORS, MINORS, AND COLLEGE RANKS FOR OVER 40 YEARS. "HANDY ANDY" WAS A PIONEER, BLAZING A RACIST-PLAGUED TRAIL THAT SOON DELIVERED THE BIG ONE -- JEWISH SUPERSTAR HANK GREENBERG.
JOYNER ©2001

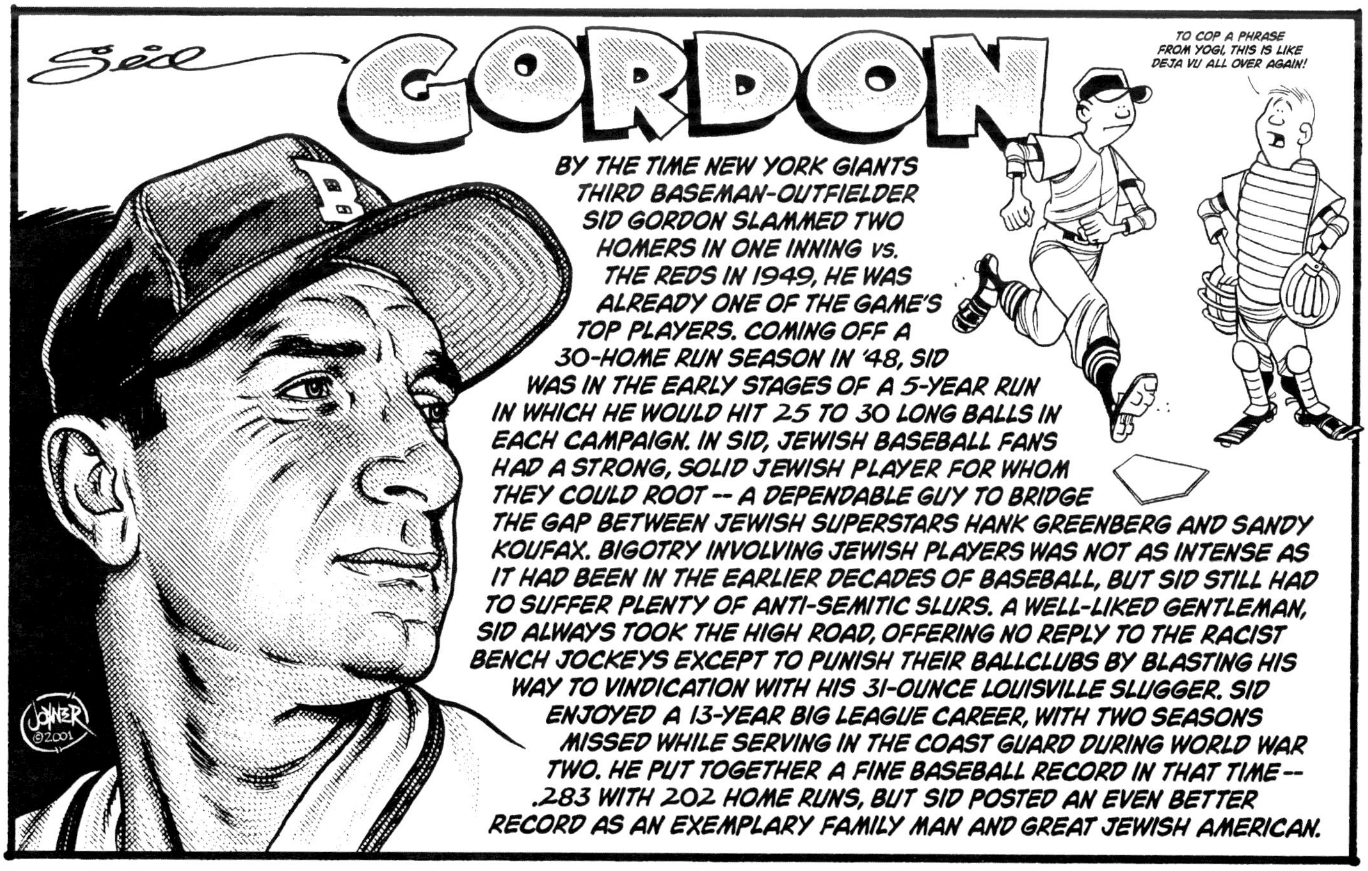
Sid
GORDON
TO COP A PHRASE FROM YOGI, THIS IS LIKE DEJA VU ALL OVER AGAIN!
BY THE TIME NEW YORK GIANTS THIRD BASEMAN-OUTFIELDER SID GORDON SLAMMED TWO HOMERS IN ONE INNING vs. THE REDS IN 1949, HE WAS ALREADY ONE OF THE GAME'S TOP PLAYERS. COMING OFF A 30-HOME RUN SEASON IN '48, SID WAS IN THE EARLY STAGES OF A 5-YEAR RUN IN WHICH HE WOULD HIT 25 TO 30 LONG BALLS IN EACH CAMPAIGN. IN SID, JEWISH BASEBALL FANS HAD A STRONG, SOLID JEWISH PLAYER FOR WHOM THEY COULD ROOT -- A DEPENDABLE GUY TO BRIDGE THE GAP BETWEEN JEWISH SUPERSTARS HANK GREENBERG AND SANDY KOUFAX. BIGOTRY INVOLVING JEWISH PLAYERS WAS NOT AS INTENSE AS IT HAD BEEN IN THE EARLIER DECADES OF BASEBALL, BUT SID STILL HAD TO SUFFER PLENTY OF ANTI-SEMITIC SLURS. A WELL-LIKED GENTLEMAN, SID ALWAYS TOOK THE HIGH ROAD, OFFERING NO REPLY TO THE RACIST BENCH JOCKEYS EXCEPT TO PUNISH THEIR BALLCLUBS BY BLASTING HIS WAY TO VINDICATION WITH HIS 31-OUNCE LOUISVILLE SLUGGER. SID ENJOYED A 13-YEAR BIG LEAGUE CAREER, WITH TWO SEASONS MISSED WHILE SERVING IN THE COAST GUARD DURING WORLD WAR TWO. HE PUT TOGETHER A FINE BASEBALL RECORD IN THAT TIME -- .283 WITH 202 HOME RUNS, BUT SID POSTED AN EVEN BETTER RECORD AS AN EXEMPLARY FAMILY MAN AND GREAT JEWISH AMERICAN.
JOYNER ©2001

Dick
KoKoS
BABY-FACED DICK WAS OFTEN DENIED ENTRY TO THE BALLPARK DURING HIS ROOKIE SEASON BY GATEKEEPERS WHO DIDN'T BELIEVE HIM WHEN HE TOLD THEM HE WAS A PLAYER!
WHO'S THE BEST RIGHTFIELDER IN THE LEAGUE? UM, THAT WOULD BE ME!
WHEN ASKED TO NAME THE "MOST CONCEITED" PLAYER IN THE AMERICAN LEAGUE, A 1954 POLL OF 100 SPORTSWRITERS RANKED ORIOLES OUTFIELDER DICK KOKOS EIGHTH! DICK HAD REASON TO BE COCKY, THOUGH! A HANDSOME KID OF 26 IN '54, HE SEEMED TO BE POISED FOR A LONG CAREER AS ONE OF THE A.L.'s ELITE POWER HITTERS! THE RIFLE-ARMED FLYCHASER BURST ON THE SCENE WITH THE ST. LOUIS BROWNS MIDWAY THROUGH THE 1948 SEASON WHEN HE SHOWED GREAT PROMISE BY BATTING .298 WITH FOUR HOMERS AND 40 RBIs IN ONLY 71 GAMES! DICK AVERAGED .261 AND 20 LONG BALLS FROM 1949 TO 1950, BUT HE THEN LOST TWO FULL YEARS TO THE KOREAN WAR! HE WASN'T QUITE THE SAME PLAYER UPON HIS RETURN TO THE BROWNIES IN 1953, SLIPPING TO .241 AND 13 HOMERS! AFTER MOVING WITH THE BROWNS TO BALTIMORE AND APPEARING IN JUST ELEVEN GAMES FOR THE '54 O's, DICK WAS BACK IN THE MINORS FOR GOOD... BUT NOT BEFORE LEAVING A STYLISH IMPRINT ON THOSE WHO WATCHED -- AND REPORTED -- ON THE GAME!
JOYNER ©2001

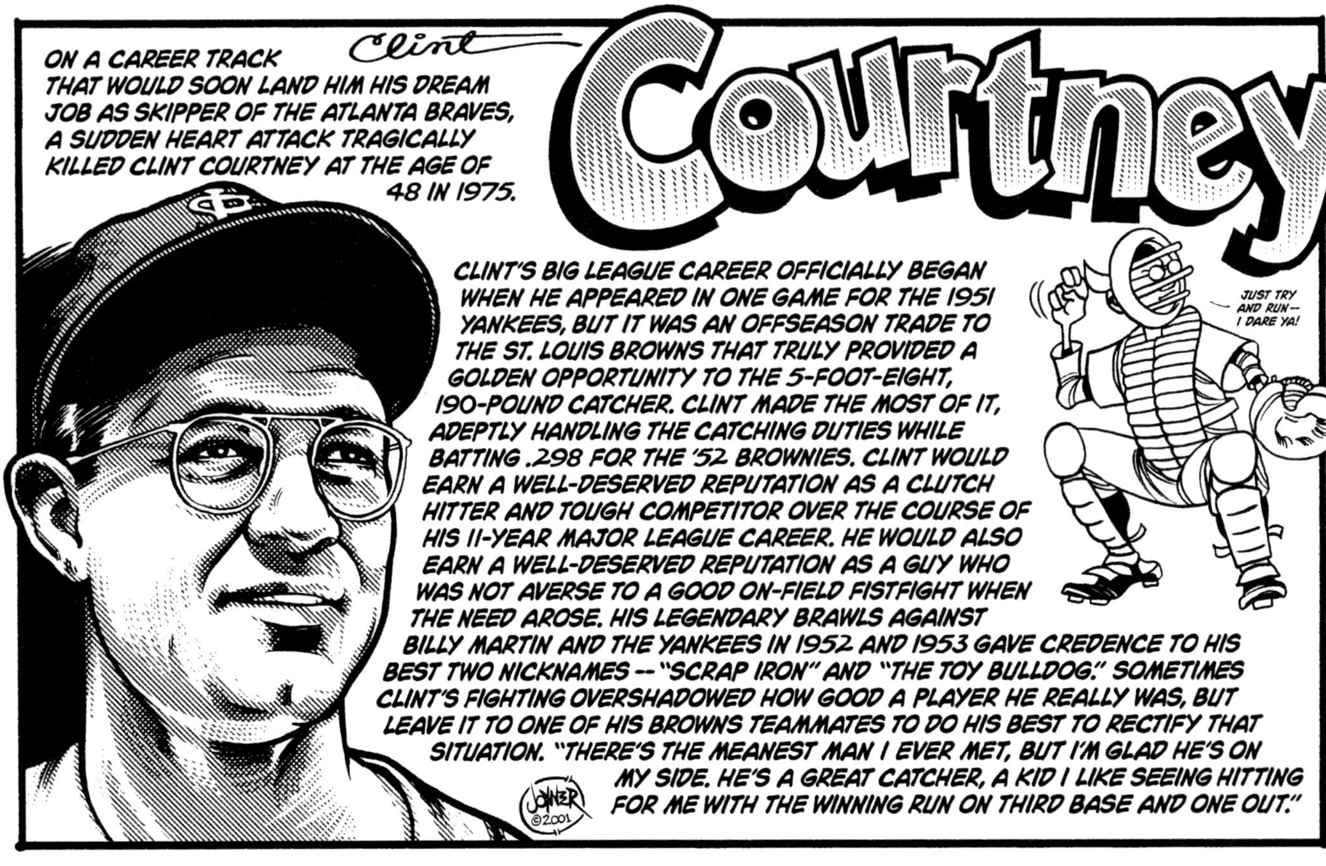
Clint
Courtney
ON A CAREER TRACK THAT WOULD SOON LAND HIM HIS DREAM JOB AS SKIPPER OF THE ATLANTA BRAVES, A SUDDEN HEART ATTACK TRAGICALLY KILLED CLINT COURTNEY AT THE AGE OF 48 IN 1975.
JUST TRY AND RUN— I DARE YA!
CLINT'S BIG LEAGUE CAREER OFFICIALLY BEGAN WHEN HE APPEARED IN ONE GAME FOR THE 1951 YANKEES, BUT IT WAS AN OFFSEASON TRADE TO THE ST. LOUIS BROWNS THAT TRULY PROVIDED A GOLDEN OPPORTUNITY TO THE 5-FOOT-EIGHT, 190-POUND CATCHER. CLINT MADE THE MOST OF IT, ADEPTLY HANDLING THE CATCHING DUTIES WHILE BATTING .298 FOR THE '52 BROWNIES. CLINT WOULD EARN A WELL-DESERVED REPUTATION AS A CLUTCH HITTER AND TOUGH COMPETITOR OVER THE COURSE OF HIS 11-YEAR MAJOR LEAGUE CAREER. HE WOULD ALSO EARN A WELL-DESERVED REPUTATION AS A GUY WHO WAS NOT AVERSE TO A GOOD ON-FIELD FISTFIGHT WHEN THE NEED AROSE. HIS LEGENDARY BRAWLS AGAINST BILLY MARTIN AND THE YANKEES IN 1952 AND 1953 GAVE CREDENCE TO HIS BEST TWO NICKNAMES -- "SCRAP IRON" AND "THE TOY BULLDOG." SOMETIMES CLINT'S FIGHTING OVERSHADOWED HOW GOOD A PLAYER HE REALLY WAS, BUT LEAVE IT TO ONE OF HIS BROWNS TEAMMATES TO DO HIS BEST TO RECTIFY THAT SITUATION. "THERE'S THE MEANEST MAN I EVER MET, BUT I'M GLAD HE'S ON MY SIDE. HE'S A GREAT CATCHER, A KID I LIKE SEEING HITTING FOR ME WITH THE WINNING RUN ON THIRD BASE AND ONE OUT."
JOYNER ©2001

Claire
SCHILLACE
IN THE MOST IMPORTANT EVENT IN WOMEN'S BASEBALL -- THE 1943 FORMATION OF THE ALL-AMERICAN GIRLS PROFESSIONAL BASEBALL LEAGUE -- CLAIRE SCHILLACE WAS THE FIRST PLAYER DRAFTED. GIVEN THE OPPORTUNITY TO CHOOSE FOR HERSELF WHICH OF THE FOUR INAUGURAL TEAMS SHE WANTED TO JOIN, CLAIRE CHOSE THE RACINE BELLES BECAUSE SHE LIKED THE NOW-ICONIC YELLOW UNIFORM. IT WAS CLAIRE'S INCREDIBLE SKILL AS A CHICAGO-BASED SOFTBALL PLAYER THAT LED A.A.G.P.B.L. OFFICIALS TO DRAFT HER WITHOUT A TRYOUT, AND THEY QUICKLY SIGNED HER TO A $75-PER-WEEK CONTRACT. "I COULDN'T BELIEVE THAT I WAS OFFERED $75 A WEEK TO DO SOMETHING I LOVED DOING," CLAIRE TOLD THE WASHINGTON POST IN 1998. "THAT WAS BIG MONEY IN THOSE DAYS." CLAIRE PLAYED FOR THE BELLES FOR FOUR YEARS, BUT THEN MOVED ON TO BEGIN A NEW LIFE AS A WIFE, MOTHER, AND TEACHER. SHE WAS A CONSULTANT ON THE 1992 FILM "A LEAGUE OF THEIR OWN," AND WAS ALSO FEATURED IN AN EXHIBIT AT THE HALL OF FAME IN COOPERSTOWN!
YEP, I THINK THE YELLOW UNIFORM WAS THE RIGHT ONE FOR ME!
JOYNER ©2002

Eleanor
ENGLE
NOTE TO SELF: DO NOT LET ANY BALLS GO BETWEEN MY LEGS!
ON JUNE 21, 1952, ELEANOR ENGLE SIGNED A CONTRACT TO PLAY SHORTSTOP FOR THE HARRISBURG SENATORS -- THE CLASS B MINOR LEAGUE AFFILIATE OF THE PHILADELPHIA A's. SLATED TO DEBUT THE NEXT DAY, ELEANOR WOULD BECOME THE FIRST WOMAN EVER TO PLAY IN MEN'S PROFESSIONAL ORGANIZED BASEBALL. A FIRESTORM OF PROTEST ERUPTED WHEN THE NEWS HIT THE PAPERS, AND WITHIN 24 HOURS A RULE WAS ENACTED THAT FORBADE WOMEN FROM PLAYING IN THE MINOR LEAGUES. ELEANOR WORKED OUT WITH THE SENATORS BEFORE THEIR GAME ON JUNE 22, BUT THE PROHIBITIVE EDICT NIXED HER DEBUT, AND SHE WATCHED THE GAME FROM THE PRESS BOX. MOST LIKELY A PUBLICITY STUNT ON THE PART OF THE SENATORS' FRONT OFFICE EXECS TO COUNTER SAGGING ATTENDANCE, THE MOST INTRIGUING PART OF THE STORY WILL REMAIN A MYSTERY -- HOW WOULD ELEANOR HAVE DONE vs. THE MEN? THERE WAS NO RECORD OF ELEANOR'S ATHLETIC ACTIVITIES OTHER THAN CLUB EXECUTIVES SAYING SHE WAS A TALENTED SOFTBALL PLAYER. AFTER WATCHING HER PRE-GAME WARMUP, ONE VETERAN SCOUT OFFERED UP THE ULTIMATE INSULT, SAYING, "SHE THREW LIKE A GIRL." WHATEVER THE CASE MAY BE, IT TOOK GUTS FOR ELEANOR TO EXPOSE HERSELF TO SUCH SCORN, AND HER ACTIONS HELPED ADVANCE THE DISCUSSION OF WOMEN IN SPORTS.
JOYNER ©2002

BLACK SOX: 1919 CHICAGO WHITE SOX

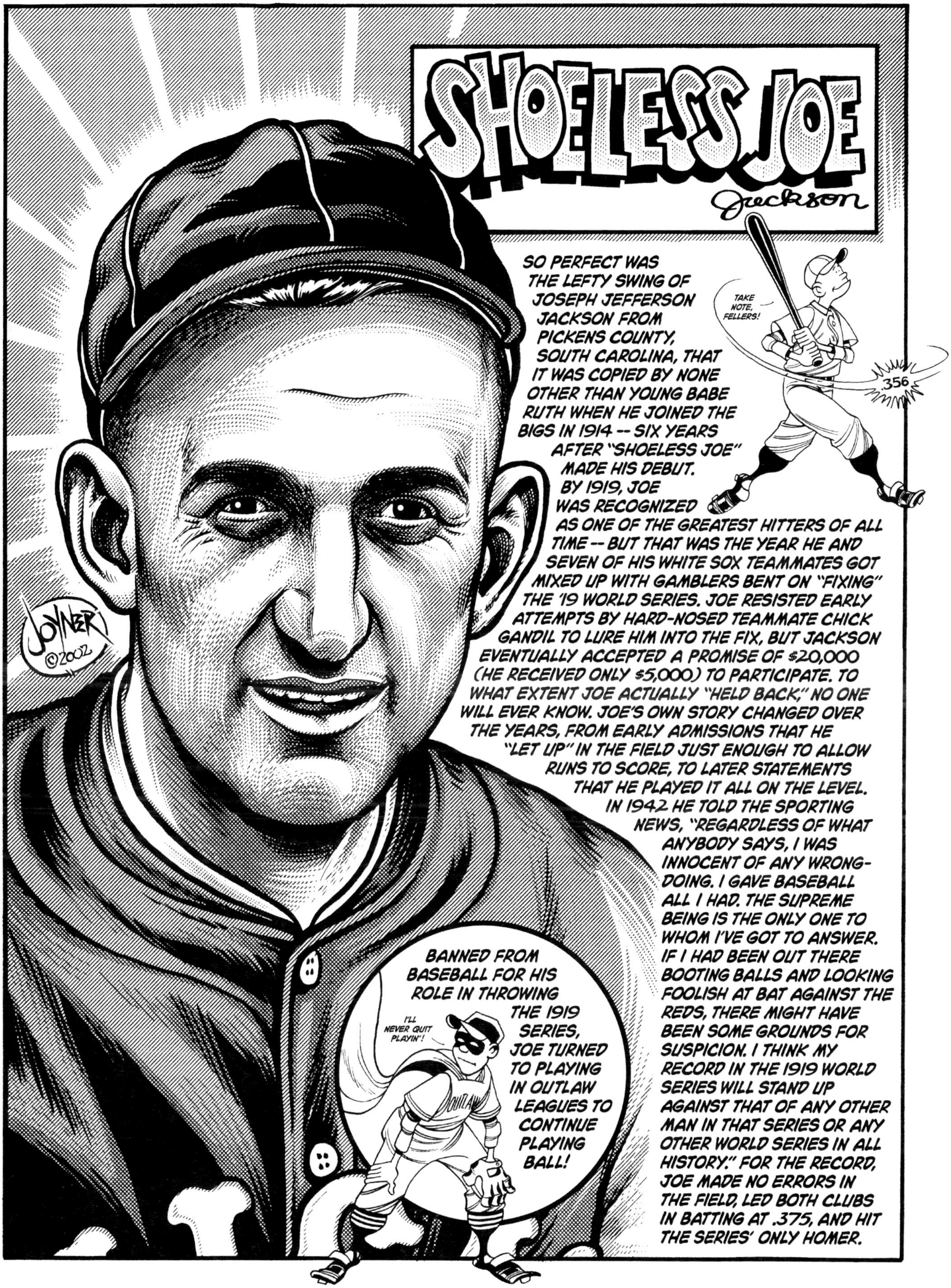
SHOELESS JOE
Jackson
SO PERFECT WAS THE LEFTY SWING OF JOSEPH JEFFERSON JACKSON FROM PICKENS COUNTY, SOUTH CAROLINA, THAT IT WAS COPIED BY NONE OTHER THAN YOUNG BABE RUTH WHEN HE JOINED THE BIGS IN 1914 -- SIX YEARS AFTER "SHOELESS JOE" MADE HIS DEBUT. BY 1919, JOE WAS RECOGNIZED AS ONE OF THE GREATEST HITTERS OF ALL TIME -- BUT THAT WAS THE YEAR HE AND SEVEN OF HIS WHITE SOX TEAMMATES GOT MIXED UP WITH GAMBLERS BENT ON "FIXING" THE '19 WORLD SERIES. JOE RESISTED EARLY ATTEMPTS BY HARD-NOSED TEAMMATE CHICK GANDIL TO LURE HIM INTO THE FIX, BUT JACKSON EVENTUALLY ACCEPTED A PROMISE OF $20,000 (HE RECEIVED ONLY $5,000) TO PARTICIPATE. TO WHAT EXTENT JOE ACTUALLY "HELD BACK," NO ONE WILL EVER KNOW. JOE'S OWN STORY CHANGED OVER THE YEARS, FROM EARLY ADMISSIONS THAT HE "LET UP" IN THE FIELD JUST ENOUGH TO ALLOW RUNS TO SCORE, TO LATER STATEMENTS THAT HE PLAYED IT ALL ON THE LEVEL. IN 1942 HE TOLD THE SPORTING NEWS, "REGARDLESS OF WHAT ANYBODY SAYS, I WAS INNOCENT OF ANY WRONG-DOING. I GAVE BASEBALL ALL I HAD. THE SUPREME BEING IS THE ONLY ONE TO WHOM I'VE GOT TO ANSWER. IF I HAD BEEN OUT THERE BOOTING BALLS AND LOOKING FOOLISH AT BAT AGAINST THE REDS, THERE MIGHT HAVE BEEN SOME GROUNDS FOR SUSPICION. I THINK MY RECORD IN THE 1919 WORLD SERIES WILL STAND UP AGAINST THAT OF ANY OTHER MAN IN THAT SERIES OR ANY OTHER WORLD SERIES IN ALL HISTORY." FOR THE RECORD, JOE MADE NO ERRORS IN THE FIELD, LED BOTH CLUBS IN BATTING AT .375, AND HIT THE SERIES' ONLY HOMER.
TAKE NOTE, FELLERS!
.356
BANNED FROM BASEBALL FOR HIS ROLE IN THROWING THE 1919 SERIES, JOE TURNED TO PLAYING IN OUTLAW LEAGUES TO CONTINUE PLAYING BALL!
I'LL NEVER QUIT PLAYIN'!
OUTLAW
JOYNER ©2002

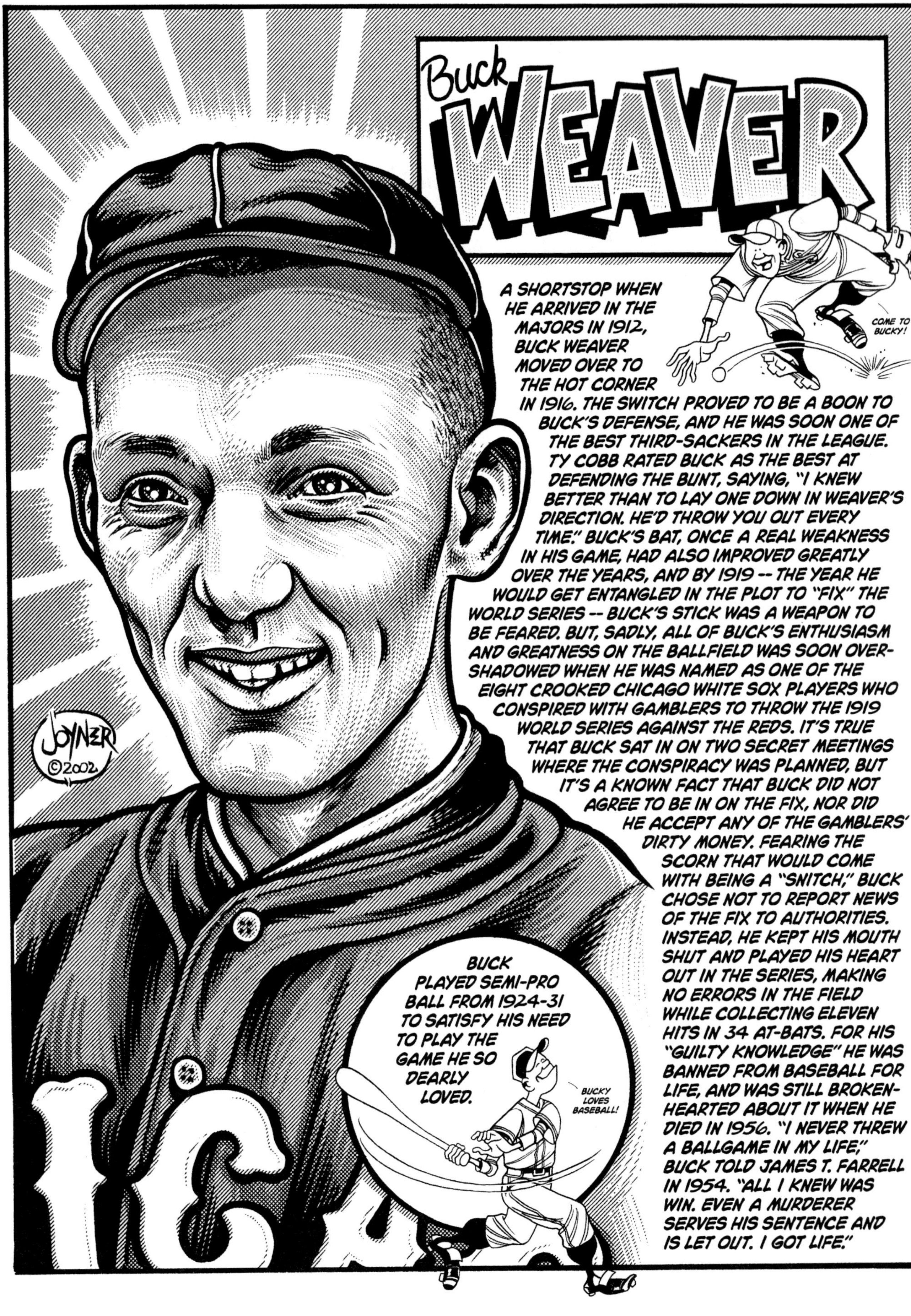
Buck WEAVER
A SHORTSTOP WHEN HE ARRIVED IN THE MAJORS IN 1912, BUCK WEAVER MOVED OVER TO THE HOT CORNER IN 1916. THE SWITCH PROVED TO BE A BOON TO BUCK'S DEFENSE, AND HE WAS SOON ONE OF THE BEST THIRD-SACKERS IN THE LEAGUE. TY COBB RATED BUCK AS THE BEST AT DEFENDING THE BUNT, SAYING, "I KNEW BETTER THAN TO LAY ONE DOWN IN WEAVER'S DIRECTION. HE'D THROW YOU OUT EVERY TIME." BUCK'S BAT, ONCE A REAL WEAKNESS IN HIS GAME, HAD ALSO IMPROVED GREATLY OVER THE YEARS, AND BY 1919 -- THE YEAR HE WOULD GET ENTANGLED IN THE PLOT TO "FIX" THE WORLD SERIES -- BUCK'S STICK WAS A WEAPON TO BE FEARED. BUT, SADLY, ALL OF BUCK'S ENTHUSIASM AND GREATNESS ON THE BALLFIELD WAS SOON OVER-SHADOWED WHEN HE WAS NAMED AS ONE OF THE EIGHT CROOKED CHICAGO WHITE SOX PLAYERS WHO CONSPIRED WITH GAMBLERS TO THROW THE 1919 WORLD SERIES AGAINST THE REDS. IT'S TRUE THAT BUCK SAT IN ON TWO SECRET MEETINGS WHERE THE CONSPIRACY WAS PLANNED, BUT IT'S A KNOWN FACT THAT BUCK DID NOT AGREE TO BE IN ON THE FIX, NOR DID HE ACCEPT ANY OF THE GAMBLERS' DIRTY MONEY. FEARING THE SCORN THAT WOULD COME WITH BEING A "SNITCH," BUCK CHOSE NOT TO REPORT NEWS OF THE FIX TO AUTHORITIES. INSTEAD, HE KEPT HIS MOUTH SHUT AND PLAYED HIS HEART OUT IN THE SERIES, MAKING NO ERRORS IN THE FIELD WHILE COLLECTING ELEVEN HITS IN 34 AT-BATS. FOR HIS "GUILTY KNOWLEDGE" HE WAS BANNED FROM BASEBALL FOR LIFE, AND WAS STILL BROKEN-HEARTED ABOUT IT WHEN HE DIED IN 1956. "I NEVER THREW A BALLGAME IN MY LIFE," BUCK TOLD JAMES T. FARRELL IN 1954. "ALL I KNEW WAS WIN. EVEN A MURDERER SERVES HIS SENTENCE AND IS LET OUT. I GOT LIFE."
COME TO BUCKY!
BUCK PLAYED SEMI-PRO BALL FROM 1924-31 TO SATISFY HIS NEED TO PLAY THE GAME HE SO DEARLY LOVED.
BUCKY LOVES BASEBALL!
JOYNER ©2002

EDDIE Cicotte

HAVING MASTERED AN ARSENAL OF MOUND OFFERINGS THAT INCLUDED TRICK PITCHES LIKE EMERY BALLS, SHINE BALLS, AND KNUCKLERS, EDDIE CICOTTE HAD EVOLVED INTO ONE OF THE LEAGUE'S BEST HURLERS BY 1919 WHEN HE GOT HIMSELF MIRED IN THE PLOT TO "FIX" THAT SEASON'S FALL CLASSIC.

THE LITTLE RIGHT-HANDER WON AN A.L. BEST 29 GAMES FOR THE CHISOX IN 1919, AND WAS POISED TO LEAD HIS TEAM TO THEIR SECOND WORLD SERIES TITLE IN THREE YEARS, BUT FINANCIAL WOES AND BITTER RESENTMENT TOWARDS TIGHT-FISTED SOX OWNER CHARLES COMISKEY CONVINCED EDDIE TO GET IN ON THE FIX. HE DEMANDED A $10,000 CASH PAYMENT UP FRONT, WHICH HE RECEIVED, AND IN EXCHANGE HE TANKED HIS PERFORMANCE IN WORLD SERIES GAMES ONE AND FOUR. AMID SWIRLING RUMORS, EDDIE LATER ADMITTED HIS ROLE IN THE FIX AND WAS SUBSEQUENTLY BANNED FROM BASEBALL FOR LIFE. "I ADMIT I DID WRONG," EDDIE SAID LATE IN HIS LIFE, "BUT I'VE PAID FOR IT. I'VE TRIED TO MAKE UP FOR IT BY LIVING AS CLEAN A LIFE AS I COULD. I'M PROUD OF THE WAY I'VE LIVED SINCE THE SCANDAL, AND I THINK MY FAMILY IS, TOO. NOBODY CAN HURT ME ANYMORE. I HAVEN'T GOT AN ENEMY IN THE WORLD. EVERYBODY WHO HAS EVER LIVED HAS COMMITTED SINS."

Lefty WILLIAMS

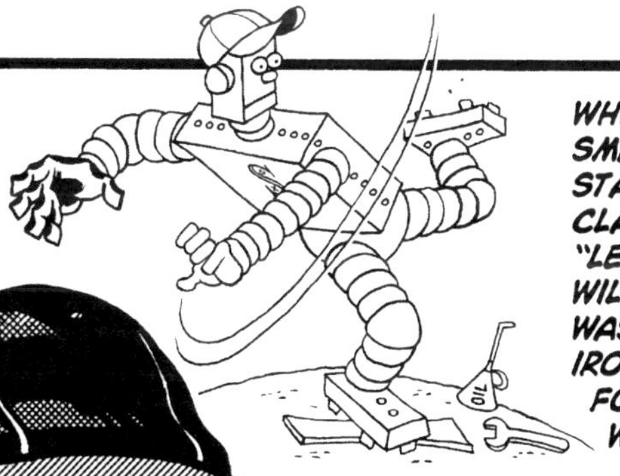

WHILE SMALL IN STATURE, CLAUDE "LEFTY" WILLIAMS WAS A REAL IRON MAN FOR THE WHITE SOX OF 1919, LEADING THE A.L. IN STARTS WHILE TOSSING 297 INNINGS. IT WAS A BREAKOUT SEASON FOR THE MISSOURI-BORN SOUTHPAW, AND HIS 23 WINS WERE A KEY REASON THE SOX CAPTURED THE 1919 A.L. PENNANT. POSITIONED TO RIDE HIS LOOPING CURVEBALL TO CHAMPIONSHIP GLORY, LEFTY WAS INSTEAD DRAWN INTO A GAMBLING CONSPIRACY TO "THROW" THE WORLD SERIES IN EXCHANGE FOR THE PROMISE OF A BIG CASH PAYOFF. "THE SITUATION WAS FIRST BROUGHT UP TO ME IN NEW YORK," LEFTY RECOUNTED IN 1920. "CHICK GANDIL CALLED ME TO ONE SIDE AND PUT THIS THING TO ME. I WAS INFORMED THAT WHETHER OR NOT I TOOK ANY ACTION, GAMES WOULD BE FIXED. SO I TOLD HIM THAT ANYTHING THEY DID WOULD BE AGREEABLE TO ME IF IT WAS GOING TO BE DONE ANYWAY. I HAD NO MONEY, SO I MIGHT AS WELL GET WHAT I COULD. I WAS SUPPOSED TO GET $10,000 AFTER THE SECOND GAME. I DIDN'T RECEIVE IT UNTIL THE FOURTH GAME, AND I GOT ONLY $5,000." LEFTY PROVED GOOD AT PITCHING BADLY, TAKING THE LOSS IN ALL THREE SERIES GAMES HE STARTED. SUBSEQUENTLY BANNED FROM BASEBALL, LEFTY PITCHED OUTLAW BALL FOR A WHILE BEFORE SETTLING WITH HIS WIFE IN CALIFORNIA WHERE HE KEPT QUIET ABOUT THE SCANDAL UNTIL HIS DEATH IN 1959. LEFTY WAS BURIED IN AN UNMARKED GRAVE IN MELROSE ABBEY MEMORIAL PARK.

Chick GANDIL

AT SIX-FOOT-TWO AND 195 POUNDS, ARNOLD "CHICK" GANDIL HONED HIS TOUGH GUY PERSONA AS A $150-PER-FIGHT HEAVYWEIGHT BOXER IN THE HARD-SCRABBLE MINING TOWN OF CANANEA, MEXICO. HE WAS ALSO HONING HIS BASEBALL SKILLS ON CANANEA'S OUTLAW BASEBALL TEAM, AND BY 1919 CHICK WAS A SEASONED BIG LEAGUE FIRST BASEMAN FOR THE CHICAGO WHITE SOX. DISGRUNTLED AT TEAM OWNER CHARLES COMISKEY'S REFUSAL TO PAY HIM A FAIR WAGE, CHICK AGREED WITH GAMBLERS TO BE THE LINCHPIN IN A PLOT TO "THROW" THE 1919 WORLD SERIES AGAINST THE UNDERDOG CINCINNATI REDS. TO SET THE RECORD (AS HE SAW IT) STRAIGHT, CHICK GAVE AN IN-DEPTH INTERVIEW TO MELVIN DURSLAG OF SPORTS ILLUSTRATED IN 1956. ON BEING BANNED FROM BASEBALL FOR LIFE, CHICK SAID, "WE GOT WHAT WE HAD COMING. I HAVE OFTEN BEEN DESCRIBED AS ONE OF THE RINGLEADERS OF THE BLACK SOX SCANDAL. THERE'S NO DOUBT ABOUT IT -- I WAS. CICOTTE AND I CALLED THE OTHER SIX TOGETHER FOR A MEETING. THEY WERE ALL INTERESTED." ON THE EVE OF THE SERIES OPENER, AMID SWIRLING RUMORS OF A "FIX," CHICK CLAIMS THE PLAYERS GOT COLD FEET. "IT WAS FINALLY DECIDED THAT THERE WAS TOO MUCH SUSPICION TO THROW THE GAMES WITHOUT GETTING CAUGHT. OUR ONLY COURSE WAS TO (DOUBLE-CROSS THE GAMBLERS AND) TRY TO WIN -- AND WE WERE CERTAIN WE COULD. I OFFER NO DEFENSE FOR THE THING WE CONSPIRED TO DO. IT WAS INEXCUSABLE. BUT I MAINTAIN THAT OUR ACTUAL LOSING OF THE SERIES WAS PURE BASEBALL FORTUNE."

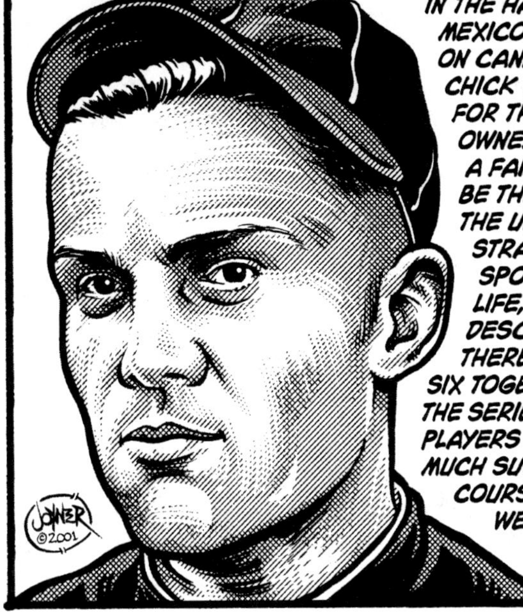

Swede RISBERG

BORN IN SUNNY CALIFORNIA, CHARLES AUGUST "SWEDE" RISBERG MADE A NAME FOR HIMSELF IN THE BAY AREA AS A HARD-THROWING SEMI-PRO PITCHER. SWEDE ALSO MADE A NOT-SO-FLATTERING NAME FOR HIMSELF, HOWEVER, AS A TOUGH, MEAN, STANDOFFISH PLAYER -- ALWAYS READY TO FIGHT. THIS REPUTATION WAS ENHANCED BY AN INCIDENT IN THE P.C.L. THAT SAW SWEDE DECK AN UMPIRE AFTER DISAGREEING WITH THE UMP'S CALLED THIRD STRIKE ON HIM. BY 1919 SWEDE WAS PLAYING SHORTSTOP WITH THE PENNANT-WINNING WHITE SOX, AND HIS SURLY DISPOSITION MADE HIM THE PERFECT RIGHT-HAND MAN TO TEAMMATE CHICK GANDIL WHO HAD HATCHED A PLOT WITH GAMBLERS TO "THROW" THE 1919 WORLD SERIES AGAINST THE CINCINNATI REDS. BANNED FROM BASEBALL FOR HIS INVOLVEMENT, SWEDE NEVER SPOKE ABOUT THE "FIX" IN HIS OLD AGE, BUT HE DID OFFER SOME BITTER INSIGHT IN 1934 WHEN HE SAID, "IF I HAD HELD UP A BANK I WOULD HAVE PAID THE PENALTY BY NOW AND WOULD BE OUT OF JAIL EARNING A LIVING. THOSE FOURTEEN YEARS PUNISHMENT WOULD SEEM TO BE ENOUGH, EVEN IF I HAD BEEN GUILTY. AT THE TIME OF THE AFFAIR I WAS GOING STRONG IN BASEBALL WITH A GOOD MANY YEARS AHEAD OF ME. I THINK I HAVE SERVED MY TERM AND PAID MY FINE, AND OUGHT TO HAVE A CHANCE TO EARN MY LIVING AGAIN IN ORGANIZED BASEBALL."

Happy FELSCH

WHITE SOX CENTERFIELDER OSCAR "HAPPY" FELSCH EARNED HIS SUNNY NICKNAME WHILE STILL AN INFANT. "HE WAS BORN WITH A SMILE," HAP'S FATHER OFTEN EXPLAINED. BUT HAP'S FRIENDLY GRIN WAS GONE BY THE SUMMER OF 1920 WHEN HE WAS BANNED FROM BASEBALL DUE TO HIS INVOLVEMENT IN THE CONSPIRACY TO "THROW" THE 1919 WORLD SERIES. IN JUST HIS FOURTH SEASON IN 1919, HAP WAS ALREADY CONSIDERED ONE OF THE BEST FLYCHASERS IN THE LEAGUE, AND HIS POWER AT THE PLATE WAS STEADILY INCREASING. TEAMMATE AND "FIX" ORGANIZER CHICK GANDIL KNEW HAP WOULD BE A KEY TO PULLING OFF THE CON, AND HE EASILY SLICK-TALKED THE AFFABLE FELSCH INTO GOING ALONG. SURE-HANDED HAP MADE SEVERAL SUSPICIOUS DEFENSIVE FLUBS IN THE SERIES WHILE HITTING FOR AN ANEMIC .192 AVERAGE. SHAMED, HE AVOIDING SPEAKING ABOUT THE SCANDAL FOR MOST OF HIS LIFE, BUT HE BEGAN OPENING UP IN HIS OLD AGE, SEEMINGLY IN AN EFFORT TO EASE THE GUILT. HE WAS VERY HELPFUL TO ELIOT ASINOF IN THE WRITING OF "EIGHT MEN OUT," BUT HIS COMMENTS TO SPORTS-WRITER HARRY REUTLINGER IN 1920 HAD ALREADY SAID IT ALL. "I GOT MY $5,000 AND I SUPPOSE THE OTHERS GOT THEIRS TOO. I'M AS GUILTY AS THE REST OF THEM. I'M GOING TO HELL, I GUESS. I WISH THAT I HADN'T GONE INTO IT. NOW I'M OUT OF BASEBALL, AND A LOT OF GAMBLERS HAVE GOTTEN RICH. THE JOKE SEEMS TO BE ON US."

FRED McMullin

WHILE HE NEVER PLAYED IN MORE THAN 70 GAMES IN ANY OF HIS FIVE SEASONS WITH CHICAGO, FRED McMULLIN POSSESSED A FINE GLOVE AND SWUNG A CAPABLE BAT WHEN BROUGHT IN OFF THE BENCH TO SPELL ONE OF THE WHITE SOX REGULARS. HE ENTERED THE 1919 SEASON WITH HIGH HOPES OF EARNING A STARTING POSITION AFTER POSTING HIS BEST SEASON THE PREVIOUS YEAR, BUT HE WAS DISAPPOINTED WHEN HE WAS AGAIN RELEGATED TO RESERVE STATUS. SOME HAVE SPECULATED THAT THIS DISAPPOINTMENT MAY HAVE LED FRED TO RECKLESSLY ENTER INTO THE GAMBLING CONSPIRACY TO "FIX" THE 1919 WORLD SERIES. WHY WOULD TEAMMATES AND GAMBLERS CUT FRED IN ON SUCH A DEAL WHEN, AS A RESERVE, FRED WOULD LIKELY HAVE LITTLE IMPACT ON THE OUTCOME? SOME SAY IT WAS BECAUSE FRED WAS ALREADY A FIXTURE AMONG THE GAMBLERS. SOME SAY FRED'S INVOLVEMENT WAS NECESSITATED AFTER HE OVERHEARD A DISCUSSION OF THE PLOT AND DEMANDED TO BE INCLUDED. NO ONE KNOWS FOR SURE BECAUSE FRED NEVER SPOKE ON THE RECORD ABOUT IT FOLLOWING HIS BANISHMENT FROM THE GAME BY COMMISSIONER LANDIS. FOR REASONS STILL UNCLEAR, FRED WAS NOT TRIED WITH THE OTHER SEVEN BLACK SOX, BUT HIS FATE WAS JUST AS SEVERE -- AN ETERNAL SPOT IN THE LINEUP OF BASEBALL INFAMY.

Kid GLEASON

WILLIAM GLEASON HAD PAID HIS DUES IN FULL BY THE TIME WHITE SOX OWNER CHARLES COMISKEY GAVE HIM HIS FIRST MANAGERIAL JOB PRIOR TO THE 1919 SEASON. CALLED "KID" BECAUSE HE STOOD ONLY 5-FOOT-7, GLEASON WAS A "BIG LEAGUE" PITCHER AND INFIELDER FROM 1888 THROUGH 1912 WHEN HE BECAME A FULL-TIME COACH FOR THE SOX. FILLED WITH OPTIMISM AT BEING HANDED THE REINS TO A BALLCLUB WITH LEGITIMATE WORLD SERIES POTENTIAL, KID'S JOY TURNED TO A LIFETIME OF PAIN WHEN HE LEARNED THAT A LARGE GROUP OF HIS PLAYERS, ANGRY AT COMISKEY FOR PAYING WHAT THEY FELT WERE UNFAIRLY LOW WAGES, SCHEMED WITH GAMBLERS TO LOSE THE 1919 SERIES TO AN UNDERDOG CINCINNATI REDS CLUB. ONE OF THE "CLEAN" SOX, SECOND BASEMAN EDDIE COLLINS, DESCRIBED KID'S SUFFERING BY SAYING, "I HAVE ALWAYS HAD GREAT ADMIRATION FOR GLEASON. HE WAS ONE OF THE BEST FRIENDS I EVER HAD. FROM THE VERY MINUTE THE SCANDAL BROKE HE WAS A CHANGED MAN. HIS SUPERB SPIRIT HAD BEEN CRUSHED. HE WAS AT MOST TIMES MOROSE AND SOMETIMES HE WAS EVEN BITTER. GLEASON REMAINED ON THE WHITE SOX BENCH THROUGH 1923, THEN SERVED AS A COACH WITH THE A's UNTIL HIS DEATH IN JANUARY 1933."

Eddie COLLINS

NEVER WAS A BASEBALL CLUB MORE VULNERABLE TO THE EVIL ENTICEMENT TO "THROW" A WORLD SERIES THAN WAS THE 1919 CHICAGO WHITE SOX -- AND THROW THE SERIES THEY DID! THE TEAM WAS PLAGUED BY DISSENSION, A FESTERING ANIMOSITY BETWEEN THE "HAVES" AND "HAVE-NOTS." THE "HAVE-NOTS" WERE A DISGRUNTLED GROUP OF UNDER-PAID, POORLY-EDUCATED PLAYERS LED BY FIRST BASEMAN CHICK GANDIL. AT THE TOP OF THE LIST OF "HAVES" WAS THE GREAT SECOND BASEMAN EDDIE COLLINS. IT'S HARD TO SAY WHETHER THE "HAVE-NOTS" DISLIKED EDDIE MORE BECAUSE OF HIS COLLEGE DEGREE OR BECAUSE OF HIS $15,000-PER-YEAR SALARY. IN ANY CASE, EDDIE WAS NOT APPROACHED BY GAMBLERS OR "SELL-OUT" PLAYERS WHEN THE PLOT TO "FIX" THE WORLD SERIES WAS CONCOCTED. EDDIE'S .226 SERIES AVERAGE AND THREE ERRORS MIGHT HAVE MADE SOME WONDER WHETHER HE WAS ONE OF THE "BLACK" SOX, BUT, TRUTH BE TOLD, "COCKY" COLLINS WAS NEVER UNDER SUSPICION. HE DID NOT LIKE DISCUSSING THE TORRID AFFAIR, BUT OFFERED SOME INSIGHT IN A 1950 ISSUE OF THE SPORTING NEWS. "THERE IS ONE THING I'M SURE OF," SAID EDDIE, "BASEBALL HAS LIVED DOWN THAT MOMENT OF INFAMY AND IS A BETTER GAME BECAUSE OF IT. AS A RESULT OF THE TREACHERY PERPETUATED BY EIGHT OF MY TEAMMATES ON THAT 1919 WHITE SOX TEAM, BASEBALL AS A SPORT HAS UNDERGONE CERTAIN REVISIONS WHICH ENABLED IT TO BE CONDUCTED ON A MUCH HIGHER LEVEL."

Ray SCHALK

DESPITE NOT LOOKING LIKE THE TYPICAL BIG LEAGUE CATCHER ("CRACKER" WAS SMALL AND NIMBLE), RAYMOND WILLIAM SCHALK WAS THE PREMIER BACKSTOP OF HIS TIME. HE EVEN BUCKED THE STEREOTYPE OF THE SLOW, PLODDING CATCHER BY BEING A GOOD BASE STEALER. RAY'S 30 STEALS IN 1916 WAS A SINGLE-SEASON RECORD FOR CATCHERS UNTIL FINALLY BROKEN IN 1982. RAY WAS IN HIS EIGHTH SEASON WITH THE WHITE SOX WHEN THE PLOT WAS HATCHED TO "FIX" THE 1919 WORLD SERIES, BUT THE GAMBLERS AND CROOKED PLAYERS KNEW BETTER THAN TO TRY AND COAX SCHALK INTO THE SCAM. RAY WAS A COMPETITOR TO HIS CORE, AND HIS INTEGRITY WAS INCORRUPTIBLE. HOPING THE RUMORS OF A FIX WERE UNTRUE, RAY ENTERED THE SERIES WITH HIGH HOPES FOR A SOX VICTORY OVER THE REDS, BUT HE QUICKLY REALIZED THE UGLY TRUTH WHEN HE WAS CONTINUALLY CROSSED UP ON PITCHES BY EDDIE CICOTTE AND LEFTY WILLIAMS. RAY WAS VERY ANGRY AT THE "BLACK" SOX, BUT HE STILL FELT SYMPATHY FOR THEM. HE RARELY SPOKE OF THEM, BUT IN 1940 SAID, "AS LONG AS I LIVE, I'LL NEVER FORGET THE DAY CHARLES A. COMISKEY CAME INTO THE CLUBHOUSE AND TOLD THE BOYS THEY HAD BEEN EXPOSED AND WERE THROUGH FOREVER. IT WAS A SHOCKING SCENE AND MY MIXED EMOTIONS NEVER HAVE BEEN STRAIGHTENED OUT SINCE I WATCHED SEVERAL OF THE RUINED ATHLETES BREAK DOWN AND CRY LIKE BABIES. I NEVER HAVE WORRIED ABOUT THE GUYS WHO WERE HARD-BOILED, BUT THOSE TEARS GOT ME."

Dickey KERR

BY THE TIME DIMINUTIVE LEFT-HANDER DICKEY KERR TOOK THE MOUND FOR HIS FIRST START IN THE 1919 WORLD SERIES, HIS HEAVILY-FAVORED WHITE SOX TRAILED THE CINCINNATI REDS TWO GAMES TO NONE. DICKEY CAME UP LARGE IN GAME THREE, PITCHING A 3-0 SHUTOUT WHILE LIMITING THE CINCY BATS TO JUST THREE HITS. SUSPICIOUS OF THE LACKLUSTER EFFORTS TURNED IN BY SOX HURLERS EDDIE CICOTTE AND LEFTY WILLIAMS IN GAMES ONE AND TWO (THERE WERE RUMORS OF A WHITE SOX "FIX" TO THROW THE SERIES), THE SPORTWRITERS HAILED LITTLE DICKEY AS A HERO FOR HIS GAME THREE PERFORMANCE, DUBBING HIM "THE NEW NAPOLEON." AFTER CICOTTE AND WILLIAMS DROPPED THE NEXT TWO GAMES, IT WAS DICKEY WHO AGAIN CAME TO THE RESCUE BY PITCHING THE SOX TO A VICTORY IN GAME SIX, CAUSING TEAMMATE RAY SCHALK TO NICKNAME HIM "THE LITTLE GIANT." DICKEY LATER SAID, "THE GAMBLERS DIDN'T COME TO ME. A NEWSMAN TIPPED ME OFF THAT THERE WAS SOMETHING FISHY GOING ON. GLEASON, OUR MANAGER, COLLINS, OUR SECOND BASEMAN, AND SCHALK, OUR CATCHER, ALSO THOUGHT SOMETHING WAS GOING ON. ANYWAY, THERE WAS NOTHING WE COULD DO ABOUT IT BECAUSE WE HAD NO PROOF." THE EFFORTS OF THE "CLEAN SOX" WERE NOT ENOUGH TO UNDO THE DAMAGE DONE BY THE "BLACK SOX," AND CHICAGO FINALLY SUCCUMBED TO THE REDS IN GAME EIGHT -- BUT LITTLE DICKEY KERR EMERGED AS A BIG MAN.

Shano COLLINS

SPEEDY RIGHTFIELDER SHANO COLLINS WAS ONE OF THE HEROES OF THE 1917 WORLD CHAMPION WHITE SOX. FIRST, HE DELIVERED THE A.L. FLAG WITH A PENNANT-CLINCHING 10TH-INNING GAME-WINNING SINGLE AGAINST THE RED SOX ON SEPTEMBER 21. SHANO THEN SPARKED CHICAGO TO A 2-1 VICTORY IN GAME ONE OF THE SERIES WITH A 3-FOR-4 PERFORMANCE AT THE PLATE. PLATOONED AGAIN WITH NEMO LEIBOLD ON THE ILL-FATED 1919 PENNANT-WINNING CHISOX CLUB, SHANO WAS A SOLID CONTRIBUTOR. IN FACT, ELIOT ASINOF, AUTHOR OF "EIGHT MEN OUT," THE BOOK THAT FIRST DETAILED THE SAD SAGA OF THE 1919 "BLACK" SOX, THOUGHT VERY HIGHLY OF SHANO'S ABILITY ON THE BALLFIELD AND WROTE THAT HE "COULD RUN, HIT, AND THROW WITH ANY BALLCLUB IN THE LEAGUE." FROM THE MOMENT HE SLAPPED THE FIRST HIT OF THE '19 WORLD SERIES TO THE LAST OUT IN THE DECIDING EIGHTH GAME, SHANO REMAINED FREE OF ANY SPECULATION THAT HE WAS ONE OF THE WHITE SOX PLAYERS WHO WERE SUSPECTED OF CONSPIRING WITH GAMBLERS TO "THROW" THE SERIES TO THE REDS. SHANO GAVE HIS ALL IN EVERY MOMENT HE SPENT ON THE DIAMOND DURING THE 1919 WORLD SERIES, AS HE ALWAYS DID, AND HAD A CLEAN CONSCIENCE WHEN HE DIED AT 69 YEARS OF AGE IN 1955.

Nemo LEIBOLD

THE BULK OF THE RIGHTFIELD DUTIES FOR THE 1919 A.L. CHAMPION CHICAGO WHITE SOX WERE PLACED IN THE VERY CAPABLE -- BUT VERY SMALL -- HANDS OF 6-YEAR BIG LEAGUE VETERAN HARRY LORAN "NEMO" LEIBOLD. AT JUST 5-FOOT-6, NEMO WAS STILL A COUPLE INCHES SHORTER THAN ANOTHER SOX SMALL FRY -- CATCHER RAY SCHALK. THE TWO BROKE INTO PRO BALL TOGETHER AT MILWAUKEE IN 1911, AND THEY MADE SUCH A SMALL TANDEM THAT THEY WERE FORCED TO SHARE ONE UPPER BERTH WHEN THE TEAM TRAVELED BY TRAIN. LEIBOLD'S SMALL STATURE EVEN EARNED HIM HIS NICKNAME, "NEMO," WHICH WAS LIFTED FROM THE CHILD PROTAGONIST IN THE COMIC STRIP "LITTLE NEMO." WHILE HE MIGHT HAVE BEEN SMALL, NEMO LEIBOLD PLAYED A BIG PART IN THE SOX'S 1919 FLAG. HE HIT .302 IN 122 GAMES FOR CHICAGO, AND WAS A VERY RELIABLE FLYCHASER. NEMO FELL ON HARD TIMES IN THE SERIES, GETTING JUST ONE HIT IN EIGHTEEN AT-BATS, BUT HE WAS ONE OF THE "SQUARE" SOX, AND WAS ASTONISHED UPON LEARNING THAT A GROUP OF TEAMMATES HAD COLLABORATED WITH GAMBLERS TO LOSE THE SERIES.

Big Bill JAMES

PLUCKED OFF WAIVERS BY THE WHITE SOX ON AUGUST 18, 1919, 6-FOOT-4 SIDE-ARMING RIGHT-HANDER WILLIAM "BIG BILL" JAMES CHIPPED IN THREE LATE-SEASON WINS IN CHICAGO'S RUN TO THE A.L. PENNANT. BILL PITCHED IN JUST ONE GAME OF THE TAINTED 1919 WORLD SERIES AND IT DIDN'T GO WELL FOR HIM. HE RELIEVED LEFTY WILLIAMS IN THE FIRST INNING OF THE EIGHTH AND FINAL GAME OF THE SERIES ONLY TO GET KNOCKED AROUND FOR EIGHT HITS AND THREE EARNED RUNS IN JUST 4-2/3 INNINGS. IN SPITE OF HIS POOR SHOWING, BIG BILL WAS ONE OF THE "SQUARE" SOX NOT IMPLICATED IN THE PLOT TO "FIX" THE WORLD SERIES. BILL WAS NOT, HOWEVER, FREE FROM INVOLVEMENT IN PREVIOUS SUSPICIOUS ACTIVITY. CHICK GANDIL AND SWEDE RISBERG ONCE TESTIFIED TO JUDGE LANDIS THAT THE 1917 WHITE SOX PAID BILL, THEN WITH DETROIT, AND THE REST OF THE TIGERS $1,100 DOLLARS TO LOSE FOUR GAMES TO THE SOX ON SEPTEMBER 2 AND 3, 1917. THE CHARGES WERE DISMISSED, BUT SUSPICION LINGERED. WHILE DOUBT STILL REMAINS AS TO WHAT REALLY WENT ON IN 1917, THERE'S NO DOUBT THAT BILL WAS RAGING MAD WHEN HE EMERGED FROM THE SHOWERS AFTER THE SOX'S LOSS IN GAME EIGHT OF THE 1919 SERIES. "LISTEN," BILL SHOUTED AT HIS TEAMMATES, "I'VE HEARD SOME THINGS ABOUT THIS SERIES, AND I GUESS YOU HAVE, TOO. IF IT'S TRUE THAT I'VE BEEN PLAYING WITH CROOKS, THEN I'LL WRING THE NECK OF EVERY FELLOW WHO'S GUILTY. GET ME. I MEAN IT. I WON'T USE A GUN OR A KNIFE. I'LL USE THESE TWO HANDS THAT HAVE KEPT ME IN THE GREATEST SPORT OF 'EM ALL."

Roy WILKINSON

WITH THE 1919 WHITE SOX ENJOYING A COMFORTABLE LATE-AUGUST LEAD IN THE A.L. PENNANT RACE, 25-YEAR-OLD ROOKIE RIGHT-HANDER ROY WILKINSON CONTINUALLY HOUNDED SOX MANAGER KID GLEASON TO LET HIM PITCH. ROY FINALLY MADE HIS SOX DEBUT ON SEPTEMBER 12 WHEN GLEASON RELENTED AND LET WILKINSON START AGAINST THE A'S AT SHIBE PARK. ALL ROY DID WAS GO OUT AND TOSS A 5-HIT SHUTOUT -- THE ONLY WHITEWASH OF HIS BIG LEAGUE CAREER. WHEN PLANS WERE MADE BETWEEN GAMBLERS AND SOME SOX PLAYERS TO "FIX" THE 1919 WORLD SERIES, ROY WAS NOT PART OF THE SCAM. HE GAVE HIS ALL DURING TWO SERIES RELIEF APPEARANCES, PITCHING TO A 3.68 E.R.A. IN 7-1/3 INNINGS. AS IT TURNS OUT, ROY WAS THE LAST HURLER FOR THE SOX TO THROW A PITCH IN THE ILL-FATED 1919 WORLD SERIES AS HE GOT EDD ROUSH TO GROUND OUT TO BUCK WEAVER TO END THE TOP OF THE 9TH IN GAME EIGHT -- THE FINAL GAME OF THE SERIES. THE SOX CAME UP EMPTY IN THE BOTTOM HALF OF THE INNING, AND IT WAS MERCIFULLY OVER. DESPITE BEING SOLD OUT BY HIS CROOKED TEAMMATES, ROY KEPT UP THE CODE OF SILENCE AND REFUSED TO TESTIFY AGAINST THEM IN THE TRIAL OF 1920.

Byrd LYNN

BYRD LYNN SPENT HIS ENTIRE 5-YEAR CAREER (1916-20) AS A CATCHER WITH THE CHICAGO WHITE SOX, BUT HE WAS CURSED BY BAD TIMING. YOU SEE, AT THAT TIME THE SOX ALREADY HAPPENED TO HAVE ONE OF THE BEST CATCHERS OF ALL TIME -- THE GREAT RAY SCHALK. THAT MEANT THAT BIRDIE SAW LITTLE ACTION, AND HE PLAYED IN JUST 116 GAMES IN HIS CAREER WITH THE CHISOX. HE'D MADE ONE APPEARANCE IN THE 1917 WORLD SERIES, AND THAT WOULD BE HIS LINE AGAIN IN THE TAINTED SERIES OF 1919. BIRDIE'S CHANCE CAME IN THE 6TH INNING OF GAME FIVE WHEN SCHALK WAS EJECTED FOR ARGUING A CLOSE PLAY. BIRDIE CAUGHT HIS ROOMIE, LEFTY WILLIAMS, FOR 2-2/3 INNINGS BEFORE LEFTY WAS SENT TO THE SHOWERS TRAILING 4-0 AFTER THE EIGHTH. AS CLOSE AS THEY WERE, BIRDIE HAD NO IDEA THAT LEFTY HAD TANKED THE GAME IN ACCORDANCE WITH AN ILLICIT PACT MADE WITH GAMBLERS (AND SOME TEAMMATES) TO "FIX" THE 1919 SERIES. IN "EIGHT MEN OUT," ELIOT ASINOF WROTE OF A LAST, CHANCE MEETING OF THESE ONCE-GREAT PALS A YEAR LATER AS LEFTY EXITED THE CRIMINAL COURTS BUILDING. "THE TWO FRIENDS STOPPED AND STARED AT EACH OTHER. IT WAS LYNN WHO FINALLY OFFERED HIS HAND. WILLIAMS ACCEPTED IT AND TRIED TO SMILE. BUT SUDDENLY TEARS STARTED ROLLING DOWN HIS CHEEKS. THEY SHOOK HANDS. THEN LYNN, ALL CHOKED UP, BACKED HURRIEDLY AWAY. THEY DID NOT SAY A WORD TO EACH OTHER AT THIS MEETING OR EVER AGAIN."

Eddie MURPHY

THE PRIDE OF HANCOCK, NEW YORK, JOHN EDWARD MURPHY ENJOYED A SOLID 11-YEAR BIG LEAGUE CAREER. BY 1919 HE WAS MERELY A UTILITY OUTFIELDER FOR THE CHICAGO WHITE SOX -- BUT ONE WHO HIT .486 IN 30 GAMES WHILE LEADING THE A.L. IN PINCH HITS WITH EIGHT! EDDIE HAD JUST TWO AT-BATS IN THE 1919 WORLD SERIES, BUT HE WAS ONE OF THE "SQUARE" SOX -- THOSE NOT IMPLICATED IN THE "FIXING" SCANDAL. FOR HIS EFFORTS, HE RECEIVED THE NICKNAME "HONEST EDDIE," AND THIS OCTOBER 2, 1920, LETTER FROM SOX OWNER CHARLES A. COMISKEY... "DEAR FRIEND: IF IT BE POSSIBLE, I REGRET MORE THAN YOU DO THE OCCURRENCES OF THE 1919 WORLD'S SERIES. THE HONEST BALL PLAYER IS STRONGER TODAY THAN EVER. AS ONE OF THE HONEST BALL PLAYERS OF THE CHICAGO WHITE SOX TEAM OF 1919, I FEEL THAT YOU WERE DEPRIVED OF THE WINNER'S SHARE OF THE WORLD'S SERIES RECEIPTS THROUGH NO FAULT OF YOURS. I DO NOT INTEND THAT YOU, AS AN HONEST BALL PLAYER, SHOULD BE PENALIZED FOR YOUR HONESTY, OR SUFFER BY REASON OF THE DISHONESTY OF OTHERS. I THEREFORE TAKE PLEASURE IN HANDING TO YOU $1,500, BEING THE DIFFERENCE BETWEEN THE WINNING AND LOSING PLAYERS SHARE. I WISH YOU ALL THE LUCK POSSIBLE, AND HOPE THAT THE FUTURE WILL BRING HAPPINESS TO YOU AND YOURS."

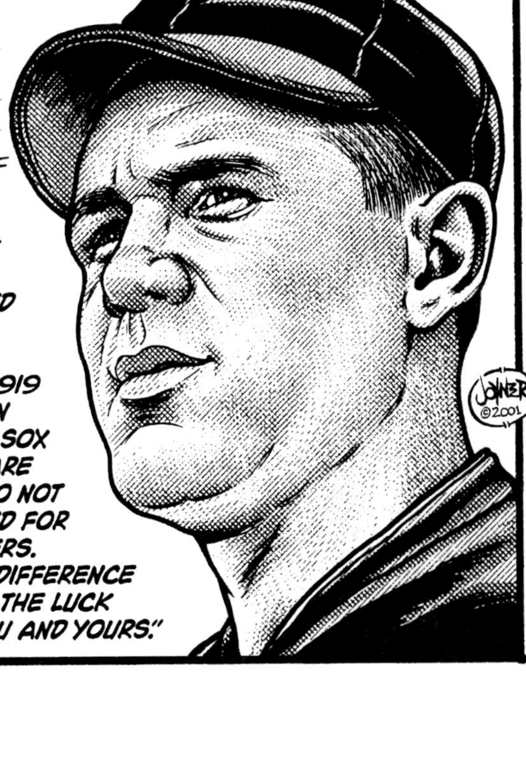

Grover LOWDERMILK

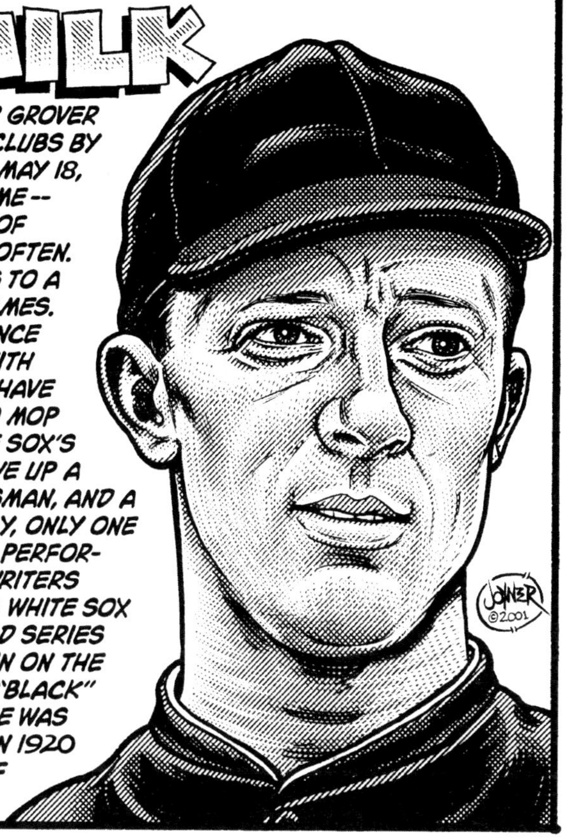

LONG AND LEAN AT 6-FOOT-4 AND 190 LBS, RIGHT-HAND PITCHER GROVER LOWDERMILK HAD WORN THE UNIFORMS OF SIX BIG LEAGUE BALLCLUBS BY THE TIME THE WHITE SOX PURCHASED HIM FROM THE BROWNS ON MAY 18, 1919. IT WAS GROVER'S HEATER -- ONE OF THE FASTEST IN THE GAME -- THAT LURED SO MANY TEAMS TO SIGN HIM, BUT IT WAS HIS LACK OF CONTROL THAT WOULD ULTIMATELY LEAD TO HIM BEING DEALT SO OFTEN.

HE SHOWED PROMISE WITH THE 1919 WHITE SOX, PITCHING TO A 5-AND-5 RECORD AND A 2.79 E.R.A. IN 20 GAMES. GROVER MADE JUST ONE APPEARANCE IN THE 1919 WORLD SERIES WITH RESULTS HE SURELY WOULD HAVE LIKED TO FORGET. BROUGHT IN TO MOP UP IN THE EIGHTH INNING OF THE SOX'S GAME ONE LOSS, GROVER GAVE UP A SINGLE, A TRIPLE, A HIT BATSMAN, AND A BASE-ON-BALLS. AMAZINGLY, ONLY ONE RUN SCORED, BUT IT WAS A PERFORMANCE THAT HAD SPORTSWRITERS ALREADY SUSPICIOUS OF A WHITE SOX PLOT TO "THROW" THE WORLD SERIES WONDERING IF GROVER WAS IN ON THE FIX. HE WAS NOT ONE OF THE "BLACK" SOX, AS IT TURNED OUT, AND HE WAS BACK WITH CHICAGO BRIEFLY IN 1920 BEFORE WILD-PITCHING HIMSELF BACK TO THE MINOR LEAGUES.

Erskine MAYER

A GRADUATE OF THE GEORGIA MILITARY ACADEMY AS A TEEN, 29-YEAR-OLD JACOB ERSKINE MAYER REPORTED FOR DUTY TO THE CHICAGO WHITE SOX IN AUGUST OF THE 1919 SEASON. ERSKINE WAS NO LONGER THE EFFECTIVE PITCHER HE'D BEEN DURING HIS CONSECUTIVE 21-WIN CAMPAIGNS WITH THE 1914-15 PHILLIES, BUT THE SOX WERE HOPING HIS EXPERIENCE WOULD HELP BOLSTER THEIR BULLPEN. IT DIDN'T QUITE WORK OUT THAT WAY, HOWEVER, AS THE SLENDER, 6-FOOT TALL RIGHT-HANDER STRUGGLED IN SIX MOUND APPEARANCES. ERSKINE WAS RESPECTABLE IN HIS ONE APPEARANCE IN THE 1919 WORLD SERIES, A MOP-UP ROLE IN THE 9TH INNING OF THE SOX'S GAME FIVE LOSS IN WHICH HE YIELDED AN UNEARNED RUN. DESPITE THE MINIMAL PART HE PLAYED IN THE SAGA OF THE '19 WHITE SOX, ERSKINE WAS UPSET WHEN HE LATER LEARNED THAT A GROUP OF TEAMMATES HAD PARTICIPATED WITH GAMBLERS IN A PLOT TO "THROW" THE WORLD SERIES. ERSKINE NEVER AGAIN PITCHED IN ORGANIZED BALL, SOMETHING HIS WIFE EXPLAINED BY SAYING, "ERK LOVED BASEBALL FOR THE TRUE SPORT IT AFFORDED, AND HE FELT IF A GAME HAD BEEN THROWN, HE WAS THROUGH WITH BASEBALL."

WHIZ KIDS:
1950
PHILADELPHIA PHILLIES

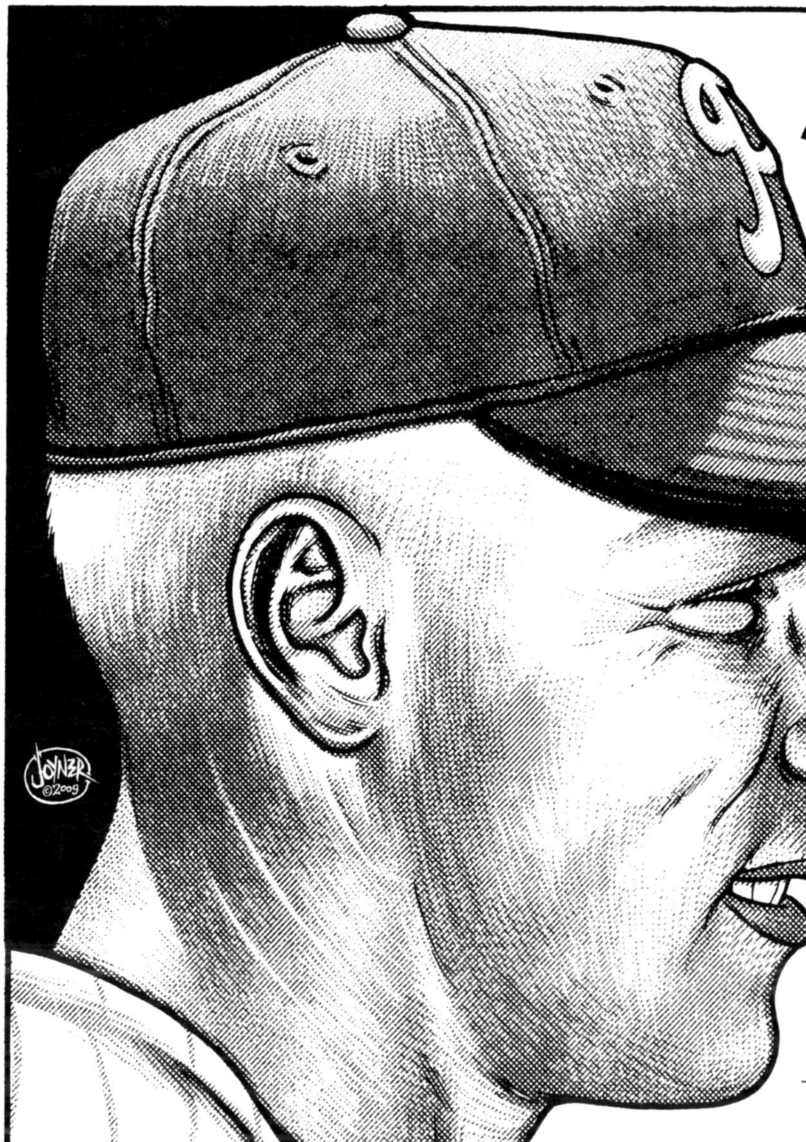

Richie ASHBURN

WITH WORLD WAR II OVER AND A FINE ROOKIE SEASON WITH THE UTICA BLUE SOX UNDER HIS BELT, 18-YEAR-OLD RICHIE ASHBURN HOPED TO CLIMB FAST AND FURIOUSLY UP THE LADDER OF THE PHILLIES MINOR LEAGUE SYSTEM! BY LATE 1945, HOWEVER, RICHIE WAS DRAFTED INTO THE ARMY WHERE HE DID AN 18-MONTH HITCH IN ALASKA!

RICHIE JOINED UTICA UPON HIS DISCHARGE IN '47 AND HAD A BANNER CAMPAIGN! RICHIE BEGAN AS A CATCHER, BUT UTICA SKIPPER EDDIE SAWYER, THE FUTURE WHIZ KIDS MANAGER, SAW THAT RICHIE'S BLAZING SPEED WAS HIS TICKET TO THE MAJORS, SO EDDIE SWITCHED THE KID TO CENTERFIELD -- A SAGE MOVE!

A SINGLES-HITTING CENTERFIELDER IN AN ERA THAT SAW THE POSITION RULED BY SLUGGERS (SEE: WILLIE, MICKEY AND DUKE), RICHIE STILL PUT TOGETHER A CAREER THAT WOULD LAND HIM IN COOPERSTOWN... ALBEIT IT BELATEDLY! OF RICHIE'S FLY-CHASING ABILITY, STAT-GEEK BILL JAMES WROTE, "ASHBURN HAS BY FAR THE GREATEST DEFENSIVE STATISTICS OF ANY OUTFIELDER IN HISTORY." A FIVE-TIME ALLSTAR, RICHIE HIT .333 AS A ROOKIE IN 1948 AND .306 AS A REGULAR WITH THE EXPANSION METS OF 1962! HE SPENT 12 OF HIS 15 SEASONS WITH THE PHILLIES AND WAS A HUGE FACTOR IN THE WHIZ KIDS' OFT-RECALLED PENNANT OF 1950! RICHIE'S GREAT PLAY, COUPLED WITH HIS WIT AND HUMOR, ENDEARED HIM TO PHILLIES FANS -- FEELINGS THAT WERE ONLY BOLSTERED WHEN HE BEGAN A DECADES-LONG RUN BROADCASTING THEIR GAMES IN 1963!

RICHIE HAD TREMENDOUS BAT CONTROL AND POSSESSED THE ABILITY TO FOUL OFF COUNTLESS PITCHES WHEN NECESSARY! ONCE WITH A COUNT OF 3-AND-2 AGAINST THE ALWAYS GRIM-FACED SAL MAGLIE, RICHIE FOULED OFF NEARLY 20 PITCHES BEFORE 'THE BARBER' GOT ASHBURN TO GROUND OUT ON A TRICK EEPHUS PITCH! "THAT WAS THE ONLY TIME I EVER SAW MAGLIE LAUGH ON A BALL FIELD," RECALLED RICHIE! ANOTHER TIME RICHIE HIT A FEMALE FAN WITH A FOUL BALL -- ONLY TO HIT HER WITH ANOTHER FOUL AS SHE WAS RECEIVING FIRST AID!

Robin
ROBERTS
ROBIN EVAN ROBERTS WAS BORN ON SEPTEMBER 30, 1926, IN SPRINGFIELD, ILLINOIS! THE ROBERTS FAMILY HAD RELOCATED THERE FROM WALES JUST FIVE YEARS EARLIER IN SEARCH OF THE AMERICAN DREAM! ROBIN'S DAD HAD SEEN TOUGH TIMES BACK IN GREAT BRITAIN AS A COAL MINER AND A SOLDIER IN WORLD WAR I! ROBIN FELL UNDER THE SPELL OF AMERICAN ATHLETICS AND BECAME A THREE-SPORT STAR IN HIGH SCHOOL, THEN A BASEBALL AND BASKETBALL STAR AT MICHIGAN STATE! THE PHILADELPHIA PHILLIES SIGNED ROBIN IN THE FALL OF 1947, GIVING THE YOUNGSTER A $25,000 BONUS WHICH HE PROMPTLY SPENT TO BUY HIS PARENTS A BRAND NEW HOME! ROBIN'S RISE TO THE TOP WAS QUICK AS HE WON 20 GAMES IN JUST HIS SECOND FULL SEASON IN THE BIGS -- 1950! THAT WAS THE YEAR OF THE LEGENDARY WHIZ KIDS, AN UPSTART BALLCLUB THAT SNATCHED THE N.L. PENNANT FROM THE DODGERS ON THE LAST GAME OF THE SEASON! DICK SISLER IS REMEMBERED AS THE HERO OF THAT GAME THANKS TO HIS 10TH-INNING GAME-WINNING LONG BALL, BUT IT WAS ROBIN WHO GOT THE WIN, PITCHING ALL 10 INNINGS WHILE ALLOWING JUST ONE DODGER TO SCORE! RELYING ON A HARD RISING FASTBALL AND PINPOINT CONTROL -- AS WELL AS HIS TOUGH, COMPETITIVE NATURE -- ROBIN WON 20 OR MORE GAMES FOR THE NEXT FIVE SEASONS! ROBIN STAYED WITH THE PHILLIES THROUGH THE 1961 SEASON, THEN PITCHED WITH BALTIMORE, HOUSTON, AND THE CUBS INTO THE MID-60s! MORE OF A FINESSE PITCHER LATER IN HIS CAREER, ROBIN PROVED HE COULD WIN IN ANY NUMBER OF DIFFERENT STYLES! THE NUMBERS PROVE IT, TOO -- 286 CAREER VICTORIES AND A 3.41 CAREER E.R.A. -- AND A TICKET TO IMMORTALITY IN THE BASEBALL HALL OF FAME IN COOPERSTOWN!
DAD, MOTHER... IT'S ALL YOURS! YOU DESERVE IT!
ROBIN WAS A REAL WORK-HORSE FOR THE PHILS, FIVE TIMES LEADING THE LEAGUE IN INNINGS PITCHED AND COMPLETE GAMES! HE TOPPED 200 INNINGS PITCHED IN 14 CAMPAIGNS -- SIX TIMES LOGGING OVER 300 FRAMES!
CLIMB ON, GUYS, I'M GONNA CARRY US!
JOYNER ©2007

Willie
PUDDINHEAD
Jones
BORN ON AUGUST 16, 1925, IN DILLON, SOUTH CAROLINA, WILLIE EDWARD JONES GREW UP IN LAUREL HILL, NORTH CAROLINA!
"HE COULDN'T SPELL CONSTANTINOPLE; DIDN'T KNOW BEANS FROM BONES. PENCILS AND BOOKS WERE NEVER MADE FOR WOODENHEAD PUDDINHEAD JONES!"
I LIKE IT!
IT'S UNCLEAR AS TO EXACTLY WHERE WILLIE PICKED UP HIS LEGENDARY NICKNAME "PUDDINHEAD," BUT MOST AGREE THAT HIS CHILDHOOD FRIENDS HUNG THE NAME ON HIM THANKS TO THE POPULARITY OF THE SONG "PUDDINHEAD JONES," A HIT RECORD FOR OZZIE NELSON IN 1933! LIKE THE CHARACTER IN THE SONG, WILLIE WAS A UNIQUE PERSONALITY! "HE WAS A GREAT GUY -- A SOUTHERN BOY WHO COULD CHARM A BULLDOG OFF A MEAT WAGON," SAID TEAMMATE RICHIE ASHBURN! AFTER SIGNING WITH THE PHILS FOR A $16,500 BONUS IN 1946, WILLIE CELEBRATED BY GAINING 25 POUNDS! UPON SEEING THE ROOKIE AT SPRING TRAINING IN 1947, PHILLIES MANAGER BEN CHAPMAN COMMENTED, "JONES MUST HAVE TRAINED ON CORN PONE AND BEANS!" BUT PUDDINHEAD WAS ALL BUSINESS WHEN HE STEPPED ON THE BALLFIELD! A TREMENDOUS GLOVEMAN, PUDDINHEAD WAS THE TOP FIELDING THIRD-SACKER OF THE 1950s! "BROOKS ROBINSON WAS THE BEST THIRD BASEMAN I EVER SAW," SAID PHILLIES GREAT ROBIN ROBERTS, "BUT PUDDINHEAD WAS VERY CLOSE TO BROOKS." HE WAS A TERROR WITH THE BAT, TOO -- EXCELLENT IN THE CLUTCH WITH GOOD POWER! ONE OF HIS BEST OFFENSIVE SEASONS CAME IN 1950 WHEN PUD CLUBBED 25 HOMERS AND HELPED THE PHILLIES TO THEIR FIRST PENNANT SINCE 1915! PUDDINHEAD PLAYED 15 SEASONS IN THE BIGS, THE BULK OF WHICH WERE SPENT IN PHILLY, AND HE STILL RANKS HIGH ON MANY OF THE PHILS' ALL-TIME OFFENSIVE AND DEFENSIVE CATEGORIES!
WHILE PUDDINHEAD IS FONDLY REMEMBERED FOR HIS GREAT HANDS, HIS FEET WERE A MUCH DIFFERENT STORY! "HE HAD THE WORST FEET I'VE EVER SEEN," SAID TEAMMATE STAN LOPATA. "HE WOULD GET UNK RUSSELL, OUR CLUBHOUSE GUY, TO GET HIM A BUCKET OF ICE WATER. PUDDINHEAD WOULD SOAK HIS FEET IN THE BUCKET -- SOCKS AND ALL! BOY, HIS FEET KILLED HIM."
OH, MY ACHIN' FEET!
JOYNER ©2009

DEL ENNIS
OUTFIELD -- PHILLIES
DELMER "DEL" ENNIS WAS BORN ON JUNE 8, 1926, IN PHILADELPHIA! POISED TO JOIN THE BIG LEAGUES AFTER A FINE YEAR AT TRENTON IN 1943, DEL INSTEAD JOINED THE NAVY! HE PLAYED ON SOME OF THE FINEST NAVY BALLCLUBS EVER ASSEMBLED IN THE SOUTH PACIFIC DURING WORLD WAR II! DEL WAS AN IMMEDIATE STAR IN HIS HOMETOWN WHEN HE BROKE IN WITH A BIG ROOKIE SEASON IN 1946 FOR THE PHILLIES THAT SAW HIM HIT .313 WITH 17 CIRCUITS AND 73 RBIs -- NUMBERS THAT EARNED HIM SELECTION TO THE 1946 N.L. ALL STAR TEAM AS WELL AS WINNING THE 1st-EVER SPORTING NEWS ROOKIE OF THE YEAR AWARD! DEL TOPPED THE 30 HOME RUN MARK TWICE IN HIS CAREER -- 30 FOR THE 1948 PHILLIES AND 31 FOR THE 1950 "WHIZ KIDS" EDITION OF THE PHILS! DEL WAS AN RBI MACHINE, 7 TIMES TOPPING THE 100 MARK!
ANOTHER BOMB FOR UNCLE SAM!
DON'T TAKE ANY WOODEN NICKELS, KID!
DEL HIT TWO GRAND SLAMS IN THREE DAYS WHEN HE BELTED ONE ON JULY 27, 1950, AND THEN LAUNCHED ANOTHER ON JULY 30! HE ENDED THE MONTH OF JULY WITH 41 RBIs -- A NEW PHILLIES RECORD, AND WOUND UP THE 1950 SEASON WITH A LEAGUE LEADING 126 DRIVEN IN!
THIS IS GETTIN' BORING!
DEL FINISHED WITH A SOLID .284 CAREER AVERAGE AND 288 HOMERS! IN 1983 HE WAS WAS NAMED TO TO THE PHILLIES CENTENNIAL TEAM!
JOYNER ©2004

Eddie WAITKUS
WAITKUS · HOBBS
I SMELL PULITZER!
WHEN BERNARD MALAMUD, IN HIS 1951 MASTERPIECE, "THE NATURAL," DESCRIBED THE SHOOTING OF ROY HOBBS BY A CRAZED FEMALE FAN, MALAMUD WAS BORROWING HEAVILY FROM THE REAL-LIFE TRAGEDY INVOLVING THE PHILLIES' ALL-STAR FIRST SACKER EDDIE WAITKUS. UNBEKNOWNST TO EDDIE, HE HAD LONG BEEN THE OBJECT OF A TWISTED OBSESSION BY RUTH STEINHAGEN, A DELUSIONAL TEENAGE FAN. THE TWO HAD NEVER MET, YET EDDIE WAS LURED TO HER HOTEL ROOM ONE NIGHT BY A MYSTERIOUS NOTE THAT PROMISED INFORMATION THAT HE'D FIND "EXTREMELY IMPORTANT." ONCE IN HER ROOM, STEINHAGEN TOLD EDDIE TO WAIT WHILE SHE WENT TO THE CLOSET TO GET A "SURPRISE" SHE HAD FOR HIM. SHE EMERGED WITH A RIFLE -- POINTED STRAIGHT AT HIS HEART. EDDIE HAD STARED DEATH IN THE FACE MANY TIMES WHILE IN COMBAT DURING HIS HIGHLY DECORATED WORLD WAR II ARMY SERVICE, BUT THIS GIRL POSED A THREAT HE'D NEVER IMAGINED. SHE SHOT HIM, THEN KNELT BY THE FALLEN PLAYER WHILE SHE HELD HIS HAND IN HER LAP. EDDIE WAS FORTUNATE TO SURVIVE THE SHOOTING, BUT HE WOULD BE FOREVER CHANGED. ONCE OUTGOING, EDDIE BECAME WITHDRAWN, AND EVENTUALLY SUFFERED FROM DEPRESSION, ALCOHOLISM, DIVORCE, AND A NERVOUS BREAKDOWN. HE FINALLY FOUND HAPPINESS WORKING WITH KIDS AT THE TED WILLIAMS BASEBALL CAMP IN THE EARLY 1970S, BUT HE SOON LOST A BATTLE WITH CANCER AND DIED AT THE AGE OF 53 IN 1972. STEINHAGEN SERVED THREE YEARS IN A STATE MENTAL INSTITUTION BEFORE BEING RELEASED AND LIVING IN TOTAL RECLUSIVE ANONYMITY EVER SINCE. THE HIGHLIGHT OF EDDIE'S CAREER, POST-SHOOTING, HAD TO BE HIS MAJOR CONTRIBUTION TO THE LEGENDARY 1950 WHIZ KIDS WHERE HE HIT .284 WHILE PLAYING EVERY GAME OF THE CAMPAIGN AT FIRST BASE! AND IT WAS THERE -- AT FIRST BASE -- THAT EDDIE'S FANS WILL ALWAYS REMEMBER HIM! GRACEFUL AND SLICK WITH THE LEATHER; IMPECCABLE FOOT-WORK -- A TRUE MAGICIAN AT THE POSITION!
ABRACADABRA -- YER OUT!
JOYNER ©2007

Mike
GOLIAT
OFTEN FORGOTTEN WHEN FANS RECALL THE GREAT PHILADELPHIA PHILLIES WHIZ KIDS OF 1950 IS THE STARTING SECOND SACKER OF THE CLUB -- MIKE GOLIAT! THE STRONG-ARMED YOUTH FROM THE COAL MINES OF PENNSYLVANIA MAY NOT HAVE POSSESSED THE GLAMOUR OF OTHER WHIZ KIDS STARS LIKE ROBIN ROBERTS, RICHIE ASHBURN, OR DEL ENNIS, BUT MIKE WAS A KEY MAN IN THE PHILLIES' FIRST PENNANT IN 35 YEARS! WHILE NOT FLASHY WITH THE GLOVE, MIKE WAS SOLID IN THE FIELD -- AND HE SWUNG THE LUMBER WITH BIG LEAGUE POWER! DESPITE BATTING JUST .234 IN 1950, MIKE WAS CHOCK FULL OF CLUTCH HITS, INCLUDING 13 ROUND-TRIPPERS! PHILS SKIPPER EDDIE SAWYER SUMMED UP MIKE THIS WAY -- "HE HIT THE BETTER PITCHERS IN THE LEAGUE. THE ONES THAT GOT HIM OUT WERE THE LESSER ONES." ONE OF THOSE "BETTER" PITCHERS WHO MIKE HIT WELL WAS DODGER ACE DON NEWCOMBE! TO SAY THAT MIKE HIT NEWCOMBE "WELL" IS ACTUALLY AN UNDERSTATEMENT! ACCORDING TO TEAMMATE ROBERTS, "GOLIAT HIT NEWCOMBE LIKE HE OWNED HIM." ONE OF MIKE'S BIGGEST OFFENSIVE DAYS OF 1950 CAME LATE IN SEPTEMBER AS THE PHILS PADDED THEIR FIRST-PLACE LEAD -- PADDING THAT WOULD BE NEEDED WHEN THE WHIZ KIDS SUFFERED A NEAR-FATAL SWOON IN THE LAST WEEK OF THE SEASON! MIKE'S BIG DAY CAME ON THE 20TH OF SEPTEMBER WHEN HE SMASHED TWO HOMERS INTO THE SHIBE PARK SEATS AS THE PHILLIES DEFEATED THE CUBS! 1950 TURNED OUT TO BE MIKE'S ONLY YEAR AS AN EVERYDAY PLAYER IN THE BIGS, AND HE WAS GONE FROM THE MAJORS BY 1953! MIKE HAD A LOT OF BASEBALL LEFT IN HIM, HOWEVER, AND HE PLAYED IN THE MINORS THROUGH THE '61 SEASON -- EVEN WINNING AN M.V.P. AWARD IN '56 WITH TORONTO OF THE INTERNATIONAL LEAGUE! MIKE LIVED A QUIET POST-BASEBALL LIFE, OPERATING A SMALL TRUCKING FIRM BEFORE JOINING THE FORD MOTOR COMPANY! FOR THE WHIZ KIDS, MIKE REPRESENTED WHAT COULD BE DONE THROUGH HARD WORK AND DETERMINATION! "HE WAS A BATTLER WHO GAVE EVERYTHING HE HAD," SAID ROBERTS, "AND HE HAD A LOT OF BIG HITS THE YEAR WE WON THE PENNANT."
GOLIAT'S MEAL TICKET
DON'T TAKE IT SO HARD, NEWK, I'LL BE OUT OF THE LEAGUE SOON!
A WHIZ KIDS SPECIAL: TWO BOMBS FOR THE PRICE OF ONE!
C'EST TOUT BON.
M.V.P. AWARD
JOYNER ©2010

THE MAD MONK

BASEBALL'S PREMIER RIGHT-HANDER IN 1949 MAY WELL HAVE BEEN THE PHILLIES' RUSS MEYER WHOSE RECORD OF 17-AND-8, ALONG WITH HIS LEAGUE LEADING 3.08 E.R.A., FIRMLY PLACED THE 25-YEAR-OLD IN AN ELITE CLASS OF UP-AND-COMING HURLERS! RUSS WOULD PITCH FOR 13 YEARS IN THE MAJORS, COMPILING A RESPECTABLE 94 WINS AGAINST JUST 73 LOSSES! WHAT RUSS COMPILED MOST, HOWEVER, WERE LEGENDARY INCIDENCES OF HIS RAGE EXPLODING AGAINST UMPS, FANS AND OPPOSING PLAYERS! RUSS WAS NICKNAMED "MONK" IN HIGH SCHOOL BECAUSE HIS GRIDIRON ABILITY REMINDED FANS OF ARMY'S GREAT HALFBACK CHARLES "MONK" MEYER! THE "MAD" PART OF RUSS' NICKNAME CAME YEARS LATER WHEN FOLKS GOT A FIRST-HAND LOOK AT HIS TEMPER ON THE DIAMOND! ONE OF HIS MOST FAMOUS MELTDOWNS HAPPENED ON THE 24TH OF MAY, 1953! FRUSTRATED BY PLATE UMP AUGIE DONATELLI'S STRIKE ZONE, RUSS BLEW A GASKET! HE STOMPED, KICKED AND CURSED -- THEN THREW THE ROSIN BAG HIGH INTO THE AIR! BEFORE OLD RUSS COULD SAY ANOTHER WORD, THE ROSIN BAG CAME DOWN RIGHT ON TOP OF HIS HEAD, PROMPTING UPROARIOUS LAUGHTER FROM THE 25,000 FANS IN ATTENDANCE! DONATELLI DIDN'T THINK IT WAS FUNNY -- HE EJECTED RUSS! THE MAD MONK WASN'T THROUGH YET, HOWEVER, AND HE GAVE AUGIE A PARTING SHOT WHEN HE REACHED THE DUGOUT -- A CROTCH-GRAB, CAPTURED BY ABC TV'S GAME-OF-THE-WEEK DUGOUT CAMERA! IT WAS SEEN NATIONWIDE, AND RUSS WAS QUICKLY FINED AND SUSPENDED!

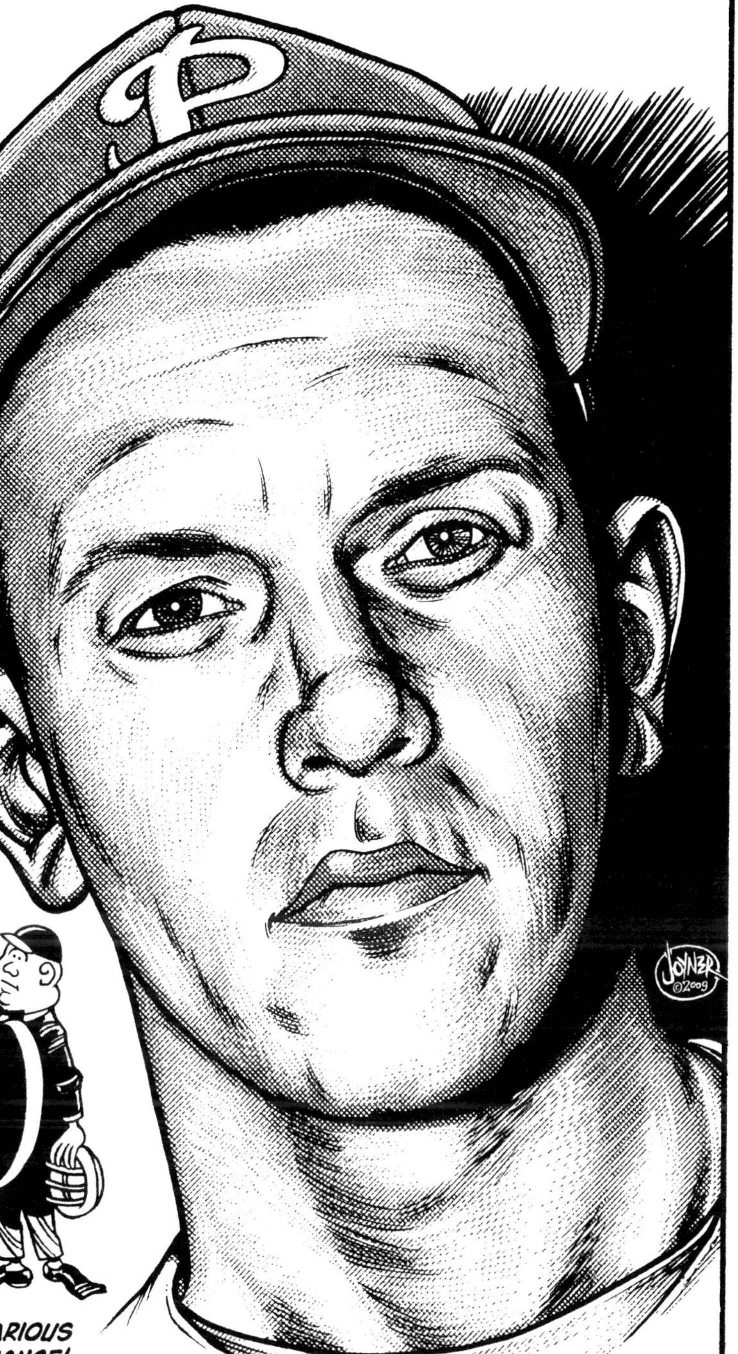

WHILE PITCHING WITH THE PHILS, RUSS RUTHLESSLY TAUNTED THE GREAT JACKIE ROBINSON -- WITH SOME OF THE JOCKEYING BEING CRUDELY RACIST! "BAD JUDGEMENT ON MY PART," RUSS WOULD LATER ADMIT, "BUT I'M NOT GOING TO DENY IT." RUSS WAS LATER TRADED TO THE DODGERS, AND HE DREADED FACING JACKIE IN THE CLUBHOUSE! RUSS' FEARS WERE ALLAYED, HOWEVER, WHEN JACKIE WAS THE FIRST TO GREET HIM -- AND THEN WARMLY WELCOMED HIM TO THE CLUB! "A HELLUVA BALLPLAYER," RUSS SAID, "AND A CLASS GUY."

Curt SIMMONS

EIGHTEEN-YEAR-OLD SOUTHPAW CURT SIMMONS HAD BEEN DAZZLING BIG LEAGUE SCOUTS FOR TWO YEARS BY HE TIME PITCHED A TEAM OF HIGH SCHOOL ALL-STARS TO A STUNNING 4-TO-4 TIE AGAINST THE PHILADELPHIA PHILLIES IN A 1947 EXHIBITION GAME! CURT STRUCK OUT ELEVEN PHILS THAT DAY, AND SO IMPRESSED THE PHILLIES' BRASS THAT THEY QUICKLY SIGNED THE KID BY OFFERING HIM A HUGE $65,000 BONUS! A FEW MONTHS LATER CURT MADE HIS MAJOR LEAGUE DEBUT, PITCHING THE PHILLIES TO A 3-TO-1 VICTORY OVER THE GIANTS IN THE LAST GAME OF THE SEASON! HIS PERFORMANCE THAT DAY WAS STELLAR -- A COMPLETE GAME 5-HITTER IN WHICH HE WHIFFED NINE GIANTS BATSMEN! IT WAS A TASTE OF THE PITCHING EXCELLENCE THAT CURT WOULD REGULARLY DELIVER FOR THE PHILLIES OVER THE COURSE OF THE NEXT 13 YEARS! 1948 AND '49 SAW CURT FLASH GLIMPSES OF THE TALENT WITH WHICH HE HAD SENT THE SCOUTS SWOONING, BUT IT WASN'T UNTIL 1950 THAT CURT MASTERED HIS CONTROL AND DELIVERED A SEASON THAT TRULY SHOWCASED HIS ABILITY! HE WENT 17-AND-8 THAT YEAR, HELPING HIS PHILLIES WIN THEIR FIRST PENNANT SINCE 1915! CURT WAS CALLED TO ACTIVE MILITARY SERVICE IN SEPTEMBER OF 1950, HOWEVER, AND WAS NOT AVAILABLE TO PLAY IN THE WORLD SERIES! THE PHILLIES, WITHOUT CURT, WERE SWEPT BY THE YANKEES, AND DID NOT RETURN TO THE FALL CLASSIC UNTIL 1980! CURT MISSED ALL OF THE '51 SEASON WHILE IN THE SERVICE, BUT RETURNED STRONG IN 1952, GOING 14-AND-8 WHILE LEADING THE LEAGUE WITH SIX SHUTOUTS! HE CONTINUED TO ROLL THROUGHOUT THE 1950s UNTIL A 1959 ARM INJURY THREATENED TO END HIS CAREER! THE PHILS BAILED ON HIM IN MAY OF 1960, RELEASING HIM OUTRIGHT! IT WAS A SHOCKING END TO A LONG AND SUCCESSFUL RELATIONSHIP! "SURE, I THOUGHT THE PHILLIES WOULD TRADE ME," CURT SAID, STUNNED, SHORTLY AFTER BEING CUT, "BUT RELEASE ME -- NO." CURT WAS SOON SIGNED BY THE CARDINALS WITH WHOM HE REBUILT HIS CAREER, WINNING 69 GAMES FROM 1960 THROUGH '66! HE MADE A POINT OF WHIPPING HIS OLD TEAM, TOO, BEATING THEM IN 17 OF 20 GAMES AFTER THEY LET HIM GO! CURT FINALLY WON THE WORLD SERIES RING THAT ELUDED HIM IN 1950 WHEN HIS CARDINALS BEAT THE YANKS IN THE '64 FALL CLASSIC!

Bill
NICHOLSON
WITHOUT A DOUBT, THE MOST DOMINANT HOME RUN SLUGGER OF THE WORLD WAR II ERA WAS THE CHICAGO CUBS' 6-FOOT, 200-POUND, LEFTY-SWINGING CLOUTER, BIG BILL NICHOLSON! BORN ON A FARM IN CHESTERTOWN, MARYLAND, ON DECEMBER 11, 1914, FAMILY LORE HAS IT THAT BABY BILL WEIGHED IN AT A WHOPPING 13 POUNDS! LIFE ON "FANCY FARM" WAS VERY GOOD TO BILL AND HELPED HIM GROW INTO A STRAPPING TEENAGER CHISELED WITH FARMWORK-GENERATED MUSCLE! HIS ATHLETIC BUILD POWERED HIM INTO A MULTI-SPORT STAR ATHLETE AT CHESTERTOWN HIGH SCHOOL, AND THEN A 3-SPORT LEGEND AT CHESTERTOWN'S WASHINGTON COLLEGE! BILL'S COLLEGIATE FENCE-BUSTING ACTIVITIES LED THE PHILADELPHIA ATHLETICS TO SIGN HIM AS SOON AS HE GRADUATED IN 1936! THEY BROUGHT HIM RIGHT UP TO THE MAJORS, BUT BILL STRUGGLED IN HIS BRIEF TRIAL AND WAS SUBSEQUENTLY FARMED OUT FOR MORE SEASONING! BILL, THIS TIME WEARING CUBBIE FLANNELS, RETURNED TO THE BIG SHOW IN MIDSEASON OF 1939, AND THIS TIME HE WAS READY! HE HOMERED IN HIS FIRST GAME WITH CHICAGO, THEN COLLECTED THREE HITS INCLUDING A 3-BAGGER IN HIS SECOND GAME! WITH THAT, BILL BECAME OFFICIALLY ENTRENCHED IN THE CUBS LINEUP, AND WOULD REMAIN THERE FOR TEN YEARS!
YOU GOTTA KEEP YOUR ELBOW UP, BILL!
NICHOLSON GARDENS
I THINK I'M GONNA LIKE IT OUT HERE!
BILL IS SOMETIMES OVERLOOKED BECAUSE HIS BIGGEST POWER SEASONS CAME IN THE ROSTER-DEPLETED WAR YEARS OF '43 AND '44, YEARS IN WHICH HE WON CONSECUTIVE HOMER TITLES! BUT A CLOSE LOOK REVEALS THAT HE WAS PROLIFIC WITH THE LONG BALL BEFORE, DURING, AND AFTER WORLD WAR II! BIG BILL JOINED THE PHILLIES IN 1949, BUT DIABETES REDUCED HIS EFFECTIVENESS! HE STILL PLAYED A VALUABLE ROLE WITH THE PHILS, HOWEVER, AND REMAINED WITH THEM FOR FIVE SEASONS! BILL RETIRED FOLLOWING THE 1953 SEASON -- A .268 HITTER WITH 235 CAREER HOME RUNS! BILL HIT 205 OF HIS ROUND-TRIPPERS WITH THE CUBS -- GOOD ENOUGH FOR 7TH ON THEIR ALL-TIME LIST! BILL TRIED VARIOUS CAREERS AFTER HIS RETIREMENT, BUT HE WAS MOST CONTENTED WHEN HE RETURNED TO HIS FARM! BILL NEVER STOPPED LOVING THE GAME, AND HE WOULD OFTEN SAY, "JUST GIVE ME GRASS, DAYLIGHT BALL, AND ANOTHER PENNANT FLYING AT WRIGLEY FIELD!"
WELCOME HOME, BILL!
JOYNER ©2008

Stan
LOPATA
STANLEY EDWARD LOPATA WAS BORN ON SEPTEMBER 12, 1925, IN DELRAY, MICHIGAN! STAN GREW UP IN THE POLISH SECTION OF DETROIT WHERE HE EXCELLED IN BASKETBALL AND BASEBALL AT SOUTHWESTERN HIGH SCHOOL! STAN'S FUTURE LAY IN BASEBALL, BUT NOT UNTIL HE FULFILLED HIS OBLIGATION TO UNCLE SAM! STAN ENTERED THE ARMY IN DECEMBER OF 1943, AND SOON FOUND HIMSELF IN EUROPE SERVING WITH THE 14TH ARMORED DIVISION! NOT ONE GIVEN TO SPEAKING ABOUT HIS BATTLEFIELD EXPERIENCES, STAN'S VALOR DURING HIS SERVICE CAN BE GLEANED FROM THE BRONZE STAR AND THE PURPLE HEART HE EARNED! STAN HIT THE PRO RANKS WITH TERRE HAUTE IN 1946 FOLLOWING HIS DISCHARGE, THEN TURNED IN AN M.V.P. SEASON WITH UTICA OF THE EASTERN LEAGUE IN '47! HE JOINED THE PHILLIES IN 1948 AS A BACKUP TO CATCHER ANDY SEMINICK AND WAS A PART OF THE WHIZ KIDS PENNANT WINNERS OF 1950! IN 1954 "STASH" RECEIVED HITTING ADVICE FROM THE GREAT ROGERS HORNSBY AND, WHEN COMBINED WITH A NEW CROUCHED STANCE, IT PROVED TO BE THE PERFECT COMBINATION TO LIFT HIS BAT OUT OF THE DOLDRUMS!
STAN BATTED .290 WITH 14 HOMERS IN JUST 84 GAMES IN 1954! HIS POWER NUMBERS IMPROVED TO 22 LONG BALLS IN 86 GAMES IN 1955, THEN CAME HIS BEST SEASON EVER AS HE BECAME THE PHILS NUMBER ONE BACKSTOP AND DELIVERED 32 ROUND-TRIPPERS IN 1956! STAN IS A MEMBER OF THE PENNSYLVANIA AND POLISH SPORTS HALLS OF FAME!
AAAAARGH! HOW'D YOU DO THAT?!
STAN WAS THE CATCHER FOR ONE OF THE MOST FAMOUS PLAYS IN PHILLIES HISTORY WHEN HE EASILY TAGGED OUT CAL ABRAMS OF THE DODGERS IN THE LAST GAME OF THE 1950 SEASON! IT WAS THE TURNING POINT OF THE GAME THAT CLINCHED THE LONG-AWAITED PENNANT FOR THE WHIZ KIDS!
JOYNER ©2008

Jocko THOMPSON

JOCKO WAS A STYLISH LEFTY WITH A HIGH LEG KICK LIKE THAT OF WARREN SPAHN!

JOHN S. "JOCKO" THOMPSON WAS A 30-YEAR OLD ROOKIE WHEN HE MADE HIS BIG LEAGUE DEBUT ON SEPTEMBER 21, 1948! WHILE HE MAY HAVE BEEN LATE GETTING TO THE SHOW, IT WASN'T FOR LACK OF A GOOD REASON! FOLLOWING HIS '41 SEASON AT GREENSBORO IN THE PIEDMONT LEAGUE, JOCKO DECIDED TO PUT HIS BASEBALL CAREER ON HOLD AND JOIN THE PARATROOPERS SO HE COULD FIGHT IN WORLD WAR II! SURVIVING MAJOR COMBAT MADE JOCKO'S BIG LEAGUE DEBUT THAT THAT MUCH SWEETER--NOT TO MENTION THE FACT THAT HE HURLED A COMPLETE GAME 6-1 VICTORY AGAINST THE REDS! NEW YORK TIMES SPORTSWRITER JAMES DAWSON WOULD LATER PAY TRIBUTE BY WRITING, "THIS WAS A WELL-DESERVED VICTORY FOR THOMPSON, A PARATROOPER WHO CAME OUT OF THE WAR WITH EVERY DECORATION SHORT OF THE CONGRESSIONAL MEDAL, TO RESUME A CAREER THAT BEGAN BACK IN 1940." ALWAYS READY FOR ANYTHING, JOCKO COULD START OR RELIEVE, AND DID SO EFFECTIVELY FOR THE PHILS FROM 1948-51!

LIEUTENANT THOMPSON WAS A PLATOON LEADER WITH COMPANY E OF THE 504TH PARACHUTE INFANTRY REGIMENT WHEN HE JUMPED INTO NAZI-OCCUPIED HOLLAND AS PART OF OPERATION MARKET GARDEN! JOCKO'S "STICK" LANDED WAY AHEAD OF THE DROP ZONE, VERY NEAR THE WELL-DEFENDED BRIDGE AT GRAVE--AN IMPORTANT OBJECTIVE IN THE HUGE AIRBORNE MISSION TO CAPTURE A SERIES OF BRIDGES WITH HOPES OF SPEEDING THE ALLIED ADVANCE INTO GERMANY! FACED WITH THE DECISION TO LEAD HIS PLATOON IN AN ATTACK ON THE BRIDGE OR WAIT FOR ADDITIONAL TROOPS, JOCKO CHOSE TO ATTACK! HIS QUICK ACTION PROVED KEY TO THE SUCCESSFUL CAPTURE OF THE BRIDGE, AND 60 YEARS LATER THE GRATEFUL PEOPLE OF HOLLAND RECOGNIZED JOCKO'S BRAVE LEADERSHIP BY RENAMING THE STRUCTURE "THE JOHN S. THOMPSON BRIDGE." TEAMMATE ROBIN ROBERTS THOUGHT HIGHLY OF JOCKO, SAYING, "WE UNDERSTOOD THAT JOCKO STILL CARRIED AROUND A CONSIDERABLE AMOUNT OF SHRAPNEL IN HIS BODY. HE HAD THE LOOK OF A CHOIRBOY, BUT HE WAS A DECORATED PARATROOPER."

Putsy
CABALLERO
I'LL DO MY BEST TO TRY AND END THIS BALLGAME BEFORE YOUR BEDTIME, KID!
WHEN 16-YEAR OLD RALPH "PUTSY" CABALLERO TROTTED OUT TO REPLACE GLEN STEWART AT THE HOT CORNER LATE IN A PHILS-GIANTS GAME ON SEPTEMBER 14, 1944, HE BECAME THE YOUNGEST PLAYER EVER TO PLAY THIRD BASE IN A BIG LEAGUE BALLGAME -- A RECORD HE HOLDS TO THIS DAY! A SUPERSTAR ATHLETE AT JESUIT HIGH SCHOOL IN NEW ORLEANS, PUTSY WAS PLANNING ON ATTENDING LOUISIANA STATE UNIVERSITY WHEN THE PHILLIES, DEPLETED BY THEIR WAR-PILLAGED ROSTER, CHANGED HIS PLANS BY OFFERING HIM A $10,000 BONUS TO SIGN RIGHT AWAY! PUTSY PROVED TO BE A VALUABLE UTILITY MAN IN 322 GAMES OVER AN 8-YEAR CAREER IN PHILLY, BUT THE THRILL OF HIS CAREER WAS BEING A PART OF THE LEGENDARY 1950 WHIZ KIDS! PHILS MANAGER EDDIE SAWYER TOOK ADVANTAGE OF PUTSY'S WHEELS TWICE IN THE 4-GAME 1950 WORLD SERIES, USING HIM TO PINCH-RUN IN GAMES TWO AND THREE! PHILLY WAS SWEPT BY THE YANKS, BUT, AS PUTSY PUT IT, "WE PLAYED THEM WELL. THEY WERE ALL GOOD GAMES. WE JUST COULDN'T GET THAT EXTRA HIT WHEN WE NEEDED IT."
PINCH-RUN, PINCH-HIT, PINCH-ANYTHING -- I DON'T CARE AS LONG AS I'M IN THE MIX!
FOLLOWING HIS PLAYING DAYS, PUTSY RETURNED TO LOUISIANA WHERE HE WAS CO-OWNER OF AN EXTERMINATION COMPANY UNTIL HIS RETIREMENT! HE LOST HIS HOME DURING HURRICANE KATRINA, BUT HIS FIGHTING SPIRIT HELPED HIM BATTLE BACK! "THE STUFF I HAD FROM BASEBALL IS ALL GONE," PUTSY SAID BACK IN '05, "BUT WHAT I HAVE TO LOOK AT IS THAT I'M IN GOOD HEALTH."
YOU'LL NEVER GET THE BEST OF ME, KATRINA -- OL' PUTSY WILL RISE AGAIN!
JOYNER ©2010

PINSTRIPERS: 2009 NEW YORK YANKEES

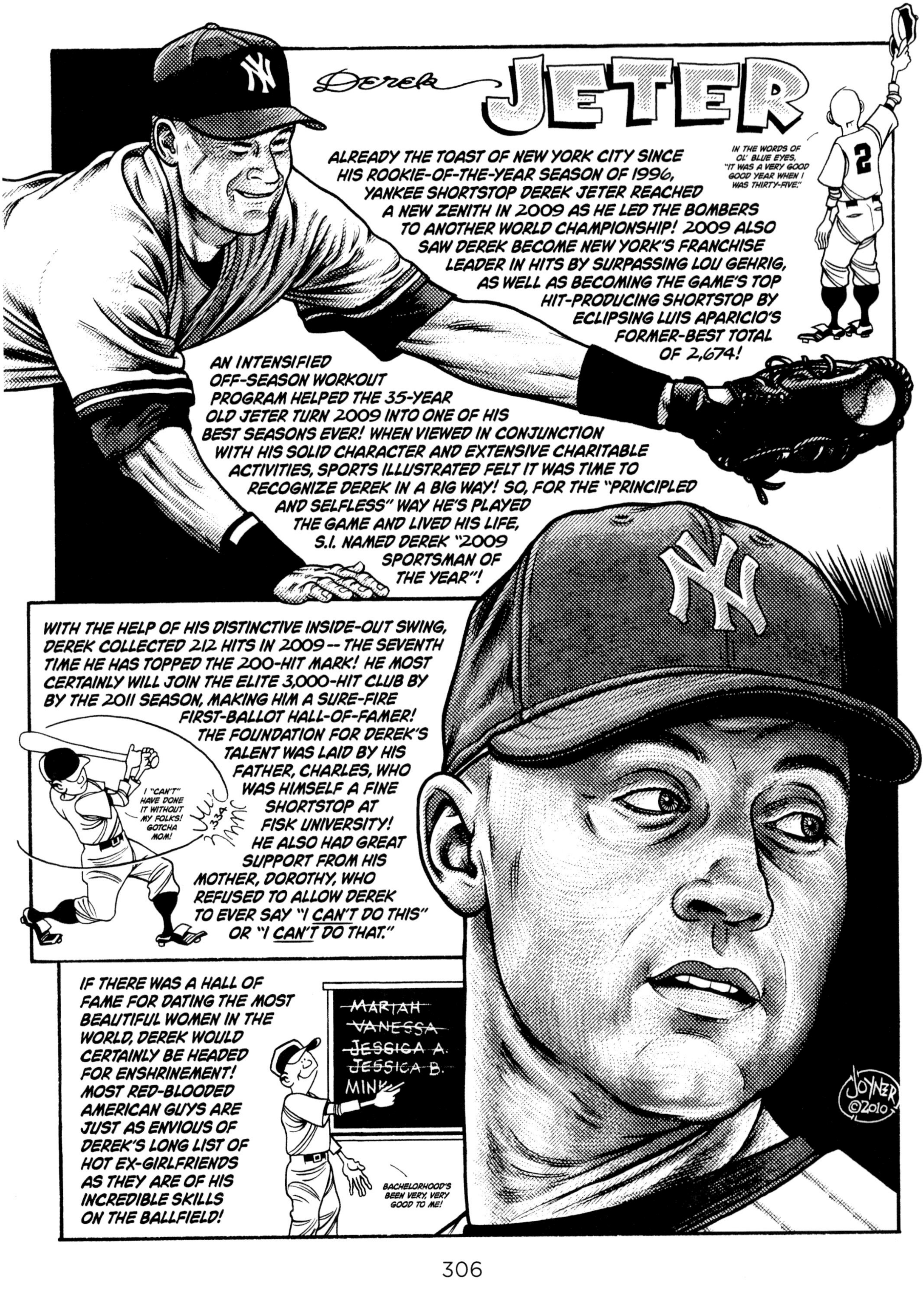
Derek JETER
IN THE WORDS OF OL' BLUE EYES, "IT WAS A VERY GOOD GOOD YEAR WHEN I WAS THIRTY-FIVE."
ALREADY THE TOAST OF NEW YORK CITY SINCE HIS ROOKIE-OF-THE-YEAR SEASON OF 1996, YANKEE SHORTSTOP DEREK JETER REACHED A NEW ZENITH IN 2009 AS HE LED THE BOMBERS TO ANOTHER WORLD CHAMPIONSHIP! 2009 ALSO SAW DEREK BECOME NEW YORK'S FRANCHISE LEADER IN HITS BY SURPASSING LOU GEHRIG, AS WELL AS BECOMING THE GAME'S TOP HIT-PRODUCING SHORTSTOP BY ECLIPSING LUIS APARICIO'S FORMER-BEST TOTAL OF 2,674!
AN INTENSIFIED OFF-SEASON WORKOUT PROGRAM HELPED THE 35-YEAR OLD JETER TURN 2009 INTO ONE OF HIS BEST SEASONS EVER! WHEN VIEWED IN CONJUNCTION WITH HIS SOLID CHARACTER AND EXTENSIVE CHARITABLE ACTIVITIES, SPORTS ILLUSTRATED FELT IT WAS TIME TO RECOGNIZE DEREK IN A BIG WAY! SO, FOR THE "PRINCIPLED AND SELFLESS" WAY HE'S PLAYED THE GAME AND LIVED HIS LIFE, S.I. NAMED DEREK "2009 SPORTSMAN OF THE YEAR"!
WITH THE HELP OF HIS DISTINCTIVE INSIDE-OUT SWING, DEREK COLLECTED 212 HITS IN 2009 -- THE SEVENTH TIME HE HAS TOPPED THE 200-HIT MARK! HE MOST CERTAINLY WILL JOIN THE ELITE 3,000-HIT CLUB BY BY THE 2011 SEASON, MAKING HIM A SURE-FIRE FIRST-BALLOT HALL-OF-FAMER! THE FOUNDATION FOR DEREK'S TALENT WAS LAID BY HIS FATHER, CHARLES, WHO WAS HIMSELF A FINE SHORTSTOP AT FISK UNIVERSITY! HE ALSO HAD GREAT SUPPORT FROM HIS MOTHER, DOROTHY, WHO REFUSED TO ALLOW DEREK TO EVER SAY "I CAN'T DO THIS" OR "I CAN'T DO THAT."
I "CAN'T" HAVE DONE IT WITHOUT MY FOLKS! GOTCHA MOM!
IF THERE WAS A HALL OF FAME FOR DATING THE MOST BEAUTIFUL WOMEN IN THE WORLD, DEREK WOULD CERTAINLY BE HEADED FOR ENSHRINEMENT! MOST RED-BLOODED AMERICAN GUYS ARE JUST AS ENVIOUS OF DEREK'S LONG LIST OF HOT EX-GIRLFRIENDS AS THEY ARE OF HIS INCREDIBLE SKILLS ON THE BALLFIELD!
MARIAH
VANESSA
JESSICA A.
JESSICA B.
MIN
BACHELORHOOD'S BEEN VERY, VERY GOOD TO ME!
JOYNER ©2010

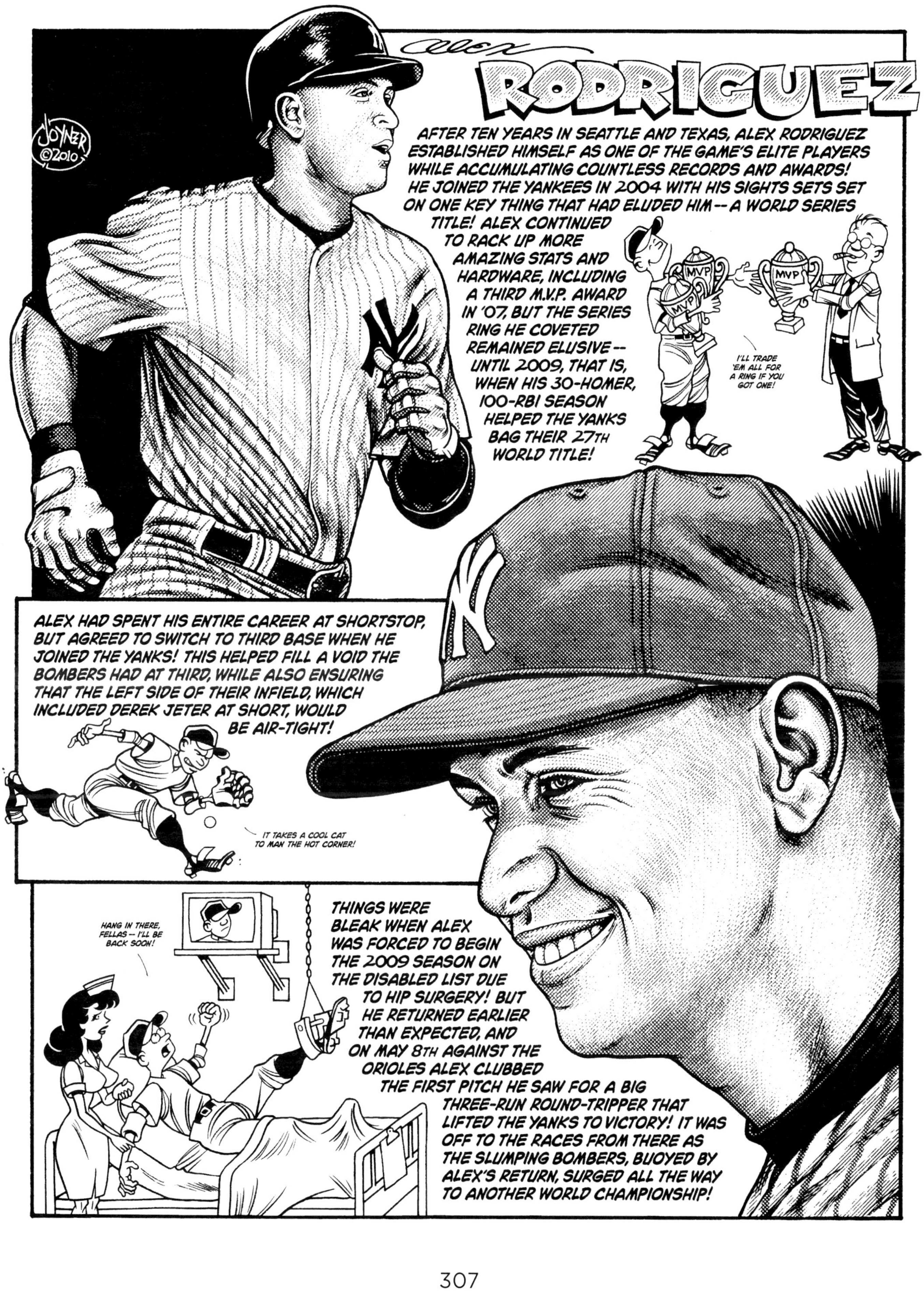
ALEX
RODRIGUEZ
JOYNER ©2010
AFTER TEN YEARS IN SEATTLE AND TEXAS, ALEX RODRIGUEZ ESTABLISHED HIMSELF AS ONE OF THE GAME'S ELITE PLAYERS WHILE ACCUMULATING COUNTLESS RECORDS AND AWARDS! HE JOINED THE YANKEES IN 2004 WITH HIS SIGHTS SETS SET ON ONE KEY THING THAT HAD ELUDED HIM -- A WORLD SERIES TITLE! ALEX CONTINUED TO RACK UP MORE AMAZING STATS AND HARDWARE, INCLUDING A THIRD M.V.P. AWARD IN '07, BUT THE SERIES RING HE COVETED REMAINED ELUSIVE -- UNTIL 2009, THAT IS, WHEN HIS 30-HOMER, 100-RBI SEASON HELPED THE YANKS BAG THEIR 27TH WORLD TITLE!
MVP
MVP
MVP
MVP
I'LL TRADE 'EM ALL FOR A RING IF YOU GOT ONE!
ALEX HAD SPENT HIS ENTIRE CAREER AT SHORTSTOP, BUT AGREED TO SWITCH TO THIRD BASE WHEN HE JOINED THE YANKS! THIS HELPED FILL A VOID THE BOMBERS HAD AT THIRD, WHILE ALSO ENSURING THAT THE LEFT SIDE OF THEIR INFIELD, WHICH INCLUDED DEREK JETER AT SHORT, WOULD BE AIR-TIGHT!
IT TAKES A COOL CAT TO MAN THE HOT CORNER!
HANG IN THERE, FELLAS -- I'LL BE BACK SOON!
THINGS WERE BLEAK WHEN ALEX WAS FORCED TO BEGIN THE 2009 SEASON ON THE DISABLED LIST DUE TO HIP SURGERY! BUT HE RETURNED EARLIER THAN EXPECTED, AND ON MAY 8TH AGAINST THE ORIOLES ALEX CLUBBED THE FIRST PITCH HE SAW FOR A BIG THREE-RUN ROUND-TRIPPER THAT LIFTED THE YANKS TO VICTORY! IT WAS OFF TO THE RACES FROM THERE AS THE SLUMPING BOMBERS, BUOYED BY ALEX'S RETURN, SURGED ALL THE WAY TO ANOTHER WORLD CHAMPIONSHIP!

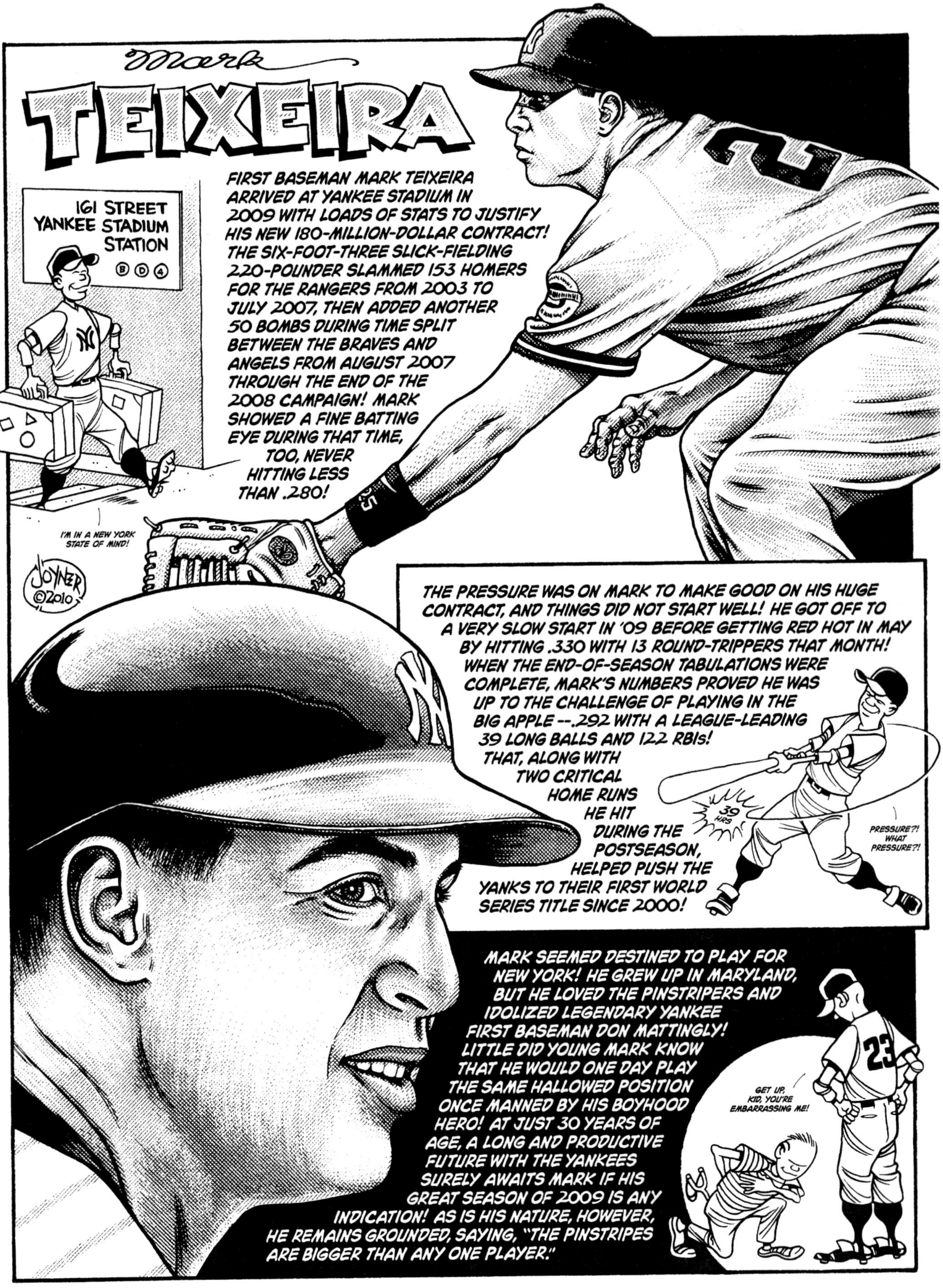
Mark
TEIXEIRA
161 STREET YANKEE STADIUM STATION
B D 4
FIRST BASEMAN MARK TEIXEIRA ARRIVED AT YANKEE STADIUM IN 2009 WITH LOADS OF STATS TO JUSTIFY HIS NEW 180-MILLION-DOLLAR CONTRACT! THE SIX-FOOT-THREE SLICK-FIELDING 220-POUNDER SLAMMED 153 HOMERS FOR THE RANGERS FROM 2003 TO JULY 2007, THEN ADDED ANOTHER 50 BOMBS DURING TIME SPLIT BETWEEN THE BRAVES AND ANGELS FROM AUGUST 2007 THROUGH THE END OF THE 2008 CAMPAIGN! MARK SHOWED A FINE BATTING EYE DURING THAT TIME, TOO, NEVER HITTING LESS THAN .280!
I'M IN A NEW YORK STATE OF MIND!
JOYNER ©2010
THE PRESSURE WAS ON MARK TO MAKE GOOD ON HIS HUGE CONTRACT, AND THINGS DID NOT START WELL! HE GOT OFF TO A VERY SLOW START IN '09 BEFORE GETTING RED HOT IN MAY BY HITTING .330 WITH 13 ROUND-TRIPPERS THAT MONTH! WHEN THE END-OF-SEASON TABULATIONS WERE COMPLETE, MARK'S NUMBERS PROVED HE WAS UP TO THE CHALLENGE OF PLAYING IN THE BIG APPLE --.292 WITH A LEAGUE-LEADING 39 LONG BALLS AND 122 RBIs! THAT, ALONG WITH TWO CRITICAL HOME RUNS HE HIT DURING THE POSTSEASON, HELPED PUSH THE YANKS TO THEIR FIRST WORLD SERIES TITLE SINCE 2000!
39 HRS
PRESSURE?! WHAT PRESSURE?!
MARK SEEMED DESTINED TO PLAY FOR NEW YORK! HE GREW UP IN MARYLAND, BUT HE LOVED THE PINSTRIPERS AND IDOLIZED LEGENDARY YANKEE FIRST BASEMAN DON MATTINGLY! LITTLE DID YOUNG MARK KNOW THAT HE WOULD ONE DAY PLAY THE SAME HALLOWED POSITION ONCE MANNED BY HIS BOYHOOD HERO! AT JUST 30 YEARS OF AGE, A LONG AND PRODUCTIVE FUTURE WITH THE YANKEES SURELY AWAITS MARK IF HIS GREAT SEASON OF 2009 IS ANY INDICATION! AS IS HIS NATURE, HOWEVER, HE REMAINS GROUNDED, SAYING, "THE PINSTRIPES ARE BIGGER THAN ANY ONE PLAYER."
GET UP, KID, YOU'RE EMBARRASSING ME!

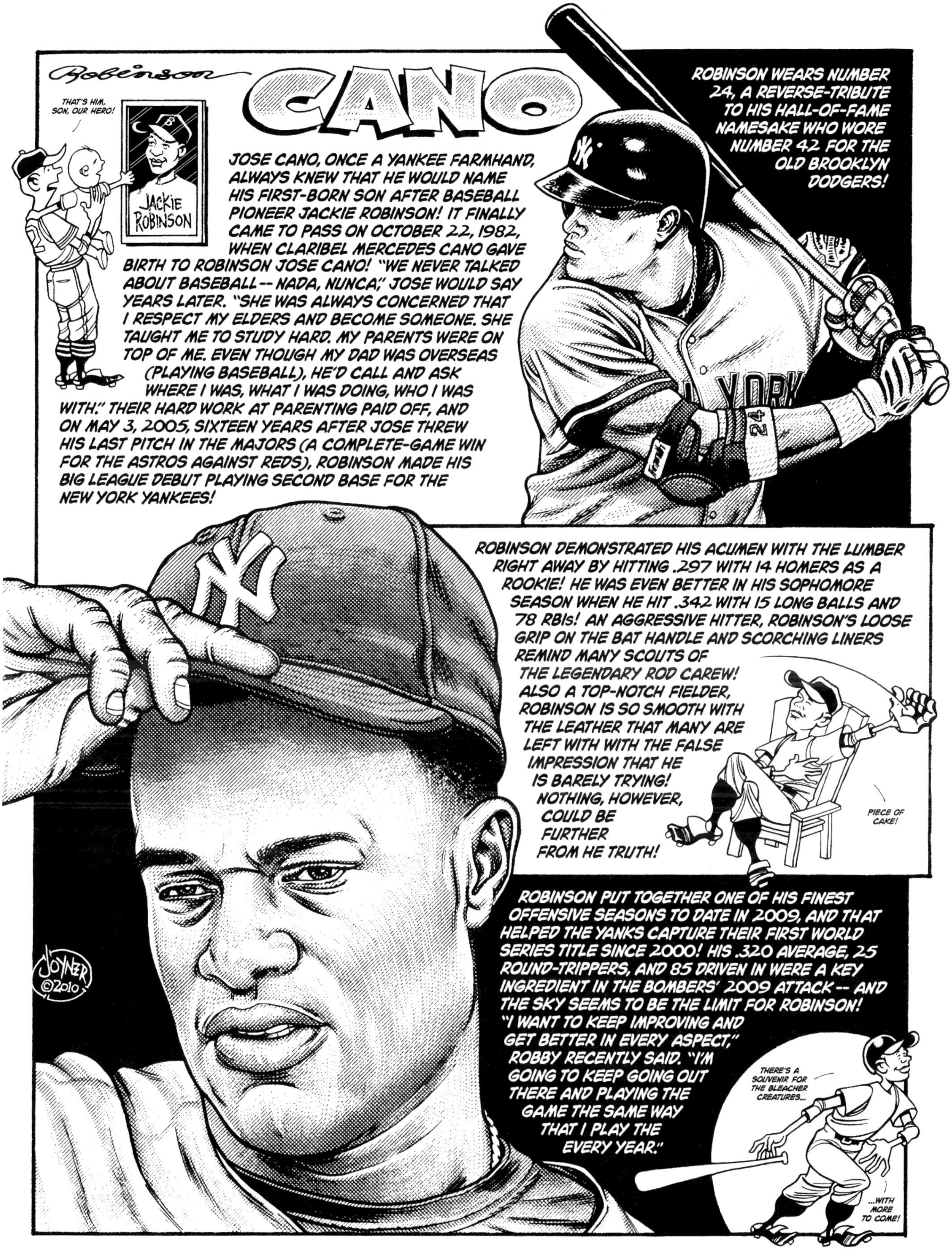
Robinson
CANO
THAT'S HIM, SON, OUR HERO!
JACKIE ROBINSON
JOSE CANO, ONCE A YANKEE FARMHAND, ALWAYS KNEW THAT HE WOULD NAME HIS FIRST-BORN SON AFTER BASEBALL PIONEER JACKIE ROBINSON! IT FINALLY CAME TO PASS ON OCTOBER 22, 1982, WHEN CLARIBEL MERCEDES CANO GAVE BIRTH TO ROBINSON JOSE CANO! "WE NEVER TALKED ABOUT BASEBALL -- NADA, NUNCA," JOSE WOULD SAY YEARS LATER. "SHE WAS ALWAYS CONCERNED THAT I RESPECT MY ELDERS AND BECOME SOMEONE. SHE TAUGHT ME TO STUDY HARD. MY PARENTS WERE ON TOP OF ME. EVEN THOUGH MY DAD WAS OVERSEAS (PLAYING BASEBALL), HE'D CALL AND ASK WHERE I WAS, WHAT I WAS DOING, WHO I WAS WITH." THEIR HARD WORK AT PARENTING PAID OFF, AND ON MAY 3, 2005, SIXTEEN YEARS AFTER JOSE THREW HIS LAST PITCH IN THE MAJORS (A COMPLETE-GAME WIN FOR THE ASTROS AGAINST REDS), ROBINSON MADE HIS BIG LEAGUE DEBUT PLAYING SECOND BASE FOR THE NEW YORK YANKEES!
ROBINSON WEARS NUMBER 24, A REVERSE-TRIBUTE TO HIS HALL-OF-FAME NAMESAKE WHO WORE NUMBER 42 FOR THE OLD BROOKLYN DODGERS!
ROBINSON DEMONSTRATED HIS ACUMEN WITH THE LUMBER RIGHT AWAY BY HITTING .297 WITH 14 HOMERS AS A ROOKIE! HE WAS EVEN BETTER IN HIS SOPHOMORE SEASON WHEN HE HIT .342 WITH 15 LONG BALLS AND 78 RBIs! AN AGGRESSIVE HITTER, ROBINSON'S LOOSE GRIP ON THE BAT HANDLE AND SCORCHING LINERS REMIND MANY SCOUTS OF THE LEGENDARY ROD CAREW! ALSO A TOP-NOTCH FIELDER, ROBINSON IS SO SMOOTH WITH THE LEATHER THAT MANY ARE LEFT WITH WITH THE FALSE IMPRESSION THAT HE IS BARELY TRYING! NOTHING, HOWEVER, COULD BE FURTHER FROM HE TRUTH!
PIECE OF CAKE!
ROBINSON PUT TOGETHER ONE OF HIS FINEST OFFENSIVE SEASONS TO DATE IN 2009, AND THAT HELPED THE YANKS CAPTURE THEIR FIRST WORLD SERIES TITLE SINCE 2000! HIS .320 AVERAGE, 25 ROUND-TRIPPERS, AND 85 DRIVEN IN WERE A KEY INGREDIENT IN THE BOMBERS' 2009 ATTACK -- AND THE SKY SEEMS TO BE THE LIMIT FOR ROBINSON! "I WANT TO KEEP IMPROVING AND GET BETTER IN EVERY ASPECT," ROBBY RECENTLY SAID. "I'M GOING TO KEEP GOING OUT THERE AND PLAYING THE GAME THE SAME WAY THAT I PLAY THE EVERY YEAR."
THERE'S A SOUVENIR FOR THE BLEACHER CREATURES...
...WITH MORE TO COME!
JOYNER ©2010

JORGE POSADA
BORN IN SANTURCE, PUERTO RICO, JORGE POSADA WAS A MULTI-SPORT STAR AT HIS HIGH SCHOOL IN SAN JUAN! IT WAS IN BASEBALL, HOWEVER, THAT JORGE TRULY DISTANCED HIMSELF FROM HIS SCHOOLMATES! HE CONTINUED TO STAR WHILE AT ALABAMA'S CALHOUN COMMUNITY COLLEGE--ON THE FIELD AND IN THE CLASSROOM! HIS EXCELLENCE ON THE DIAMOND RESULTED IN HIS BEING DRAFTED BY THE NEW YORK YANKEES, WHILE HIS APTITUDE WITH THE BOOKS EARNED HIM THE TITLE OF 1991 CALHOUN COLLEGE CLASS VALEDICTORIAN!
I CRACK HOMERS -- AND BOOKS!
DIPLOMA
JORGE ALREADY HAD FOUR WORLD SERIES RINGS BY THE TIME THE 2009 SEASON BEGAN, BUT HE WAS DETERMINED TO HELP THE YANKS WIN ANOTHER! WITH THAT IN MIND, JORGE SET ABOUT PUTTING TOGETHER ANOTHER SOLID OFFENSIVE SEASON TO GO WITH HIS CONTINUING FINE WORK BEHIND THE DISH! THE YANKS WERE QUITE PROLIFIC WITH HOME-FIELD DINGERS DURING THE DEBUT SEASON OF THE NEW YANKEE STADIUM, AND JORGE STARTED IT ALL BY LAUNCHING THE BALLPARK'S FIRST HOMER ON APRIL 16, 2009!
THERE'S NO PLACE LIKE HOME PLATE!
JORGE, AS USUAL, TURNED OUT TO BE A KEY MAN IN HELPING THE YANKEES WIN ANOTHER WORLD SERIES IN 2009! HIS CLUTCH HOMER AGAINST THE TWINS IN THE DIVISIONAL SERIES WAS A DAGGER FOR MINNESOTA FANS, AS WAS HIS BIG HOMER AGAINST THE ANGELS IN THE A.L.C.S! JORGE HAS PILED UP IMPRESSIVE NUMBERS DURING HIS 15 YEARS IN PINSTRIPES! IN '03 HE JOINED YOGI BERRA AS THE ONLY OTHER YANKS CATCHER TO HIT 30 HOMERS IN A SEASON... MAYBE ONE DAY HE'LL JOIN YOGI IN THE HALL OF FAME!
I'LL LEAVE THE LIGHT ON FOR YOU IN COOPERSTOWN, KID!
THANKS, YOGI!
JOYNER ©2010

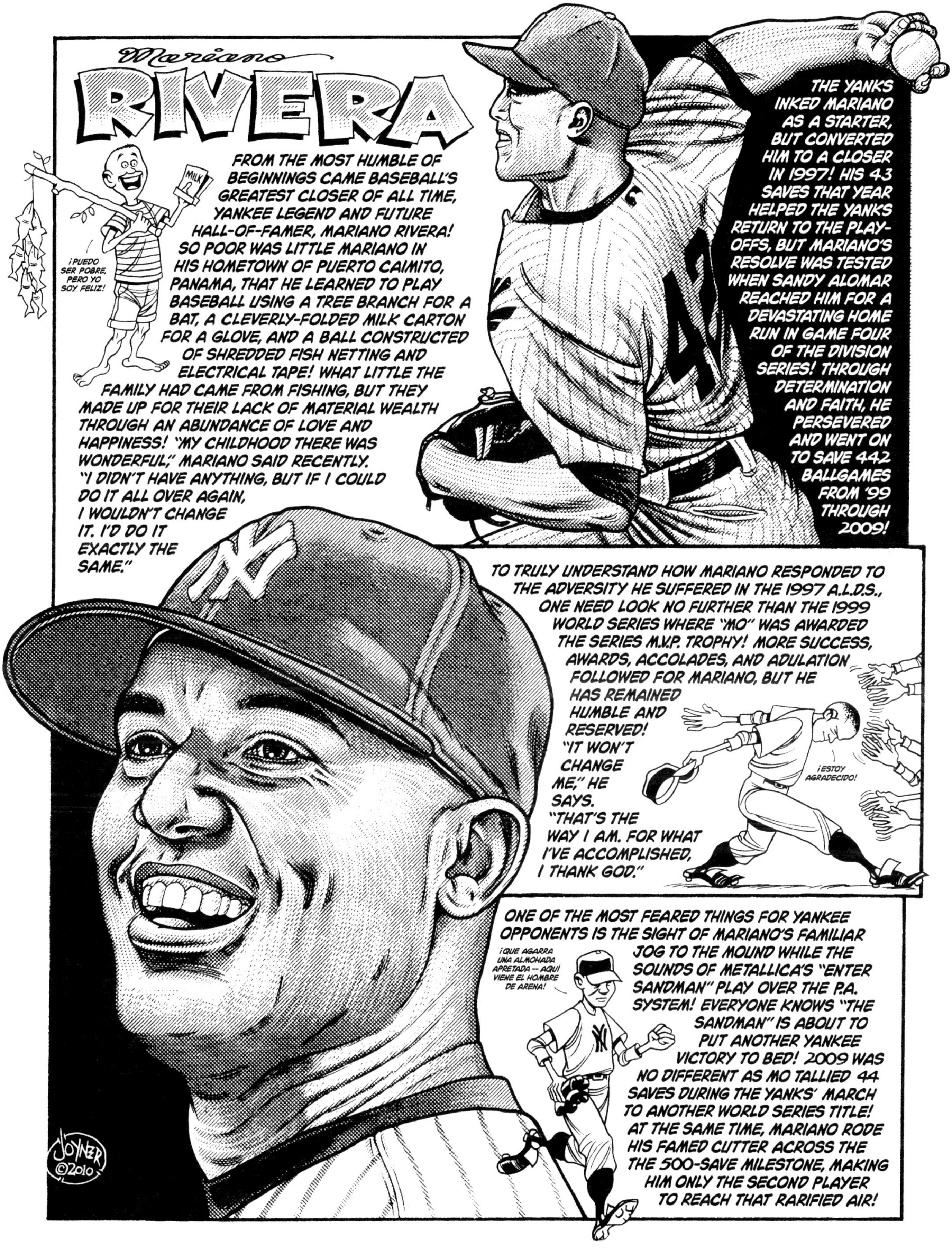
Mariano
RIVERA
FROM THE MOST HUMBLE OF BEGINNINGS CAME BASEBALL'S GREATEST CLOSER OF ALL TIME, YANKEE LEGEND AND FUTURE HALL-OF-FAMER, MARIANO RIVERA! SO POOR WAS LITTLE MARIANO IN HIS HOMETOWN OF PUERTO CAIMITO, PANAMA, THAT HE LEARNED TO PLAY BASEBALL USING A TREE BRANCH FOR A BAT, A CLEVERLY-FOLDED MILK CARTON FOR A GLOVE, AND A BALL CONSTRUCTED OF SHREDDED FISH NETTING AND ELECTRICAL TAPE! WHAT LITTLE THE FAMILY HAD CAME FROM FISHING, BUT THEY MADE UP FOR THEIR LACK OF MATERIAL WEALTH THROUGH AN ABUNDANCE OF LOVE AND HAPPINESS! "MY CHILDHOOD THERE WAS WONDERFUL," MARIANO SAID RECENTLY. "I DIDN'T HAVE ANYTHING, BUT IF I COULD DO IT ALL OVER AGAIN, I WOULDN'T CHANGE IT. I'D DO IT EXACTLY THE SAME."
MILK
¡PUEDO SER POBRE, PERO YO SOY FELIZ!
THE YANKS INKED MARIANO AS A STARTER, BUT CONVERTED HIM TO A CLOSER IN 1997! HIS 43 SAVES THAT YEAR HELPED THE YANKS RETURN TO THE PLAY-OFFS, BUT MARIANO'S RESOLVE WAS TESTED WHEN SANDY ALOMAR REACHED HIM FOR A DEVASTATING HOME RUN IN GAME FOUR OF THE DIVISION SERIES! THROUGH DETERMINATION AND FAITH, HE PERSEVERED AND WENT ON TO SAVE 442 BALLGAMES FROM '99 THROUGH 2009!
TO TRULY UNDERSTAND HOW MARIANO RESPONDED TO THE ADVERSITY HE SUFFERED IN THE 1997 A.L.D.S., ONE NEED LOOK NO FURTHER THAN THE 1999 WORLD SERIES WHERE "MO" WAS AWARDED THE SERIES M.V.P. TROPHY! MORE SUCCESS, AWARDS, ACCOLADES, AND ADULATION FOLLOWED FOR MARIANO, BUT HE HAS REMAINED HUMBLE AND RESERVED! "IT WON'T CHANGE ME," HE SAYS. "THAT'S THE WAY I AM. FOR WHAT I'VE ACCOMPLISHED, I THANK GOD."
¡ESTOY AGRADECIDO!
ONE OF THE MOST FEARED THINGS FOR YANKEE OPPONENTS IS THE SIGHT OF MARIANO'S FAMILIAR JOG TO THE MOUND WHILE THE SOUNDS OF METALLICA'S "ENTER SANDMAN" PLAY OVER THE P.A. SYSTEM! EVERYONE KNOWS "THE SANDMAN" IS ABOUT TO PUT ANOTHER YANKEE VICTORY TO BED! 2009 WAS NO DIFFERENT AS MO TALLIED 44 SAVES DURING THE YANKS' MARCH TO ANOTHER WORLD SERIES TITLE! AT THE SAME TIME, MARIANO RODE HIS FAMED CUTTER ACROSS THE THE 500-SAVE MILESTONE, MAKING HIM ONLY THE SECOND PLAYER TO REACH THAT RARIFIED AIR!
¡QUE AGARRA UNA ALMOHADA APRETADA -- AQUÍ VIENE EL HOMBRE DE ARENA!
JOYNER ©2010

Johnny DAMON
AFTER TOILING SIX YEARS IN KANSAS CITY AND ONE YEAR IN OAKLAND, HUSTLING LEFTFIELDER JOHNNY DAMON HEADED FOR THE BIG TIME WHEN HE JOINED THE RED SOX IN 2002! SPORTING HIS SHAGGY "CAVEMAN" LOOK, JOHNNY HELPED LEAD THE 2004 SOX TO THEIR FIRST WORLD SERIES TITLE SINCE 1918! JOHNNY'S CLUTCH TWO-HOMER OUTBURST IN GAME SEVEN OF THAT YEAR'S A.L.C.S. SANK THE YANKEES AND CATAPULTED BOSTON TO ULTIMATE GLORY! JOHNNY TRADED HIS RED SOCKS FOR YANKEE PINSTRIPES IN 2006 WITH HOPES OF DOING FOR THE BOMBERS WHAT HE'D HELPED DO FOR BOSTON! BUT FIRST THINGS FIRST -- JOHNNY MET WITH A BARBER ON DECEMBER 22, 2005, AND SHED HIS CAVEMAN LOOK IN ORDER TO MEET THE YANKS' STRICT DRESS CODE!
CAN I GET HAZARDOUS DUTY PAY FOR THIS?!
JOYNER ©2010
FROM 2006-08 JOHNNY WAS A REAL SPARKPLUG FOR THE YANKS, HITTING .286 WITH 53 HOMERS AND 87 STOLEN BASES -- BUT HIS CONTRIBUTION DID NOT TRANSLATE TO A CHAMPIONSHIP! UNTIL 2009, THAT IS! JOHNNY POSTED A FINE YEAR IN '09, BATTING .282 WITH 24 HOMERS AND 82 RBIs! THAT HELPED THE YANKS RETURN TO THE POSTSEASON AFTER MISSING OUT IN '08! JOHNNY THEN PROVIDED THE POSTSEASON PLAY OF THE YEAR WHEN HE SWIPED TWO BASES ON ONE PITCH IN GAME FOUR OF THE WORLD SERIES AGAINST THE PHILLIES! HIS HEADS-UP BASERUNNING IGNITED THE YANKS, LEADING THEM TO A CRITICAL GAME FOUR WIN AND, FINALLY, A WORLD SERIES CROWN!
TWO FOR THE ROAD, PLEASE!
WITH ANOTHER TITLE NOW UNDER HIS BELT, JOHNNY IS ON THE MOVE AGAIN! THIS TIME HE IS OFF TO DETROIT FOR THE 2010 SEASON WITH HOPES OF HELPING THE TIGERS RETURN TO THE PROMISED LAND! YANKS FANS WILL WISH HIM WELL, FOR SURE, AND ALWAYS HOLD HIM DEAR FOR HIS PART IN RETURNING THEM TO GLORY!
THANKS FOR A WILD RIDE, NEW YORK!

Nick SWISHER
"I'VE BEEN BLESSED TO BE IN SUCH A WONDERFUL SITUATION HERE WITH THE YANKEES." THOSE WERE THE WORDS OF SLUGGING RIGHTFIELDER NICK SWISHER FOLLOWING HIS TRADE TO NEW YORK ON NOVEMBER 13, 2008! THE YANKS WON THE WORLD SERIES ELEVEN MONTHS LATER, AND NICK'S 29 HOMERS AND 82 RBIs WERE A KEY FACTOR IN THE BOMBERS' GOOD FORTUNE! THE VERSATILE FLYCHASER EVEN SPELLED THE BULLPEN ONCE BY PITCHING A SCORELESS INNING AT TAMPA BAY ON APRIL 13, 2009! NICK ENDURED A POSTSEASON SLUMP, BUT BROKE OUT OF IT IN A BIG WAY WHEN HIS DOUBLE AND ROUND-TRIPPER HELPED LEAD THE YANKS TO VICTORY OVER THE PHILLIES IN GAME THREE OF THE 2009 WORLD SERIES!
ANYTHING TO HELP THE TEAM WIN!
AN ALL-AROUND ATHLETE AT PARKERSBURG HIGH IN WEST VIRGINIA, NICK SERIOUSLY CONSIDERED ACCEPTING AN OFFER TO PLAY FOOTBALL FOR NOTRE DAME! NICK INSTEAD OPTED TO PLAY BASEBALL FOR OHIO STATE WHERE HE WON THE BIG TEN FRESHMAN OF THE YEAR AWARD IN 2000, THEN FOLLOWED THAT BY EARNING ALL BIG TEN HONORS IN 2001 AND 2002! BASEBALL IS HIS TRUE CALLING, BUT NICK WILL ALWAYS BE FOOTBALL CRAZY. "I'D BE LYING IF I TOLD YOU I DON'T HAVE THAT FOOTBALL BUG IN ME," HE SAID. "THERE'S NOTHING LIKE BIG TEN FOOTBALL-- IT'S AWESOME."
THIS ONE'S FOR THE OLD BUCKEYES!
NICK'S HARD WORK, BIG PLAYS, AND COLORFUL DEMEANOR HAVE ENDEARED HIM TO YANKEE STADIUM'S "BLEACHER CREATURES" WHO SIT BEHIND HIM IN RIGHTFIELD! NICK REWARDS THEIR AFFECTION BY TURNING AND OFFERING UP THE "SWISH SALUTE" DURING THEIR TRADITIONAL TOP-OF-THE-FIRST ROLL CALL! NICK HAS JUST THE RIGHT ATTITUDE FOR A LONG, BRIGHT CAREER! "EVERY TIME I COME TO THE BALLPARK, I WANT TO HAVE AS MUCH FUN AS I CAN."
SWISHER REPORTING FOR DUTY!
314
33
JOYNER ©2010

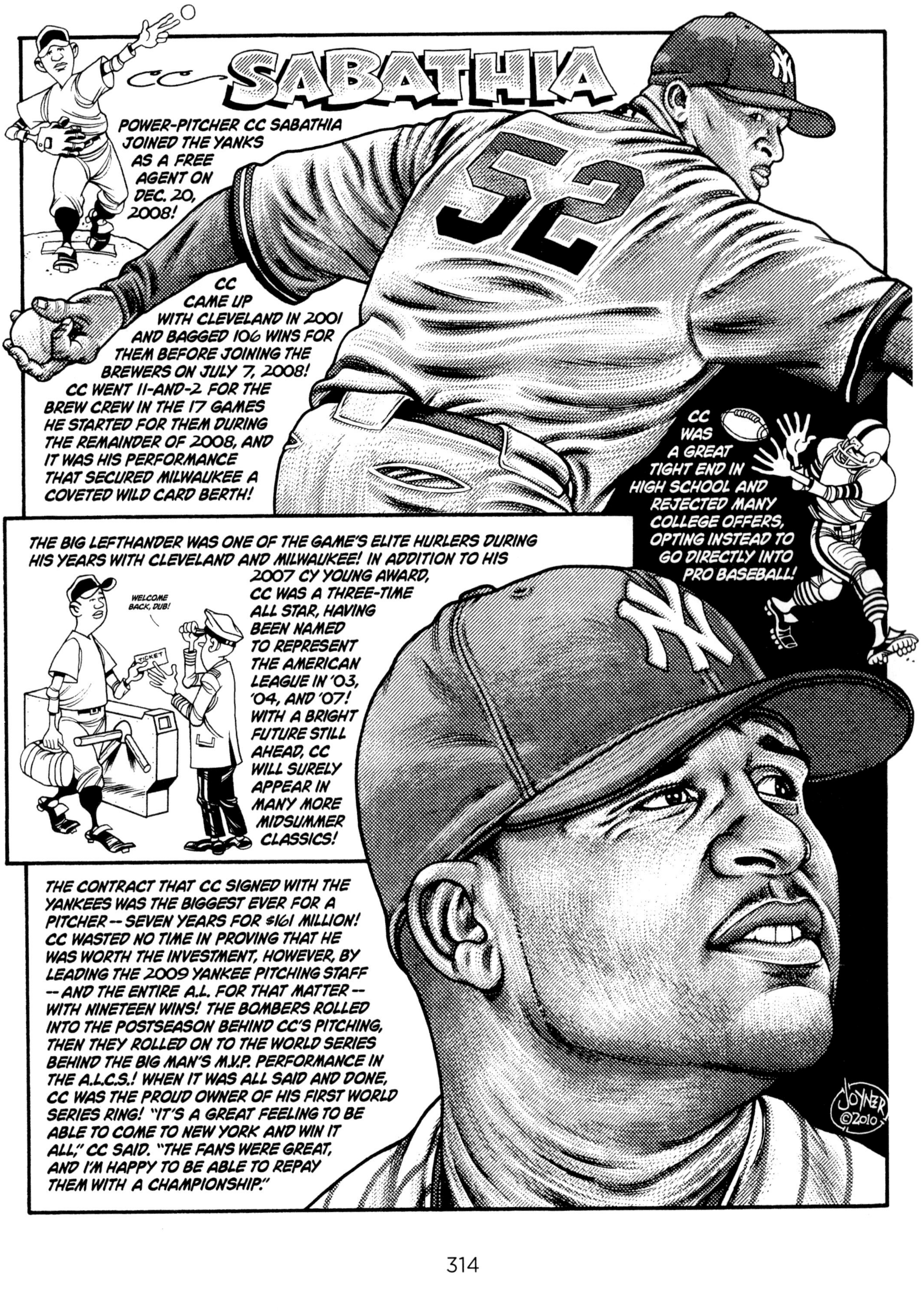
CC SABATHIA
POWER-PITCHER CC SABATHIA JOINED THE YANKS AS A FREE AGENT ON DEC. 20, 2008!
CC CAME UP WITH CLEVELAND IN 2001 AND BAGGED 106 WINS FOR THEM BEFORE JOINING THE BREWERS ON JULY 7, 2008! CC WENT 11-AND-2 FOR THE BREW CREW IN THE 17 GAMES HE STARTED FOR THEM DURING THE REMAINDER OF 2008, AND IT WAS HIS PERFORMANCE THAT SECURED MILWAUKEE A COVETED WILD CARD BERTH!
CC WAS A GREAT TIGHT END IN HIGH SCHOOL AND REJECTED MANY COLLEGE OFFERS, OPTING INSTEAD TO GO DIRECTLY INTO PRO BASEBALL!
THE BIG LEFTHANDER WAS ONE OF THE GAME'S ELITE HURLERS DURING HIS YEARS WITH CLEVELAND AND MILWAUKEE! IN ADDITION TO HIS 2007 CY YOUNG AWARD, CC WAS A THREE-TIME ALL STAR, HAVING BEEN NAMED TO REPRESENT THE AMERICAN LEAGUE IN '03, '04, AND '07! WITH A BRIGHT FUTURE STILL AHEAD, CC WILL SURELY APPEAR IN MANY MORE MIDSUMMER CLASSICS!
WELCOME BACK, DUB!
TICKET
THE CONTRACT THAT CC SIGNED WITH THE YANKEES WAS THE BIGGEST EVER FOR A PITCHER -- SEVEN YEARS FOR $161 MILLION! CC WASTED NO TIME IN PROVING THAT HE WAS WORTH THE INVESTMENT, HOWEVER, BY LEADING THE 2009 YANKEE PITCHING STAFF -- AND THE ENTIRE A.L. FOR THAT MATTER -- WITH NINETEEN WINS! THE BOMBERS ROLLED INTO THE POSTSEASON BEHIND CC'S PITCHING, THEN THEY ROLLED ON TO THE WORLD SERIES BEHIND THE BIG MAN'S M.V.P. PERFORMANCE IN THE A.L.C.S.! WHEN IT WAS ALL SAID AND DONE, CC WAS THE PROUD OWNER OF HIS FIRST WORLD SERIES RING! "IT'S A GREAT FEELING TO BE ABLE TO COME TO NEW YORK AND WIN IT ALL," CC SAID. "THE FANS WERE GREAT, AND I'M HAPPY TO BE ABLE TO REPAY THEM WITH A CHAMPIONSHIP."
JOYNER ©2010

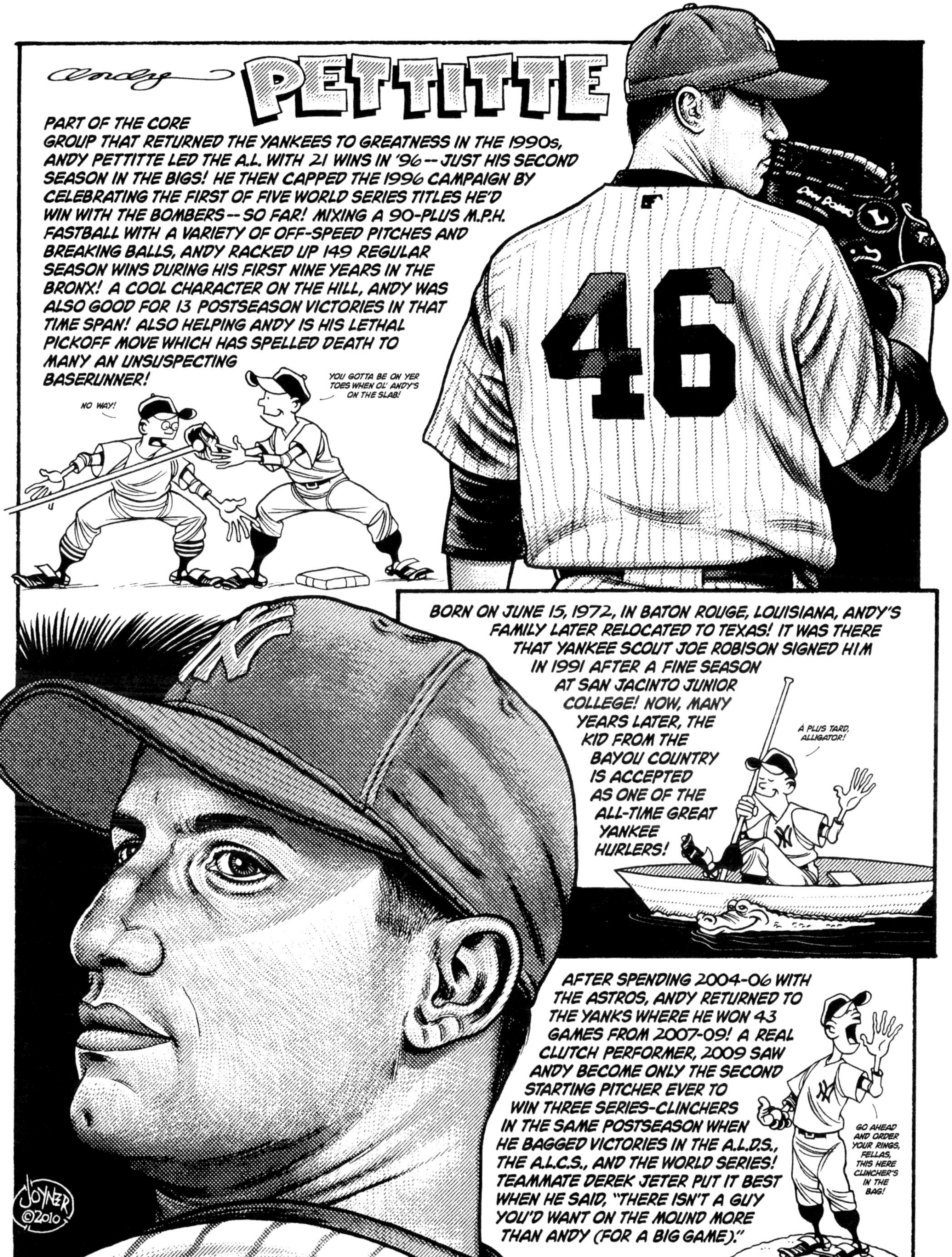
Andy PETTITTE
PART OF THE CORE GROUP THAT RETURNED THE YANKEES TO GREATNESS IN THE 1990s, ANDY PETTITTE LED THE A.L. WITH 21 WINS IN '96 -- JUST HIS SECOND SEASON IN THE BIGS! HE THEN CAPPED THE 1996 CAMPAIGN BY CELEBRATING THE FIRST OF FIVE WORLD SERIES TITLES HE'D WIN WITH THE BOMBERS -- SO FAR! MIXING A 90-PLUS M.P.H. FASTBALL WITH A VARIETY OF OFF-SPEED PITCHES AND BREAKING BALLS, ANDY RACKED UP 149 REGULAR SEASON WINS DURING HIS FIRST NINE YEARS IN THE BRONX! A COOL CHARACTER ON THE HILL, ANDY WAS ALSO GOOD FOR 13 POSTSEASON VICTORIES IN THAT TIME SPAN! ALSO HELPING ANDY IS HIS LETHAL PICKOFF MOVE WHICH HAS SPELLED DEATH TO MANY AN UNSUSPECTING BASERUNNER!
YOU GOTTA BE ON YER TOES WHEN OL' ANDY'S ON THE SLAB!
NO WAY!
46
BORN ON JUNE 15, 1972, IN BATON ROUGE, LOUISIANA, ANDY'S FAMILY LATER RELOCATED TO TEXAS! IT WAS THERE THAT YANKEE SCOUT JOE ROBISON SIGNED HIM IN 1991 AFTER A FINE SEASON AT SAN JACINTO JUNIOR COLLEGE! NOW, MANY YEARS LATER, THE KID FROM THE BAYOU COUNTRY IS ACCEPTED AS ONE OF THE ALL-TIME GREAT YANKEE HURLERS!
A PLUS TARD, ALLIGATOR!
AFTER SPENDING 2004-06 WITH THE ASTROS, ANDY RETURNED TO THE YANKS WHERE HE WON 43 GAMES FROM 2007-09! A REAL CLUTCH PERFORMER, 2009 SAW ANDY BECOME ONLY THE SECOND STARTING PITCHER EVER TO WIN THREE SERIES-CLINCHERS IN THE SAME POSTSEASON WHEN HE BAGGED VICTORIES IN THE A.L.D.S., THE A.L.C.S., AND THE WORLD SERIES! TEAMMATE DEREK JETER PUT IT BEST WHEN HE SAID, "THERE ISN'T A GUY YOU'D WANT ON THE MOUND MORE THAN ANDY (FOR A BIG GAME)."
GO AHEAD AND ORDER YOUR RINGS, FELLAS, THIS HERE CLINCHER'S IN THE BAG!
JOYNER ©2010

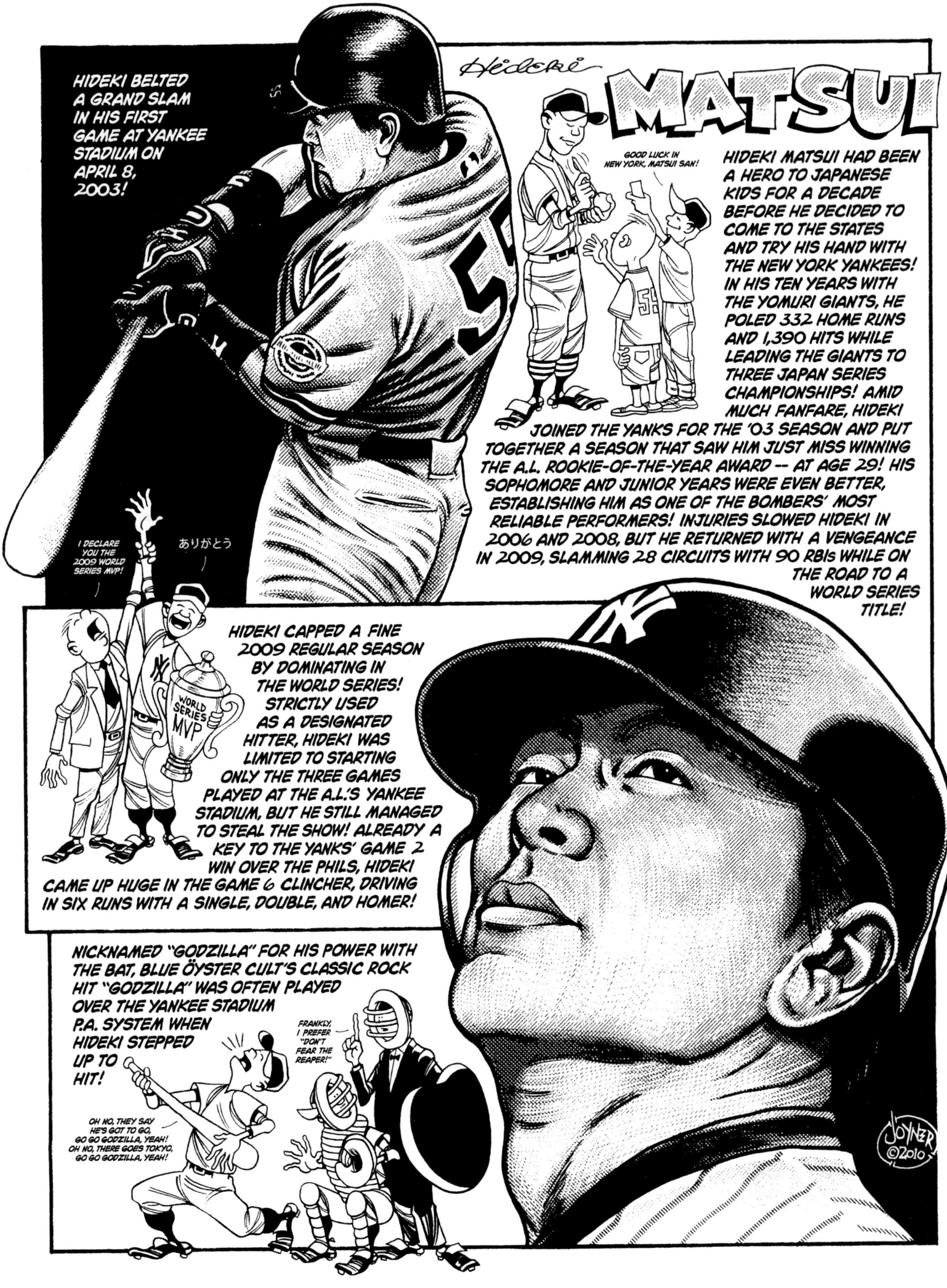

Hideki
MATSUI
HIDEKI BELTED A GRAND SLAM IN HIS FIRST GAME AT YANKEE STADIUM ON APRIL 8, 2003!
GOOD LUCK IN NEW YORK, MATSUI SAN!
HIDEKI MATSUI HAD BEEN A HERO TO JAPANESE KIDS FOR A DECADE BEFORE HE DECIDED TO COME TO THE STATES AND TRY HIS HAND WITH THE NEW YORK YANKEES! IN HIS TEN YEARS WITH THE YOMURI GIANTS, HE POLED 332 HOME RUNS AND 1,390 HITS WHILE LEADING THE GIANTS TO THREE JAPAN SERIES CHAMPIONSHIPS! AMID MUCH FANFARE, HIDEKI JOINED THE YANKS FOR THE '03 SEASON AND PUT TOGETHER A SEASON THAT SAW HIM JUST MISS WINNING THE A.L. ROOKIE-OF-THE-YEAR AWARD -- AT AGE 29! HIS SOPHOMORE AND JUNIOR YEARS WERE EVEN BETTER, ESTABLISHING HIM AS ONE OF THE BOMBERS' MOST RELIABLE PERFORMERS! INJURIES SLOWED HIDEKI IN 2006 AND 2008, BUT HE RETURNED WITH A VENGEANCE IN 2009, SLAMMING 28 CIRCUITS WITH 90 RBIs WHILE ON THE ROAD TO A WORLD SERIES TITLE!
I DECLARE YOU THE 2009 WORLD SERIES MVP!
ありがとう
WORLD SERIES MVP
HIDEKI CAPPED A FINE 2009 REGULAR SEASON BY DOMINATING IN THE WORLD SERIES! STRICTLY USED AS A DESIGNATED HITTER, HIDEKI WAS LIMITED TO STARTING ONLY THE THREE GAMES PLAYED AT THE A.L.'S YANKEE STADIUM, BUT HE STILL MANAGED TO STEAL THE SHOW! ALREADY A KEY TO THE YANKS' GAME 2 WIN OVER THE PHILS, HIDEKI CAME UP HUGE IN THE GAME 6 CLINCHER, DRIVING IN SIX RUNS WITH A SINGLE, DOUBLE, AND HOMER!
NICKNAMED "GODZILLA" FOR HIS POWER WITH THE BAT, BLUE ÖYSTER CULT'S CLASSIC ROCK HIT "GODZILLA" WAS OFTEN PLAYED OVER THE YANKEE STADIUM P.A. SYSTEM WHEN HIDEKI STEPPED UP TO HIT!
OH NO, THEY SAY HE'S GOT TO GO, GO GO GODZILLA, YEAH! OH NO, THERE GOES TOKYO, GO GO GODZILLA, YEAH!
FRANKLY, I PREFER "DON'T FEAR THE REAPER!"
JOYNER ©2010

Melky
CABRERA
WHEN THE YANKEES CAPTURED THE 2009 WORLD SERIES CROWN, A GOOD CHUNK OF THE CREDIT FOR THEIR VICTORY WAS OWED TO THEIR EXCITING DOMINICAN-BORN CENTERFIELDER, 25-YEAR-OLD MELKY CABRERA! SWITCH-HITTING MELKY WON A STARTING SPOT IN LATE APRIL AND QUICKLY ESTABLISHED HIMSELF AS A RELIABLE MAN IN THE PINCH BY RAPPING OUT A WALK-OFF HIT ON APRIL 22 AGAINST THE A's! TWO MORE WALK-OFF HITS THE NEXT MONTH RESULTED IN MELKY BEING NAMED THE MAJOR LEAGUE BASEBALL CLUTCH PLAYER OF THE MONTH OF MAY! MELKY SETTLED IN TO BAT A RESPECTABLE .274 WITH 13 HOMERS AND 68 RBIs ON THE YEAR, THEREBY MAKING A VALUABLE CONTRIBUTION TO THE BOMBERS' 103-WIN REGULAR SEASON! HIS POSTSEASON WAS BITTERSWEET, HOWEVER, BECAUSE WHILE THE YANKS WOULD WIN IT ALL, MELKY'S SEASON ENDED PREMATURELY AFTER PULLING UP LAME WITH A BAD HAMSTRING IN WORLD SERIES GAME FOUR!
¡PERO QUIERO PAGAR!
NEW YORK
NEW YORK
JOYNER ©2010
ONE OF THE GREATEST DAYS IN THE 2009 SEASON OF MELKY CABRERA WAS AUGUST 2 WHEN HE HIT FOR THE CYCLE AGAINST THE WHITE SOX IN AN 8-5 YANKEE WIN! IN DOING SO, MELKY BECAME THE FIRST YANKEE TO ACCOMPLISH THE DEED SINCE 1995, AND JUST THE FIFTH PINSTRIPER TO DO IT IN THE CLUB'S STORIED HISTORY! MELKY, WHO HAD NO TRIPLES TO THAT POINT IN THE SEASON, NEEDED A NINTH-INNING THREE-BAGGER TO COMPLETE HIS CYCLE -- AND HE GOT IT THANKS TO A QUIRKY BOUNCE OFF THE OUTFIELD PADDING! AS MELKY STOOD TRIUMPHANTLY ON THIRD BASE, HE PLAYFULLY CLAPPED, STUCK OUT HIS TONGUE, AND POINTED TO HIS TEAMMATES IN THE DUGOUT!
¡ESTO ES DIVERTIDO!
DEALT TO THE BRAVES ON DECEMBER 22, 2009, MELKY WILL BE MISSED BY YANKEE FANS -- NOT JUST FOR THE LOSS OF HIS HUSTLE AND ENTHUSIASM, BUT ALSO FOR THE LOSS OF HIS GREAT NAME! THE NAME "MELKY" LED TO FUN WORD PLAYS LIKE "MELKY WAY CABRERA" (COURTESY OF ESPN'S CHRIS BERMAN), "THE MELK MAN ALWAYS RINGS TWICE," AND "THE MELK MAN DELIVERS" (BOTH COURTESY OF YANKEE BROADCASTER JOHN STERLING)!
MILK
¿TOMO LECHE?

A.J. BURNETT
AFTER SPENDING THE FIRST TEN YEARS OF HIS CAREER WITH THE MARLINS AND BLUE JAYS, RIGHT-HANDER A.J. BURNETT SIGNED A BIG FIVE-YEAR DEAL WITH THE YANKEES ON DECEMBER 18, 2008! THE BENEFITS TO BOTH THE YANKS AND A.J. WERE IMMEDIATE! LEANING HEAVILY ON HIS MID-90s TAILING FASTBALL AND HIS CURVE, A.J. WON 13 GAMES, WHICH HELPED THE BOMBERS RETURN TO THE POSTSEASON AFTER MISSING OUT IN '08! A.J. THEN PUT HIS STAMP ON NEW YORK'S SUBSEQUENT CHAMPIONSHIP BY TOSSING A 7-INNING, 9-STRIKEOUT VICTORY OVER THE PHILLIES IN GAME TWO OF THE 2009 WORLD SERIES!
AS I THINK, SO SHALL I BECOME... AS LONG AS I CAN PAINT THE BLACK!
A.J. IS ONE OF THE GAME'S UNIQUE CHARACTERS, AND PLAYS WITH VISIBLE PASSION AND EMOTION! WHEN ASKED TO NAME THE THREE PEOPLE HE'D MOST LIKE TO HAVE AS DINNER GUESTS, A.J. SAID, "MY GRANDPA, BRUCE LEE, AND THE MAN UPSTAIRS." A.J.'S FONDNESS FOR LEE IS WELL KNOWN BECAUSE HE SPORTS A TATTOO OF THE MARTIAL ARTS LEGEND ON HIS LEFT ARM! HEARTS LEAPT IN THE CHESTS OF YANKEE FANS DURING SPRING TRAINING WHEN A.J. WAS STRUCK BY A LINE DRIVE -- DIRECTLY ON HIS BRUCE LEE TATTOO! UNFAZED AND DRAWING POWER FROM THE LATE, GREAT MASTER, A.J. SAID, "IT'S A GOOD THING I HAVE BRUCE LEE."
EMBRACING THE MODERN TRADITION OF THE POST-GAME CELEBRATORY SHAVING CREAM PIE TO THE FACE, A.J. TOOK IT UPON HIMSELF TO LEAD THE 2009 YANKS IN DISPENSING PIES TO HIS TEAMMATES! MOST NOTABLE AMONG HIS MANY "VICTIMS" WERE A-ROD, DAMON, CANO, TEIXEIRA, MATSUI, POSADA, AND EVEN MANAGER JOE GIRARDI!
LET ME TELL YOU EXACTLY HOW I WON THE GAME...
JOYNER ©2010

Joba
CHAMBERLAIN
STANDING SIX-FOOT-TWO AND WEIGHING IN AT 230 POUNDS, JOBA CHAMBERLAIN MAKES FOR QUITE AN IMPOSING SIGHT WHEN GAZED UPON BY OPPOSITION BATSMEN! ANY HOPES THAT THE HULKING RIGHT-HANDER IS ONLY A PAPER GIANT ARE IMMEDIATELY DISMISSED WHEN JOBA'S HEATER POPS THE CATCHER'S MITT -- OCCASIONALLY AT SPEEDS REACHING 100 MPH! NEEDLESS TO SAY, HE'S A FORCE TO BE RECKONED WITH!
JOBA WENT TO THE UNIVERSITY OF NEBRASKA WHERE HIS BRILLIANT 10-AND-2 RECORD HELPED THE CORNHUSKERS REACH THE 2005 COLLEGE WORLD SERIES!
62
THE YANKS MADE JOBA THE 41ST PLAYER CHOSEN IN THE 2006 DRAFT WHEN THEY SELECTED HIM ON JUNE 6TH OF THAT YEAR! HE MADE HIS DEBUT 14 MONTHS LATER BY STRIKING OUT THE FIRST MAN HE FACED -- BLUE JAYS PINCH-HITTER RAY OLMEDO!
IMPOSING AS HE MAY BE TO LOOK AT ON THE SLAB, JOBA IS A GENTLE GIANT, AND HAPPY AS A KID WHEN HE'S PLAYING "GUITAR HERO," ONE OF HIS FAVORITE ACTIVITIES!
LOVE IN AN ELEVATOR! LOVIN' IT UP WHEN YOU'RE GOIN' DOWN... ON STRIKES!
JOBA SUFFERED FROM ARM TENDONITIS IN 2006, SO THE YANKEES WERE VERY PROTECTIVE OF HIM WHEN THEY BROUGHT HIM UP IN '07! THE SPECIFICS OF HIS USAGE WERE OUTLINED IN A COMPLICATED SET OF GUIDELINES THAT CAME TO BE CALLED "THE JOBA RULES." THE PHRASE TOOK ON AN ENTIRELY NEW MEANING AS JOBA BEGAN TO MOW DOWN ENEMY HITTERS WITH INCREASING REGULARITY! THEN, IN THE BLINK OF AN EYE, THOUSANDS OF YANKEE FANS STARTED SHOWING UP AT THE STADIUM PROUDLY WEARING T-SHIRTS THAT READ "JOBA RULES!"
I'M JUST CHECKING TO MAKE SURE I'M ALLOWED TO THROW A SLIDER WITH A 1-AND-2 COUNT!
JOBA CONTRIBUTED NINE WINS TO THE YANKS' 2009 REGULAR SEASON, THEN PICKED UP THE VICTORY IN GAME FOUR OF THE WORLD SERIES AGAINST PHILADELPHIA! INCIDENTALLY, JOBA RECORDED THE LAST STRIKEOUT AT THE OLD STADIUM WHEN HE FANNED AUBREY HUFF ON SEPTEMBER 21, 2008! AS A SOUVENIR, JOBA TOOK A BAG OF DIRT FROM THE HALLOWED MOUND WHERE LEGENDS LIKE RUTH, RUFFING, FORD, AND GUIDRY ONCE TOED THE RUBBER!
GOODBYE, OLD FRIEND -- IT'S BEEN NICE KNOWIN' YOU!
JOYNER ©2010

JOE GIRARDI
GIRARDI * CUBS
EIGHT YEAR OLD JOE GIRARDI WAS ALREADY HIGHLY FOCUSED WHEN HE WROTE IN A THIRD GRADE ESSAY THAT HE WANTED PLAY BASEBALL FOR HIS HOME TEAM CHICAGO CUBS! SIXTEEN YEARS LATER, JOE REALIZED HIS GOAL WHEN HE MADE HIS BIG LEAGUE DEBUT AS THE CUBBIES' CATCHER ON APRIL 4, 1989! THE DAY WAS MADE THAT MUCH SWEETER WHEN JOE GOT A HIT IN HIS FIRST AT-BAT -- A SINGLE OFF PHILLIES' RIGHT-HANDER FLOYD YOUMANS! JOE MADE IT TO THE WORLD SERIES IN 1996 DURING HIS FIRST SEASON PLAYING WITH THE YANKS! HIS BIG TRIPLE IN GAME SIX HELPED THE BOMBERS WIN THE GAME AND THE SERIES -- THEIR FIRST SINCE '78! OF THE RBI THREE-BAGGER, JOE SAYS, "IT WAS THE BIGGEST HIT OF MY CAREER IN THE BIGGEST GAME OF MY CAREER." JOE LEFT THE YANKS TO REJOIN THE CUBS IN 2000, THEN WRAPPED UP HIS PLAYING DAYS WITH THE CARDINALS IN 2003! HE CAME BACK TO NEW YORK IN 2008 WHEN HE SUCCEEDED JOE TORRE AS YANKEE SKIPPER!
ONE DAY!
27 THIS YEAR, 28 NEXT YEAR!
THRILLED TO BE MANAGING THE YANKS, JOE WAS CONFIDENT HE COULD LEAD THE CLUB BACK TO THE WORLD SERIES! IN FACT, JOE EVEN CHOSE TO WEAR JERSEY NO. 27 -- A DAILY REMINDER OF HIS GOAL TO HELP THE FRANCHISE WIN THEIR 27TH WORLD SERIES TITLE! JOE REACHED THAT GOAL IN JUST HIS SECOND SEASON AT THE HELM WHEN HIS YANKEES DEFEATED A POWERFUL PHILADELPHIA PHILLIES TEAM IN THE 2009 SERIES!
JOYNER ©2010
ALL IN A DAY'S WORK MA'AM!
WHILE DRIVING HOME FROM THE 2009 WORLD SERIES FINALE, SUPER-JOE HELPED RESCUE A MOTORIST FROM A CRASH ON NEW YORK'S CROSS COUNTY PARKWAY! WHEN ASKED ABOUT HIS POST-GAME GOOD SAMARITANISM, JOE SAID, "I THINK THE MOST IMPORTANT THING IS THAT, OBVIOUSLY, THERE'S A LOT OF JOY IN WHAT WE DO, BUT WE CAN'T FORGET TO BE HUMAN BEINGS WHEN WE HELP OTHERS OUT." JOE IS A DEVOUT CHRISTIAN, AND TRIES TO LEAD OTHERS BY SETTING A GOOD EXAMPLE!

INDEX

Page numbers in ***bold italics*** indicate player bio-illustrations.